Mike Holt's Illustrated Guide to

Understanding the
NATIONAL
ELECTRICAL CODE®

Volume 1 • Articles 90 - 480

Based on the 2014 NEC®

Mike Holt Enterprises, Inc.
888.NEC.CODE (632.2633) • www.MikeHolt.com

NOTICE TO THE READER

Mike Holt's Illustrated Guide to Understanding the National Electrical Code®, Volume 1, based on the 2014 NEC®

First Printing: February 2014

Author: Mike Holt
Technical Illustrator: Mike Culbreath
Cover Design: Madalina Iordache-Levay
Layout Design and Typesetting: Cathleen Kwas

COPYRIGHT © 2014 Charles Michael Holt
ISBN 978-1-932685-76-3

Produced and Printed in the USA

For more information, call 888.NEC.CODE (632.2633), or e-mail Info@MikeHolt.com.

This logo is a registered trademark of Mike Holt Enterprises, Inc.

If you are an instructor and would like to request an examination copy of this or other Mike Holt Publications:

Call: 888.NEC.CODE (632.2633) • Fax: 352.360.0983
E-mail: Info@MikeHolt.com • Visit: www.MikeHolt.com

You can download a sample PDF of all our publications by visiting www.MikeHolt.com

I dedicate this book to the
Lord Jesus Christ, my mentor and teacher

Mike Holt

Our Commitment

We are committed to serving the electrical industry with integrity and respect by always searching for the most accurate interpretation of the NEC® and creating the highest quality instructional material that makes learning easy.

We are invested in the idea of changing lives, and build our products with the goal of not only helping you meet your licensing requirements, but also with the goal that this knowledge will improve your expertise in the field and help you throughout your career.

We are committed to building a life-long relationship with you, and to helping you in each stage of your electrical career. Whether you are an apprentice just getting started in the industry, or an electrician preparing to take an exam, we are here to help you. When you need Continuing Education credits to renew your license, we will do everything we can to get our online courses and seminars approved in your state. Or if you are a contractor looking to train your team, we have a solution for you. And if you have advanced to the point where you are now teaching others, we are here to help you build your program and provide tools to make that task easier.

We genuinely care about providing quality electrical training that will help you take your skills to the next level.

Thanks for choosing Mike Holt Enterprises for your electrical training needs. We are here to help you every step of the way and encourage you to contact us so we can be a part of your success.

God bless,

Mike Holt

TABLE OF CONTENTS

Table of Contents

Table of Contents

CHAPTER 3—WIRING METHODS AND MATERIALS

Table of Contents

Table of Contents

ABOUT THIS TEXTBOOK

Mike Holt's Illustrated Guide to Understanding the National Electrical Code®, Volume 1, based on the 2014 NEC®

This edition of *Mike Holt's Illustrated Guide to Understanding the National Electrical Code®, Volume 1* textbook is intended to provide you with the tools necessary to understand the technical requirements of the *National Electrical Code (NEC)*.

The writing style of this textbook is meant to be informative, practical, useful, easy to read, and applicable for everyday use. Just like all of Mike Holt's textbooks, this one contains hundreds of full-color illustrations showing the safety requirements of the *National Electrical Code* in practical use, helping you visualize the *Code* in today's electrical installations.

This illustrated textbook contains cautions regarding possible conflicts or confusing *NEC* requirements, tips on proper electrical installations, and warnings of dangers related to improper electrical installations. In spite of this effort, some rules may still seem unclear or need additional editorial improvement.

We can't eliminate confusing, conflicting, or controversial *Code* requirements, but we do try to put them into sharper focus to help you understand their intended purpose. Sometimes a requirement is confusing and it might be hard to understand its actual application. When this occurs, this textbook will point the situation out in an upfront and straightforward manner. We apologize in advance if that ever seems disrespectful, but our intention is to help the industry understand the current *NEC* as best as possible, point out areas that need refinement, and encourage *Code* users to be a part of the change process that creates a better *NEC* for the future.

The Scope of this Textbook

This textbook, *Mike Holt's Illustrated Guide to Understanding the National Electrical Code, Volume 1* covers the general installation requirements contained in Articles 90 through 480 (*NEC* Chapters 1 through 4), and is written with these stipulations:

1. **Power Systems and Voltage.** All power-supply systems are assumed to be one of the following, unless identified otherwise:

   - 2-wire, single-phase, 120V
   - 3-wire, single-phase, 120/240V
   - 4-wire, three-phase, 120/240V Delta
   - 4-wire, three-phase, 120/208V or 277/480V Wye

2. **Electrical Calculations.** Unless the questions or examples specify three-phase, they're based on a single-phase power supply. In addition, all amperage calculations are rounded to the nearest ampere in accordance with Section 220.5(B).

3. **Conductor Material.** Conductors are assumed to be copper, unless aluminum is identified or specified.

4. **Conductor Sizing.** Conductors are sized based on a THHN/THWN-2 copper conductor terminating on a 75°C terminal in accordance with 110.14(C), unless the question or example indicates otherwise.

5. **Overcurrent Device.** The term "overcurrent device" refers to a molded-case circuit breaker, unless specified otherwise. Where a fuse is specified, it's a single-element type fuse, also known as a "one-time fuse," unless the text specifies otherwise.

This textbook is to be used along with the *NEC*, not as a replacement for it. Be sure to have a copy of the 2014 *National Electrical Code* handy. Compare what's being explained in this textbook to what the *Code* book says, and discuss with others any topics that you find difficult to understand.

You'll notice that we've paraphrased a great deal of the *NEC* wording, and some of the article and section titles appear different from the text in the actual *Code* book. We believe doing so makes it easier to understand the content of the rule, so keep this in mind when comparing this textbook to the actual *NEC*.

This textbook follows the *NEC* format, but it doesn't cover every *Code* requirement. For example, it doesn't include every article, section, subsection, exception, or Informational Note. So don't be concerned if you see that the textbook contains Exception 1 and Exception 3, but not Exception 2.

We hope that as you read through this textbook, you'll allow sufficient time to review the text along with the outstanding graphics and examples, which are invaluable to your understanding.

How to Use This Textbook

The layout of this textbook incorporates special features designed not only to help you navigate easily through the material but to enhance your understanding as well.

Graphics with an icon and green border contain a 2014 *Code* change, with *NEC* text changes underlined in green. Green-bordered graphics with no green underlined text most likely indicate that the change is the removal of some text. Graphics without a colored border support the concept being discussed, but nothing in the graphic was affected by a change for 2014.

Bolded Author's Comments are intended to help you understand the *NEC* material and background information.

Text that's underlined in the chapter color denotes a change in the *Code* for 2014.

Color coding and a modular format make it easy to navigate through each section of the textbook.

Framed white notes contain examples and practical application questions and answers. **Formulas** are easily identifiable in green text in the gray bar.

Light gray sections with a border in the chapter color contain additional background information.

A QR code under the article number can be scanned with a smartphone app to take you to a sample video clip so you can watch Mike and the DVD panel discuss this topic.

Danger, Caution, and Warning icons highlight areas of concern.

Cross-References, Notes, and Exceptions

Cross-References. This textbook contains several *NEC* cross-references to other related *Code* requirements to help you develop a better understanding of how the *NEC* rules relate to one another. These cross-references are indicated by *Code* section numbers in brackets, an example of which is "[90.4]."

Informational Notes. Informational Notes contained in the *NEC* will be identified in this textbook as "Note."

Exceptions. Exceptions contained in this textbook will be identified as "Ex" and not spelled out.

Textbook Corrections

We're committed to providing you the finest product with the fewest errors. We take great care in researching the *NEC* requirements to ensure this textbook is correct, but we're realistic and know that there'll be errors found and reported after this textbook is printed. This can occur because the *NEC* is dramatically changed each *Code* cycle; new articles are added, some are deleted, some are relocated, and many are renumbered.

The last thing we want is for you to have problems finding, communicating, or accessing this information. Any errors found after printing are listed on our website, so if you find an error, first check to see if it's already been corrected by going to www.MikeHolt.com, click on "Books," and then click on "Corrections" (www.MikeHolt.com/book-corrections.htm).

If you believe that there's an error of any kind (typographical, grammatical, technical, or anything else) in this textbook or in the Answer Key and it isn't already listed on the website, e-mail Corrections@MikeHolt.com. Be sure to include the textbook title, page number, and any other pertinent information.

If you have adopted Mike Holt textbooks for use in your classroom you can register for up-to-date Answer Keys that can be downloaded from our website. To register and receive a log-in password, go to our website www.MikeHolt.com, click on "Instructors" in the sidebar of links, and then click on "Answer Keys." On this same page you'll also find instructions for accessing and downloading these Answer Keys. Please note that this feature will only work after you've received a log-in password.

Technical Questions

As you progress through this textbook, you might find that you don't understand every explanation, example, calculation, or comment. Don't become frustrated, and don't get down on yourself. Remember, this is the *National Electrical Code*, and sometimes the best attempt to explain a concept isn't enough to make it perfectly clear. If you're still confused, visit www.MikeHolt.com, and post your question on our free Code Forum for help. The forum is a moderated community of electrical professionals where you can exchange ideas and post technical questions that will be answered by your peers.

QR Codes

What's this symbol? It's a QR code and gives you the ability to use your smartphone to scan the image (using a barcode reader app) and be directed to a website. For example, the QR code to the right (when captured) will direct your smartphone to the Mike Holt Enterprises website. We've included these in various places in our textbook to make it easier for you to go directly to the website page referenced.

Follow the QR Code! When you see a QR code next to a section in the text, scan it with your smartphone to bring it to life. You will be able to watch a video clip that shows Mike and his panel of experts discussing this topic.

These video clips are samples from the DVDs that were created for this book. Whether you're a visual or an auditory learner, watching the DVDs will enhance your knowledge and understanding as you read through the textbook.

Try it here! Scan this QR code and watch the Bloopers clip from the recording of the DVDs to accompany this textbook.

To order the DVDs that accompany this textbook at a discounted price, call our office at 888.632.2633.

Additional Products to Help You Learn

Understanding the 2014 NEC, Volume 1 DVDs

One of the best ways to get the most out of this textbook is to use it in conjunction with the corresponding DVDs. Mike Holt's DVDs provide a 360° view of each topic with specialized commentary from Mike and his panel of industry experts.

To order your copy of the DVDs at a discounted price, call our office at 888.632.2633.

Workbook to Accompany Understanding the National Electrical Code, Volume 1

Mike Holt's study programs are designed to maximize your learning and retention. The additional practice questions and quizzes (over 1,300) in this workbook will solidify your knowledge and give you the confidence you need on the job, or in preparation for your exam.

To order, visit www.MikeHolt.com/14code.

Theory Library

Understanding electrical theory is critical for anyone who works with electricity. This textbook teaches the fundamentals that you need in order to understand and comply with *NEC* rules that govern installations—starting from basic scientific principles, to electrical formulas, to practical applications of electricity.

This library includes:

- *Basic Electrical Theory* textbook
- Electrical Fundamentals and Basic Electricity DVD
- Electrical Circuits, Systems, and Protection DVD
- Alternating Current, Motors, Generators, and Transformers DVD

To order, visit www.MikeHolt.com/theory.

Calculations Library

You must master electrical calculations to be successful in the electrical trade. The textbook contains clear, easy-to-understand graphics that help you fully understand the concepts behind electrical calculations. The detailed DVDs take you step-by-step through the calculations.

This library includes:

- *Electrical Calculations* textbook
- Raceway and Box Calculations DVD
- Conductor Sizing and Protection Calculations DVD
- Motor and Air-Conditioning Calculations DVD
- Voltage-Drop Calculations DVD
- Dwelling Unit Calculations DVD
- Multifamily Dwelling Calculations DVD
- Commercial Calculations DVD
- Transformer Calculations DVD

To order, visit www.MikeHolt.com/calculations.

2014 *Code* Book and Tabs

Whether you prefer the softbound, spiral bound, or the loose-leaf version, everyone should have an updated *Code* book for accurate reference. Placing tabs on *Code* articles, sections, and tables will make it easier for you to use the *NEC*. However, too many tabs will defeat the purpose. Mike's best-selling tabs make organizing your *Code* book easy.

To order your *Code* book and set of tabs visit www.MikeHolt.com/14code, or call 1.888.NEC.CODE (632.2633).

ABOUT THE
NATIONAL ELECTRICAL CODE

The *National Electrical Code* is written for persons who understand electrical terms, theory, safety procedures, and electrical trade practices. These individuals include electricians, electrical contractors, electrical inspectors, electrical engineers, designers, and other qualified persons. The *Code* isn't written to serve as an instructional or teaching manual for untrained individuals [90.1(A)].

Learning to use the *NEC* can be likened to learning the strategy needed to play the game of chess well; it's a great game if you enjoy mental warfare. When learning to play chess, you must first learn the names of the game pieces, how they're placed on the board, and how each one is moved.

Once you understand the fundamentals, you're ready to start playing the game. Unfortunately, at this point all you can do is make crude moves, because you really don't understand how all the information works together. To play chess well, you'll need to learn how to use your knowledge by working on subtle strategies before you can work your way up to the more intriguing and complicated moves.

The *Code* is updated every three years to accommodate new electrical products and materials, changing technologies, improved installation techniques, and to make editorial refinements to improve readability and application. While the uniform adoption of each new edition of the *NEC* is the best approach for all involved in the electrical industry, many inspection jurisdictions modify the *Code* when it's adopted. To further complicate this situation, the *NEC* allows the authority having jurisdiction, typically the "Electrical Inspector," the flexibility to waive specific *Code* requirements, and to permit alternative methods. This is only allowed when he or she is assured the completed electrical installation is equivalent in establishing and maintaining effective safety [90.4].

Keeping up with requirements of the *Code* should be the goal of everyone involved in the safety of electrical installations. This includes electrical installers, contractors, owners, inspectors, engineers, instructors, and others concerned with electrical installations.

About the 2014 *NEC*

The actual process of changing the *Code* takes about two years, and it involves hundreds of individuals making an effort to have the *NEC* as current and accurate as possible. Let's review how this process works:

Step 1. Proposals—November, 2011. Anybody can submit a proposal to change the *Code* before the proposal closing date. Thousands of proposals were submitted to modify the 2011 *NEC* and create the 2014 *Code*. Of these proposals, several hundred rules were revised that significantly affect the electrical industry. Some changes were editorial revisions, while others were more significant, such as new articles, sections, exceptions, and Informational Notes.

Step 2. *Code*-Making Panel(s) Review Proposals—January, 2012. All *Code* change proposals were reviewed by *Code*-Making Panels. There were 19 panels in the 2014 revision process who voted to accept, reject, or modify proposals.

Step 3. Report on Proposals (ROP)—July, 2012. The voting of the *Code*-Making Panels on the proposals was published for public review in a document called the "Report on Proposals," frequently referred to as the "ROP."

Step 4. Public Comments—October, 2012. Once the ROP was available, public comments were submitted asking the *Code*-Making Panel members to revise their earlier actions on change proposals, based on new information. The closing date for "Comments" was October, 2012.

Step 5. Comments Reviewed by *Code* Panels—December, 2012. The *Code*-Making Panels met again to review, discuss, and vote on public comments.

Step 6. Report on Comments (ROC)—March, 2013. The voting on the "Comments" was published for public review in a document called the "Report on Comments," frequently referred to as the "ROC."

Step 7. Electrical Section—June, 2013. The NFPA Electrical Section discussed and reviewed the work of the *Code*-Making Panels. The Electrical Section developed recommendations on last-minute motions to revise the proposed *NEC* draft that would be presented at the NFPA's annual meeting.

Step 8. NFPA Annual Meeting—June, 2013. The 2014 *NEC* was voted by the NFPA members to approve the action of the *Code*-Making Panels at the annual meeting, after a number of motions (often called "floor actions" or "NITMAMs") were voted on.

Step 9. Standards Council Review Appeals and Approves the 2014 *NEC*—July, 2013. The NFPA Standards Council reviewed the record of the *Code*-making process and approved publication of the 2014 *NEC*.

Step 10. 2014 *NEC* Published—September, 2013. The 2014 *National Electrical Code* was published, following the NFPA Board of Directors review of appeals.

> **Author's Comment:** Proposals and comments can be submitted online at the NFPA website (www.nfpa.org). From the homepage, click on "Codes and Standards", then find NFPA 70 (*National Electrical Code*). From there, follow the on screen instructions to download the proposal form. The deadline for proposals to create the 2017 *National Electrical Code* will be around November of 2014. If you would like to see something changed in the *Code*, you're encouraged to participate in the process.

Not a Game

Electrical work isn't a game, and it must be taken very seriously. Learning the basics of electricity, important terms and concepts, as well as the basic layout of the *NEC* gives you just enough knowledge to be dangerous. There are thousands of specific and unique applications of electrical installations, and the *Code* doesn't cover every one of them. To safely apply the *NEC*, you must understand the purpose of a rule and how it affects the safety aspects of the installation.

NEC Terms and Concepts

The *NEC* contains many technical terms, so it's crucial for *Code* users to understand their meanings and their applications. If you don't understand a term used in a *Code* rule, it will be impossible to properly apply the *NEC* requirement. Be sure you understand that Article 100 defines the terms that apply to two or more *Code* articles. For example, the term "Dwelling Unit" is found in many articles; if you don't know what a dwelling unit is, how can you apply the requirements for it?

In addition, many articles have terms unique for that specific article and definitions of those terms are only applicable for that given article. For example, Section 250.2 contains the definitions of terms that only apply to Article 250—Grounding and Bonding.

Small Words, Grammar, and Punctuation

It's not only the technical words that require close attention, because even the simplest of words can make a big difference to the application of a rule. The word "or" can imply alternate choices for wiring methods, while "and" can mean an additional requirement. Let's not forget about grammar and punctuation. The location of a comma can dramatically change the requirement of a rule.

Slang Terms or Technical Jargon

Electricians, engineers, and other trade-related professionals use slang terms or technical jargon that isn't shared by all. This makes it very difficult to communicate because not everybody understands the intent or application of those slang terms. So where possible, be sure you use the proper word, and don't use a word if you don't understand its definition and application. For example, lots of electricians use the term "pigtail" when describing the short conductor for the connection of a receptacle, switch, luminaire, or equipment. Although they may understand it, not everyone does.

NEC Style and Layout

Before we get into the details of the *NEC*, we need to take a few moments to understand its style and layout. Understanding the structure and writing style of the *Code* is very important before it can be used and applied effectively. The *National Electrical Code* is organized into ten major components.

1. Table of Contents
2. Article 90 (Introduction to the *Code*)
3. Chapters 1 through 9 (major categories)
4. Articles 90 through 840 (individual subjects)
5. Parts (divisions of an article)
6. Sections and Tables (*NEC* requirements)
7. Exceptions (*Code* permissions)
8. Informational Notes (explanatory material)
9. Annexes (information)
10. Index

1. Table of Contents. The Table of Contents displays the layout of the chapters, articles, and parts as well as the page numbers. It's an excellent resource and should be referred to periodically to observe the interrelationship of the various *NEC* components. When attempting to locate the rules for a particular situation, knowledgeable *Code* users often go first to the Table of Contents to quickly find the specific *NEC* Part that applies.

2. Introduction. The *NEC* begins with Article 90, the introduction to the *Code*. It contains the purpose of the *NEC*, what's covered and what isn't covered along with how the *Code* is arranged. It also gives information on enforcement and how mandatory and permissive rules are written as well as how explanatory material is included. Article 90 also includes information on formal interpretations, examination of equipment for safety, wiring planning, and information about formatting units of measurement.

3. Chapters. There are nine chapters, each of which is divided into articles. The articles fall into one of four groupings: General Requirements (Chapters 1 through 4), Specific Requirements (Chapters 5 through 7), Communications Systems (Chapter 8), and Tables (Chapter 9).

Chapter 1—General
Chapter 2—Wiring and Protection
Chapter 3—Wiring Methods and Materials
Chapter 4—Equipment for General Use
Chapter 5—Special Occupancies
Chapter 6—Special Equipment
Chapter 7—Special Conditions
Chapter 8—Communications Systems (Telephone, Data, Satellite, Cable TV and Broadband)
Chapter 9—Tables–Conductor and Raceway Specifications

4. Articles. The *NEC* contains approximately 140 articles, each of which covers a specific subject. For example:

Article 110—General Requirements
Article 250—Grounding and Bonding
Article 300—General Requirements for Wiring Methods and Materials
Article 430—Motors and Motor Controllers
Article 500—Hazardous (Classified) Locations
Article 680—Swimming Pools, Fountains, and Similar Installations
Article 725—Remote-Control, Signaling, and Power-Limited Circuits
Article 800—Communications Circuits

5. Parts. Larger articles are subdivided into parts. Because the parts of a *Code* article aren't included in the section numbers, we have a tendency to forget what "part" the *NEC* rule is relating to. For example, Table 110.34(A) contains working space clearances for electrical equipment. If we aren't careful, we might think this table applies to all electrical installations, but Table 110.34(A) is located in Part III, which only contains requirements for "Over 600 Volts, Nominal" installations. The rules for working clearances for electrical equipment for systems 600V, nominal, or less are contained in Table 110.26(A)(1), which is located in Part II—600 Volts, Nominal, or Less.

6. Sections and Tables.

Sections. Each *NEC* rule is called a "*Code* Section." A *Code* section may be broken down into subsections by letters in parentheses (A), (B), and so on. Numbers in parentheses (1), (2), and so forth, may further break down a subsection, and lowercase letters (a), (b), and so on, further break the rule down to the third level. For example, the rule requiring all receptacles in a dwelling unit bathroom to be GFCI protected is contained in Section 210.8(A)(1). Section 210.8(A)(1) is located in Chapter 2, Article 210, Section 8, Subsection (A), Sub-subsection (1).

Many in the industry incorrectly use the term "Article" when referring to a *Code* section. For example, they say "Article 210.8," when they should say "Section 210.8." Section numbers in this textbook are shown without the word "Section," unless they begin a sentence. For example, Section 210.8(A) is shown as simply 210.8(A).

Tables. Many *NEC* requirements are contained within tables, which are lists of *Code* rules placed in a systematic arrangement. The titles of the tables are extremely important; you must read them carefully in order to understand the contents, applications, limitations, and so forth, of each table in the *NEC*. Many times notes are provided in or below a table; be sure to read them as well since they're also part of the requirement. For example, Note 1 for Table 300.5 explains how to measure the cover when burying cables and raceways, and Note 5 explains what to do if solid rock is encountered.

7. Exceptions. Exceptions are *Code* requirements or permissions that provide an alternative method to a specific rule. There are two types of exceptions—mandatory and permissive. When a rule has several exceptions, those exceptions with mandatory requirements are listed before the permissive exceptions.

Mandatory Exceptions. A mandatory exception uses the words "shall" or "shall not." The word "shall" in an exception means that if you're using the exception, you're required to do it in a particular way. The phrase "shall not" means it isn't permitted.

Permissive Exceptions. A permissive exception uses words such as "shall be permitted," which means it's acceptable (but not mandatory) to do it in this way.

8. Informational Notes. An Informational Note contains explanatory material intended to clarify a rule or give assistance, but it isn't a *Code* requirement.

9. Annexes. Annexes aren't a part of the *NEC* requirements, and are included in the *Code* for informational purposes only.

Annex A. Product Safety Standards

Annex B. Application Information for Ampacity Calculation

Annex C. Raceway Fill Tables for Conductors and Fixture Wires of the Same Size

Annex D. Examples

Annex E. Types of Construction

Annex F. Critical Operations Power Systems (COPS)

Annex G. Supervisory Control and Data Acquisition (SCADA)

Annex H. Administration and Enforcement

Annex I. Recommended Tightening Torques

Annex J. ADA Standards for Accessible Design

10. Index. The Index at the back of the *Code* book is helpful in locating a specific rule.

Changes to the *NEC* since the previous edition(s), are identified by shading, but rules that have been relocated aren't identified as a change. A bullet symbol "•" is located on the margin to indicate the location of a rule that was deleted from a previous edition. New articles contain a vertical line in the margin of the page.

Different Interpretations

Some electricians, contractors, instructors, inspectors, engineers, and others enjoy the challenge of discussing the *NEC* requirements, hopefully in a positive and productive manner. This give-and-take is important to the process of better understanding the *Code* requirements and application(s). However, if you're going to participate in an *NEC* discussion, please don't spout out what you think without having the actual *Code* book in your hand. The professional way of discussing an *NEC* requirement is by referring to a specific section, rather than talking in vague generalities.

How to Locate a Specific Requirement

How to go about finding what you're looking for in the *Code* book depends, to some degree, on your experience with the *NEC*. *Code* experts typically know the requirements so well they just go to the correct rule without any outside assistance. The Table of Contents might be the only thing very experienced *NEC* users need to locate the requirement they're looking for. On the other hand, average *Code* users should

use all of the tools at their disposal, including the Table of Contents and the Index.

Table of Contents. Let's work out a simple example: What *NEC* rule specifies the maximum number of disconnects permitted for a service? If you're an experienced *Code* user, you'll know Article 230 applies to "Services," and because this article is so large, it's divided up into multiple parts (actually eight parts). With this knowledge, you can quickly go to the Table of Contents and see it lists the Service Equipment Disconnecting Means requirements in Part VI.

> **Author's Comment:** The number 70 precedes all page numbers because the *NEC* is NFPA Standard Number 70.

Index. If you use the Index, which lists subjects in alphabetical order, to look up the term "service disconnect," you'll see there's no listing. If you try "disconnecting means," then "services," you'll find that the Index indicates that the rule is located in Article 230, Part VI. Because the *NEC* doesn't give a page number in the Index, you'll need to use the Table of Contents to find it, or flip through the *Code* book to Article 230, then continue to flip through pages until you find Part VI.

Many people complain that the *NEC* only confuses them by taking them in circles. As you gain experience in using the *Code* and deepen your understanding of words, terms, principles, and practices, you'll find the *NEC* much easier to understand and use than you originally thought.

Customizing Your *Code* Book

One way to increase your comfort level with the *Code* book is to customize it to meet your needs. You can do this by highlighting and underlining important *NEC* requirements, and by attaching tabs to important pages. Be aware that if you're using your *Code* book to take an exam, some exam centers don't allow markings of any type.

Highlighting. As you read through this textbook, be sure you highlight those requirements in the *Code* that are the most important or relevant to you. Use one color for general interest and a different one for important requirements you want to find quickly. Be sure to highlight terms in the Index and the Table of Contents as you use them.

Underlining. Underline or circle key words and phrases in the *NEC* with a red pen (not a lead pencil) and use a short ruler or other straightedge to keep lines straight and neat. This is a very handy way to make important requirements stand out. A short ruler or other straightedge also comes in handy for locating specific information in the many *Code* tables.

ABOUT THE AUTHOR

Mike Holt—Author

Founder and President
Mike Holt Enterprises
Groveland, FL
www.MikeHolt.com

Mike Holt worked his way up through the electrical trade. He began as an apprentice electrician and became one of the most recognized experts in the world as it relates to electrical power installations. He's worked as a journeyman electrician, master electrician, and electrical contractor. Mike's experience in the real world gives him a unique understanding of how the *NEC* relates to electrical installations from a practical standpoint. You'll find his writing style to be direct, nontechnical, and powerful.

Did you know Mike didn't finish high school? So if you struggled in high school or didn't finish at all, don't let it get you down. However, realizing that success depends on one's continuing pursuit of education, Mike immediately attained his GED, and ultimately attended the University of Miami's Graduate School for a Master's degree in Business Administration.

Mike resides in Central Florida, is the father of seven children, has five grandchildren, and enjoys many outside interests and activities. He's a nine-time National Barefoot Water-Ski Champion (1988, 1999, 2005–2009, 2012–2013). He's set many national records and continues to train year-round at a World competition level (www.barefootwaterskier.com).

What sets him apart from some is his commitment to living a balanced lifestyle; placing God first, family, career, then self.

Special Acknowledgments—First, I want to thank God for my godly wife who's always by my side and my children, Belynda, Melissa, Autumn, Steven, Michael, Meghan, and Brittney.

A special thank you must be sent to the staff at the National Fire Protection Association (NFPA), publishers of the *NEC*—in particular Jeff Sargent for his assistance in answering my many *Code* questions over the years. Jeff, you're a "first class" guy, and I admire your dedication and commitment to helping others understand the *NEC*. Other former NFPA staff members I would like to thank include John Caloggero, Joe Ross, and Dick Murray for their help in the past.

A personal thank you goes to Sarina, my long-time friend and office manager. It's been wonderful working side-by-side with you for over 25 years nurturing this company's growth from its small beginnings.

ABOUT THE ILLUSTRATOR

Mike Culbreath—Illustrator

Graphic Illustrator
Alden, MI
www.MikeHolt.com

Mike Culbreath devoted his career to the electrical industry and worked his way up from an apprentice electrician to master electrician. He started in the electrical field doing residential and light commercial construction. He later did service work and custom electrical installations. While working as a journeyman electrician, he suffered a serious on-the-job knee injury. As part of his rehabilitation, Mike completed courses at Mike Holt Enterprises. and then passed the exam to receive his Master Electrician's license. In 1986, with a keen interest in continuing education for electricians, he joined the staff to update material and began illustrating Mike Holt's textbooks and magazine articles.

He started with simple hand-drawn diagrams and cut-and-paste graphics. When frustrated by the limitations of that style of illustrating, he took a company computer home to learn how to operate some basic computer graphic software. Becoming aware that computer graphics offered a lot of flexibility for creating illustrations, Mike took every computer graphics class and seminar he could to help develop his computer graphic skills. He's now worked as an illustrator and editor with the company for over 25 years and, as Mike Holt has proudly acknowledged, has helped to transform his words and visions into lifelike graphics.

Originally from South Florida, Mike now lives in northern lower Michigan where he enjoys kayaking, photography, and cooking, but his real passion is his horses.

Mike loves spending time with his children Dawn and Mac and his grandchildren Jonah and Kieley.

Special Acknowledgments—I would like to thank Ryan Jackson, an outstanding and very knowledgeable *Code* guy, and Eric Stromberg, an electrical engineer and super geek (and I mean that in the most complimentary manner, this guy is brilliant), for helping me keep our graphics as technically correct as possible.

I also want to give a special thank you to Cathleen Kwas for making me look good with her outstanding layout design and typesetting skills and Toni Culbreath who proofreads all of my material. I would also like to acknowledge Belynda Holt Pinto, our Chief Operations Officer and the rest of the outstanding staff at Mike Holt Enterprises, for all the hard work they do to help produce and distribute these outstanding products.

And last but not least, I need to give a special thank you to Mike Holt for not firing me over 25 years ago when I "borrowed" one of his computers and took it home to begin the process of learning how to do computer illustrations. He gave me the opportunity and time needed to develop my computer graphic skills. He's been an amazing friend and mentor since I met him as a student many years ago. Thanks for believing in me and allowing me to be part of the Mike Holt Enterprises family.

Editorial and Production Team

A special thanks goes to **Toni Culbreath** for her outstanding contribution to this project. She worked tirelessly to proofread and edit this publication. Her attention to detail and dedication is irreplaceable.

Many thanks to **Cathleen Kwas** who did the design, layout, and production of this book. Her desire to create the best possible product for our customers is greatly appreciated.

Also, thanks to **Paula Birchfield** who was the Production Coordinator of the textbook. She helped keep everything flowing and tied up all the loose ends.

Thanks to **Bruce Marcho** for doing such an excellent job recording, editing, and producing our DVDs. Bruce has played a vital role in the production of our products for over 25 years.

Video Team

Victor Ammons

Senior Electrical Engineer
Hillsborough, NJ

Victor Ammons was born in North Carolina, but has lived primarily in New Jersey since the age of five. He spent his high school and college vacation times working in a small, family owned electrical contracting firm. Vic married his high school sweetheart after sophomore year at North Carolina State University, from which both graduated with honors two years later. After four years in the Army, during which time their first child was born in Germany, Vic and Anne alternated getting MBA degrees. They now have three married children and five grandchildren.

After a number of years of running the family contracting business while his father's health declined, Vic trained and turned the business over to his brother-in-law. He then returned to the engineering field in which he had trained. Vic is a registered Professional Engineer in New Jersey and has served in an engineering management role for several engineering and architectural/engineering firms. He is now a senior electrical engineer for Jacobs in Morristown, New Jersey.

Vic and Anne now reside in west central New Jersey in an area with a few dozen families among over a thousand acres of woodlands. Yes, there are still woodlands in New Jersey; we haven't gotten around to paving them all yet. Vic and Anne, who will celebrate their 45th anniversary in 2014, are avid square and round dancers, and are active in several clubs. Vic is also a woodworker and an amateur beekeeper. Both are active in several capacities in their church.

Daniel Brian House

Dan House Electric, Inc.
Ocala, FL
www.DanHouseElectric.com

Brian House is a high-energy entrepreneur with a passion for doing business the right way. Brian is currently the CEO of Dan House Electric, Inc., an unlimited electrical contracting company based in Florida and working throughout the southeast United States.

Brian has been involved in varying aspects of electrical contracting and energy conservation since the 1990s. He has a passion for constantly improving the combinations of technology offered to his customers, whether it is designing energy-efficient lighting retrofits, exploring "green" biomass generators, or partnering with solar energy companies as their preferred installer. Brian has experienced the ups and downs of electrical contracting and enjoys the challenges of design build projects.

Passionate about helping others, he regularly engages with the youth of the local community to motivate them into exploring their future.

Brian and his wife Carissa have shared the joy of their four children and over 30 foster children during a happy 16 years of marriage. When not at work or church, he can be found racing mountain bikes with his kids or on the action-packed intercoastals as an avid fly fisherman.

Ryan Jackson

Electrical Inspector
Draper City, UT

Ryan Jackson is an electrical consultant in the Salt Lake City, Utah, area who began his career as a carpenter while in high school. He began doing electrical work when he was 18 and, at the age of 23, Ryan landed his first job as an electrical inspector and subsequently became certified in building, plumbing, and mechanical inspection (commercial and residential), as well as building and electrical plan review. Two years after becoming an inspector, he was approached by a friend in the area asking him to fill in for him at an electrical seminar. After his first class Ryan was hooked, and is now a highly sought after seminar instructor. He's taught in several states, and loves helping people increase their understanding of the *Code*.

Ryan met Mike in 2005 and helped with his 2005 *Understanding the NEC, Volume 2* videos and textbooks. He believes there are only a few opportunities that can change a person's life and career—and meeting Mike was one of them.

When Ryan isn't working, he can often be found in his garage turning wood on his lathe, or in the kitchen where he enjoys wine making. Ryan married his high school sweetheart, Sharie, and they have two beautiful children together: Kaitlynn and Aaron.

Eric Stromberg

Electrical Engineer/Instructor
Stromberg Engineering, Inc.
Los Alamos, NM
www.strombergengineering.com.

Eric Stromberg worked as a journeyman electrician, before and during the time he attended college. When he graduated with a degree in Electrical Engineering in 1982, he took a job as an electronics technician. Eric became a licensed fire alarm installation superintendent and spent the next seven years installing and maintaining life safety systems in high-rise buildings.

In 1989, he went to work for Dow Chemical, where he designed power distribution systems for world-class industrial facilities. Eric began teaching *National Electrical Code* classes to engineers in 1997. He received his professional engineering license, for the State of Texas, in 2003 and, in 2005, started Stromberg Engineering.

In 2013, Eric retired from Dow Chemical and now lives in the mountains of northern New Mexico. Eric's oldest daughter, Ainsley, lives in Boston, Massachusetts with her husband Nathan. His son, Austin, is in the Air Force and is stationed at Minot, North Dakota. His youngest daughter, Brieanna, is a singer/songwriter who lives in Austin, Texas.

ARTICLE
90

INTRODUCTION TO THE
NATIONAL ELECTRICAL CODE

Introduction to Article 90—Introduction to the *National Electrical Code*

Many *NEC* violations and misunderstandings wouldn't occur if people doing the work simply understood Article 90. For example, many people see *Code* requirements as performance standards. In fact, the *NEC* requirements are bare minimums for safety. This is exactly the stance electrical inspectors, insurance companies, and courts take when making a decision regarding electrical design or installation.

Article 90 opens by saying the *NEC* isn't intended as a design specification or instruction manual. The *National Electrical Code* has one purpose only, and that's the "practical safeguarding of persons and property from hazards arising from the use of electricity." The necessity of carefully studying the *NEC* rules can't be overemphasized, and the role of textbooks such as this one is to help in that undertaking. Understanding where to find the rules in the *Code* that apply to the installation is invaluable. Rules in several different articles often apply to even a simple installation.

Article 90 then describes the scope and arrangement of the *NEC*. The balance of this article provides the reader with information essential to understanding the *Code* rules.

Typically, electrical work requires you to understand the first four chapters of the *NEC* which apply generally, plus have a working knowledge of the Chapter 9 tables. That understanding begins with Article 90. Chapters 5, 6, and 7 make up a large portion of the *Code*, but they apply to special occupancies, special equipment, or other special conditions. They build on, modify, or amend the rules in the first four chapters. Chapter 8 contains the requirements for communications systems, such as telephone systems, antenna wiring, CATV, and network-powered broadband systems. Communications systems aren't subject to the general requirements of Chapters 1 through 4, or the special requirements of Chapters 5 through 7, unless there's a specific reference in Chapter 8 to a rule in Chapters 1 through 7.

90.1 Purpose of the *NEC*

(A) Practical Safeguarding. The purpose of the *NEC* is to ensure that electrical systems are installed in a manner that protects people and property by minimizing the risks associated with the use of electricity. It isn't a design specification standard or instruction manual for the untrained and unqualified. Figure 90–1

Author's Comment:

- The *Code* is intended to be used by those skilled and knowledgeable in electrical theory, electrical systems, construction, and the installation and operation of electrical equipment.

(B) Adequacy. The *Code* contains requirements considered necessary for a safe electrical installation. If an electrical system is installed in compliance with the *NEC*, it'll be essentially free from electrical hazards. The *Code* is a safety standard, not a design guide.

Figure 90–1

Figure 90–3

NEC requirements aren't intended to ensure the electrical installation will be efficient, convenient, adequate for good service, or suitable for future expansion. Specific items of concern, such as electrical energy management, maintenance, and power quality issues aren't within the scope of the *Code*. Figure 90–2

Figure 90–2

Note: Hazards in electrical systems often occur because circuits are overloaded or not properly installed in accordance with the *NEC*. These often occur if the initial wiring didn't provide reasonable provisions for system changes or for the increase in the use of electricity. **Figure 90–3**

Author's Comment:

- See the definition of "Overload" in Article 100.

- The *NEC* doesn't require electrical systems to be designed or installed to accommodate future loads. However, the electrical designer (typically an electrical engineer) is concerned with not only ensuring electrical safety (*Code* compliance), but also with ensuring the system meets the customers' needs, both of today and in the near future. To satisfy customers' needs, electrical systems are often designed and installed above the minimum requirements contained in the *NEC*. But just remember, if you're taking an exam, licensing exams are based on your understanding of the minimum *Code* requirements.

(C) Relation to International Standards. The requirements of the *NEC* address the fundamental safety principles contained in the International Electrotechnical Commission (IEC) standards, including protection against electric shock, adverse thermal effects, overcurrent, fault currents, and overvoltage. Figure 90–4

Author's Comment:

- The *NEC* is used in Chile, Ecuador, Peru, and the Philippines. It's also the *Electrical Code* for Colombia, Costa Rica, Mexico, Panama, Puerto Rico, and Venezuela. Because of these adoptions, it's available in Spanish from the National Fire Protection Association, 617.770.3000, or www.NFPA.org.

NEC Relation to International Standards
90.1(C) and Note

The *NEC* addresses the safety principles contained in the IEC standard such as:
• Protection against electric shock
• Adverse thermal effects
• Overcurrent
• Fault currents
• Overvoltage

Figure 90–4

90.2 Scope of the *NEC*

(A) What Is Covered. The *NEC* contains requirements necessary for the proper installation of electrical conductors, equipment, cables, and raceways for power, signaling, fire alarm, optical cable, and communications systems for: Figure 90–5

Scope of the *NEC*
90.2(A)

The *NEC* contains requirements for the installation of electrical conductors, equipment, cables, and raceways for power, signaling, fire alarm, optical cable, and communications systems.

Figure 90–5

(1) Public and private premises, including buildings, mobile homes, recreational vehicles, and floating buildings. Figure 90–6

Scope of the *NEC* - Public and Private Premises
90.2(A)(1) and (2)

Public lighting on private property must be installed in accordance with the *NEC* even if installed by an electric utility.

The *NEC* covers installations in or on:
(1) Public and private premises, and
(2) Yards, lots, parking lots, carnivals and industrial structures.

Figure 90–6

(2) Yards, lots, parking lots, carnivals, and industrial substations.

(3) Conductors and equipment connected to the utility supply.

(4) Installations used by an electric utility, such as office buildings, warehouses, garages, machine shops, recreational buildings, and other electric utility buildings that aren't an integral part of a utility's generating plant, substation, or control center. Figure 90–7

Scope of the *NEC* - Utility Buildings
90.2(A)(4)

Generating Plant

Warehouse

Business Office

Buildings used by the electric utility, such as offices, warehouses, garages, and machine shops are covered by the *Code*.

Figure 90–7

(B) What Isn't Covered. The *NEC* doesn't apply to:

(1) Transportation Vehicles. The *NEC* doesn't apply to installations in cars, trucks, boats, ships and watercraft, planes, electric trains, or underground mines.

(2) Mining Equipment. The *NEC* doesn't apply to installations underground in mines and self-propelled mobile surface mining machinery and its attendant electrical trailing cables.

(3) Railways. The *NEC* doesn't apply to railway power, signaling, and communications wiring.

(4) Communications Utilities. If the installation is under the exclusive control of the communications utility, the installation requirements of the *NEC* don't apply to the communications (telephone), Community Antenna Television (CATV), or network-powered broadband utility equipment located in building spaces used exclusively for these purposes, or located outdoors if the installation is under the exclusive control of the communications utility. Figures 90–8 and 90–9

Figure 90–8

Author's Comment:

- Interior wiring for communications systems, not in building spaces used exclusively for these purposes, must be installed in accordance with the following Chapter 8 Articles:

  □ Telephone and Data, Article 800
  □ CATV, Article 820
  □ Network-Powered Broadband, Article 830

Figure 90–9

(5) Electric Utilities. The *NEC* doesn't apply to electrical installations under the exclusive control of an electric utility where such installations:

  a. Consist of utility installed service drops or service laterals under their exclusive control. Figure 90–10

Figure 90–10

  b. Are on property owned or leased by the electric utility for the purpose of generation, transformation, transmission, distribution, or metering of electric energy. Figure 90–11

Figure 90–11

Author's Comment:

■ Luminaires located in legally established easements, or rights-of-way, such as at poles supporting transmission or distribution lines, are exempt from the *NEC*. However, if the electric utility provides site and public lighting on private property, then the installation must comply with the *Code* [90.2(A)(4)].

c. Are located on legally established easements, or rights-of-way. Figure 90–12

Figure 90–12

d. Are located by other written agreements either designated by or recognized by public service commissions, utility commissions, or other regulatory agencies having jurisdiction for such installations; limited to installations for the purpose of communications, metering, generation, control, transformation, transmission, or distribution of electric energy where legally established easements or rights-of-way can't be obtained. These installations are limited to federal lands, Native American reservations through the U.S. Department of the Interior Bureau of Indian Affairs, military bases, lands controlled by port authorities and state agencies and departments, and lands owned by railroads.

Note to 90.2(B)(4) and (5): Utilities include entities that install, operate, and maintain communications systems (telephone, CATV, Internet, satellite, or data services) or electric supply (generation, transmission, or distribution systems) and are designated or recognized by governmental law or regulation by public service/utility commissions. Utilities may be subject to compliance with codes and standards covering their regulated activities as adopted under governmental law or regulation.

90.3 *Code* Arrangement

The *Code* is divided into an introduction and nine chapters. Figure 90–13

Code Arrangement 90.3

General Requirements
- Ch 1 - General
- Ch 2 - Wiring and Protection
- Ch 3 - Wiring Methods & Materials
- Ch 4 - Equipment for General Use

Chapters 1 through 4 generally apply to all applications.

Special Requirements
- Chapter 5 - Special Occupancies
- Chapter 6 - Special Equipment
- Chapter 7 - Special Conditions

Chs 5 through 7 can supplement or modify the general requirements of Chapters 1 through 4.

- Ch 8 - Communications Systems
Ch 8 requirements aren't subject to requirements in Chapters 1 through 7, unless there's a specific reference in Ch 8 to a rule in Chapters 1 through 7.

- Chapter 9 - Tables
Ch 9 tables are applicable as referenced in the *NEC* and are used for calculating raceway sizes, conductor fill, and voltage drop.

- Annexes A through J
Annexes are for information only and aren't enforceable.

The *NEC* is divided into an introduction and nine chapters, followed by informational annexes.

Copyright 2014, www.MikeHolt.com

Figure 90–13

General Requirements. The requirements contained in Chapters 1, 2, 3, and 4 apply to all installations.

Author's Comment:

■ These first four chapters may be thought of as the foundation for the rest of the *Code*, and are the main focus of this textbook.

Special Requirements. The requirements contained in Chapters 5, 6, and 7 apply to special occupancies, special equipment, or other special conditions. These chapters can supplement or modify the requirements in Chapters 1 through 4.

Communications Systems. Chapter 8 contains the requirements for communications systems, such as telephone systems, antenna wiring, CATV, and network-powered broadband systems. Communications systems aren't subject to the general requirements of Chapters 1 through 4, or the special requirements of Chapters 5 through 7, unless there's a specific reference in Chapter 8 to a rule in Chapters 1 through 7.

Author's Comment:

■ An example of how Chapter 8 works is in the rules for working space about equipment. The typical 3 ft working space isn't required in front of communications equipment, because Table 110.26(A)(1) isn't referenced in Chapter 8.

Tables. Chapter 9 consists of tables applicable as referenced in the *NEC*. The tables are used to calculate raceway sizing, conductor fill, the radius of raceway bends, and conductor voltage drop.

Annexes. Annexes aren't part of the *Code*, but are included for informational purposes. There are ten Annexes:

- Annex A. Product Safety Standards
- Annex B. Application Information for Ampacity Calculation
- Annex C. Raceway Fill Tables for Conductors and Fixture Wires of the Same Size
- Annex D. Examples
- Annex E. Types of Construction
- Annex F. Critical Operations Power Systems (COPS)
- Annex G. Supervisory Control and Data Acquisition (SCADA)
- Annex H. Administration and Enforcement
- Annex I. Recommended Tightening Torques
- Annex J. ADA Standards for Accessible Design

90.4 Enforcement

The *Code* is intended to be suitable for enforcement by governmental bodies that exercise legal jurisdiction over electrical installations for power, lighting, signaling circuits, and communications systems, such as: Figure 90–14

Figure 90–14

Signaling circuits which include:

- Article 725 Class 1, Class 2, and Class 3 Remote-Control, Signaling, and Power-Limited Circuits
- Article 760 Fire Alarm Systems
- Article 770 Optical Fiber Cables and Raceways

Communications systems which include:

- Article 810 Radio and Television Equipment (satellite dish and antenna)
- Article 820 Community Antenna Television and Radio Distribution Systems (coaxial cable)

Author's Comment:

■ The installation requirements for signaling circuits and communications circuits are covered in Mike Holt's *Understanding the National Electrical Code, Volume 2* textbook.

The enforcement of the *NEC* is the responsibility of the authority having jurisdiction (AHJ), who is responsible for interpreting requirements, approving equipment and materials, waiving *Code* requirements, and ensuring equipment is installed in accordance with listing instructions.

Author's Comment:

- See the definition of "Authority Having Jurisdiction" in Article 100.

Interpretation of the Requirements. The authority having jurisdiction is responsible for interpreting the *NEC*, but his or her decisions must be based on a specific *Code* requirement. If an installation is rejected, the authority having jurisdiction is legally responsible for informing the installer of the specific *NEC* rule that was violated. Figure 90–15

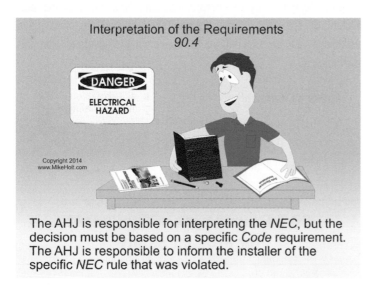

The AHJ is responsible for interpreting the *NEC*, but the decision must be based on a specific *Code* requirement. The AHJ is responsible to inform the installer of the specific *NEC* rule that was violated.

Figure 90–15

Author's Comment:

- The art of getting along with the authority having jurisdiction consists of doing good work and knowing what the *Code* actually says (as opposed to what you only think it says). It's also useful to know how to choose your battles when the inevitable disagreement does occur.

Approval of Equipment and Materials. Only the authority having jurisdiction has authority to approve the installation of equipment and materials. Typically, the authority having jurisdiction will approve equipment listed by a product testing organization, such as Underwriters Laboratories, Inc. (UL). The *NEC* doesn't require all equipment to be listed, but many state and local AHJs do. See 90.7, 110.2, 110.3, and the definitions for "Approved," "Identified," "Labeled," and "Listed" in Article 100. Figure 90–16

Only the AHJ has the authority to approve equipment and materials. Approval is typically based on product listing.

Figure 90–16

Author's Comment:

- According to the *NEC*, the authority having jurisdiction determines the approval of equipment. This means he or she can reject an installation of listed equipment and can approve the use of unlisted equipment. Given our highly litigious society, approval of unlisted equipment is becoming increasingly difficult to obtain.

Approval of Alternate Means. By special permission, the authority having jurisdiction may approve alternate methods where it's assured equivalent safety can be achieved and maintained.

Author's Comment:

- Special permission is defined in Article 100 as the written consent of the authority having jurisdiction.

Waiver of New Product Requirements. If the current *NEC* requires products that aren't yet available at the time the *Code* is adopted, the authority having jurisdiction can allow products that were acceptable in the previous *Code* to continue to be used.

Author's Comment:

■ Sometimes it takes years before testing laboratories establish product standards for new *NEC* requirements, and then it takes time before manufacturers can design, manufacture, and distribute those products to the marketplace.

90.5 Mandatory Requirements and Explanatory Material

(A) Mandatory Requirements. In the *NEC* the words "shall" or "shall not," indicate a mandatory requirement.

Author's Comment:

■ For the ease of reading this textbook, the word "shall" has been replaced with the word "must," and the words "shall not" have been replaced with "must not." Remember that in many places, we'll paraphrase the *Code* instead of providing exact quotes, to make it easier to read and understand.

(B) Permissive Requirements. When the *Code* uses "shall be permitted" it means the identified actions are permitted but not required, and the authority having jurisdiction isn't permitted to restrict an installation from being completed in that manner. A permissive rule is often an exception to the general requirement.

Author's Comment:

■ For ease of reading, the phrase "shall be permitted," as used in the *Code*, has been replaced in this textbook with the phrase "is permitted" or "are permitted."

(C) Explanatory Material. References to other standards or sections of the *NEC*, or information related to a *Code* rule, are included in the form of Informational Notes. Such notes are for information only and aren't enforceable as requirements of the *NEC*.

For example, Informational Note 4 in 210.19(A)(1) recommends that the voltage drop of a circuit not exceed 3 percent. This isn't a requirement; it's just a recommendation.

Author's Comment:

■ For convenience and ease of reading in this textbook, Informational Notes will simply be identified as "Note."

■ Informational Notes aren't enforceable, but Table Notes are. This textbook will call notes found in a table "Table Notes."

(D) Informative Annexes. Nonmandatory information annexes contained in the back of the *Code* book are for information only and aren't enforceable as requirements of the *NEC*.

90.6 Formal Interpretations

To promote uniformity of interpretation and application of the provisions of the *NEC*, formal interpretation procedures have been established and are found in the NFPA Regulations Governing Committee Projects.

Author's Comment:

■ This is rarely done because it's a very time-consuming process, and formal interpretations from the NFPA aren't binding on the authority having jurisdiction.

90.7 Examination of Equipment for Product Safety

Product evaluation for safety is typically performed by a testing laboratory, which publishes a list of equipment that meets a nationally recognized test standard. Products and materials that are listed, labeled, or identified by a testing laboratory are generally approved by the authority having jurisdiction.

Author's Comment:

■ See Article 100 for the definition of "Approved."

Except to detect alterations or damage, listed factory-installed internal wiring and construction of equipment needn't be inspected at the time of installation [300.1(B)]. Figure 90–17

Figure 90–17

90.9 Units of Measurement

(B) Dual Systems of Units. Both the metric and inch-pound measurement systems are shown in the *NEC*, with the metric units appearing first and the inch-pound system immediately following in parentheses.

Author's Comment:

- This is the standard practice in all NFPA standards, even though the U.S. construction industry uses inch-pound units of measurement. You'll need to be cautious when using the tables in the *Code* because the additional units can make the tables more complex and more difficult to read.

(D) Compliance. Installing electrical systems in accordance with the metric system or the inch-pound system is considered to comply with the *Code*.

Author's Comment:

- Since the use of either the metric or the inch-pound system of measurement constitutes compliance with the *NEC*, this textbook uses only inch-pound units.

ARTICLE 90 PRACTICE QUESTIONS

Please use the 2014 *Code* book to answer the following questions.

1. The *NEC* is _____.

   (a) intended to be a design manual
   (b) meant to be used as an instruction guide for untrained persons
   (c) for the practical safeguarding of persons and property
   (d) published by the Bureau of Standards

2. Compliance with the provisions of the *NEC* will result in _____.

   (a) good electrical service
   (b) an efficient electrical system
   (c) an electrical system essentially free from hazard
   (d) all of these

3. Hazards often occur because of _____.

   (a) overloading of wiring systems by methods or usage not in conformity with the *NEC*
   (b) initial wiring not providing for increases in the use of electricity
   (c) a and b
   (d) none of these

4. The *NEC* applies to the installation of _____.

   (a) electrical conductors and equipment within or on public and private buildings
   (b) outside conductors and equipment on the premises
   (c) optical fiber cables and raceways
   (d) all of these

5. The *NEC* does not cover electrical installations in ships, watercraft, railway rolling stock, aircraft, or automotive vehicles.

   (a) True
   (b) False

6. Installations of communications equipment that are under the exclusive control of communications utilities, and located outdoors or in building spaces used exclusively for such installations _____ covered by the *NEC*.

   (a) are
   (b) are sometimes
   (c) are not
   (d) may be

7. Utilities may be subject to compliance with codes and standards covering their regulated activities as adopted under governmental law or regulation.

   (a) True
   (b) False

8. Utilities may include entities that are designated or recognized by governmental law or regulation by public service/utility commissions.

   (a) True
   (b) False

9. Chapters 1 through 4 of the *NEC* apply _____.

    (a) generally to all electrical installations
    (b) only to special occupancies and conditions
    (c) only to special equipment and material
    (d) all of these

10. The authority having jurisdiction shall not be allowed to enforce any requirements of Chapter 7 (Special Conditions) or Chapter 8 (Communications Systems).

    (a) True
    (b) False

11. By special permission, the authority having jurisdiction may waive specific requirements in this *Code* where it is assured that equivalent objectives can be achieved by establishing and maintaining effective safety.

    (a) True
    (b) False

12. If the *NEC* requires new products that are not yet available at the time a new edition is adopted, the _____ may permit the use of the products that comply with the most recent previous edition of the *Code* adopted by that jurisdiction.

    (a) electrical engineer
    (b) master electrician
    (c) authority having jurisdiction
    (d) permit holder

13. When the *Code* uses "_____," it means the identified actions are allowed but not required, and they may be options or alternative methods.

    (a) shall
    (b) shall not
    (c) shall be permitted
    (d) a or b

14. Nonmandatory Informative Annexes contained in the back of the *Code* book _____.

    (a) are for information only
    (b) aren't enforceable as a requirement of the *Code*
    (c) are enforceable as a requirement of the *Code*
    (d) a and b

Notes

CHAPTER 1

GENERAL

Introduction to Chapter 1—General

Before you can make sense of the *Code*, you must become familiar with a few basic rules, concepts, definitions, and requirements. As you study the *NEC*, you'll see that these are the foundation for a proper understanding of the *Code*.

Chapter 1 consists of two topics. Article 100 provides definitions so people can understand one another when trying to communicate about *Code*-related matters and Article 110 provides the general requirements needed to correctly apply the rest of the *NEC*.

Time spent learning this general material is a great investment. After understanding Chapter 1, some of the *Code* requirements that seem confusing to other people will become increasingly clear to you. The requirements will begin to make sense because you'll have the foundation from which to understand and apply them. When you read the *NEC* requirements in later chapters, you'll understand the principles upon which many of them are based, and not be surprised at all. You'll read them and feel like you already know them.

- **Article 100—Definitions.** Part I of Article 100 contains the definitions of terms used throughout the *Code* for systems that operate at 600V, nominal, or less. The definitions of terms in Part II apply to systems that operate at over 600V, nominal.

Definitions of standard terms, such as volt, voltage drop, ampere, impedance, and resistance, aren't listed in Article 100. If the *NEC* doesn't define a term, then a dictionary suitable to the authority having jurisdiction should be consulted. A building code glossary might provide better definitions than a dictionary found at your home or school.

Definitions located at the beginning of an article apply only to that specific article. For example, the definition of a swimming "Pool" is contained in 680.2, because this term applies only to the requirements contained in Article 680—Swimming Pools, Fountains, and Similar Installations. As soon as a defined term is used in two or more articles, its definition should be included in Article 100.

- **Article 110—Requirements for Electrical Installations.** This article contains general requirements for electrical installations for the following:
  - Part I. General
  - Part II. 600V, Nominal, Or Less

ARTICLE 100

DEFINITIONS

Introduction to Article 100—Definitions

Have you ever had a conversation with someone, only to discover that what you said and what he or she heard were completely different? This often happens when people in a conversation don't understand the definitions of the words being used, and that's why the definitions of key terms are located right at the beginning of the *NEC* (Article 100), or at the beginning of each article. If we can all agree on important definitions, then we speak the same language and avoid misunderstandings. Because the *Code* exists to protect people and property, it's very important to know the definitions presented in Article 100.

Here are a few tips for learning the many definitions in the *Code*:

- – Break the task down. Study a few words at a time, rather than trying to learn them all at one sitting.
- – Review the graphics in the textbook. These will help you see how a term is applied.
- – Relate the definitions to your work. As you read a word, think about how it applies to the work you're doing. This'll provide a natural reinforcement to the learning process.

Definitions

Accessible (as it applies to wiring methods). Not permanently closed in by the building structure or finish and capable of being removed or exposed without damaging the building structure or finish. Figure 100–1

Author's Comment:

- ■ Conductors in a concealed raceway are considered concealed, even though they may become accessible by withdrawing them from the raceway. See the Note to the definition of "Concealed" in this article.

- ■ Raceways, cables, and enclosures installed above a suspended ceiling or within a raised floor are considered accessible, because the wiring methods can be accessed without damaging the building structure. See the definitions of "Concealed" and "Exposed" in this article. Figure 100–2

Figure 100–1

Figure 100–2

 Scan this QR code for a video of the following *Code* rule. See page xix for information on how to use the QR codes.

Accessible, Readily (Readily Accessible). Capable of being reached quickly without having to climb over or remove obstacles, resort to portable ladders, or use tools. Figure 100–3

Figure 100–3

Adjustable Speed Drive. A piece of equipment that provides a way to adjust the speed of an electric motor.

Author's Comment:

■ Adjustable-speed drives are often referred to as "variable-speed drives" or "variable-frequency drives (VFDs)."

Note: A variable frequency drive is one type of electronic adjustable speed drive that controls the speed of an AC motor by changing the frequency and voltage of the motor's power supply.

Adjustable Speed Drive System. A combination of an adjustable speed drive, its associated motor(s), and any other equipment associated with the two.

Ampacity. The maximum current, in amperes, a conductor can carry continuously, under the conditions of use without exceeding its temperature rating.

Author's Comment:

■ See 310.10 and 310.15 for details and examples. Figure 100–4

Figure 100–4

Appliance [Article 422]. Electrical equipment, other than industrial equipment, built in standardized sizes, such as ranges, ovens, cooktops, refrigerators, drinking water coolers, or beverage dispensers.

Approved. Acceptable to the authority having jurisdiction, usually the electrical inspector. Figure 100–5

Figure 100–5

Figure 100–7

Author's Comment:

- Product listing doesn't mean the product is approved, but it can be a basis for approval. See 90.4, 90.7, 110.2, and the definitions in this article for "Authority Having Jurisdiction," "Identified," "Labeled," and "Listed."

Arc-Fault Circuit Interrupter (AFCI). An arc-fault circuit interrupter is a device intended to de-energize the circuit when it detects the current waveform characteristics unique to an arcing fault. Figures 100–6 and 100–7

Attachment Plug (Plug Cap), (Plug) [Article 406]. A wiring device at the end of a flexible cord intended to be inserted into a receptacle in order to make an electrical connection. Figure 100–8

Figure 100–8

Figure 100–6

Author's Comment:

- The use of cords with attachment plugs is limited by 210.50(A), 400.7, 410.24, 410.62, 422.16, 422.33, 590.4, 645.5 and other sections.

Authority Having Jurisdiction (AHJ). The organization, office, or individual responsible for approving equipment, materials, an installation, or a procedure. See 90.4 and 90.7 for more information.

Note: The authority having jurisdiction may be a federal, state, or local government department or an individual, such as a fire chief, fire marshal, chief of a fire prevention bureau or labor department or health department, a building official or electrical inspector, or others having statutory authority. In some circumstances, the property owner or his/her agent assumes the role, and at government installations, the commanding officer, or departmental official may be the authority having jurisdiction.

Author's Comment:

- Typically, the authority having jurisdiction is the electrical inspector who has legal statutory authority. In the absence of federal, state, or local regulations, the operator of the facility or his or her agent, such as an architect or engineer of the facility, can assume the role.

- Some believe the authority having jurisdiction should have a strong background in the electrical field, such as having studied electrical engineering or having obtained an electrical contractor's license, and in a few states this is a legal requirement. Memberships, certifications, and active participation in electrical organizations, such as the International Association of Electrical Inspectors (IAEI), speak to an individual's qualifications. Visit www.IAEI.org for more information about that organization.

Automatic. Functioning without the necessity of human intervention.

Bathroom. A bathroom is an area that includes a basin as well as one or more of the following: a toilet, urinal, tub, shower, bidet, or similar plumbing fixture. Figure 100–9

Author's Comment:

- All 15A and 20A, 125V receptacles located in bathrooms must be GFCI protected [210.8(A)(1) and 210.8(B)(1)].

Battery System. An interconnection of one or more storage batteries and their chargers. It can also include converters, inverters, and other associated equipment. Figure 100–10

Bonded (Bonding). Connected to establish electrical continuity and conductivity. Figure 100–11

Figure 100–9

Figure 100–10

Author's Comment:

- The purpose of bonding is to connect two or more conductive objects together to ensure the electrical continuity of the fault current path, provide the capacity and ability to conduct safely any fault current likely to be imposed, and to minimize potential differences (voltage) between conductive components. Figures 100–12 and 100–13

Figure 100–11

Figure 100–13

Figure 100–12

Figure 100–14

Bonding Conductor or Jumper. A conductor that ensures electrical conductivity between metal parts of the electrical installation. Figure 100–14

Bonding Jumper, Main. A conductor, screw, or strap that connects the circuit equipment grounding conductor to the neutral conductor at service equipment in accordance with 250.24(B) [250.24(A)(4), 250.28, and 408.3(C)]. Figure 100–15

Bonding Jumper, System. The connection between the neutral conductor and the supply-side bonding jumper or equipment grounding conductor, or both, at a separately derived system. Figure 100–16

Branch Circuit [Article 210]. The conductors between the final overcurrent device and the receptacle outlets, lighting outlets, or other outlets as defined in this article. Figure 100–17

Branch Circuit, Individual. A branch circuit that only supplies one load.

Figure 100–15

Figure 100–17

Figure 100–16

Figure 100–18

Branch Circuit, Multiwire. A branch circuit that consists of two or more ungrounded circuit conductors with a common neutral conductor. There must be a voltage between the ungrounded conductors and an equal difference of voltage from each ungrounded conductor to the common neutral conductor. Figure 100–18

Author's Comment:

■ Multiwire branch circuits offer the advantage of fewer conductors in a raceway, smaller raceway sizing, and a reduction of material and labor costs. In addition, multiwire branch circuits can reduce circuit voltage drop by as much as 50 percent. However, because of the dangers associated with multiwire branch circuits, the *NEC* contains additional requirements to ensure a safe installation. See 210.4, 300.13(B), and 408.41 in this textbook for details.

Building. A structure that stands alone or is cut off from other structures by fire walls with all openings protected by fire doors approved by the authority having jurisdiction. Figure 100–19

Figure 100–19

Author's Comment:

■ Not all fire-rated walls are fire walls. Building codes describe fire barriers, fire partitions and other fire-rated walls, in addition to fire walls. Check with your local building inspector to determine if a rated wall creates a separate building (fire wall).

Cabinet [Article 312]. An enclosure for either surface mounting or flush mounting provided with a frame in which a door can be hung. Figure 100–20

Author's Comment:

■ Cabinets are used to enclose panelboards. See the definition of "Panelboard" in this article.

Cable Routing Assembly. A channel or channels, with their fittings, that support and route communications wires and cables, optical fiber cables, data cables, Class 2 and Class 3 cables, and power-limited fire alarm cables. Figure 100–21

Figure 100–20

Figure 100–21

Author's Comment:

■ A cable routing assembly is typically a "U" shaped trough, with or without covers, designed to hold cables, and it isn't a raceway.

Charge Controller. Equipment that controls dc voltage or dc current, or both, and is used to charge a battery or other energy storage device. Figure 100–22

Figure 100–22

Circuit Breaker. A device designed to be opened and closed manually, and which opens automatically on a predetermined overcurrent without damage to itself. Circuit breakers are available in different configurations, such as inverse time, adjustable trip (electronically controlled), and instantaneous trip/motor-circuit protectors. Figure 100–23

Figure 100–23

Inverse Time. Inverse time breakers operate on the principle that as the current increases, the time it takes for the devices to open decreases. This type of breaker provides overcurrent protection (overload, short circuit, and ground fault). This is the most common type of circuit breaker that you'll buy over-the-counter.

Adjustable Trip. Adjustable trip breakers permit the thermal trip setting to be adjusted. The adjustment is often necessary to coordinate the operation of the circuit breakers with other overcurrent devices.

Author's Comment:

- Coordination means that the devices with the lowest ratings, closest to the fault, operate and isolate the fault and minimize disruption so the rest of the system can remain energized and functional. This sounds simple, but large systems (especially emergency systems) may require an expensive engineering study; so if you're responsible for bidding a project, be aware of this requirement.

Instantaneous Trip. Instantaneous trip breakers operate on the principle of electromagnetism only and are used for motors. Sometimes these devices are called motor-circuit protectors. This type of overcurrent device doesn't provide overload protection. It only provides short-circuit and ground-fault protection; overload protection must be provided separately.

Author's Comment:

- Instantaneous trip circuit breakers have no intentional time delay and are sensitive to current inrush, and to vibration and shock. Consequently, they shouldn't be used where these factors are known to exist.

Clothes Closet. A non-habitable room or space intended primarily for the storage of garments and apparel. Figure 100–24

Author's Comment:

- The definition of "Clothes Closet" provides clarification in the application of overcurrent devices [240.24(D)] and luminaires [410.16] in clothes closets.

Communications Equipment. Electronic telecommunications equipment used for the transmission of audio, video, and data, including support equipment such as computers, as well as the conductors that are used solely for the operation of the equipment. Figure 100–25

Figure 100–24

Figure 100–26

Figure 100–25

Figure 100–27

Communications Raceway. An enclosed channel of nonmetallic materials designed for holding communications wires and cables in plenum, riser, and general-purpose applications. Figure 100–26

Concealed. Rendered inaccessible by the structure or finish of the building.

Note: Conductors in a concealed raceway are considered concealed, even though they may be made accessible by withdrawing them from the raceway. Figure 100–27

Author's Comment:

■ Wiring behind panels designed to allow access, such as removable ceiling tile, is considered exposed.

Conduit Body. A fitting that's installed in a conduit or tubing system and provides access to conductors through a removable cover. Figure 100–28

Connector, Pressure (Solderless). A device that establishes a conductive connection between conductors or between a conductor and a terminal by the means of mechanical pressure.

Figure 100–28

Figure 100–30

Continuous Load. A load where the maximum current is expected to exist for 3 hours or more continuously, such as store or parking lot lighting.

Control Circuit. The circuit of a control apparatus or system that carries the electric signals directing the performance of the controller but doesn't carry the main power current. Figure 100–29

Figure 100–29

Controller. A device that controls the electric power delivered to electrical equipment in some predetermined manner. This includes time clocks, lighting contactors, photocells, and equipment with similar functions. Figure 100–30

Author's Comment:

■ For the definition of "Motor Controller," see 430.2.

Coordination (Selective). Localization of an overcurrent condition to restrict outages to the circuit or equipment affected, accomplished by the choice of overcurrent devices. Selective coordination includes all currents, from overloads to short circuits. Figure 100–31

Figure 100–31

Author's Comment:

■ Selective coordination means the overcurrent protection scheme confines the interruption to a particular area rather than to the whole system. For example, if someone plugs in a space heater and raises the total demand on a 20A circuit to 25A, or if a short circuit or ground fault occurs with selective coordination, the only breaker or fuse that'll open is the one protecting just that branch circuit. Without selective coordination, an entire building can go dark!

Demand Factor. The ratio of the maximum demand to the total connected load.

Author's Comment:

- This definition is primarily used in the application of the requirements of Article 220—Branch-Circuit, Feeder, and Service Calculations.

Device. A component of an electrical installation, <u>other than a conductor,</u> intended to carry or control electric energy as its principal function. Figure 100–32

Figure 100–32

Author's Comment:

- Devices include busbars, receptacles, switches, illuminated switches, circuit breakers, fuses, time clocks, controllers, and so forth, but not locknuts or other mechanical fittings. A device may consume very small amounts of energy, such as an illuminated switch, but still be classified as a device based on its principal function.

Disconnecting Means. A device that opens all of the ungrounded circuit conductors from their power source. This includes devices such as switches, attachment plugs and receptacles, and circuit breakers. Figure 100–33

Figure 100–33

Author's Comment:

- Review the following for the specific requirements for equipment disconnecting means:

  - ☐ Air-conditioning and refrigeration equipment, 440.14
  - ☐ Appliances, Article 422, Part III
  - ☐ Buildings supplied by a feeder, Article 225, Part II
  - ☐ Electric space-heating equipment, 424.19
  - ☐ Electric duct heaters, 424.65
  - ☐ Luminaires, 410.130(G)
  - ☐ Motor control conductors, 430.75
  - ☐ Motor controllers, 430.102(A)
  - ☐ Motors, 430.102(B)(1)
  - ☐ Refrigeration equipment, 440.14
  - ☐ Services, Article 230, Part VI
  - ☐ Swimming pool, spa, hot tub, and fountain equipment, 680.12
  - ☐ Solar PV, 690.13, 690.14, 690.15, 690.16, and 690.17

Dusttight. Constructed so that dust won't enter the enclosure or case under specified test conditions.

Duty, Continuous. Operation at a substantially constant load for an indefinitely long time.

Duty, Varying. Operation at loads, and for intervals of time, which may both be subject to wide variation.

Dwelling Unit. A space that provides independent living facilities, with space for eating, living, and sleeping; as well as permanent facilities for cooking and sanitation. Figure 100–34

Dwelling Unit
Article 100 Definition

A single unit that provides permanent provisions for living, sleeping, cooking, and sanitation.

Figure 100–34

Dwelling, Multifamily. A building that contains three or more dwelling units. Figure 100–35

Effective Ground-Fault Current Path. An intentionally constructed low-impedance conductive path designed to carry fault current from the point of a ground fault to the source for the purpose of opening the circuit overcurrent protective device. Figure 100–36

Author's Comment:

■ In Figure 100–36, "EGC" represents the equipment grounding conductor [259.118], "MBJ" represents the main bonding jumper, "SNC" represents the service neutral conductor (grounded service conductor), and "GEC" represents the grounding electrode conductor.

Dwelling, Multifamily
Article 100 Definition

A building with 3 or more dwelling units. Examples include apartment buildings, condominiums, and some hotels and motels.

Figure 100–35

Effective Ground-Fault Current Path
Article 100 Definition

An intentionally constructed, low-impedance, electrically conductive path designed to carry fault current from the point of a ground fault to the supply source.

Figure 100–36

The current path shown between the supply source grounding electrode and the grounding electrode at the service main shows that some current will flow through the earth but the earth isn't part of the effective ground-fault current path.

The effective ground-fault current path is intended to help remove dangerous voltage from a ground fault by opening the circuit overcurrent device. Figure 100–37

Electric-Discharge Lighting. Systems of illumination utilizing fluorescent lamps, high-intensity discharge (HID) lamps, or neon tubing. Figure 100–38

Figure 100–37

Figure 100–39

Figure 100–38

Electric Sign [Article 600]. A fixed, stationary, or portable self-contained, electrically illuminated piece of equipment with words or symbols designed to convey information or attract attention.

Enclosed. Surrounded by a case, housing, fence, or wall(s) that prevents accidental contact with energized parts.

Energized. Electrically connected to a source of voltage.

Equipment. A general term including fittings, devices, appliances, luminaires, machinery, and the like. Figure 100–39

Explosionproof Equipment. Equipment capable of withstanding an explosion that may occur within it, and of preventing the ignition of gas or vapor surrounding the enclosure by sparks, flashes, or an explosion within, and that operates at such an external temperature that surrounding flammable atmosphere won't be ignited by its heat. Figure 100–40

Figure 100–40

Exposed (as applied to live parts). Capable of being accidentally touched or approached to an unsafe distance.

Note: This term applies to parts that aren't suitably guarded, isolated, or insulated.

Exposed (as applied to wiring methods). On or attached to the surface of a building, or behind panels designed to allow access. Figure 100–41

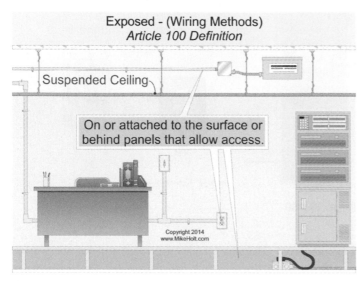

Figure 100–41

Feeder [Article 215]. The conductors between the service equipment, a separately derived system, or other power supply and the final branch-circuit overcurrent device. Figure 100–42

Conductors between service equipment, a separately derived system, or other power supply, and the final branch-circuit overcurrent device.

Figure 100–42

Author's Comment:

■ An "other power source" includes a solar energy (photo-voltaic) system.

■ To have a better understanding of what a feeder is, be sure to review the definitions of "Service Equipment" and "Separately Derived System."

Fitting. An accessory, such as a locknut, intended to perform a mechanical function.

Garage. A building or portion of a building where self-propelled vehicles can be kept.

Ground. The earth. Figure 100–43

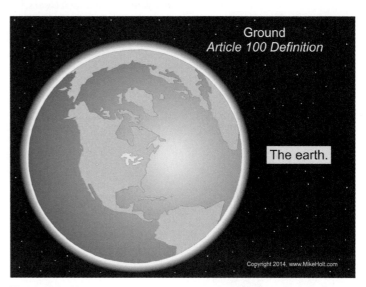

Figure 100–43

Ground Fault. An unintentional electrical connection between an ungrounded conductor and the metal parts of enclosures, raceways, or equipment. Figure 100–44

Grounded (Grounding). Connected to ground or to a conductive body that extends the ground connection.

Author's Comment:

■ An example of a "body that extends the ground (earth) connection" is the termination to structural steel that's connected to the earth either directly or by the termination to another grounding electrode in accordance with 250.52. Figure 100–45

Grounded System, Solidly. A power supply system connected to ground (earth) without inserting any resistor or impedance device between the system and ground. Figure 100–46

Figure 100-44

Figure 100-46

Figure 100-45

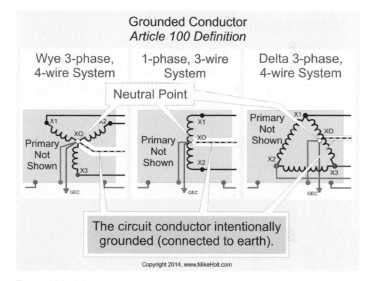

Figure 100-47

Grounded Conductor [Article 200]. The system or circuit conductor that's intentionally grounded (connected to the earth). Figure 100-47

Author's Comment:

- Because the neutral conductor of a solidly grounded system is always grounded (connected to the earth), it's also called a "grounded conductor." To make it easier for the reader of this textbook, we'll refer to the "grounded" conductor of a solidly grounded system as the "neutral" conductor, except for the applications contained in Article 690—Solar PV Systems.

Ground-Fault Circuit Interrupter (GFCI). A device intended to protect people by de-energizing a circuit when a current imbalance has been detected that exceeds the value established for a "Class A" device.

Note: A "Class A" ground-fault circuit interrupter opens the circuit when the imbalance current has a value of 6 mA or higher and doesn't trip when the current to ground is less than 4 mA. **Figure 100-48**

Figure 100–48

Author's Comment:

- A GFCI operates on the principle of monitoring the unbalanced current between the current-carrying circuit conductors. On a 120V circuit, the GFCI will monitor the unbalanced current between the ungrounded and neutral conductors; on 240V GFCIs, this monitoring is between ungrounded conductors. GFCI-protective devices are commercially available in receptacles, circuit breakers, cord sets, and other types of devices. Figure 100–49

Figure 100–49

Ground-Fault Protection of Equipment. A system intended to provide protection of equipment from damaging ground-fault currents by opening all ungrounded conductors of the faulted circuit. This protection is provided at current levels less than those required to protect conductors from damage through the operation of a supply circuit overcurrent device [215.10, 230.95, and 240.13].

Author's Comment:

- This type of protective device isn't intended to protect people and trips at a higher level than required for "Class A" GFCIs. This type of device is typically referred to as ground-fault protection for equipment, or GFPE, but should never be called a GFCI.

Grounding Conductor, Equipment (EGC). The conductive path(s) that provides a ground-fault current path and connects metal parts of equipment to the system neutral conductor, to the grounding electrode conductor, or both [250.110 through 250.126]. Figure 100–50

Figure 100–50

Note 1: The circuit equipment grounding conductor also performs bonding.

Author's Comment:

- To quickly remove dangerous touch voltage on metal parts from a ground fault, the equipment grounding conductor must be connected to the system neutral conductor at the source, and have low enough impedance so that fault current will quickly rise to a level that'll open the circuit's overcurrent device [250.2 and 250.4(A)(3)].

Note 2: An equipment grounding conductor can be any one or a combination of the types listed in 250.118. **Figure 100–51**

Figure 100–51

Author's Comment:

- Equipment grounding conductors include:

    □ A bare or insulated conductor

    □ Rigid Metal Conduit

    □ Intermediate Metal Conduit

    □ Electrical Metallic Tubing

    □ Listed Flexible Metal Conduit as limited by 250.118(5)

    □ Listed Liquidtight Flexible Metal Conduit as limited by 250.118(6)

    □ Armored Cable

    □ Copper metal sheath of Mineral Insulated Cable

    □ Metal-Clad Cable as limited by 250.118(10)

    □ Metallic cable trays as limited by 250.118(11) and 392.60

    □ Electrically continuous metal raceways listed for grounding

    □ Surface Metal Raceways listed for grounding

Grounding Electrode. A conducting object used to make a direct electrical connection to the earth [250.50 through 250.70]. Figure 100–52

Grounding Electrode Conductor (GEC). The conductor used to connect the system grounded (neutral) conductor to a grounding electrode. Figure 100–53

Figure 100–52

Figure 100–53

Author's Comment:

- For services see 250.24(A), for separately derived systems see 250.30(A), and for buildings supplied by a feeder see 250.32(A).

Guest Room. An accommodation that combines living, sleeping, sanitary, and storage facilities. Figure 100–54

Guest Suite. An accommodation with two or more contiguous rooms comprising a compartment, with or without doors between such rooms, that provides living, sleeping, sanitary, and storage facilities.

Figure 100–54

Handhole Enclosure. An enclosure for underground system use sized to allow personnel to reach into it for the purpose of installing or maintaining equipment or wiring. It may have an open or closed bottom. Figure 100–55

Figure 100–55

Author's Comment:

- See 314.30 for the installation requirements for handhole enclosures.

Hermetic Refrigerant Motor-Compressor. A compressor and motor enclosed in the same housing, operating in the refrigerant.

Hoistway. A vertical opening or space in which an elevator is designed to operate. Figure 100–56

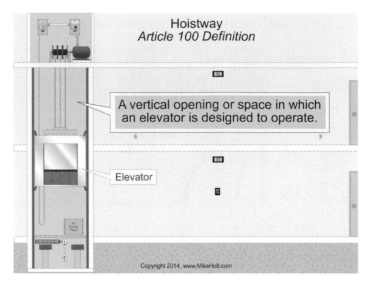

Figure 100–56

Hybrid System. A system comprised of multiple power sources, such as photovoltaic, wind, micro-hydro generators, engine-driven generators, and others, but not the utility power system. Figure 100–57

Figure 100–57

Identified Equipment. Recognized as suitable for a specific purpose, function, or environment by listing, labeling, or other means approved by the authority having jurisdiction.

Author's Comment:

- See 90.4, 90.7, 110.3(A)(1), and the definitions for "Approved," "Labeled," and "Listed" in this article.

In Sight From (Within Sight). Visible and not more than 50 ft away from the equipment. Figure 100–58

Figure 100–58

Interrupting Rating. The highest short-circuit current at rated voltage the device is identified to interrupt under standard test conditions.

Author's Comment:

- For more information, see 110.9 in this textbook.

Intersystem Bonding Termination. A device that provides a means to connect intersystem bonding conductors for communications systems to the grounding electrode system, in accordance with 250.94. Figure 100–59

Isolated. Not readily accessible to persons unless special means for access are used.

Kitchen. An area with a sink and permanent provisions for food preparation and cooking. Figure 100–60

Figure 100–59

Figure 100–60

Labeled. Equipment or materials that have a label, symbol, or other identifying mark in the form of a sticker, decal, printed label, or molded or stamped into the product by a testing laboratory acceptable to the authority having jurisdiction. Figure 100–61

Author's Comment:

- Labeling and listing of equipment typically provides the basis for equipment approval by the authority having jurisdiction [90.4, 90.7, 110.2, and 110.3].

Figure 100–61

Lighting Outlet. An outlet for the connection of a lampholder or luminaire. Figure 100–62

Figure 100–62

Listed. Equipment or materials included in a list published by a testing laboratory acceptable to the authority having jurisdiction. The listing organization must periodically inspect the production of listed equipment or material to ensure the equipment or material meets appropriate designated standards and is suitable for a specified purpose.

Author's Comment:

- The *NEC* doesn't require all electrical equipment to be listed, but some *Code* requirements do specifically require product listing. Organizations such as OSHA increasingly require that listed equipment be used when such equipment is available [90.7, 110.2, and 110.3].

Lighting Track (Track Lighting). This is a manufactured assembly designed to support and energize luminaires that can be readily repositioned on the track, and whose length may be altered by the addition or subtraction of sections of track. Figure 100–63

Figure 100–63

Location, Damp. Locations protected from weather and not subject to saturation with water or other liquids.

Note: This includes locations partially protected under canopies, marquees, roofed open porches, and interior locations subject to moderate degrees of moisture, such as some basements, barns, and cold-storage warehouses. Figure 100–64

Location, Dry. An area not normally subjected to dampness or wetness, but which may temporarily be subjected to dampness or wetness, such as a building under construction.

Location, Wet. An installation underground, in concrete slabs in direct contact with the earth, as well as locations subject to saturation with water, and unprotected locations exposed to weather. Figures 100–65 and 100–66

Figure 100–64

Figure 100–66

Figure 100–65

Figure 100–67

Author's Comment:

■ The interior of a raceway installed in wet locations is considered to be a wet location, and the conductors used must be suitable for wet locations [300.5(B) and 300.9].

Luminaire [Article 410]. A complete lighting unit consisting of a light source with the parts designed to position the light source and connect it to the power supply and distribute the light. A lampholder by itself isn't a luminaire. Figure 100–67

Multioutlet Assembly [Article 380]. A surface, flush, or freestanding raceway designed to hold conductors and receptacles. Figure 100–68

Neutral Conductor. The conductor connected to the neutral point of a system that's intended to carry current under normal conditions. Figure 100–69

Author's Comment:

■ The neutral conductor of a solidly grounded system is required to be grounded (connected to the earth), therefore this conductor is also called a "grounded conductor."

Figure 100–68

Figure 100–70

Figure 100–69

Figure 100–71

Neutral Point. The common point of a 4-wire, three-phase, wye-connected system; the midpoint of a 3-wire, single-phase system; or the midpoint of the single-phase portion of a three-phase, delta-connected system. Figure 100–70

Nonautomatic. Requiring human intervention to perform a function.

Nonlinear Load. A load where the current waveform doesn't follow the applied sinusoidal voltage waveform. Figure 100–71

Note: Single-phase nonlinear loads include electronic equipment, such as copy machines, laser printers, and electric-discharge lighting. Three-phase nonlinear loads include uninterruptible power supplies, induction motors, and electronic switching devices, such as adjustable speed drives (variable frequency drives). Figure 100–72

Author's Comment:

■ The subject of nonlinear loads is beyond the scope of this textbook. For more information on this topic, visit www.Mike-Holt.com, click on the "Technical" link, then on the "Power Quality" link.

Figure 100–72

Figure 100–74

Outlet. A point in the wiring system where electric current is taken to supply a load (utilization equipment). This includes receptacle outlets and lighting outlets, as well as outlets for ceiling paddle fans and smoke alarms. Figure 100–73

Figure 100–73

Outline Lighting [Article 600]. An arrangement of incandescent lamps, electric-discharge lighting, or other electrically powered light sources to outline or call attention to certain features such as the shape of a building or the decoration of a window. Figure 100–74

Overcurrent. Current, in amperes, greater than the rated current of the equipment or conductors resulting from an overload, short circuit, or ground fault. Figure 100–75

Figure 100–75

Author's Comment:

- See the definitions of "Ground Fault" in 250.2 and "Overload" in this article.

Overcurrent Protective Device, Supplementary. A device intended to provide limited overcurrent protection for specific applications and utilization equipment, such as luminaires and appliances. This limited protection is in addition to the required protection provided in the branch circuit by the branch-circuit overcurrent device. Figure 100–76

Figure 100–76

Overload. The operation of equipment above its current rating, or current in excess of conductor ampacity. When an overload condition persists for a sufficient length of time, it can result in equipment failure or in a fire from damaging or dangerous overheating. A fault, such as a short circuit or ground fault, isn't an overload.

Panelboard [Article 408]. A distribution point containing overcurrent devices and designed to be installed in a cabinet. Figure 100–77

Author's Comment:

- See the definition of "Cabinet" in this article.

- The slang term in the electrical field for a panelboard is "the guts." This is the interior of the panelboard assembly and is covered by Article 408, while the cabinet is covered by Article 312.

Photovoltaic (PV) System. The combination of all components and subsystems that convert solar energy into electrical energy. Figure 100–78

Figure 100–77

Figure 100–78

Premises Wiring. The interior and exterior wiring, including power, lighting, control, and signal circuits, and all associated hardware, fittings, and wiring devices. This includes both permanently and temporarily installed wiring from the service point to the outlets, or where there's no service point, wiring from and including the power source, such as a generator, transformer, or PV system to the outlets. Figure 100–79

Premises wiring doesn't include the internal wiring of electrical equipment and appliances, such as luminaires, dishwashers, water heaters, motors, controllers, motor control centers, air-conditioning equipment, and so on [90.7 and 300.1(B)]. Figure 100–80

Premises Wiring
Article 100 Definition

Power, lighting, control, and signal circuit wiring from the service point to the outlets or from and including the power source to the outlets where there is no service point.

Figure 100–79

Qualified Person
Article 100 Definition

A person with the skills and knowledge related to the construction, operation, and installation of electrical equipment, including safety training to recognize and avoid electrical hazards.

Figure 100–81

Premises Wiring
Article 100 Definition

Premises wiring doesn't include the internal wiring of electrical equipment and appliances, such as luminaires, dishwashers, water heaters, motors, controllers, motor control centers, air-onditioning equipment, and so on.

Premises Wiring

Figure 100–80

Note: Power sources include, but aren't limited to, interconnected or stand-alone batteries, PV systems, other distributed generation systems, or generators.

Qualified Person. A person who has the skill and knowledge related to the construction and operation of electrical equipment and its installation. This person must have received safety training to recognize and avoid the hazards involved with electrical systems. Figure 100–81

Note: NFPA 70E, *Standard for Electrical Safety in the Workplace*, provides information on safety training requirements expected of a "qualified person."

Author's Comment:

■ Examples of this safety training include, but aren't limited to, training in the use of special precautionary techniques, of personal protective equipment (PPE), of insulating and shielding materials, and of using insulated tools and test equipment when working on or near exposed conductors or circuit parts that can become energized.

■ In many parts of the United States, electricians, electrical contractors, electrical inspectors, and electrical engineers must complete from 6 to 24 hours of *NEC* review each year as a requirement to maintain licensing. This in itself doesn't make one qualified to deal with the specific hazards involved with electrical systems.

Raceway. An enclosure designed for the installation of conductors, cables, or busbars. Raceways in the *NEC* include:

Note: Each raceway is defined in the 3xx.2 section of its own article.

Author's Comment:

■ A cable tray system isn't a raceway; it's a support system for cables and raceways [392.2].

Raceway Type	Article
Busways	368
Electrical Metallic Tubing	358
Electrical Nonmetallic Tubing	362
Flexible Metal Conduit	348
Intermediate Metal Conduit	342
Liquidtight Flexible Metal Conduit	350
Liquidtight Flexible Nonmetallic Conduit	356
Metal Wireways	376
Multioutlet Assembly	380
Rigid Metal Conduit	344
PVC Conduit	352
Surface Metal Raceways	386
Surface Nonmetallic Raceways	388

Figure 100–82

Rainproof. Constructed, protected, or treated so as to prevent rain from interfering with the successful operation of the apparatus under specified test conditions.

Raintight. A raintight enclosure is constructed or protected so that exposure to a beating rain won't result in the entrance of water under specified test conditions.

Receptacle [Article 406]. A contact device installed at an outlet for the connection of an attachment plug. A single receptacle contains one device on a strap (mounting yoke), and a multiple receptacle contains more than one device on a common yoke. Figure 100–82

Receptacle Outlet. An opening in an outlet box where receptacles have been installed.

Remote-Control Circuit [Article 725]. An electric circuit that controls another circuit by a relay or equivalent device installed in accordance with Article 725. Figure 100–83

Retrofit Kit. An assembly of parts for the field conversion of utilization equipment.

Sealable Equipment. Equipment enclosed with a means of sealing or locking so that live parts can't be made accessible without opening the enclosure.

Note: The equipment may or may not be operable without opening the enclosure.

Figure 100–83

Separately Derived System. An electrical source, other than a service, having no direct connection(s) to circuit conductors of any other electrical source other than those established by grounding and bonding connections. Figures 100–84, 100–85 and 100–86

Author's Comment:

■ Separately derived systems are actually much more complicated than the above definition suggests, and understanding them requires additional study. For more information, see 250.30.

Figure 100–84

Figure 100–86

Figure 100–85

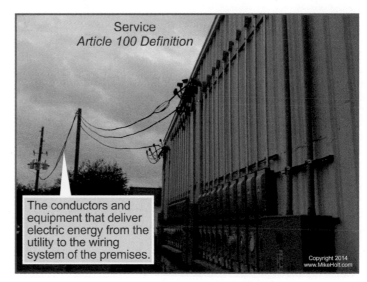

Figure 100–87

Service [Article 230]. The conductors from the electric utility that deliver electric energy to the wiring system of the premises. Figure 100–87

Author's Comment:

■ Conductors from a UPS system, solar PV system, generator, or transformer aren't service conductors. See the definitions of "Feeder" and "Service Conductors" in this article.

Service Conductors. The conductors from the service point to the service disconnecting means. Figure 100–88

Author's Comment:

■ These conductors fall within the requirements of Article 230, since they're owned by the customer.

■ "Service Conductors" is a term that can include service lateral and service-entrance conductors.

Service Conductors, Overhead. Overhead conductors between the service point and the first point of connection to the service-entrance conductors at the building. Figure 100–89

Figure 100–88

Figure 100–90

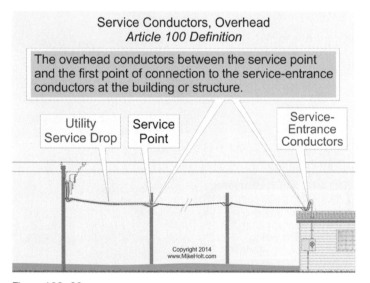

Figure 100–89

Author's Comment:

- These conductors fall within the requirements of Article 230, since they aren't under the exclusive control of the electric utility.

Service Conductors, Underground. Underground conductors between the service point and the first point of connection to the service-entrance conductors in a terminal box, meter, or other enclosure, inside or outside the building wall. Figure 100–90

Author's Comment:

- These conductors fall within the requirements of Article 230, since they aren't under the exclusive control of the electric utility.

Note: Where there's no terminal box, meter, or other enclosure, the point of connection is the point of entrance of the service conductors into the building.

Service Drop. Overhead conductors between the utility electric supply and the service point. Figure 100–91

Figure 100–91

Author's Comment:

- These conductors don't fall within the requirements of Article 230, since they're under the exclusive control of the electric utility.

Service-Entrance Conductors, Overhead System. The conductors between the terminals of service equipment and service drop or overhead service conductors. Figure 100–92

Figure 100–92

Author's Comment:

- These conductors fall within the requirements of Article 230, since they aren't under the exclusive control of the electric utility.

Service-Entrance Conductors, Underground System. The conductors between the terminals of service equipment and service lateral or underground service conductors.

Author's Comment:

- These conductors fall within the requirements of Article 230, since they aren't under the exclusive control of the electric utility.

Service Equipment [Article 230]. Circuit breaker(s) or switch(es) connected to the load end of service conductors, intended to control and cut off the service supply to the buildings. Figure 100–93

Figure 100–93

Author's Comment:

- It's important to know where a service begins and where it ends in order to properly apply the *NEC* requirements. Sometimes the service ends before the metering equipment. Figure 100–94

Figure 100–94

- Service equipment is often referred to as the "service disconnect" or "service disconnecting means."

Service Lateral. Underground conductors between the utility electric supply and the service point. Figure 100–95

Figure 100–95

Author's Comment:

■ These conductors don't fall within the requirements of Article 230, since they're under the exclusive control of the electric utility.

Service Point [Article 230]. The point where the electrical utility conductors make contact with premises wiring. Figure 100–96

Figure 100–96

Note: The service point is the point where the serving utility ends and the premises wiring begins.

Author's Comment:

■ For utility-owned transformers, the service point will be at the utility transformer secondary terminals, at the service drop, or the meter socket enclosure, depending on where the utility conductors terminate. Figure 100–97

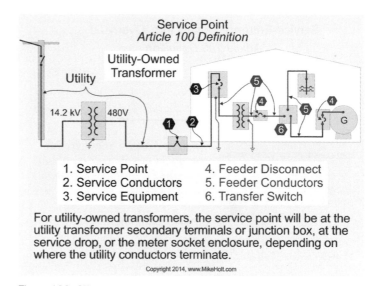

Figure 100–97

■ For customer-owned transformers, the service point will be at the termination of the utility conductors, often at the utility pole. Figure 100–98

Short-Circuit Current Rating. The prospective symmetrical fault current at a nominal voltage that electrical equipment is able to be connected to without sustaining damage exceeding defined acceptance criteria.

Signaling Circuit [Article 725]. A circuit that energizes signaling equipment. Figure 100–99

Special Permission. Written consent from the authority having jurisdiction.

Author's Comment:

■ See the definition of "Authority Having Jurisdiction."

Structure. That which is built or constructed.

Figure 100–98

Figure 100–100

Figure 100–99

Figure 100–101

Surge Protective Device (SPD) [Article 285]. A protective device intended to limit transient voltages by diverting or limiting surge current and preventing the continued flow of current while remaining capable of repeating these functions. Figure 100–100

Type 1. A permanently connected surge protective device listed for installation between the utility transformer and the service equipment. Figure 100–101

Type 2. A permanently connected surge protective device listed for installation on the load side of the service disconnecting means. Figure 100–102

Type 3. A surge protective device listed for installation on branch circuits.

Author's Comment:

■ Type 3 surge protective devices can be installed anywhere on the load side of branch-circuit overcurrent protection up to the equipment served, provided there's a minimum of 30 ft of conductor length between the connection and the service or separately derived system [285.25].

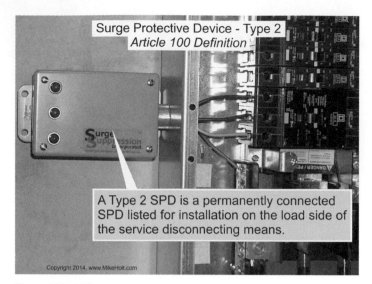

Figure 100–102

Type 4. A component surge protective device; this includes those installed in receptacles and relocatable power taps (plug strips). Figure 100–103

Figure 100–103

Note: For further information see UL 1449, *Standard for Surge Protective Devices.*

Switch, General-Use Snap. A switch constructed to be installed in a device box or a box cover.

Ungrounded System. An electrical power system that's not connected to the ground (earth) or a conductive body that extends the ground (earth) connection. Figure 100–104

Figure 100–104

Utilization Equipment. Equipment that utilizes electricity for electronic, electromechanical, chemical, heating, lighting, or similar purposes.

Voltage of a Circuit. The greatest effective root-mean-square difference of potential between any two conductors of the circuit.

Voltage, Nominal. A value assigned for the purpose of conveniently designating voltage classes, such as 120/240V, 120/208V, or 277/480V [220.5(A)]. Figure 100–105

> **Note 1:** The actual voltage at which a circuit operates can vary from the nominal within a range that permits satisfactory operation of equipment.

Author's Comment:

- Common voltage ratings of electrical equipment are 115V, 200V, 208V, 230V, and 460V. The electrical power supplied might be at the 240V, nominal voltage, but the voltage at the equipment will be less. Therefore, electrical equipment is rated at a value less than the nominal system voltage.

Figure 100–105

Figure 100–106

Voltage-to-Ground. The greatest difference of potential (RMS) between an ungrounded conductor and the neutral point of the circuit that's grounded. Figure 100–106

Watertight. Constructed so that moisture won't enter the enclosure under specific test conditions.

Weatherproof. Constructed or protected so that exposure to the weather won't interfere with successful operation.

ARTICLE 110
REQUIREMENTS FOR ELECTRICAL INSTALLATIONS

Introduction to Article 110—Requirements for Electrical Installations

Article 110 sets the stage for how you'll implement the rest of the *NEC*. This article contains a few of the most important and yet neglected parts of the *Code*. For example:

- How should conductors be terminated?
- What kinds of warnings, markings, and identification does a given installation require?
- What's the right working clearance for a given installation?
- What do the temperature limitations at terminals mean?
- What are the *NEC* requirements for dealing with flash protection?

It's critical that you master Article 110, and that's exactly what this *Illustrated Guide to Understanding the National Electrical Code* is designed for. As you read this article, you're building your foundation for correctly applying the *NEC*. In fact, this article itself is a foundation for much of the *Code*. The purpose for the *National Electrical Code* is to provide a safe installation, but Article 110 is perhaps focused a little more on providing an installation that's safe for the installer and maintenance electrician, so time spent in this article is time well spent.

Part I. General Requirements

110.1 Scope

Article 110 covers the general requirements for the examination and approval, installation and use, access to and spaces about electrical equipment; as well as general requirements for enclosures intended for personnel entry (manholes, vaults, and tunnels).

Note: See Annex J for information regarding ADA accessibility design.

Author's Comment:

- Requirements for people with disabilities include things like mounting heights for switches and receptacles, and requirements for the distance that objects such as wall sconces protrude from a wall.

110.2 Approval of Conductors and Equipment

The authority having jurisdiction must approve all electrical conductors and equipment. Figure 110–1

Author's Comment:

- For a better understanding of product approval, review 90.4, 90.7, 110.3 and the definitions for "Approved," "Identified," "Labeled," and "Listed" in Article 100.

Figure 110–1

110.3 Examination, Identification, Installation, and Use of Equipment

(A) Guidelines for Approval. The authority having jurisdiction must approve equipment. In doing so, consideration must be given to the following:

(1) Suitability for installation and use in accordance with the *NEC*

Note: Suitability of equipment use may be identified by a description marked on or provided with a product to identify the suitability of the product for a specific purpose, environment, or application. Special conditions of use or other limitations may be marked on the equipment, in the product instructions, or appropriate listing and labeling information. Suitability of equipment may be evidenced by listing or labeling.

(2) Mechanical strength and durability

(3) Wire-bending and connection space

(4) Electrical insulation

(5) Heating effects under all conditions of use

(6) Arcing effects

(7) Classification by type, size, voltage, current capacity, and specific use

(8) Other factors contributing to the practical safeguarding of persons using or in contact with the equipment

(B) Installation and Use. Equipment must be installed and used in accordance with any instructions included in the listing or labeling requirements. Figure 110–2

Figure 110–2

Author's Comment:

- See the definitions of "Labeling" and "Listing" in Article 100.

- Failure to follow product listing instructions, such as the torquing of terminals and the sizing of conductors, is a violation of this *Code* rule. Figure 110–3

Figure 110–3

■ When an air conditioner nameplate specifies "Maximum Fuse Size," one-time or dual-element fuses must be used to protect the equipment. Figure 110–4

Figure 110–4

110.4 Voltages

The voltage rating of electrical equipment is not permitted to be less than the nominal voltage of a circuit to which it's connected. Figure 110–5

Figure 110–5

110.5 Copper Conductors

When the conductor material (copper/aluminum) isn't specified in a rule, the material and sizes are based on a copper conductor.

110.6 Conductor Sizes

Conductor sizes are expressed in American Wire Gage (AWG), typically from 18 AWG up to 4/0 AWG. Conductor sizes larger than 4/0 AWG are expressed in kcmil (thousand circular mils). Figure 110–6

Figure 110–6

110.7 Wiring Integrity

Completed installations must be free from short circuits, ground faults, or any connections to ground unless required or permitted by the *Code*. Figure 110–7

110.8 Suitable Wiring Methods

Only wiring methods recognized as suitable are included in the *NEC*, and they must be installed in accordance with the *Code*. Figure 110–8

Figure 110–7

Figure 110–9

Figure 110–8

Author's Comment:

- See Chapter 3 for power and lighting wiring methods, Chapter 7 for signaling, remote-control, and power-limited circuits, and Chapter 8 for communications circuits.

110.9 Interrupting Protection Rating

Overcurrent devices such as circuit breakers and fuses are intended to interrupt the circuit, and they must have an interrupting rating <u>sufficient for the nominal circuit voltage</u> and the current that's available at the line terminals of the equipment. Figure 110–9

Author's Comment:

- See the definition of "Interrupting Rating" in Article 100.

- Unless marked otherwise, the ampere interrupting rating for circuit breakers is 5,000A [240.83(C)], and for fuses it's 10,000A [240.60(C)(3)]. **Figure 110–10**

Figure 110–10

Available Short-Circuit Current

Available short-circuit current is the current, in amperes, available at a given point in the electrical system. This available short-circuit current is first determined at the secondary terminals of the utility transformer. Thereafter, the available short-circuit current is calculated at the terminals of service equipment, then at branch-circuit panelboards and other equipment. The available short-circuit current is different at each point of the electrical system. It's highest at the utility transformer and lowest at the branch-circuit load.

The available short-circuit current depends on the impedance of the circuit. The greater the circuit impedance (utility transformer and the additive impedances of the circuit conductors), the lower the available short-circuit current. Figure 110–11

Available Short-Circuit Current

As the electrical system's impedance increases, short-circuit amperes (SCA) decrease

| SCA=46,263A | SCA=34,338A | SCA=17,447A | SCA=3,949A |

Utility Transformer
Copyright 2014 www.MikeHolt.com

Service   Branch Panel

Overcurrent devices must be rated for the available fault current [110.9].

Conductors and equipment must have a current rating sufficient to withstand the available fault current [110.10].

Figure 110–11

The factors that affect the available short-circuit current at the utility transformer include the system voltage, the transformer kVA rating, and the circuit impedance (expressed in a percentage on the equipment nameplate). Properties that have an impact on the impedance of the circuit include the conductor material (copper versus aluminum), conductor size, conductor length, and motor-operated equipment supplied by the circuit.

DANGER: *Extremely high values of current flow (caused by short circuits or ground faults) produce tremendously destructive thermal and magnetic forces. Overcurrent protection devices not rated to interrupt the current at the available fault values at its listed voltage rating can explode while attempting to open the circuit overcurrent device from a short circuit or ground fault, which can cause serious injury or death, as well as property damage.* Figure 110–12

Improper Amperes Interrupting Rating (AIC)
110.9

10,000 AIR (AIC)
Danger: The overcurrent device isn't suitable for the available fault current.

16,000A Fault Current   Copyright 2014, www.MikeHolt.com

Overcurrent protection not properly rated for the available short-circuit and ground-fault values of the circuit can explode while it's attempting to open.

Figure 110–12

110.10 Circuit Impedance, Short-Circuit Current Rating, and Other Characteristics

Electrical equipment must have a short-circuit current rating that permits the circuit protective device to open from a short circuit or ground fault without extensive damage to the electrical equipment of the circuit. This fault is assumed to be either between two or more of the circuit conductors or between any circuit conductor and the equipment grounding conductor(s) permitted in 250.118. Listed equipment applied in accordance with their listing is considered to have met the requirements of this section.

Author's Comment:

- For example, a motor controller must have a sufficient short-circuit rating for the available fault current. If the fault current exceeds the controller's short-circuit current rating, the controller can explode, endangering persons and property. Figure 110–13

Figure 110–13

Author's Comment:

- Conductors must not be exposed to ultraviolet rays from the sun unless identified for the purpose [310.10(D)].

Note 1: Raceways, cable trays, cablebus, cable armor, boxes, cable sheathing, cabinets, elbows, couplings, fittings, supports, and support hardware must be of materials that are suitable for the environment in which they're to be installed, in accordance with 300.6.

Note 2: Some cleaning and lubricating compounds contain chemicals that can cause deterioration of the plastic used for insulating and structural applications in equipment.

Equipment not identified for outdoor use and equipment identified only for indoor use must be protected against damage from the weather during construction.

Note 3: See *NEC* Table 110.28 for appropriate enclosure-type designations.

110.11 Deteriorating Agents

Electrical equipment and conductors must be suitable for the environment and conditions of use. Consideration must also be given to the presence of corrosive gases, fumes, vapors, liquids, or other substances that can have a deteriorating effect on the conductors or equipment. Figure 110–14

110.12 Mechanical Execution of Work

Electrical equipment must be installed in a neat and workmanlike manner. Figure 110–15

Figure 110–14

Figure 110–15

(A) Unused Openings. Unused openings, other than those intended for the operation of equipment or for mounting purposes, or those that are part of the design for listed products, must be closed by fittings that provide protection substantially equivalent to the wall of the equipment. Figure 110–16

Figure 110–16

Note: Accepted industry practices are described in ANSI/NECA 1, *Standard Practices for Good Workmanship in Electrical Construction.*

Author's Comment:

■ The National Electrical Contractors Association (NECA) created a series of National Electrical Installation Standards (NEIS)® that established the industry's first quality guidelines for electrical installations. These standards define a benchmark or baseline of quality and workmanship for installing electrical products and systems. They explain what installing electrical products and systems in a "neat and workmanlike manner" means. For more information about these standards, visit www.NECA-NEIS.org.

(B) Integrity of Electrical Equipment. Internal parts of electrical equipment must not be damaged or contaminated by foreign material, such as paint, plaster, cleaners, and so forth.

Author's Comment:

■ Precautions must be taken to provide protection from contamination of the internal parts of panelboards and receptacles during building construction. Make sure that electrical equipment is properly masked and protected before painting or other phases of the project take place that can cause damage. Figure 110–17

Figure 110–17

Electrical equipment that contains damaged parts may adversely affect safe operation or mechanical strength of the equipment and must not be installed. This includes parts that are broken, bent, cut, or deteriorated by corrosion, chemical action, or overheating. Figure 110–18

Author's Comment:

■ Damaged parts include cracked insulators, arc shields not in place, overheated fuse clips, and damaged or missing switch handles or circuit-breaker handles. Figure 110–19

Figure 110–18

Figure 110–20

Figure 110–19

110.13 Mounting and Cooling of Equipment

(A) Mounting. Electrical equipment must be firmly secured to the surface on which it's mounted. Figure 110–20

110.14 Conductor Termination and Splicing

Conductor terminal and splicing devices must be identified for the conductor material and they must be properly installed and used. Figure 110–21

Figure 110–21

Author's Comment:

- Switches and receptacles marked CO/ALR are designed to ensure a good connection through the use of a larger contact area and compatible materials. The terminal screws are plated with the element called "Indium." Indium is an extremely soft metal that forms a gas-sealed connection with the aluminum conductor.

Connectors and terminals for conductors more finely stranded than Class B and Class C, as shown in Table 10 of Chapter 9, must be identified for the use of finely stranded conductors. Figure 110–22

Finely Stranded Flexible Conductor Termination 110.14

Connectors and terminations for conductors more finely stranded than Class B and Class C stranding must be identified for the conductor class [Chapter 9, Table 10].

Figure 110–22

Author's Comment:

- According to UL Standard 486 A-B, a terminal/lug/connector must be listed and marked for use with other than Class B stranded conductors. With no marking or factory literature/instructions to the contrary, terminals may only be used with Class B stranded conductors.

- See the definition of "Identified" in Article 100.

- Conductor terminations must comply with the manufacturer's instructions as required by 110.3(B). For example, if the instructions for the device state "Suitable for 18-12 AWG Stranded," then only stranded conductors can be used with the terminating device. If the instructions state "Suitable for 18-12 AWG Solid," then only solid conductors are permitted, and if the instructions state "Suitable for 18-12 AWG," then either solid or stranded conductors can be used with the terminating device.

Copper and Aluminum Mixed. Copper and aluminum conductors must not make contact with each other in a device unless the device is listed and identified for this purpose.

Author's Comment:

- Few terminations are listed for the mixing of aluminum and copper conductors, but if they are, that'll be marked on the product package or terminal device. The reason copper and aluminum shouldn't be in contact with each other is because corrosion develops between the two different metals due to galvanic action, resulting in increased contact resistance at the splicing device. This increased resistance can cause the splice to overheat and cause a fire.

Note: Many terminations and equipment are either marked with a tightening torque or have the torque values included in the product's instructions. Figure 110–23

Conductor Termination Manufacturer's Torque Specifications 110.14 Note

Many terminations and equipment are either marked with a tightening torque or have the torque values included in the installation instructions.

Figure 110–23

Author's Comment:

■ Conductors must terminate in devices that have been properly tightened in accordance with the manufacturer's torque specifications included with equipment instructions. Failure to torque terminals can result in excessive heating of terminals or splicing devices due to a loose connection. A loose connection can also lead to arcing which increases the heating effect and may also lead to a short circuit or ground fault. Any of these can result in a fire or other failure, including an arc-flash event. In addition, this is a violation of 110.3(B), which requires all equipment to be installed in accordance with listing or labeling instructions.

> **Question:** *What do you do if the torque value isn't provided with the device?*
>
> **Answer:** *In the absence of connector or equipment manufacturer's recommended torque values, Table I.1, Table I.2, and Table I.3 contained in Annex I may be used to correctly tighten screw-type connections for power and lighting circuits.*

Author's Comment:

■ Terminating conductors without a torque tool can result in an improper and unsafe installation. If a torque screwdriver isn't used, there's a good chance the conductors aren't properly terminated.

(A) Terminations. Conductor terminals must ensure a good connection without damaging the conductors and must be made by pressure connectors (including set screw type) or splices to flexible leads. Figure 110–24

Author's Comment:

■ See the definition of "Connector, Pressure" in Article 100.

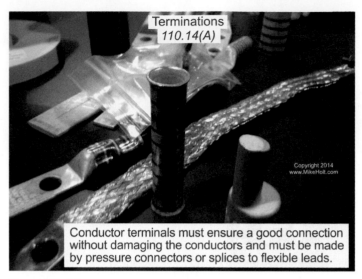

Conductor terminals must ensure a good connection without damaging the conductors and must be made by pressure connectors or splices to flexible leads.

Figure 110–24

> **Question:** *What if the conductor is larger than the terminal device?*
>
> **Answer:** *This condition needs to be anticipated in advance, and the equipment should be ordered with terminals that'll accommodate the larger conductor. However, if you're in the field, you should:*
> - *Contact the manufacturer and have them express deliver you the proper terminals, bolts, washers, and nuts, or*
> - *Order a terminal device that crimps on the end of the larger conductor and reduces the termination size.*

Terminals for more than one conductor and terminals used for aluminum conductors must be identified for this purpose, either within the equipment instructions or on the terminal itself. Figure 110–25

Author's Comment:

■ Split-bolt connectors are commonly listed for only two conductors, although some are listed for three conductors. However, it's a common industry practice to terminate as many conductors as possible within a split-bolt connector, even though this violates the *NEC.* Figure 110–26

(B) Conductor Splices. Conductors must be spliced by a splicing device identified for the purpose or by exothermic welding.

Figure 110–25

Figure 110–27

Unless marked otherwise, terminals are listed for one wire.

Figure 110–26

Figure 110–28

Author's Comment:

■ Conductors aren't required to be twisted together prior to the installation of a twist-on wire connector, unless specifically required in the installation instructions. Figure 110–27

Unused circuit conductors aren't required to be removed. However, to prevent an electrical hazard, the free ends of the conductors must be insulated to prevent the exposed end of the conductor from touching energized parts. This requirement can be met by the use of an insulated twist-on or push-on wire connector. Figure 110–28

Author's Comment:

■ See the definition of "Energized" in Article 100.

Underground Splices:

Single Conductors. Single direct burial conductors of types UF or USE can be spliced underground without a junction box, but the conductors must be spliced with a device listed for direct burial [300.5(E) and 300.15(G)]. Figure 110–29

Figure 110–29

Figure 110–30

Multiconductor Cable. Multiconductor UF or USE cable can have the individual conductors spliced underground without a junction box as long as a listed splice kit that encapsulates the conductors as well as the cable jacket is used.

(C) Temperature Limitations (Conductor Size). Conductors are to be sized using their ampacity from the insulation temperature rating column of Table 310.15(B)(16) that corresponds to the lowest temperature rating of any terminal, device, or conductor of the circuit.

Author's Comment:

- Conductors with insulation temperature ratings higher than the termination's temperature rating can be used for ampacity adjustment, correction, or both. Figure 110–30

(1) Equipment Temperature Rating Provisions. Unless the equipment is listed and marked otherwise, conductor sizing for equipment terminations must be based on Table 310.15(B)(16) in accordance with (a) or (b):

(a) Equipment Rated 100A or Less.

(1) Conductors must be sized using the 60°C temperature column of Table 310.15(B)(16). Figure 110–31

(3) Conductors terminating on terminals rated 75°C are sized in accordance with the ampacities listed in the 75°C temperature column of Table 310.15(B)(16). Figure 110–32

Figure 110–31

(4) Motors marked with design letters B, C, or D, conductors having an insulation rating of 75°C or higher can be used, provided the ampacity of such conductors doesn't exceed the 75°C ampacity. Figure 110–33

(b) Equipment Rated Over 100A.

(1) Conductors must be sized using the 75°C temperature column of Table 310.15(B)(16). Figure 110–34

Conductor Sizing - Equipment Rated 100A or Less
110.14(C)(1)(a)(3)

Terminals Rated 75°C

Conductors terminating on equipment rated 75°C are sized in accordance with the ampacities listed in the 75°C temperature column of Table 310.15(B)(16), provided the conductors have an insulation rating of at least 75°C.

Figure 110–32

Conductor Sizing - Equipment Over 100A
110.14(C)(1)(b)(1)

Unless listed and marked otherwise, conductors must be sized using the 75°C column of Table 310.15(B)(16).

Inverter

Figure 110–34

Conductor Sizing Motors Marked With Designed Letters B, C, or D
110.14(C)(1)(a)(4)

Motors marked with design letters B, C, or D can use the 75°C column of Table 310.15(B)(16) for conductor sizing.

Figure 110–33

Separately Installed Connectors
110.14(C)(2)

Conductors terminating on separately installed connectors can be sized to the 90°C column of Table 310.15(B)(16) if the conductors and connectors are rated at least 90°C.

Figure 110–35

(2) Separate Connector Provisions. Conductors can be sized to the 90°C column of Table 310.15(B)(16) if the conductors and pressure connectors are rated at least 90°C. Figure 110–35

Note: Equipment markings or listing information may restrict the sizing and temperature ratings of connected conductors.

110.15 High-Leg Conductor Identification

On a 4-wire, delta-connected, three-phase system, where the mid-point of one phase winding of the secondary is grounded (a high-leg system), the conductor with 208V to ground must be durably and permanently marked by an outer finish orange in color, or other effective means. Such identification must be placed at each point on the system where a connection is made if the neutral conductor is present [230.56]. Figure 110–36

Figure 110–36

□ **Disconnects.** The *NEC* doesn't specify the termination location for the high-leg conductor in switch equipment (Switches—Article 404), but the generally accepted practice is to terminate this conductor to the "B" phase.

□ **Utility Equipment.** The ANSI standard for meter equipment requires the high-leg conductor (208V to neutral) to terminate on the "C" (right) phase of the meter socket enclosure. This is because the demand meter needs 120V, and it obtains that voltage from the "B" phase. Figure 110–37

Figure 110–37

Author's Comment:

■ The high-leg conductor is also called the "wild leg," "stinger leg," or "bastard leg."

■ Other important *NEC* rules relating to the high leg are as follows:

□ **Panelboards.** Since 1975, panelboards supplied by a 4-wire, delta-connected, three-phase system must have the high-leg conductor terminate to the "B" phase of a panelboard [408.3(E)]. Section 408.3(F)(1) requires panelboards to be field-marked with "Caution Phase B Has 208V to Ground."

■ Also hope the utility lineman isn't color blind and doesn't inadvertently cross the "orange" high-leg conductor (208V) with the red (120V) service conductor at the weatherhead. It's happened before…

⚠ **WARNING:** *When replacing equipment in existing facilities that contain a high-leg conductor, care must be taken to ensure the high-leg conductor is replaced in its original location. Prior to 1975, the high-leg conductor was required to terminate on the "C" phase of panelboards and switchboards. Failure to re-terminate the high leg in accordance with the existing installation can result in 120V circuits being inadvertently connected to the 208V high leg, with disastrous results.*

110.16 Arc-Flash Hazard Warning

Electrical equipment such as switchboards, <u>switchgear,</u> panelboards, industrial control panels, meter socket enclosures, and motor control centers in other than dwelling units that are likely to require examination, adjustment, servicing, or maintenance while energized must be marked to warn qualified persons of the danger associated with an arc flash from short circuits or ground faults. The marking <u>can be made in the</u> field <u>or the factory, must not be handwritten, must be permanently affixed, be of sufficient durability to withstand the environment involved [110.21(B)]</u>, and be clearly visible to qualified persons before they examine, adjust, service, or perform maintenance on the equipment. Figure 110–38

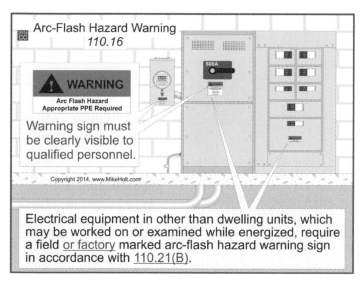

Figure 110–38

Author's Comment:

- See the definition of "Qualified Person" in Article 100.

- This rule is meant to warn qualified persons who work on energized electrical systems that an arc flash hazard exists so they'll select proper personal protective equipment (PPE) in accordance with industry accepted safe work practice standards.

Note 1: NFPA 70E, *Standard for Electrical Safety in the Workplace,* provides assistance in determining the severity of potential exposure, planning safe work practices, <u>arc-flash labeling,</u> and selecting personal protective equipment.

110.21 Markings

(A) Manufacturer's Markings. The manufacturer's name, trademark, or other descriptive marking must be placed on all electrical equipment and, where required by the *Code*, markings such as voltage, current, wattage, or other ratings must be provided. All marking must have sufficient durability to withstand the environment involved.

(B) Field-Applied Hazard Markings. Where caution, warning, or danger signs or labels are required, the labels must meet the following:

(1) The markings must use words, colors, or symbols that effectively warn personnel. Figure 110–39

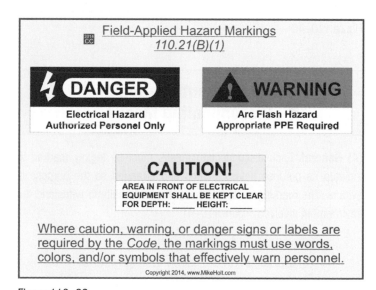

Figure 110–39

Note: ANSI Z535.4, *Product Safety Signs and Labels,* provides guidelines for the design and durability of signs and labels.

(2) The label can't be handwritten, and it must be permanently affixed to the equipment. Figure 110–40

Ex to (2): Labels that contain information that's likely to change can be handwritten, if it's legible.

Author's Comment:

- A permanently affixed sign would include a sticker, but not a piece of paper taped to the equipment.

(3) The marking must be of sufficient durability to withstand the environment involved.

Figure 110–40

110.22 Identification of Disconnecting Means

(A) General. Each disconnecting means must be legibly marked to indicate its purpose unless located and arranged so the purpose is evident. The marking must be of sufficient durability to withstand the environment involved. Figure 110–41

Figure 110–41

(C) Tested Series Combination Systems. Tested series-rated installations must be legibly field-marked in accordance with 240.86(B) with a permanently affixed label that's not <u>handwritten of sufficient durability to withstand the environment involved</u> [110.21(B)] to indicate the equipment has been applied with a series combination rating.

110.24 Available Fault Current

(A) Field Marking. Service equipment in other than dwelling units must be legibly field marked with the maximum available fault current, including the date the fault current calculation was performed, and be of sufficient durability to withstand the environment involved. Figure 110–42

Figure 110–42

Note: The fault current markings required by this section are to ensure compliance with 110.9 and 110.10. They're not intended to be used for arc flash analysis. Arc flash hazard information is available in NFPA 70E, *Standard for Electrical Safety in the Workplace.*

(B) Modifications. When modifications to the electrical installation affect the maximum available fault current at the service, the maximum available fault current must be recalculated to ensure the service equipment ratings are sufficient for the maximum available fault current at the line terminals of the equipment. The required field marking(s) in 110.24(A) must be adjusted to reflect the new level of maximum available fault current.

Ex: Field markings aren't required for industrial installations where conditions of maintenance and supervision ensure that only qualified persons service the equipment.

110.25 Lockable Disconnecting Means

Where the *Code* requires that a disconnecting means is lockable in the open position, the provisions for locking must remain in place whether the lock is installed or not. Figure 110–43

Figure 110–43

Ex: Locking provisions for cord-and-plug connected equipment don't need to remain in place without the lock installed.

Part II. 600V, Nominal, or Less

110.26 Spaces About Electrical Equipment

 Scan this QR code for a video of this *Code* rule. See page xix for information on how to use the QR codes.

For the purpose of safe operation and maintenance of equipment, access and working space must be provided about all electrical equipment.

(A) Working Space. Equipment that may need examination, adjustment, servicing, or maintenance while energized must have working space provided in accordance with (1), (2), and (3):

Author's Comment:

- The phrase "while energized" is the root of many debates. As always, check with the AHJ to see what equipment he or she believes needs a clear working space.

Figure 110–44

(1) Depth of Working Space. The working space, which is measured from the enclosure front, must not be less than the distances contained in Table 110.26(A)(1). Figure 110–44

Table 110.26(A)(1) Working Space			
Voltage–to–Ground	Condition 1	Condition 2	Condition 3
0–150V	3 ft	3 ft	3 ft
151–600V	3 ft	3½ft	4 ft

- **Condition 1**—*Exposed live parts on one side of the working space and no live or grounded parts, including concrete, brick, or tile walls are on the other side of the working space.*
- **Condition 2**—*Exposed live parts on one side of the working space and grounded parts, including concrete, brick, or tile walls are on the other side of the working space.*
- **Condition 3**—*Exposed live parts on both sides of the working space.*

(a) Rear and Sides. Working space isn't required for the back or sides of assemblies where all connections and all renewable or adjustable parts are accessible from the front. Figure 110–45

Working Space - Back or Sides of Equipment
110.26(A)(1)(a)

Working Space Not Required

Equipment Assembly

Work Space

Copyright 2014
www.MikeHolt.com

Working space isn't required for the back or sides of assemblies where all connections are accessible from the front.

Figure 110–45

(b) Low Voltage. If special permission is granted in accordance with 90.4, working space for equipment that operates at not more than 30V ac or 60V dc can be less than the distance in Table 110.26(A)(1). Figure 110–46

Working Space - Low-Voltage Systems
110.26(A)(1)(b)

Fire Alarm Panel

Working Space Required

Copyright 2014
www.MikeHolt.com

CATV [Art. 820]

Working space isn't required for Communications Systems [90.3].

Telephone [Art. 800]

Broadband [Art. 830]

Where special permission is granted, working space for equipment operating at not more than 30V ac or 60V dc can be smaller than the distance in Table 110.26(A)(1).

Figure 110–46

Author's Comment:

- See the definition of "Special Permission" in Article 100.

(c) Existing Buildings. If electrical equipment is being replaced, Condition 2 working space is permitted between dead-front switchboards, **switchgear**, panelboards, or motor control centers located across the aisle from each other where conditions of maintenance and supervision ensure that written procedures have been adopted to prohibit equipment on both sides of the aisle from being open at the same time, and only authorized, qualified persons will service the installation.

Author's Comment:

- The working space requirements of 110.26 don't apply to equipment included in Chapter 8—Communications Circuits [90.3].

(2) Width of Working Space. The width of the working space must be a minimum of 30 in., but in no case less than the width of the equipment. Figure 110–47

Working Space - Width
110.26(A)(2)

Equipment 30 In. or Less

Equipment Over 30 In.

30 in. Wide

Width of Equipment

Copyright 2014, www.MikeHolt.com

The width of the working space must be a minimum of 30 in., but in no case less than the width of the equipment, whichever is greater.

Figure 110–47

Author's Comment:

- The width of the working space can be measured from left-to-right, from right-to-left, or simply centered on the equipment, and the working space can overlap the working space for other electrical equipment. Figure 110–48

Figure 110–48

Figure 110–50

In all cases, the working space must be of sufficient width, depth, and height to permit all equipment doors to open 90 degrees. Figure 110–49

Equipment such as raceways, cables, wireways, cabinets, panels, and so on, can be located above or below electrical equipment, but must not extend more than 6 in. into the equipment's working space. Figure 110–51

Figure 110–49

Figure 110–51

(3) Height of Working Space (Headroom). The height of the working space in front of equipment must not be less than 6½ ft, measured from the grade, floor, platform, or the equipment height, whichever is greater. Figure 110–50

Ex 1: The minimum headroom requirement doesn't apply to service equipment or panelboards rated 200A or less located in an existing dwelling unit.

Author's Comment:

■ See the definition of "Dwelling Unit" in Article 100.

Ex 2: Meters are permitted to extend beyond the other equipment.

(B) Clear Working Space. The working space required by this section must be clear at all times. Therefore, this space isn't permitted for storage. Figure 110–52

Figure 110–52

When normally enclosed live parts are exposed for inspection or servicing, the working space, if in a passageway or general open space, must be suitably guarded.

Author's Comment:

- When working in a passageway, the working space should be guarded from occupants using it. When working on electrical equipment in a passageway one must be mindful of a fire alarm evacuation with numerous occupants congregated and moving through the area.

⚠ **CAUTION:** *It's very dangerous to service energized parts in the first place, and it's unacceptable to be subjected to additional dangers by working around bicycles, boxes, crates, appliances, and other impediments.*

Author's Comment:

- Signaling and communications equipment must not be installed in a manner that encroaches on the working space of the electrical equipment. Figure 110–53

Figure 110–53

(C) Entrance to and Egress from Working Space.

(1) Minimum Required. At least one entrance of sufficient area must provide access to and egress from the working space.

Author's Comment:

- Check to see what the authority having jurisdiction considers "Sufficient Area." Building codes contain minimum dimensions for doors and openings for personnel travel.

(2) Large Equipment. An entrance to and egress from each end of the working space of electrical equipment rated 1,200A or more that's over 6 ft wide is required. The opening must be a minimum of 24 in. wide and 6½ ft high. Figure 110–54

A single entrance to and egress from the required working space is permitted where either of the following conditions is met:

(a) Unobstructed Egress. Only one entrance is required where the location permits a continuous and unobstructed way of egress travel. Figure 110–55

(b) Double Workspace. Only one entrance is required where the required working space depth is doubled, and the equipment is located so the edge of the entrance is no closer than the required working space distance. Figure 110–56

Figure 110–54

For equipment rated 1,200A or more and over 6 ft wide, an entrance to and egress from (2 ft wide x 6 ½ ft wide) is required at each end of the working space.

Figure 110–56

One entrance/egress is permitted where the required working space is doubled, and equipment is located so the edge of the entrance is no closer than the required working space distance.

Figure 110–55

Figure 110–57

For equipment rated 800A or more, personnel door(s) located less than 25 ft from the nearest edge of the working space must open in the direction of egress and have listed panic hardware.

(3) Personnel Doors. If equipment with overcurrent or switching devices rated 800A or more is installed, personnel door(s) for entrance to and egress from the working space located less than 25 ft from the nearest edge of the working space must have the door(s) open in the direction of egress and be equipped with listed panic hardware. Figure 110–57

Author's Comment:

■ History has shown that electricians who suffer burns on their hands in electrical arc flash or arc blast events often can't open doors equipped with knobs that must be turned.

■ Since this requirement is in the *NEC*, the electrical contractor is responsible for ensuring that panic hardware is installed where required. Some electrical contractors are offended at being held liable for nonelectrical responsibilities, but this rule is designed to save the lives of electricians. For this and other reasons, many construction professionals routinely hold "pre-construction" or "pre-con" meetings to review potential opportunities for miscommunication—before the work begins.

(D) Illumination. Service equipment, switchboards, <u>switchgear,</u> and panelboards, as well as motor control centers located indoors must have illumination located indoors and must not be controlled by automatic means only. Figure 110–58

Figure 110–58

Author's Comment:

■ The *Code* doesn't provide the minimum foot-candles required to provide proper illumination. Proper illumination of electrical equipment rooms is essential for the safety of those qualified to work on such equipment.

(E) Dedicated Equipment Space. Switchboards, <u>switchgear,</u> panelboards, and motor control centers must have dedicated equipment space as follows:

(1) Indoors.

(a) Dedicated Electrical Space. The footprint space (width and depth of the equipment) extending from the floor to a height of 6 ft above the equipment or to the structural ceiling, whichever is lower, must be dedicated for the electrical installation, Figure 110–59.

No piping, ducts, or other equipment foreign to the electrical installation can be installed in this dedicated footprint space. Figure 110–60

Ex: Suspended ceilings with removable panels can be within the dedicated footprint space [110.26(E)(1)(d)].

Figure 110–59

Figure 110–60

Author's Comment:

■ Electrical raceways and cables not associated with the dedicated space can be within the dedicated space. These aren't considered "equipment foreign to the electrical installation." Figure 110–61

(b) Foreign Systems. Foreign systems can be located above the dedicated space if protection is installed to prevent damage to the electrical equipment from condensation, leaks, or breaks in the foreign systems, which can be as simple as a drip-pan. Figure 110–62

Figure 110–61

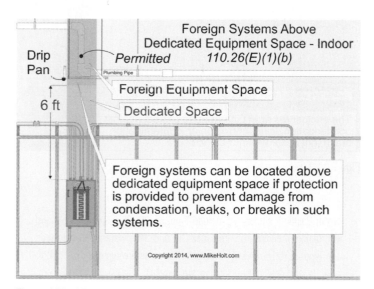

Figure 110–62

(c) Sprinkler Protection. Sprinkler protection piping isn't permitted in the dedicated space, but the *NEC* doesn't prohibit sprinklers from spraying water on electrical equipment.

(d) Suspended Ceilings. A dropped, suspended, or similar ceiling isn't considered a structural ceiling. Figure 110–63

(2) Outdoor. Outdoor installations must comply with 110.26(E)(2)(a) and (b).

(a) Installation Requirements. Outdoor electrical equipment must be installed in suitable enclosures and be protected from accidental contact by unauthorized personnel, or by vehicular traffic, or by accidental spillage or leakage from piping systems.

Figure 110–63

(b) Dedicated Electrical Space. The footprint space (width and depth of the equipment) extending from the floor to a height of 6 ft above the equipment must be dedicated for the electrical installation. No piping, ducts, or other equipment foreign to the electrical installation can be installed in this dedicated footprint space. Figure 110–64

Figure 110–64

Author's Comment:

■ See the definition of "Accessible as it applies to equipment" in Article 100.

110.27 Guarding

(A) Guarding Live Parts. Live parts of electrical equipment operating at 50V or more must be guarded against accidental contact. This can be done by:

(1) Locating them in a separate room, vault, or enclosure.

(2) Guarding with a partition or screen.

(3) Locating them on a balcony or platform.

(4) Elevating them above the floor or working surface, <u>in accordance with the following:</u>

<u>(a)</u> <u>8 ft for 50V through 300V.</u>

<u>(b)</u> <u>8½ ft for 301V through 600V.</u>

(B) Prevent Physical Damage. Electrical equipment must not be installed where subject to physical damage, unless enclosures or guards are arranged and they're of sufficient strength to prevent damage. Figure 110–65

Figure 110–65

(C) Warning Signs. Entrances to rooms and other guarded locations containing exposed live parts must be marked with conspicuous signs forbidding unqualified persons from entering.

110.28 Enclosure Types

Enclosures must be marked with an enclosure-type number and be suitable for the location in accordance with Table 110.28.

The enclosures aren't intended to protect against condensation, icing, corrosion, or contamination that might occur within the enclosure or that enters via the raceway or unsealed openings. Figure 110–66

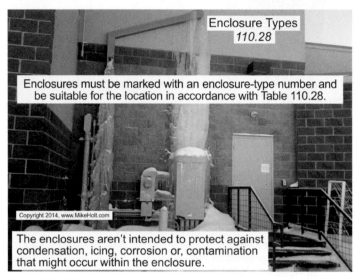

Figure 110–66

Note: Raintight enclosures include Types 3, 3S, 3SX, 3X, 4, 4X, 6, and 6P; rainproof enclosures are Types 3R, and 3RX; watertight enclosures are Types 4, 4X, 6, and 6P; driptight enclosures are Types 2, 5, 12, 12K, and 13; and dusttight enclosures are Types 3, 3S, 3SX, 3X, 5, 12, 12K, and 13.

CHAPTER 1 PRACTICE QUESTIONS

Please use the 2014 *Code* book to answer the following questions.

1. The *NEC* is _____.

   (a) intended to be a design manual
   (b) meant to be used as an instruction guide for untrained persons
   (c) for the practical safeguarding of persons and property
   (d) published by the Bureau of Standards

2. The following systems shall be installed in accordance with the *NEC* requirements:

   (a) signaling conductors, equipment, and raceways
   (b) communications conductors, equipment, and raceways
   (c) electrical conductors, equipment, and raceways
   (d) all of these

3. The *NEC* applies to the installation of _____.

   (a) electrical conductors and equipment within or on public and private buildings
   (b) outside conductors and equipment on the premises
   (c) optical fiber cables and raceways
   (d) all of these

4. Installations of communications equipment that are under the exclusive control of communications utilities, and located outdoors or in building spaces used exclusively for such installations _____ covered by the *NEC*.

   (a) are
   (b) are sometimes
   (c) are not
   (d) may be

5. Electric utilities may include entities that install, operate, and maintain _____.

   (a) communications systems (telephone, CATV, Internet, satellite, or data services)
   (b) electric supply systems (generation, transmission, or distribution systems)
   (c) local area network wiring on the premises
   (d) a or b

6. Communications wiring such as telephone, antenna, and CATV wiring within a building shall not be required to comply with the installation requirements of Chapters 1 through 7, except where specifically referenced in Chapter 8.

   (a) True
   (b) False

7. Chapters 1 through 4 of the *NEC* apply _____.

   (a) generally to all electrical installations
   (b) only to special occupancies and conditions
   (c) only to special equipment and material
   (d) all of these

8. By special permission, the authority having jurisdiction may waive specific requirements in this *Code* where it is assured that equivalent objectives can be achieved by establishing and maintaining effective safety.

   (a) True
   (b) False

9. Explanatory material, such as references to other standards, references to related sections of the *NEC*, or information related to a *Code* rule, are included in the form of Informational Notes.

   (a) True
   (b) False

10. Nonmandatory Informative Annexes contained in the back of the *Code* book _____.

    (a) are for information only
    (b) aren't enforceable as a requirement of the *Code*
    (c) are enforceable as a requirement of the *Code*
    (d) a and b

11. Admitting close approach not guarded by locked doors, elevation, or other effective means, is referred to as _____.

    (a) accessible (as applied to equipment)
    (b) accessible (as applied to wiring methods)
    (c) accessible, readily
    (d) all of these

12. "_____" means acceptable to the authority having jurisdiction.

    (a) Identified
    (b) Listed
    (c) Approved
    (d) Labeled

13. An arc-fault circuit interrupter is a device intended to de-energize the circuit when it recognizes characteristics unique to _____.

    (a) overcurrent
    (b) arcing
    (c) a ground fault
    (d) harmonic fundamental

14. A _____ is an area that includes a basin with a toilet, urinal, tub, shower, bidet, or similar plumbing fixtures.

    (a) bath area
    (b) bathroom
    (c) rest area
    (d) none of these

15. A battery system includes storage batteries and battery chargers, and can include inverters, converters, and associated electrical equipment.

    (a) True
    (b) False

16. The connection between the grounded circuit conductor and the supply-side bonding jumper or equipment grounding conductor, or both, at a _____ is called a "system bonding jumper."

    (a) service disconnect
    (b) separately derived system
    (c) motor control center
    (d) separate building or structure disconnect

17. The circuit conductors between the final overcurrent device protecting the circuit and the outlet(s) are known as "_____ conductors."

    (a) feeder
    (b) branch-circuit
    (c) home run
    (d) none of these

18. A cable routing assembly is composed of single or connected multiple channels as well as associated fittings, forming a structural system to _____ high densities of wires and cables, typically communications wires and cables, optical fiber and data (Class 2 and Class 3) cables.

    (a) support
    (b) route
    (c) protect
    (d) a and b

19. A circuit breaker is a device designed to _____ the circuit automatically on a predetermined overcurrent without damage to itself when properly applied within its rating.

    (a) energize
    (b) reset
    (c) connect
    (d) open

20. A communications raceway is an enclosed channel of nonmetallic materials designed for holding communications wires and cables in _____ applications.

    (a) plenum
    (b) riser
    (c) general-purpose
    (d) all of these

21. A separate portion of a raceway system that provides access through a removable cover(s) to the interior of the system, defines the term _____.

    (a) junction box
    (b) accessible raceway
    (c) conduit body
    (d) cutout box

22. The selection and installation of overcurrent devices so that an overcurrent condition will be localized and restrict outages to the circuit or equipment affected, is called "_____."

    (a) overcurrent protection
    (b) interrupting capacity
    (c) selective coordination
    (d) overload protection

23. "Varying duty" is defined as _____.

    (a) intermittent operation in which the load conditions are regularly recurrent
    (b) operation at a substantially constant load for an indefinite length of time
    (c) operation for alternate intervals of load and rest, or load, no load, and rest
    (d) operation at loads, and for intervals of time, both of which may be subject to wide variation

24. A _____ is a single unit that provides independent living facilities for one or more persons, including permanent provisions for living, sleeping, cooking, and sanitation.

    (a) one-family dwelling
    (b) two-family dwelling
    (c) dwelling unit
    (d) multifamily dwelling

25. Surrounded by a case, housing, fence, or wall(s) that prevents persons from accidentally contacting energized parts is called "_____."

    (a) guarded
    (b) covered
    (c) protection
    (d) enclosed

26. As used in the *NEC*, equipment includes _____.

    (a) fittings
    (b) appliances
    (c) machinery
    (d) all of these

27. The *NEC* defines a "_____" as all circuit conductors between the service equipment, the source of a separately derived system, or other power supply source and the final branch-circuit overcurrent device.

    (a) service
    (b) feeder
    (c) branch circuit
    (d) all of these

28. Connected to ground or to a conductive body that extends the ground connection is called "_____."

    (a) equipment grounding
    (b) bonded
    (c) grounded
    (d) all of these

29. The installed conductive path(s) that provide(s) a ground-fault current path and connects normally noncurrent-carrying metal parts of equipment together and to the system grounded conductor or to the grounding electrode conductor, or both, is known as a(n) _____.

    (a) grounding electrode conductor
    (b) grounding conductor
    (c) equipment grounding conductor
    (d) none of these

30. A handhole enclosure is an enclosure for use in underground systems, provided with an open or closed bottom, and sized to allow personnel to _____.

    (a) enter and exit freely
    (b) reach into but not enter
    (c) have full working space
    (d) examine it visually

31. Within sight means visible and not more than _____ ft distant from the equipment.

    (a) 10
    (b) 20
    (c) 25
    (d) 50

32. Equipment or materials to which a label, symbol, or other identifying mark of a product evaluation organization that is acceptable to the authority having jurisdiction has been attached is known as "_____."

    (a) listed
    (b) labeled
    (c) approved
    (d) identified

33. A _____ location is protected from weather and not subject to saturation with water or other liquids.

    (a) dry
    (b) damp
    (c) wet
    (d) moist

34. A(n) _____ is intended to provide limited overcurrent protection for specific applications and utilization equipment such as luminaires and appliances. This limited protection is in addition to the protection provided by the required branch-circuit overcurrent protective device.

    (a) supplementary overcurrent device
    (b) surge protection device
    (c) arc-fault circuit interrupter
    (d) Class A GFCI

35. NFPA 70E—*Standard for Electrical Safety in the Workplace*, provides information to help determine the electrical safety training requirements expected of a qualified person.

    (a) True
    (b) False

36. A single receptacle is a single contact device with no other contact device on the same _____.

    (a) circuit
    (b) yoke
    (c) run
    (d) equipment

37. The conductors and equipment from the electric utility that deliver electric energy to the wiring system of the premises is called a "_____."

    (a) branch circuit
    (b) feeder
    (c) service
    (d) none of these

38. The overhead system service-entrance conductors are the service conductors between the terminals of _____ and a point where they are joined by a tap or splice to the service drop or overhead service conductors.

    (a) service equipment
    (b) service point
    (c) grounding electrode
    (d) equipment grounding conductor

39. The prospective symmetrical fault current at a nominal voltage to which an apparatus or system is able to be connected without sustaining damage exceeding defined acceptance criteria is known as the "_____."

    (a) short-circuit current rating
    (b) arc flash rating
    (c) overcurrent rating
    (d) available fault current

40. A switch constructed so that it can be installed in device boxes or on box covers, or otherwise used in conjunction with wiring systems recognized by the *NEC* is called a "_____ switch."

    (a) transfer
    (b) motor-circuit
    (c) general-use snap
    (d) bypass isolation

41. An enclosure constructed so that moisture will not enter the enclosure under specific test conditions is called "_____."

    (a) watertight
    (b) moistureproof
    (c) waterproof
    (d) rainproof

42. Conductors normally used to carry current shall be _____ unless otherwise provided in this *Code*.

    (a) bare
    (b) stranded
    (c) of copper
    (d) of aluminum

43. Unless identified for use in the operating environment, no conductors or equipment shall be _____ having a deteriorating effect on the conductors or equipment.

    (a) located in damp or wet locations
    (b) exposed to fumes, vapors, liquids, or gases
    (c) exposed to excessive temperatures
    (d) all of these

44. Conductor terminal and splicing devices must be _____ for the conductor material and they must be properly installed and used.

    (a) listed
    (b) approved
    (c) identified
    (d) all of these

45. Conductor ampacity shall be determined using the _____ column of Table 310.15(B)(16) for circuits rated 100A or less or marked for 14 AWG through 1 AWG conductors, unless the equipment terminals are listed for use with conductors that have higher temperature ratings.

    (a) 30°C
    (b) 60°C
    (c) 75°C
    (d) 90°C

46. Each disconnecting means shall be legibly marked to indicate its purpose unless located and arranged so _____.

    (a) that it can be locked out and tagged
    (b) it is not readily accessible
    (c) the purpose is evident
    (d) that it operates at less than 300 volts-to-ground

47. Access and _____ shall be provided and maintained about all electrical equipment to permit ready and safe operation and maintenance of such equipment.

    (a) ventilation
    (b) cleanliness
    (c) circulation
    (d) working space

48. The required working space for access to live parts operating at 300 volts-to-ground, where there are exposed live parts on both sides of the workspace is _____.

    (a) 3 ft
    (b) 3½ ft
    (c) 4 ft
    (d) 4½ ft

49. The minimum height of dedicated equipment space for motor control centers installed indoors is _____ above the enclosure, or to the structural ceiling, whichever is lower.

    (a) 3 ft
    (b) 5 ft
    (c) 6 ft
    (d) 6½ ft

50. To guard live parts operating at 50V must be guarded by being
_____.

   (a) located in a room accessible only to qualified persons
   (b) located on a balcony accessible only to qualified persons
   (c) elevated 8 ft or more above the floor or other working sur-
      face for 50V to 300V
   (d) any of these

CHAPTER 2

WIRING AND PROTECTION

Introduction to Chapter 2—Wiring and Protection

Chapter 2 provides general rules for wiring and for the protection of conductors. The rules in this chapter apply to all electrical installations covered by the *NEC*—except as modified in Chapters 5, 6, and 7 [90.3].

Communications systems (Chapter 8 systems) aren't subject to the general requirements of Chapters 1 through 4, or the special requirements of Chapters 5 through 7, unless there's a specific reference in Chapter 8 to a rule in Chapters 1 through 7 [90.3].

As you go through Chapter 2, remember its purpose. It's primarily concerned with correctly sizing and protecting circuits. Every article in this chapter deals with a different aspect of this purpose. This differs from the purpose of Chapter 3, which is to correctly install the conductors that make up those circuits.

Chapter 1 introduced you to the *NEC* and provided a solid foundation for understanding the *Code*. Chapters 2 (Wiring and Protection) and 3 (Wiring Methods and Materials) continue building the foundation for applying the *NEC*. Chapter 4 applies the preceding chapters to general equipment. It's beneficial to learn the first four chapters of the *Code* in a sequential manner because each of the first four chapters builds on the one before it. Once you've become familiar with the first four chapters, you can learn the next four in any order you wish.

- **Article 200—Use and Identification of Grounded [Neutral] Conductors.** This article contains the requirements for the use and identification of the grounded conductor and its terminals.

  ### Author's Comment:
  - Throughout this textbook, we'll use the term "neutral" when referring to the grounded conductor when the application isn't related to PV systems or corner-grounded delta-connected systems.

- **Article 210—Branch Circuits.** Article 210 contains the requirements for branch circuits, such as conductor sizing, identification, and GFCI protection, as well as receptacle and lighting outlet requirements.

- **Article 215—Feeders.** This article covers the requirements for the installation and ampacity of feeders.

■ **Article 220—Branch-Circuit, Feeder, and Service Calculations.** Article 220 provides the requirements for calculating the minimum size for branch circuits, feeders, and services. This article also aids in determining related factors such as the number of receptacles on a circuit in nondwelling installations, and the minimum number of branch circuits required.

■ **Article 225—Outside Branch Circuits and Feeders.** This article covers the installation requirements for equipment, including branch circuits and feeders located outside (overhead and underground) that run on or between buildings, poles, and other structures on the premises.

■ **Article 230—Services.** Article 230 covers the installation requirements for service conductors and equipment. It's very important to know where the service begins and ends when applying Article 230.

Author's Comment:

■ Conductors from a battery, uninterruptible power supply, solar PV system, generator, or transformer aren't service conductors; they're feeder conductors.

■ **Article 240—Overcurrent Protection.** This article provides the requirements for overcurrent protection and overcurrent devices. Overcurrent protection for conductors and equipment is provided to open the circuit if the current reaches a value that'll cause an excessive or dangerous temperature on the conductors or conductor insulation.

■ **Article 250—Grounding and Bonding.** Article 250 covers the grounding requirements for providing a path to the earth to reduce overvoltage from lightning, and the bonding requirements for a low-impedance fault current path necessary to facilitate the operation of overcurrent devices in the event of a ground fault.

■ **Article 285—Surge Protective Devices (SPDs).** This article covers the general, installation, and connection requirements for surge protective devices (SPDs) permanently installed on both the line side and load side of service equipment.

ARTICLE 200

USE AND IDENTIFICATION OF GROUNDED [NEUTRAL] CONDUCTORS

Introduction to Article 200—Use and Identification of Grounded [Neutral] Conductors

This article contains the requirements for the identification of the grounded [neutral] conductor and its terminals. Article 100 contains definitions for both "Grounded Conductor" and "Neutral Conductor." In some cases, both of these terms apply to the same conductor. Figures 200–1 and 200–2

In a system that produces direct current, such as a PV system, the "grounded conductor" isn't a neutral conductor. Figure 200–3

Author's Comment:

- Throughout this textbook, we'll use the term "neutral" when referring to the grounded conductor when the application isn't related to PV systems or corner-grounded delta-connected systems.

Figure 200–1

Figure 200–2

Figure 200–3

Figure 200–4

Part I. General

200.1 Scope

Article 200 contains requirements for the use and identification of grounded [neutral] conductors and terminals.

200.2 General

(B) Continuity. The continuity of the grounded [neutral] conductor isn't permitted to be dependent on metal enclosures, raceways, or cable armor. Figure 200–4

Author's Comment:

■ This requirement prohibits the practice of terminating the grounded [neutral] conductor on the enclosure of a panel or other equipment, rather than on the neutral terminal bar. This ensures the metallic panelboard, raceway, or cable armor doesn't carry neutral current. Some panelboards have two terminal bars, one on either side of the panelboard with a strap connecting the terminal bars together. Caution must be taken to terminate the neutral conductor to the neutral terminal, not to the equipment grounding conductor terminal.

200.4 Neutral Conductors

Neutral conductors must comply with (A) and (B).

(A) Installation. A single neutral conductor can't be used for more than one branch circuit. Figure 200–5

Figure 200–5

(B) Grouping. The ungrounded and neutral conductors of multiple branch circuits must be identified or grouped together by cable ties or similar means in every enclosure. Figure 200–6

Figure 200–6

Figure 200–7

Ex 1: Grouping isn't required where the circuit conductors are contained in a single raceway or cable unique to that circuit that makes the grouping obvious.

Ex 2: Grouping isn't required if the conductors pass through a box or conduit body without any splices or terminations, or if the conductors don't have a loop as described in 314.16(B)(1).

Author's Comment:

- 210.4(D) contains a similar requirement for branch circuit conductors.

200.6 Neutral Conductor Identification

(A) Size 6 AWG or Smaller. Neutral conductors 6 AWG and smaller must be identified by one of the following means: Figure 200–7

(1) A continuous white outer finish.

(2) A continuous gray outer finish.

(3) Three continuous white or gray stripes along its entire length on other than green insulation.

(4) Wires that have their outer covering finished to show a white or gray color but have colored tracer threads in the braid identifying the source of manufacture are considered to meet the provisions of this section.

Author's Comment:

- The use of white tape, paint, or other methods of identification aren't permitted for neutral conductors 6 AWG and smaller. Figure 200–8

White tape, paint, or other methods of identification aren't permitted for neutral conductors 6 AWG and smaller.

Figure 200–8

(6) A single-conductor, sunlight-resistant, outdoor-rated cable used as the grounded conductor in PV power systems as permitted by 690.31(B) can be identified by distinctive white marking at all terminations. Figure 200–9

Figure 200–9

(B) Size 4 AWG or Larger. Neutral conductors 4 AWG or larger must be identified by one of the following means: Figure 200–10

Figure 200–10

(1) A continuous white outer finish along its entire length.

(2) A continuous gray outer finish along its entire length.

(3) Three continuous white or gray stripes along its length.

(4) White or gray tape or markings at the terminations.

(D) Neutral Conductors of Different Systems. If neutral conductors of different voltage systems are installed in the same raceway, cable, or enclosure, each system neutral conductor must be identified by:

(1) A continuous white or gray outer finish along its entire length. Figure 200–11

Figure 200–11

(2) The neutral conductor of the other system must have a different outer covering of continuous white or gray outer finish along its entire length or by an outer covering of white or gray with a readily distinguishable color stripe (other than green) along its entire length. Figure 200–12

(3) Other identification allowed by 200.6(A) or (B) that distinguishes the neutral conductor from other systems.

200.7 Use of White or Gray Color

(C) Circuits of 50V or More. A conductor with white or gray insulation can only be used for the ungrounded conductor as follows:

Mixing Neutral Conductors of Different Systems
In the Same Raceway or Enclosure
200.6(D)(2)

| Gray | White |

| White or Gray | White/Gray with a Colored Stripe |

Copyright 2014, www.MikeHolt.com

The neutral conductor of the different systems must have an outer covering of continuous white or gray finish along its entire length or by an outer covering of white or gray with a readily distinguishable colored stripe (other than green) along its entire length.

Figure 200–12

(1) Cable Assembly. The white or gray conductor within a cable can be used for the ungrounded conductor, if permanently reidentified by marking tape, painting, or other effective means at each location where the conductor is visible to indicate its use as an ungrounded conductor. Identification must encircle the insulation and must be a color other than white, gray, or green. Figure 200–13

Use of White Conductor
Cable Assemblies
200.7(C)(1)

240V
Outlet

Copyright 2014
www.MikeHolt.com

The white or gray conductor within a cable can be used for the ungrounded conductor if permanently reidentified by means such as marking tape or painting where the conductor is visible.

Figure 200–13

The white or gray conductor within a cable can be used to supply power to single-pole, 3-way, and 4-way switch loops, as well as travelers for 3-way and 4-way switching If permanently reidentified at each location where the conductor is visible to indicate its use as an ungrounded conductor. Figures 200–14 and 200–15

White Conductor in Cable Assemblies at Switches
200.7(C)(1)

A white conductor can be used to supply a switch if it's permanently reidentified.

Switch Leg

Copyright 2014, www.MikeHolt.com

The white or gray conductor within a cable can be used for single-pole switch loops if permanently identified at each location where the conductor is visible to indicate its use as an ungrounded conductor.

Figure 200–14

White Conductor in Cable Assemblies at Switches
200.7(C)(1)

Traveler

White wire can be used for
3-way or 4-way switch travelers,
if permanently reidentified.

The white or gray conductor within a cable can be used for 3-way or 4-way switch travelers if permanently identified at each location where the conductor is visible to indicate its use as an ungrounded conductor.

Copyright 2014, www.MikeHolt.com

Figure 200–15

Author's Comment:

- Because 404.2(C) requires a neutral conductor at nearly every switch point, the allowance to re-identify a white conductor (such as a traveler) will only be used when the neutral conductor isn't required at the switch by that section.

(2) Flexible Cord. The white or gray conductor within a flexible cord can be used for the ungrounded conductor for connecting an appliance or equipment as permitted by 400.7.

Note: Care should be taken when working on existing systems because a gray insulated conductor may have been used in the past as an ungrounded conductor.

Author's Comment:

- The *NEC* doesn't permit the use of white or gray conductor insulation for ungrounded conductors in a raceway, even if the conductors are permanently reidentified. Figure 200–16

Figure 200–16

200.9 Terminal Identification

The terminal for the grounded [neutral] conductor must be colored white (actually silver). The terminal for the ungrounded conductor must be a color readily distinguishable from white (brass or copper).

Author's Comment:

- Terminals for the circuit equipment grounding conductor must be green [250.126 and 406.10(B)].

200.10 Identification of Terminals

(B) Receptacles, Plugs, and Connectors. Receptacles must have the terminal intended for connection to the grounded [neutral] conductor identified by:

(1) A metal or metal coating that's substantially white in color or marked by the word white or the letter W.

(2) If the terminal isn't visible, the conductor entrance hole must be marked with the word white or the letter W.

(C) Screw Shell. To prevent electric shock, the screw shell of a luminaire or lampholder must be connected to the grounded [neutral] conductor [410.90]. Figure 200–17

Figure 200–17

Author's Comment:

- See the definition of "Luminaire" in Article 100.

200.11 Polarity

A grounded [neutral] conductor must not be connected to terminals or leads that will cause reversed polarity [410.50].

ARTICLE 210
BRANCH CIRCUITS

Introduction to Article 210—Branch Circuits

This article contains the requirements for branch circuits, such as conductor sizing and identification, GFCI protection, and receptacle and lighting outlet requirements. It consists of three parts:

- Part I. General Provisions
- Part II. Branch-Circuit Ratings
- Part III. Required Outlets

Table 210.2 of this article identifies specific-purpose branch circuits. The provisions for branch circuits that supply equipment listed in Table 210.2 amend or supplement the provisions given in Article 210 for branch circuits, so it's important to be aware of the contents of this table.

The following sections contain a few key items on which to spend extra time as you study Article 210:

- **210.4—Multiwire Branch Circuits.** The conductors of these circuits must originate from the same panel.

- **210.8—GFCI Protection.** Crawl spaces, unfinished basements, and boathouses are just some of the many locations that require GFCI protection.

- **210.11—Branch Circuits Required.** With three subheadings, 210.11 gives summarized requirements for the number of branch circuits in certain situations, states that a load calculated on a VA per area basis must be evenly proportioned, and covers some minimum branch circuit rules for dwelling units.

- **210.12—Arc-Fault Circuit-Interrupter Protection.** An arc-fault circuit interrupter (AFCI) is a device intended to de-energize a circuit when it detects the current waveform characteristics unique to an arcing fault. The purpose of an AFCI is to protect against a fire hazard, whereas the purpose of a GFCI is to protect people against electrocution.

- **210.19—Conductors—Minimum Ampacity and Size.** This section covers the basic rules for sizing branch-circuit conductors, including continuous and noncontinuous loads.

- **210.21—Outlet Devices.** Outlet devices must have an ampere rating at least as large as the load to be served, as well as following the other rules of this section.

- **210.22 and 210.23—Permissible Loads.** This is intended to prevent a circuit overload from occurring because of an improper design and planning of circuitry.

■ **210.52—Dwelling Unit Receptacle Outlets.** There are some specific receptacle spacing rules and branch-circuit requirements for dwelling units that don't apply to other occupancies.

Mastering the branch-circuit requirements in Article 210 will give you a jump-start toward completing installations that are free of *Code* violations.

Part I. General Provisions

210.1 Scope

Article 210 contains the requirements for conductor sizing, overcurrent protection, identification, and GFCI protection of branch circuits, as well as receptacle outlets and lighting outlet requirements.

Author's Comment:

■ Article 100 defines a "branch circuit" as the conductors between the final overcurrent device and the receptacle outlets, lighting outlets, or other outlets. Figure 210–1

Figure 210–1

210.2 Other Articles

Other *NEC* sections that have specific requirements for branch circuits include:

- Air-Conditioning and Refrigeration, 440.6, 440.31, and 440.32
- Appliances, 422.10
- Data Processing (Information Technology) Equipment, 645.5
- Electric Space-Heating Equipment, 424.3(B)
- Generators, 445.20
- Motors, 430.22
- Signs, 600.5

210.3 Branch-Circuit Rating

The rating of a branch circuit is determined by the rating of the branch-circuit overcurrent device, not the conductor size.

Author's Comment:

■ For example, the branch-circuit ampere rating of a 10 THHN conductor on a 20A circuit breaker is 20A. Figure 210–2

Figure 210–2

210.4 Multiwire Branch Circuits

Author's Comment:

■ A multiwire branch circuit consists of two or more ungrounded circuit conductors with a common neutral conductor. There must be a difference of potential (voltage) between the ungrounded conductors and an equal difference of potential (voltage) from each ungrounded conductor to the common neutral conductor. Figure 210–3

Branch Circuit, Multiwire
Article 100 Definition

Neutral Conductor
L1
120V
120V   240V
L2

Copyright 2014
www.MikeHolt.com

A branch circuit with two or more ungrounded conductors having a voltage between them, with equal voltage between the ungrounded conductors and the neutral conductor.

Figure 210–3

(A) General. A multiwire branch circuit can be considered a single circuit or a multiple circuit.

To prevent inductive heating and to reduce conductor impedance for fault currents, all conductors of a multiwire branch circuit must originate from the same panelboard.

Author's Comment:

■ For more information on the inductive heating of metal parts, see 300.3(B), 300.5(I), and 300.20.

Note 1: Unwanted and potentially hazardous harmonic neutral currents can cause additional heating of the neutral conductor of a 4-wire, three-phase, 120/208V or 277/480V wye-connected system, which supplies nonlinear loads. To prevent fire or equipment damage from excessive harmonic neutral currents, the designer should consider: (1) increasing the size of the neutral conductor, or (2) installing a separate neutral for each phase. See 220.61(C)(2) and 310.15(B)(5)(c) in this textbook for additional information. Figures 210–4 and 210–5

Multiwire Branch Circuits
Harmonic Neutral Conductor Current
210.4(A) Note 1

L1   L2   16 Amps
16 Amps   16A   16A
          Nonlinear Nonlinear

Primary
Not
Shown   32 Amps   Neutral
                    Conductor   16A
L3   Nonlinear

16 Amps

Copyright 2014, www.MikeHolt.com

Potentially hazardous harmonic currents can add to the neutral conductor of a 3-phase, 120/208V or 277/480V, 4-wire, wye-connected power system.

Figure 210–4

Neutral Triplen Currents

Single-Phase Loads With
Odd Triplen Harmonics

60 Hz Fundamental
— 3rd Harmonic
Phase A

120°
Phase B

120°
Phase C

Neutral
Triplen
Current

Copyright 2014
www.MikeHolt.com

Odd triplen harmonics added to the neutral.

Figure 210–5

Author's Comment:

- See the definition of "Nonlinear Load" in Article 100.

- For more information, please visit www.MikeHolt.com. Click on "Technical Information" on the left side of the page, and then select "Power Quality."

Note 2: See 300.13(B) for the requirements relating to the continuity of the neutral conductor on multiwire branch circuits. Figure 210–6

Figure 210–6

Continuity of the neutral conductor of a multiwire branch circuit must not be interrupted by the removal of a wiring device.

⚠️ **CAUTION:** *If the continuity of the neutral conductor of a multiwire circuit is interrupted (opened), the resultant over- or undervoltage can cause a fire and/or destruction of electrical equipment. For details on how this occurs, see 300.13(B) in this textbook.* Figures 210–7 *and* 210–8

(B) Disconnecting Means. Each multiwire branch circuit must have a means to simultaneously disconnect all ungrounded conductors at the point where the branch circuit originates. Figure 210–9

Note: Individual single-pole circuit breakers with handle ties identified for the purpose can be used for this application [240.15(B)(1)]. Figure 210–10

Figure 210–7

Figure 210–8

⚠️ **CAUTION:** *This rule is intended to prevent people from working on energized circuits they thought were disconnected.*

(C) Line-to-Neutral Loads. Multiwire branch circuits must supply only line-to-neutral loads.

Ex 1: A multiwire branch circuit is permitted to supply an individual piece of line-to-line utilization equipment, such as a range or dryer. Figure 210–11

Figure 210–9

Figure 210–11

Figure 210–10

Figure 210–12

Ex 2: A multiwire branch circuit is permitted to supply both line-to-line and line-to-neutral loads if the circuit is protected by a device such as a multipole circuit breaker with a common internal trip that opens all ungrounded conductors of the multiwire branch circuit simultaneously under a fault condition. Figure 210–12

(D) Grouping. The ungrounded and neutral conductors of a multiwire branch circuit must be grouped together by cable ties or similar means at the point of origination. Figure 210–13

Figure 210–13

Ex: Grouping isn't required where the circuit conductors are contained in a single raceway or cable unique to that circuit that makes the grouping obvious, or if the conductors have circuit number tags on them. Figure 210–14

Figure 210–14

Author's Comment:

- Grouping all associated conductors of a multiwire branch circuit together by cable ties or other means within the point of origination makes it easier to visually identify the conductors of the multiwire branch circuit. The grouping will assist in making sure that the correct neutral is used at junction points and in connecting multiwire branch-circuit conductors to circuit breakers correctly, particularly where twin breakers are used. If proper diligence isn't exercised when making these connections, two circuit conductors can be accidentally connected to the same phase or line.

⚠ **CAUTION:** *If the ungrounded conductors of a multiwire circuit aren't terminated to different phases or lines, the currents on the neutral conductor won't cancel, which can cause an overload on the neutral conductor.* Figure 210–15

Caution: If the ungrounded conductors of a multiwire circuit aren't terminated to different phases or lines, the currents on the neutral conductor won't cancel, but will add, which can cause a dangerous overload on the neutral conductor.

Figure 210–15

210.5 Identification for Branch Circuits

(A) Neutral Conductor. The neutral conductor of a branch circuit must be identified in accordance with 200.6.

(B) Equipment Grounding Conductor. Equipment grounding conductors can be bare, covered, or insulated. Insulated equipment grounding conductors size 6 AWG and smaller must have a continuous outer finish either green or green with one or more yellow stripes [250.119]. Figure 210–16

Figure 210–16

On equipment grounding conductors 4 AWG and larger, insulation can be permanently reidentified with green marking at the time of installation at every point where the conductor is accessible [250.119(A)].

(C) Identification of Ungrounded Conductors. Ungrounded conductors must be identified as follows:

(1) More Than One Voltage System. If the premises wiring system contains branch circuits supplied from more than one voltage system, each ungrounded conductor must be identified by phase and system at all termination, connection, and splice points in accordance with 210.5(C)(1)(a) and (b). Figure 210–17

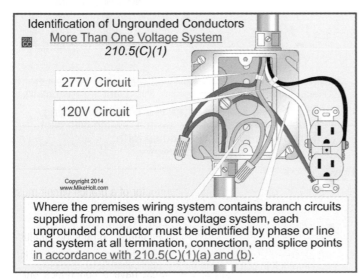

Figure 210–17

(a) Means of Identification. Identification can be by color coding, marking tape, tagging, or other means approved by the authority having jurisdiction. Figure 210–18

Figure 210–18

(b) Posting. The method of identification must be documented in a manner that's readily available or permanently posted at each branch-circuit panelboard. Figure 210–19

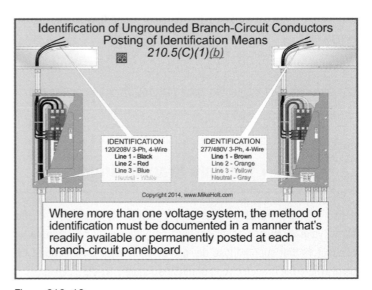

Figure 210–19

Author's Comment:

- When a premises has more than one voltage system supplying branch circuits, the ungrounded conductors must be identified by phase and system. This can be done by permanently posting an identification legend that describes the method used, such as color-coded marking tape or color-coded insulation.

- Conductors with insulation that's green or green with one or more yellow stripes can't be used for an ungrounded or neutral conductor [250.119].

- Although the *NEC* doesn't require a specific color code for ungrounded conductors, electricians often use the following color system for power and lighting conductor identification:

  - 120/240V, single-phase—black, red, and white
  - 120/208V, three-phase—black, red, blue, and white
  - 120/240V, three-phase—black, orange, blue, and white
  - 277/480V, three-phase—brown, orange, yellow, and gray; or, brown, purple, yellow, and gray

210.6 Branch-Circuit Voltage Limitations

(A) Occupancy Limitation. In dwelling units, the voltage between conductors must not exceed 120V, nominal, when they supply the terminals of:

(1) Luminaires.

(2) Cord-and-plug-connected loads of 1,440 VA or less or less than ¼ hp.

210.7 Multiple Branch Circuits

If two or more branch circuits supply devices or equipment on the same yoke, a means to disconnect simultaneously all ungrounded conductors that supply those devices or equipment is required at the point where the branch circuit originates. Figure 210–20

Figure 210–20

Author's Comment:

- A yoke, also called a strap, is the metal mounting structure for a receptacle, switch, switch with pilot light, switch-receptacle, and so forth. Figure 210–21

Figure 210–21

- Individual single-pole circuit breakers with handle ties identified for the purpose, or a circuit breaker with a common internal trip, can be used for this application [240.15(B)(1)].

210.8 GFCI Protection

Ground-fault circuit interruption for personnel must be provided as required in 210.8(A) through (D). The ground-fault circuit-interrupter device must be installed at a readily accessible location. Figure 210–22

Figure 210–22

Author's Comment:

■ According to Article 100, "readily accessible" means capable of being reached quickly without having to climb over or remove obstacles, or resort to portable ladders.

(A) Dwelling Units. GFCI protection is required for all 15A and 20A, 125V receptacles installed in the following locations:

Author's Comment:

■ See the definitions of "GFCI" and "Dwelling Unit" in Article 100.

(1) Bathroom Area. GFCI protection is required for all 15A and 20A, 125V receptacles in the bathroom area of a dwelling unit. Figure 210–23

Author's Comment:

■ See the definition of "Bathroom" in Article 100.

Figure 210–23

■ In the continued interests of safety, proposals to allow receptacles for dedicated equipment in the bathroom area to be exempted from the GFCI protection requirements have been rejected.

(2) Garages and Accessory Buildings. GFCI protection is required for all 15A and 20A, 125V receptacles in garages, and in grade-level portions of accessory buildings used for storage or work areas of a dwelling unit. Figure 210–24

Figure 210–24

Author's Comment:

- See the definition of "Garage" in Article 100.

- A receptacle outlet is required in a dwelling unit attached garage [210.52(G)(1)], but a receptacle outlet isn't required in an accessory building or a detached garage without power. If a 15A or 20A, 125V receptacle is installed in an accessory building, it must be GFCI protected. Figure 210–25

Figure 210–25

(3) Outdoors. All 15A and 20A, 125V receptacles located outdoors of dwelling units, including receptacles installed under the eaves of roofs, must be GFCI protected. Figure 210–26

Author's Comment:

- Each dwelling unit of a multifamily dwelling that has an individual entrance at grade level must have at least one GFCI-protected receptacle outlet accessible from grade level located not more than 6½ ft above grade [210.52(E)(2)].

- Balconies, decks, and porches that are attached to the dwelling unit and are accessible from inside the dwelling must have at least one GFCI-protected receptacle outlet accessible from the balcony, deck, or porch [210.52(E)(3)].

Figure 210–26

Ex: GFCI protection isn't required for a receptacle that's supplied by a branch circuit dedicated to fixed electric snow-melting or deicing or pipeline and vessel heating equipment, if the receptacle isn't readily accessible and the equipment or receptacle has ground-fault protection of equipment (GFPE) [426.28 and 427.22]. Figure 210–27

GFCI protection isn't required for a receptacle supplied by a branch circuit dedicated to fixed electric snow-melting or deicing or pipeline and vessel heating equipment, if the receptacle isn't readily accessible and the equipment or receptacle has GFPE [426.28, 427.22].

Figure 210–27

(4) Crawl Spaces. All 15A and 20A, 125V receptacles installed in crawl spaces at or below grade of a dwelling unit must be GFCI protected.

Author's Comment:

- The *Code* doesn't require a receptacle to be installed in a crawl space, except when heating, air-conditioning, and refrigeration equipment is installed there [210.63].

(5) Unfinished Basements. GFCI protection is required for all 15A and 20A, 125V receptacles located in the unfinished portion of a basement not intended as a habitable room and limited to storage and work areas. Figure 210–28

Figure 210–28

Ex: A receptacle supplying only a permanently installed fire alarm or burglar alarm system isn't required to be GFCI protected [760.41(B) and 760.121(B)].

Author's Comment:

- A receptacle outlet is required in each unfinished portion of a dwelling unit basement [210.52(G)(3)].

(6) Kitchen Countertop Surfaces. GFCI protection is required for all 15A and 20A, 125V receptacles that serve countertop surfaces in a dwelling unit. Figure 210–29

Author's Comment:

- GFCI protection is required for all receptacles that serve countertop surfaces, but GFCI protection isn't required for receptacles that serve built-in appliances, such as dishwashers, trash compactors, exhaust fans, or kitchen waste disposals.

Figure 210–29

- See 210.52(C) for the location requirements of countertop receptacles.

(7) Sinks. GFCI protection is required for all 15A and 20A, 125V receptacles located within an arc measurement of 6 ft from the outside edge of a sink. Figures 210–30 and 210–31

Figure 210–30

Figure 210–31

Figure 210–33

(8) Boathouses. GFCI protection is required for all 15A and 20A, 125V receptacles located in a dwelling unit boathouse. Figure 210–32

(10) Laundry Areas. All 15A and 20A, 125V receptacles installed in laundry areas of a dwelling unit must be GFCI protected. Figure 210–34

Figure 210–32

Figure 210–34

Author's Comment:

■ The *Code* doesn't require a 15A or 20A, 125V receptacle to be installed in a boathouse, but if one is installed, it must be GFCI protected.

(9) Bathtubs or Shower Stalls. GFCI protection is required for all 15A and 20A, 125V receptacles located within 6 ft of the outside edge of a bathtub or shower stall. Figure 210–33

(B) Other than Dwelling Units. GFCI protection is required for all 15A and 20A, 125V receptacles installed in the following commercial/industrial locations:

(1) Bathrooms. All 15A and 20A, 125V receptacles installed in commercial or industrial bathrooms must be GFCI protected. Figure 210–35

Figure 210–35

Author's Comment:

- See the definition of "Bathroom" in Article 100.

- A 15A or 20A, 125V receptacle isn't required in a commercial or industrial bathroom, but if one is installed, it must be GFCI protected.

(2) Kitchens. All 15A and 20A, 125V receptacles installed in a kitchen, even those that don't supply the countertop surface, must be GFCI protected. Figure 210–36

Figure 210–36

Author's Comment:

- A kitchen is an area with a sink and permanent provisions for food preparation and cooking [Article 100]

- GFCI protection isn't required for receptacles rated other than 15A and 20A, 125V in these locations.

- GFCI protection isn't required for hard-wired equipment in these locations.

- An area such an employee break room with a sink and cord-and-plug-connected cooking appliance such as a microwave oven isn't considered a kitchen. Figure 210–37

Figure 210–37

(3) Rooftops. All 15A and 20A, 125V receptacles installed on rooftops must be GFCI protected. Figure 210–38

Author's Comment:

- A 15A or 20A, 125V receptacle outlet must be installed within 25 ft of heating, air-conditioning, and refrigeration equipment [210.63].

Figure 210–38

Figure 210–40

Ex 1 to (3): Receptacles on rooftops aren't required to be readily accessible other than from the rooftop. Figure 210–39

(5) Sinks. All 15A and 20A, 125V receptacles installed within 6 ft of the outside edge of a sink must be GFCI protected. Figure 210–41

Figure 210–39

Figure 210–41

(4) Outdoors. All 15A and 20A, 125V receptacles installed outdoors must be GFCI protected. Figure 210–40

Ex 2 to (3) and (4): GFCI protection isn't required for a receptacle that's supplied by a branch circuit dedicated to fixed electric snow-melting or deicing or pipeline and vessel heating equipment, if the receptacle isn't readily accessible and the equipment or receptacle has ground-fault protection of equipment (GFPE) [426.28 and 427.22].

Ex 1: In industrial laboratories, receptacles used to supply equipment where removal of power would introduce a greater hazard aren't required to be GFCI protected.

Ex 2: Receptacles located in patient bed locations of general care or critical care areas of health care facilities aren't required to be GFCI protected.

(6) Indoor Wet Locations. All 15A and 20A, 125V receptacles installed indoors in wet locations must be GFCI protected.

(7) Locker Rooms. All 15A and 20A, 125V receptacles installed in locker rooms with associated showering facilities must be GFCI protected.

(8) Garages. All 15A and 20A, 125V receptacles installed in garages, service bays, and similar areas must be GFCI protected, unless they're in show rooms or exhibition halls. Figure 210–42

Figure 210–42

(C) Boat Hoists. GFCI protection is required for outlets supplying boat hoists in dwelling unit locations. Figure 210–43

Author's Comment:

- See the definition of "Outlet" in Article 100.

- This ensures GFCI protection regardless of whether the boat hoist is cord-and-plug-connected or hard-wired.

(D) Dwelling Unit Dishwashers. Outlets supplying dishwashers in a dwelling unit must be GFCI protected. Figure 210–44

Figure 210–43

Figure 210–44

210.11 Branch Circuits Required

(A) Number of Branch Circuits. The minimum number of general lighting and general-use receptacle branch circuits must be determined by dividing the total calculated load in amperes by the ampere rating of the circuits used.

Question: *How many 15A, 120V circuits are required for the general lighting and general-use receptacles for a dwelling having floor area of 1,500 ft², exclusive of an unfinished cellar not adaptable for future use [Example D1(a) in Annex D]?* Figure 210–45

(a) 1   (b) 2   (c) 3   (d) 4

Answer: *(c) 3*

Step 1: *Determine the total VA load:*

$$VA = 1,500 \text{ sq ft} \times 3 \text{ VA per sq ft [Table 220.12]}$$

VA = 4,500 VA

Step 2: *Determine the amperes:*

$$I = VA/E$$

I = 4,500VA/120V

I = 38A

Step 3: *Determine the number of circuits:*

Number of Circuits = 38A/15A

Number of Circuits = Three 15A, or two 20A, 120V

Number of General Lighting and General-Use Receptacle Circuits - Dwelling Unit
210.11(A) and Annex D, Example D1(a)

1,500 sq ft Dwelling

Number of Circuits:
Step 1: 1,500 sq ft x 3 VA = 4,500 VA
Step 2: 4,500 VA/120V = 38A
Step 3: 38A/15A = 2.5 = 3- 15A (or 2- 20A circuits)

Copyright 2014
www.MikeHolt.com

Figure 210–45

Author's Comment:

■ There's no limit to the number of receptacles on a circuit in a dwelling unit.

(B) Load Evenly Proportioned Among Branch Circuits. If the load is calculated on the volt-amperes/square foot, the wiring system must be provided to serve the calculated load, with the loads evenly proportioned among multioutlet branch circuits within the panelboard. Figure 210–46

Load Evenly Proportioned Among Branch Circuits
210.11(B)

Copyright 2014
www.MikeHolt.com

Square foot of garage and open porches not counted [220.12].

House = 2,148 square feet
2,148 sq ft x 3 VA = 6444 VA/120V = 53.7A/15A = 3.58
3.58 = Minimum of four 15A general lighting and general-use receptacle circuits

If the load is calculated on the volt-amperes/square foot, the wiring system must be provided to serve the calculated load, with the loads evenly proportioned among multioutlet branch circuits within the panelboard.

Figure 210–46

(C) Dwelling Unit.

(1) Small-Appliance Branch Circuits. Two or more 20A, 120V small-appliance receptacle branch circuits are required for the 15A or 20A receptacle outlets in a dwelling unit kitchen, dining room, breakfast room, pantry, or in similar dining areas as required by 210.52(B). Figure 210–47

Author's Comment:

■ See the definition of "Receptacle Outlet" in Article 100.

■ A 15A, 125V receptacle is rated for 20A feed-through, so it can be used for this purpose [210.21(B)(3)].

■ Lighting outlets or receptacles located in other areas of a dwelling unit must not be connected to the small-appliance branch circuit [210.52(B)(2)].

■ The two 20A small-appliance branch circuits can be supplied by one 3-wire multiwire circuit or by two separate 120V circuits [210.4(A)].

Figure 210–47

Figure 210–49

(2) Laundry Branch Circuit. One 20A, 120V branch circuit must be provided for the receptacle outlets required by 210.52(F) for a dwelling unit laundry room. The 20A laundry room receptacle circuit is permitted to supply more than one receptacle in the laundry room. The 20A laundry receptacle must not serve any other outlets, such as the laundry room lighting or receptacles in other rooms. Figure 210–48

- A 15A receptacle is rated for 20A feed-through, so it can be used for this purpose [210.21(B)(3)].

- GFCI protection is required for 15A and 20A, 125V receptacles located in a laundry room [210.8(A)(10)]. Figure 210–50

Figure 210–48

Figure 210–50

Author's Comment:

- The 20A, 120V laundry branch circuit is required, even if the laundry appliance installed is a 30A, 230V combination washer/dryer. Figure 210–49

(3) Bathroom Branch Circuit. One 20A, 120V branch circuit must be provided for the receptacle outlets required by 210.52(D) for a dwelling unit bathroom. This 20A bathroom receptacle circuit must not serve any other outlet, such as bathroom lighting outlets or receptacles in other rooms. Figure 210–51

Figure 210–51

A minimum of one 20A circuit is required to supply the required bathroom receptacles. Other outlets aren't permitted on the bathroom receptacle circuit.

Figure 210–51

Author's Comment:

■ A 15A, 125V receptacle is rated for 20A feed-through, so it can be used for this purpose [210.21(B)(3)].

Ex: A single 20A, 120V branch circuit is permitted to supply all of the outlets in a single bathroom, as long as no single load fastened in place is rated more than 10A [210.23(A)]. Figure 210–52

A single 20A, 120V circuit can supply all of the outlets in a single bathroom, as long as no single load exceeds 10A [210.23(A)(2)].

Figure 210–52

Question: *Can a luminaire, ceiling fan, or bath fan be connected to the 20A, 120V branch circuit that supplies only one bathroom?*

Answer: *Yes.*

210.12 Arc-Fault Circuit-Interrupter Protection

Arc-fault circuit-interrupter protection must be provided in accordance with 210.12(A), (B) and (C). AFCI devices must be installed in readily accessible locations.

(A) Where Required. All 15A or 20A, 120V branch circuits in dwelling units supplying outlets or devices in kitchens, family rooms, dining rooms, living rooms, parlors, libraries, dens, bedrooms, sunrooms, recreation rooms, closets, hallways, laundry areas, or similar rooms or areas must be protected by one of the following: Figure 210–53

Figure 210–53

(1) A listed combination type AFCI, installed to provide protection of the entire branch circuit.

(2) A listed branch/feeder type AFCI at the origin of the branch circuit, plus a listed outlet branch-circuit AFCI installed at the first outlet box of the branch circuit. The outlet box must be marked to indicate that it's the first outlet box of the circuit.

---

(3) A listed supplemental arc protection circuit breaker installed at the origin of the branch circuit, plus a listed outlet branch-circuit type AFCI installed at the first outlet box on the branch circuit. When using this option, the following must be met:

(a) The branch-circuit wiring must be continuous from the branch circuit overcurrent device to the AFCI device.

(b) The maximum length of the branch circuit to the AFCI is 50 ft for 14 AWG conductors or 70 ft for 12 AWG conductors.

(c) The first outlet box in the circuit must be marked.

(4) A regular fuse or circuit breaker, plus a listed outlet branch-circuit type AFCI installed at the first outlet of the branch circuit. When using this option, the following must be met:

(a) The branch-circuit wiring must be continuous from the branch-circuit overcurrent device to the AFCI device.

(b) The maximum length of the branch circuit to the AFCI is 50 ft for 14 AWG conductors or 70 ft for 12 AWG conductors.

(c) The first outlet box in the circuit must be marked.

(d) The combination of the branch-circuit overcurrent device and the AFCI must be listed and identified as meeting the requirements for a "System Combination" type AFCI.

(5) A listed outlet branch-circuit type AFCI at the first outlet can be used, if the wiring between the overcurrent device and the AFCI contains all metal boxes and is installed using any (or a combination) of the following: RMC, IMC, EMT, Type MC, Type AC cables meeting the requirements of 250.118, metal wireways, or metal auxiliary gutters.

(6) A listed outlet branch-circuit type AFCI at the first outlet of the circuit can be used, if the wiring between the overcurrent device and the AFCI is in a raceway with 2 in. of concrete encasement.

Author's Comment:

■ The combination AFCI is a circuit breaker that protects downstream branch-circuit wiring as well as cord sets and power-supply cords; an outlet branch-circuit AFCI (receptacle) is installed as the first outlet in a branch circuit to protect downstream branch-circuit wiring, cord sets, and power-supply cords.

■ The 120V circuit limitation means AFCI protection isn't required for equipment rated 230V, such as a baseboard heater or room air conditioner. For more information, visit www.MikeHolt.com, click on the "Search" link, and then search for "AFCI."

Ex: AFCI protection can be omitted for an individual branch circuit to a fire alarm system in accordance with 760.41(B) and 760.121(B), if the circuit conductors are installed in metal wireways, metal auxiliary gutters, RMC, IMC, EMT, or steel sheath Type AC or MC cable that qualifies as an equipment grounding conductor in accordance with 250.118, with metal outlet and junction boxes.

Note 3: See 760.41(B) and 760.121(B) for power-supply requirements for fire alarm systems.

Author's Comment:

■ Smoke alarms connected to a 15A or 20A circuit in a dwelling unit must be AFCI protected if the smoke alarm is located in one of the areas specified in 210.12(A). The exemption from AFCI protection for the "fire alarm circuit" contained in 760.41(B) and 760.121(B) doesn't apply to the single- or multiple-station smoke alarm circuit typically installed in dwelling unit bedroom areas. This is because a smoke alarm circuit isn't a fire alarm circuit as defined in NFPA 72, *National Fire Alarm Code*. Unlike single- or multiple-station smoke alarms, fire alarm systems are managed by a fire alarm control panel. Figure 210–54

Figure 210–54

(B) Branch-Circuit Extensions or Modifications—Dwelling Units. Where branch-circuit wiring is modified, replaced, or extended in any of the areas specified in 210.12(A), the branch circuit must be protected by:

(1) A listed combination AFCI located at the origin of the branch circuit; or

(2) A listed outlet branch circuit AFCI located at the first receptacle outlet of the existing branch circuit.

Ex: AFCI protection isn't required for extensions less than 6 ft long, as long as there are no outlets or devices added.

(C) Dormitory Units. All 120V, single phase, 15A and 20A branch circuits supplying outlets installed in dormitory unit bedrooms, living rooms, hallways, closets, and similar rooms must be AFCI protected by one of the methods discussed in 210.12(A)(1) through (6).

210.17 Electric Vehicle Branch Circuit

Electric vehicle charging outlets must be supplied by a circuit that has no other outlets. Figure 210–55

Note: See 625.2 for the definition of "Electrical Vehicle."

Figure 210–55

210.18 Guest Rooms and Guest Suites

Guest rooms and guest suites provided with permanent provisions for cooking must have branch circuits installed in accordance with the dwelling unit requirements of 210.11. Figure 210–56

A guest room or suite with permanent provisions for cooking must follow the branch circuit rules for a dwelling unit.

Figure 210–56

Author's Comment:

■ See the definitions of "Guest Room" and "Guest Suite" in Article 100.

Part II. Branch-Circuit Ratings

210.19 Conductor Sizing

(A) Branch Circuits.

(1) General. Branch-circuit conductors must have an ampacity of not less than the maximum load to be served. The conductor must be the larger of (a) or (b).

(a) Conductors must be sized no less than 125 percent of the continuous loads, plus 100 percent of the noncontinuous loads, based on the terminal temperature rating ampacities as listed in Table 310.15(B)(16). Figure 210–57

(b) Conductors must be sized to the maximum load to be served after the application of any adjustment or correction factors. Figure 210–58

Ex 1: If the assembly and the overcurrent device are both listed for operation at 100 percent of its rating, the conductors can be sized at 100 percent of the continuous load.

Figure 210–57

Figure 210–58

Author's Comment:

- Equipment suitable for 100 percent continuous loading is rarely available in ratings under 400A.

- See the definition of "Continuous Load" in Article 100.

- See 210.20 for the sizing requirements for the branch-circuit overcurrent device for continuous and noncontinuous loads.

Question: *What size branch-circuit conductors are required for a 4-wire circuit of a 45A nonlinear continuous load, if the equipment terminals are rated 75°C?*

(a) 10 AWG   (b) 8 AWG   (c) 6 AWG   (d) 4 AWG

Answer: *(c) 6 AWG*

Since the load is 45A continuous, the conductors must be sized to have an ampacity of not less than 56A (45A x 1.25). According to the 75°C column of Table 310.15(B)(16), a 6 AWG conductor is suitable, because it has an ampere rating of 65A at 75°C. This satisfies the portion of the calculation discussed in 210.19(A)(1)(a).

For 210.19(A)(1)(b), we've to address ambient temperature and conductor bundling.

Because the neutral in this example is considered a current-carrying conductor [310.15(B)(5)(c)], there are four current-carrying conductors. Table 310.15(B)(3)(a) requires an adjustment factor of 80% for this example.

6 AWG rated 75A at 90°C x 0.80 = 60A after adjustment factors which is adequate for the 45A load, Figure 210–59. If we'd selected an 8 AWG rated 55A at 90°C, based on the 45A load, it would be too small for the load after applying the adjustment factor (55A x 0.80 = 44A).

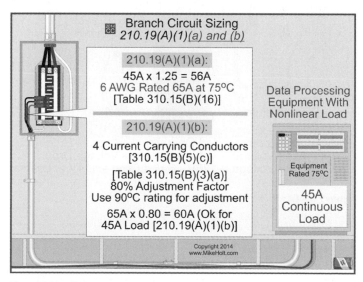

Figure 210–59

Note 4: To provide reasonable efficiency of operation of electrical equipment, branch-circuit conductors should be sized to prevent a voltage drop not to exceed 3 percent. In addition, the maximum total voltage drop on both feeders and branch circuits shouldn't exceed 5 percent. Figures 210–60 and 210–61

Figure 210–60

Figure 210–61

Author's Comment:

- Many believe the *NEC* requires conductor voltage drop, as per Note 4 to be applied when sizing conductors. Although this is often a good practice, it's not a *Code* requirement because Notes are only advisory statements [90.5(C)]. Figure 210–62

Many believe the *NEC* requires conductor voltage drop to be applied when sizing conductors. Although this is often a good practice, it's not a *Code* requirement.

Figure 210–62

- The *NEC* doesn't consider voltage drop to be a safety issue, except for sensitive electronic equipment [647.4(D)] and fire pumps [695.7].

(2) Branch Circuits Supplying More than One Receptacle. Branch circuits that supply more than one receptacle must have an ampacity not less than the rating of the circuit overcurrent device [210.3].

(3) Household Ranges and Cooking Appliances. Branch-circuit conductors that supply household ranges, wall-mounted ovens or counter-mounted cooking units must have an ampacity not less than the rating of the branch circuit, and not less than the maximum load to be served. For ranges of 8¾ kW or more rating, the minimum branch-circuit ampere rating is 40A.

Ex 1: Conductors tapped from a 50A branch circuit for electric ranges, wall-mounted electric ovens and counter-mounted electric cooking units must have an ampacity not less than 20A, and must have sufficient ampacity for the load to be served. The taps must not be longer than necessary for servicing the appliances. Figure 210–63

Figure 210–63

210.20 Overcurrent Protection

(A) Continuous and Noncontinuous Loads. Branch-circuit overcurrent devices must have a rating of not less than 125 percent of the continuous loads, plus 100 percent of the noncontinuous loads. Figure 210–64

Figure 210–64

Author's Comment:

■ See 210.19(A)(1) for branch-circuit conductor sizing requirements.

Ex: If the assembly and the overcurrent devices are both listed for operation at 100 percent of their rating, the branch-circuit overcurrent device can be sized at 100 percent of the continuous load.

Author's Comment:

■ Equipment suitable for 100 percent continuous loading is rarely available in ratings under 400A.

(B) Conductor Protection. Branch-circuit conductors must be protected against overcurrent in accordance with 240.4.

(C) Equipment Protection. Branch-circuit equipment must be protected in accordance with 240.3.

210.21 Outlet Device Rating

(A) Lampholder Ratings. Lampholders connected to a branch circuit rated over 20A must be of the heavy-duty type.

Author's Comment:

■ Fluorescent lampholders aren't rated heavy duty, so fluorescent luminaires must not be installed on circuits rated over 20A.

(B) Receptacle Ratings and Loadings.

(1) Single Receptacles. A single receptacle on an individual branch circuit must have an ampacity not less than the rating of the overcurrent device. Figure 210–65

Note: A single receptacle has only one contact device on its yoke [Article 100]; this means a duplex receptacle is considered as two receptacles.

(2) Multiple Receptacle Loading. If connected to a branch circuit that supplies two or more receptacles, the total cord-and-plug-connected load must not exceed 80 percent of the receptacle rating.

Author's Comment:

■ A duplex receptacle has two contact devices on the same yoke [Article 100]. This means even one duplex receptacle on a circuit makes that circuit a multioutlet branch circuit.

A single receptacle on an individual branch circuit must have an ampere rating of not less than the rating of the circuit overcurrent device.

Figure 210–65

(3) Multiple Receptacle Rating. If connected to a branch circuit that supplies two or more receptacles, receptacles must have an ampere rating in accordance with the values listed in Table 210.21(B)(3). Figure 210–66

Figure 210–66

Table 210.21(B)(3) Receptacle Ratings	
Circuit Rating	Receptacle Rating
15A	15A
20A	15A or 20A
30A	30A
40A	40A or 50A
50A	50A

210.22 Permissible Loads, Individual Branch Circuits

An individual branch circuit is permitted to supply any load that doesn't exceed the ampere rating of the branch-circuit. Figure 210–67

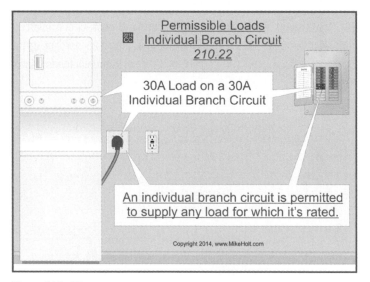

Figure 210–67

210.23 Permissible Loads, Multiple-Outlet Branch Circuits

In no case is the load permitted to exceed the branch-circuit ampere rating.

Branch circuits rated 15A or 20A supplying two or more outlets must only supply loads in accordance with 210.23(A).

(A) 15A and 20A Circuit. A 15A or 20A branch circuit is permitted to supply lighting, equipment, or any combination of both.

Author's Comment:

■ Except for temporary installations [590.4(D)], 15A or 20A circuits can be used to supply both lighting and receptacles on the same circuit. Figure 210–68

Figure 210–68

(1) Cord-and-Plug-Connected Equipment Not Fastened in Place. Cord-and-plug-connected equipment not fastened in place, such as a drill press or table saw, must not have an ampere rating more than 80 percent of the branch-circuit rating. Figure 210–69

Author's Comment:

■ UL and other testing laboratories list portable equipment (such as hair dryers) up to 100 percent of the circuit rating. The *NEC* is an installation standard, not a product standard, so it can't prohibit this practice. There really is no way to limit the load to 80 percent of the branch-circuit rating if testing laboratories permit equipment to be listed for 100 percent of the circuit rating.

(2) Fixed Equipment. Equipment fastened in place (other than luminaires) must not be rated more than 50 percent of the branch-circuit ampere rating if this circuit supplies luminaires, receptacles, or both. Figure 210–70

Figure 210–69

Figure 210–70

> **Question:** *Can a whole house (central) vacuum motor rated 13A be installed on an existing 20A circuit that supplies more than one receptacle outlet?*
>
> **Answer:** *No, an individual 15A or 20A branch circuit will be required.*

210.25 Branch Circuits in Buildings with Multiple Occupancies

(A) Dwelling Unit Branch Circuits. Dwelling unit branch circuits are only permitted to supply loads within or associated with the dwelling unit.

(B) Common Area Branch Circuits. Branch circuits installed for public or common areas of a multi-occupancy building aren't permitted to originate from equipment that supplies an individual dwelling unit or tenant space.

Author's Comment:

- This rule prohibits common area branch circuits from being supplied from an individual dwelling unit or tenant space to prevent common area circuits from being turned off by tenants or by the utility due to nonpayment of electric bills.

Part III. Required Outlets

210.50 General

Receptacle outlets must be installed in accordance with 210.52 through 210.64.

Note: See Annex J for information regarding ADA accessibility design.

Author's Comment:

- Many places don't use the *Americans with Disabilities Act Accessibility Guidelines* (ADAAG); they use ICC A117.1 *Accessible and Usable Buildings and Facilities.* These documents are very similar, and both are ways of satisfying the Americans with Disabilities Act (ADA).

(A) Cord Pendant Receptacle Outlet. A permanently installed flexible cord pendant receptacle is considered a receptacle outlet. Figure 210–71

Author's Comment:

- Only cords identified for use as pendants in Table 400.4 may be used for pendants,, also see 314.23(H) for the requirements for boxes at pendant outlets.

Figure 210–71

(C) Appliance Receptacle Outlets. Receptacle outlets installed in a dwelling unit for a specific appliance, such as a clothes washer, dryer, range, garage door opener or refrigerator, must be within 6 ft of the intended location of the appliance. Figure 210–72

Figure 210–72

210.52 Dwelling Unit Receptacle Outlet Requirements

This section provides requirements for 15A and 20A, 125V receptacle outlets. The receptacles required by this section are in addition to any receptacle that's:

(1) Part of a luminaire or appliance,

(2) Controlled by a wall switch in accordance with 210.70(A)(1), Ex 1. Figure 210–73

Dwelling Unit Receptacles Switched Receptacle
210.52(2)

6 ft

15A or 20A, 125V Duplex Receptacle

Copyright 2014 www.MikeHolt.com

Switching one receptacle of a duplex receptacle meets the lighting requirements of 210.70(A)(1) and the receptacle placement requirements of 210.52(A)(1).

Figure 210–73

(3) Located within cabinets or cupboards, or

(4) Located more than 5½ ft above the floor.

(A) General Requirements—Dwelling Unit. A receptacle outlet must be installed in every kitchen, family room, dining room, living room, sunroom, parlor, library, den, bedroom, recreation room, and similar room or area in accordance with (1), (2),(3) and (4):

(1) Receptacle Placement. A receptacle outlet must be installed so that no point along the floor line of any wall is more than 6 ft, measured horizontally along the floor line, from a receptacle outlet. Figure 210–74

Author's Comment:

■ The purpose of this rule is to ensure that a general-purpose receptacle is conveniently located to reduce the chance that an extension cord will be used.

Dwelling Unit Receptacle Outlet Spacing
210.52(A)(1)

Fixed Panel
2 Ft or More Wall Space
Bedroom
Closet — Hall
Bedroom
Bath
Foyer
Laundry
Dining Room
Kitchen
Rail (wall space)
Living Room (Sunken)
Fireplace
Garage

Copyright 2014 www.MikeHolt.com

A receptacle outlet must be installed in every kitchen, family room, dining room, living room, den, bedroom, or recreation room so no point along the wall space will be more than 6 ft from a receptacle outlet.

Figure 210–74

(2) Definition of Wall Space.

(1) Any space 2 ft or more in width, unbroken along the floor line by doorways and similar openings, fireplaces, and fixed cabinets. Figure 210–75

Dwelling Unit Receptacle Outlet Requirements
210.52(A)(2)(1)

6 ft Max. — 6 ft Max.

Wall space behind a door is part of the measurement to determine the location of a receptacle.

6 ft Max.

2 ft

Fixed Cabinet

Any space 2 ft or more in width, unbroken along the floor line by doorways and similar openings, fireplaces, and fixed cabinets.

2 ft

Closet

6 ft Max.

Copyright 2014, www.MikeHolt.com

12 ft Max. — 6 ft Max.

Figure 210–75

(2) The space occupied by fixed panels in exterior walls.

(3) The space occupied by fixed room dividers, such as freestanding bar-type counters or guard rails.

(3) Floor Receptacle Outlets. Floor receptacle outlets aren't counted as the required receptacle wall outlet if they're located more than 18 in. from the wall. Figure 210–76

Figure 210–76

(4) Countertop Receptacles. Receptacles installed for countertop surfaces as required by 210.52(C), can't be used to meet the receptacle requirements for wall space as required by 210.52(A). Figure 210–77

Figure 210–77

(B) Small-Appliance Circuits.

(1) Receptacle Outlets. The two or more 20A, 120V small-appliance branch circuits serving the kitchen, pantry, breakfast room, and dining room area of a dwelling unit [210.11(C)(1)] must serve all wall, floor and countertop receptacle outlets [210.52(C)], and the receptacle outlet for refrigeration equipment. Figure 210–78

Figure 210–78

Ex 2: The receptacle outlet for refrigeration equipment can be supplied from an individual branch circuit rated 15A or greater. Figure 210–79

Figure 210–79

(2) Not Supply Other Outlets. The 20A, 120V small-appliance circuits required by 210.11(C)(1) must not supply outlets for luminaires or appliances.

Ex 1: The 20A, 120V small-appliance branch circuit can be used to supply a receptacle for an electric clock.

Ex 2: A receptacle can be connected to the small-appliance branch circuit to supply a gas-fired range, oven, or counter-mounted cooking unit. Figure 210–80

Figure 210–80

Author's Comment:

■ A range hood or above the range microwave listed as a range hood that's cord and plug connected must be supplied by an individual branch circuit [422.16(B)(4)(5)].

(C) Countertop Receptacles. In kitchens, pantries, breakfast rooms, dining rooms, and similar areas of dwelling units, receptacle outlets for countertop spaces must be installed according to (1) through (5) below.

(1) Wall Countertop Spaces. A receptacle outlet must be installed for each kitchen and dining area countertop wall space 1 ft or wider, and receptacles must be placed so that no point along the countertop wall space is more than 2 ft, measured horizontally, from a receptacle outlet. Figure 210–81

Ex: A receptacle outlet isn't required on a wall directly behind a range, counter-mounted cooking unit, or sink, in accordance with Figure 210.52(C)(1) in the NEC. Figure 210–82

Figure 210–81

Figure 210–82

Author's Comment:

■ If the countertop space behind a range or sink is larger than the dimensions noted in Figure 210.52(C)(1) of the *NEC*, then a GFCI-protected receptacle must be installed in that space. This is because, for all practical purposes, if there's sufficient space for an appliance, an appliance will be placed there.

(2) Island Countertop Spaces. At least one receptacle outlet must be installed at each island countertop space with a long dimension of 2 ft or more, and a short dimension of 1 ft or more. Figure 210–83

Figure 210–83

(3) Peninsular Countertop Spaces. At least one receptacle outlet must be installed at each peninsular countertop with a long dimension of 2 ft or more, and a short dimension of 1 ft or more, measured from the connecting edge. Figure 210–84

Figure 210–84

Author's Comment:

■ The *Code* doesn't require more than one receptacle outlet in an island or peninsular countertop space, regardless of the length of the countertop, unless the countertop is broken as described in 210.52(C)(4).

(4) Separate Countertop Spaces. When breaks occur in countertop spaces for rangetops, refrigerators, or sinks, each countertop space is considered as a separate countertop for determining receptacle placement. Figure 210–85

Figure 210–85

If a range, counter-mounted cooking unit, or sink is installed in an island or peninsular countertop, and the depth of the counter behind the range, counter-mounted cooking unit, or sink is less than 12 in., the countertop space is considered to be two separate countertop spaces. Figure 210–86

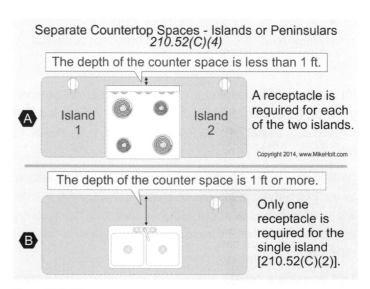

Figure 210–86

Author's Comment:

- GFCI protection is required for all 15A and 20A, 125V receptacles that supply kitchen countertop surfaces [210.8(A)(6)].

(5) Receptacle Location. Receptacle outlets required by 210.52(C)(1) for the countertop space must be located on or above, but not more than 20 in. above, the countertop surface. Figure 210–87

Figure 210–87

Receptacle outlet assemblies listed for the application can be installed in countertops. Figure 210–88

Figure 210–88

Note: Receptacles must not be installed in a face-up position in countertops or similar work surface areas in a dwelling unit [406.5(E)].

Ex: The receptacle outlet for the countertop space can be installed below the countertop only for construction for the physically impaired or when wall space or a backsplash isn't available, such as in an island or peninsular counter. Under these conditions, the required receptacle(s) must be located no more than 1 ft below the countertop surface and no more than 6 in. from the countertop edge, measured horizontally. Figure 210–89

Figure 210–89

Receptacle outlets rendered not readily accessible by appliances fastened in place, located in an appliance garage, behind sinks, or rangetops [210.52(C)(1) Ex], or supplying appliances that occupy dedicated space don't count as the required countertop receptacles.

Author's Comment:

- An "appliance garage" is an enclosed area on the countertop where an appliance can be stored and hidden from view when not in use. If a receptacle is installed inside an appliance garage, it doesn't count as a required countertop receptacle outlet.

(D) Dwelling Unit Bathroom Receptacles. In dwelling units, not less than one 15A or 20A, 125V receptacle outlet must be installed within 3 ft from the outside edge of each bathroom basin. Figure 210–90

A 15A or 20A, 125V receptacle outlet must be installed within 3 ft of the outside edge of each basin.

Figure 210–90

The receptacle outlet must be located on a wall or partition adjacent to the basin counter surface, or on the side or face of the basin cabinet. In no case can the receptacle be located more than 12 in. below the top of the basin.

Receptacle outlet assemblies listed for the application can be installed in countertops. Figure 210–91

The required bathroom receptacle outlet can be located on the countertop or on the side or face of the basin cabinet. In no case can the receptacle be located more than 12 in. below the top of the basin.

Figure 210–91

Note: Receptacles must not be installed in a face-up position in countertops or similar work surface areas [406.5(E)].

Author's Comment:

■ One receptacle outlet can be located between two basins to meet this requirement, but only if it's located within 3 ft of the outside edge of each basin. Figure 210–92

One 15A or 20A, 125V receptacle outlet must be installed within 3 ft from the outside edge of each bathroom basin.

Figure 210–92

■ The bathroom receptacles must be GFCI protected [210.8(A)(1)].

(E) Dwelling Unit Outdoor Receptacles. Outdoor receptacles must comply with the following:

Note: See 210.8(A)(3).

(1) One- and Two-Family Dwellings. Two GFCI-protected 15A or 20A, 125V receptacle outlets that are readily accessible from grade must be installed outdoors for each dwelling unit, one at the front and one at the back, no more than 6½ ft above grade. Figure 210–93

(2) Multifamily Dwelling. Each dwelling unit of a multifamily dwelling that has an individual entrance at grade level must have at least one GFCI-protected 15A or 20A, 125V receptacle outlet readily accessible from grade located not more than 6½ ft above grade. Figure 210–94

(3) Balconies, Decks, and Porches. At least one 15A or 20A, 125V receptacle outlet must be installed not more than 6½ ft above any balcony, deck, or porch surface that's attached to, and accessible from, the inside of a dwelling unit. The receptacle must be accessible from the deck, balcony, or porch surface. Figure 210–95

Figure 210–93

Figure 210–95

Figure 210–94

Figure 210–96

Author's Comment:

- These receptacles must be GFCI protected [210.8(A)(3)].

(F) Dwelling Unit Laundry Area Receptacles. Each dwelling unit must have not less than one 15A or 20A, 125V receptacle installed in the area where laundry equipment is intended to be installed. The receptacle(s) must be supplied by the 20A, 120V laundry branch circuit, which must not supply any other outlets [210.11(C)(2)]. Figure 210–96

Author's Comment:

- Receptacles located within 6 ft of a laundry room sink require GFCI protection [210.8(A)(7)].

Ex 1: A laundry receptacle outlet isn't required in a dwelling unit located in a multifamily dwelling unit with laundry facilities available to all occupants.

(G) Dwelling Unit Garage, Basement, and Accessory Building Receptacles. For single family dwellings, at least one receptacle must be installed in accordance with (1) through (3). The receptacle must be in addition to any receptacles supplied for specific equipment.

(1) Garages. A 15A or 20A, 125V receptacle is required in each attached garage and in each detached garage with electric power. The branch circuit supplying this receptacle(s) must not supply outlets outside of the garage. At least one receptacle must be provided for each car space. Figure 210–97

Figure 210–98

Figure 210–97

Author's Comment:

- The required garage receptacle circuit can't supply other loads commonly seen on this circuit, such as the exterior lights and receptacles for the house.

(2) Accessory Buildings. A 15A or 20A, 125V receptacle is required in each accessory building with electric power. Figure 210–98

Author's Comment:

- GFCI protection is required for all 15A or 20A, 125V receptacles installed in unfinished basements [210.8(A)(5)], garages, and accessory buildings [210.8(A)(2)] of dwelling units.

(3) Basements. Each unfinished portion of a basement must have a 15A or 20A, 125V receptacle outlet installed. Figure 210–99

Author's Comment:

- One 15A or 20A, 125V receptacle outlet is required in a dwelling unit basement even if no portion has been finished into a habitable room.

Figure 210–99

- The purpose of this requirement is to prevent an extension cord from a non-GFCI-protected receptacle from being used to supply power to loads in the unfinished portion of the basement.

(H) Dwelling Unit Hallway Receptacles. One 15A or 20A, 125V receptacle outlet must be installed in each hallway that's at least 10 ft long, measured along the centerline of the hallway without passing through a doorway. Figure 210–100

One 15A or 20A, 125V receptacle outlet must be installed in each hallway that's at least 10 ft long (measured along the centerline without passing through a doorway).

Figure 210–100

(I) Foyer Receptacles. Foyers that aren't part of a hallway [210.52(H)] having an area greater than 60 sq ft must have a receptacle located on any wall space 3 ft or more in width and unbroken by doorways, windows next to doors that extend to the floor, and similar openings. Figure 210–101

Foyers with an area greater than 60 ft² must have a receptacle in each wall space 3 ft or wider and unbroken by doorways, windows next to doors that extend to the floor, and similar openings.

Figure 210–101

210.60 Receptacles in Guest Rooms, Guest Suites, Dormitories, and Similar Occupancies

(A) General Requirements. Guest rooms or guest suites in hotels, motels, and sleeping rooms in dormitories and similar occupancies, must have receptacle outlets installed in accordance with all the requirements for a dwelling unit as described in 210.52(A) and 210.52(D).

Guest rooms with permanent provisions for living, sleeping, cooking, and sanitation must have receptacles installed in accordance with the dwelling unit requirements of 210.52.

(B) Receptacle Placement. The number of receptacle outlets required for guest rooms must not be less than that required for a dwelling unit, in accordance with 210.52(A). To eliminate the need for extension cords by guests for ironing, computers, refrigerators, and so forth, receptacles can be located to be convenient for permanent furniture layout, but not less than two receptacle outlets must be readily accessible.

Receptacle outlets behind a bed must be located so the bed won't make contact with the attachment plug, or the receptacle must be provided with a suitable guard. Figure 210–102

Receptacle outlets behind a bed must be located so the bed won't make contact with an attachment plug, or the receptacle must be provided with a suitable guard.

Figure 210–102

Author's Comment:

■ See the definition of "Attachment Plug" in Article 100.

210.62 Show Windows

At least one <u>125V, 15A or 20A</u> receptacle outlet must be installed within 18 in. of the top of a show window for each 12 linear feet or major fraction thereof measured horizontally at its maximum width. Figure 210–103

Show-Window Receptacle Outlet
210.62

Show-Window Lighting

At least one <u>125V, 15A or 20A</u> receptacle outlet must be installed within 18 in. of the top of a show window for each 12 linear feet or major fraction thereof measured horizontally at its maximum width.

Copyright 2014, www.MikeHolt.com

Figure 210–103

Author's Comment:

■ See the definition of "Show Window" in Article 100.

210.63 Heating, Air-Conditioning, and Refrigeration (HACR) Equipment

A 15A or 20A, 125V receptacle outlet must be installed at an accessible location for the servicing of heating, air-conditioning, and refrigeration equipment. The receptacle must be located within 25 ft of, and on the same level as, the heating, air-conditioning, and refrigeration equipment. Figure 210–104

Author's Comment:

■ A receptacle outlet isn't required for ventilation equipment, because it's not heating, air-conditioning, or refrigeration equipment.

Heating, Air-Conditioning, and Refrigeration Receptacle
210.63

A 15A or 20A, 125V receptacle is required within 25 ft of heat, A/C, and refrigeration equipment.

Copyright 2014 www.MikeHolt.com

GFCI protection is required [210.8].

Figure 210–104

■ The HACR receptacle must be GFCI protected if located outdoors [210.8(A)(3) and 210.8(B)(5)] or in the crawl space or unfinished basement of a dwelling unit [210.8(A)(4) and 210.8(A)(5)].

■ The outdoor 15A or 20A, 125V receptacle outlet required for dwelling units [210.52(E)(1)] can be used to satisfy this requirement. Figure 210–105

Heating, Air-Conditioning, and Refrigeration Receptacle
210.63

Heating or A/C Unit

GFCI

Dwelling Unit

Copyright 2014 www.MikeHolt.com

GFCI

One of the outside receptacles required by 210.52(E) can be used as the air-conditioning or heat servicing receptacle if it meets all the requirements of 210.63.

Figure 210–105

Ex: A receptacle outlet isn't required at one- and two-family dwellings for the service of evaporative coolers.

210.64 Electrical Service Areas

At least one 15A or 20A, 125V receptacle outlet must be installed within 50 ft of the electrical service equipment. Figures 210–106 and 210–107

Figure 210–106

Figure 210–107

Ex: The receptacle outlet isn't required for one- and two-family dwellings.

210.70 Lighting Outlet Requirements

(A) Dwelling Unit Lighting Outlets. Lighting outlets must be installed in:

(1) Habitable Rooms. At least one wall switch-controlled lighting outlet must be installed in every habitable room and bathroom of a dwelling unit. Figure 210–108

Figure 210–108

Author's Comment:

■ See the definition of "Lighting Outlet" in Article 100.

Ex 1: In other than kitchens and bathrooms, a receptacle controlled by a wall switch can be used instead of a lighting outlet. Figure 210–109

Ex 2: Lighting outlets can be controlled by occupancy sensors equipped with a manual override that permits the sensor to function as a wall switch. Figure 210–110

Figure 210–109

Figure 210–111

Figure 210–110

Author's Comment:

- The *Code* specifies the location of the wall switch-controlled lighting outlet, but it doesn't specify the switch location. Naturally, you wouldn't want to install a switch behind a door or other inconvenient location, but the *NEC* doesn't require you to relocate the switch to suit the swing of the door. When in doubt as to the best location to place a light switch, consult the job plans or ask the customer. Figure 210–111

(2) Other Areas.

(a) Hallways, Stairways, and Garages. In dwelling units, not less than one wall switch-controlled lighting outlet must be installed in hallways, stairways, attached garages, and detached garages with electric power.

(b) Exterior Entrances. At least one wall switch-controlled lighting outlet must provide illumination on the exterior side of outdoor entrances or exits of dwelling units with grade-level access. Figure 210–112

Figure 210–112

Author's Comment:

- The *NEC* doesn't require a switch adjacent to each outdoor entrance or exit. The *Code* considers switch location a "design issue" which is beyond the purpose of the *NEC* [90.1(A)]. For this reason, proposals to mandate switch locations have been rejected.

- A lighting outlet isn't required to provide illumination on the exterior side of outdoor entrances or exits for a commercial or industrial occupancy.

(c) Stairway. If the stairway between floor levels has six risers or more, a wall switch must be located at each floor level and at each landing level that includes an entryway to control the illumination for the stairway. Figure 210–113

Figure 210–113

Ex to (a), (b), and (c): Lighting outlets for hallways, stairways, and outdoor entrances can be switched by a remote, central, or automatic control device. Figure 210–114

(3) Storage and Equipment Rooms. At least one lighting outlet that contains a switch or is controlled by a wall switch must be installed in attics, underfloor spaces, utility rooms, and basements used for storage or containing equipment that requires servicing. The switch must be located at the usual point of entry to these spaces, and the lighting outlet must be located at or near the equipment that requires servicing. Figure 210–115

Figure 210–114

Figure 210–115

(B) Guest Rooms or Guest Suites. At least one wall switch-controlled lighting outlet must be installed in every habitable room and bathroom of a guest room or guest suite of hotels, motels, and similar occupancies.

Ex 1: In other than bathrooms and kitchens, a receptacle controlled by a wall switch is permitted in lieu of lighting outlets. Figure 210–116

Ex 2: Lighting outlets can be controlled by occupancy sensors equipped with a manual override that permits the sensor to function as a wall switch.

Lighting Outlets - Guest Rooms or Guest Suites
210.70(B) Ex 1

Bathroom and kitchen areas must have a wall switch-controlled lighting outlet [210.70(B)].

In other than bathrooms and kitchens, one or more wall switch-controlled receptacle(s) can be used instead of lighting outlets.

GFCI

Copyright 2014
www.MikeHolt.com

Figure 210–116

(C) Other Than Dwelling Units. At least one lighting outlet that contains a switch or is controlled by a wall switch must be installed in attics and underfloor spaces containing equipment that requires servicing. The switch must be located at the usual point of entry to these spaces, and the lighting outlet must be located at or near the equipment requiring servicing.

Author's Comment:

■ A 15A or 20A, 125V receptacle must be installed within 25 ft of HACR equipment [210.63].

ARTICLE
215
FEEDERS

Introduction to Article 215—Feeders

Article 215 covers the rules for the installation and ampacity of feeders. The requirements for feeders have some similarities to those for branch circuits, but in some ways, feeders bear a resemblance to service conductors. It's important to understand the distinct differences between these three types of circuits in order to correctly apply the *Code* requirements.

Feeders are the conductors between the service equipment, the separately derived system, or other supply source, and the final branch-circuit overcurrent device. Conductors past the final overcurrent device protecting the circuit and the outlet are branch-circuit conductors and fall within the scope of Article 210 [Article 100 Definitions].

Service conductors are the conductors from the service point of the electric utility to the service disconnecting means [Article 100 Definition]. If there's no serving utility, and the electrical power is derived from a generator or other on-site power source, then the conductors from the supply source are defined as feeders and there are no service conductors.

It's easy to be confused between feeder, branch circuit, and service conductors, so it's important to evaluate each installation carefully using the Article 100 Definitions to be sure the correct *NEC* rules are followed.

215.1 Scope

Article 215 covers the installation, conductor sizing, and protection requirements for feeders.

Author's Comment:

- Article 100 defines feeders as the conductors between service equipment, a separately derived system, or other power supply, and the final branch-circuit overcurrent device. Figure 215–1

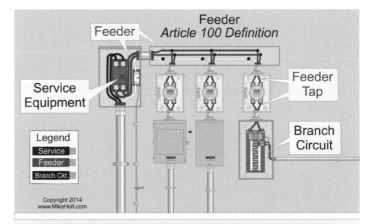

Conductors between service equipment, a separately derived system, or other power supply, and the final branch-circuit overcurrent device.

Figure 215–1

215.2 Minimum Rating

(A) Feeder Conductor Size.

(1) General. Feeders must be sized to carry the calculated load from Parts III, IV, and V of Article 220. The feeder conductors must be the larger of (a) or (b):

(a) The minimum feeder conductor ampacity must be no less than 125 percent of the continuous load, plus 100 percent of the noncontinuous load, based on the terminal temperature rating ampacities as listed in Table 310.15(B)(16) [110.14(C)(1)]. Figure 215–2

Figure 215–2

(b) The feeder ampacity must be not less than the maximum load to be served after the application of any adjustment or correction factors. Figure 215–3

Figure 215–3

Author's Comment:

■ See 215.3 for the feeder overcurrent device sizing requirements for continuous and noncontinuous loads.

Note 2: To provide reasonable efficiency of operation of electrical equipment, feeder conductors should be sized to prevent a voltage drop not to exceed 3 percent. In addition, the maximum total voltage drop on both feeders and branch circuits shouldn't exceed 5 percent.

Note 3: See 210.19(A), Note 4, for voltage drop for branch circuits.

Ex 1: If the assembly and the overcurrent device are both listed for operation at 100 percent of their rating, the conductors can be sized at 100 percent of the continuous load.

Author's Comment:

■ Equipment suitable for 100 percent continuous loading is rarely available in ratings under 400A.

Ex 2: Neutral conductors can be sized at 100 percent of the continuous and noncontinuous load.

Question: *What size feeder conductors are required for a 200A continuous load if the terminals are rated 75ºC?* Figure 215–4

(a) *2/0 AWG ungrounded conductors and a 1/0 AWG neutral conductor*

(b) *3/0 AWG ungrounded conductors and a 1/0 AWG neutral conductor*

(c) *4/0 AWG ungrounded conductors and a 1/0 AWG neutral conductor*

(d) *250 kcmil ungrounded conductors and a 3/0 AWG neutral conductor*

Answer: *(d) 250 kcmil AWG ungrounded conductors and a 3/0 AWG neutral conductor*

Since the load is 200A continuous, the feeder conductors must have an ampacity of not less than 250A (200A x 1.25). The neutral conductor is sized to the 200A continuous load according to the 75ºC column of Table 310.15(B)(16). According to the 75ºC column of Table 310.15(B)(16), 250 kcmil has an ampacity of 255A, and 3/0 has an ampacity of 200A.

(2) Neutral Conductor Size. The feeder neutral conductor must be sized to carry the maximum unbalanced load in accordance with 220.61, and must not be smaller than listed in 250.122, based on the rating of the feeder overcurrent device. The sizing requirements of 250.122(F) for parallel conductors don't apply.

Question: *What size neutral conductor is required for a feeder consisting of 250 kcmil ungrounded conductors and one neutral conductor protected by a 250A overcurrent device, where the unbalanced load is only 50A, with 75ºC terminals?* Figure 215–5

(a) *6 AWG*   (b) *4 AWG*   (c) *1/0 AWG*   (d) *3/0 AWG*

Answer: *(b) 4 AWG [based on Table 250.122]*

Table 310.15(B)(16) and 220.61 permit an 8 AWG neutral conductor, rated 50A at 75ºC to carry the 50A unbalanced load, but the neutral conductor isn't permitted to be smaller than 4 AWG, as listed in Table 250.122, based on the 250A overcurrent device.

Feeder Neutral Conductor Size
215.2(A)(1) Ex 2

250A Overcurrent Device [215.3]

200A Continuous Load

Ungrounded Conductor 250 kcmil Rated 255A at 75ºC [Tbl 310.15(B)(16)]

Neutral Conductor 3/0 AWG Rated 200A at 75ºC [Tbl 310.15(B)(16)]

Copyright 2014 www.MikeHolt.com

The neutral conductor is permitted to be sized at 100% of the continuous/noncontinuous load.

Figure 215–4

Feeder Neutral Conductor Size
215.2(A)(2)

250A Feeder Overcurrent Device

250 kcmil

Unbalanced Load is 50A

Copyright 2014 www.MikeHolt.com

An 8 AWG rated 50A at 75ºC will carry the load but Table 250.122 requires a 4 AWG for the 250A protection device.

The size of the neutral conductor must carry the maximum unbalanced load and not be smaller than required by 250.122, based on the rating of the feeder overcurrent device.

Figure 215–5

215.3 Overcurrent Protection Sizing

Feeder overcurrent devices must have a rating of not less than 125 percent of the continuous loads, plus 100 percent of the noncontinuous loads. Figure 215–6

Figure 215–6

Author's Comment:

■ See 215.2(A)(1) for feeder conductor sizing requirements.

Ex: If the assembly and the overcurrent device are both listed for operation at 100 percent of its rating, the overcurrent device can be sized at 100 percent of the continuous load.

Author's Comment:

■ Equipment suitable for 100 percent continuous loading is rarely available in ratings under 400A.

215.4 Feeders with Common Neutral Conductor

(A) Feeders with Common Neutral. Up to three sets of 3-wire feeders or two sets of 4-wire feeders can use the same neutral conductor.

Author's Comment:

■ The neutral conductor must be sized to carry the total unbalanced load for all feeders as determined in Article 220, see 220.61.

215.6 Equipment Grounding Conductor

Feeder circuits must include or provide an equipment grounding conductor of a type listed in 250.118, and it must terminate in a manner so that branch-circuit equipment grounding conductors can be connected to it, and installed in accordance with 250.134. Figure 215–7

Figure 215–7

215.10 Ground-Fault Protection of Equipment

Each feeder disconnecting means rated 1,000A or more supplied by a 4-wire, three-phase, 277/480V wye-connected system must be provided with ground-fault protection of equipment in accordance with 230.95 and 240.13.

Author's Comment:

■ See the definition of "Ground-Fault Protection of Equipment" in Article 100.

Ex 2. Equipment ground-fault protection isn't required if ground-fault protection of equipment is provided on the supply side of the feeder and on the load side of the transformer supplying the feeder.

Author's Comment:

■ Ground-fault protection of equipment isn't permitted for fire pumps [695.6(G)], and it's not required for emergency systems [700.26] or legally required standby systems [701.17].

215.12 Conductor Identification

(A) Neutral Conductor. The neutral conductor of a feeder must be identified in accordance with 200.6.

(B) Equipment Grounding Conductor. Equipment grounding conductors can be bare, and individually covered or insulated equipment grounding conductors sized 6 AWG and smaller must have a continuous outer finish either green or green with one or more yellow stripes [250.119]. Figure 215–8

Identification of Equipment Grounding Conductor
6 AWG or Smaller
250.119

The equipment grounding conductor can be bare or have continuous insulation that's green or green with one or more yellow stripe.

Copyright 2014, www.MikeHolt.com

Figure 215–8

Insulated equipment grounding conductors 4 AWG and larger can be permanently reidentified with green marking at the time of installation at every point where the conductor is accessible [250.119(A)]. Figure 215–9

Identifying Equipment Grounding Conductor
4 AWG and Larger
250.119(A)(1)

Insulated equipment grounding conductors 4 AWG and larger can be reidentified with green marking at every point where the conductor is accessible.

Copyright 2014, www.MikeHolt.com

Figure 215–9

(C) Ungrounded Conductors. Ungrounded feeder conductors must be identified in accordance with (1) or (2).

(1) Multiple Voltage Systems. If the premises wiring system contains feeders supplied from more than one voltage system, each ungrounded conductor, at all termination, connection, and splice points, must be identified by phase or line and system, in accordance with (a) and (b).

(a) Identification Method. Identification can be by color coding, marking tape, tagging, or other means approved by the authority having jurisdiction. Figure 215–10

Multiple Voltage Systems
Identification Method
215.12(C)(1)(a)

Identification can be by color coding, marking tape, tagging, or other means approved by the authority having jurisdiction.

Copyright 2014
www.MikeHolt.com

Where the premises wiring system contains feeders supplied from more than one voltage system, each ungrounded conductor must be identified by phase or line and system at termination, connection, and splice points [215.12(C)(1)].

Figure 215–10

(b) Posting of Identification Method. Such identification must be documented in a manner that's readily available, or it must be permanently posted at each panelboard. Figure 215–11

Author's Comment:

■ Although the *NEC* doesn't require a specific color code for ungrounded conductors, electricians often use the following color system for power and lighting conductor identification:

☐ 120/240V, single-phase—black, red, and white

☐ 120/208V, three-phase—black, red, blue, and white

☐ 120/240V, three-phase—black, orange, blue, and white

☐ 277/480V, three-phase—brown, orange, yellow, and gray; or, brown, purple, yellow, and gray

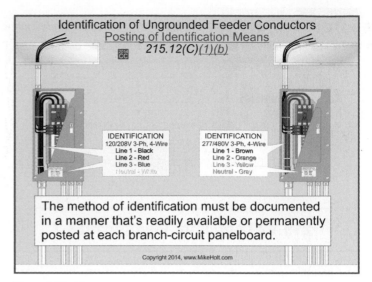

Figure 215–11

BRANCH-CIRCUIT, FEEDER, AND SERVICE CALCULATIONS

Introduction to Article 220—Branch-Circuit, Feeder, and Service Calculations

This five-part article focuses on the requirements for calculating the minimum size of branch circuit, feeder, and service conductors.

Part I describes the layout of Article 220 and provides a table of where other types of load calculations can be found in the *NEC*. Part II provides requirements for branch-circuit calculations and for specific types of branch circuits. Part III covers the requirements for feeder and service calculations, using what's commonly called the "standard method of calculation." Part IV provides optional calculations that can be used in place of the standard calculations provided in Parts II and III—if your installation meets certain requirements. Farm Load Calculations are discussed in Part V of the article.

In many cases, either the standard method (Part III) or the optional method (Part IV) can be used; however, these two methods don't yield identical results. In fact, sometimes these two answers may be diverse enough to call for different service sizes. There's nothing to say that either answer is right or wrong. If taking an exam, read the instructions carefully to be sure which method the test wants you to use. As you work through Article 220, be sure to study the illustrations to help you fully understand it. Also be sure to review the examples in Annex D of the *NEC* to provide more practice with these calculations.

Part I. General

220.1 Scope

This article contains the requirements necessary for calculating branch circuits, feeders, and services. In addition, this article can be used to determine the number of receptacles on a circuit and the number of general-purpose branch circuits required.

220.3 Application of Other Articles

Other articles contain calculations that are in addition to, or modify, those contained within Article 220. Take a moment to review the following additional calculation requirements found in these sections:

- Air-Conditioning and Refrigeration Equipment, 440.6, 440.21, 440.22, 440.31, 440.32, and 440.62
- Appliances, 422.10 and 422.11
- Branch Circuits, 210.19 and 210.20(A)
- Computers (Data Processing Equipment), 645.4 and 645.5(A)
- Conductors, 310.15
- Electric Vehicle Charging Systems, 625.14
- Feeders, 215.2(B) and 215.3
- Fire Pumps, 695.7
- Fixed Electric Space-Heating Equipment, 424.3(B)
- Marinas, 555.12, 555.19(A)(4), and 555.19(B)
- Mobile Homes and Manufactured Homes, 550.12 and 550.18
- Motors, 430.6(A), 430.22, 430.24, 430.52, and 430.62
- Overcurrent Protection, 240.4 and 240.15

- Refrigeration (Hermetic), 440.6 and Part IV of Article 440
- Recreational Vehicle Parks, 551.73(A)
- Electronic Equipment, 647.4(D)
- Services, 230.42(A) and 230.79
- Signs, 600.5
- Transformers, 450.3

220.5 Calculations

(A) Voltage Used for Calculations. Unless other voltages are specified, branch-circuit, feeder, and service loads must be calculated on nominal system voltages, such as 120V, 120/240V, 120/208V, 240V, 277/480V, or 480V. Figure 220–1

Figure 220–1

Unless other voltages are specified, loads must be calculated on nominal system voltage; 120/240V, 120/208V, or 277/480V is typically used for commercial occupancies.

Author's Comment:

■ A nominal value is assigned to a circuit for the purpose of convenient circuit identification. The actual voltage at which a circuit operates can vary from the nominal within a range that permits satisfactory operation of equipment [Article 100]. Figure 220–2

(B) Fractions of an Ampere (Rounding Amperes). Calculations can be rounded to the nearest whole number and fractions less than 0.50A can be dropped.

Figure 220–2

Author's Comment:

■ When do you round—after each calculation, or at the final calculation? The *NEC* isn't specific on this issue, but rounding at each calculation can lead to accumulated errors that can be an issue with the authority having jurisdiction.

Question: *According to 424.3(B), the branch-circuit conductors and overcurrent device for electric space-heating equipment must be sized at no less than 125 percent of the total load. What size conductor is required to supply a 9.60 kW (40A), 240V, single-phase fixed space heater with a 3A blower motor, if the equipment terminals are rated 75°C?* Figure 220–3

(a) 10 AWG   *(b) 8 AWG*   *(c) 6 AWG*   *(d) 4 AWG*

Answer: *(c) 6 AWG*

Step 1: *Determine the load for the heater:*

$$I = VA/E$$

I = 9,600 VA/240V
I = 40A

Step 2: *Conductor size at 125% of the load:*
Conductor Size = (40A + 3A) x 1.25
Conductor Size = 53.75A, round up to 54A

Article 220 calculations can be rounded to the nearest whole number, with fractions smaller than 0.50A dropped.

9.6 kW heat strip, 3A blower, 240V

I = (9,600W/240V) + 3A = 43A
43A x 125% [424.3(B)] = 53.75A, Round up to 54A
Table 310.15(B)(16), 6 AWG rated 65A at 75°C

Figure 220–3

Part II. Branch-Circuit Load Calculations

220.12 General Lighting

The general lighting load specified in Table 220.12 must be calculated from the outside dimensions of the building or area involved. Figure 220–4

General Lighting and Receptacles Table 220.12

Open Porch

40 ft Outside Dimension

2,000 sq ft based on the outside dimensions.

Garage, carport, or spaces not adaptable for future use.

50 ft Outside Dimension

General Lighting and General-Use Receptacle Load
2,000 sq ft x 3 VA = 6,000 VA

Figure 220–4

Table 220.12 General Lighting VA per Square Foot	
Occupancy	VA/Sq. Ft
Armories and auditoriums	1
Assembly halls and auditoriums	1
Banks	3½b
Barber shops and beauty parlors	3
Churches	1
Clubs	2
Courtrooms	2
Dwelling units	3a
Garages—commercial (storage)	½
Halls, corridors, closets, stairways	½
Hospitals	2
Hotels and motels without cooking facilities	2
Industrial commercial (loft buildings)	2
Lodge rooms	1½
Office buildings	3½b
Restaurants	2
Schools	3
Storage spaces	¼
Stores	3
Warehouses (storage)	¼

Table Note a: *The VA load for general–use receptacles, bathroom receptacles [220.14(J)(1) and 210.11(C)(3)], outside receptacles, as well as garage, basement receptacles [220.14(J)(2), 210.52(E) and (G)], and lighting outlets [220.14(J)(3), 210.70(A) and (B)] in a dwelling unit are included in the 3 VA per–square–foot general lighting [220.14(J)].*

Table Note b: *The receptacle calculated load for banks and office buildings is the largest calculation of either (1) or (2) [220.14(K)].*

For dwelling units, the calculated floor area don't include open porches, garages, or unused or unfinished spaces not adaptable for future use. Figure 220–5

Ex: Where the adopted energy code requires a smaller value for lighting loads, the energy code values can be used if the following requirements are met:

Figure 220–5

Figure 220–6

(1) A power monitoring system that provides continuous information on the lighting load of the building must be installed.

(2) The power monitoring system must have an alarm that alerts the building owner or manager if the lighting load exceeds the values set by the energy code.

(3) The lighting load demand factors in 220.42 can't be used.

220.14 Other Loads—All Occupancies

The minimum VA load for each outlet must comply with (A) through (L).

(A) Specific Equipment. The branch-circuit VA load for equipment and appliance outlets must be calculated on the VA rating of the equipment or appliance.

(B) Electric Dryers and Electric Cooking Appliances in Dwelling Units and Household Cooking Appliances used in Instructional Programs. The branch-circuit VA load for household electric dryers must comply with 220.54, and household electric ranges and other cooking appliances must comply with 220.55.

(C) Motor Outlets. The motor branch-circuit VA load must be determined by multiplying the motor full-load current (FLC) listed in Table 430.248 or 430.250 by the motor table voltage, in accordance with 430.22 [430.6(A)(1)]. Figure 220–6

(D) Luminaires. The branch-circuit VA load for recessed luminaires must be calculated based on the maximum VA rating for which the luminaires are rated.

(E) Heavy-Duty Lampholders. The branch-circuit VA load for heavy-duty lampholders must be calculated at a minimum of 600 VA.

(F) Sign Outlet. Each commercial occupancy that's accessible to pedestrians must have at least one 20A sign outlet [600.5(A)], which must have a minimum branch-circuit load of 1,200 VA. Figure 220–7

Figure 220–7

(G) Show Windows. The branch-circuit VA load for show-window lighting must be calculated in accordance with (1) or (2):

(1) 180 VA for each outlet in accordance with 220.14(L), or

(2) 200 VA for each linear foot of show-window lighting [220.43]. Figure 220–8

50 linear ft of show-window lighting x 200 VA per ft = 10,000 VA lighting load

Continuous loads at 125% [215.2(A)(1)]

10,000 VA x 1.25 = 12,500 VA lighting load

Copyright 2014, www.MikeHolt.com

Figure 220–8

(H) Fixed Multioutlet Assemblies. Fixed multioutlet assemblies in commercial occupancies used in other than dwelling units, or in the guest rooms of hotels or motels, must be calculated in accordance with (1) or (2). Figure 220–9

Fixed multioutlet assemblies in commercial occupancies must be calculated in accordance with (1) or (2).
(1) Each 5 ft or fraction is equal to 180 VA.
(2) Simultaneous use; each 1 ft or fraction equals 180 VA.

Figure 220–9

(1) If appliances are unlikely to be used simultaneously, each 5 ft or fraction of 5 ft of multioutlet assembly is considered as one outlet of 180 VA. Figure 220–10

2 sections x 180 VA = 360 VA

Copyright 2014, www.MikeHolt.com

Figure 220–10

(2) If appliances are likely to be used simultaneously, each 1 ft or fraction of a foot of multioutlet assembly is considered as one outlet of 180 VA. Figure 220–11

3 x 180 VA per ft = 540 VA

Copyright 2014, www.MikeHolt.com

Figure 220–11

Author's Comment:

■ See the definition of "Multioutlet Assembly" in Article 100.

■ The feeder or service calculated load for fixed multioutlet assemblies can be calculated in accordance with the demand factors contained in 220.44.

(I) Receptacle Outlets. 180 VA per mounting strap for each 15A or 20A, 125V general-use receptacle outlet, except as covered in 200.14(J) and (K). Figure 220–12

Figure 220–12

A single device consisting of four or more receptacles is considered as 90 VA for each receptacle (360 VA for a quad receptacle). Figure 220–13

Question: What's the maximum number of 15A or 20A, 125V receptacle outlets permitted on a 20A, 120V general-purpose branch circuit in a commercial occupancy? Figure 220–14

(a) 4   (b) 6   (c) 10   (d) 13

Answer: (d) 13

Circuit VA = Volts x Amperes

Circuit VA = 120V x 20A
Circuit VA = 2,400 VA

Number of Receptacles = 2,400 VA/180 VA
Number of Receptacles = 13

Figure 220–13

Figure 220–14

Author's Comment:

■ According to the *NEC* Handbook, published by the NFPA, general-purpose receptacles aren't considered a continuous load.

(J) Residential Receptacle Load. In one-family, two-family, and multifamily dwellings, and in guest rooms of hotels and motels, the outlets specified in (1), (2), and (3) are included in the general lighting load calculations of 220.12.

(1) General-use receptacle outlets, including the receptacles connected to the 20A bathroom circuit [210.11(C)(3)].

(2) Outdoor, garage, and basement receptacle outlets [210.52(E) and (G)].

(3) Lighting outlets [210.70(A) and (B)].

Author's Comment:

■ There's no VA load for 15A and 20A, 125V general-use receptacle outlets, because the loads for these devices are part of the 3 VA per-square-foot for general lighting as listed in Table 220.12 for dwelling units.

■ The *NEC* doesn't limit the number of receptacle outlets on a general-purpose branch circuit in a dwelling unit. See the *NEC Handbook* for more information. Figure 220–15

Number of Outlets Per Circuit - Dwelling Unit
220.14(J)

Copyright 2014, www.MikeHolt.com

The *NEC* doesn't limit the number of receptacle and lighting outlets on a general-purpose circuit in a dwelling unit.

Figure 220–15

Question: *What's the maximum number of 15A or 20A, 125V receptacle outlets permitted on a 15A or 20A, 120V general-purpose branch circuit in a dwelling unit?*

(a) 4   (b) 6   (c) 8   (d) No limit

Answer: *(d) No limit*

⚠ CAUTION: *There might be a local Code requirement that limits the number of receptacle outlets on a general-purpose branch circuit.*

Author's Comment:

■ Although there's no limit on the number of receptacle outlets on dwelling general-purpose branch circuits, the *NEC* does require a minimum number of circuits to be installed for general-purpose receptacles and lighting outlets [210.11(A)]. In addition, the receptacle and lighting loads must be evenly distributed among the required circuits [210.11(B)].

(K) Banks and Office Buildings. The receptacle calculated load for banks and office buildings is the largest calculation of either (1) or (2).

(1) Determine the receptacle calculated load at 180 VA per receptacle yoke [220.14(I)], then apply the demand factor from Table 220.44, or

(2) Determine the receptacle load at 1 VA per sq ft.

Bank or Office General Lighting and Receptacle—Example 1

Question: *What's the calculated receptacle load for an 18,000 sq ft bank with 160 15A, 125V receptacles?* Figure 220–16

(a) 15,400 VA   (b) 19,400 VA   (c) 28,800 VA   (d) 142 kVA

Answer: *(b) 19,400 VA*

[220.14(K)(1) and 220.14(I)]
160 Receptacles x 180 VA = 28,800 VA
First 10,000 at 100% =   − 10,000 VA x 1.00 =   10,000 VA
Remainder at 50% =   18,800 VA x 0.50 = + 9,400 VA
Receptacle Calculated Load =   19,400 VA

[220.14(K)(2)]
18,000 x 1 VA per sq ft   18,000 VA
                                                  (smaller, omit)

Bank/Office Building - Receptacle Calculated Load
220.14(K)

Bank - 18,000 sq ft
160 Receptacles

The larger of 220.14(K)(1) and (K)(2):

220.14(K)(1) [220.44],
160 receptacles x 180 VA = 28,800 VA
First 10,000 VA at 100% - 10,000 VA = 10,000 VA
Remainder at 50%   18,800 VA = + 9,400 VA
Receptacle Calculated Load   19,400 VA

220.14(K)(2), 18,000 sq ft x 1 VA per ft = 18,000 VA

Figure 220–16

Bank/Office Building - Receptacle Calculated Load
220.14(K)

Bank - 18,000 sq ft
140 Receptacles

The larger of 220.14(K)(1) and (K)(2):

220.14(K)(1) [220.44],
140 receptacles x 180 VA = 25,200 VA
First 10,000 VA at 100%   -10,000 VA = 10,000 VA
Remainder at 50%   15,200 VA = 7,600 VA
Receptacle Calculated Load   17,600 VA

220.14(K)(2), 18,000 sq ft x 1 VA per ft = 18,000 VA

Figure 220–17

Bank or Office General Lighting and Receptacle—Example 2

Question: *What's the receptacle calculated load for an 18,000 sq ft bank with 140 15A, 125V receptacles? Figure 220–17*

(a) 15,000 VA   (b) 18,000 VA   (c) 23,000 VA   (d) 31,000 VA

Answer: *(b) 18,000 VA*

[220.14(K)(1) and 220.14(l)]
140 Receptacles x 180 VA =   25,200 VA
First 10,000 at 100% =   −10,000 VA x 1.00 = 10,000 VA
Remainder at 50% =   15,200 VA x 0.50 = + 7,600 VA
Receptacle Calculated Load =   17,600 VA
                                  (smaller, omit)

[220.14(K)(2)]
18,000 x 1 VA per sq ft =   18,000 VA

(L) Other Outlets. 180 VA for each receptacle and lighting outlet not covered in (A) through (K).

220.18 Maximum Load on a Branch Circuit

(A) Motor Operated Loads. Branch circuits that supply motor loads must be sized not less than 125 percent of the motor FLC, in accordance with 430.6(A) and 430.22.

Question: *What's the minimum size branch-circuit conductor for a 2 hp, 230V motor, where the conductor terminals are rated 75°C? Figure 220–18*

(a) 14 AWG   (b) 12 AWG   (c) 10 AWG   (d) 8 AWG

Answer: *(a) 14 AWG*

Step 1: *Determine the motor full-load current: [Table 430.248] 2 hp FLC = 12A*

Step 2: *Size the branch-circuit conductors at 125 percent of the FLC in accordance with Table 310.15(B)(16) [430.22]:*
Branch-Circuit Conductors = 12A x 1.25
Branch-Circuit Conductors = 15A, 14 AWG rated 20A at 75°C.

Motor Branch Circuit
220.18(A)

12A x 1.25 = 15A [430.22]
14 AWG Rated 20A at 75ºC

2 hp, 230V
Sump Pump
FLC = 12A

Copyright 2014
www.MikeHolt.com

Branch circuits that supply motor loads must have
an ampacity not less than 125% of the motor FLC.

Figure 220–18

(B) Inductive and LED Lighting Loads. Branch circuits that supply inductive and LED driver lighting loads must be sized to the total ampere rating of the luminaire, not to the total wattage of the lamps. Figure 220–19

Branch-Circuit Loads - Inductive and LED Lighting
220.18(B)

Branch circuits for inductive luminaires or LED
drivers must be sized to the total ampere rating of
the luminaire, not the total wattage of the lamps.

Copyright 2014, www.MikeHolt.com

Figure 220–19

Question: *What's the maximum number of 1.34A fluorescent luminaires permitted on a 20A circuit if the luminaires operate for more than 3 hours?*

(a) 8   (b) 11   (c) 13   (d) 15

Answer: *(b) 11*

The maximum continuous load must not exceed 80 percent of the circuit rating [210.19(A)(1)].

Maximum Load = 20A x 0.80
Maximum Load = 16A

Luminaires on Circuit = 16A/1.34A
Luminaires on Circuit = 11.94 or 11 luminaires

Author's Comment:

■ Because of power factor (inductive luminaires), the input VA of each luminaire is 162 VA (120V x 1.34A), which is greater than the 136W (34W x 4 lamps) of the lamps. This may seem complicated, but just remember—size all circuits that supply lighting loads to the ampere rating of the luminaire, not to the wattage of the lamps.

(C) Household Cooking Appliances. Branch-circuit conductors for household cooking appliances can be sized in accordance with Table 220.55; specifically, Table Note 4 for branch circuits.

Author's Comment:

■ For ranges rated 8.75 kW or more, the minimum branch-circuit rating is 40A [210.19(A)(3)].

Part III. Feeder and Service Calculations

220.40 General

The calculated load for a feeder or service must not be less than the sum of the branch-circuit loads, as determined by Part II of this article, as adjusted for the demand factors contained in Parts III, IV, or V.

Note: See Examples D1(a) through D10 in Annex D.

220.42 General Lighting Demand Factors

The *Code* recognizes that not all luminaires will be on at the same time, and it permits the following demand factors to be applied to the general lighting load as determined in Table 220.42.

Table 220.42 General Lighting Demand Factors

Type of Occupancy	Lighting VA Load	Demand Factor
Dwelling Units	First 3,000 VA Next 117,000 VA Remainder at	100% 35% 25%
Hotels/motels without provision for cooking	First 20,000 VA Next 80,000 VA Remainder at	50% 40% 30%
Warehouses (storage)	First 12,500 VA Remainder at	100% 50%
All others	Total VA	100%

Question: *What's the general lighting and receptacle calculated load, after demand factors, for a 40 x 50 ft (2,000 sq ft) dwelling unit?* Figure 220–20

(a) 2,050 VA   (b) 3,050 VA   (c) 4,050 VA   (d) 5,050 VA

Answer: *(c) 4,050 VA*

General Lighting = 40 x 50 ft
General Lighting = 2,000 sq ft x 3 VA per sq ft
General Lighting = 6,000 VA

First 3,000 VA at 100% 3,000 VA x 1.00 =	*3,000 VA*
Next 117,000 VA at 35% 3,000 VA x 0.35 =	*+ 1,050 VA*

General Lighting and General-Use Receptacles
Calculated Load =   *4,050 VA*

Author's Comment:

■ For commercial occupancies, the VA load for receptacles [220.14(I)] and fixed multioutlet assemblies [220.14(H)] can be added to the general lighting load and subjected to the demand factors of Table 220.42 [220.44].

General Lighting and Receptacle Calculated Load
Table 220.42

2,000 sq ft based on the outside dimensions. (40 x 50 = 2000)

Garage, carport, or spaces not adaptable for future use. Do NOT Count.

Open Porch Does NOT Count

40 ft Outside Dimension

50 ft Outside Dimension

Copyright 2014, www.MikeHolt.com

2,000 sq ft x 3 VA per sq ft = 6,000 VA
1st 3,000 VA at 100%   - 3,000 VA x 1.00 = 3,000 VA
Next 117,000 VA at 35%   3,000 VA x 0.35 = 1,050 VA
General lighting & general-use receptacle load = 4,050 VA

Figure 220–20

220.43 Commercial—Show Window and Track Lighting Load

(A) Show Windows. The feeder/service VA load must not be less than 200 VA per linear foot.

(B) Track Lighting. The feeder/service VA load must not be less than 150 VA for every 2 ft of track lighting or fraction of that length. Figure 220–21

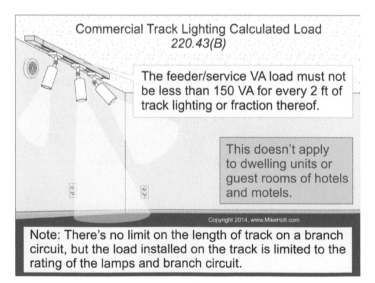

Commercial Track Lighting Calculated Load
220.43(B)

The feeder/service VA load must not be less than 150 VA for every 2 ft of track lighting or fraction thereof.

This doesn't apply to dwelling units or guest rooms of hotels and motels.

Copyright 2014, www.MikeHolt.com

Note: There's no limit on the length of track on a branch circuit, but the load installed on the track is limited to the rating of the lamps and branch circuit.

Figure 220–21

Ex: Track lighting supplied through a device that limits the current to the track can have the load calculated based on the current rating of the limiting device.

Author's Comment:

■ There's no limit on the length of track that can be supplied by a single branch circuit.

■ If a feeder or service supplies continuous loads, the minimum feeder or service conductor ampacity, before the application of ambient temperature correction [310.15(B)(2)(a)], conductor bundling adjustment [310.15(B)(3)(a)], or both, must have an allowable ampacity of at least 125 percent of the continuous load [215.2(A)(1) for feeders and 230.42(A) for services].

Question: *What's the approximate feeder/service calculated load for conductor sizing for 150 ft of track lighting in a commercial occupancy?*

(a) 10,000 VA   (b) 12,000 VA   (c) 14,000 VA   (d) 16,000 VA

Answer: *(c) 14,000 VA*

Feeder Calculated Load = 150 ft/2 ft
Feeder Calculated Load = 5 units x 150 VA x 1.25
 (continuous load)
Feeder Calculated Load = 14,063 VA

Author's Comment:

■ This rule doesn't apply to branch circuits. Therefore, the maximum number of lampholders permitted on a track lighting system is based on the wattage rating of the lamps and the voltage and ampere rating of the circuit [410.151(B)]. Because lighting is a continuous load, the maximum load on a branch circuit must not exceed 80 percent of the circuit rating [210.19(A)(1)].

Question: *How many 75W lampholders can be installed on a 20A, 120V track lighting circuit in a commercial occupancy if the track is 32 ft long?*

(a) 10   (b) 15   (c) 20   (d) 25

Answer: *(d) 25*

Maximum Load Permitted on Circuit = 20A x 0.80
Maximum Load Permitted on Circuit = 16A

Maximum Load in VA = 120V x 16A
Maximum Load in VA = 1,920 VA

Number of Lampholders = 1,920 VA/75 VA
Number of Lampholders = 25.60

Author's Comment:

■ There's no limit on the length of track lighting that can be supplied by a branch circuit.

■ The total wattage of the lamps on the track isn't permitted to exceed the rating of the track [410.151(B)].

220.44 Other than Dwelling Unit—Receptacle Load

The feeder/service VA load for general-purpose receptacles [220.14(I)] and fixed multioutlet assemblies [220.14(H)] is determined by:

• Adding the receptacle and fixed multioutlet assembly VA load with the general lighting load [Table 220.12] and adjusting this VA value by the demand factors contained in Table 220.42, or

• Applying a 50 percent demand factor to that portion of the receptacle and fixed multioutlet receptacle load that exceeds 10 kVA.

Question: *What's the calculated feeder/service VA load, after demand factors, for 150 general-purpose receptacles and 100 ft of fixed multioutlet assembly in a commercial occupancy? The appliances powered by the multioutlet assembly aren't used simultaneously.* Figure 220–22

(a) 8,500 VA   (b) 10,000 VA   (c) 20,300 VA   (d) 27,000 VA

Answer: *(c) 20,300 VA*

Step 1: *Determine the total connected load:*

> *Receptacle Load = 150 receptacles x 180 VA*
> *Receptacle Load = 27,000 VA [220.14(I)]*
>
> *Multioutlet Load = 100 ft/5 ft*
> *Multioutlet Load = 20 sections x 180 VA*
> *Multioutlet Load = 3,600 VA [220.14(H)]*

Step 2: *Apply Table 220.44 demand factor:*

> *Total Connected Load = 30,600 VA*
> *First 10,000 VA at 100% =*
> *10,000 VA x 1.00 =*   *10,000 VA*
> *Remainder at 50% = 20,600 VA x 0.50 =*   *+10,300 VA*
> *Receptacle Calculated Load =*   *20,300 VA*

Receptacle Calculated Load
220.44

Building contains:
- 150 Receptacles
- 100 ft of Multioutlet Assembly

Copyright 2014
www.MikeHolt.com

150 receptacles x 180 VA = 27,000 VA [220.14(I)]
100 ft/5 ft = 20 sections x 180 VA = 3,600 VA [220.14(H)]
Total Connected Load = 30,600 VA
1st 10,000 VA at 100% = -10,000 VA x 1.00 = 10,000 VA
Remainder at 50% = 20,600 VA x 0.50 = +10,300 VA
Receptacle Calculated Load = 20,300 VA

Figure 220–22

220.50 Motor Load

The feeder/service load for motors must be sized not less than 125 percent of the largest motor load, plus the sum of the other motor loads. See 430.24 for example.

220.51 Fixed Electric Space-Heating Load

The feeder/service load for fixed electric space-heating equipment must be calculated at 100 percent of the total connected load.

220.52 Dwelling Unit— Small-Appliance and Laundry Load

(A) Small-Appliance Circuit Load. The feeder/service VA load for each 20A small-appliance circuit covered by 210.11(C)(1) is 1,500 VA, and this load can be subjected to the general lighting demand factors contained in Table 220.42.

Author's Comment:

- Each dwelling unit must have a minimum of two 20A, 120V small-appliance branch circuits for the kitchen and dining room receptacles [210.11(C)(1)].

- The bathroom circuit covered by 210.11(C)(3) isn't included in the service/feeder calculations.

(B) Laundry Circuit Load. The feeder/service VA load for each 20A laundry circuit covered by 210.11(C)(2) is 1,500 VA, and this load can be subjected to the general lighting demand factors contained in Table 220.42.

Author's Comment:

- A laundry circuit isn't required in each dwelling unit of a multifamily building if laundry facilities are provided on the premises for all building occupants [210.52(F) Ex 1].

220.53 Dwelling Unit—Appliance Load

A demand factor of 75 percent can be applied to the total connected load of four or more appliances on the same feeder/service. This demand factor doesn't apply to electric space-heating equipment [220.51], electric clothes dryers [220.54], electric ranges [220.55], electric air-conditioning equipment [Article 440, Part IV], or motors [220.50].

Question: *What's the feeder/service appliance calculated load for a dwelling unit that contains a 1,000 VA disposal, a 1,500 VA dishwasher, and a 4,500 VA water heater?* Figure 220–23

(a) 3,000 VA   (b) 4,500 VA   (c) 6,000 VA   (d) 7,000 VA

Answer: *(d) 7,000 VA*

No demand factor applies for three appliances.

Appliance Calculated Load for Service
220.53

Waste disposer	900 VA
Dishwasher	1,200 VA
Water heater	5,000 VA
Connected load =	7,100 VA

Calculated Load: 7,100 VA x 35 units x 0.75 = 186,375 VA

Figure 220–23

Question: *What's the feeder/service appliance calculated load, after demand factors, for a 12-unit multifamily dwelling if each unit contains a 1,000 VA disposal, a 1,500 VA dishwasher, and a 4,500 VA water heater?*

(a) 23,000 VA   (b) 43,500 VA   (c) 63,000 VA   (d) 71,000 VA

Answer: *(c) 63,000 VA*

Calculated Load = 7,000 VA x 12 units x 0.75*
Calculated Load = 63,000 VA

*Each dwelling unit has only three appliances, but the feeder supplies a total of 36 appliances (12 units x 3 appliances).

220.54 Dwelling Unit—Electric Clothes Dryer Load

The feeder/service load for electric clothes dryers located in a dwelling unit must not be less than 5,000W (5,000 VA), or the nameplate rating of the equipment if more than 5,000W (5,000 VA). Kilovolt-amperes (kVA) is considered equivalent to kilowatts (kW) for loads calculated in this section. Figure 220–24

Dryer Calculated Load - Dwelling Unit
220.54

The feeder/service calculated load is based on the nameplate value but 5,000W (or 5,000 VA) is the minimum.

kVA is considered the same as kW for loads calculated using this section.

Figure 220–24

When a building contains five or more dryers, it's permissible to apply the demand factors listed in Table 220.54 to the total connected dryer load.

Author's Comment:

- A clothes dryer load isn't required if the dwelling unit doesn't have an electric clothes dryer circuit receptacle outlet.

Table 220.54 Dwelling Unit Dryer Demand Factors

Number of Dryers	Demand Factor(Percent)
1–4	100%
5	85%
6	75%
7	65%
8	60%
9	55%
10	50%
11	47%
12–23	47% minus 1% for each dryer exceeding 11
24–42	35% minus 0.50% for each dryer exceeding 23
43 and over	25%

Question: What's the feeder/service calculated load for a 10-unit multifamily building that contains a 5 kW dryer in each unit?

(a) 25,000W   (b) 43,500W   (c) 63,000W   (d) 71,000W

Answer: (a) 25,000W

Table 220.54 demand factor for 10 units is 50%

Calculated Load = 10 units x 5,000W x 0.50
Calculated Load = 25,000W

220.55 Electric Ranges and Cooking Appliances in Dwelling Units and Household Cooking Appliances Used in Instructional Programs

Household cooking appliances rated over 1.75 kW can have the feeder/service load calculated according to the demand factors of Table 220.55. See the *NEC* for the actual Table.

Table Note 1: For identically sized ranges individually rated more than 12 kW, the maximum demand in Column C must be increased 5 percent for each additional kilowatt of rating, or major fraction thereof, by which the rating of individual ranges exceeds 12 kW.

Question: What's the feeder/service calculated load for three 15.60 kVA ranges?

(a) 14 kVA   (b) 15 kVA   (c) 17 kVA   (d) 21 kVA

Answer: (c) 17 kVA (closest answer)

Step 1: Determine the Column C demand load for 3 units: 1 4 kVA.

Step 2: Because each 15.60 kVA range exceeds 12 kVA by 3.60 kVA, increase the Column C demand load by 5% for each kVA or major fraction of kVA in excess of 12 kVA.

Step 3: Because 3.60 kVA is 3 kVA plus a major fraction of a kVA, increase the Column C value by 4 x 5% = 20%

Increase the Column C load (14 kVA) by 20%:
14 kVA x 1.20 = 16.80 kVA.

Table Note 2: For ranges individually rated more than 8.75 kW, but none exceeding 27 kW, and of different ratings, an average rating must be calculated by adding together the ratings of all ranges to obtain the total connected load (using 12 kW for any range rated less than 12 kW) and dividing this total by the number of ranges. Then the maximum demand in Column C must be increased 5 percent for each kilowatt, or major fraction thereof, by which this average value exceeds 12 kW.

Question: What's the feeder/service calculated load for three ranges rated 9 kVA and three ranges rated 14 kVA?

(a) 22 kVA   (b) 36 kVA   c) 42 kVA   (d) 78 kVA

Answer: (a) 22 kVA

Step 1: Determine the total connected load:

9 kVA (minimum 12 kVA); 3 Ranges x 12 kVA =	36 kVA
14 kVA; 3 Ranges x 14 kVA =	+ 42 kVA
Total Connected Load =	78 kVA

(continued)

Step 2: Determine the average of range ratings:

78 kVA/6 units = 13 kVA average rating

Step 3: Demand load from Table 220.55 Column C:

6 ranges = 21 kVA

Step 4: Because the average of the ranges (13 kVA) exceeds 12 kVA by 1 kVA, increase the Column C demand load (21 kVA) by 5%:

Calculated Load = 21 kVA x 1.05
Calculated Load = 22.05 kVA

Table Note 3: Over 1¾ kW through 8¾ kW. In lieu of the method provided in Column C, you are permissible to add the nameplate ratings of all household cooking appliances rated more than 1¾ kW but not more than 8¾ kW and multiply the sum by the demand factors specified in Column A or Column B for the given number of appliances. Where the rating of cooking appliances falls under both Column A and Column B, the demand factors for each column can be applied to the appliances for that column, and the results added together. Figure 220–25

Table Note 4: It's permissible to compute the branch-circuit load for one range in accordance with Table 220.55.

Question: What's the branch-circuit calculated load in amperes for a single 12 kW range connected on a 120/240V circuit? Figure 220–26

(a) 20A   (b) 33A   (c) 41A   (d) 50A

Answer: (b) 33A

Column C Calculated Load = 8 kW

Branch-Circuit Load in Amperes, I = P/E

P = 8,000W

E = 240V

I = 8,000W/240V
I = 33.33A

Table Note 4: The branch-circuit load for one wall-mounted oven or one counter-mounted cooking unit must be the nameplate rating of the appliance.

Figure 220–26

Column A applies to the 3 kW ovens.
Column B applies to the 6 kW cooktop.

Column A demand: (3 kW x 2 units) x 0.75 demand = 4.5 kW
Column B demand: 6 kW x 0.8 demand   = +4.8 kW
Total Service/Feeder Calculated Load   9.3 kW

Figure 220–25

Question: What size branch-circuit conductors are required for a 6 kW wall-mounted oven with 75°C terminals connected on a 120/240V circuit? **Figure 220–27**

(a) 14 AWG   (b) 12 AWG   (c) 10 AWG   (d) 8 AWG

Answer: (c) 10 AWG

Branch-Circuit Load in Amperes, I = P/E

$P = 6,000W$

$E = 240V$

$I = 6,000W/240V$

$I = 25A$, 10 AWG rated 35A at 75°C, [Table 310.15(B)(16) and 110.14(C)(1)]

Table Note 4: The branch-circuit load for one counter-mounted cooking unit and up to two wall-mounted ovens is determined by adding the nameplate ratings together and treating that value as a single range.

Oven Branch Circuit
Dwelling Unit
Table 220.55, Note 4

6 kW, 120/240V
Wall-Mounted Oven

Table 310.15(B)(16)
10 AWG Rated
30A at 60°C

Oven = Nameplate Value for Branch Circuit

$$I = \frac{VA}{E} = \frac{6,000W}{240V} = 25A$$

Copyright 2014, www.MikeHolt.com

Figure 220–27

Question: What size branch circuit is required for one 6 kW counter-mounted cooking unit and two 3 kW wall-mounted ovens connected on a 120/240V circuit? The cooking unit and ovens all have 60°C terminals. **Figure 220–28**

(a) 14 AWG   (b) 12 AWG   (c) 10 AWG   (d) 8 AWG

Answer: (d) 8 AWG

Step 1: Determine the total connected load:

     Total Connected Load = (6 kW + 3 kW + 3 kW).
     Total Connected Load = 12 kW

Step 2: Determine the calculated VA load as a single 12 kW range:

     Table 220.55 Column C = 8 kW

Step 3: Determine the branch-circuit load in amperes:

Branch-Circuit Load in Amperes, I = P/E

$P = 8,000W$

$E = 240V$

$I = 8,000W/240V$

$I = 33.33A$, 8 AWG rated 40A at 60°C [Table 310.15(B)(16) and 110.14(C)(1)]

Branch Circuit for One Cooktop & Two Ovens - Dwelling
Table 220.55, Note 4

Add the *nameplate* ratings of all units then size as *one unit* according to Table 220.55.

Treat As One Unit
6 kW Cooktop

3 kW Oven

3 kW Oven

Taps, See
210.19(A)(3) Ex 1

8 AWG Branch Circuit

Copyright 2014, www.MikeHolt.com

Step 1: Total nameplate of all three units,
6 kW + 3 kW + 3 kW = 12 kW
Step 2: Table 220.55, Column C, 8 kW
Step 3: I = P/E = 8,000W/240V = 33.33A
40A is minimum circuit rating [210.19(A)(3)]
Table 310.15(B)(16), 8 AWG rated 40A at 60°C

Figure 220–28

Author's Comment:

■   For ranges rated 8.75 kW or more, the minimum branch-circuit rating is 40A [210.19(A)(3)].

220.56 Commercial—Kitchen Equipment Load

Table 220.56 can be used to calculate the feeder/service load for thermostat-controlled or intermittently used commercial electric cooking equipment, such as dishwasher booster heaters, water heaters, and other kitchen loads. The kitchen equipment feeder/service calculated load must not be less than the sum of the two largest kitchen equipment loads. Table 220.56 demand factors don't apply to space-heating, ventilating, or air-conditioning equipment.

Question: What's the feeder/service calculated load for one 15 kW booster water heater, one 15 kW water heater, one 3 kW oven, and one 2 kW deep fryer in a commercial kitchen? Figure 220–29

(a) 15 kW   (b) 20 kW   (c) 26 kW   (d) 30 kW

Answer: (d) 30 kW

Step 1: Determine the total connected load:

Total Connected Load = 15 kW + 15 kW + 3 kW + 2 kW

Total Connected Load = 35 kW

Step 2: Determine the feeder/service calculated load:

35 kW x 0.80 = 28 kW, but it must not be less than the sum of the two largest appliances, or 30 kW.

Table 220.56, 4 units, 80% of connected load.

Water Heater	15.00 kW*	*The calculated load can't
Booster Heater	15.00 kW*	be less than the sum of the
Oven	3.00 kW	two largest appliances.
Deep fryer	2.00 kW	
Total Connected	35.00 kW x 0.80 DF = *28 kW Demand	

*Two Largest Appliances:

Water Heater	15.00 kW
Booster Heater	15.00 kW
	30.00 kW which exceeds 28 kW

Feeder/Service Calculated Load = 30 kW

Figure 220–29

220.60 Noncoincident Loads

If it's unlikely that two or more loads will be used at the same time, only the largest load(s) must be used to determine the feeder/service VA calculated load. Figure 220–30

Figure 220–30

Question: What's the feeder/service calculated load for an air conditioner having a rated load current of 14A at 240V as compared to a 9.6 kW electric space heater with 3A fan at 240V? Figure 220–31

(a) 5,000W   (b) 6,000W   (c) 7,500W   (d) 9,000W

Answer: (d) 9,000W

Air-Conditioning VA = 240V x 14A

Air-Conditioning VA = 3,360 VA (omit, smaller than 9,000W)

Electric Space Heating Load = 9,600W + 3A x 240V

Electric Space Heating Load = 9,600W + (3A x 240V)

Electric Space Heating Load = 10,320 VA [220.51]

Figure 220–31

Figure 220–32

220.61 Feeder/Service Neutral Unbalanced Load

(A) Basic Calculation. The calculated neutral load for feeders/services is the maximum calculated load between the neutral conductor and any one ungrounded conductor. Line-to-line loads don't place any load on the neutral conductor, therefore they aren't considered.

> **Question:** What's the minimum neutral conductor size for a 200A feeder, of which 100A is line-to-line loads with a maximum unbalanced neutral load of 100A? Figure 220–32
>
> (a) 3/0 AWG   (b) 1/0 AWG   (c) 1 AWG   (d) 3 AWG
>
> **Answer:** (d) 3 AWG
>
> 200A total load less 100A line-to-line loads = 100A neutral load
>
> Table 310.15(B)(16), 75°C column, 3 AWG rated 100A

(B) Permitted Reductions.

(1) Dwelling Unit Cooking and Dryer Load.

Cooking Load. The feeder/service neutral calculated load for household electric ranges, wall-mounted ovens, or counter-mounted cooking units can be calculated at 70 percent of the cooking equipment calculated load in accordance with Table 220.55.

> **Question:** What's the feeder/service calculated neutral load for nine 12 kW household ranges?
>
> (a) 13 kW   (b) 14.70 kW   (c) 16.80 kW   (d) 24 kW
>
> **Answer:** (c) 16.80 kW
>
> **Step 1:** Table 220.55 Column C = 24 kW
>
> **Step 2:** Neutral Load = 24 kW x 0.70
>   Neutral Load = 16.80 kW

Dryer Load. The feeder/service neutral calculated load for household electric dryers can be calculated at 70 percent of the dryer calculated load in accordance with Table 220.54.

> **Question:** A 10-unit multifamily building has a 5 kW electric clothes dryer in each unit. What's the feeder/service neutral load for these dryers?
>
> (a) 17.50 kW   (b) 23.50 kW   (c) 33 kW   (d) 41 kW
>
> **Answer:** (a) 17.50 kW
>
> **Step 1:** Table 220.54 = 10 units x 5 kW x 0.50
>   Table 220.54 = 25 kW
>
> **Step 2:** Neutral Load = 25 kW x 0.70
>   Neutral Load = 17.50 kW

(2) Over 200A Neutral Reduction. The feeder/service calculated neutral load for a 3-wire, single-phase, or 4-wire, three-phase system, can be reduced for that portion of the unbalanced load over 200A by a multiplier of 70 percent.

Question: *What's the feeder/service neutral calculated load for the following? The voltage system is 120/240V, single phase.* Figure 220–33

- *100A of line-to-line loads*
- *100A of household ranges*
- *50A of household dryers*
- *350A of line-to-neutral loads*

(a) 200A   (b) 379A   (c) 455A   (d) 600A

Answer: *(b) 379A*

Step 1: *Determine the total feeder/service neutral load:*

Line-to-line	*100A*	*0A*
Ranges	*100A*	*70A (100A x 0.70)*
Dryers	*50A*	*35A (50A x 0.70)*
Line-to-neutral	*+ 350A*	*+ 350A*
Total Load =	*600A*	*455A*

Step 2: *Determine the demand feeder/service neutral load:*

Total Neutral Load	*455A*	
First 200A at 100%	*− 200A*	*x 1.00 = 200A*
Remainder at 70%	*255A*	*x 0.70 = +179A*
Total Demand Neutral Load =		*379A*

(C) Prohibited Reductions. No reduction of the neutral conductor calculated feeder/service load is permitted for the following:

(1) 3-Wire Circuits from 4-Wire Wye-Connected Systems. The feeder/service neutral calculated load must not be reduced for 3-wire circuits that consist of two ungrounded conductors and a neutral conductor supplied from a 4-wire, three-phase, 120/208V or 277/480V wye-connected system. This is because the neutral load on the 3-wire circuit will carry approximately the same amount of line-to-neutral current as the ungrounded conductors [310.15(B)(5)(c)].

Question: *What's the current on the neutral conductor of a 3-wire feeder supplied from a 4-wire, three-phase, 120/208V or 277/480V wye-connected system? The ungrounded conductors carry 200A of line-to-neutral loads.* Figure 220–34

(a) 200A   (b) 379A   (c) 455A   (d) 600A

Answer: *(a) 200A*

$$I_N = \sqrt{(I_{Line1}^2 + I_{Line2}^2) - (I_{Line1} \times I_{Line}^2)}$$
$$I_N = \sqrt{200A^2 + 200A^2 - (200A \times 200A)}$$
$$I_N = \sqrt{80,000 - 40,000}$$
$$I_N = \sqrt{40,000}$$
$$I_N = 200A$$

Over 200A Neutral Reduction
220.61(B)(2)

Multifamily Building Service

	Service/Feeder	Neutral
240V Loads	100A	0A
Range Loads	100A	70A
Dryer Loads	50A	35A
120V Loads	350A	350A
Total Loads	600A	455A

Total Neutral Load   455A
1st 200A at 100%   - 200A x 1.0 = 200A
Remainder at 70%   255A x 0.7 = 179A
Total Neutral Calculated Load   = 379A

Copyright 2014, www.MikeHolt.com

Figure 220–33

Over 200A Neutral Reduction Not Permitted
220.61(C)(1)

120/208V or 277/480V

3-wire feed from a 4-wire, three-phase, wye system.

The calculated neutral load must not be reduced for 3-wire circuits that consist of two ungrounded conductors and a neutral conductor supplied from a 4-wire, three-phase, wye-connected system.

Copyright 2014 www.MikeHolt.com

Figure 220–34

---

(2) Nonlinear Loads. The feeder/service neutral calculated load must not be reduced for nonlinear loads supplied from a 4-wire, three-phase, 120/208V or 277/480V wye-connected system.

Question: *What's the feeder/service neutral calculated load for the following?*

- *200A of line-to-line loads*
- *200A of line-to-neutral nonlinear loads*
- *200A of line-to-neutral linear loads*

(a) 200A   (b) 400A   (c) 500A   (d) 600A

Answer: *(d) 400A*

	Feeder/ Service	Neutral Load
Line-to-Line Loads	200A	0A
Nonlinear Line-to-Neutral Loads	200A	200A
Linear Line-to-Neutral Loads	200A	200A
Total Calculated Load	600A	400A

Part IV. Optional Calculations for Computing Feeder and Service Loads

220.82 Dwelling Unit— Optional Load Calculation

(A) Feeder/Service Load. The 3-wire feeder/service load for a dwelling unit can be calculated by adding the calculated loads from 220.82(B) and (C). The feeder/service neutral calculated load must be determined in accordance with 220.61.

(B) General Loads. The feeder/service calculated load must not be less than 100 percent of the first 10 kVA, plus 40 percent of the remainder of the following:

(1) General Lighting. The general lighting load is based on 3 VA per sq ft for general lighting and general-use receptacles. The floor area is calculated from the outside dimensions of the dwelling unit, not including open porches, garages, or unused or unfinished spaces not adaptable for future use.

(2) Small-Appliance and Laundry Circuits. A load of 1,500 VA for each 20A small-appliance and laundry branch circuit [220.11(C)(1) and (2)]. Since a minimum of two small-appliance circuits and a laundry circuit are required, the minimum load for calculation purposes is 4,500 VA.

(3) Appliances. The nameplate rating of the following:

 a. Appliances fastened in place, permanently connected or located to be on a specific circuit

 b. Ranges, wall-mounted ovens, counter-mounted cooking units

 c. Clothes dryers

 d. Water heaters

(4) Motor VA. The VA nameplate rating of all motors not part of an appliance.

(C) Air-Conditioning and Heating Equipment. The larger of (1) through (6):

(1) Air-Conditioning Equipment. 100 percent of the nameplate rating(s).

(2) Heat-Pump Compressor without Supplemental Heating. 100 percent of the heat-pump nameplate rating.

(3) Heat-Pump Compressor and Supplemental Heating. 100 percent of the nameplate rating of the heat pump and 65 percent of the supplemental electric heating. If the heat-pump compressor is prevented from operating at the same time as the supplementary heat, it can be omitted in the calculation.

(4) Space-Heating Units (three or fewer units). 65 percent of the space-heating nameplate rating.

(5) Space-Heating Units (four or more units). 40 percent of the space-heating nameplate rating.

(6) Thermal Storage Heating. 100 percent of the thermal storage heating nameplate rating.

Author's Comment:

- One form of thermal storage heating involves heating bricks or water at night when the electric rates are lower. Then during the day, the building uses the thermally stored heat.

Question: Using the optional calculation method, what size 3-wire, single-phase, 120/240V feeder/service ungrounded conductors are required for a 1,500 sq ft dwelling unit that contains the following loads?

- Dishwasher   1,200 VA
- Disposal   900 VA
- Cooktop   6,000 VA
- Oven   3,000 VA
- Dryer   4,000 VA
- Water heater   4,500 VA
- Heat-pump compressor having a rating of 5 hp, with supplemental electric heat having a rating of 7 kW.

(a) 100A (b) 110A   (c) 125A   (d) 150A

Answer: (c) 125A

Step 1: Determine the total feeder/service calculated load:

Lighting, receptacles, and appliance calculated load [220.82(B)]

Small appliance	1,500 VA x 2 =	3,000 VA
Laundry	1,500 VA x 1 =	1,500 VA
General lighting	1,500 sq ft x 3 VA/sq ft =	4,500 VA
Dishwasher	1,200 VA x 1 =	1,200 VA
Disposal	900 VA x 1 =	900 VA
Cooktop	6,000 VA x 1 =	6,000 VA
Oven	3,000 VA x 1 =	3,000 VA
Dryer	4,000 VA x 1 =	4,000 VA
Water heater	4,500 VA x 1 =	+ 4,500 VA
		28,600 VA

First 10,000 VA at 100%
10,000 VA x 1.00 =   10,000 VA
Remainder at 40% 18,600 VA x 0.40 =   + 7,440 VA
220.82(B) Calculated Load =   17,440 VA

Largest of Air-Conditioning or Heat [220.82(C)]
Heat pump 5 hp compressor at 100%
230V x 28A =   6,440 VA

Supplemental heat at 65% =
7,000 VA x 0.65 =   + 4,550 VA

Total Calculated Load 220.82(B) and (C)
17,440 VA + 6,440 VA + 4,550 VA =   28,430 VA

(continued)

Step 2: Determine the feeder/service calculated load in amperes:

$$I = VA/E$$

I = 28,430 VA/240V
I = 119A, 2 AWG [215.2(A)(4) and 310.15(B)(7)]

220.83 Existing Dwelling Unit Calculations

It's permissible to calculate the total load in accordance with 220.83(A) or (B).

(B) If Additional Air-Conditioning Equipment or Electric Space-Heating Equipment Is to Be Installed. The larger of the air-conditioning or space-heating load, plus the first 8 kVA of the following loads (1 through 3) at 100 percent, and the remainder of the loads at 40 percent:

(1) General lighting and general-use receptacles 3 volt-amperes/ft^2 as per 220.12

(2) 1,500 VA for 20A small-appliance and laundry branch circuits as per 210.11(C)(1) and (C)(2)

(3) The nameplate rating of:

    a. All appliances that are fastened in place, permanently connected, or located to be on a specific circuit

    b. Ranges, wall-mounted ovens, counter-mounted cooking units

    c. Clothes dryers

    d. Water heaters

Question: *For an existing dwelling, what size 3-wire, single-phase, 120/240V feeder/service ungrounded conductors are required for a 1,500 sq ft dwelling unit that contains the following loads?*

- *Dishwasher*   *1,200 VA*
- *Disposal*   *900 VA*
- *Cooktop*   *6,000 VA*
- *Oven*   *3,000 VA*
- *Dryer*   *4,000 VA*
- *Water heater*   *4,500 VA*
- *Air-Conditioning compressor having a rating of 5 hp, with electric heat having a rating of 7 kW.*

(a) 100A (b) 110A   *(c) 125A*   *(d) 150A*

Answer: *(c) 125A*

Step 1: *Determine the total feeder/service calculated load:*

(1) General Lighting at 3 VA/sq ft

1,500 sq ft x 3 VA/sq ft =	*4,500 VA*

(2) Small and Laundry Appliance Circuits

Small appliance	*1,500 VA x 2 =*	*3,000 VA*
Laundry	*1,500 VA x 1 =*	*1,500 VA*

(3) Nameplate of all appliances

Dishwasher	*1,200 VA x 1 =*	*1,200 VA*
Disposal	*900 VA x 1 =*	*900 VA*
Cooktop	*6,000 VA x 1 =*	*6,000 VA*
Oven	*3,000 VA x 1 =*	*3,000 VA*
Dryer	*4,000 VA x 1 =*	*4,000 VA*
Water heater	*4,500 VA x 1 =*	*+ 4,500 VA*
		28,600 VA

First 8,000 VA at 100%

8,000 VA x 1.00 =	*8,000 VA*
Remainder at 40% 20,600 VA x 0.40 =	*+ 8,240 VA*
220.82(B) Calculated Load =	*16,240 VA*

Largest of Air-Conditioning or Heat [220.82(C)]
Air-Conditioner,

5 hp compressor at 100% 230V x 28A =	*6,440 VA*
Heat at 100% =	*7,000 VA*

Total Calculated Load

16,240 VA + 7,000 VA =	*23,240 VA*

(continued)

Step 2: *Determine the feeder/service calculated load in amperes:*

$$I = VA/E$$

I = 23,240 VA/240V

I = 97A, 4 AWG [215.2(A)(4) and 310.15(B)(7)]

220.84 Multifamily—Optional Load Calculation

(A) Feeder or Service Load. The feeder/service calculated load for a building with three or more dwelling units equipped with electric cooking equipment, and either electric space heating or air-conditioning, can be in accordance with the demand factors of Table 220.84, based on the number of dwelling units. The feeder/service neutral calculated load must be determined in accordance with 220.61.

(B) House Loads. House loads are calculated in accordance with Part III of Article 220, and then added to the Table 220.84 calculated load.

Author's Comment:

- House loads are those not directly associated with the individual dwelling units of a multifamily dwelling. Some examples of house loads are landscape and parking lot lighting, common area lighting, common laundry facilities, common pool and recreation areas, and so on.

(C) Connected Loads. The connected loads from all of the dwelling units are added together, and then the Table 220.84 demand factors are applied to determine the calculated load.

(1) 3 VA per sq ft for general lighting and general-use receptacles.

(2) 1,500 VA for each 20A small-appliance circuit as required by 210.11(C)(1) (a minimum of two circuits per dwelling unit), and 1,500 VA for each 20A laundry circuit as required by 210.11(C)(2).

Author's Comment:

- A laundry circuit isn't required in an individual unit of a multifamily dwelling if common laundry facilities are provided [210.52(F) Ex 1].

(3) Appliances. The nameplate rating of the following:

a. Appliances fastened in place, permanently connected or located to be on a specific circuit

b. Ranges, wall-mounted ovens, counter-mounted cooking units

c. Clothes dryers not connected to the required laundry circuit specified in 210.11(C)(2)

d. Water heaters

(4) The nameplate rating of all motors not part of an appliance.

(5) The larger of the air-conditioning load or fixed electric space-heating load.

Question: What size 4-wire, three-phase, 120/208V service is required for a multifamily building with twenty 1,500 sq ft dwelling units, where each unit contains the following loads?

- Dishwasher   1,200 VA
- Water heater   4,500 VA
- Disposal   900 VA
- Dryer   4,000 VA
- Cooktop   6,000 VA
- Oven   3,000 VA
- Heat   7,000 VA
- Air-Conditioning, 5 hp compressor   6,440 VA

(a) 400A   (b) 600A   (c) 800A   (d) 1,200A

Answer: (c) 800A [240.4 and 240.6(A)]

Step 1: Determine the dwelling unit connected load:

General lighting	1,500 sq ft x 3 VA/sq ft =	4,500 VA
Small appliance	1500VA x 2 =	3,000 VA
Laundry	1,500 VA x 1 =	1,500 VA
Dishwasher	1,200 VA x 1 =	1,200 VA
Water heater	4,500 VA x 1 =	4,500 VA
Disposal	900 VA x 1 =	900 VA
Dryer	4,000 VA x 1 =	4,000 VA
Cooktop	6,000 VA x 1 =	6,000 VA
Oven	3,000 VA x 1 =	3,000 VA
Air-Conditioning		
5 hp (omit)	0 VA x 1 =	0 VA
Heat =		+ 7,000 VA
Total Dwelling Unit Load =		35,600 VA

(continued)

Step 2: Determine the calculated load for the multifamily building:
Demand Factor for 20 units = 0.38
[Table 220.84]
35,600 VA x 20 x 0.38 =   270,560 VA

Step 3: Determine feeder/service conductor size:

$I = VA/(E \times \sqrt{3})$

$I = 270,560 \, VA/(208V \times 1.732)$

$I = 751A$

I of Each Conductor Parallel Set = 751A/2 conductors

I of Each Conductor Parallel Set = 376A

Conductor = 500 kcmil, rated 380A at 75°C x 2

Conductor = 760A, Table 310.15(B)(16)

220.85 Optional Calculation— Two Dwelling Units

If two dwelling units are supplied by a single feeder, and where the standard calculated load in accordance with Part II of this article exceeds that for three identical units calculated in accordance with 220.84, the lesser of the two calculated loads may be used. Figure 220–35

Figure 220–35

220.87 Determining Existing Loads

The calculation of a feeder or service load for existing installations can be based on 125 percent of the maximum demand data for one year.

Ex: If the maximum demand data for one year isn't available, the maximum power demand over a 15-minute period continuously recorded over a minimum 30-day period using a recording ammeter or power meter connected to the highest loaded phase, based on the initial loading at the start of the recording is permitted. The recording must be taken when the building or space is occupied based on the larger of the heating or cooling equipment load. Figure 220–36

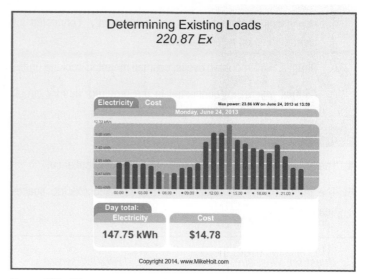

Figure 220–36

ARTICLE 225

OUTSIDE BRANCH CIRCUITS AND FEEDERS

Introduction to Article 225—Outside Branch Circuits and Feeders

This article covers the installation requirements for equipment, including branch circuit and feeder conductors (overhead and underground), located outdoors on or between buildings, poles, and other structures on the premises. Conductors installed outdoors can serve many purposes such as area lighting, power for outdoor equipment, or providing power to a separate building or structure. It's important to remember that the power supply for buildings isn't always a service conductor, but in many cases may be feeders or branch-circuit conductors originating in another building. Be careful not to assume that the conductors supplying power to a building are service conductors until you've identified where the utility service point is and reviewed the Article 100 Definitions for feeders, branch circuits, and service conductors. If they're service conductors, use Article 230. For outside branch-circuit and feeder conductors, whatever they feed, use this article.

Table 225.3 shows other articles that may furnish additional requirements, then Part I of Article 225 goes on to address installation methods intended to provide a secure installation of outside conductors while providing sufficient conductor size, support, attachment means, and maintaining safe clearances.

Part II of this article limits the number of supplies (branch circuits or feeders) permitted to a building or structure and provides rules regarding disconnects for them. These rules include the disconnect rating, construction characteristics, labeling, and where to locate the disconnecting means and the grouping of multiple disconnects.

Outside branch circuits and feeders over 1,000V are the focus of Part III of Article 225.

Part I. General

225.1 Scope

Article 225 contains the installation requirements for outside branch circuits and feeders installed on or between buildings, structures, or poles. Figure 225–1

Author's Comment:

- Review the following definitions in Article 100:
    - "Branch Circuit"
    - "Building"
    - "Feeder"
    - "Structure"

Figure 225–1

225.2 Other Articles

Other articles containing important requirements include:

- Branch Circuits, Article 210
- Class 1, Class 2, and Class 3 Remote-Control, Signaling, and Power-Limited Circuits, Article 725
- Communications Circuits, Article 800
- Community Antenna Television and Radio Distribution Systems, Article 820
- Conductors for General Wiring, Article 310
- Electric Signs and Outline Lighting, Article 600
- Feeders, Article 215
- Floating Buildings, Article 553
- Grounding and Bonding, Article 250
- Marinas and Boatyards, Article 555
- Radio and Television Equipment, Article 810
- Services, Article 230
- Solar PV Systems, Article 690
- Swimming Pools, Fountains, and Similar Installations, Article 680

225.6 Minimum Size of Conductors

(A) Overhead Spans.

(1) Conductor Size. Conductors 10 AWG and larger are permitted for overhead spans up to 50 ft long. For spans over 50 ft in length, the minimum size conductor is 8 AWG, unless supported by a messenger wire. Figure 225–2

Figure 225–2

(B) Festoon Lighting. Overhead conductors for festoon lighting must not be smaller than 12 AWG, unless messenger wires support the conductors. The overhead conductors must be supported by messenger wire, with strain insulators, whenever the spans exceed 40 ft in length. Figure 225–3

Figure 225–3

225.7 Luminaires Installed Outdoors

(C) 277V to Ground Circuits. 277V and 480V branch circuits are permitted to supply luminaires for lighting outdoor areas of industrial establishments, office buildings, schools, stores, and other commercial or public buildings. Figure 225–4

Figure 225–4

225.15 Supports Over Buildings

Conductor spans over a building must be securely supported by substantial structures. If practicable, such supports must be independent of the building [230.29].

225.16 Attachment

(A) Point of Attachment. The point of attachment for overhead conductors must not be less than 10 ft above the finished grade, and it must be located so the minimum conductor clearance required by 225.18 can be maintained. Figure 225–5

Figure 225–5

⚠ **CAUTION:** *Conductors might need to have the point of attachment raised so the overhead conductors will comply with the clearances from building openings and other building areas required by 225.19.*

(B) Means of Attachment to Buildings. Open conductors must be attached to fittings identified for use with conductors, or to noncombustible, nonabsorbent insulators securely attached to the building or other structure.

225.17 Masts as Supports

Only branch-circuit or feeder conductors can be attached to the mast. Figure 225–6

Figure 225–6

Masts used for the support of final spans of feeders or branch circuits must be installed in accordance with (A) and (B).

Author's Comment:

- Aerial cables and antennas for radio and TV equipment must not be attached to the feeder or branch-circuit mast [810.12]. In addition, 800.133(B) prohibits communications cables from being attached to raceways, including a mast for power conductors.

(A) Strength. If a mast is used for overhead conductor support, it must have adequate mechanical strength, braces, or guy wires to withstand the strain caused by the conductors. Conduit hubs must be identified for use with a mast. Figure 225–7

(B) Attachment. Conductors can't be attached to a mast between a weatherhead or end of the conduit and a coupling if the coupling is above the last conduit support, or if the coupling is above the building or structure. Figure 225–8

Figure 225–7

Figure 225–8

225.18 Clearance for Overhead Conductors

Overhead conductor spans must maintain vertical clearances as follows: Figure 225–9

(1) 10 ft above finished grade, sidewalks, platforms, or projections from which they might be accessible to pedestrians for 120V, 120/208V, 120/240V, or 240V circuits.

Overhead Conductor Clearance
225.18

Overhead conductors must have a minimum clearance of:
(1) 10 ft above finished grade, sidewalks, platforms or projections from which they might be accessible to pedestrians
(2) 12 ft above residential property and driveways

Figure 225–9

Clearance Above Roofs
225.19(A)

Minimum Clearance Over a Roof is 8 Ft

8 ft

Overhead conductors must maintain a vertical clearance of 8 ft above the surface of a roof that must be maintained for a distance of not less than 3 ft from the edge of the roof.

Figure 225–10

(2) 12 ft above residential property and driveways, and those commercial areas not subject to truck traffic for 120V, 120/208V, 120/240V, 240V, 277V, 277/480V, or 480V circuits.

(4) 18 ft over public streets, alleys, roads, parking areas subject to truck traffic, driveways on other than residential property, and other areas traversed by vehicles (such as those used for cultivation, grazing, forestry, and orchards).

(5) 24½ ft over track rails of railroads.

Author's Comment:

■ Overhead conductors located above pools, outdoor spas, outdoor hot tubs, diving structures, observation stands, towers, or platforms must be installed in accordance with the clearance requirements in 680.8.

225.19 Clearances from Buildings

(A) Above Roofs. Overhead conductors must maintain a vertical clearance of 8 ft above the surface of a roof and must be maintained for a distance of at least 3 ft from the edge of the roof. Figure 225–10

Ex 2: The overhead conductor clearances from the roof can be reduced from 8 ft to 3 ft if the slope of the roof meets or exceeds 4 in. of vertical rise for every 12 in. of horizontal run.

Ex 3: For 120/208V or 120/240V circuits, the conductor clearance over the roof overhang can be reduced from 8 ft to 18 in., if no more than 6 ft of conductor passes over no more than 4 ft of roof. Figure 225–11

Clearance Above Roof
225.19(A) Ex 3

Maximum 6 ft of Conductors Over Roof

18 in. Minimum

Maximum 4 ft Over Roof

For 120/208V or 120/240V circuits, conductor clearance can be 18 in., if no more than 6 ft of conductor pass over no more than 4 ft of roof.

Figure 225–11

Ex 4: The 3 ft clearance from the roof edge doesn't apply when the point of attachment is on the side of the building below the roof.

(B) From Other Structures. Overhead conductors must maintain a clearance of at least 3 ft from signs, chimneys, radio and television antennas, tanks, and other nonbuilding or nonbridge structures.

(D) Final Span Clearance.

(1) Clearance from Windows. Overhead conductors must maintain a clearance of 3 ft from windows that open, doors, porches, balconies, ladders, stairs, fire escapes, or similar locations. Figure 225–12

Figure 225–12

Ex: Overhead conductors installed above a window aren't required to maintain the 3 ft distance from the window.

(2) Vertical Clearance. Overhead conductors must maintain a vertical clearance of at least 10 ft above platforms, projections, or surfaces from which they might be reached. This vertical clearance must be maintained for 3 ft, measured horizontally from the platforms, projections, or surfaces from which they might be reached.

(3) Below Openings. Overhead conductors must not be installed under an opening through which materials might pass, and they must not be installed where they'll obstruct an entrance to building openings. Figure 225–13

225.22 Raceways on Exterior Surfaces of Buildings or Other Structures

Raceways on exterior surfaces of buildings or other structures must be arranged to drain, and be suitable for use in wet locations.

Figure 225–13

Author's Comment:

- A "Wet Location" is an area subject to saturation with water and unprotected locations exposed to weather [Article 100].

225.26 Trees for Conductor Support

Trees or other vegetation must not be used for the support of overhead conductor spans. Figure 225–14

Figure 225–14

Author's Comment:

- Overhead conductor spans for services [230.10] and temporary wiring [590.4(J)] aren't permitted to be supported by vegetation.

225.27 Raceway Seals

Underground raceways (used or unused) entering buildings must be sealed or plugged to prevent moisture from contacting energized live parts [300.5(G)]. To ensure that the conductors or cables aren't damaged, sealants must be identified for use with the conductor or cable in the raceway. Figure 225–15

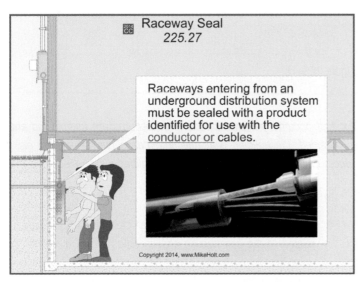

Figure 225–15

Part II. Buildings or Other Structures Supplied by a Feeder(s) or Branch Circuit(s)

225.30 Number of Supplies

If more than one building or other structure is on the same property, each building must be served by no more than one feeder or single or multiwire branch circuit, except as permitted in (A) through (E).

Author's Comment:

- Article 100 defines a "Structure" as, "That which is built or constructed."

(A) Special Conditions. Additional supplies are permitted for:

(1) Fire pumps

(2) Emergency systems

(3) Legally required standby systems

(4) Optional standby systems

(5) Parallel power production systems

(6) Systems designed for connection to multiple sources of supply for the purpose of enhanced reliability.

Author's Comment:

- To minimize the possibility of simultaneous interruption, the disconnecting means for the fire pump or standby power must be located remotely away from the normal power disconnect [225.34(B)].

(B) Special Occupancies. By special permission, additional supplies are permitted for:

(1) Multiple-occupancy buildings where there's no available space for supply equipment accessible to all occupants, or

(2) A building so large that two or more supplies are necessary.

(C) Capacity Requirements. Additional supplies are permitted for a building where the capacity requirements exceed 2,000A.

(D) Different Characteristics. Additional supplies are permitted for different voltages, frequencies, or uses, such as control of outside lighting from multiple locations.

(E) Documented Switching Procedures. Additional supplies are permitted where documented safe switching procedures are established and maintained for disconnection.

225.31 Disconnecting Means

A disconnect is required for all conductors that enter a building. Figure 225–16

Figure 225–16

225.32 Disconnect Location

The disconnecting means for a building must be installed at a readily accessible location either outside or inside nearest the point of entrance of the conductors. Figure 225–17

Figure 225–17

Supply conductors are considered outside of a building or other structure where they're encased or installed under not less than 2 in. of concrete or brick [230.6]. Figure 225–18

Figure 225–18

Ex 1: If documented safe switching procedures are established and maintained, the building disconnecting means can be located elsewhere on the premises, if monitored by qualified persons.

Author's Comment:

- A "Qualified Person" is one who has skills and knowledge related to the construction and operation of the electrical equipment and installation, and has received safety training to recognize and avoid the hazards involved with electrical systems [Article 100].

Ex 3: A disconnecting means isn't required within sight of poles that support luminaires. Figure 225–19

Author's Comment:

- According to Article 100, within sight means that it's visible and not more than 50 ft from one to the other.

Ex 4: The disconnecting means for a sign must be controlled by an externally operable switch or circuit breaker that opens all ungrounded conductors to the sign. The sign disconnecting means must be within sight of the sign, or the disconnecting means must be capable of being locked in the open position [600.6(A)]. Figure 225–20

Figure 225–19

Figure 225–20

225.33 Maximum Number of Disconnects

(A) General. The building disconnecting means can consist of no more than six switches or six circuit breakers in a single enclosure, or separate enclosures for each supply grouped in one location as permitted by 225.30. Figure 225–21

Figure 225–21

225.34 Grouping of Disconnects

(A) General. The building disconnecting means must be grouped in one location, and they must be marked to indicate the loads they serve [110.22].

(B) Additional Disconnects. To minimize the possibility of accidental interruption of the critical power systems, the disconnecting means for a fire pump or for standby power must be located remotely away from the normal power disconnect.

225.35 Access to Occupants

In a multiple-occupancy building, each occupant must have access to the disconnecting means for their occupancy.

Ex: The occupant's disconnecting means can be accessible to only building management, if electrical maintenance under continuous supervision is provided by the building management.

225.36 Type

The building disconnecting means can be comprised of a circuit breaker, molded case switch, general-use switch, snap switch, or other approved means. If an existing building uses the neutral conductor for the bonding of metal parts [250.32(B) Ex], the disconnect must be listed as suitable for use as service equipment. Figure 225–22

Figure 225–22

Author's Comment:

■ "Suitable for use as service equipment" means, among other things, that the service disconnecting means is supplied with a main bonding jumper so a neutral-to-case connection can be made, as required in 250.24(C) and 250.142(A).

225.37 Identification of Multiple Feeders

If a building is fed by more than one supply, a permanent plaque or directory must be installed at each feeder disconnect location denoting all other feeders or branch circuits that supply that building, and the area served by each.

225.38 Disconnect Construction

(A) Manual or Power-Operated Circuit Breakers. The building disconnecting means can consist of either a manual switch or a power-operated switch or circuit breaker capable of being operated manually.

Author's Comment:

■ A shunt-trip pushbutton can be used to open a power-operated circuit breaker. The circuit breaker is the disconnecting means, not the pushbutton.

(D) Indicating. The disconnecting means for a building supplied by a feeder must plainly indicate whether it's in the open or closed position.

225.39 Rating of Disconnecting Means

A single disconnecting means for a building must have an ampere rating not less than the calculated load as determined by Article 220. If the disconnecting means consists of more than one switch or circuit breaker, the combined ratings of the circuit breakers must not be less than the calculated load as determined by Article 220. In addition, the disconnecting means must not be rated lower than:

(A) One-Circuit Installation. For installations consisting of a single branch circuit, the disconnecting means must have a rating of not less than 15A.

(B) Two-Circuit Installation. For installations consisting of two 2-wire branch circuits, the feeder disconnecting means must have a rating of not less than 30A.

(C) One-Family Dwelling. For a one-family dwelling, the feeder disconnecting means must have a rating of not less than 100A, 3-wire.

(D) All Others. For all other installations, the feeder or branch-circuit disconnecting means must have a rating of not less than 60A.

ARTICLE 230

SERVICES

Introduction to Article 230—Services

This article covers the installation requirements for service conductors and service equipment. The requirements for service conductors differ from those for other conductors. For one thing, service conductors for one building can't pass through the interior of another building or structure [230.3], and you apply different rules depending on whether a service conductor is inside or outside a building. When are they "outside" as opposed to "inside?" The answer may seem obvious, but 230.6 should be consulted before making this decision.

Let's review the following definitions in Article 100 to understand when the requirements of Article 230 apply:

- **Service Point.** The point of connection between the serving utility and the premises wiring.

- **Service Conductors.** The conductors from the service point to the service disconnecting means. Service-entrance conductors can either be overhead or underground.

- **Service Equipment.** The necessary equipment, usually consisting of circuit breakers or switches and fuses and their accessories, connected to the load end of service conductors at a building or other structure, and intended to constitute the main control and cutoff of the electrical supply. Service equipment doesn't include individual meter socket enclosures [230.66].

After reviewing these definitions, you should understand that service conductors originate at the serving utility (service point) and terminate on the line side of the service disconnecting means. Conductors and equipment on the load side of service equipment are considered feeder conductors or branch circuits, and must be installed in accordance with Articles 210 and 215. They must also comply with Article 225 if they're outside branch circuits and feeders, such as the supply to a building. Feeder conductors include: Figures 230–1 and 230–2

- Secondary conductors from customer-owned transformers,
- Conductors from generators, UPS systems, or PV systems, and
- Conductors to remote buildings

Service
Article 230

1. Service Point
2. Service Conductors
3. Service Equipment
4. Feeder Disconnect
5. Feeder Conductors
6. Transfer Switch

Copyright 2014, www.MikeHolt.com

Figure 230–1

Article 230 consists of seven parts:

- Part I. General
- Part II. Overhead Service Conductors
- Part III. Underground Service Conductors
- Part IV. Service-Entrance Conductors
- Part V. Service Equipment
- Part VI. Disconnecting Means
- Part VIII. Overcurrent Protection

1. Service Point
2. Service Conductors
3. Service Equipment
4. Feeder Disconnect
5. Feeder Conductors
6. Transfer Switch

Figure 230–2

Part I. General

230.1 Scope

Article 230 covers the installation requirements for service conductors and service equipment.

230.2 Number of Services

A building can only be served by one service drop or service lateral, except as permitted by (A) through (D). Figure 230–3

(A) Special Conditions. Additional services are permitted for the following:

(1) Fire pumps

(2) Emergency systems

(3) Legally required standby systems

Author's Comment:

- A separate service for emergency and legally required systems is permitted only when approved by the authority having jurisdiction [700.12(D) and 701.11(D)].

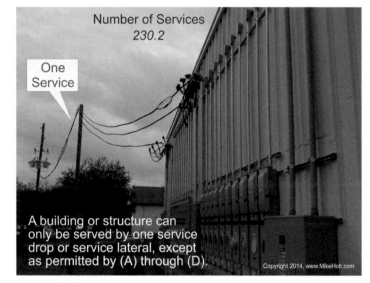

Figure 230–3

(4) Optional standby power

(5) Parallel power production systems

(6) Systems designed for connection to multiple sources of supply for the purpose of enhanced reliability.

Author's Comment:

■ To minimize the possibility of simultaneous interruption, the disconnecting means for the fire pump, emergency system, or standby power system must be located remotely away from the normal power disconnect [230.72(B)].

(B) Special Occupancies. By special permission, additional services are permitted for:

(1) Multiple-occupancy buildings where there's no available space for supply equipment accessible to all occupants, or

(2) A building or other structure so large that two or more supplies are necessary.

(C) Capacity Requirements. Additional services are permitted:

(1) If the capacity requirements exceed 2,000A, or

(2) If the load requirements of a single-phase installation exceed the utility's capacity, or

(3) By special permission.

Author's Comment:

■ Special permission is defined in Article 100 as "the written consent of the authority having jurisdiction."

(D) Different Characteristics. Additional services are permitted for different voltages, frequencies, or phases, or for different uses, such as for different electricity rate schedules.

(E) Identification of Multiple Services. If a building is supplied by more than one service, or a combination of feeders and services, a permanent plaque or directory must be installed at each service and feeder disconnect location to denote all other services and feeders supplying that building, and the area served by each. Figure 230–4

230.3 Not to Pass Through a Building

Service conductors must not pass through the interior of another building or other structure.

Figure 230–4

230.6 Conductors Considered Outside a Building

Conductors are considered outside of a building when they're installed:

(1) Under not less than 2 in. of concrete beneath a building. Figure 230–5

Figure 230–5

(2) Within a building in a raceway encased in not less than 2 in. of concrete or brick.

(3) In a vault that meets the construction requirements of Article 450, Part III.

(4) In a raceway under not less than 18 in. of the earth beneath a building.

(5) Within rigid or intermediate metal conduit that passes directly through an eave but not a wall of a building. Figure 230–6

Figure 230–6

230.7 Service Conductors Separate from Other Conductors

Service conductors must not be installed in the same raceway or cable with feeder or branch-circuit conductors. Figure 230–7

⚠️ **WARNING:** *Overcurrent protection for the feeder or branch-circuit conductors can be bypassed if service conductors are mixed with feeder or branch-circuit conductors in the same raceway and a fault occurs between the service and feeder or branch-circuit conductors. Figure 230–8*

Figure 230–7

Figure 230–8

Author's Comment:

■ This rule doesn't prohibit the mixing of service, feeder, and branch-circuit conductors in the same service equipment enclosure.

■ This requirement may be the root of the misconception that "line" and "load" conductors must not be installed in the same raceway. It's true that service conductors must not be installed in the same raceway with feeder or branch-circuit conductors, but line and load conductors for feeders and branch circuits can be in the same raceway or enclosure. Figure 230–9

Figure 230–9

230.8 Raceway Seals

Underground raceways (used or unused) entering buildings must be sealed or plugged to prevent moisture from contacting energized live parts [300.5(G)]. Figure 230–10

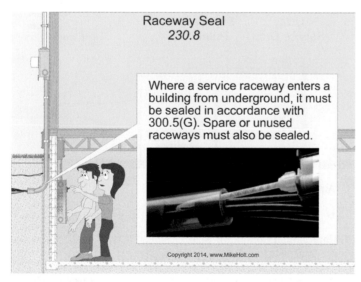

Figure 230–10

230.9 Clearance from Building Openings

(A) Clearance. Overhead service conductors must maintain a clearance of 3 ft from windows that open, doors, porches, balconies, ladders, stairs, fire escapes, or similar locations. Figure 230–11

Figure 230–11

Ex: Overhead conductors installed above a window aren't required to maintain the 3 ft distance.

(B) Vertical Clearance. Overhead service conductors must maintain a vertical clearance not less than 10 ft above platforms, projections, or surfaces from which they might be reached [230.24(B)]. This vertical clearance must be maintained for 3 ft, measured horizontally from the platform, projections, or surfaces from which people might reach them.

(C) Below Openings. Service conductors must not be installed under an opening through which materials might pass, and they must not be installed where they'll obstruct entrance to building openings. Figure 230–12

Figure 230–12

230.10 Vegetation as Support

Trees or other vegetation must not be used for the support of overhead service conductor spans. Figure 230–13

Figure 230–13

■ Service-drop conductors installed by the electric utility must comply with the *National Electrical Safety Code* (NESC), not the *National Electrical Code* [90.2(B)(5)]. Overhead service conductors that aren't under the exclusive control of the electric utility must be installed in accordance with the *NEC*.

Part II. Overhead Service Conductors

230.23 Overhead Service Conductor Size and Rating

(A) General. Overhead service conductors must have adequate mechanical strength, and they must have sufficient ampacity to carry the load as calculated in accordance with Article 220. Figure 230–14

Overhead Service Conductors - General
230.23(A)

Overhead service conductors must have adequate mechanical strength, and must have sufficient ampacity to carry the load calculated in accordance with Art. 220.

Utility Service Drop | Service Point | Service-Entrance Conductors

Copyright 2014
www.MikeHolt.com

Figure 230–14

(B) Ungrounded Conductor Size. Overhead service conductors must not be smaller than 8 AWG copper or 6 AWG aluminum.

Ex: Overhead service conductors can be as small as 12 AWG for limited-load installations.

(C) Neutral Conductor Size. The neutral overhead service conductor must be sized to carry the maximum unbalanced load, in accordance with 220.61, and it must not be sized smaller than required by 250.24(C).

WARNING: *In all cases, the service neutral conductor size must not be smaller than required by 250.24(C) to ensure that it has sufficiently low impedance and current-carrying capacity to safely carry fault current in order to facilitate the operation of the overcurrent device.*

Question: *What size neutral conductor is required for a structure with a 400A service supplied with 500 kcmil conductors if the maximum line-to-neutral load is no more than 100A?*

(a) 3 AWG   (b) 2 AWG   (c) 1 AWG   (d) 1/0 AWG

Answer: *(d) 1/0 AWG*

According to Table 310.15(B)(16), 3 AWG rated 100A at 75°C [110.14(C)(1)] is sufficient to carry 100A of neutral current. However, the service neutral conductor must be sized not smaller than 1/0 AWG, in accordance with Table 250.102(C)(1), based on the area of the service conductor [250.24(C)].

Figure 230–15

(B) Vertical Clearance for Overhead Service Conductors. Overhead service conductor spans must maintain the following vertical clearances: Figure 230–16

230.24 Vertical Clearance for Overhead Service Conductors

Overhead service conductor spans must maintain the vertical clearances as follows:

(A) Above Roofs. A minimum of 8 ft above the surface of a roof for a minimum distance of 3 ft in all directions from the edge of the roof.

Ex 2: If the slope of the roof exceeds 4 in. of vertical rise for every 12 in. of horizontal run, 120/208V or 120/240V overhead service conductor clearances can be reduced to 3 ft over the roof.

Ex 3: If no more than 6 ft of conductors pass over no more than 4 ft of roof, 120/208V or 120/240V overhead service conductor clearances over the roof overhang can be reduced to 18 in. Figure 230–15

Ex 4: The 3 ft vertical clearance for overhead service conductors that extends from the roof doesn't apply when the point of attachment is on the side of the building below the roof.

Ex 5: If the voltage between conductors doesn't exceed 300V and the roof area is guarded or isolated, a reduction in clearance to 3 ft is permitted.

Figure 230–16

(1) 10 ft above finished grade, sidewalks, or platforms or projections from which they might be accessible to pedestrians for 120/208V or 120/240V circuits.

(2) 12 ft above residential property and driveways, and those commercial areas not subject to truck traffic for 120/208V, 120/240V, or 277/480V circuits.

(4) 18 ft over public streets, alleys, roads, parking areas subject to truck traffic, driveways on other than residential property, and other areas traversed by vehicles, such as those used for cultivation, grazing, forestry, and orchards.

Author's Comment:

- Department of Transportation (DOT) type right-of-ways in rural areas are often used by slow-moving and tall farming machinery to avoid impeding road traffic.

(D) Swimming Pools. Overhead service conductors that aren't under the exclusive control of the electric utility located above pools, outdoor spas, outdoor hot tubs, diving structures, observation stands, towers, or platforms must be installed in accordance with the clearance requirements contained in 680.8.

(E) Clearance from Communications Cables. Where communications cables and electric light or power conductors are supported by the same pole, communications cables must have a minimum separation of 12 in. at any point in the span, including the point of attachment to the building [800.44(A)(4)].

230.26 Point of Attachment

The point of attachment for <u>overhead service</u> conductors must not be less than 10 ft above the finished grade, and it must be located so that the minimum service conductor clearances required by 230.9 and 230.24 can be maintained. Figure 230–17

⚠️ **CAUTION:** *The point of attachment for conductors might need to be raised so the overhead service conductors will comply with the clearances from building openings required by 230.9 and from other areas by 230.24.*

230.27 Means of Attachment

Multiconductor cables used for overhead service conductors must be attached to buildings or other structures by fittings identified for use with service conductors.

Figure 230–17

Open conductors must be attached to fittings identified for use with service conductors or to noncombustible, nonabsorbent insulators securely attached to the building or other structure.

230.28 Service Masts Used as Supports

<u>Masts used for the support of overhead service conductors or service drops must be installed in accordance with (A) and (B). Only these conductors can be attached to the mast.</u>

Author's Comment:

- Sections 810.12 and 820.44(C) specify that aerial cables for radio, TV, or CATV must not be attached to the service mast, and 810.12 prohibits antennas from being attached to the service mast. In addition, 800.133(B) and 830.133(B) prohibit broadband communications cables from being attached to raceways, including a service mast. Figure 230–18

(A) Strength. <u>If a mast is used for overhead conductor support,</u> it must have adequate mechanical strength, braces, or guy wires to withstand the strain caused by the conductors. <u>Conduit hubs must be identified for use with a mast.</u> Figure 230–19

(B) Attachment. <u>Conductors can't be attached to a mast between a weatherhead or end of the conduit and a coupling if the coupling is above the last conduit support, or if the coupling is above the building or structure.</u> Figure 230–20

Figure 230–18

Figure 230–20

Figure 230–19

Author's Comment:

■ Some local codes require a minimum trade size 2 rigid metal conduit for the service mast. In addition, many electric utilities contain specific requirements for the installation of the service mast.

Part III. Underground Service Conductors

230.31 Underground Service Conductor Size and Rating

Author's Comment:

■ Underground service conductors installed by the electric utility must comply with the *National Electrical Safety Code* (NESC), not the *National Electrical Code* [90.2(B)(5)]. Underground conductors that aren't under the exclusive control of the electric utility must be installed in accordance with the *NEC*.

(A) General. Underground service conductors must have sufficient ampacity to carry the load as calculated in accordance with Article 220. Figure 230–21

(B) Ungrounded Conductor Size. Underground service conductors must not be smaller than 8 AWG copper or 6 AWG aluminum.

Ex: Underground service conductors can be as small as 12 AWG for limited-load installations.

(C) Neutral Conductor Size. The neutral conductor must be sized to carry the maximum unbalanced load in accordance with 220.61, and it must not be sized smaller than required by 250.24(C).

Figure 230–21

Author's Comment:

■ 250.24(C) requires the service neutral conductor to be sized no smaller than Table 250.102(C)(1).

230.32 Protection Against Damage

Underground service conductors must be installed in accordance with 300.5, and have minimum cover in accordance with Table 300.5.

Part IV. Service-Entrance Conductors

230.40 Number of Service-Entrance Conductor Sets

Each service drop, service lateral, or set of underground or overhead service conductors may only supply one set of service entrance conductors.

Ex 2: Service conductors can supply two to six service disconnecting means as permitted in 230.71(A).

Ex 3: A single-family dwelling unit and its accessory structure(s) can have one set of service conductors run to each structure.

Ex 4: Two-family dwellings, multifamily dwellings, and multiple occupancy buildings are permitted to have one set of service conductors to supply branch circuits for public or common areas.

Ex 5: One set of service-entrance conductors connected to the supply side of the normal service disconnecting means can supply standby power systems, fire pump equipment, and fire and sprinkler alarms [230.82(5)] as well as Solar PV systems. Figure 230–22

Figure 230–22

230.42 Size and Rating

(A) Load Calculations. Service-entrance conductors must have sufficient ampacity for the loads to be served in accordance with Parts III, IV, or V of Article 220. The ampacity must not be less than (1), (2), or (3).

(1) 125 percent of the continuous loads, plus 100 percent of the noncontinuous loads.

Author's Comment:

■ See 215.3 for the sizing requirements of feeder overcurrent devices for continuous and noncontinuous loads.

Question: *What size service-entrance conductors are required for a 200A continuous three-phase load, if the terminals are rated 75°C?* Figure 230–23

(a) 2/0 AWG   (b) 3/0 AWG   (c) 4/0 AWG   (d) 250 kcmil

Answer: *(d) 250 kcmil*

Since the load is 200A continuous, the service-entrance conductors must have an ampacity not less than 250A (200A x 1.25). According to the 75°C column of Table 310.15(B)(16), 250 kcmil conductors are suitable because they have an ampere rating of 255A at 75°C.

Figure 230–24

Figure 230–23

(2) The sum of the noncontinuous load plus the continuous load after the application of any adjustment of correction factors. Figure 230–24

(3) 100 percent of the continuous and noncontinuous load, if the conductors terminate to an overcurrent device listed for 100 percent of its rating.

(C) Neutral Conductor Size. The service neutral conductor must be sized to carry the maximum unbalanced load in accordance with 220.61, and must not be sized smaller than required by 250.24(C).

WARNING: *In all cases the service neutral conductor size must not be smaller than required by 250.24(C) to ensure that it has sufficiently low impedance and current-carrying capacity to safely carry fault current in order to facilitate the operation of the overcurrent device.*

230.43 Wiring Methods

Service-entrance conductors must be installed with one of the following wiring methods:

(1) Open wiring on insulators

(3) Rigid metal conduit (RMC)

(4) Intermediate metal conduit (IMC)

(5) Electrical metallic tubing (EMT)

(6) Electrical nonmetallic tubing (ENT)

(7) Service-entrance cables

(8) Wireways

(9) Busways

(11) PVC Conduit

(13) Type MC Cable

(15) Flexible metal conduit (FMC) or liquidtight flexible metal conduit (LFMC) not longer than 6 ft

(16) Liquidtight flexible nonmetallic conduit (LFNC)

(17) High-Density Polyethylene Conduit (HDPE)

(18) Nonmetallic Underground Conduit with Conductors (NUCC)

(19) Reinforced Thermosetting Resin Conduit (RTRC)

230.46 Spliced Conductors

Service-entrance conductors can be spliced or tapped in accordance with 110.14, 300.5(E), 300.13, and 300.15. Figure 230–25

Figure 230–25

230.50 Protection Against Physical Damage

(A) Underground Service-Entrance Conductors. Underground service-entrance conductors must be protected against physical damage in accordance with 300.5. Figure 230–26

(B) All Other Service-Entrance Conductors.

(1) Service-Entrance Cables. Service-entrance cables that are subject to physical damage must be protected by one of the following: Figure 230–27

(1) Rigid metal conduit (RMC)

(2) Intermediate metal conduit (IMC)

Figure 230–26

Figure 230–27

(3) Schedule 80 PVC conduit

Author's Comment:

■ If the authority having jurisdiction determines the raceway isn't subject to physical damage, Schedule 40 PVC conduit can be used. Figure 230–28

(4) Electrical metallic tubing (EMT)

(5) Reinforced Thermosetting Resin Conduit (RTRC)

(6) Other means approved by the authority having jurisdiction

Figure 230–28

Figure 230–29

(2) Other Than Service-Entrance Cable. Individual open conductors and cables, other than service-entrance cables, must not be installed within 10 ft of grade level or where exposed to physical damage.

230.51 Cable Supports

(A) Service-Entrance Cable Supports. Service-entrance cable must be supported within 1 ft of the weatherhead, raceway connections or enclosure, and at intervals not exceeding 30 in.

230.54 Overhead Service Locations

(A) Service Head. Raceways for overhead service drops or overhead service conductors must have a weatherhead listed for wet locations.

(B) Service-Entrance Cable. Service-entrance cables must be equipped with a weatherhead listed for wet locations.

Ex: SE cable can be formed into a gooseneck and taped with self-sealing weather-resistant thermoplastic.

(C) Above the Point of Attachment. Service heads and goosenecks must be located above the point of attachment for service-drop or overhead service conductors. See 230.26. Figure 230–29

Ex: If it's impractical to locate the service head above the point of attachment, it must be located within 2 ft of the point of attachment.

(D) Secured. Service-entrance cables must be held securely in place.

(E) Opposite Polarity Through Separately Bushed Holes. Service heads must provide a bushed opening, and ungrounded conductors must be in separate openings.

(F) Drip Loops. Drip loop conductors must be connected to the service-drop or overhead service conductors below the service head or termination of the service-entrance cable sheath.

(G) Arranged so Water Won't Enter. Service entrance and overhead service conductors must be arranged to prevent water from entering service equipment.

230.56 High-Leg Identification

On a 4-wire, delta-connected, three-phase system, where the midpoint of one phase winding is grounded (high-leg system), the conductor with the higher phase voltage-to-ground (208V) must be durably and permanently marked by an outer finish that's orange in color, or by other effective means. Such identification must be placed at each point on the system where a connection is made if the neutral conductor is present [110.15]. Figure 230–30

Author's Comment:

■ The high-leg conductor is also called the "wild leg," "stinger leg," or "bastard leg."

High-Leg Conductor Identification
230.56

Delta High-Leg 3-Phase, 4-Wire System

Copyright 2014, www.MikeHolt.com

The high-leg conductor must be identified by an orange color at each point in the system where both a connection is made and the neutral conductor is present.

Figure 230–30

- Since 1975, panelboards supplied by a 4-wire, delta-connected, three-phase system must have the high-leg conductor (208V) terminate to the "B" (center) phase of a panelboard [408.3(E)].

- The ANSI standard for meter equipment requires the high-leg conductor (208V to neutral) to terminate on the "C" (right) phase of the meter socket enclosure. This is because the demand meter needs 120V and it gets this from the "B" phase. Hopefully, the utility lineman isn't colorblind and doesn't inadvertently cross the "orange" high-leg conductor (208V) with the red (120V) service conductor at the weather-head. It's happened before… Figure 230–31

High-Leg Conductor Termination
230.56

Delta High-Leg
3-Phase, 4-Wire System

The high leg must terminate on the "B" phase [408.3(E)(1)].

Copyright 2014
www.MikeHolt.com

CAUTION: Utilities require the high-leg conductor in meters be located on the "C" phase.

Figure 230–31

Part V. Service Equipment—General

230.66 Listed as Suitable for Service Equipment

The service disconnecting means must be listed as suitable for use as service equipment. Figure 230–32

Disconnect - Suitable as Service Equipment
230.66

Copyright 2014
www.MikeHolt.com

The service disconnecting means must be listed as suitable for use as service equipment.

Figure 230–32

Author's Comment:

- "Suitable for use as service equipment" means, among other things, that the service disconnecting means is supplied with a main bonding jumper so a neutral-to-case connection can be made, as required in 250.24(C) and 250.142(A).

Part VI. Service Equipment—Disconnecting Means

230.70 Disconnect Requirements

The service disconnecting means must open all service-entrance conductors from the building premises wiring.

(A) Location.

(1) Readily Accessible. The service disconnecting means must be placed at a readily accessible location either outside the building, or inside nearest the point of service conductor entry. Figure 230–33

Figure 230–33

> ⚠️ **WARNING:** *Because service-entrance conductors don't have short-circuit or ground-fault protection, they must be limited in length when installed inside a building. Some local jurisdictions have a specific requirement as to the maximum length permitted within a building.*

(2) Bathrooms. The service disconnecting means isn't permitted to be installed in a bathroom. Figure 230–34

Author's Comment:

■ Overcurrent devices must not be located in the bathrooms of dwelling units, or guest rooms or guest suites of hotels or motels [240.24(E)].

(3) Remote Control. If a remote-control device (such as a pushbutton for a shunt-trip breaker) is used to actuate the service disconnecting means, the service disconnecting means must still be at a readily accessible location either outside the building, or nearest the point of entry of the service conductors as required by 230.70(A)(1). Figure 230–35

Figure 230–34

Figure 230–35

Author's Comment:

■ See the definition of "Remote Control" in Article 100.

■ The service disconnecting means must consist of a manually operated switch, a power-operated switch, or a circuit breaker that's also capable of being operated manually [230.76].

(B) Disconnect Identification. Each service disconnecting means must be permanently marked to identify it as part of the service disconnecting means. Figure 230–36

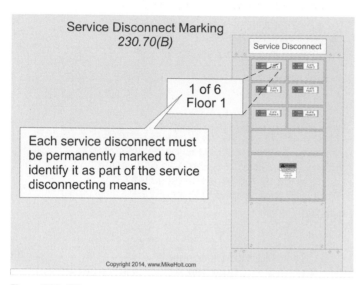

Figure 230–36

Author's Comment:

■ When a building has multiple services and/or feeders, a plaque is required at each service or feeder disconnect location to show the location of the other service or feeder disconnect locations. See≠ 230.2(E).

(C) Suitable for Use. Each service disconnecting means must be suitable for the prevailing conditions.

230.71 Number of Disconnects

(A) Maximum. There must be no more than six service disconnects for each service permitted by 230.2, or each set of service-entrance conductors permitted by 230.40 Ex 1, 3, 4, or 5. Figures 230–37 and 230–38

The service disconnecting means can consist of up to six switches or six circuit breakers mounted in a single enclosure, in a group of separate enclosures, or in or on a switchboard, or in switchgear.

Figure 230–37

Figure 230–38

⚠ **CAUTION:** *The rule is six disconnecting means for each service, not for each building. If the building has two services, then there can be a total of 12 service disconnects (six disconnects per service).* Figure 230–39

Service Disconnect - Maximum Number
230.71(A)

There must be no more than six disconnects
for each service permitted by 230.2.

Figure 230–39

230.72 Grouping of Disconnects

(A) Two to Six Disconnects. The service disconnecting means for each service must be grouped.

(B) Additional Service Disconnecting Means. To minimize the possibility of simultaneous interruption of power, the disconnecting means for fire pumps [Article 695], emergency [Article 700], legally required standby [Article 701], or optional standby [Article 702] systems must be located remote from the one to six service disconnects for normal service.

Author's Comment:

■ Because emergency systems are just as important as fire pumps and standby systems, they need to have the same safety precautions to prevent unintended interruption of the supply of electricity.

(C) Access to Occupants. In a multiple-occupancy building, each occupant must have access to their service disconnecting means.

Ex: In multiple-occupancy buildings where electrical maintenance is provided by continuous building management, the service disconnecting means can be accessible only to building management personnel.

230.76 Manual or Power Operated

The service disconnecting means can consist of:

(1) A manually operable switch or circuit breaker equipped with a handle or other suitable operating means.

(2) A power-operated switch or circuit breaker, provided it can be opened by hand in the event of a power supply failure. Figure 230–40

Service Disconnect
Manually or Power Operated
230.76

The service disconnect must be either:
(1) a manually operable switch or circuit breaker with a handle
(2) A power-operable switch or circuit breaker that can be opened by hand.

A shunt-trip control pushbutton isn't a disconnect.

Figure 230–40

230.77 Indicating

The service disconnecting means must indicate whether it's in the off (open) or (closed) position.

230.79 Rating of Disconnect

The service disconnecting means for a building must have an ampere rating of not less than the calculated load according to Article 220, and in no case less than:

(A) One-Circuit Installation. For installations consisting of a single branch circuit, the disconnecting means must have a rating not less than 15A.

(B) Two-Circuit Installation. For installations consisting of two 2-wire branch circuits, the disconnecting means must have a rating not less than 30A.

(C) One-Family Dwelling. For a one-family dwelling, the disconnecting means must have a rating not less than 100A, 3-wire.

(D) All Others. For all other installations, the disconnecting means must have a rating not less than 60A.

Author's Comment:

■ A shunt-trip button doesn't qualify as a service disconnect because it doesn't meet any of the above requirements.

230.81 Connection to Terminals

The service conductors must be connected to the service disconnecting means by pressure connectors, clamps, or other means approved by the authority having jurisdiction. Connections must not be made using solder.

230.82 Connected on Supply Side of the Service Disconnect

Electrical equipment must not be connected to the supply side of the service disconnect enclosure, except for the following:

(2) Meters and meter sockets can be connected to the supply side of the service disconnect enclosure.

(3) `Meter disconnect switches that have a short-circuit and interrupting current rating are permitted to be connected to the supply side of the service disconnect. The meter disconnect must be legibly field marked on its exterior in a manner suitable for the environment as follows: Figure 230–41

METER DISCONNECT

NOT SERVICE EQUIPMENT

Author's Comment:

■ Electric utilities often require a meter disconnect switch for 277/480V services to enhance safety for utility personnel when they install or remove a meter.

Figure 230–41

(4) Type 1 surge protective devices can be connected to the supply side of the service disconnect enclosure. Figure 230–42

Figure 230–42

Author's Comment:

■ A Type 1 surge protective device is listed to be permanently connected on the line side of service equipment [285.23].

(5) Taps used to supply legally required and optional standby power systems, fire pump equipment, fire and sprinkler alarms, and load (energy) management devices can be connected to the supply side of the service disconnect enclosure.

Author's Comment:

■ Emergency standby power must not be supplied by a connection ahead of service equipment [700.12].

(6) Solar PV systems can be connected to the supply side of the service disconnect enclosure in accordance with 705.12(A). Figure 230–43

Figure 230–43

Author's Comment:

■ In general transfer switches for generators aren't permitted ahead of the service disconnect unless rated as the service disconnect in accordance with 230.66.

Part VII. Service Equipment Overcurrent Protection

230.90 Overload Protection Required

Each ungrounded service conductor must have overload protection [240.21(D)]. Figure 230–44

Author's Comment:

■ The *NEC* doesn't require service conductors to be provided with short-circuit or ground-fault protection, but the feeder overcurrent device provides overload protection for the service conductors.

Figure 230–44

(A) Overcurrent Device Rating. The rating of the overcurrent device must not be more than the ampacity of the conductors.

Ex 2: If the ampacity of the ungrounded conductors doesn't correspond with the standard rating of overcurrent devices as listed in 240.6(A), the next higher overcurrent device can be used, if it doesn't exceed 800A [240.4(B)]. Figure 230–45

Where the ampacity of the ungrounded conductors doesn't correspond with the standard rating of the overcurrent device, the next higher overcurrent device can be used, if it doesn't exceed 800A [240.4(B)].

Figure 230–45

Ex 3: The combined ratings of two to six service disconnecting means can exceed the ampacity of the service conductors provided the calculated load, in accordance with Article 220, doesn't exceed the ampacity of the service conductors. Figure 230–46

Figure 230–46

Ex 5: Overload protection for 3-wire, single-phase, 120/240V dwelling unit service conductors can be in accordance with 310.15(B)(7). Figure 230–47

Figure 230–47

ARTICLE
240

OVERCURRENT PROTECTION

Introduction to Article 240—Overcurrent Protection

This article provides the requirements for selecting and installing overcurrent devices. Overcurrent exists when current exceeds the rating of equipment or the ampacity of a conductor, due to an overload, short circuit, or ground fault [Article 100].

■ **Overload.** An overload is a condition where equipment or conductors carry current exceeding their current rating [Article 100]. A fault, such as a short circuit or ground fault, isn't an overload. An example of an overload is plugging two 12.50A (1,500W) hair dryers into a 20A branch circuit.

■ **Short Circuit.** A short circuit is the unintentional electrical connection between any two normally current-carrying conductors of an electrical circuit, either line-to-line or line-to-neutral.

■ **Ground Fault.** A ground fault is an unintentional, electrically conducting connection between an ungrounded conductor of an electrical circuit and the normally noncurrent-carrying conductors, metallic enclosures, metallic raceways, metallic equipment, or the earth [Article 100]. During the period of a ground fault, dangerous voltages will be present on metal parts until the circuit overcurrent device opens.

Overcurrent devices protect conductors and equipment. Selecting the proper overcurrent protection for a specific circuit can become more complicated than it sounds. The general rule for overcurrent protection is that conductors must be protected in accordance with their ampacities at the point where they receive their supply [240.4 and 240.21]. There are many special cases that deviate from this basic rule, such as the overcurrent protection limitations for small conductors [240.4(D)] and the rules for specific conductor applications found in other articles, as listed in Table 240.4(G). There are also a number of rules allowing tap conductors in specific situations [240.21(B)]. Article 240 even has limits on where overcurrent devices are allowed to be located [240.24].

An overcurrent protection device must be capable of opening a circuit when an overcurrent situation occurs, and must also have an interrupting rating sufficient to avoid damage in fault conditions [110.9]. Carefully study the provisions of this article to be sure you provide sufficient overcurrent protection in the correct location.

Part I. General

240.1 Scope

Article 240 covers the general requirements for overcurrent protection and the installation requirements of overcurrent devices. Figure 240–1

Figure 240–1

Author's Comment:

- Overcurrent is a condition where the current exceeds the rating of equipment or ampacity of a conductor due to overload, short circuit, or ground fault [Article 100]. Figure 240–2

Figure 240–2

Note: An overcurrent device protects the circuit by opening the device when the current reaches a value that'll cause excessive or dangerous temperature rise (overheating) in conductors. Overcurrent devices must have an interrupting rating sufficient for the maximum possible fault current available on the line-side terminals of the equipment [110.9]. Electrical equipment must have a short-circuit current rating that permits the circuit's overcurrent device to clear short circuits or ground faults without extensive damage to the circuit's electrical components [110.10].

240.2 Definitions

Current-Limiting Overcurrent Device. An overcurrent device (typically a fast-acting fuse) that reduces the fault current to a magnitude substantially less than that obtainable in the same circuit if the current-limiting device wasn't used. See 240.40 and 240.60(B). Figure 240–3

Figure 240–3

Author's Comment:

- A current-limiting fuse is a type of fuse designed for operations related to short circuits only. When a fuse operates in its current-limiting range, it'll begin to melt in less than a quarter of a cycle, and it'll open a bolted short circuit in less than half a cycle. This type of fuse limits the instantaneous peak let-through current to a value substantially less than what will occur in the same circuit if the fuse is replaced with a solid conductor of equal impedance. If the available short-circuit current exceeds the equipment/conductor short-circuit current rating, then the thermal and magnetic forces can cause the equipment circuit conductors, as well as the circuit equipment grounding conductors, to vaporize. The only solutions to the problem of excessive available fault current are to:

- Install equipment with a higher short-circuit rating, or

- Protect the components of the circuit by a current-limiting overcurrent device such as a fast-clearing fuse, which can reduce the let-through energy.

A breaker or a fuse does limit current, but it may not be listed as a current-limiting device. A thermal-magnetic circuit breaker typically clears fault current in less than three to five cycles when subjected to a short circuit or ground fault of 20 times its rating. A standard fuse will clear the same fault in less than one cycle and a current-limiting fuse in less than half of a cycle.

Tap Conductors. A conductor, other than a service conductor, that has overcurrent protection rated more than the ampacity of a conductor. See 240.21(A) and 240.21(B) for details. Figure 240–4

240.3 Protection of Equipment

The following equipment and their conductors are protected against overcurrent in accordance with the article that covers the type of equipment:

Conductors, other than service conductors, that have overcurrent protection ahead of the point of supply that exceeds the value permitted for similar conductors.

Figure 240–4

Table 240.3—Other Articles		
Equipment	Article	Section
Air–Conditioning and Refrigeration Equipment	440	440.22
Appliances	422	All
Audio Circuits	640	640.9
Branch Circuits	210	210.20
Class 1, 2, and 3 Circuits	725	All
Feeder Conductors	215	215.3
Flexible Cords	240	240.5(B)(1)
Fire Alarms	760	All
Fire Pumps	695	All
Fixed Electric Space–Heating Equipment	424	424.3(B)
Fixture Wire	240	240.5(B)(2)
Panelboards	408	408.36
Service Conductors	230	230.90(A)
Transformers	450	450.3

240.4 Protection of Conductors

Except as permitted by (A) through (G), conductors must be protected against overcurrent in accordance with their ampacity after ampacity correction and adjustment as specified in 310.15. Figure 240–5

Protection of Conductors
240.4

1/0 AWG Rated 150A at 75°C Protected by a 150A Device

6 AWG Rated 55A at 60°C Protected by a 50A Device

Except as permitted by 240.4(A) through (G), conductors must be protected against overcurrent in accordance with their ampacity.

Copyright 2014, www.MikeHolt.com

Figure 240–5

(A) Power Loss Hazard. Conductor overload protection isn't required, but short-circuit protection is required where the interruption of the circuit will create a hazard; such as in a material-handling electromagnet circuit or fire pump circuit.

(B) Overcurrent Devices Rated 800A or Less. The next higher standard rating of overcurrent device listed in 240.6 (above the ampacity of the ungrounded conductors being protected) is permitted, provided all of the following conditions are met:

(1) The conductors aren't part of a branch circuit supplying more than one receptacle for cord-and-plug-connected loads.

(2) The ampacity of a conductor, after the application of ambient temperature correction [310.15(B)(2)(a)], conductor bundling adjustment [310.15(B)(3)(a)], or both, doesn't correspond with the standard rating of a fuse or circuit breaker in 240.6(A).

(3) The overcurrent device rating doesn't exceed 800A. Figure 240–6

Author's Comment:

■ This "next size up" rule doesn't apply to feeder tap conductors [240.21(B)] or transformer secondary conductors [240.21(C)].

Overcurrent Devices - Not Over 800A
Next Size Up
240.4(B)(3)

Where the conductor ampacity doesn't correspond with a standard overcurrent device rating, the next higher rated device can be used if it's not over 800A.

400A [240.6]

370A Calculated Load Use 500 kcmil Rated 380A at 75°C

Copyright 2014, www.MikeHolt.com

Figure 240–6

(C) Overcurrent Devices Rated Over 800A. If the circuit's overcurrent device exceeds 800A, the conductor ampacity, after the application of ambient temperature correction [310.15(B)(2)(a)], conductor bundling adjustment [310.15(B)(3)(a)], or both, must have a rating of not less than the rating of the overcurrent device defined in 240.6. Figure 240–7

Overcurrent Device - Over 800A
240.4(C)

1,200A/3 sets = 400A
600 kcmil, rated 420A
Table 310.15(B)(16), 75°C

1,200A

If the circuit's overcurrent device exceeds 800A, the conductor must have an ampacity not less than the overcurrent device rating.

Copyright 2014, www.MikeHolt.com

Figure 240–7

(D) Small Conductors. Unless specifically permitted in 240.4(E) or (G), overcurrent protection must not exceed the following: Figure 240–8

(1) 18 AWG Copper—7A

Figure 240–8

(2) 16 AWG Copper—10A

(3) 14 AWG Copper—15A

(4) 12 AWG Aluminum/Copper-Clad Aluminum—15A

(5) 12 AWG Copper—20A

(6) 10 AWG Aluminum/Copper-Clad Aluminum—25A

(7) 10 AWG Copper—30A

(E) Tap Conductors. Tap conductors must be protected against overcurrent as follows:

(1) Household Ranges and Cooking Appliances and Other Loads, 210.19(A)(3) and (4)

(2) Fixture Wire, 240.5(B)(2)

(3) Location in Circuit, 240.21

(4) Reduction in Ampacity Size of Busway, 368.17(B)

(5) Feeder or Branch Circuits (busway taps), 368.17(C)

(6) Single Motor Taps, 430.53(D)

(F) Transformer Secondary Conductors. The primary overcurrent device sized in accordance with 450.3(B) is considered suitable to protect the secondary conductors of a 2-wire (single voltage) system, provided the primary overcurrent device doesn't exceed the value determined by multiplying the secondary conductor ampacity by the secondary-to-primary transformer voltage ratio.

Question: *What's the minimum secondary conductor size required for a 2-wire, 480V to 120V transformer rated 1.50 kVA with 60°C terminals?* Figure 240–9

(a) 16 AWG   *(b) 14 AWG*   *(c) 12 AWG*   *(d) 10 AWG*

Answer: *(c) 12 AWG*

Primary Current = VA/E

VA = 1,500 VA
E = 480V

Primary Current = 1,500 VA/480V
Primary Current = 3.13A

Primary Protection [450.3(B)] = 3.13A x 1.67
Primary Protection = 5.22A or 5A Fuse

Secondary Current = 1,500 VA/120V
Secondary Current = 12.50A

Secondary Conductor = 12 AWG, rated 20A at 60°C, [Table 310.15(B)(16)]

The 5A primary overcurrent device can be used to protect 12 AWG secondary conductors because it doesn't exceed the value determined by multiplying the secondary conductor ampacity by the secondary-to-primary transformer voltage ratio.

5A< or = 20A x 120V/480V
5A< or = 20A x (0.25)
5A< or = 5A

Transformer Secondary Conductor Protection
240.4(F)

The primary overcurrent device can protect the secondary conductors of a 2-wire system if the primary device doesn't exceed the value determined by multiplying the secondary conductor ampacity by the secondary-to-primary voltage ratio.

Figure 240–9

(G) Overcurrent Protection for Specific Applications. Overcurrent protection for specific equipment and conductors must comply with the requirements referenced in Table 240.4(G).

Air-Conditioning and Refrigeration [Article 440]. Air-conditioning and refrigeration equipment, and their circuit conductors, must be protected against overcurrent in accordance with 440.22.

Author's Comment:

- Typically, the branch-circuit ampacity and protection size is marked on the equipment nameplate [440.4(A)].

Question: What size branch-circuit overcurrent device is required for an air conditioner (18A) when the nameplate indicates the minimum circuit ampacity is 23A, with maximum overcurrent protection of 40A? The nameplate specifies 60°C terminals. Figure 240–10

(a) 12 AWG, 40A protection   (b) 12 AWG, 50A protection
(c) 12 AWG, 60A protection   (d) 12 AWG, 70A protection

Answer: (a) 12 AWG, 40A protection

Protection of
Air-Conditioning Circuits
240.4(G)
and 440.22(A)

40A Protection

12 AWG
Rated 25A at 60°C

Copyright 2014, www.MikeHolt.com

Air-conditioning and refrigeration equipment must be protected against overcurrent in accordance with 440.22.

Figure 240–10

Author's Comment:

- Air-conditioning and refrigeration nameplate values are calculated by the manufacturer according to the following:

  □ Branch-Circuit Conductor Size [440.32]
  18A x 1.25 = 22.50A, 12 AWG rated 25A at 75°C

□ Branch-Circuit Protection Size [440.22(A)]
18A x 2.25 = 40.50A, 40A maximum overcurrent protection size [240.6(A)]

□ Motors [Article 430]. Motor circuit conductors must be protected against short circuits and ground faults in accordance with 430.52 and 430.62 [430.51].

If the nameplate calls for fuses, fuses must be used to comply with the manufacturer's instructions [110.3(B)].

Question: What size branch-circuit conductor and overcurrent device (circuit breaker) is required for a 7½ hp, 230V, three-phase motor with 75°C terminals? Figure 240–11

(a) 10 AWG, 50A breaker   (b) 10 AWG, 60A breaker
(c) a or b   (d) none of these

Answer: (c) a or b

Step 1: Determine the branch-circuit conductor size [Table 310.15(B)(16), 430.22, and Table 430.250]:

FLC = 28A [Table 430.250]
22A x 1.25 = 28A, 10 AWG, rated 35A at 75°C

Step 2: Determine the branch-circuit protection size [240.6(A), 430.52(C)(1) Ex 1, and Table 430.250].

Inverse Time Breaker: 22A x 2.50 = 55A
Next size up = 60A

Motor circuit conductors must be protected against short circuits and ground faults in accordance with 430.52.

Figure 240–11

Motor Control [Article 430]. Motor control circuit conductors must be sized and protected in accordance with 430.72.

Remote-Control, Signaling, and Power-Limited Circuits [Article 725]. Remote-control, signaling, and power-limited circuit conductors must be protected against overcurrent in accordance with 725.43.

240.5 Protection of Flexible Cords and Fixture Wires

(A) Ampacities. Flexible cord must be protected by an overcurrent device in accordance with its ampacity as specified in Table 400.5(A)(1) or Table 400.5(A)(2). Fixture wires must be protected against overcurrent in accordance with their ampacity as specified in Table 402.5. Supplementary overcurrent protection, as discussed in 240.10, is permitted to provide this protection.

(B) Branch-Circuit Overcurrent Protection.

(1) Cords for Listed Appliances or Luminaires. If flexible cord is used with a specific listed appliance or luminaire, the conductors are considered protected against overcurrent when used within the appliance or luminaire listing requirements.

Author's Comment:

- The *NEC* only applies to premises wiring, not to the supply cords of listed appliances and luminaires.

(2) Fixture Wire. Fixture wires can be tapped to the following circuits:

(1) 20A–18 AWG, up to 50 ft of run length

(2) 20A–16 AWG, up to 100 ft of run length

(3) 20A–14 AWG and larger

(3) Extension Cord Sets. Flexible cord used in listed extension cord sets is considered protected against overcurrent when used within the extension cord's listing requirements. Figure 240–12

Protection of Extension Cords
240.5(B)(3)

Flexible cord used in listed extension cords are considered protected by the circuit they're plugged into if used in accordance with listing and labeling instructions.

Listed Extension Cord

Copyright 2014, www.MikeHolt.com

Figure 240–12

240.6 Standard Ampere Ratings

(A) Fuses and Fixed-Trip Circuit Breakers. The standard ratings in amperes for fuses and inverse time breakers are: 15, 20, 25, 30, 35, 40, 45, 50, 60, 70, 80, 90, 100, 110, 125, 150, 175, 200, 225, 250, 300, 350, 400, 450, 500, 600, 700, 800, 1,000, 1,200, 1,600, 2,000, 2,500, 3,000, 4,000, 5,000 and 6,000. Figure 240–13

Standard Overcurrent Device Ratings
240.6(A)

30A   20A

30 AMP
DE Fuse
250V
10,000A Max. R.M.S

INTERRUPTING RATING
10,000 AMPS
MAX. RMS SYM.
120/240 VOLTS AC

Copyright 2014, www.MikeHolt.com

The standard ratings for fuses and inverse-time breakers include: 15, 20, 25, 30, 35, 40, 45, 50, 60, 70, 80, 90, 100, 110, 125, 150, 175, 200, 225, 250, 300, 350, 400, 450, 500, 600, 700, 800, 1,000, 1,200, 1,600, 2,000, 2,500, 3,000, 4,000, 5,000, and 6,000A.

Figure 240–13

Additional standard ampere ratings for fuses include 1, 3, 6, 10, and 601.

Author's Comment:

■ Fuses rated less than 15A are sometimes required for the protection of fractional horsepower motor circuits [430.52], motor control circuits [430.72], small transformers [450.3(B)], and remote-control circuit conductors [725.43].

(B) Adjustable Circuit Breakers. The ampere rating of an adjustable circuit breaker is equal to its maximum long-time pickup current setting.

(C) Restricted Access, Adjustable-Trip Circuit Breakers. The ampere rating of adjustable-trip circuit breakers that have restricted access to the adjusting means is equal to their adjusted long-time pickup current settings.

240.10 Supplementary Overcurrent Protection

Supplementary overcurrent devices must not be used as the required branch-circuit overcurrent device. Figure 240–14

Supplementary overcurrent devices can't be used as the required circuit overcurrent device.

Figure 240–14

A supplementary overcurrent device isn't required to be readily accessible [240.24(A)(2)].

Author's Comment:

■ Article 100 defines a "Supplementary Overcurrent Device" as a device intended to provide limited overcurrent protection for specific applications and utilization equipment. This limited protection is in addition to the protection provided in the required branch circuit by the branch-circuit overcurrent device.

240.13 Ground-Fault Protection of Equipment

Service disconnects and feeder circuits rated 1,000A or more, supplied from a 4-wire, three-phase, 277/480V wye-connected system must be protected against ground faults in accordance with 230.95 [215.10 and 230.95].

The requirement for ground-fault protection of equipment doesn't apply to:

(1) Continuous industrial processes where a nonorderly shutdown will introduce additional or increased hazards.

(2) Installations where ground-fault protection of equipment is already provided.

(3) Fire pumps [695.6(H)].

Author's Comment:

■ Article 100 defines "Ground-Fault Protection of Equipment" as a system intended to provide protection of equipment from ground faults by opening the overcurrent device at current levels less than those required to protect conductors from damage. This type of protective system isn't intended to protect people, only connected equipment. See 215.10 and 230.95 for similar requirements for feeders and services.

■ Ground-fault protection of equipment isn't required for emergency power systems [700.26] or legally required standby power systems [701.17].

240.15 Ungrounded Conductors

(A) Overcurrent Device Required. A fuse or circuit breaker must be connected in series with each ungrounded conductor.

(B) Circuit Breaker as an Overcurrent Device. Circuit breakers must automatically (and manually) open all ungrounded conductors of the circuit, except as follows:

(1) Multiwire Branch Circuits. Individual single-pole breakers with identified handle ties are permitted for a multiwire branch circuit that only supplies line-to-neutral loads. Figure 240–15

Figure 240–15

Author's Comment:

- According to Article 100, "Identified" means recognized as suitable for a specific purpose, function, or environment by listing, labeling, or other means approved by the authority having jurisdiction. This means handle ties made from nails, screws, wires, or other nonconforming materials aren't suitable. Figure 240–16

- Single-pole AFCI or GFCI circuit breakers aren't suitable for protecting multiwire branch circuits. AFCI or GFCI circuit breakers for multiwire branch circuits must be of the 2-pole type. Figure 240–17

Handle ties must be identified for the purpose, which means that handle ties made from nails, screws, wires, or other nonconforming material aren't permitted.

Figure 240–16

AFCI or GFCI circuit breakers must be of the 2-pole type if they are used to protect multiwire branch circuits.

Figure 240–17

(2) Single-Phase, Line-to-Line Loads. Individual single-pole circuit breakers rated 120/240V with handle ties identified for the purpose are permitted on each ungrounded conductor of a branch circuit that supplies single-phase, line-to-line loads. Figure 240–18

(3) Three-Phase, Line-to-Line Loads. Individual single-pole breakers rated 120/240V with handle ties identified for the purpose are permitted on each ungrounded conductor of a branch circuit that serves three-phase, line-to-line loads on systems not exceeding 120V to ground. Figure 240–19

Figure 240–18

Figure 240–20

Figure 240–19

Part II. Location

240.21 Overcurrent Protection Location in Circuit

Except as permitted by (A) through (H), overcurrent devices must be placed at the point where the branch-circuit or feeder conductors receive their power. Taps and transformer secondary conductors aren't permitted to supply another conductor (tapping a tap isn't permitted). Figure 240–20

(A) Branch-Circuit Taps. Branch-circuit taps are permitted in accordance with 210.19.

(B) Feeder Taps. Conductors can be tapped to a feeder as specified in 240.21(B)(1) through (B)(5). The "next size up protection rule" of 240.4(B) isn't permitted for tap conductors. Figure 240–21

Figure 240–21

(1) 10-Foot Feeder Tap. Feeder tap conductors up to 10 ft long are permitted without overcurrent protection at the tap location if the tap conductors comply with the following:

(1) The ampacity of the tap conductor must not be less than: Figure 240–22

Figure 240–22

a. The calculated load in accordance with Article 220, and

b. The rating of the overcurrent device supplied by the tap conductors.

Ex: Listed equipment, such as a surge protection device, can have their conductors sized in accordance with the manufacturer's instructions.

(2) The tap conductors must not extend beyond the equipment they supply.

(3) The tap conductors are installed in a raceway when they leave the enclosure.

(4) The tap conductors must have an ampacity not less than 10 percent of the rating of the overcurrent device that protects the feeder. Figure 240–23

Note: See 408.36 for the overcurrent protection requirements for panelboards.

Figure 240–23

Ten-Foot Tap Rule

Example: *A 400A breaker protects a set of 500 kcmil feeder conductors. There are three taps fed from the 500 kcmil feeder that supply disconnects with 200A, 150A, and 30A overcurrent devices. What are the minimum size conductors for these taps?* Figure 240–24

- *200A: 3/0 AWG is rated 200A at 75°C, and is greater than 10 percent of the rating of the overcurrent device (400A).*

- *150A: 1/0 AWG is rated 150A at 75°C, and is greater than 10 percent of the rating of the overcurrent device (400A).*

- *30A: 8 AWG rated 40A at 60°C. The tap conductors from the 400A feeder to the 30A overcurrent device can't be less than 40A (10 percent of the rating of the 400A feeder overcurrent device.*

Figure 240–24

Figure 240–26

(2) 25-Foot Feeder Tap. Feeder tap conductors up to 25 ft long are permitted without overcurrent protection at the tap location if the tap conductors comply with the following: Figures 240–25 and 240–26

(5) Outside Feeder Taps of Unlimited Length. Outside feeder tap conductors can be of unlimited length, without overcurrent protection at the point they receive their supply, if they comply with the following: Figure 240–27

Figure 240–25

Figure 240–27

(1) The ampacity of the tap conductors must not be less than one-third the rating of the overcurrent device that protects the feeder.

(2) The tap conductors terminate in an overcurrent device rated no more than the tap conductor ampacity in accordance with 310.15.

(1) The tap conductors are suitably protected from physical damage in a raceway or manner approved by the authority having jurisdiction.

(2) The tap conductors must terminate at a single circuit breaker or a single set of fuses that limits the load to the ampacity of the conductors.

(3) The overcurrent device for the tap conductors is an integral part of the disconnecting means, or it's located immediately adjacent to it.

(4) The disconnecting means is located at a readily accessible location, either outside the building, or nearest the point of entry of the conductors.

(C) Transformer Secondary Conductors. A set of conductors supplying single or separate loads is permitted to be connected to a transformer secondary without overcurrent protection in accordance with (1) through (6).

The permission of the "next size up" protection rule when the conductor ampacity doesn't correspond with the standard size overcurrent protection device of 240.4(B) doesn't apply to transformer secondary conductors. Figure 240–28

Figure 240–28

(1) Protection by Primary Overcurrent Device. The primary overcurrent device sized in accordance with 450.3(B) is considered suitable to protect the secondary conductors of a 2-wire (single-voltage) system, provided the primary overcurrent device doesn't exceed the value determined by multiplying the secondary conductor ampacity by the secondary-to-primary transformer voltage ratio.

Question: *What's the minimum size secondary conductor required for a 2-wire, 480V to 120V transformer rated 1.50 kVA with 60ºC terminals?* Figure 240–29

(a) 16 AWG   *(b) 14 AWG*   *(c) 12 AWG*   *(d) 10 AWG*

Answer: *(c) 12 AWG*

Primary Current = VA/E

VA = 1,500 VA
E = 480V

Primary Current = 1,500 VA/480V
Primary Current = 3.13A

Primary Protection [450.3(B)] = 3.13A x 1.67
Primary Protection [450.3(B)] = 5.22A or 5A Fuse

Secondary Current = 1,500 VA/120V
Secondary Current = 12.50A

Secondary Conductor = 12 AWG, rated 20A at 60ºC,
[Table 310.15(B)(16)]

The 5A primary overcurrent device can be used to protect 12 AWG secondary conductors because it doesn't exceed the value determined by multiplying the secondary conductor ampacity by the secondary-to-primary transformer voltage ratio.

5A< or = 20A x 120V/480V
5A< or = 20A x (0.25)
5A< or = 5A

Figure 240–29

(2) 10 Ft Secondary Conductors. Secondary conductors can be run up to 10 ft without overcurrent protection if installed as follows:

(1) The ampacity of the secondary conductor must not be less than: Figure 240–30

Figure 240–30

a. The calculated load in accordance with Article 220, and

b. The rating of the overcurrent device at the termination of the secondary conductors

Ex: Listed equipment, such as a surge protection device, can have their conductors sized in accordance with the manufacturer's instructions.

(2) The secondary conductors must not extend beyond the switchboard, switchgear, panelboard, disconnecting means, or control devices they supply.

(3) The secondary conductors are enclosed in a raceway.

(4) Not less than 10 percent of the rating of the overcurrent device protecting the primary of the transformer, multiplied by the primary-to-secondary transformer voltage ratio.

(4) Outside Secondary Conductors of Unlimited Length. Outside secondary conductors can be of unlimited length, without overcurrent protection at the point they receive their supply, if they're installed as follows: Figure 240–31

(1) The conductors are suitably protected from physical damage in a raceway or manner approved by the authority having jurisdiction.

Figure 240–31

(2) The conductors must terminate at a single circuit breaker or a single set of fuses that limit the load to the ampacity of the conductors.

(3) The overcurrent device for the ungrounded conductors is an integral part of a disconnecting means or it's located immediately adjacent thereto.

(4) The disconnecting means is located at a readily accessible location that complies with one of the following:

a. Outside of a building.

b. Inside, nearest the point of entrance of the conductors.

c. If installed in accordance with 230.6, nearest the point of entrance of the conductors.

(5) Secondary Conductors from a Feeder Tapped Transformer. Transformer secondary conductors must be installed in accordance with 240.21(B)(3).

(6) 25-Foot Secondary Conductor. Secondary conductors can be run up to 25 ft without overcurrent protection if they comply with all of the following: Figure 240–32

(1) The secondary conductors have an ampacity not less than the value of the primary-to-secondary voltage ratio multiplied by one-third of the rating of the overcurrent device that protects the primary of the transformer.

Secondary Conductors Not Over 25 Ft
240.21(C)(6)

Secondary Conductors

Secondary conductors must:
• Have an ampacity not less than the primary-to-secondary voltage ratio multiplied by 1/3 the rating of the primary overcurrent device.
• Terminate in a single overcurrent device that limits the load to the conductor ampacity.

Copyright 2014
www.MikeHolt.com

Figure 240–32

Location of Overcurrent Devices
Readily Accessible
240.24(A)

Overcurrent devices must be:
• Readily accessible.
• Not more than 6 ft 7 in. above the floor or platform.

VIOLATION

Copyright 2014
www.MikeHolt.com

Readily accessible means capable of being reached quickly without having to climb over or remove obstacles, or without having to use portable ladders or use tools [Art. 100 Def].

Figure 240–33

(2) Secondary conductors terminate in a single circuit breaker or set of fuses rated no more than the tap conductor ampacity in accordance with 310.15 [Table 310.15(B)(16)].

(3) The secondary conductors are protected from physical damage by being enclosed in a manner approved by the authority having jurisdiction, such as within a raceway.

(D) Service Conductors. Service conductors must be protected against overload in accordance with 230.90 and 91.

(H) Battery Conductors. Overcurrent protection is installed as close as practicable to the storage battery terminals.

240.24 Location of Overcurrent Devices

(A) Readily Accessible. Circuit breakers and fuses must be readily accessible, and they must be installed so the center of the grip of the operating handle of the fuse switch or circuit breaker, when in its highest position, isn't more than 6 ft 7 in. above the floor or working platform, unless the installation is for: Figure 240–33

(1) Busways, as provided in 368.17(C).

(2) Supplementary overcurrent devices aren't required to be readily accessible [240.10]. Figure 240–34

(3) For overcurrent devices, as described in 225.40 and 230.92.

Location of Supplementary
Overcurrent Protective Device
240.24(A)(2)

Please Keep Door Closed

Supplementary Overcurrent Device

Supplementary overcurrent devices, such as those provided for luminaires, aren't required to be readily accessible [240.10].

Copyright 2014
www.MikeHolt.com

Figure 240–34

(4) Overcurrent devices located next to equipment can be mounted above 6 ft 7 in., if accessible by portable means [404.8(A) Ex 2]. Figure 240–35

(C) Not Exposed to Physical Damage. Overcurrent devices must not be exposed to physical damage. Figure 240–36

Figure 240–35

Figure 240–37

Figure 240–36

Figure 240–38

Note: Electrical equipment must be suitable for the environment, and consideration must be given to the presence of corrosive gases, fumes, vapors, liquids, or chemicals that have a deteriorating effect on conductors or equipment [110.11]. Figure 240–37

(D) Not in Vicinity of Easily Ignitible Material. Overcurrent devices must not be located near easily ignitible material, such as in clothes closets. Figure 240–38

(E) Not in Bathrooms. Overcurrent devices aren't permitted to be located in the bathrooms of dwelling units, dormitories, or guest rooms or guest suites of hotels or motels. Figure 240–39

Author's Comment:

■ The service disconnecting means must not be located in a bathroom, even in commercial or industrial facilities [230.70(A)(2)].

(F) Over Steps. Overcurrent devices must not be located over the steps of a stairway. Figure 240–40

Author's Comment:

■ Clearly, it's difficult for electricians to safely work on electrical equipment that's located on uneven surfaces such as over stairways.

Overcurrent devices must not be located in the bathrooms of dwelling units, dormitories, guest rooms, or guest suites.

Figure 240–39

Figure 240–40

Part III. Enclosures

240.32 Damp or Wet Locations

In damp or wet locations, enclosures containing overcurrent devices must prevent moisture or water from entering or accumulating within the enclosure. When the enclosure is surface mounted in a wet location, it must be mounted with not less than ¼ in. of air space between it and the mounting surface. See 312.2.

240.33 Vertical Position

Enclosures containing overcurrent devices must be mounted in a vertical position unless this isn't practical. Circuit-breaker enclosures can be mounted horizontally if the circuit breaker is installed in accordance with 240.81. Figure 240–41

Figure 240–41

Author's Comment:

■ Section 240.81 specifies that where circuit-breaker handles are operated vertically, the "up" position of the handle must be in the "on" position. So, in effect, an enclosure that contains one row of circuit breakers can be mounted horizontally, but an enclosure that contains a panelboard with multiple circuit breakers on opposite sides of each other will have to be mounted vertically.

Part V. Plug Fuses, Fuseholders, and Adapters

240.50 General

(A) Maximum Voltage. Plug fuses are permitted to be used only when:

(1) The circuit voltage doesn't exceed 125 volts between conductors.

(2) The circuits are supplied by a system with a line-to-neutral voltage not exceeding 150V.

(C) Hexagon Configuration. Plug fuses of 15A or lower rating must be identified by a hexagonal configuration of the window, cap or other prominent part.

240.51 Edison-Base Fuses

(A) Classification. Edison-base fuses are classified to operate at not more than 125V and have an ampere rating of not more than 30A.

(B) Replacement Only. Edison-base fuses are permitted only for replacement in an existing installation where there's no evidence of tampering or overfusing.

240.52 Edison-Base Fuseholders

Edison-base fuseholders must be used only if they're made to accept Type S fuses by the use of adapters.

240.53 Type S Fuses

(A) Classification. Type S fuses operate at not more than 125V and have ampere ratings of 15A, 20A, and 30A. Figure 240–42

(B) Not Interchangeable. Type S fuses are made so different ampere ratings aren't interchangeable.

240.54 Type S Fuses, Adapters, and Fuseholders

(A) Type S Adapters. Type S adapters are designed to fit Edison-base fuseholders.

(B) Prevent Edison-Base Fuses. Type S fuseholders and adapters are designed for Type S fuses only.

(C) Nonremovable Adapters. Type S adapters are designed so they can't be removed once installed.

Type S Plug Fuses
240.53(A)

Type S fuses are classified to operate at not more than 125V and have an ampere rating of 15A, 20A, or 30A.

Copyright 2014, www.MikeHolt.com

Figure 240–42

(D) Nontamperable. Type S fuses, fuseholders and adapters must be designed so that tampering or shunting would be difficult.

(E) Interchangeability. Dimensions of Type S fuses, fuseholders, and adapters shall be standardized to permit interchangeability regardless of the manufacturer.

Part VI. Cartridge Fuses and Fuseholders

240.60 General

Author's Comment:

■ There are two basic designs of cartridge fuses, the ferrule type with a maximum rating of 60A and the knife-blade type rated over 60A. The fuse length and diameter varies with the voltage and current rating. Figure 240–43

(A) Maximum Voltage—300V Type. Cartridge fuses and fuseholders of the 300V type can only be used for:

• Circuits not exceeding 300V between conductors.
• Circuits not exceeding 300V from any ungrounded conductor to the neutral point.

(B) Noninterchangeable Fuseholders. Fuseholders must be designed to make it difficult to interchange fuses of any given class for different voltages and current ratings.

Cartridge Fuses
240.60

Ferrule-Type
Cartridge Fuse

30 AMP
DE Fuse
250V

100
AMPS

Knife-Blade Type
Cartridge Fuse

Copyright 2014, www.MikeHolt.com

There are two basic designs of cartridge fuses, the ferrule type (maximum 60A) and the knife-blade type. The length and diameter of the fuse varies with the fuse voltage and current rating.

Figure 240–43

Fuseholders for current-limiting fuses must be designed so only current-limiting fuses can be inserted.

Author's Comment:

- A current-limiting fuse is a fast-clearing overcurrent device that reduces the fault current to a magnitude substantially lower than that obtainable in the same circuit if the current-limiting device isn't used [240.2].

(C) Marking. Cartridge fuses have an interrupting rating of 10,000A, unless marked otherwise. They must be marked with:

(1) Ampere rating

(2) Voltage rating

(3) Interrupting rating if not 10,000A

(4) Current limiting if applicable

(5) Name or trademark of manufacturer

⚠️ **WARNING:** *Fuses must have an interrupting rating sufficient for the short-circuit current available at the line terminals of the equipment. Using a fuse with an inadequate interrupting current rating can cause equipment to be destroyed from a line-to-line or ground fault, and result in death or serious injury. See 110.9 for more details.* Figure 240–44

Fuse - Interrupting Rating
240.60(C)

Fuse Rated 200,000 AIC

Fuse Rated 10,000 AIC

Cartridge fuses have an interrupting rating of 10,000A, unless marked otherwise.

Care should be taken to ensure that fuses have sufficient interrupting rating for the available fault current [110.9].

16,000A
Fault Current

Copyright 2014, www.MikeHolt.com

Figure 240–44

240.61 Classification

Cartridge fuses and fuseholders are classified according to voltage and amperage ranges. Fuses rated 1,000V, nominal, or less are permitted for voltages at or below their ratings.

Part VII. Circuit Breakers

240.80 Method of Operation

Circuit breakers must be capable of being opened and closed by hand. Nonmanual means of operating a circuit breaker, such as electrical shunt trip or pneumatic operation, are permitted as long as the circuit breaker can also be manually operated.

240.81 Indicating

Circuit breakers must clearly indicate whether they're in the open "off" or closed "on" position. When the handle of a circuit breaker is operated vertically, the "up" position of the handle must be the "on" position. See 240.33 and 404.6(C). Figure 240–45

Circuit Breaker
Indicating On or Off
240.81

VIOLATION

Circuit breakers must indicate whether they're in the "off" or "on" position. When the handle is operated vertically, the "up" position of the handle must be the "on" position.

Copyright 2014, www.MikeHolt.com

Figure 240–45

Circuit Breaker - Interrupting Rating
240.83(C)

DANGER
5,000 AIC Rating

OKAY
22,000 AIC Rating

Copyright 2014
www.MikeHolt.com

Circuit breakers have an interrupting rating of 5,000A unless marked otherwise.

16,000A Fault Current

CAUTION: Overcurrent devices must have an interrupting rating not less than the nominal circuit voltage and the current that's available at the line terminals of the equipment [110.9].

Figure 240–46

240.82 Nontamperable

A circuit breaker must be designed so that any alteration of its trip point (calibration) or the time required for its operation requires dismantling of the device or breaking of a seal for other than intended adjustments.

240.83 Markings

(A) Durable and Visible. Circuit breakers must be marked with their ampere rating in a manner that's durable and visible after installation. Such marking is permitted to be made visible by removal of a trim or cover.

(C) Interrupting Rating. Circuit breakers have an interrupting rating of 5,000A unless marked otherwise.

⚠ **WARNING:** *Take care to ensure the circuit breaker has an interrupting rating sufficient for the short-circuit current available at the line terminals of the equipment. Using a circuit breaker with an inadequate interrupting current rating can cause equipment to be destroyed from a line-to-line or ground fault, and result in death or serious injury. See 110.9 for more details.* Figure 240–46

(D) Used as Switches. Circuit breakers used to switch 120V or 277V fluorescent lighting circuits must be listed and marked "SWD" or "HID." Circuit breakers used to switch high-intensity discharge lighting circuits must be listed and marked "HID." Figure 240–47

Circuit Breakers Used as Switches
240.83(D)

HID
Breaker

SWD
Breaker

Circuit breakers used to switch 120V or 277V fluorescent lighting circuits must be listed and marked "SWD" or "HID." Circuit breakers used to switch high-intensity discharge lighting circuits must be listed and marked "HID."

Copyright 2014, www.MikeHolt.com

Figure 240–47

Author's Comment:

■ This rule applies only when the circuit breaker is used as the switch. If a general-use snap switch or contactor is used to control the lighting, this rule doesn't apply.

■ UL 489, *Standard for Molded Case Circuit Breakers*, permits "HID" breakers to be rated up to 50A, whereas an "SWD" breaker can only be rated up to 20A. The tests for "HID" breakers include an endurance test at 75 percent power factor, whereas "SWD" breakers are endurance-tested at 100 percent power factor. The contacts and the spring of an "HID" breaker are of a heavier-duty material to dissipate the increased heat caused by the increased current flow in the circuit, because the "HID" luminaire takes a minute or two to ignite the lamp.

(E) Voltage Markings. Circuit breakers must be marked with a voltage rating that corresponds with their interrupting rating. See 240.85.

240.85 Applications

Straight Voltage Rating. A circuit breaker with a straight voltage rating, such as 240V or 480V, is permitted on a circuit where the nominal voltage between any two conductors (line-to-neutral or line-to-line) doesn't exceed the circuit breaker's voltage rating. Figures 240–48 and 240–49

Figure 240–49

Slash Voltage Rating. A circuit breaker with a slash rating, such as 120/240V or 277/480V, is permitted on a solidly grounded system where the nominal voltage of any one conductor to ground doesn't exceed the lower of the two values, and the nominal voltage between any two conductors doesn't exceed the higher value. Figure 240–50

Figure 240–48

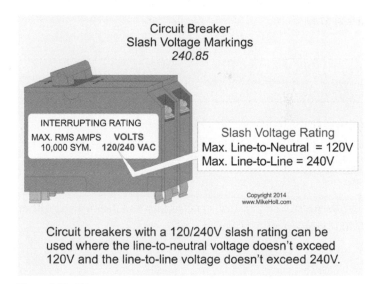

Figure 240–50

⚠️ **CAUTION:** *A 120/240V slash circuit breaker must not be used on the high leg of a solidly grounded 4-wire, three-phase, 120/240V delta-connected system, because the line-to-ground voltage of the high leg is 208V, which exceeds the 120V line-to-ground voltage rating of the breaker.* Figure 240–51

Note: When installing circuit breakers on corner-grounded delta systems, consideration needs to be given to the circuit breakers' individual pole-interrupting capability.

Figure 240–51

ARTICLE 250

GROUNDING AND BONDING

Introduction to Article 250—Grounding and Bonding

No other article can match Article 250 for misapplication, violation, and misinterpretation. Terminology used in this article has been a source for much confusion, but that has improved during the last few *NEC* revisions. It's very important to understand the difference between grounding and bonding in order to correctly apply the provisions of Article 250. Pay careful attention to the definitions that apply to grounding and bonding both here and in Article 100 as you begin the study of this important article. Article 250 covers the grounding requirements for providing a path to the earth to reduce overvoltage from lightning, and the bonding requirements for a low-impedance fault current path back to the source of the electrical supply to facilitate the operation of overcurrent devices in the event of a ground fault.

Over the past several *Code* cycles, this article was extensively revised to organize it better and make it easier to understand and implement. It's arranged in a logical manner, so it's a good idea to just read through Article 250 to get a big picture view—after you review the definitions. Next, study the article closely so you understand the details. The illustrations will help you understand the key points.

Part I. General

250.1 Scope

Article 250 contains the following grounding and bonding requirements:

(1) What systems and equipment are required to be grounded.

(3) Location of grounding connections.

(4) Types of electrodes and sizes of grounding and bonding conductors.

(5) Methods of grounding and bonding.

250.2 Definition

Bonding Jumper, Supply-Side. The conductor on the supply side of the service or separately derived system overcurrent protection device that ensures electrical conductivity between metal parts and the grounded conductor. Figures 250–1 and 250–2

250.4 General Requirements for Grounding and Bonding

 Scan this QR code for a video of this *Code* rule. See page xix for information on how to use the QR codes.

(A) Solidly Grounded Systems.

(1) Electrical System Grounding. Electrical power systems are grounded (connected to the earth) to limit the voltage induced by lightning, line surges, or unintentional contact by higher-voltage lines. Figure 250–3

Bonding Jumper, Supply-Side - Service
250.2 Definition

Supply-Side
Bonding Jumper

The conductor on the supply side of the service overcurrent protection device that ensures the required electrical conductivity between metal parts required to be connected.

Figure 250–1

Electrical System Grounding
250.4(A)(1)

Electrical power systems are grounded (connected to the earth) to limit the voltage induced by lightning, line surges, or unintentional contact by higher-voltage lines.

Figure 250–3

Bonding Jumper, Supply-Side - SDS
250.2 Definition

The conductor on the supply side of the separately derived system overcurrent protection device that ensures the required electrical conductivity between metal parts required to be electrically connected.

System Bonding Jumper

Figure 250–2

Electrical System Grounding
250.4(A)(1)

Solidly Grounded System

System grounding helps reduce fires in buildings as well as voltage stress on electrical insulation, thereby ensuring longer insulation life for motors, transformers, and other system components.

Figure 250–4

Author's Comment:

▪ System grounding helps reduce fires in buildings as well as voltage stress on electrical insulation, thereby ensuring longer insulation life for motors, transformers, and other system components. Figure 250–4

Note: To limit imposed voltage, the grounding electrode conductors shouldn't be any longer than necessary and unnecessary bends and loops should be avoided. Figure 250–5

(2) Equipment Grounding. Metal parts of electrical equipment are grounded to reduce arcing within the buildings/structures from induced voltage from indirect lightning strikes. Figure 250–6

⚠️ **DANGER:** *Failure to ground metal parts to earth can result in induced voltage on metal parts from an indirect lightning strike seeking a path to the earth within the building—possibly resulting in a fire and/or electric shock from a sideflash.* Figure 250–7

Figure 250–5

Figure 250–7

Figure 250–6

DANGER: *Because the contact resistance of an electrode to the earth is so high, very little fault current returns to the power supply if the earth is the only fault current return path. Result—the circuit overcurrent device won't open and clear the ground fault, and all metal parts associated with the electrical installation, metal piping, and structural building steel will become and remain energized.* Figure 250–8

Figure 250–8

Author's Comment:

■ Grounding metal parts helps drain off static electricity charges before flashover potential is reached. Static grounding is often used in areas where the discharge (arcing) of the voltage buildup (static) can cause dangerous or undesirable conditions [500.4 Note 3].

(3) Equipment Bonding. Metal parts of electrical raceways, cables, enclosures, and equipment must be connected to the supply source via an effective ground-fault current path. Figure 250–9

Figure 250–9

Author's Comment:

■ To quickly remove dangerous voltage on metal parts from a ground fault, the effective ground-fault current path must have sufficiently low impedance to the source so that fault current will quickly rise to a level that'll open the branch-circuit overcurrent device. Figure 250–10

Figure 250–10

■ The time it takes for an overcurrent device to open is inversely proportional to the magnitude of the fault current. This means the higher the ground-fault current value, the less time it'll take for the overcurrent device to open and clear the fault. For example, a 20A circuit with an overload of 40A (two times the 20A rating) takes 25 to 150 seconds to open the circuit overcurrent device. At 100A (five times the 20A rating) the 20A breaker trips in 5 to 20 seconds.

(4) Bonding Conductive Materials. Electrically conductive materials likely to become energized, such as metal water piping systems, metal sprinkler piping, metal gas piping, and other metal-piping systems, as well as exposed structural steel members, must be connected to the supply source via an effective ground-fault current path. Figure 250–11

Figure 250–11

Author's Comment:

■ The phrase "likely to become energized" is subject to interpretation by the authority having jurisdiction.

(5) Effective Ground-Fault Current Path. Metal parts of electrical raceways, cables, enclosures, or equipment must be bonded together and to the supply source in a manner that creates a low-impedance path for ground-fault current that facilitates the operation of the circuit overcurrent device. Figure 250–12

Effective Ground-Fault Current Path
250.4(A)(5)

Effective Ground-Fault
Current Path

Metal parts of electrical equipment must be
bonded to the supply source in a manner that
creates a low-impedance path for ground-fault
current to open the circuit overcurrent device.

Figure 250–12

Author's Comment:

- To ensure a low-impedance ground-fault current path, all circuit conductors must be grouped together in the same raceway, cable, or trench [300.3(B), 300.5(I), and 300.20(A)]. Figure 250–13

All Conductors Must be Grouped
300.3(B)

VIOLATION
Conductor Must be Inside Raceway

To help ensure a low-impedance effective ground-fault
path, all circuit conductors must be grouped together in
the same raceway, cable, or trench [300.5(I), 300.20(A)].

Figure 250–13

Because the earth isn't suitable to serve as the required effective ground-fault current path, an equipment grounding conductor is required to be installed with all circuits. Figure 250–14

Effective Ground-Fault Current Path
250.4(A)(5)

Because the earth isn't suitable to
serve as the required effective ground-
fault current path, an equipment
grounding conductor is required to be
installed with all circuits.

A ground rod serves no purpose,
but is permitted by 250.54.

Figure 250–14

Question: What's the maximum fault current that can flow through the earth to the power supply from a 120V ground fault to metal parts of a light pole without an equipment grounding conductor that's grounded (connected to the earth) via a rod having a contact resistance to the earth of 25 ohms? Figure 250–15

(a) 4.80A   (b) 20A   (c) 40A   (d) 100A

Answer: (a) 4.80A

$$I = E/R$$

I = 120V/25 ohms
I = 4.80A

Figure 250–15

Figure 250–17

⚠️ **DANGER:** *Because the contact resistance of an electrode to the earth is so high, very little fault current returns to the power supply if the earth is the only fault current return path.* Figure 250–16

Result—the circuit overcurrent device won't open and all metal parts associated with the electrical installation, metal piping, and structural building steel will become and remain energized. Figure 250–17

Figure 250–16

Earth Shells

According to ANSI/IEEE 142, *Recommended Practice for Grounding of Industrial and Commercial Power Systems* (Green Book) [4.1.1], the resistance of the soil outward from a rod is equal to the sum of the series resistances of the earth shells. The shell nearest the rod has the highest resistance and each successive shell has progressively larger areas and progressively lower resistances. Don't be concerned if you don't understand this statement; just review the table below. Figure 250–18

Figure 250–18

Distance from Rod	Soil Contact Resistance
1 ft (Shell 1)	68% of total contact resistance
3 ft (Shells 1 and 2)	75% of total contact resistance
5 ft (Shells 1, 2, and 3)	86% of total contact resistance

Since voltage is directly proportional to resistance, the voltage gradient of the earth around an energized rod will be as follows, assuming a 120V ground fault:

Distance from Rod	Soil Contact Resistance	Voltage Gradient
1 ft (Shell 1)	68%	82V
3 ft (Shells 1 and 2)	75%	90V
5 ft (Shells 1, 2, and 3)	86%	103V

(B) Ungrounded Systems.

Author's Comment:

- Ungrounded systems are those systems with no connection to the ground or to a conductive body that extends the ground connection [Article 100]. **Figure 250–19**

Figure 250–19

(1) Equipment Grounding. Metal parts of electrical equipment are grounded (connected to the earth) to reduce induced voltage on metal parts from lightning so as to prevent fires from an arc within the buildings. Figure 250–20

Figure 250–20

Author's Comment:

- Grounding metal parts helps drain off static electricity charges before an electric arc takes place (flashover potential). Static grounding is often used in areas where the discharge (arcing) of the voltage buildup (static) can cause dangerous or undesirable conditions [500.4 Note 3].

 CAUTION: *Connecting metal parts to the earth (grounding) serves no purpose in electrical shock protection.*

(2) Equipment Bonding. Metal parts of electrical raceways, cables, enclosures, or equipment must be bonded together in a manner that creates a low-impedance path for ground-fault current to facilitate the operation of the circuit overcurrent device.

The fault current path must be capable of safely carrying the maximum ground-fault current likely to be imposed on it from any point on the wiring system where a ground fault may occur to the electrical supply source.

(3) Bonding Conductive Materials. Conductive materials such as metal water piping systems, metal sprinkler piping, metal gas piping, and other metal-piping systems, as well as exposed structural steel members likely to become energized must be bonded together in a manner that creates a low-impedance fault current path that's capable of carrying the maximum fault current likely to be imposed on it. Figure 250–21

Figure 250–21

Author's Comment:

- The phrase "likely to become energized" is subject to interpretation by the authority having jurisdiction.

(4) Fault Current Path. Electrical equipment, wiring, and other electrically conductive material likely to become energized must be installed in a manner that creates a low-impedance fault current path to facilitate the operation of overcurrent devices should a second ground fault from a different phase occur. Figure 250–22

Author's Comment:

- A single ground fault can't be cleared on an ungrounded system because there's no low-impedance fault current path to the power source. The first ground fault simply grounds the system and initiates the ground detector. However, a second ground fault on a different phase results in a line-to-line short circuit between the two ground faults. The

Figure 250–22

conductive path, between the ground faults, provides the low-impedance fault current path necessary so the overcurrent device will open.

250.6 Objectionable Current

 Scan this QR code for a video of this *Code* rule. See page xix for information on how to use the QR codes.

(A) Preventing Objectionable Current. To prevent a fire, electric shock, or improper operation of circuit overcurrent devices or electronic equipment, electrical systems and equipment must be installed in a manner that prevents objectionable neutral current from flowing on metal parts. Figure 250–23

(C) Temporary Currents Not Classified as Objectionable Currents. Temporary currents from abnormal conditions, such as ground faults, aren't to be classified as objectionable current. Figure 250–24

(D) Limitations to Permissible Alterations. Currents that introduce noise or data errors in electronic equipment aren't considered objectionable currents for the purposes of this section. Circuits that supply electronic equipment must be connected to an equipment grounding conductor.

Objectionable Current
250.6(A)

To prevent a fire, electric shock, or improper operation of circuit overcurrent devices or electronic equipment, electrical systems and equipment must be installed in a manner that prevents objectionable neutral current from flowing on metal parts.

Copyright 2014, www.MikeHolt.com

Figure 250–23

Objectionable Current
250.6(C)

The overcurrent device opens to remove dangerous voltage.

Ground Fault

120V

20A

600 Amps

120V Load

SBJ

SSBJ

EGC

Temporary currents from ground faults aren't classified as objectionable current.

Copyright 2014, www.MikeHolt.com

Figure 250–24

Objectionable Current

Objectionable neutral current occurs because of improper neutral-to-case connections or wiring errors that violate 250.142(B).

Improper Neutral-to-Case Connection [250.142]

Panelboards. Objectionable neutral current will flow on metal parts and the equipment grounding conductor when the neutral conductor is connected to the metal case of a panelboard on the load side of service equipment. Figure 250–25

Objectionable Current
Improper Neutral Connection

Service

Panelboard

Objectionable Current

VIOLATION [250.24(A)(5)]
A neutral-to-case connection on the load side of the service equipment.

Objectionable neutral current will flow on the equipment grounding conductor when the neutral conductor is connected to the metal case of a panelboard on the load side of service equipment.

Copyright 2014, www.MikeHolt.com

Figure 250–25

Separately Derived Systems. Objectionable neutral current will flow on metal parts if the neutral conductor is connected to the circuit equipment grounding conductor on the load side of the system bonding jumper for a separately derived system. Figure 250–26

Objectionable Current
Improper Neutral Connection

Neutral Current

VIOLATION
A neutral-to-case connection at both the transformer and the panel creates a parallel path for neutral current.

Objectionable Current

Neutral Current

Copyright 2014 www.MikeHolt.com

Figure 250–26

Generator. Objectionable neutral current will flow on metal parts and the equipment grounding conductor if a generator is connected to a transfer switch with a solidly connected neutral and a neutral-to-case connection is made at the generator. Figure 250–27

Figure 250–27

Figure 250–29

Disconnects. Objectionable neutral current will flow on metal parts and the equipment grounding conductor when the neutral conductor is connected to the metal case of a disconnecting means that's not part of the service equipment. Figure 250–28

- A 230V time-clock motor is replaced with a 115V time-clock motor, and the circuit equipment grounding conductor is used for neutral return current.

- A 115V water filter is wired to a 240V well-pump motor circuit, and the circuit equipment grounding conductor is used for neutral return current. Figure 250–30

Figure 250–28

Figure 250–30

Wiring Errors. Objectionable neutral current will flow on metal parts and equipment grounding conductors when the neutral conductor from one system is used as the neutral conductor for a different system. Figure 250–29

Objectionable neutral current will flow on the equipment grounding conductor when the circuit equipment grounding conductor is used as a neutral conductor such as where:

- The circuit equipment grounding conductor is used for neutral return current. Figure 250–31

Figure 250–31

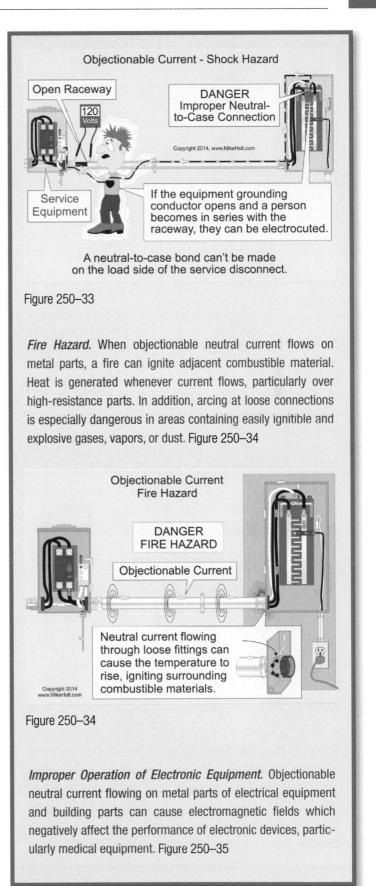

Figure 250–33

Fire Hazard. When objectionable neutral current flows on metal parts, a fire can ignite adjacent combustible material. Heat is generated whenever current flows, particularly over high-resistance parts. In addition, arcing at loose connections is especially dangerous in areas containing easily ignitible and explosive gases, vapors, or dust. Figure 250–34

Dangers of Objectionable Current

Objectionable neutral current on metal parts can cause electric shock, fires, and improper operation of electronic equipment and overcurrent devices such as GFPs, GFCIs, and AFCIs.

Shock Hazard. When objectionable neutral current flows on metal parts or the equipment grounding conductor, electric shock and even death can occur from the elevated voltage on those metal parts. Figures 250–32 and 250–33

Figure 250–32

Improper Operation of Electronic Equipment. Objectionable neutral current flowing on metal parts of electrical equipment and building parts can cause electromagnetic fields which negatively affect the performance of electronic devices, particularly medical equipment. Figure 250–35

Figure 250–34

Figure 250–35

For more information, visit www.MikeHolt.com, click on the "Technical Link," and then on "Power Quality."

When a solidly grounded system is properly bonded, the voltage of all metal parts to the earth and to each other will be zero. Figure 250–36

Figure 250–36

When objectionable neutral current travels on metal parts and equipment grounding conductors because of the improper bonding of the neutral to metal parts, a difference of potential will exist between all metal parts. This situation can cause some electronic equipment to operate improperly. Figure 250–37

Figure 250–37

Operation of Overcurrent Devices. When objectionable neutral current travels on metal parts, tripping of electronic overcurrent devices equipped with ground-fault protection can occur because some neutral current flows on the circuit equipment grounding conductor instead of the neutral conductor.

250.8 Termination of Grounding and Bonding Conductors

(A) Permitted Methods. Equipment grounding conductors, grounding electrode conductors, and bonding jumpers must terminate in one or more of the following methods:

(1) Listed pressure connectors

(2) Terminal bars

(3) Pressure connectors listed for grounding and bonding

(4) Exothermic welding

(5) Machine screws that engage at least two threads or are secured with a nut Figure 250–38

(6) Self-tapping machine screws that engage at least two threads

(7) Connections that are part of a listed assembly

(8) Other listed means

Figure 250–38

Author's Comment:

■ Grounding and bonding fittings can be buried or encased in concrete if they're installed in accordance with 250.53(G), 250.68(A) Ex 1, and 250.70.

250.12 Clean Surfaces

Nonconductive coatings, such as paint, must be removed to ensure good electrical continuity, or the termination fittings must be designed so as to make such removal unnecessary [250.53(A) and 250.96(A)].

Author's Comment:

■ Tarnish on copper water pipe needn't be removed before making a termination.

(B) Methods Not Permitted. Connection devices or fittings that depend solely on solder aren't allowed.

Part II. System Grounding and Bonding

250.10 Protection of Fittings

250.20 Systems Required to be Grounded

Where subject to physical damage, grounding and bonding fittings must be protected by enclosing the fittings in metal, wood, or an equivalent protective covering. Figure 250–39

(A) Systems Below 50V. Systems operating below 50V aren't required to be grounded or bonded in accordance with 250.30 unless the transformer's primary supply is from: Figure 250–40

Figure 250–39

Figure 250–40

(1) A 277V or 480V system.

(2) An ungrounded system.

(B) Systems Over 50V. The following systems must be grounded (connected to the earth):

(1) Single-phase systems where the neutral conductor is used as a circuit conductor. Figure 250–41

Figure 250–41

(2) Three-phase, wye-connected systems where the neutral conductor is used as a circuit conductor. Figure 250–42

Figure 250–42

(3) Three-phase, high-leg delta-connected systems where the neutral conductor is used as a circuit conductor. Figure 250–43

Figure 250–43

250.21 Ungrounded Systems

(B) Ground Detectors.

(1) Systems that aren't required to be grounded in accordance with 250.20(B) [250.21(A)(4)] must have ground detectors installed.

(2) The ground detection sensing equipment must be connected as close as practicable to where the system receives its supply.

(C) Marking. Ungrounded systems must be legibly marked "Caution Ungrounded System Operating — _____ Volts Between Conductors" at the source or first disconnecting means of the system, with sufficient durability to withstand the environment involved. Figure 250–44

250.24 Service Equipment— Grounding and Bonding

(A) Grounded System. Service equipment supplied from a grounded system must have the grounding electrode conductor terminate in accordance with (1) through (5).

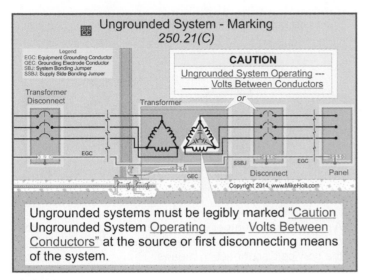

Figure 250–44

(1) Grounding Location. A grounding electrode conductor must connect the service neutral conductor to the grounding electrode at any accessible location, from the load end of the <u>overhead service conductors,</u> service drop<u>, underground service conductors,</u> or service lateral, up to and including the service disconnecting means. Figure 250–45

Figure 250–45

Author's Comment:

■ Some inspectors require the service neutral conductor to be grounded (connected to the earth) from the meter socket enclosure, while other inspectors insist that it be grounded

(connected to the earth) only from the service disconnect. Grounding at either location complies with this rule.

(4) Grounding Termination. When the service neutral conductor is connected to the service disconnecting means [250.24(B)] by a wire or busbar [250.28], the grounding electrode conductor is permitted to terminate to either the neutral terminal or the equipment grounding terminal within the service disconnect.

(5) Neutral-to-Case Connection. A neutral-to-case connection isn't permitted on the load side of service equipment, except as permitted by 250.142(B). Figure 250–46

Figure 250–46

Author's Comment:

■ If a neutral-to-case connection is made on the load side of service equipment, dangerous objectionable neutral current will flow on conductive metal parts of electrical equipment [250.6(A)]. Objectionable neutral current on metal parts of electrical equipment can cause electric shock and even death from ventricular fibrillation, as well as a fire. Figures 250–47 and 250–48

(B) Main Bonding Jumper. A main bonding jumper [250.28] is required to connect the neutral conductor to the equipment grounding conductor within the service disconnecting means. Figures 250–49 and 250–50

Load Side Neutral-to-Case Connection
250.24(A)(5)

Open Raceway

120 Volts

DANGER
Improper Neutral-
to-Case Connection

Service
Equipment

If the equipment grounding
conductor opens, a person
who is in series with the
raceway can be electrocuted.

A neutral-to-case bond can't be made
on the load side of the service disconnect.

Copyright 2014, www.MikeHolt.com

Figure 250–47

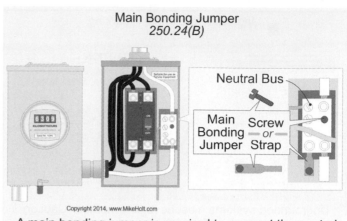

Main Bonding Jumper
250.24(B)

Neutral Bus

Main
Bonding
Jumper

Screw
or
Strap

Copyright 2014, www.MikeHolt.com

A main bonding jumper is required to connect the neutral
conductor to the equipment grounding conductor within
the service disconnecting means.

Figure 250–49

Load Side Neutral-to-Case Connection
250.24(A)(5)

DANGER
FIRE HAZARD

Objectionable Current

Copyright 2014
www.MikeHolt.com

Neutral current flowing
through loose fittings can
cause the temperature to
rise, igniting surrounding
combustible materials.

Figure 250–48

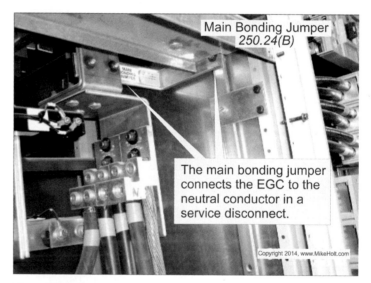

Main Bonding Jumper
250.24(B)

The main bonding jumper
connects the EGC to the
neutral conductor in a
service disconnect.

Copyright 2014, www.MikeHolt.com

Figure 250–50

(C) Neutral Conductor Brought to Service Equipment. A service
neutral conductor must be run from the electric utility supply with the
ungrounded conductors and terminate to the service disconnect neutral terminal. A main bonding jumper [250.24(B)] must be installed
between the service neutral terminal and the service disconnecting
means enclosure [250.28]. Figures 250–51 and 250–52

Author's Comment:

■ The service neutral conductor provides the effective
ground-fault current path to the power supply to ensure
that dangerous voltage from a ground fault will be quickly
removed by opening the overcurrent device [250.4(A)(3) and
250.4(A)(5)]. Figure 250–53

Figure 250–51

Figure 250–53

Figure 250–52

Figure 250–54

DANGER: *Dangerous voltage from a ground fault won't be removed from metal parts, metal piping, and structural steel if the service disconnecting means enclosure isn't connected to the service neutral conductor. This is because the contact resistance of a grounding electrode to the earth is so great that insufficient fault current returns to the power supply if the earth is the only fault current return path to open the circuit overcurrent device.* Figure 250–54

Author's Comment:

■ If the neutral conductor is opened, dangerous voltage will be present on metal parts under normal conditions, providing the potential for electric shock. If the earth's ground resistance is 25 ohms and the load's resistance is 25 ohms, the voltage drop across each of these resistors will be half of the voltage source. Since the neutral is connected to the service disconnect, all metal parts will be elevated to 60V above the earth's potential for a 120/240V system. **Figure 250–55**

Figure 250–55

- To determine the actual voltage on the metal parts from an open service neutral conductor, you need to do some complex calculations. Visit www.MikeHolt.com and go to the "Free Resources" link to download a spreadsheet for this purpose.

(1) Single Raceway. Because the service neutral conductor serves as the effective ground-fault current path to the source for ground faults, the neutral conductor must be sized so it can safely carry the maximum fault current likely to be imposed on it [110.10 and 250.4(A)(5)]. This is accomplished by sizing the neutral conductor not smaller than specified in Table 250.102(C)(1), based on the cross-sectional area of the largest ungrounded service conductor. Figure 250–56

Figure 250–56

Author's Comment:

- In addition, the neutral conductors must have the capacity to carry the maximum unbalanced neutral current in accordance with 220.61.

Question: *What's the minimum size service neutral conductor required where the ungrounded service conductors are 350 kcmil and the maximum unbalanced load is 100A?* **Figure 250–57**

(a) 3 AWG   *(b) 2 AWG*   *(c) 1 AWG*   *(d) 1/0 AWG*

Answer: *(b) 2 AWG [Table 250.102(C)(1)]*

The unbalanced load of 100A requires a 3 AWG service neutral conductor, which is rated 100A at 75°C in accordance with Table 310.15(B)(16) [220.61], but the neutral conductor can be smaller than 2 AWG to carry fault current, based on the 350 kcmil ungrounded conductors [Table 250.102(C)(1)].

Figure 250–57

(2) Parallel Conductors in Two or More Raceways. If service conductors are paralleled in two or more raceways, a neutral conductor must be installed in each of the parallel raceways. The size of the neutral conductor in each raceway must not be smaller than specified in Table 250.102(C)(1), based on the cross-sectional area of the largest ungrounded service conductor in each raceway. In no case can the neutral conductor in each parallel set be sized smaller than 1/0 AWG [310.10(H)(1)].

Author's Comment:

- In addition, the neutral conductors must have the capacity to carry the maximum unbalanced neutral current in accordance with 220.61.

Question: *What's the minimum size service neutral conductor required for each of two raceways, where the ungrounded service conductors in each of the raceways are 350 kcmil and the maximum unbalanced load is 100A?* Figure 250–58

(a) 3 AWG   *(b) 2 AWG*   *(c) 1 AWG*   *(d) 1/0 AWG*

Answer: *(d) 1/0 AWG per raceway [Table 250.102(C)(1) and 310.10(H)]*

The unbalanced load of 50A in each raceway requires an 8 AWG service neutral conductor, which is rated 50A at 75°C in accordance with Table 310.15(B)(16) [220.61]. Also, Table 250.102(C)(1) requires a minimum of 2 AWG in each raceway, however, 1/0 AWG is the smallest conductor permitted to be parallel [310.10(H) and Table 310.15(B)(16)].

Service Neutral Size
Parallel Conductors in Two or More Raceways
250.24(C)(2)

350 kcmil ungrounded service conductors are in each raceway.
Minimum 1/0 AWG Service Neutral per Raceway

Service Equipment

Copyright 2014, www.MikeHolt.com

The service neutral conductor in each raceway must not be smaller than specified in Table 250.102(C)(1) based on the size of the largest ungrounded conductor in each raceway, but can't be smaller than 1/0 AWG [310.10(H)].

Figure 250–58

(D) Grounding Electrode Conductor. A grounding electrode conductor, sized in accordance with 250.66 based on the area of the ungrounded service conductor, must connect the neutral conductor and metal parts of service equipment enclosures to a grounding electrode in accordance with Part III of Article 250.

Question: *What's the minimum size grounding electrode conductor for a 400A service where the ungrounded service conductors are sized at 500 kcmil?* Figure 250–59

(a) 3 AWG   *(b) 2 AWG*   *(c) 1 AWG*   *(d) 1/0 AWG*

Answer: *(d) 1/0 AWG [Table 250.66]*

Grounding Electrode Conductor Sizing
250.24(D)

400A Service

500 kcmil Service Conductors

1/0 AWG Grounding Electrode Conductor [Table 250.66]

Copyright 2014 www.MikeHolt.com

Figure 250–59

Author's Comment:

- If the grounding electrode conductor is connected to a rod(s), the portion of the conductor that's the sole connection to the rod(s) isn't required to be larger than 6 AWG copper [250.66(A)]. Figure 250–60

- If the grounding electrode conductor is connected to a concrete-encased electrode(s), the portion of the conductor that's the sole connection to the concrete-encased electrode(s) isn't required to be larger than 4 AWG copper [250.66(B)]. Figure 250–61

Figure 250–60

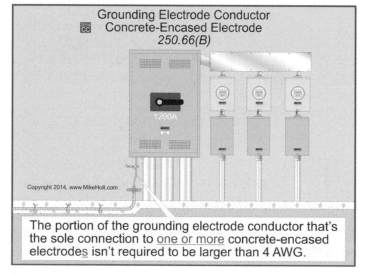

Figure 250–61

250.28 Main Bonding Jumper and System Bonding Jumper

Main and system bonding jumpers must be installed as follows:

Author's Comment:

■ **Main Bonding Jumper.** At service equipment, a main bonding jumper must be installed to electrically connect the neutral conductor to the service disconnect enclosure [250.24(B)]. **Figure 250–62**

Figure 250–62

DANGER: *Metal parts of the electrical installation, as well as metal piping and structural steel, will become and remain energized with dangerous voltage from a ground fault if a main bonding jumper isn't installed at service equipment.* Figure 250–63

Figure 250–63

■ **System Bonding Jumper.** A system bonding jumper must be installed between the neutral terminal of a separately derived system and the circuit equipment grounding conductor [Article 100 Bonding Jumper, System and 250.30(A)(1)].

DANGER: *Metal parts of the electrical installation, as well as metal piping and structural steel, will become and remain energized with dangerous voltage from a ground fault if a system bonding jumper isn't installed for a separately derived system.* Figure 250–64

Figure 250–64

(A) Material. The bonding jumper can be a wire, bus, or screw.

(B) Construction. If the bonding jumper is a screw, it must be identified with a green finish visible with the screw installed.

(C) Attachment. Main and system bonding jumpers must terminate by one of the following means in accordance with 250.8(A):

- Listed pressure connectors
- Terminal bars
- Pressure connectors listed as grounding and bonding equipment
- Exothermic welding
- Machine screw-type fasteners that engage not less than two threads or are secured with a nut
- Thread-forming machine screws that engage not less than two threads in the enclosure
- Connections that are part of a listed assembly
- Other listed means

(D) Size.

(1) Main and system bonding jumpers must be sized not smaller than the sizes shown in Table 250.102(C)(1). Figure 250–65

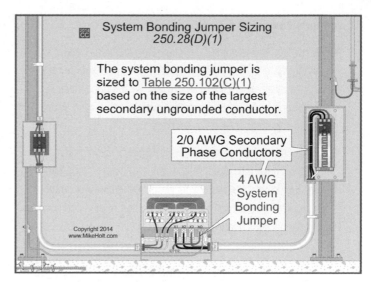

Figure 250–65

250.30 Separately Derived Systems— Grounding and Bonding

Note 1: An alternate alternating-current power source such as an on-site generator isn't a separately derived system if the neutral conductor is solidly interconnected to a service-supplied system neutral conductor. An example is a generator provided with a transfer switch that includes a neutral conductor that's not switched. Figure 250–66

Figure 250–66

Author's Comment:

- According to Article 100, a separately derived system is a wiring system whose power is derived from a source, other than a utility, where there's no direct electrical connection to the supply conductors of another system, other than through grounding and bonding connections.

- Transformers are separately derived when the primary conductors have no direct electrical connection from circuit conductors of one system to circuit conductors of another system, other than connections through grounding and bonding connections. Figure 250–67

Figure 250–67

- A generator having transfer equipment that switches the neutral conductor, or one that has no neutral conductor at all, is a separately derived system and must be grounded and bonded in accordance with 250.30(A). Figure 250–68

Note 2: For nonseparately derived systems, see 445.13 for the minimum size neutral conductors necessary to carry fault current. Figures 250–69 and 250–70

(A) Grounded Systems. Separately derived systems must be grounded and bonded in accordance with (A)(1) through (A)(8).

A neutral-to-case connection must not be made on the load side of the system bonding jumper, except as permitted by 250.142(B).

Figure 250–68

Figure 250–69

(1) System Bonding Jumper. A system bonding jumper must be installed at the same location where the grounding electrode conductor terminates to the neutral terminal of the separately derived system; either at the separately derived system or the system disconnecting means, but not at both locations [250.30(A)(5)].

(a) System Bonding Jumper at Source. Where the system bonding jumper is installed at the source of the separately derived system, the system bonding jumper must connect the neutral conductor of the derived system to the metal enclosure of the derived system. Figure 250–71

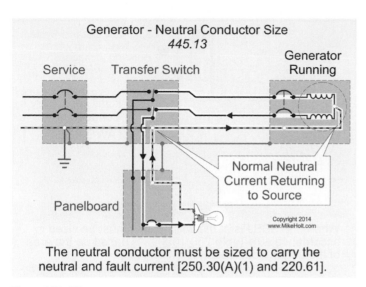

Figure 250–70

The neutral conductor must be sized to carry the neutral and fault current [250.30(A)(1) and 220.61].

Where the system bonding jumper is installed at the first disconnect, the system bonding jumper must connect the neutral conductor of the derived system to the metal disconnecting means enclosure.

Figure 250–72

Where the system bonding jumper is installed at the source, the system bonding jumper must connect the neutral conductor of the derived system to the metal enclosure of the derived system.

Figure 250–71

(b) System Bonding Jumper at Disconnecting Means. Where the system bonding jumper is installed at the first disconnecting means of a separately derived system, the system bonding jumper must connect the neutral conductor of the derived system to the metal disconnecting means enclosure. Figure 250–72

Author's Comment:

■ A system bonding jumper is a conductor, screw, or strap that bonds the metal parts of a separately derived system to the system neutral point [Article 100 Bonding Jumper, System], and it's sized to Table 250.102(C)(1) in accordance with 250.28(D).

DANGER: *During a ground fault, metal parts of electrical equipment, as well as metal piping and structural steel, will become and remain energized providing the potential for electric shock and fire if the system bonding jumper isn't installed.* Figure 250–73

DANGER: If a system bonding jumper isn't installed, metal parts remain energized providing the potential for electric shock.

Figure 250–73

⚠️ **CAUTION:** *Dangerous objectionable neutral current will flow on conductive metal parts of electrical equipment as well as metal piping and structural steel, in violation of 250.6(A), if more than one system bonding jumper is installed, or if it's not located where the grounding electrode conductor terminates to the neutral conductor.* Figure 250–74

Figure 250–74

(2) Supply-Side Bonding Jumper to Disconnect. A supply-side bonding jumper (nonflexible metal raceway or wire) must be run from the derived system to the derived system disconnecting means.

(a) If the supply-side bonding jumper is of the wire type, it must be sized in accordance with Table 250.102(C)(1), based on the area of the largest ungrounded derived system conductor in the raceway or cable.

Question: What size supply-side bonding jumper is required for flexible metal conduit containing 300 kcmil secondary conductors? Figure 250–75

(a) 3 AWG   (b) 2 AWG   (c) 1 AWG   (d) 1/0 AWG

Answer: *(b) 2 AWG [Table 250.102(C)(1)]*

Where the SSBJ is of the wire type, it must be sized in accordance with Table 250.102(C)(1) based on the area of the ungrounded secondary conductor.

Figure 250–75

(3) System Bonding Jumper at Disconnect—Neutral Conductor Size. If the system bonding jumper is installed at the disconnecting means instead of at the source, the following requirements apply:

(a) Sizing for Single Raceway. The neutral conductor must be routed with the ungrounded conductors of the derived system to the disconnecting means and be sized not smaller than specified in Table 250.102(C)(1), based on the area of the ungrounded conductor of the derived system. Figure 250–76

The neutral conductor must be routed with the ungrounded conductors of the derived system to the disconnecting means and be sized not smaller than specified in Table 250.102(C)(1).

Figure 250–76

(b) Parallel Conductors in Two or More Raceways. If the conductors from the derived system are installed in parallel in two or more raceways, the neutral conductor of the derived system in each raceway or cable must be sized not smaller than specified in Table 250.102(C)(1), based on the area of the largest ungrounded conductor of the derived system in the raceway or cable. In no case is the neutral conductor of the derived system permitted to be smaller than 1/0 AWG [310.10(H)].

Author's Comment:

- If the system bonding jumper is installed at the disconnecting means instead of at the source, a supply side bonding jumper must connect the metal parts of the separately derived system to the neutral conductor at the disconnecting means [250.30(A)(2)].

(4) Grounding Electrode. The grounding electrode for a separately derived system must be as near as practicable, and preferably in the same area where the system bonding jumper is installed and be one of the following: Figure 250–77

Figure 250–77

(1) Metal water pipe electrode, within 5 ft of the entry to the building [250.52(A)(1)].

(2) Metal building frame electrode [250.52(A)(2)].

Ex 1: If the water pipe or structural metal electrode aren't available, one of the following electrodes can be used:

- *A concrete-encased electrode encased by not less than 2 in. of concrete, located horizontally or vertically, and within that portion of concrete foundation or footing that's in direct contact with the earth [250.52(A)(3)].*

- *A ground ring electrode encircling the building, buried not less than 30 in. below grade, consisting of at least 20 ft of bare copper conductor not smaller than 2 AWG [250.52(A)(4) and 250.53(F)].*

- *A rod electrode having not less than 8 ft of contact with the soil meeting the requirements of 250.52(A)(5) and 250.53(G).*

- *Other metal underground systems, piping systems, or underground tanks [250.52(A)(8)].*

Note 1: Interior metal water piping in the area served by separately derived systems must be bonded to the separately derived system in accordance with 250.104(D).

(5) Grounding Electrode Conductor, Single Separately Derived System. The grounding electrode conductor must be sized in accordance with 250.66, based on the area of the largest ungrounded conductor of the derived system. A grounding electrode conductor must terminate to the neutral at the same point on the separately derived system where the system bonding jumper is connected. Figure 250–78

Figure 250–78

Author's Comment:

■ System grounding helps reduce fires in buildings as well as voltage stress on electrical insulation, thereby ensuring longer insulation life for motors, transformers, and other system components. Figure 250–79

Figure 250–79

■ To prevent objectionable neutral current from flowing [250.6] onto metal parts, the grounding electrode conductor must originate at the same point on the separately derived system where the system bonding jumper is connected [250.30(A)(1)].

Ex 1: The grounding electrode conductor is permitted to terminate to the equipment grounding terminal at the derived system or first system disconnecting means in accordance with 250.30(A)(1). Figure 250–80

Ex 3: Separately derived systems rated 1 kVA or less aren't required to be grounded (connected to the earth).

(6) Grounding Electrode Conductor, Multiple Separately Derived Systems. Where there are multiple separately derived systems, a grounding electrode conductor tap from each separately derived system to a common grounding electrode conductor is permitted. This connection is to be made at the same point on the separately derived system where the system bonding jumper is connected [250.30(A)(1)]. Figure 250–81

The GEC is permitted to terminate to the equipment grounding terminal at the derived system or first system disconnecting means in accordance with 250.30(A)(1).

Figure 250–80

Figure 250–81

Ex 1: If the system bonding jumper is a wire or busbar, the grounding electrode conductor tap can terminate to either the neutral terminal or the equipment grounding terminal, bar, or bus in accordance with 250.30(A)(1).

Ex 2: Separately derived systems rated 1 kVA or less aren't required to be grounded (connected to the earth).

(a) Common Grounding Electrode Conductor. The common grounding electrode conductor can be one of the following:

(1) A conductor not smaller than 3/0 AWG copper or 250 kcmil aluminum.

(2) The metal frame of the buildings that complies with 250.52(A)(2) or is connected to the grounding electrode system by a conductor not smaller than 3/0 AWG copper or 250 kcmil aluminum.

(b) Tap Conductor Size. Grounding electrode conductor taps must be sized in accordance with Table 250.66, based on the area of the largest ungrounded conductor of the given derived system.

(c) Connections. All tap connections to the common grounding electrode conductor must be made at an accessible location by one of the following methods:

(1) A connector listed as grounding and bonding equipment.

(2) Listed connections to aluminum or copper busbars not less than ¼ in. in depth x 2 in. in width

(3) Exothermic welding.

Grounding electrode conductor taps must be connected to the common grounding electrode conductor so the common grounding electrode conductor isn't spliced.

(7) Installation. The grounding electrode conductor must comply with the following:

- Be of copper where within 18 in. of the earth [250.64(A)].

- Be securely fastened to the surface on which it's carried [250.64(B)].

- Be adequately protected if exposed to physical damage [250.64(B)].

- Metal enclosures enclosing a grounding electrode conductor must be made electrically continuous from the point of attachment to cabinets or equipment to the grounding electrode [250.64(E)].

(8) Structural Steel and Metal Piping. To ensure dangerous voltage from a ground fault is removed quickly, structural steel and metal piping in the area served by a separately derived system must be connected to the neutral conductor at the separately derived system in accordance with 250.104(D).

(C) Outdoor Source. Separately derived systems located outside the building must have the grounding electrode connection made at the separately derived system location. Figure 250–82

Figure 250–82

250.32 Buildings Supplied by a Feeder

(A) Equipment Grounding Electrode. Building feeder disconnects must be connected to a grounding electrode to reduce induced voltages on the metal parts from nearby lightning strikes. Figure 250–83

Figure 250–83

Author's Comment:

- The *Code* prohibits the use of the earth to serve as an effective ground-fault current path [250.4(A)(5) and 250.4(B)(4)].

Ex: A grounding electrode is not required for a building disconnect supplied by a branch circuit. Figure 250–84

Figure 250–84

(B) Equipment Grounding Conductor.

(1) Building Supplied by a Feeder. To quickly clear a ground fault and remove dangerous voltage from metal parts, the building disconnecting means must be connected to the circuit equipment grounding conductor, of the type(s) described in 250.118. If the supply circuit equipment grounding conductor is of the wire type, it must be sized in accordance with 250.122, based on the rating of the overcurrent device. Figure 250–85

⚠️ **CAUTION:** *To prevent dangerous objectionable neutral current from flowing on metal parts [250.6(A)], the supply circuit neutral conductor isn't permitted to be connected to the remote building disconnecting means [250.142(B)].* Figure 250–86

To clear a ground fault and remove dangerous voltage from metal parts, the building disconnecting means must be connected to the circuit equipment grounding conductor.

Figure 250–85

The equipment grounding conductor and metal water pipe carry neutral current.

Figure 250–86

Ex 1: The neutral conductor can serve as the ground-fault return path for the building disconnecting means for existing installations in compliance with previous editions of the Code where there are no continuous metallic paths between buildings and structures, ground-fault protection of equipment isn't installed on the supply side of the circuit, and the neutral conductor is sized no smaller than the larger of:

(1) The maximum unbalanced neutral load in accordance with 220.61.

(2) The minimum equipment grounding conductor size in accordance with 250.122.

(2) Building Supplied by Separately Derived System.

(a) With Feeder Overcurrent Protection. If overcurrent protection is provided for the feeders from the separately derived system to the building, the supply conductors must contain an equipment grounding conductor in accordance with 250.32(B)(1).

(b) Without Feeder Overcurrent Protection. If overcurrent protection isn't provided for the feeder conductors supplying the building as permitted by 240.21(C)(4), grounding and bonded must be in accordance with 250.30(A). Figure 250–87

Figure 250–87

(E) Grounding Electrode Conductor Size. The grounding electrode conductor must terminate to the equipment grounding terminal of the disconnecting means (not neutral terminal), and it must be sized in accordance with 250.66, based on the conductor area of the ungrounded feeder conductor.

> **Question:** What size grounding electrode conductor is required for a building disconnect supplied with a 3/0 AWG feeder? Figure 250–88
>
> (a) 4 AWG   (b) 3 AWG   (c) 2 AWG   (d) 1 AWG
>
> **Answer:** (a) 4 AWG [Table 250.66]

Figure 250–88

Author's Comment:

- If the grounding electrode conductor is connected to a rod(s), the portion of the conductor that's the sole connection to the rod(s) isn't required to be larger than 6 AWG copper [250.66(A)]. If the grounding electrode conductor is connected to a concrete-encased electrode(s), the portion of the conductor that's the sole connection to the concrete-encased electrode(s) isn't required to be larger than 4 AWG copper [250.66(B)].

250.34 Generators—Portable and Vehicle-Mounted

(A) Portable Generators. A portable generator isn't required to be grounded (connected to the earth) if: Figure 250–89

(1) The generator only supplies equipment or receptacles mounted on the generator, and

(2) The metal parts of the generator and the receptacle grounding terminal are connected to the generator frame.

(B) Vehicle-Mounted Generators. A vehicle-mounted generator isn't required to be grounded (connected to the earth) if: Figure 250–90

(1) The generator frame is bonded to the vehicle frame,

Figure 250–89

Figure 250–91

Figure 250–90

(2) The generator only supplies equipment or receptacles mounted on the vehicle or generator, and

(3) The metal parts of the generator and the receptacle grounding terminal are connected to the generator frame.

250.35 Permanently Installed Generators

(A) Separately Derived System. If the generator is installed as a separately derived system, the system must be grounded (connected to the earth) and bonded in accordance with 250.30. Figure 250–91

250.36 High-Impedance Grounded Systems

High-impedance grounded systems are only permitted for three-phase systems where all of the following conditions are met: Figure 250–92

Figure 250–92

(1) Conditions of maintenance and supervision ensure that only qualified persons service the installation.

(2) Ground detectors are installed on the system [250.21(B)].

(3) Line-to-neutral loads aren't served.

Author's Comment:

- High-impedance grounded systems are generally referred to as "high-resistance grounded systems" in the industry.

(A) Grounding Impedance Location. To limit fault current to a very low value, high-impedance grounded systems must have a resistor installed between the neutral point of the derived system and the grounding electrode conductor. Figure 250–93

High-impedance grounded systems have a resistor installed between the neutral point of the derived system and the grounding electrode conductor.

Figure 250–93

Note: For more information on this topic see IEEE 142—*Recommended Practice for Grounding of Industrial and Commercial Power Systems* (Green Book).

Part III. Grounding Electrode System and Grounding Electrode Conductor

250.50 Grounding Electrode System

Any grounding electrode described in 250.52(A)(1) through (A)(7) that's present at a building must be bonded together to form the grounding electrode system. Figure 250–94

- Underground metal water pipe [250.52(A)(1)]
- Metal frame of the buildings [250.52(A)(2)]

The following grounding electrodes that are present must be connected together to form the grounding electrode system:
1. Metal underground water pipe
2. Metal frame of building/structure
3. Concrete-encased electrode (Ufer)
4. Ground ring
5. Ground rod
6. Other listed electrode

Figure 250–94

- Concrete-encased electrode [250.52(A)(3)]
- Ground ring [250.52(A)(4)]
- Rod [250.52(A)(5)]
- Other listed electrodes [250.52(A)(6)]
- Grounding plate [250.52(A)(7)]

Ex: Concrete-encased electrodes aren't required for existing buildings where the conductive steel reinforcing bars aren't accessible without chipping up the concrete. Figure 250–95

Concrete-encased electrodes aren't required for existing buildings or structures where the conductive steel reinforcing bars aren't accessible without chipping up the concrete.

Figure 250–95

Author's Comment:

- When a concrete-encased electrode is used at a building that doesn't have an underground metal water pipe electrode, no additional electrode is required. Figure 250–96

Figure 250–96

250.52 Grounding Electrode Types

(A) Electrodes Permitted for Grounding.

(1) Underground Metal Water Pipe Electrode. Underground metal water pipe in direct contact with the earth for 10 ft or more can serve as a grounding electrode. Figure 250–97

Author's Comment:

- Controversy about using metal underground water piping as a grounding electrode has existed since the early 1900s. The water industry believes that neutral current flowing on water piping corrodes the metal. For more information, contact the American Water Works Association about their report—*Effects of Electrical Grounding on Pipe Integrity and Shock Hazard*, Catalog No. 90702, 1.800.926.7337. Figure 250–98

(2) Metal Frame Electrode. The metal frame of a building can serve as a grounding electrode when it meets at least one of the following conditions:

Figure 250–97

Figure 250–98

(1) At least one structural metal member is in direct contact with the earth for 10 ft or more, with or without concrete encasement.

(2) The hold-down bolts securing the structural steel are connected to a concrete-encased electrode [250.52(A)(3)] by welding, exothermic welding, steel tie wires, or other approved means. Figure 250–99

(3) Concrete-Encased Electrode. Figure 250–100

(1) One or more electrically conductive steel reinforcing bars of not less than ½ in. diameter, mechanically connected together by steel tie wires, or other effective means to create a 20 ft or greater length can serve as a grounding electrode.

Figure 250–99

Figure 250–100

(2) Bare copper conductor not smaller than 4 AWG of 20 ft or greater length.

The reinforcing bars or bare copper conductor must be encased by at least 2 in. of concrete located horizontally of a concrete footing or vertically within a concrete foundation that's in direct contact with the earth can serve as a grounding electrode.

Where multiple concrete-encased electrodes are present at a building, only one is required to serve as a grounding electrode. Figure 250–101

Figure 250–101

Note: : Concrete separated from the earth because of insulation, vapor barriers, or similar items isn't considered to be in direct contract with the earth. Figure 250–102

Figure 250–102

Author's Comment:

■ The grounding electrode conductor to a concrete-encased grounding electrode isn't required to be larger than 4 AWG copper [250.66(B)].

■ The concrete-encased grounding electrode is also called a "Ufer Ground," named after a consultant working for the U.S. Army during World War II. The technique Mr. Ufer came up with was necessary because the site needing grounding had no underground water table and little rainfall. The desert site was a series of bomb storage vaults in the area of Flagstaff, Arizona. This type of grounding electrode generally offers the lowest ground resistance for the cost.

(4) Ground Ring Electrode. A ground ring consisting of at least 20 ft of bare copper conductor not smaller than 2 AWG buried in the earth encircling a building, can serve as a grounding electrode. Figure 250–103

Figure 250–103

Author's Comment:

■ The ground ring must be buried not less than 30 in. [250.53(F)], and the grounding electrode conductor to a ground ring isn't required to be larger than the ground ring conductor size [250.66(C)].

(5) Rod Electrode. Rod electrodes must have at less 8 ft in length in contact with the earth [250.53(G)].

(b) Rod-type electrodes must have a diameter of at least ⅝ in., unless listed. Figure 250–104

Figure 250–104

Author's Comment:

■ The grounding electrode conductor, if it's the sole connection to the rod(s), isn't required to be larger than 6 AWG copper [250.66(A)].

■ The diameter of a rod has an insignificant effect on the contact resistance of a rod(s) to the earth. However, larger diameter rods (¾ in. and 1 in.) are sometimes installed where mechanical strength is desired, or to compensate for the loss of the electrode's metal due to corrosion.

(6) Listed Electrode. Other listed grounding electrodes can serve as a grounding electrode.

(7) Ground Plate Electrode. A bare or conductively coated iron or steel plate with not less than ¼ in. of thickness, or a solid uncoated copper metal plate not less than 0.06 in. of thickness, with an exposed surface area of not less than 2 sq ft can serve as a grounding electrode.

(8) Metal Underground Piping Electrode. Metal underground piping and well casings can serve as a grounding electrode. Figure 250–105

Author's Comment:

■ The grounding electrode conductor to the metal underground system must be sized in accordance with Table 250.66.

(B) Not Permitted for Use as a Grounding Electrode.

(1) Underground metal gas-piping systems aren't permitted to be used as a grounding electrode. Figure 250–106

Figure 250–105

Figure 250–106

250.53 Grounding Electrode Installation Requirements

(A) Rod Electrodes.

(1) Below Permanent Moisture Level. If practicable, pipe electrodes must be embedded below the permanent moisture level and be free from nonconductive coatings such as paint or enamel.

(2) Supplemental Electrode. A rod electrode must be supplemented by an additional electrode that's bonded to: Figure 250–107

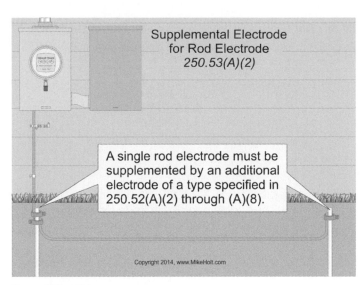

Figure 250–107

(1) Another rod electrode

(2) The grounding electrode conductor

(3) The service neutral conductor

(4) Nonflexible metal service raceway

(5) The service disconnect

Ex: A single rod electrode having a contact resistance to the earth of 25 ohms or less is not required to have a supplemental electrode. Figure 250–108

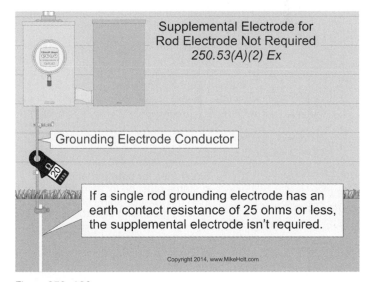

Figure 250–108

(3) Spacing. The supplemental electrode for a rod electrode must be installed not less than 6 ft from the rod electrode. Figure 250–109

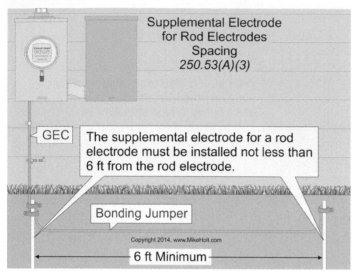

Figure 250–109

(B) Electrode Spacing. Electrodes for premises systems must be located no closer than 6 ft from lightning protection system grounding electrodes. Two or more grounding electrodes that are bonded together are considered a single grounding electrode system. Figure 250–110

Figure 250–110

(C) Grounding Electrode Bonding Jumper. Grounding electrode bonding jumpers must be copper when within 18 in. of the earth [250.64(A)], be securely fastened to the surface, and be protected from physical damage [250.64(B)]. The bonding jumper to each electrode must be sized in accordance with 250.66. Figure 250–111

Figure 250–111

The grounding electrode bonding jumpers must terminate by one of the following means in accordance with 250.8(A): Figure 250–112

- Listed pressure connectors
- Terminal bars
- Pressure connectors listed as grounding and bonding equipment
- Exothermic welding
- Machine screw-type fasteners that engage not less than two threads or are secured with a nut
- Thread-forming machine screws that engage not less than two threads in the enclosure
- Connections that are part of a listed assembly
- Other listed means

When the termination is encased in concrete or buried, the termination fittings must be listed for this purpose [250.70].

(D) Underground Metal Water Pipe Electrode.

(1) Interior Metal Water Piping. The bonding connection for the interior metal water piping system, as required by 250.104(A), must not be dependent on water meters, filtering devices, or similar equipment likely to be disconnected for repairs or replacement. When necessary,

Figure 250–112

Figure 250–114

a bonding jumper must be installed around insulated joints and equipment likely to be disconnected for repairs or replacement. Figure 250–113

- Rod electrode [250.52(A)(5)]
- Other listed electrode [250.52(A)(6)]
- Metal underground piping electrode [250.52(A)(8)]

The supplemental grounding electrode conductor must terminate to one of the following: Figure 250–115

Figure 250–113

Figure 250–115

(2) Underground Metal Water Pipe Supplemental Electrode. When an underground metal water pipe grounding electrode is present, it must be used as part of the grounding electrode system [250.52(A)(1)], and it must be supplemented by one of the following electrodes:

- Metal frame of the building electrode [250.52(A)(2)]
- Concrete-encased electrode [250.52(A)(3)] Figure 250–114
- Ground ring electrode [250.52(A)(4)]

(1) Grounding electrode conductor

(2) Service neutral conductor

(3) Metal service raceway

(4) Service equipment enclosure

Ex: The supplemental electrode is permitted to be bonded to interior metal water piping located not more than 5 ft from the point of entrance to the building [250.68(C)(1)].

(E) Supplemental Rod Electrode. The grounding electrode conductor to a rod(s) that serves as a supplemental electrode, isn't required to be larger than 6 AWG copper.

(F) Ground Ring. A ground ring electrode (conductor) that encircling the building, consisting of at least 20 ft of bare copper conductor not smaller than 2 AWG, must be buried not less than 30 in. [250.52(A)(4)]. Figure 250–116

Ground Ring
250.53(F)

A ground ring encircling the building or structure, consisting of at least 20 ft of bare copper conductor not smaller than 2 AWG, must be buried at a depth of not less than 30 in.

Copyright 2014
www.MikeHolt.com

Figure 250–116

(G) Rod Electrodes. Rod electrodes must be installed so that not less than 8 ft of length is in contact with the soil. If rock bottom is encountered, the rod must be driven at an angle not to exceed 45 degrees from vertical. If rock bottom is encountered at an angle up to 45 degrees from vertical, the rod can be buried in a minimum 30 in. deep trench. Figure 250–117

The upper end of the rod must be flush with or underground unless the grounding electrode conductor attachment is protected against physical damage as specified in 250.10.

Author's Comment:

■ When the grounding electrode attachment fitting is located underground, it must be listed for direct soil burial [250.68(A) Ex 1 and 250.70].

Ground Rod Electrode Installation
250.53(G)

45°

Ⓐ 8 ft Minimum

Ⓑ

Ⓒ 2½ ft Minimum

Copyright 2014, www.MikeHolt.com

Rock Bottom

Clamps must be suitable for direct burial [250.70].

A minimum of 8 ft of a rod electrode must be in contact with the soil. The upper end of the ground rod must be flush with or below ground level unless protected from physical damage.

Figure 250–117

Measuring the Ground Resistance

A ground resistance clamp meter, or a three-point fall of potential ground resistance meter, can be used to measure the contact resistance of a grounding electrode to the earth.

Ground Clamp Meter. The ground resistance clamp meter measures the contact resistance of the grounding electrode system to the earth by injecting a high-frequency signal via the service neutral conductor to the utility grounding connection, and then measuring the strength of the return signal through the earth to the grounding electrode being measured. Figure 250–118

Measuring Contact Resistance
Ground Clamp Meter

Employees Only

Clamp Meter

Copyright 2014
www.MikeHolt.com

The clamp meter measures the contact resistance to the earth of the grounding electrode system by injecting a high-frequency signal to the utility ground, then measuring the strength of the return signal.

Figure 250–118

Fall of Potential Ground Resistance Meter. The three-point fall of potential ground resistance meter determines the contact resistance of a single grounding electrode to the earth by using Ohm's Law: R=E/I. Figure 250–119

Figure 250–119

This meter divides the voltage difference between the electrode to be measured and a driven potential test stake (P) by the current flowing between the electrode to be measured and a driven current test stake (C). The test stakes are typically made of ¼ in. diameter steel rods, 24 in. long, driven two-thirds of their length into the earth.

The distance and alignment between the potential and current test stakes, and the electrode, is extremely important to the validity of the earth contact resistance measurements. For an 8 ft rod, the accepted practice is to space the current test stake (C) 80 ft from the electrode to be measured.

The potential test stake (P) is positioned in a straight line between the electrode to be measured and the current test stake (C). The potential test stake should be located at approximately 62 percent of the distance the current test stake is located from the electrode. Since the current test stake (C) for an 8 ft rod is located 80 ft from the grounding electrode, the potential test stake (P) will be about 50 ft from the electrode to be measured.

Question: *If the voltage between the rod and the potential test stake (P) is 3V and the current between the rod and the current test stake (C) is 0.20A, then the earth contact resistance of the electrode to the earth will be _____.* Figure 250–120

(a) 5 ohms   (b) 10 ohms   (c) 15 ohms   (d) 25 ohms

Answer: (c) 15 ohms

Resistance = Voltage/Current

E (Voltage) = 3V
I (Current) = 0.20A

R = E/I

Resistance = 3V/0.20A
Resistance = 15 ohms

Figure 250–120

Author's Comment:

- The three-point fall of potential meter should only be used to measure the contact resistance of one electrode to the earth at a time, and this electrode must be independent and not connected to any part of the electrical system. The contact resistance of two electrodes bonded together must not be measured until they've been separated. The contact resistance of two separate electrodes to the earth can be thought of as two resistors in parallel, if they're outside each other's sphere of influence.

Soil Resistivity

The earth's ground resistance is directly impacted by soil resistivity, which varies throughout the world. Soil resistivity is influenced by electrolytes, which consist of moisture, minerals, and dissolved salts. Because soil resistivity changes with moisture content, the resistance of any grounding system varies with the seasons of the year. Since moisture is stable at greater distances below the surface of the earth, grounding systems are generally more effective if the grounding electrode can reach the water table. In addition, placing the grounding electrode below the frost line helps to ensure less deviation in the system's contact resistance to the earth year round.

The contact resistance to the earth can be lowered by chemically treating the earth around the grounding electrodes with electrolytes designed for this purpose.

250.54 Auxiliary Grounding Electrodes

 Scan this QR code for a video of this *Code* rule. See page xix for information on how to use the QR codes.

Auxiliary electrodes are permitted, but they have no requirements since they serve no useful purpose related to electrical safety addressed by the *NEC*. Figure 250–121

Figure 250–121

If an auxiliary electrode is installed, it's not required to be bonded to the building grounding electrode system, required to have the grounding conductor sized to 250.66, or comply with the 25-ohm requirement of 250.53(A)(2) Ex. Figure 250–122

Figure 250–122

CAUTION: *An auxiliary electrode typically serves no useful purpose, and in some cases it may actually cause equipment failures by providing a path for lightning to travel through electronic equipment.* Figure 250–123

Figure 250–123

DANGER: *Because the contact resistance of an electrode to the earth is so great, very little fault current returns to the power supply if the earth is the only fault current return path. Result—the circuit overcurrent device won't open and clear the ground fault, and all metal parts associated with the electrical installation, metal piping, and structural building steel will become and remain energized.*

250.60 Lightning Protection Electrode

A lightning protection system in accordance with NFPA 780 is intended to protect the structure from lighting damage. Figure 250–124

Figure 250–124

The lightning protection electrode is not permitted to be used for the electrical power grounding electrode system. Figure 250–125

Note 2: If a lightning protection system is installed, the lightning protection system must be bonded to the building grounding electrode system so as to limit potential difference between it and the electrical system wiring in accordance with 250.106. **Figure 250–126**

Figure 250–125

Figure 250–126

250.62 Grounding Electrode Conductor

Grounding electrode conductors of the wire type must be solid or stranded, insulated or bare, and must be copper if within 18 in. of the earth [250.64(A)]. Figure 250–127

Figure 250–127

Figure 250–128

250.64 Grounding Electrode Conductor Installation

Grounding electrode conductors must be installed as specified in (A) through (F).

(A) Aluminum Conductors. Aluminum grounding electrode conductors must not be in contact with masonry, subject to corrosive conditions, or within 18 in. of the earth.

(B) Conductor Protection. Where installed exposed, grounding electrode conductors must be protected where subject to physical damage and are permitted to be installed on or through framing members. Grounding electrode conductors 6 AWG and larger can be installed exposed along the surface of the building if securely fastened and not subject to physical damage. Figure 250–128

Grounding electrode conductors sized 8 AWG must be protected by installing them in rigid metal conduit, intermediate metal conduit, PVC conduit, electrical metallic tubing, or reinforced thermosetting resin conduit.

Author's Comment:

- A ferrous metal raceway containing a grounding electrode conductor must be made electrically continuous by bonding each end of the raceway to the grounding electrode conductor [250.64(E)], so it's best to use nonmetallic conduit.

Grounding electrode conductors and bonding jumpers located underground, aren't required to comply with the cover requirements of 300.5. Figure 250–129

Figure 250–129

(C) Continuous. Grounding electrode conductor(s) must be installed without a splice or joint except by:

(1) Irreversible compression-type connectors or exothermic welding.

(2) Busbars connected together.

(3) Bolted, riveted, or welded connections of structural metal frames of buildings.

(4) Threaded, welded, brazed, soldered or bolted-flange connections of metal water piping.

(D) Grounding Electrode Conductor for Multiple Building or Structure Disconnects. If a service or building disconnect consists of more than a single enclosure, grounding electrode connections must be made in one of the following methods:

(1) Common Grounding Electrode Conductor and Taps. A grounding electrode conductor tap must extend to the inside of each disconnecting means enclosure.

The common grounding electrode conductor must be sized in accordance with 250.66, based on the sum of the circular mil area of the largest ungrounded conductor supplying the equipment. Figure 250–130

Figure 250–130

A grounding electrode conductor must extend from each disconnecting means, sized no smaller than specified in Table 250.66, based on the area of the largest ungrounded conductor for each disconnecting means.

The grounding electrode tap conductors must be connected to the common grounding electrode conductor, without splicing the common grounding electrode conductor, by one of the following methods:

(1) Exothermic welding.

(2) Connectors listed as grounding and bonding equipment.

(3) Connections to a busbar of sufficient length and not less than ¼ in. thick × 2 in. wide that's securely fastened and installed in an accessible location.

(2) Individual Grounding Electrode Conductors. A grounding electrode conductor, sized in accordance with 250.66 based on the ungrounded conductor(s) supplying the individual disconnecting means, must be connected between the grounding electrode system and one or more of the following:

(1) The service neutral conductor, Figure 250–131

Figure 250–131

(2) The equipment grounding conductor of the feeder circuit,

(3) The supply-side bonding jumper.

(3) Common Grounding Electrode Conductor Location. A single grounding electrode conductor, sized not smaller than specified in Table 250.66, based on the area of the ungrounded conductor at the location, must connect the grounding electrode system to one or more of the following locations:

(1) The service neutral conductor, Figure 250–132

(2) The equipment grounding conductor of the feeder circuit,

(3) The supply-side bonding jumper.

(E) Ferrous Enclosures and Raceways Containing Grounding Electrode Conductor.

Figure 250–132

(1) General. To prevent inductive choking of grounding electrode conductors, ferrous raceways and enclosures containing grounding electrode conductors must have each end of the raceway or enclosure bonded to the grounding electrode or grounding electrode conductor. Figure 250–133

Figure 250–133

(2) Methods. Bonding must be done by one of the methods discussed in 250.92(B)(2) through (B)(4).

(3) Size. Bonding jumpers must be the same size or larger than the required size of the grounding electrode conductor in the raceway or other enclosure.

(4) Wiring Methods. When a raceway is used for a grounding electrode conductor, it must meet all of the requirements for the raceway, such as securing and supporting, number of bends, conductor fill, and so forth.

Author's Comment:

■ Nonferrous metal raceways, such as aluminum rigid metal conduit, enclosing the grounding electrode conductor aren't required to meet the "bonding each end of the raceway to the grounding electrode conductor" provisions of this section.

⚠ **CAUTION:** *The effectiveness of a grounding electrode is significantly reduced if a ferrous metal raceway containing a grounding electrode conductor isn't bonded to the ferrous metal raceway at both ends. This is because a single conductor carrying high-frequency induced lightning current in a ferrous raceway causes the raceway to act as an inductor, which severely limits (chokes) the current flow through the grounding electrode conductor. ANSI/IEEE 142— Recommended Practice for Grounding of Industrial and Commercial Power Systems (Green Book) states: "An inductive choke can reduce the current flow by 97 percent."*

Author's Comment:

■ To save a lot of time and effort, install the grounding electrode conductor exposed if it's not subject to physical damage [250.64(B)], or enclose it in nonmetallic conduit suitable for the application [352.10(F)].

(F) Termination to Grounding Electrode.

(1) Single Grounding Electrode Conductor. A single grounding electrode conductor is permitted to terminate to any grounding electrode of the grounding electrode system. Figure 250–134

(2) Multiple Grounding Electrode Conductors. When multiple grounding electrode conductors are installed [250.64(D)(2)], each grounding electrode conductor is permitted to terminate to any grounding electrode of the grounding electrode system. Figure 250–135

Figure 250–134

Figure 250–136

Figure 250–135

(3) Termination to Busbar. Grounding electrode conductors and grounding electrode bonding jumpers are permitted to terminate to a busbar sized not less than ¼ in. × 2 in. that's securely fastened at an accessible location. The terminations to the busbar must be made by a listed connector or by exothermic welding. Figure 250–136

250.66 Sizing Grounding Electrode Conductor

Except as permitted in (A) through (C), the grounding electrode conductor must be sized in accordance with Table 250.66.

(A) Rod. If the grounding electrode conductor is connected to <u>one or more</u> rods, as permitted in 250.52(A)(5), that portion of the grounding electrode conductor that's the sole connection to the rod(s) isn't required to be larger than 6 AWG copper. Figure 250–137

Figure 250–137

(B) Concrete-Encased Grounding Electrode. If the grounding electrode conductor is connected to <u>one or more</u> concrete-encased electrode<u>s,</u> as permitted in 250.52(A)(3), that portion of the grounding electrode conductor that's the sole connection to the concrete-encased electrode<u>(s)</u> isn't required to be larger than 4 AWG copper. Figure 250–138

The portion of the grounding electrode conductor that's the sole connection to <u>one or more</u> concrete-encased electrode<u>s</u> isn't required to be larger than 4 AWG.

Figure 250–138

(C) Ground Ring. If the grounding electrode conductor is connected to a ground ring, the portion of the conductor that's the sole connection to the ground ring isn't required to be larger than the conductor used for the ground ring.

Author's Comment:

- A ground ring encircling the buildings in direct contact with the earth must consist of at least 20 ft of bare copper conductor not smaller than 2 AWG [250.52(A)(4)]. See 250.53(F) for the installation requirements for a ground ring.

- Table 250.66 is used to size the grounding electrode conductor when the conditions of 250.66(A), (B), or (C) don't apply. Figure 250–139

The grounding electrode conductor is sized using Table 250.66 based on the largest service-entrance conductor or equivalent area for parallel conductors.

Figure 250–139

Table 250.66 Sizing Grounding Electrode Conductor	
Conductor or Area of Parallel Conductors	Copper Grounding Electrode Conductor
12 through 2 AWG	8 AWG
1 or 1/0 AWG	6 AWG
2/0 or 3/0 AWG	4 AWG
Over 3/0 through 350 kcmil	2 AWG
Over 350 through 600 kcmil	1/0 AWG
Over 600 through 1,100 kcmil	2/0 AWG
Over 1,100 kcmil	3/0 AWG

250.68 Termination to the Grounding Electrode

(A) Accessibility. The mechanical elements used to terminate a grounding electrode conductor or bonding jumper to a grounding electrode must be accessible. Figure 250–140

Ex 1: The termination isn't required to be accessible if the termination to the electrode is encased in concrete or buried in the earth. Figure 250–141

Figure 250–140

Figure 250–141

Author's Comment:

- If the grounding electrode attachment fitting is encased in concrete or buried in the earth, it must be listed for direct soil burial or concrete encasement [250.70].

Ex 2: Exothermic or irreversible compression connections, together with the mechanical means used to attach to fireproofed structural metal, aren't required to be accessible.

(B) Integrity of Underground Metal Water Pipe Electrode. A bonding jumper must be installed around insulated joints and equipment likely to be disconnected for repairs or replacement for an underground metal water piping system used as a grounding electrode. The bonding jumper must be of sufficient length to allow the removal of such equipment while retaining the integrity of the grounding path. Figure 250–142

Figure 250–142

(C) Grounding Electrode Connections.

(1) Interior metal water piping located not more than 5 ft from the point of entrance to the building can serve as a grounding electrode conductor.

(2) The metal frame of a building can serve as a grounding electrode conductor. Figure 250–143

(3) A concrete-encased electrode can be extended from the concrete to an accessible location above the concrete. Figure 250–144

Figure 250–143

Figure 250–144

250.70 Grounding Electrode Conductor Termination Fittings

The grounding electrode conductor must terminate to the grounding electrode by exothermic welding, listed lugs, listed pressure connectors, listed clamps, or other listed means. In addition, fittings terminating to a grounding electrode must be listed for the materials of the grounding electrode.

When the termination to a grounding electrode is encased in concrete or buried in the earth, the termination fitting must be listed for direct soil burial or concrete encasement. No more than one conductor can terminate on a single clamp or fitting unless the clamp or fitting is listed for multiple connections. Figure 250–145

Figure 250–145

Part IV. Grounding Enclosure, Raceway, and Service Cable Connections

250.80 Service Raceways and Enclosures

Metal enclosures and raceways containing service conductors must be connected to the neutral conductor at service equipment if the electrical system is grounded, or to the grounding electrode conductor for electrical systems that aren't grounded.

Ex: Metal elbows having a minimum of 18 in. of cover installed in an underground nonmetallic raceway system aren't required to be connected to the service neutral or grounding electrode conductor. Figure 250–146

250.86 Other Enclosures

Metal raceways and enclosures containing electrical conductors operating at 50V or more [250.20(A)] must be connected to the circuit equipment grounding conductor. Figure 250–147

Figure 250–146

Figure 250–148

Figure 250–147

Ex 2: Short sections of metal raceways used for the support or physical protection of cables aren't required to be connected to the circuit equipment grounding conductor. Figure 250–148

Ex 3: A metal elbow installed in a run of underground nonmetallic raceway having a minimum of 18 in. of cover or encased in not less than 2 in. of concrete aren't required to be connected to the circuit equipment grounding conductor.

Part V. Bonding

250.90 General

Bonding must be provided to ensure electrical continuity and the capacity to conduct safely any fault current likely to be imposed.

250.92 Bonding Equipment for Services

(A) Bonding Requirements for Equipment for Services. The metal parts of equipment indicated below must be bonded together in accordance with 250.92(B). Figure 250–149

(1) Metal raceways containing service conductors.

(2) Metal enclosures containing service conductors.

Author's Comment:

■ Metal raceways or metal enclosures containing feeder and branch-circuit conductors are required to be connected to the circuit equipment grounding conductor in accordance with 250.86. Figure 250–150

Figure 250–149

Figure 250–151

Figure 250–150

Figure 250–152

(B) Methods of Bonding. Bonding jumpers around reducing washers or oversized, concentric, or eccentric knockouts are required. Figure 250–151

Standard locknuts are permitted to make a mechanical connection of the raceway(s), but they can't serve as the bonding means required by this section. Figure 250–152

Electrical continuity at service equipment, service raceways, and service conductor enclosures must be ensured by one of the following methods:

(1) Bonding the metal parts to the service neutral conductor. Figure 250–153

Author's Comment:

■ A main bonding jumper is required to bond the service disconnect to the service neutral conductor [250.24(B) and 250.28].

■ At service equipment, the service neutral conductor provides the effective ground-fault current path to the power supply [250.24(C)]; therefore, an equipment grounding conductor isn't required to be installed within PVC conduit containing service-entrance conductors [250.142(A)(1) and 352.60 Ex 2]. Figure 250–154

Figure 250–153

Figure 250–155

Figure 250–154

Figure 250–156

(2) Terminating metal raceways to metal enclosures by threaded hubs on enclosures if made up wrenchtight. Figure 250–155

(3) Terminating metal raceways to metal enclosures by threadless fittings if made up tight. Figure 250–156

(4) Other listed devices, such as bonding-type locknuts, bushings, wedges, or bushings with bonding jumpers.

Author's Comment:

■ A listed bonding wedge or bushing with a bonding jumper to the service neutral conductor is required when a metal raceway containing service conductors terminates to a ringed knockout. **Figure 250–157**

■ The bonding jumper used for this purpose must be sized in accordance with Table 250.102(C)(1), based on the area of the largest ungrounded service conductors within the raceway [250.102(C)].

Methods of Bonding at Service - Ringed Knockout Entry
250.92(B)(4)

A listed bonding fitting with a bonding jumper to the service neutral conductor is required when a metal raceway terminates to a ringed knockout.

Figure 250–157

■ A bonding-type locknut can be used for a metal raceway containing service conductors that terminates to an enclosure without a ringed knockout. Figure 250–158

Methods of Bonding at Service
No Ringed Knockout Entry
250.92(B)(4)

A bonding-type locknut can be used for a metal raceway terminating to an enclosure without a ringed knockout.

Figure 250–158

■ A bonding locknut differs from a standard locknut in that it contains a bonding screw with a sharp point that drives into the metal enclosure to ensure a solid connection.

■ Bonding one end of a service raceway to the service neutral provides the low-impedance fault current path to the source. Figure 250–159

Methods of Bonding at Service
250.92(B)(4)

Bonding at only one end of a service raceway provides the low-impedance path for fault current to flow back to the power supply.

Figure 250–159

250.94 Intersystem Bonding Termination

An external accessible intersystem bonding termination for the connection of communications systems bonding conductors must be provided at service equipment and disconnecting means for buildings supplied by a feeder. Figure 250–160

An external accessible intersystem bonding termination must be provided at service equipment and disconnecting means for buildings supplied by a feeder.

Figure 250–160

The intersystem bonding termination must:

(1) Be accessible for connection and inspection. Figure 250–161

Figure 250-161

(2) Consist of a set of terminals with the capacity for connection of not less than three intersystem bonding conductors.

(3) Not interfere with opening the enclosure for a service, building disconnecting means, or metering equipment.

(4) Be securely mounted and electrically connected to service equipment, the meter enclosure, or exposed nonflexible metallic service raceway, or be mounted at one of these enclosures and be connected to the enclosure or grounding electrode conductor with a minimum 6 AWG copper conductor.

(5) Be securely mounted to the building's disconnecting means, or be mounted at the disconnecting means and be connected to the metallic enclosure or grounding electrode conductor with a minimum 6 AWG copper conductor.

(6) The terminals must be listed as grounding and bonding equipment.

Author's Comment:

■ According to Article 100, an intersystem bonding termination is a device that provides a means to connect communications systems bonding conductors to the building grounding electrode system.

Ex: At existing buildings, an external accessible means for bonding communications systems together can be by the use of a:

(1) Nonflexible metallic raceway,

(2) Grounding electrode conductor, or

(3) Connection approved by the authority having jurisdiction.

Note 2: Communications systems must be bonded to the intersystem bonding termination in accordance with the following requirements: Figure 250-162

- Antennas/Satellite Dishes, 810.15 and 810.21
- CATV, 820.100
- Telephone Circuits, 800.100

Figure 250-162

Author's Comment:

■ All external communications systems must be connected to the intersystem bonding termination to minimize the damage to them from induced potential (voltage) differences between the systems from a lightning event. Figure 250-163

Figure 250-163

250.96 Bonding Other Enclosures

(A) Maintaining Effective Ground-Fault Current Path. Metal parts intended to serve as equipment grounding conductors, including raceways, cables, equipment, and enclosures, must be bonded together to ensure they have the capacity to conduct safely any fault current likely to be imposed on them [110.10, 250.4(A)(5), and Note to Table 250.122].

Nonconductive coatings such as paint, lacquer, and enamel on equipment must be removed to ensure an effective ground-fault current path, or the termination fittings must be designed so as to make such removal unnecessary [250.12].

Author's Comment:

■ The practice of driving a locknut tight with a screwdriver and pliers is considered sufficient in removing paint and other nonconductive finishes to ensure an effective ground-fault current path.

250.97 Bonding Metal Parts Containing 277V and 480V Circuits

Metal raceways or cables containing 277V and/or 480V feeder or branch circuits terminating at ringed knockouts must be bonded to the metal enclosure with a bonding jumper sized in accordance with 250.122, based on the rating of the circuit overcurrent device [250.102(D)]. Figure 250–164

Author's Comment:

■ Bonding jumpers for raceways and cables containing 277V or 480V circuits are required at ringed knockout terminations to ensure the ground-fault current path has the capacity to safely conduct the maximum ground-fault current likely to be imposed [110.10, 250.4(A)(5), and 250.96(A)].

■ Ringed knockouts aren't listed to withstand the heat generated by a 277V ground fault, which generates five times as much heat as a 120V ground fault. Figure 250–165

277V/480V Circuit Bonding
250.97

No Ringed Knockouts: Standard Locknut Okay

Ringed Knockouts: Bonding Jumper Required

Metal raceways or cables containing 277V or 480V circuits terminating at ringed knockouts must be bonded with a bonding jumper.

Figure 250–164

277V/480V Circuit Bonding
250.97

Heat generated from a 120V fault, based on resistance of 1 ohm

$I = E/R$
$I = 120V/1\Omega$
$I = 120A$

$P = I^2 \times R$
$P = 120A^2 \times 1\Omega$
$P = 14,400W$

Heat generated from a 277V fault, based on resistance of 1 ohm

$I = E/R$
$I = 277V/1\Omega$
$I = 277A$

$P = I^2 \times R$
$P = 277A^2 \times 1\Omega$
$P = 76,729W$

A 277V ground fault generates over 5 times the heat of a 120V ground fault.

Figure 250–165

Ex: A bonding jumper isn't required where ringed knockouts aren't encountered, knockouts are totally punched out, or where the box is listed to provide a reliable bonding connection. Figure 250–166

250.98 Bonding Loosely Jointed Metal Raceways

Expansion fittings and telescoping sections of metal raceways must electrically continuous by equipment bonding jumpers. Figure 250–167

Figure 250–166

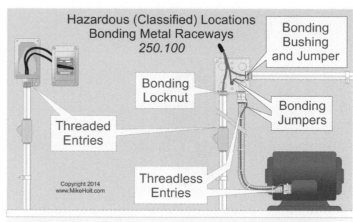

One or more of the above bonding methods [250.92(B)(2) through (B)(4)] are required whether or not equipment grounding conductors of the wire type are installed.

Figure 250–168

Figure 250–167

250.100 Bonding in Hazardous (Classified) Locations

Regardless of the circuit voltage, electrical continuity of metal parts of equipment and raceways in hazardous (classified) locations must be ensured by bonding-type locknuts, bushings, wedges, or bushings with bonding jumpers [250.92(B)(2) through (B)(4)]; whether or not equipment grounding conductors of the wire type are installed in the raceway. Figure 250–168

Note: See 501.30, 502.30, or 503.30 for specific bonding requirements.

250.102 Bonding Conductors and Jumpers

(A) Material. Equipment bonding jumpers must be copper or aluminum of the wire type or other corrosion-resistant material for bus or screw.

(B) Termination. Equipment bonding jumpers must terminate by one of the following means in accordance with 250.8(A):

- Listed pressure connectors
- Terminal bars
- Pressure connectors listed as grounding and bonding equipment
- Exothermic welding
- Machine screw-type fasteners that engage not less than two threads or are secured with a nut
- Thread-forming machine screws that engage not less than two threads in the enclosure
- Connections that are part of a listed assembly
- Other listed means

(C) Supply-Side Bonding Jumper Sizing.

(1) Single Raceway Installations. The supply-side bonding jumper is sized in accordance with Table 250.102(C)(1), based on the largest ungrounded conductor within the raceway. Figure 250–169

Figure 250–169

(2) Parallel Conductor Installations. If the ungrounded supply conductors are paralleled in two or more raceways or cables, the size of the supply-side bonding jumper for each raceway or cable is sized in accordance with Table 250.102(C)(1), based on the size of the largest ungrounded conductors in each raceway or cable.

> **Question:** What size single supply-side bonding jumper is required for three metal raceways, each containing 400 kcmil service conductors? Figure 250– 170
>
> (a) 1 AWG   (b) 1/0 AWG   (c) 2/0 AWG   (d) 300 AWG
>
> **Answer:** (b) 1/0 AWG [Table 250.102(C)(1)]

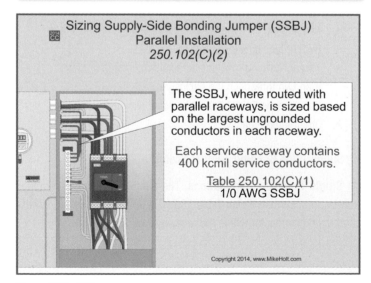

Figure 250–170

Table 250.102(C)(1). Grounded Conductor, Main Bonding Jumper, System Bonding Jumper, and Supply-Side Bonding Jumper Alternating-Current Systems

Size of Largest Ungrounded Conductor Per Raceway		Size of Conductor or Bonding Jumper
Copper	Aluminum or Copper-Clad Aluminum	Copper
2 or smaller	1/0 or smaller	8
1 or 1/0	2/0 or 3/0	6
2/0 or 3/0	Over 3/0 250 kcmil	4
Over 3/0 through 350 kcmil	Over 250 through 500 kcmil	2
Over 350 through 600 kcmil	Over 500 through 900 kcmil	1/0

(D) Load Side Bonding Jumper Sizing. Bonding jumpers on the load side of feeder and branch-circuit overcurrent devices are sized in accordance with 250.122, based on the rating of the circuit overcurrent device.

> **Question:** What size equipment bonding jumper is required for each metal raceway where the circuit conductors are protected by a 1,200A overcurrent device? Figure 250–171
>
> (a) 1 AWG   (b) 1/0 AWG   (c) 2/0 AWG   (d) 3/0 AWG
>
> **Answer:** (d) 3/0 AWG [Table 250.122]
>
> If a single bonding jumper is used to bond two or more raceways, it must be sized in accordance with 250.122, based on the rating of the largest circuit overcurrent device. Figure 250–172

(E) Installation of Bonding Jumpers.

(1) Inside Raceway. Bonding jumpers installed inside a raceway must be identified in accordance with 250.119 and must terminate to the enclosure in accordance with 250.148.

(2) Outside Raceway. Bonding jumpers installed outside a raceway must be routed with the raceway and can't exceed 6 ft in length. Figure 250–173

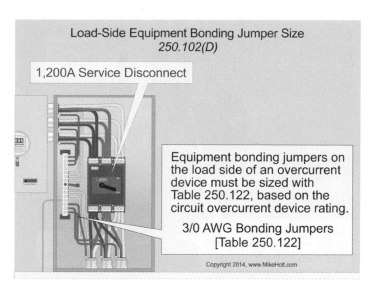

Load-Side Equipment Bonding Jumper Size
250.102(D)

1,200A Service Disconnect

Equipment bonding jumpers on the load side of an overcurrent device must be sized with Table 250.122, based on the circuit overcurrent device rating.

3/0 AWG Bonding Jumpers
[Table 250.122]

Copyright 2014, www.MikeHolt.com

Figure 250–171

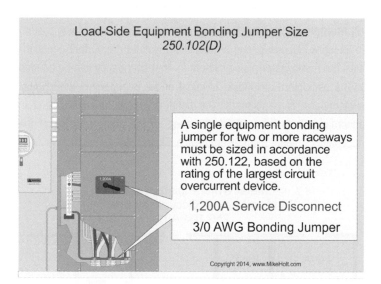

Load-Side Equipment Bonding Jumper Size
250.102(D)

A single equipment bonding jumper for two or more raceways must be sized in accordance with 250.122, based on the rating of the largest circuit overcurrent device.

1,200A Service Disconnect

3/0 AWG Bonding Jumper

Copyright 2014, www.MikeHolt.com

Figure 250–172

250.104 Bonding of Piping Systems and Exposed Structural Metal

Author's Comment:

■ To remove dangerous voltage on metal parts from a ground fault, electrically conductive metal water piping systems, metal sprinkler piping, metal gas piping, as well as exposed structural metal members likely to become energized, must be connected to an effective ground-fault current path [250.4(A)(4)].

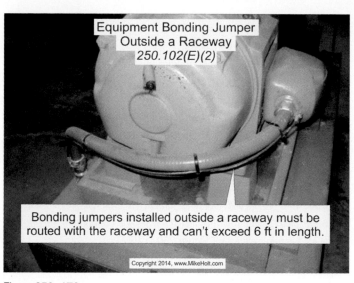

Equipment Bonding Jumper Outside a Raceway
250.102(E)(2)

Bonding jumpers installed outside a raceway must be routed with the raceway and can't exceed 6 ft in length.

Copyright 2014, www.MikeHolt.com

Figure 250–173

(A) Metal Water Piping System. Metal water piping systems that are interconnected to form a mechanically and electrically continuous system must be bonded in accordance with 250.104(A)(1), (A)(2), or (A)(3). The bonding jumper must be copper where within 18 in. of the earth [250.64(A)], securely fastened to the surface on which it's mounted [250.64(B)], and adequately protected if exposed to physical damage [250.64(B)]. In addition, all points of attachment must be accessible, except as permitted in 250.68(A) Ex.

(1) Buildings Supplied by a Service. The metal water piping system, including the metal sprinkler water piping system of a building, supplied with service conductors must be bonded to one of the following: Figure 250–174

Metal Water Piping System - Bonding Requirements
250.104(A)(1)

Metal water piping systems, including the sprinkler system, must be bonded to one of the following:
(1) Service enclosure
(2) Service neutral conductor
(3) Grounding electrode conductor
(4) Grounding electrode

Service Disconnect

Copyright 2014 www.MikeHolt.com

Figure 250–174

- Service equipment enclosure,
- Service neutral conductor,
- Grounding electrode conductor of sufficient size, or
- Grounding electrode system.

The metal water piping system bonding jumper must be sized in accordance with Table 250.66, based on the cross-sectional area of the ungrounded service conductors.

Question: *What size bonding jumper is required for a metal water piping system, if the 300 kcmil service conductors are paralleled in two raceways?* Figure 250–175

(a) 6 AWG   (b) 4 AWG   (c) 2 AWG   (d) 1/0 AWG

Answer: *(d) 1/0 AWG, based on 600 kcmil conductors, in accordance with Table 250.66*

Figure 250–175

Author's Comment:

- If hot and cold metal water pipes are electrically connected, only one bonding jumper is required, either to the cold or hot water pipe. Bonding isn't required for isolated sections of metal water piping connected to a nonmetallic water piping system. Figure 250–176

Figure 250–176

(2) Multiple Occupancy Building. When a metal water piping system in an individual occupancy is metallically isolated from other occupancies, the metal water piping system for that occupancy can be bonded to the equipment grounding terminal of the occupancy's switchgear, switchboard, or panelboard. The bonding jumper must be sized in accordance with Table 250.122, based on the ampere rating of the occupancy's feeder overcurrent device. Figure 250–177

Figure 250–177

(3) Buildings Supplied by a Feeder. The metal water piping system of a building supplied by a feeder must be bonded to one of the following:

- The equipment grounding terminal of the building disconnect enclosure,
- The feeder equipment grounding conductor, or
- The grounding electrode system.

The bonding jumper is sized to Table 250.66, based on the cross-sectional area of the ungrounded feeder conductor.

(B) Other Metal-Piping Systems. Metal-piping systems such as gas or air that are likely to become energized are permitted to be bonded to the equipment grounding conductor for the circuit that's likely to energize the piping. Figure 250–178

Figure 250–178

Note 1: Bonding all piping and metal air ducts within the premises will provide additional safety. Figure 250–179

Note 2: The *National Fuel Gas Code*, NFPA 54, Section 7.13 contains further information about bonding gas piping. Figure 250–180

Author's Comment

- Informational Notes in the *NEC* are for information purposes only and aren't enforceable as a requirement of the *Code* [90.5(C)].

Figure 250–179

Figure 250–180

(C) Structural Metal. An exposed metal structural building frame that's likely to become energized must be bonded to the: Figure 250–181

- Service equipment enclosure,
- Service neutral conductor,
- Building disconnecting means for buildings supplied by a feeder,
- Grounding electrode conductor if of sufficient size, or
- Grounding electrode system.

Figure 250–181

Figure 250–182

Author's Comment:

- This rule doesn't require the bonding of sheet metal framing members (studs) or the metal skin of a wood-frame building.

The bonding jumper must be sized in accordance with Table 250.66, based on the area of the ungrounded supply conductors. The bonding jumper must be copper where within 18 in. of the earth [250.64(A)], securely fastened to the surface on which it's carried [250.64(B)], and adequately protected if exposed to physical damage [250.64(B)]. In addition, all points of attachment must be accessible, except as permitted in 250.68(A) Ex.

(D) Separately Derived Systems. Metal water piping systems and structural metal that forms a building frame must be bonded as required in (D)(1) through (D)(3).

(1) Metal Water Pipe. The nearest available point of the metal water piping system in the area served by a separately derived system must be bonded to the neutral point of the separately derived system where the grounding electrode conductor is connected. Figure 250–182

The bonding jumper must be sized in accordance with Table 250.66, based on the area of the ungrounded conductor of the derived system.

Ex 2: The metal water piping system is permitted to be bonded to the structural metal building frame if it serves as the grounding electrode [250.52(A)(1)] for the separately derived system. Figure 250–183

Figure 250–183

(2) Structural Metal. Exposed structural metal interconnected to form the building frame must be bonded to the neutral point of each separately derived system where the grounding electrode conductor is connected.

The bonding jumper must be sized in accordance with Table 250.66, based on the area of the ungrounded conductors of the derived system.

Ex 1: Bonding to the separately derived system isn't required if the metal structural frame serves as the grounding electrode [250.52(A)(2)] for the separately derived system.

250.106 Lightning Protection System

When a lightning protection system is installed in accordance with NFPA 780, the lightning protection electrode (ground terminals) must be bonded to the building grounding electrode system. Figure 250–184

Figure 250–184

Author's Comment:

- The grounding electrode for a lightning protection system must not be used as the required grounding electrode system for the building [250.60]. Figure 250–185

Note 1: See NFPA 780—*Standard for the Installation of Lightning Protection Systems,* which contains detailed information on grounding, bonding, and sideflash distance from lightning protection systems.

Note 2: To minimize the likelihood of arcing between metal parts because of induced voltage, metal raceways, enclosures, and other metal parts of electrical equipment may require bonding or spacing from the lightning protection conductors in accordance with NFPA 780—*Standard for the Installation of Lightning Protection Systems.*

Figure 250–185

Part VI. Equipment Grounding and Equipment Grounding Conductors

250.110 Fixed Equipment Connected by Permanent Wiring Methods—General

Exposed metal parts of fixed equipment likely to become energized must be connected to the circuit equipment grounding conductor where the equipment is:

(1) Within 8 ft vertically or 5 ft horizontally of the earth or a grounded metal object

(2) Located in a wet or damp location

(3) In electrical contact with metal

(4) In a hazardous (classified) location [Articles 500 through 517]

(5) Supplied by a wiring method that provides an equipment grounding conductor

(6) Supplied by a 277V or 480V circuit

Ex 3: Listed double-insulated equipment isn't required to be connected to the circuit equipment grounding conductor.

250.112 Specific Equipment Fastened in Place or Connected by Permanent Wiring Methods

To remove dangerous voltage from a ground fault, metal parts must be connected to the circuit equipment grounding conductor. Figure 250–186

Figure 250–186

(I) Remote-Control, Signaling, and Fire Alarm Circuits. Equipment supplied by circuits operating at 50V or less isn't required to be connected to the circuit equipment grounding conductor. Figure 250–187

Author's Comment:

- Class 1 power-limited circuits, Class 2, and Class 3 remote-control and signaling circuits, and fire alarm circuits operating at 50V or less don't need to have any metal parts connected to an equipment grounding conductor.

(K) Skid-Mounted Equipment. Electrical equipment permanently mounted on skids, and the skids themselves, must be connected to the equipment grounding conductor sized as required by 250.122.

Figure 250–187

250.114 Cord-and-Plug-Connected Equipment

To remove dangerous voltage from a ground fault, metal parts must be connected to the circuit equipment grounding conductor. Figure 250–188

Figure 250–188

Ex: Listed double-insulated equipment isn't required to be connected to the circuit equipment grounding conductor.

250.118 Types of Equipment Grounding Conductors

An equipment grounding conductor can be any one or a combination of the following: Figure 250–189

Figure 250–189

Note: The equipment grounding conductor is intended to serve as part of the effective ground-fault current path. See 250.2. Figure 250–190

Figure 250–190

Author's Comment:

■ The effective ground-fault path is an intentionally constructed low-impedance conductive path designed to carry fault current from the point of a ground fault on a wiring system to the electrical supply source. Its purpose is to quickly remove dangerous voltage from a ground fault by opening the circuit overcurrent device [250.2]. Figure 250–191

Figure 250–191

(1) An equipment grounding conductor of the wire type is permitted to be bare or insulated copper or aluminum conductor. Figure 250–192

Figure 250–192

(2) Rigid metal conduit (RMC) can serve as an equipment grounding conductor.

(3) Intermediate metal conduit (IMC) can serve as an equipment grounding conductor.

(4) Electrical metallic tubing (EMT) can serve as an equipment grounding conductor.

(5) Listed flexible metal conduit (FMC) can serve as an equipment grounding conductor where: Figure 250–193

Figure 250–193

a. The raceway terminates in listed fittings.

b. The circuit conductors are protected by an overcurrent device rated 20A or less.

c. The combined length of the flexible conduit in the same ground-fault current path doesn't exceed 6 ft.

d. If flexibility is required to minimize the transmission of vibration from equipment or to provide flexibility for equipment that requires movement after installation, an equipment grounding conductor of the wire type must be installed with the circuit conductors in accordance with 250.102(E), and it must be sized in accordance with 250.122, based on the rating of the circuit overcurrent device. Figure 250–194

Figure 250–194

(6) Listed liquidtight flexible metal conduit (LFMC) can serve as an equipment grounding conductor where: Figure 250–195

Figure 250–195

a. The raceway terminates in listed fittings.

b. For ⅜ in. through ½ in., the circuit conductors are protected by an overcurrent device rated 20A or less.

c. For ¾ in. through 1¼ in., the circuit conductors are protected by an overcurrent device rated 60A or less.

d. The combined length of the flexible conduit in the same ground-fault current path doesn't exceed 6 ft.

e. If flexibility is required to minimize the transmission of vibration from equipment or to provide flexibility for equipment that requires movement after installation, an equipment grounding conductor of the wire type must be installed with the circuit conductors in accordance with 250.102(E), and it must be sized in accordance with 250.122, based on the rating of the circuit overcurrent device.

(8) The sheath of Type AC cable containing an aluminum bonding strip can serve as an equipment grounding conductor. Figure 250–196

Figure 250–196

Author's Comment:

- The internal aluminum bonding strip isn't an equipment grounding conductor, but it allows the interlocked armor to serve as an equipment grounding conductor because it reduces the impedance of the armored spirals to ensure that a ground fault will be cleared. It's the aluminum bonding strip in combination with the cable armor that creates the circuit equipment grounding conductor. Once the bonding strip exits the cable, it can be cut off because it no longer serves any purpose.

- The effective ground-fault current path must be maintained by the use of fittings specifically listed for Type AC cable [320.40]. See 300.12, 300.15, and 320.100.

(9) The copper sheath of Type MI cable can serve as an equipment grounding conductor.

(10) Type MC cable

a. The interlock type cable contains an insulated or uninsulated equipment grounding conductor in compliance with 250.118(1) can serve as an equipment grounding conductor. Figure 250–197

Figure 250–197

b. The combined metallic sheath and uninsulated equipment grounding/bonding conductor of interlocked metal is listed and identified as an equipment grounding conductor can serve as an equipment grounding conductor. Figure 250–198

Figure 250–198

Author's Comment:

- Once the bare aluminum grounding/bonding conductor exits the cable, it can be cut off because it no longer serves any purpose. The effective ground-fault current path must be maintained by the use of fittings specifically listed for Type MCAP® cable [330.40]. See 300.12, 300.15, and 330.100. Figure 250–199

Figure 250–200

Figure 250–199

c. The metallic sheath of the smooth or corrugated tube-type MC cable that's listed and identified as an equipment grounding conductor can serve as an equipment grounding conductor.

(11) Metallic cable trays can serve as an equipment grounding conductor where continuous maintenance and supervision ensure only qualified persons will service the cable tray, with cable tray and fittings identified for grounding and the cable tray, fittings [392.10], and raceways are bonded using bolted mechanical connectors or bonding jumpers sized and installed in accordance with 250.102 [392.60]. Figure 250–200

(13) Listed electrically continuous metal raceways, such as metal wireways [Article 376] or strut-type channel raceways [384.60] can serve as an equipment grounding conductor.

(14) Surface metal raceways listed for grounding [Article 386] can serve as an equipment grounding conductor.

250.119 Identification of Equipment Grounding Conductors

Unless required to be insulated, equipment grounding conductors can be bare or covered. Insulated equipment grounding conductors must have a continuous outer finish that's either green or green with one or more yellow stripes. Figure 250–201

Figure 250–201

Conductors with insulation that's green, or green with one or more yellow stripes, aren't permitted be used for an ungrounded or neutral conductor. Figure 250–202

Figure 250–202

Author's Comment:

- The *NEC* neither requires nor prohibits the use of the color green for the identification of grounding electrode conductors. Figure 250–203

Figure 250–203

Ex 3: Conductors with green insulation can be used as ungrounded signal conductors for traffic signal control and traffic signal indicating heads. The circuit must still include an equipment grounding conductor, and if it's of the wire type it must be bare or green with one or more yellow stripes.

(A) Conductors 4 AWG and Larger.

(1) Identified if Accessible. Insulated equipment grounding conductors 4 AWG and larger can be permanently reidentified at the time of installation at every point where the conductor is accessible. Figure 250–204

Figure 250–204

Ex: Identification of equipment grounding conductors 4 AWG and larger in conduit bodies isn't required.

(2) Identification Method. Figure 250–205

Figure 250–205

a. Removing the insulation at termination

b. Coloring the insulation green at termination

c. Marking the insulation at termination with green tape or green adhesive labels

250.120 Equipment Grounding Conductor Installation

An equipment grounding conductor must be installed as follows:

(A) Raceway, Cable Trays, Cable Armor, Cablebus, or Cable Sheaths. If it consists of a raceway, cable tray, cable armor, cablebus framework, or cable sheath, fittings for joints and terminations must be made tight using suitable tools.

(C) Equipment Grounding Conductors Smaller Than 6 AWG. If not routed with circuit conductors as permitted in 250.130(C) and 250.134(B) Ex 2, equipment grounding conductors smaller than 6 AWG must be installed in a raceway or cable if subject to physical damage. Figure 250–206

Figure 250–206

250.121 Use of Equipment Grounding Conductors

An equipment grounding conductor isn't permitted to be used as a grounding electrode conductor. Figure 250–207

Figure 250–207

Ex: Equipment grounding conductors of the wire type can be used as a grounding electrode conductor, provided they meet all of the rules for both.

Author's Comment:

■ For PV systems, 690.47(C) permits a combined equipment grounding/grounding electrode conductor if sized to the larger of 250.122 or 250.166 and installed in accordance with 250.64(E). Figure 250–208

Figure 250–208

250.122 Sizing Equipment Grounding Conductor

(A) General. Equipment grounding conductors of the wire type must be sized not smaller than shown in Table 250.122, based on the rating of the circuit overcurrent device; however, the circuit equipment grounding conductor isn't required to be larger than the circuit conductors. Figure 250–209

Table 250.122 Sizing Equipment Grounding Conductor

Overcurrent Device Rating	Copper Conductor
15A	14 AWG
20A	12 AWG
25A—60A	10 AWG
70A—100A	8 AWG
110A—200A	6 AWG
225A—300A	4 AWG
350A—400A	3 AWG
450A—500A	2 AWG
600A	1 AWG
700A—800A	1/0 AWG
1,000A	2/0 AWG
1,200A	3/0 AWG

(B) Increased in Size. If ungrounded conductors are increased in size from the minimum ampacity that'd be required for the load, wire type equipment grounding conductors must be proportionately increased in size according to the circular mil area of the ungrounded conductors.

Author's Comment:

- Ungrounded conductors are sometimes increased in size to accommodate conductor voltage drop, harmonic current heating, short-circuit rating, or simply for future capacity.

Sizing Equipment Grounding Conductor Of the Wire Type 250.122(A)

125A Feeder Protection

40A Branch-Circuit Protection

6 AWG

10 AWG

An equipment grounding conductor is sized to the circuit's overcurrent device rating in accordance with Table 250.122.

Copyright 2014, www.MikeHolt.com

Figure 250–209

Question: If the ungrounded conductors for a 40A circuit (with 75°C terminals) are increased in size from 8 AWG to 6 AWG due to voltage drop, the circuit equipment grounding conductor must be increased in size from 10 AWG to _____. Figure 250–210

(a) 10 AWG   (b) 8 AWG   (c) 6 AWG   (d) 4 AWG

Answer: (b) 8 AWG

The circular mil area of 6 AWG is 59 percent more than 8 AWG (26,240 Cmil/16,510 Cmil) [Chapter 9, Table 8].

According to Table 250.122, the circuit equipment grounding conductor for a 40A overcurrent device will be 10 AWG (10,380 Cmil), but the circuit equipment grounding conductor for this circuit must be increased in size by a multiplier of 1.59.

Conductor Size = 10,380 Cmil x 1.59
Conductor Size = 16,504 Cmil
Conductor Size = 8 AWG, Chapter 9, Table 8

Figure 250–210

Figure 250–211

Question: *If the ungrounded conductors for a 40A circuit (with 60°C terminals) are increased in size from 8 AWG to 6 AWG due to having four current-carrying conductors in a raceway, the circuit equipment grounding conductor must be increased in size from 10 AWG to _____.*

(a) An increase isn't required   *(b) 8 AWG*
(c) 6 AWG   *(d) 4 AWG*

Answer: *(a) An increase isn't required*

The equipment grounding conductor doesn't need to be increased in size in this example, because the 6 AWG is the smallest size ungrounded conductor allowed by the Code.

8 AWG rated 40A at 60°C x 0.80 = 32A after adjustment factors is too small for the circuit example. 6 AWG rated 55A at 60°C, is required (55A x 0.80 = 44A).

(C) Multiple Circuits. When multiple circuits are installed in the same raceway, cable, or cable tray, one equipment grounding conductor sized in accordance with 250.122, based on the rating of the largest circuit overcurrent device is sufficient. Figure 250–211

(D) Motor Branch Circuits.

(1) General. The equipment grounding conductor of the wire type must be sized in accordance with Table 250.122, based on the rating of the motor circuit branch-circuit short-circuit and ground-fault overcurrent device, but this conductor isn't required to be larger than the circuit conductors [250.122(A)].

Question: *What size equipment grounding conductor is required for a 2 hp, 230V, single-phase motor?* Figure 250–212

(a) 14 AWG   *(b) 12 AWG*   *(c) 10 AWG*   *(d) 8 AWG*

Answer: *(a) 14 AWG*

Step 1: *Determine the branch-circuit conductor size [430.22(A) and Table 310.15(B)(16)]*

2 hp, 230V Motor FLC = 12A [Table 430.248]

12A x 1.25 = 15A, 14 AWG, rated 20A at 75°C [Table 310.15(B)(16)]

Step 2: *Determine the branch-circuit protection [240.6(A), 430.52(C)(1), and Table 430.248]*

12A x 2.50 = 30A

Step 3: *The circuit equipment grounding conductor must be sized to the 30A overcurrent device—10 AWG [Table 250.122], but it's not required to be sized larger than the circuit conductors—14 AWG.*

(F) Parallel Runs. If circuit conductors are installed in parallel in separate raceways or cable as permitted by 310.10(H), an equipment grounding conductor must be installed for each parallel conductor set. The equipment grounding conductor in each raceway or cable must be sized in accordance with Table 250.122, based on the rating of the circuit overcurrent device, but it's not required to be larger than the circuit conductors [250.122(A)]. Figure 250–213

Figure 250–212

Figure 250–214

Figure 250–213

(G) Feeder Tap Conductors. Equipment grounding conductors for feeder taps must be sized in accordance with Table 250.122, based on the ampere rating of the overcurrent device ahead of the feeder, but in no case is it required to be larger than the feeder tap conductors. Figure 250–214

Part VII. Methods of Equipment Grounding

250.130 Equipment Grounding Conductor Connections

(C) Nongrounding Receptacle Replacement or Branch-Circuit Extension. If a grounding-type receptacle is installed or a branch circuit extension is made from an outlet box that doesn't contain an equipment grounding conductor, the grounding contacts of a grounding-type receptacle must be connected to one of the following: Figures 250–215 and 250–216

Figure 250–215

Figure 250–216

(1) The grounding electrode system [250.50]

(2) The grounding electrode conductor

(3) The panelboard equipment grounding terminal

(4) An equipment grounding conductor that's part of a different circuit, if both circuits originate from the same panel

(5) The service neutral conductor

Note: A grounding-type receptacle can replace a nongrounding-type receptacle, without having the grounding terminal connected to an equipment grounding conductor, if the receptacle is GFCI protected and marked in accordance with 406.4(D)(2). Figure 250–217

Figure 250–217

250.134 Equipment Connected by Permanent Wiring Methods

Except as permitted for services or separately derived systems [250.142(A)], metal parts of equipment, raceways, and enclosures must be connected to an equipment grounding conductor by one of the following methods:

(A) Equipment Grounding Conductor Types. By connecting to one of the equipment grounding conductors identified in 250.118.

(B) With Circuit Conductors. If an equipment grounding conductor of the wire type is installed, it must be in the same raceway, cable tray, trench, cable, or cord with the circuit conductors in accordance with 300.3(B).

Author's Comment:

- All conductors of a circuit must be installed in the same raceway, cable, trench, cord, or cable tray to minimize induction of the heating of ferrous metal raceways and enclosures, and to maintain a low-impedance ground-fault current path [250.4(A)(3)]. Figure 250–218

Figure 250–218

250.136 Equipment Considered Grounded

(A) Equipment Secured to Grounded Metal Supports. The structural metal frame of a building must not be used as the required equipment grounding conductor.

250.138 Cord-and-Plug-Connected Equipment

(A) Equipment Grounding Conductor. Metal parts of cord-and-plug-connected equipment must be connected to an equipment grounding conductor that terminates to a grounding-type attachment plug.

250.140 Ranges, Ovens, and Clothes Dryers

The frames of electric ranges, wall-mounted ovens, counter-mounted cooking units, clothes dryers, and outlet boxes that are part of the circuit for these appliances must be connected to the equipment grounding conductor [250.134(A)]. Figure 250–219

Neutral Not Permitted for Equipment Grounding
250.140

Neutral Conductor

Proper Installation

VIOLATION

Copyright 2014, www.MikeHolt.com

The neutral conductor can't be used for equipment grounding. This means that 4-wire cords and receptacles are required for ranges, dryers, and ovens.

Figure 250–219

⚠ **CAUTION:** *Ranges, dryers, and ovens have their metal cases connected to the neutral conductor at the factory. This neutral-to-case connection must be removed when these appliances are installed in new construction, and a 4-wire cord and receptacle must be used [250.142(B)].*

Ex: For existing installations if an equipment grounding conductor isn't present in the outlet box, the frames of electric ranges, wall-mounted ovens, counter-mounted cooking units, clothes dryers, and outlet boxes that are part of the circuit for these appliances may be connected to the neutral conductor. Figure 250–220

Grounding Ranges, Ovens, and Clothes Dryers
Existing Installations
250.140 Ex

A circuit without an equipment grounding conductor.

Neutral Conductor, 10 AWG or Larger

Copyright 2014, www.MikeHolt.com

For existing branch circuit installations, where an equipment grounding conductor isn't present in the outlet box, the frames and outlet boxes that are part of the circuit can be connected to the circuit neutral conductor.

Figure 250–220

250.142 Use of Neutral Conductor for Equipment Grounding

(A) Supply-Side Equipment.

(1) Service Equipment. The neutral conductor can be used as the circuit equipment grounding conductor on the supply side or within the enclosure of the service disconnect in accordance with 250.24(B). Figure 250–221

Neutral-to-Case Connection
Service Equipment
250.142(A)(1)

Main Bonding Jumper

Service Neutral Conductor

Copyright 2014, www.MikeHolt.com

The service neutral conductor must be connected to the equipment grounding conductor at service equipment in accordance with 250.24(B).

Figure 250–221

(3) Separately Derived Systems. The neutral conductor can be used as the circuit equipment grounding conductor at the source of a separately derived system or within the enclosure of the system disconnecting means in accordance with 250.30(A)(1).

⚠️ **DANGER:** *Failure to install the system bonding jumper as required by 250.30(A)(1) creates a condition where dangerous touch voltage from a ground fault won't be removed.*

(B) Load-Side Equipment. Except as permitted in 250.30(A)(1) for separately derived systems and 250.32(B) Ex, for separate buildings/structures, the neutral conductor isn't permitted to serve as an equipment grounding conductor on the load side of service equipment.

Ex 1: In existing installations, the frames of ranges, wall-mounted ovens, counter-mounted cooking units, and clothes dryers can be connected to the neutral conductor in accordance with 250.140 Ex.

Ex 2: The neutral conductor can be connected to meter socket enclosures on the load side of the service disconnecting means if:

(1) Ground-fault protection isn't provided on service equipment,

(2) Meter socket enclosures are immediately adjacent to the service disconnecting means, and

(3) The neutral conductor is sized in accordance with 250.122, based on the ampere rating of the occupancy's feeder overcurrent device.

250.146 Connecting Receptacle Grounding Terminal to Metal Enclosure

Except as permitted for (A) through (D), an equipment bonding jumper sized in accordance with 250.122, based on the rating of the circuit overcurrent device, must connect the grounding terminal of a receptacle to a metal box. Figure 250–222

Author's Comment:

- The *NEC* doesn't restrict the position of the receptacle grounding terminal; it can be up, down, or sideways. *Code* proposals to specify the mounting position of receptacles have always been rejected. Figure 250–223

An equipment bonding jumper, sized in accordance with 250.122, must connect the grounding terminal of the receptacle to the metal box.

Figure 250–222

Figure 250–223

(A) Surface-Mounted Box. An equipment bonding jumper from a receptacle to a metal box that's surface mounted isn't required if there's direct metal-to-metal contact between the device yoke and the metal box. To ensure a suitable bonding path between the device yoke and a metal box, at least one of the insulating retaining washers on the yoke screw must be removed. Figure 250–224

An equipment bonding jumper isn't required for receptacles attached to listed exposed work covers when the receptacle is attached to the cover with at least two fasteners that have a thread locking or screw or nut locking means, and the cover mounting holes are located on a flat non-raised portion of the cover. Figure 250–225

Figure 250–224

Figure 250–226

Figure 250–225

Figure 250–227

(B) Self-Grounding Receptacles. Receptacle yokes listed as self-grounding are designed to establish the equipment bonding between the device yoke and a metal box via the metal mounting screws. Figure 250–226

(C) Floor Boxes. Listed floor boxes are designed to establish the bonding path between the device yoke and a metal box.

(D) Isolated Ground Receptacles. The grounding terminal of an isolated ground receptacle must be connected to an insulated equipment grounding conductor run with the circuit conductors. Figure 250–227

The circuit equipment grounding conductor is permitted to pass through panelboards [408.40 Ex], boxes, wireways, or other enclosures without a connection to the enclosure [250.148 Ex].

⚠️ **CAUTION:** *Type AC Cable—Type AC cable containing an insulated equipment grounding conductor of the wire type can be used to supply receptacles having insulated grounding terminals because the metal armor of the cable is listed as an equipment grounding conductor [250.118(8)].* Figure 250–228

Type MC Cable—The metal armor sheath of interlocked Type MC cable containing an insulated equipment grounding conductor isn't listed as an equipment grounding conductor. Therefore, this wiring method with a single equipment grounding conductor can't supply an isolated ground receptacle installed in a metal box (because the box isn't connected to an equipment grounding conductor). However, Type MC cable with two insulated equipment grounding conductors is acceptable, since one equipment grounding conductor connects to the metal box and the other to the isolated ground receptacle. See Figure 250–228

The armor assembly of interlocked Type MC^{AP®} cable with a 10 AWG bare aluminum grounding/bonding conductor running just below the metal armor is listed to serve as an equipment grounding conductor in accordance with 250.118(10)(b).

Figure 250–228

Author's Comment:

■ When should an isolated ground receptacle be installed and how should the isolated ground system be designed? These questions are design issues and must not be answered based on the *NEC* alone [90.1(A)]. In most cases, using

isolated ground receptacles is a waste of money. For example, IEEE 1100—*Powering and Grounding Electronic Equipment* (Emerald Book) states: "The results from the use of the isolated ground method range from no observable effects, the desired effects, or worse noise conditions than when standard equipment bonding configurations are used to serve electronic load equipment [8.5.3.2]."

■ In reality, few electrical installations truly require an isolated ground system. For those systems that can benefit from an isolated ground system, engineering opinions differ as to what's a proper design. Making matters worse—of those properly designed, few are correctly installed and even fewer are properly maintained. For more information on how to properly ground electronic equipment, go to: www.MikeHolt.com, click on the "Technical" link, and then visit the "Power Quality" page.

250.148 Continuity and Attachment of Equipment Grounding Conductors in Metal Boxes

If circuit conductors are spliced or terminated on equipment within a metal box, the equipment grounding conductor associated with those circuits must be connected to the box in accordance with the following: Figure 250–229

Figure 250–229

Ex: The circuit equipment grounding conductor for an isolated ground receptacle installed in accordance with 250.146(D) isn't required to terminate to a metal box. Figure 250–230

Figure 250–230

(A) Splicing. Equipment grounding conductors must be spliced together with a device listed for the purpose [110.14(B)]. Figure 250–231

Figure 250–231

Author's Comment:

- Wire connectors of any color can be used with equipment grounding conductor splices, but green wire connectors can only be used with equipment grounding conductors since they're only tested for that application.

(B) Grounding Continuity. Equipment grounding conductors must terminate in a manner such that the disconnection or the removal of a receptacle, luminaire, or other device won't interrupt the grounding continuity. Figure 250–232

Figure 250–232

(C) Metal Boxes. Terminating equipment grounding conductors within metal boxes must be with a grounding screw that's not used for any other purpose, a fitting listed for grounding, or a listed grounding device such as a ground clip. Figure 250–233

Author's Comment:

- Equipment grounding conductors aren't permitted to terminate to a screw that secures a plaster ring. Figure 250–234

Terminating Equipment Grounding Conductors in Metal Box
250.148(C)

Equipment grounding conductors must be connected to a metal box by a grounding screw that's not used for any other purpose or a listed grounding device.

Figure 250–233

Terminating Equipment Grounding Conductors in a Metal Box
250.148(C)

VIOLATION

Equipment grounding conductors must be connected to a metal box by a screw or fitting that's not used for any other purpose.

Figure 250–234

Part VIII. Direct-Current Systems

250.166 Sizing Grounding Electrode Conductor

Except as permitted in (C) through (E), the grounding electrode conductor must be sized in accordance with 250.166(A) and (B), but not required to be larger than 3/0 copper or 250 kcmil aluminum.

(B) Not Smaller Than 8 AWG. The grounding electrode conductor is not permitted to be smaller than the largest ungrounded dc conductor, and not smaller than 8 AWG copper.

(C) Rod. If the grounding electrode conductor is connected to one or more rods as permitted in 250.52(A)(5), that portion of the grounding electrode conductor that's the sole connection to the rod(s) isn't required to be larger than 6 AWG copper. Figure 250–235

Ground Rod
250.166(C)

Array

If the grounding electrode conductor is connected to one or more ground rods as permitted in 250.52(A)(5), that portion of the grounding electrode conductor that's the sole connection to the ground rod(s) isn't required to be larger than 6 AWG copper.

Figure 250–235

(D) Concrete-Encased Grounding Electrode. If the grounding electrode conductor is connected to one or more concrete-encased electrodes as permitted in 250.52(A)(3), that portion of the grounding electrode conductor that's the sole connection to the concrete-encased electrode(s) isn't required to be larger than 4 AWG copper. Figure 250–236

Concrete-Encased Grounding Electrode
250.166(D)

Array

If the GEC is connected to one or more concrete-encased electrodes as permitted in 250.52(A)(3), that portion of the GEC that's the sole connection to the concrete-encased electrode(s) isn't required to be larger than 4 AWG copper.

Figure 250–236

ARTICLE 285

SURGE PROTECTIVE DEVICES (SPDS)

Introduction to Article 285—Surge Protective Devices (SPDs)

This article covers the general requirements, installation requirements, and connection requirements for surge protective devices (SPDs) rated 1kV or less that are permanently installed on premises wiring systems. The *NEC* doesn't require surge protective devices to be installed, but if they are, they must comply with this article.

Surge protective devices are designed to reduce transient voltages present on premises power distribution wiring and load-side equipment, particularly electronic equipment such as computers, telecommunications equipment, security systems, and electronic appliances.

These transient voltages can originate from a number of sources, including anything from lightning to laser printers. The best line of defense for all types of electronic equipment may be the installation of surge protective devices at the electrical service and source of power, as well as at the location of the utilization equipment. Figures 285–1 and 285–2

The intent of a surge protection device is to limit transient voltages by diverting or limiting surge current and preventing continued flow of current while remaining capable of repeating these functions [Article 100]. Figure 285–3

Voltage spikes/transients caused by the switching of utility power lines or power factor correction capacitors, or lightning can reach thousands of volts and amperes.

Figure 285–1

Voltage spikes (transients) produced by premises equipment such as photocopiers, laser printers, and other high reactive loads cycling off, can be in the hundreds of volts.

Figure 285–2

Figure 285–3

Part I. General

285.1 Scope

This article covers the installation and connection requirements for permanently installed surge protective devices. Figure 285–4

Figure 285–4

Note: Surge arresters rated less than 1,000V are known as Type 1 surge protective devices.

285.3 Uses Not Permitted

A surge protective device must not be used in:

(1) Circuits that exceed 1,000V.

(2) Ungrounded systems, impedance grounded systems, or corner-grounded delta systems, unless listed specifically for use on these systems.

(3) If the voltage rating of the surge protective device is less than the maximum continuous phase-to-ground voltage available at the point of connection.

285.4 Number Required

If used, the surge protective device must be connected to each ungrounded conductor of the circuit. Figure 285–5

Figure 285–5

285.5 Listing

Surge protective devices must be listed.

Author's Comment:

■ According to UL 1449, *Standard for Surge Protective Devices*, these units are intended to limit the maximum amplitude of transient voltage surges on power lines to specified values.

They aren't intended to function as lightning arresters. The adequacy of the voltage suppression level to protect connected equipment from voltage surges hasn't been evaluated.

285.6 Short-Circuit Current Rating

Surge protective devices must be marked with their short-circuit current rating, and they must not be installed if the available fault current exceeds that rating. This short-circuit current marking requirement doesn't apply to receptacles containing surge protective device protection.

⚠️ **WARNING:** *Surge protective devices of the series type are susceptible to failure at high fault currents. A hazardous condition is present if the surge protective device short-circuit current rating is less than the available fault current.*

Part II. Installation

285.11 Location

Surge protective devices can be located indoors or outdoors and be made inaccessible to unqualified persons, unless listed for installation in accessible locations.

285.12 Routing of Conductors

Surge protective device conductors must not be any longer than necessary, and unnecessary bends must be avoided. Figure 285–6

285.13 Type 4 and Other Component Type SPDs

Type 4 component assemblies and other component type SPDs can only be installed by the manufacturer.

Routing of SPD Conductors
285.12

SPD conductors must not be any longer than necessary, and unnecessary bends must be avoided.

Copyright 2014, www.MikeHolt.com

Figure 285–6

Part III. Connecting Surge protective Devices

285.23 Type 1 SPD—Line Side of Service Equipment

(A) Installation. Type 1 surge protective devices can be connected as follows:

(1) Supply side of service equipment [230.82(4)]. Figure 285–7

Type 1 Surge Protective Device
285.23(A)

Copyright 2014
www.MikeHolt.com

Type 1 SPDs are rated less than 1,000V and are listed to be installed on the line or load side of the service equipment.

Figure 285–7

(2) Load side of service equipment in accordance with 285.24.

(B) Grounding. Type 1 surge protective devices located at service equipment must be connected to one of the following: Figure 285–8

Figure 285–8

Figure 285–9

(1) Service neutral conductor,

(2) Grounding electrode conductor,

(3) Grounding electrode for the service, or

(4) Equipment grounding terminal in the service equipment.

Author's Comment:

- Only one conductor can be connected to a terminal, unless the terminal is identified for multiple conductors [110.14(A)]. Figure 285–9

- The definition of a Type 1 surge protection device in Article 100 states that it's a permanently connected surge protective device listed for installation between the utility transformer and the service equipment. Figure 285–10

Figure 285–10

285.24 Type 2 SPD—Feeder Circuits

(A) Service Equipment. Type 2 surge protective devices can be connected to the load side of service equipment. Figure 285–11

Author's Comment:

- Only one conductor can be connected to a terminal, unless the terminal is identified for multiple conductors [110.14(A)]. Figure 285–12

- The definition of a Type 2 surge protection device in Article 100 states that it's a permanently connected surge protective device listed for installation on the load side of the service disconnecting means. Figure 285–13

(B) Feeder-Supplied Buildings. Type 2 surge protective devices can be connected anywhere on the load side of the building overcurrent device.

Type 2 Surge Protective Device
285.24(A)

Type 2 SPD

Type 2 SPDs are listed to be installed on the load side of service equipment.

Copyright 2014, www.MikeHolt.com

Figure 285–11

Surge Protective Device - Type 2
Article 100 Definition

A Type 2 SPD is a permanently connected SPD listed for installation on the load side of the service disconnecting means.

Copyright 2014, www.MikeHolt.com

Figure 285–13

Connecting Type 2 SPDs
Load Side of Service
285.24(A)

VIOLATION
Terminals are listed for one wire unless marked otherwise [110.14(A)].

Copyright 2014, www.MikeHolt.com

Figure 285–12

Surge-Protective Devices (SPDs)
285.25

Type 3 SPD (TVSS)

Type 3 SPD protective devices can be installed on the load side of branch-circuit overcurrent protection up to the equipment served. If included in the manufacturer's instructions, the Type 3 SPD connection must be a minimum of 30 ft of conductor distance from service or separately derived system disconnect.

Copyright 2014, www.MikeHolt.com

Figure 285–14

(C) Separately Derived Systems. Type 2 surge protective devices can be connected anywhere on the premises wiring of the separately derived system.

285.25 Type 3 SPDs—Branch Circuits

Type 3 surge protective devices can be installed on the load side of a branch-circuit overcurrent device. If included in the manufacturer's instructions, the Type 3 SPD connection must be a minimum 30 ft of conductor distance from the service or separately derived system disconnect. Figure 285–14

Author's Comment:

■ The definition of a Type 3 surge protection device in Article 100 states it's a surge protective device listed for installation on branch circuits.

CHAPTER 2 PRACTICE QUESTIONS

Please use the 2014 *Code* book to answer the following questions.

1. The continuity of a grounded conductor shall not depend on a connection to a _____.

   (a) metallic enclosure
   (b) raceway
   (c) cable armor
   (d) all of these

2. The GFCI protection required by 210.8(A), (B), (C), and (D) must be ____.

   (a) the circuit breaker type only
   (b) accessible
   (c) readily accessible
   (d) concealed

3. All 15A and 20A, 125V receptacles installed in bathrooms of _____ shall have ground-fault circuit-interrupter (GFCI) protection for personnel.

   (a) guest rooms in hotels/motels
   (b) dwelling units
   (c) office buildings
   (d) all of these

4. GFCI protection shall be provided for all 15A and 20A, 125V receptacles installed in a dwelling unit _____.

   (a) attic
   (b) garage
   (c) laundry room
   (d) all of these

5. Two or more _____ small-appliance branch circuits shall be provided to supply power for receptacle outlets in the dwelling unit kitchen, dining room, breakfast room, pantry, or similar dining areas.

   (a) 15A
   (b) 20A
   (c) 30A
   (d) either 20A or 30A

6. There shall be a minimum of one _____ branch circuit for the laundry outlet(s) required by 210.52(F).

   (a) 15A
   (b) 20A
   (c) 30A
   (d) b and c

7. An individual 20A branch circuit can supply a single dwelling unit bathroom for receptacle outlet(s) and other equipment within the same bathroom.

   (a) True
   (b) False

8. A receptacle connected to one of the dwelling unit small-appliance branch circuits can be used to supply an electric clock.

   (a) True
   (b) False

9. A receptacle connected to a dwelling unit small-appliance circuit can supply gas-fired ranges, ovens, or counter-mounted cooking units.

(a) True
(b) False

10. A receptacle outlet shall be installed at each dwelling unit kitchen wall countertop space that is 12 in. or wider and receptacle outlets shall be installed so that no point along the wall line is more than _____ in., measured horizontally from a receptacle outlet in that space.

(a) 10
(b) 12
(c) 16
(d) 24

11. Receptacles installed behind a bed in the guest rooms in hotels and motels shall be located to prevent the bed from contacting an attachment plug, or the receptacle shall be provided with a suitable guard.

(a) True
(b) False

12. The number of receptacle outlets for guest rooms in hotels and motels shall not be less than that required for a dwelling unit. These receptacles can be located to be convenient for permanent furniture layout, but at least _____ receptacle outlet(s) shall be readily accessible.

(a) one
(b) two
(c) three
(d) four

13. At least one 125V, 15A or 20A receptacle outlet shall be installed within 18 in. of the top of a show window for each _____ linear ft, or major fraction thereof, of show-window area measured horizontally at its maximum width.

(a) 10
(b) 12
(c) 18
(d) 24

14. When calculations in Article 220 result in a fraction of an ampere that is less than _____, such fractions can be dropped.

(a) 0.49
(b) 0.50
(c) 0.51
(d) 0.80

15. The 3 VA per-square-foot general lighting load for dwelling units does not include _____.

(a) open porches
(b) garages
(c) unused or unfinished spaces not adaptable for future use
(d) all of these

16. Where fixed multioutlet assemblies are used in other than dwelling units or the guest rooms of hotels or motels, each _____ or fraction thereof of each separate and continuous length shall be considered as one outlet of not less than 180 VA where appliances are unlikely to be used simultaneously.

(a) 5 ft
(b) 5½ ft
(c) 6 ft
(d) 6½ ft

17. There shall be no reduction in the size of the neutral or grounded conductor on _____ loads supplied from a 4-wire, wye-connected, three-phase system.

(a) dwelling unit
(b) hospital
(c) nonlinear
(d) motel

18. Under the optional method for calculating a single-family dwelling service, general loads beyond the initial 10 kVA are assessed at a _____ percent demand factor.

(a) 40
(b) 50
(c) 60
(d) 75

19. There shall be no more than _____ switches or circuit breakers to serve as the disconnecting means for a building supplied by a feeder.

    (a) two
    (b) four
    (c) six
    (d) eight

20. The two to six disconnects for a disconnecting means for a building supplied by a feeder shall be _____.

    (a) the same size
    (b) grouped
    (c) in the same enclosure
    (d) none of these

21. In a multiple-occupancy building, each occupant shall have access to his or her own _____.

    (a) disconnecting means
    (b) building drops
    (c) building-entrance assembly
    (d) lateral conductors

22. Overhead service conductors can be supported to hardwood trees.

    (a) True
    (b) False

23. Service-drop conductors shall have _____.

    (a) sufficient ampacity to carry the load
    (b) adequate mechanical strength
    (c) a or b
    (d) a and b

24. The minimum size service-drop conductor permitted is _____ AWG copper or _____ AWG aluminum or copper-clad aluminum.

    (a) 8, 8
    (b) 8, 6
    (c) 6, 8
    (d) 6, 6

25. One set of service-entrance conductors connected to the supply side of the normal service disconnecting means shall be permitted to supply standby power systems, fire pump equipment, and fire and sprinkler alarms covered by 230.82(5).

    (a) True
    (b) False

26. Ungrounded service-entrance conductors shall be sized not less than _____ percent of the continuous load, plus 100 percent of the noncontinuous load.

    (a) 100
    (b) 115
    (c) 125
    (d) 150

27. Wiring methods permitted for service-entrance conductors include _____.

    (a) rigid metal conduit
    (b) electrical metallic tubing
    (c) PVC conduit
    (d) all of these

28. Each service disconnecting means shall be suitable for _____.

    (a) hazardous (classified) locations
    (b) wet locations
    (c) dry locations
    (d) the prevailing conditions

29. There shall be no more than _____ disconnects installed for each service or for each set of service-entrance conductors as permitted in 230.2 and 230.40.

    (a) two
    (b) four
    (c) six
    (d) eight

30. When the service contains two to six service disconnecting means, they shall be _____.

    (a) the same size
    (b) grouped
    (c) in the same enclosure
    (d) none of these

31. Flexible cords approved for and used with a specific listed appliance or luminaire shall be considered to be protected by the branch-circuit overcurrent device when _____.

    (a) not more than 6 ft in length
    (b) 20 AWG and larger
    (c) applied within the listing requirements
    (d) 16 AWG and larger

32. Flexible cord used in listed extension cord sets shall be considered protected against overcurrent when used _____.

    (a) in indoor installations
    (b) in unclassified locations
    (c) within the extension cord's listing requirements
    (d) within 50 ft of the branch-circuit panelboard

33. Plug fuses of the Edison-base type shall have a maximum rating of _____.

    (a) 20A
    (b) 30A
    (c) 40A
    (d) 50A

34. Plug fuses of the Edison-base type shall be used _____.

    (a) where overfusing is necessary
    (b) as a replacement in existing installations
    (c) as a replacement for Type S fuses
    (d) 50A and above

35. Ground clamps and fittings that are exposed to physical damage shall be enclosed in _____.

    (a) metal
    (b) wood
    (c) the equivalent of a or b
    (d) none of these

36. _____ on equipment to be grounded shall be removed from contact surfaces to ensure good electrical continuity.

    (a) Paint
    (b) Lacquer
    (c) Enamel
    (d) any of these

37. Main bonding jumpers and system bonding jumpers shall not be smaller than specified in _____.

    (a) Table 250.102(C)(1)
    (b) Table 250.122
    (c) Table 310.15(B)(16)
    (d) Chapter 9, Table 8

38. Where the supply conductors are larger than 1,100 kcmil copper or 1,750 kcmil aluminum, the main bonding jumper shall have an area that is _____ the area of the largest phase conductor when of the same material.

    (a) at least equal to
    (b) at least 50 percent of
    (c) not less than 12½ percent of
    (d) not more than 12½ percent of

39. When a permanently installed generator _____, the requirements of 250.30 apply.

    (a) is a separately derived system
    (b) is not a separately derived system
    (c) supplies only cord and plug connected loads
    (d) none of these

40. High-impedance grounded neutral systems shall be permitted for three-phase ac systems of 480V to 1,000V where _____.

    (a) the conditions of maintenance ensure that only qualified persons service the installation
    (b) ground detectors are installed on the system
    (c) line-to-neutral loads are not served
    (d) all of these

41. The upper end of a ground rod electrode shall be _____ ground level unless the aboveground end and the grounding electrode conductor attachment are protected against physical damage.

    (a) above
    (b) flush with
    (c) below
    (d) b or c

42. Where rock bottom is encountered when driving a ground rod at an angle up to 45 degrees, the electrode can be buried in a trench that is at least _____ deep.

    (a) 18 in.
    (b) 30 in.
    (c) 4 ft
    (d) 8 ft

43. The connection of the grounding electrode conductor to a buried grounding electrode (driven ground rod) shall be made with a listed terminal device that is accessible.

    (a) True
    (b) False

44. Exothermic or irreversible compression connections, together with the mechanical means used to attach to fireproofed structural metal, shall not be required to be accessible.

    (a) True
    (b) False

45. Equipment bonding jumpers on the supply side of the service shall be no smaller than the sizes shown in _____.

    (a) Table 250.102(C)(1)
    (b) Table 250.122
    (c) Table 310.15(B)(16)
    (d) Table 310.15(B)(6)

46. The supply-side bonding jumper on the supply side of services shall be sized according to the _____.

    (a) overcurrent device rating
    (b) ungrounded supply conductor size
    (c) service-drop size
    (d) load to be served

47. The armor of Type AC cable containing an aluminum bonding strip is recognized by the *NEC* as an equipment grounding conductor.

    (a) True
    (b) False

48. Type MC cable provides an effective ground-fault current path and is recognized by the *NEC* as an equipment grounding conductor when _____.

    (a) it contains an insulated or uninsulated equipment grounding conductor in compliance with 250.118(1)
    (b) the combined metallic sheath and uninsulated equipment grounding/bonding conductor of interlocked metal tape–type MC cable is listed and identified as an equipment grounding conductor
    (c) only when it is hospital grade Type MC cable
    (d) a or b

49. Where circuit conductors are spliced or terminated on equipment within a box, any equipment grounding conductors associated with those circuit conductors shall be connected to the box with devices suitable for the use.

    (a) True
    (b) False

50. The arrangement of grounding connections shall be such that the disconnection or the removal of a receptacle, luminaire, or other device fed from the box does not interrupt the grounding continuity.

    (a) True
    (b) False

CHAPTER 3

WIRING METHODS AND MATERIALS

Introduction to Chapter 3—Wiring Methods and Materials

Chapter 3 covers wiring methods and materials, and provides some very specific installation requirements for conductors, cables, boxes, raceways, and fittings. This chapter includes detailed information about the installation and restrictions involved with wiring methods.

It may be because of those details that many people incorrectly apply the rules from this chapter. Be sure to pay careful attention to the details, and be sure that you make your installation comply with the rules in the *NEC*, not just completing it in the manner that you may have been taught or because "it's always been done that way." This is especially true when it comes to applying the Tables.

Violations of the rules for wiring methods found in Chapter 3 can result in problems with power quality and can lead to fire, shock, and other hazards.

The type of wiring method you'll use depends on several factors; job specifications, *Code* requirements, the environment, need, and cost are among them.

Chapter 3 begins with rules that are common to most wiring methods [Article 300]. It then covers conductors [Article 310] and enclosures [Articles 312 and 314]. The articles that follow become more specific and deal more in-depth with individual wiring methods such as specific types of cables [Articles 320 through 340] and various raceways [Articles 342 through 390]. The chapter winds up with Article 392, a support system, and the final articles [Articles 394 through 398] for open wiring.

Notice as you read through the various wiring methods that the *Code* attempts to use similar subsection numbering for similar topics from one article to the next, using the same digits after the decimal point in the section number for the same topic. This makes it easier to locate specific requirements in a particular article. For example, the rules for securing and supporting can be found in the section that ends with .30 of each article. In addition to this, you'll find a "uses permitted" and "uses not permitted" section in nearly every article.

Wiring Method Articles

- **Article 300—General Requirements for Wiring Methods and Materials.** Article 300 contains the general requirements for all wiring methods included in the *NEC*, except for signaling and communications systems, which are covered in Chapters 7 and 8.

- **Article 310—Conductors for General Wiring.** This article contains the general requirements for conductors, such as insulation markings, ampacity ratings, and conductor use. Article 310 doesn't apply to conductors that are part of flexible cords, fixture wires, or conductors that are an integral part of equipment [90.6 and 300.1(B)].

- **Article 312—Cabinet.** Article 312 covers the installation and construction specifications for cabinet.

- **Article 314—Outlet, Device, Pull, and Junction Boxes, Conduit Bodies, Fittings, and Handhole Enclosures.** Installation requirements for outlet boxes, pull and junction boxes, as well as conduit bodies, and handhole enclosures are contained in this article.

Cable Articles

Articles 320 through 340 address specific types of cables. If you take the time to become familiar with the various types of cables, you'll:

- Understand what's available for doing the work.
- Recognize cable types that have special *NEC* requirements.
- Avoid buying cable that you can't install due to *Code* requirements you can't meet with that particular wiring method.

Here's a brief overview of each one:

- **Article 320—Armored Cable (Type AC).** Armored cable is an assembly of insulated conductors, 14 AWG through 1 AWG, individually wrapped with waxed paper. The conductors are contained within a flexible spiral metal (steel or aluminum) sheath that interlocks at the edges. Armored cable looks like flexible metal conduit. Many electricians call this metal cable "BX®."

- **Article 330—Metal-Clad Cable (Type MC).** Metal-clad cable encloses insulated conductors in a metal sheath of either corrugated or smooth copper or aluminum tubing, or spiral interlocked steel or aluminum. The physical characteristics of Type MC cable make it a versatile wiring method permitted in almost any location and for almost any application. The most commonly used Type MC cable is the interlocking kind, which looks similar to armored cable or flexible metal conduit.

- **Article 334—Nonmetallic-Sheathed Cable (Type NM).** Nonmetallic-sheathed cable encloses two, three, or four insulated conductors, 14 AWG through 2 AWG, within a nonmetallic outer jacket. Because this cable is nonmetallic, it contains a separate equipment grounding conductor. Nonmetallic-sheathed cable is a common wiring method used for residential and commercial branch circuits. Many electricians call this plastic-sheathed cable "Romex®."

- **Article 336—Power and Control Tray Cable (Type TC).** Power and control tray cable is a factory assembly of two or more insulated conductors under a nonmetallic sheath for installation in cable trays, in raceways, or supported by a messenger wire.

- **Article 338—Service-Entrance Cable (Types SE and USE).** Service-entrance cable can be a single-conductor or a multiconductor assembly within an overall nonmetallic covering. This cable is used primarily for services not over 600V, but is also permitted for feeders and branch circuits.

■ **Article 340—Underground Feeder and Branch-Circuit Cable (Type UF).** Underground feeder cable is a moisture-, fungus-, and corrosion-resistant cable suitable for direct burial in the earth, and it comes in sizes 14 AWG through 4/0 AWG [340.104]. Multiconductor UF cable is covered in molded plastic that surrounds the insulated conductors.

Raceway Articles

Articles 342 through 390 address specific types of raceways. Refer to Article 100 for the definition of a raceway. If you take the time to become familiar with the various types of raceways, you'll:

- Understand what's available for doing the work.
- Recognize raceway types that have special *Code* requirements.
- Avoid buying a raceway that you can't install due to *NEC* requirements you can't meet with that particular wiring method.

Here's a brief overview of each one:

■ **Article 342—Intermediate Metal Conduit (Type IMC).** Intermediate metal conduit is a circular metal raceway with the same outside diameter as rigid metal conduit. The wall thickness of intermediate metal conduit is less than that of rigid metal conduit, so it has a greater interior cross-sectional area for holding conductors. Intermediate metal conduit is lighter and less expensive than rigid metal conduit, but it's permitted in all the same locations as rigid metal conduit. Intermediate metal conduit also uses a different steel alloy, which makes it stronger than rigid metal conduit, even though the walls are thinner.

■ **Article 344—Rigid Metal Conduit (Type RMC).** Rigid metal conduit is similar to intermediate metal conduit, except the wall thickness is greater, so it has a smaller interior cross-sectional area. Rigid metal conduit is heavier than intermediate metal conduit and it's permitted to be installed in any location, just like intermediate metal conduit.

■ **Article 348—Flexible Metal Conduit (Type FMC).** Flexible metal conduit is a raceway of circular cross section made of a helically wound, interlocked metal strip of either steel or aluminum. It's commonly called "Greenfield" or "Flex."

■ **Article 350—Liquidtight Flexible Metal Conduit (Type LFMC).** Liquidtight flexible metal conduit is a raceway of circular cross section with an outer liquidtight, nonmetallic, sunlight-resistant jacket over an inner flexible metal core, with associated couplings, connectors, and fittings. It's listed for the installation of electrical conductors. Liquidtight flexible metal conduit is commonly called "Sealtite®" or simply "liquidtight." Liquidtight flexible metal conduit is of similar construction to flexible metal conduit, but it has an outer thermoplastic covering.

■ **Article 352—Rigid Polyvinyl Chloride Conduit (Type PVC).** Rigid polyvinyl chloride conduit is a nonmetallic raceway of circular cross section with integral or associated couplings, connectors, and fittings. It's listed for the installation of electrical conductors.

- **Article 356—Liquidtight Flexible Nonmetallic Conduit (Type LFNC).** Liquidtight flexible nonmetallic conduit is a raceway of circular cross section with an outer liquidtight, nonmetallic, sunlight-resistant jacket over an inner flexible core, with associated couplings, connectors, and fittings.

  - Type LFNC-A (orange). A smooth seamless inner core and cover bonded together with reinforcement layers inserted between the core and covers.
  - Type LFNC-B (gray). A smooth inner surface with integral reinforcement within the conduit wall.
  - Type LFNC-C (black). A corrugated internal and external surface without integral reinforcement within the conduit wall.

- **Article 358—Electrical Metallic Tubing (EMT).** Electrical metallic tubing is a nonthreaded thinwall raceway of circular cross section designed for the physical protection and routing of conductors and cables. Compared to rigid metal conduit and intermediate metal conduit, electrical metallic tubing is relatively easy to bend, cut, and ream. EMT isn't threaded, so all connectors and couplings are of the threadless type. Today, it's available in a range of colors, such as red and blue.

- **Article 362—Electrical Nonmetallic Tubing (ENT).** Electrical nonmetallic tubing is a pliable, corrugated, circular raceway made of PVC. It's often called "Smurf Pipe" or "Smurf Tube," because it was available only in blue when it came out and at the time the children's cartoon characters "The Smurfs" were popular. It's now available in multiple colors such as red and yellow as well as blue.

- **Article 376—Metal Wireways.** A metal wireway is a sheet metal trough with hinged or removable covers for housing and protecting electrical conductors and cable, in which conductors are placed after the wireway has been installed as a complete system.

- **Article 380—Multioutlet Assemblies.** A multioutlet assembly is a surface, flush, or freestanding raceway designed to hold conductors and receptacles. It's assembled in the field or at the factory.

- **Article 386—Surface Metal Raceways.** A surface metal raceway is a metallic raceway intended to be mounted to the surface with associated accessories, in which conductors are placed after the raceway has been installed as a complete system.

- **Article 388—Surface Nonmetallic Raceways.** A surface nonmetallic raceway is intended to be surface mounted with associated accessories. Conductors are placed inside after the raceway has been installed as a complete system.

Cable Tray

- **Article 392—Cable Trays.** A cable tray system is a unit or assembly of units or sections with associated fittings that form a structural system used to securely fasten or support cables and raceways. A cable tray isn't a raceway; it's a support system for raceways, cables, and enclosures.

GENERAL REQUIREMENTS FOR WIRING METHODS AND MATERIALS

Introduction to Article 300—General Requirements for Wiring Methods and Materials

Article 300 contains the general requirements for all wiring methods included in the *NEC*. However, the article doesn't apply to communications systems, which are covered in Chapter 8, except when Article 300 is specifically referenced in Chapter 8.

This article is primarily concerned with how to install, route, splice, protect, and secure conductors and raceways. How well you conform to the requirements of Article 300 will generally be evident in the finished work, because many of the requirements tend to determine the appearance of the installation. Because of this, it's often easy to spot Article 300 problems if you're looking for *Code* violations. For example, you can easily see when someone runs an equipment grounding conductor outside a raceway instead of grouping all conductors of a circuit together, as required by 300.3(B).

A good understanding of Article 300 will start you on the path to correctly installing the wiring methods included in Chapter 3. Be sure to carefully consider the accompanying illustrations, and refer to the definitions in Article 100 as needed.

Part I. General

300.1 Scope

(A) Wiring Installations. Article 300 contains the general requirements for wiring methods and materials for power and lighting.

Author's Comment:

- The requirements contained in Article 300 don't apply to the wiring methods for signaling and communications systems, except where there's a specific reference in Chapter 7 or 8 to a rule in Article 300.

  □ CATV, 820.3
  □ Class 2 and 3 Circuits, 725.3
  □ Communications Cables and Raceways, 800.133(A)(2)
  □ Fire Alarm Circuits, 760.3

(B) Integral Parts of Equipment. The requirements contained in Article 300 don't apply to the internal parts of electrical equipment. Figure 300–1

Integral Parts of Equipment
300.1(B)

The requirements contained in Article 300 don't apply to the internal parts of electrical equipment.

Copyright 2014, www.MikeHolt.com

Figure 300–1

(C) Trade Sizes. Designators for raceway trade sizes are given in Table 300.1(C).

Author's Comment:

- Industry practice is to describe raceways using inch sizes, such as ½ in., 2 in., and so on; however, the proper reference (2005 *NEC* change) is to use "Trade Size ½," or "Trade Size 2." In this textbook we use the term "Trade Size."

300.3 Conductors

(A) Conductors. Single conductors must be installed within a Chapter 3 wiring method, such as a raceway, cable, or enclosure. Figure 300–2

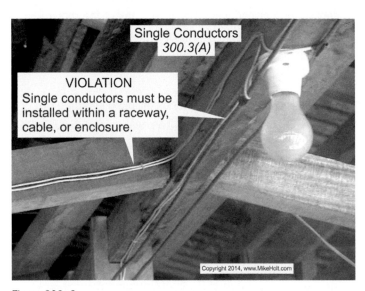

Figure 300–2

Ex: Overhead conductors can be installed in accordance with 225.6.

(B) Circuit Conductors Grouped Together. All conductors of a circuit and, where used, the neutral and equipment grounding and bonding conductors must be installed in the same raceway, cable, trench, cord, or cable tray, except as permitted by (1) through (4). Figure 300–3

(1) Paralleled Installations. Conductors installed in parallel in accordance with 310.10(H) must have all circuit conductors within the same raceway, cable tray, trench, or cable. Figure 300–4

Figure 300–3

Figure 300–4

Ex: Parallel conductors run underground can be installed in different raceways (Phase A in raceway 1, Phase B in raceway 2, and so forth), if the raceways are nonmetallic or nonmagnetic and the installation complies with 300.20(B). See 300.5(I) Ex 2.

Author's Comment:

- All conductors of a circuit must be installed in the same raceway, cable, trench, cord, or cable tray to minimize induction of the heating of ferrous metal raceways and enclosures, and to maintain a low-impedance ground-fault current path [250.4(A)(3)].

(2) Grounding and Bonding Conductors. Equipment grounding jumpers can be located outside of a flexible raceway if the bonding jumper is installed in accordance with 250.102(E)(2). Figure 300–5

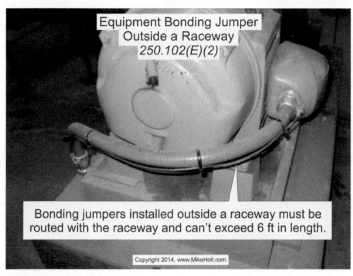

Figure 300–5

For dc circuits, the equipment grounding conductor is permitted to be run separately from the circuit conductors in accordance with 250.134(B) Ex 2. Figure 300–6

Figure 300–6

(3) Nonferrous Wiring Methods. Circuit conductors can be installed in different raceways (Phase A in raceway 1, Phase B in raceway 2, and so on) if, in order to reduce or eliminate inductive heating, the raceway is nonmetallic or nonmagnetic and the installation complies with 300.20(B). See 300.3(B)(1) and 300.5(I) Ex 2.

(C) Conductors of Different Systems.

(1) Mixing. Power conductors of alternating-current and direct-current systems rated 600V or less can occupy the same raceway, cable, or enclosure if all conductors have an insulation voltage rating not less than the maximum circuit voltage. Figure 300–7

Figure 300–7

Author's Comment:

- Control, signal, and communications wiring must be separated from power and lighting circuits so the higher-voltage conductors don't accidentally energize the control, signal, or communications wiring: Figure 300–8

    □ CATV Coaxial Cable, 820.133(A)
    □ Class 1 control circuits, 725.48
    □ Class 2 and Class 3 Control Circuits, 725.136(A)
    □ Communications Circuits, 800.133(A)(1)(c)
    □ Fire Alarm Circuits, 760.136(A)
    □ Instrumentation Tray Cable, 727.5
    □ Sound Circuits, 640.9(C)

Figure 300–8

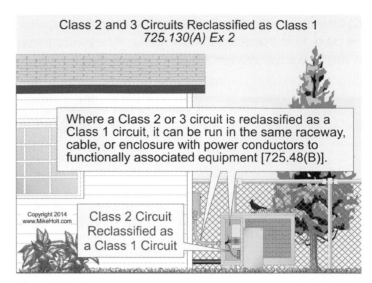

Figure 300–10

■ Class 1 circuit conductors can be installed with associated power conductors [725.48(B)(1)] if all conductors have an insulation voltage rating not less than the maximum circuit voltage [300.3(C)(1)]. Figure 300–9

Note 2: PV system conductors, both direct current and alternating current, are permitted to be installed in the same raceways, outlet and junction boxes, or similar fittings with each other, but they must be kept entirely independent of all other non-PV system wiring [690.31(B)]. Figure 300–11

Figure 300–9

Figure 300–11

■ A Class 2 circuit that's been reclassified as a Class 1 circuit [725.130(A) Ex 2] can be installed with associated power conductors [725.48(B)(1)] if all conductors have an insulation voltage rating not less than the maximum circuit voltage [300.3(C)(1)]. Figure 300–10

300.4 Protection Against Physical Damage

Conductors, raceways, and cables must be protected against physical damage [110.27(B)].

(A) Cables and Raceways Through Wood Members. When the following wiring methods are installed through wood members, they must comply with (1) and (2). Figure 300–12

Figure 300–12

- Armored Cable, Article 320
- Electrical Nonmetallic Tubing, Article 362
- Flexible Metal Conduit, Article 348
- Liquidtight Flexible Metal Conduit, Article 350
- Liquidtight Flexible Nonmetallic Conduit, Article 356
- Metal-Clad Cable, Article 330
- Nonmetallic-Sheathed Cable, Article 334
- Service-Entrance Cable, Article 338
- Underground Feeder and Branch-Circuit Cable, Article 340

(1) Holes in Wood Members. Holes through wood framing members for the above cables or raceways must be not less than 1¼ in. from the edge of the wood member. If the edge of the hole is less than 1¼ in. from the edge, a ¹⁄₁₆ in. thick steel plate of sufficient length and width must be installed to protect the wiring method from screws and nails.

Ex 1: A steel plate isn't required to protect rigid metal conduit, intermediate metal conduit, PVC conduit, or electrical metallic tubing.

Ex 2: A listed and marked steel plate less than $\frac{1}{16}$ in. thick that provides equal or better protection against nail or screw penetration is permitted. Figure 300–13

Figure 300–13

Author's Comment:

- Hardened steel plates thinner than ¹⁄₁₆ in. have been tested and found to provide better protection from screw and nail penetration than the thicker plates.

(2) Notches in Wood Members. If notching of wood framing members for cables and raceways are permitted by the building *Code*, a ¹⁄₁₆ in. thick steel plate of sufficient length and width must be installed to protect the wiring method laid in these wood notches from screws and nails.

⚠ **CAUTION:** *When drilling or notching wood members, be sure to check with the building inspector to ensure you don't damage or weaken the structure and violate the building Code.*

Ex 1: A steel plate isn't required to protect rigid metal conduit, intermediate metal conduit, PVC conduit, or electrical metallic tubing.

Ex 2: A listed and marked steel plate less than $\frac{1}{16}$ in. thick that provides equal or better protection against nail or screw penetration is permitted. Figure 300–14

Figure 300–14

(B) Nonmetallic-Sheathed Cable and Electrical Nonmetallic Tubing Through Metal Framing Members.

(1) Nonmetallic-Sheathed Cable (NM). If Type NM cables pass through factory or field openings in metal framing members, the cable must be protected by listed bushings or listed grommets that cover all metal edges. The protection fitting must be securely fastened in the opening before the installation of the cable. Figure 300–15

Figure 300–15

(2) Type NM Cable and Electrical Nonmetallic Tubing. If nails or screws are likely to penetrate Type NM cable or electrical nonmetallic tubing, a steel sleeve, steel plate, or steel clip not less than 1/16 in. in thickness must be installed to protect the cable or tubing.

Ex: A listed and marked steel plate less than 1/16 in. thick that provides equal or better protection against nail or screw penetration is permitted.

(C) Behind Suspended Ceilings. Wiring methods, such as boxes, enclosures cables or raceways, installed behind panels designed to allow access must be supported in accordance with its applicable article and 300.11(A). Figure 300–16

Figure 300–16

Author's Comment:

- Similar requirements are contained in Chapters 6, 7, and 8 as follows:

  □ Audio Cable, 640.6(B)
  □ CATV Coaxial Cable, 820.21 and 820.24
  □ Communications (twisted pair) Cable, 800.21
  □ Control and Signaling Cable, 725.21 and 725.24
  □ Fire Alarm Cable, 760.7 and 760.8
  □ Optical Fiber Cable, 770.21 and 770.24

(D) Cables and Raceways Parallel to Framing Members and Furring Strips. Cables or raceways run parallel to framing members or furring strips must be protected if they're likely to be penetrated by nails or screws, by installing the wiring method so it isn't less than 1¼ in. from the nearest edge of the framing member or furring strip. If the edge of the framing member or furring strip is less than 1¼ in. away, a ¹⁄₁₆ in. thick steel plate of sufficient length and width must be installed to protect the wiring method from screws and nails. Figure 300–17

Figure 300–17

Author's Comment:

- This rule doesn't apply to control, signaling, and communications cables, but similar requirements are contained in Chapters 6, 7, and 8 as follows:

  - CATV Coaxial Cable, 820.24
  - Communications Cable, 800.24
  - Control and Signaling Cable, 725.24
  - Optical Fiber Cable, 770.24
  - Fire Alarm Cable, 760.8
  - Audio Cable, 640.6(B)

Ex 1: Protection isn't required for rigid metal conduit, intermediate metal conduit, PVC conduit, or electrical metallic tubing.

Ex 2: For concealed work in finished buildings, or finished panels for prefabricated buildings if such supporting is impracticable, the cables can be fished between access points.

Ex 3: A listed and marked steel plate less than ¹⁄₁₆ in. thick that provides equal or better protection against nail or screw penetration is permitted.

(E) Wiring Under Roof Decking. Cables, raceways, and enclosures under metal-corrugated sheet roof decking must not be located within 1½ in. of the roof decking, measured from the lowest surface of the roof decking to the top of the cable, raceway, or box. In addition, cables, raceways, and enclosures aren't permitted in concealed locations of metal-corrugated sheet decking type roofing. Figure 300–18

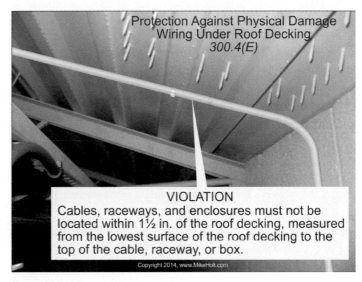

Figure 300–18

Author's Comment:

- This requirement also applies to luminaires installed in or under roof decking [410.10(F)].

Note: Roof decking material will be installed or replaced after the initial raceway or cabling which may be penetrated by the screws or other mechanical devices designed to provide "hold down" strength of the waterproof membrane or roof insulating material.

Ex: Spacing from roof decking doesn't apply to rigid metal conduit and intermediate metal conduit.

(F) Cables and Raceways Installed in Grooves. Cables and raceways installed in a groove must be protected by a ¹⁄₁₆ in. thick steel plate or sleeve, or by 1¼ in. of free space.

Author's Comment:

- An example is Type NM cable installed in a groove cut into the Styrofoam-type insulation building block structure and then covered with wallboard.

Ex 1: Protection isn't required if the cable is installed in rigid metal conduit, intermediate metal conduit, PVC conduit, or electrical metallic tubing.

Ex 2: A listed and marked steel plate less than 1/16 in. thick that provides equal or better protection against nail or screw penetration is permitted.

(G) Insulating Fittings. If raceways contain insulated circuit conductors 4 AWG and larger that enter an enclosure, the conductors must be protected from abrasion during and after installation by a fitting identified to provide a smooth, rounded insulating surface, such as an insulating bushing. Figure 300–19

Figure 300–19

Author's Comment:

- If IMC or RMC conduit enters an enclosure without a connector, a bushing must be provided, regardless of the conductor size [342.46 and 344.46].

- An insulated fitting isn't required for a bare grounding electrode conductor. Figure 300–20

Ex: Insulating bushings aren't required if a raceway terminates in a threaded raceway entry that provides a smooth, rounded, or flared surface for the conductors, such as a hub.

Figure 300–20

(H) Structural Joints. A listed expansion/deflection fitting or other means approved by the authority having jurisdiction must be used where a raceway crosses a structural joint intended for expansion, contraction or deflection.

300.5 Underground Installations

(A) Minimum Burial Depths. When cables or raceways are installed underground, they must have a minimum "cover" in accordance with Table 300.5. Figure 300–21

Underground Installations - Minimum Cover Depths
Table 300.5

	UF or USE Cables or Conductors	RMC or IMC	PVC not Encased in Concrete	Residential 15A & 20A GFCI 120V Branch Ckts
Street Driveway Parking Lot	24 in.	24 in.	24 in.	24 in.
Driveways One - Two Family	18 in.	18 in.	18 in.	12 in.
Solid Rock With not Less than 2 in. of Concrete	Raceway Only			Raceway Only
Other Applications	24 in.	6 in.	18 in.	12 in.

Figure 300–21

Table 300.5 Minimum Cover Requirements in Inches

Location	Buried Cables	Metal Raceway	Nonmetallic Raceway
Under Building	0	0	0
Dwelling Unit	24/12*	6	18
Dwelling Unit Driveway	18/12*	6	18/12*
Under Roadway	24	24	24
Other Locations	24	6	18

*Residential branch circuits rated 120V or less with GFCI protection and maximum overcurrent protection of 20A.

Note: This is a summary of the NEC's Table 300.5. See the table in the NEC for full details.

Note 1 to Table 300.5 defines "Cover" as the distance from the top of the underground cable or raceway to the top surface of finished grade. Figure 300–22

Figure 300–23

Figure 300–22

Author's Comment:

■ The cover requirements contained in 300.5 don't apply to signaling, communications, and other power-limited wiring systems: Figure 300–23

  □ CATV, 90.3
  □ Class 2 and 3 Circuits, 725.3
  □ Communications Cables and Raceways, 90.3
  □ Fire Alarm Circuits, 760.3
  □ Optical Fiber Cables and Raceways, 770.3

(B) Wet Locations. The interior of enclosures or raceways installed in an underground installation are considered to be a wet location. Cables and insulated conductors installed in underground enclosures or raceways must comply with 310.10(C). Splices within an underground enclosure must be listed as suitable for wet locations [110.14(B)]. Figure 300–24

Figure 300–24

Author's Comment:

- The definition of a "Wet Location" as contained in Article 100, includes installations underground, in concrete slabs in direct contact with the earth, locations subject to saturation with water, and unprotected locations exposed to weather. If raceways are installed in wet locations above grade, the interior of these raceways is also considered to be a wet location [300.9].

(C) Cables and Conductors Under Buildings. Cables and conductors installed under a building must be installed in a raceway that extends past the outside walls of the building. Figure 300–25

Figure 300–25

Ex 2: Type MC Cable listed for direct burial is permitted under a building without installation in a raceway [330.10(A)(5)]. Figure 300–26

(D) Protecting Underground Cables and Conductors. Direct-buried conductors and cables such as Types MC, UF, and USE installed underground must be protected from damage in accordance with (1) through (4).

(1) Emerging from Grade. Direct-buried cables or conductors that emerge from grade must be installed in an enclosure or raceway to protect against physical damage. Protection isn't required to extend more than 18 in. below grade, and protection above ground must extend to a height of not less than 8 ft. Figure 300–27

Figure 300–26

Figure 300–27

(2) Conductors Entering Buildings. Underground conductors and cables that enter a building must be protected to the point of entrance.

(3) Service Conductors. Underground service conductors must have their location identified by a warning ribbon placed in the trench at least 12 in. above the underground conductor installation. Figure 300–28

(E) Underground Splices and Taps. Direct-buried conductors or cables can be spliced or tapped underground without a splice box [300.15(G)], if the splice or tap is made in accordance with 110.14(B). Figure 300–29

Figure 300–28

Figure 300–29

(F) Backfill. Backfill material for underground wiring must not damage the underground cable or raceway, or contribute to the corrosion of the metal raceway.

Author's Comment:

- Large rocks, chunks of concrete, steel rods, mesh, and other sharp-edged objects must not be used for backfill material, because they can damage the underground conductors, cables, or raceways.

(G) Raceway Seals. If moisture could enter an underground raceway and contact energized live parts, a seal must be installed at one or both ends of the raceway. Figure 300–30

Figure 300–30

Author's Comment:

- This is a common problem for equipment located downhill from the supply, or in underground equipment rooms. See 230.8 for service raceway seals and 300.7(A) for different temperature area seals.

Note: Hazardous explosive gases or vapors make it necessary to seal underground raceways that enter the building in accordance with 501.15.

Author's Comment:

- It isn't the intent of this Note to imply that sealing fittings of the types required in hazardous locations be installed in unclassified locations, except as required in Chapter 5. This also doesn't imply that the sealing material provides a watertight seal, but only that it prevents moisture from entering the raceways.

(H) Bushing. Raceways that terminate underground must have a bushing or fitting at the end of the raceway to protect emerging cables or conductors.

(I) Conductors Grouped Together. All underground conductors of the same circuit, including the equipment grounding conductor, must be inside the same raceway, or in close proximity to each other in the same trench. See 300.3(B). Figure 300–31

Figure 300–31

Figure 300–32

Ex 1: Conductors can be installed in parallel in raceways, multiconductor cables, or direct-buried single-conductor cables. Each raceway or multiconductor cable must contain all conductors of the same circuit including the equipment grounding conductor. Each direct-buried single-conductor cable must be located in close proximity in the trench to the other single conductor cables in the same parallel set of conductors, including equipment grounding conductors.

Ex 2: Parallel circuit conductors installed in accordance with 310.10(H) of the same phase or neutral can be installed in underground PVC conduits, if inductive heating at raceway terminations is reduced by the use of aluminum locknuts and cutting a slot between the individual holes through which the conductors pass as required by 300.20(B). Figure 300–32

Author's Comment:

- Installing ungrounded and neutral conductors in different PVC conduits makes it easier to terminate larger parallel sets of conductors, but it'll result in higher levels of electromagnetic fields (EMF).

(J) Earth Movement. Direct-buried conductors, cables, or raceways that are subject to movement by settlement or frost must be arranged to prevent damage to conductors or equipment connected to the wiring.

(K) Directional Boring. Cables or raceways installed using directional boring equipment must be approved by the authority having jurisdiction for this purpose.

Author's Comment:

- Directional boring technology uses a directional drill, which is steered continuously from point "A" to point "B." When the drill head comes out of the earth at point "B," it's replaced with a back-reamer and the duct or raceway being installed is attached to it. The size of the boring rig (hp, torque, and pull-back power) comes into play, along with the types of soil, in determining the type of raceways required. For telecommunications work, multiple poly innerducts are pulled in at one time. At major crossings, such as expressways, railroads, or rivers, outerduct may be installed to create a permanent sleeve for the innerducts.

  "Innerduct" and "outerduct" are terms usually associated with optical fiber cable installations, while "unitduct" comes with factory installed conductors. All of these come in various sizes. Galvanized rigid metal conduit, Schedule 40 and Schedule 80 PVC, HDPE conduit and nonmetallic underground conduit with conductors (NUCC) are common wiring methods used with directional boring installations.

300.6 Protection Against Corrosion and Deterioration

Raceways, cable trays, cablebus, cable armor, boxes, cable sheathing, cabinets, elbows, couplings, fittings, supports, and support hardware must be suitable for the environment. Figure 300–33

Figure 300–33

(A) Ferrous Metal Equipment. Ferrous metal raceways, enclosures, cables, cable trays, fittings, and support hardware must be protected against corrosion by a coating of listed corrosion-resistant material. Where conduit is threaded in the field, the threads must be coated with an approved electrically conductive, corrosion-resistant compound, such as cold zinc.

Note: Field-cut threads are those threads that are cut anywhere other than at the factory.

Author's Comment:

■ Nonferrous metal raceways, such as aluminum rigid metal conduit, don't have to meet the provisions of this section.

(1) Protected from Corrosion Solely by Enamel. If ferrous metal parts are protected from corrosion solely by enamel, they must not be used outdoors or in wet locations as described in 300.6(D).

(2) Organic Coatings on Boxes or Cabinets. Boxes or cabinets having a system of organic coatings marked "Raintight," "Rainproof," or "Outdoor Type," can be installed outdoors.

(3) In Concrete or in Direct Contact with the Earth. Ferrous metal raceways, cable armor, boxes, cable sheathing, cabinets, elbows, couplings, nipples, fittings, supports, and support hardware can be installed in concrete or in direct contact with the earth, or in areas subject to severe corrosive influences if made of material approved for the condition, or if provided with corrosion protection approved for the condition.

Author's Comment:

■ Galvanized electrical metallic tubing can be installed in concrete at grade level and in direct contact with the earth, but supplementary corrosion protection is usually required (UL White Book, *Guide Information for Electrical Equipment*). Electrical metallic tubing can be installed in concrete above the ground floor slab generally without supplementary corrosion protection. Figure 300–34

Figure 300–34

(B) Aluminum Equipment. Aluminum raceways, cable trays, cablebus, cable armor, boxes, cable sheathing, cabinets, elbows, couplings, nipples, fittings, supports, and support hardware embedded or encased in concrete or in direct contact with the earth must be provided with supplementary corrosion protection.

(C) Nonmetallic Equipment. Nonmetallic raceways, cable trays, cablebus, boxes, cables with a nonmetallic outer jacket and internal metal armor or jacket, cable sheathing, cabinets, elbows, couplings, nipples, fittings, supports, and support hardware must be made of material identified for the condition, and must comply with (1) and (2). Figure 300–35

Figure 300–35

(1) Exposed to Sunlight. If exposed to sunlight, the materials must be listed or identified as sunlight resistant.

(2) Chemical Exposure. If subject to exposure to chemical solvents, vapors, splashing, or immersion, materials or coatings must either be inherently resistant to chemicals based upon their listing, or be identified for the specific chemical.

(D) Indoor Wet Locations. In portions of dairy processing facilities, laundries, canneries, and other indoor wet locations, and in locations where walls are frequently washed or where there are surfaces of absorbent materials, such as damp paper or wood, the entire wiring system, where installed exposed, including all boxes, fittings, raceways, and cables, must be mounted so there's at least ¼ in. of airspace between it and the wall or supporting surface.

Author's Comment:

- See the definitions of "Exposed" and "Location, Wet" in Article 100.

Ex: Nonmetallic raceways, boxes, and fittings are permitted without the airspace on a concrete, masonry, tile, or similar surface.

Note: Areas where acids and alkali chemicals are handled and stored may present corrosive conditions, particularly when wet or damp. Severe corrosive conditions may also be present in portions of meatpacking plants, tanneries, glue houses, and some stables; in installations immediately adjacent to a seashore or swimming pool, spa, hot tub, and fountain areas; in areas where chemical deicers are used; and in storage cellars or rooms for hides, casings, fertilizer, salt, and bulk chemicals.

300.7 Raceways Exposed to Different Temperatures

(A) Sealing. If a raceway is subjected to different temperatures, and where condensation is known to be a problem, the raceway must be filled with a material approved by the authority having jurisdiction that'll prevent the circulation of warm air to a colder section of the raceway. An explosionproof seal isn't required for this purpose. Figure 300–36

Raceways must be sealed to prevent the circulation of warm air to a colder section of the raceway or sleeve.

Figure 300–36

(B) Expansion Fittings. Raceways must be provided with expansion fittings where necessary to compensate for thermal expansion and contraction. Figure 300–37

Figure 300–37

Note: Table 352.44 provides the expansion characteristics for PVC conduit. The expansion characteristics for steel conduit are determined by multiplying the values from Table 352.44 by 0.20, and the expansion characteristics for aluminum raceways are determined by multiplying the values from Table 352.44 by 0.40. Table 354.44 provides the expansion characteristics for reinforced thermosetting resin conduit (RTRC). Figure 300–38

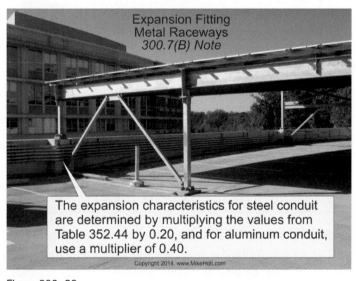

Figure 300–38

300.8 Not Permitted in Raceways

Raceways are designed for the exclusive use of electrical conductors and cables, and aren't permitted to contain nonelectrical components, such as pipes or tubes for steam, water, air, gas, drainage, and so forth. Figures 300–39 and 300–40

Figure 300–39

Figure 300–40

300.9 Raceways in Wet Locations Above Grade

Insulated conductors and cables installed in raceways in aboveground wet locations must be listed for use in wet locations according to 310.10(C). Figure 300–41

Raceways in Wet Locations Abovegrade
300.9

VIOLATION
NM cable isn't suitable for a wet location [334.12(B)(4)].

Insulated conductors and cables installed in raceways located in wet locations must be listed for use in wet locations.

Copyright 2014, www.MikeHolt.com

Figure 300–41

300.10 Electrical Continuity

Metal raceways and enclosures for conductors must be metallically joined together to form an effective ground-fault current path to facilitate the operation of the circuit overcurrent protection device [110.10 and 250.4(A)(3)]. Figure 300–42

Raceways and cable assemblies must be mechanically secured to boxes, fittings, cabinets, and other enclosures.

Ex 1: Short lengths of metal raceways used for the support or protection of cables aren't required to be electrically continuous, nor are they required to be connected to an equipment grounding conductor [250.86 Ex 2 and 300.12 Ex]. Figure 300–43

Electrical Continuity
300.10

Utility Source | Meter | Main | Panel | Outlet

Copyright 2014 www.MikeHolt.com

Effective Ground-Fault Current Path

Ground Fault

Metal raceways and enclosures for conductors must be metallically joined together to form an effective ground-fault current path to facilitate the operation of the circuit overcurrent protection device.

Figure 300–42

Electrical Continuity - Short Sections of Raceways
300.10 Ex 1

Short sections of raceways used for support or protection of cables aren't required to be electrically continuous.

Copyright 2014 www.MikeHolt.com

Figure 300–43

300.11 Securing and Supporting

(A) Secured in Place. Raceways, cable assemblies, and enclosures must be securely fastened in place. The ceiling-support wires or ceiling grid must not be used to support raceways and cables (power, signaling, or communications). However, independent support wires that are secured at both ends and provide secure support are permitted. Figure 300–44

Figure 300–44

Figure 300–45

Author's Comment:

- Outlet boxes [314.23(D)] and luminaires can be secured to the suspended-ceiling grid if securely fastened to the ceiling-framing members by mechanical means such as bolts, screws, or rivets, or by the use of clips or other securing means identified for use with the type of ceiling-framing member(s) used [410.36(B)].

(1) Fire-Rated Ceiling Assembly. Electrical wiring within the cavity of a fire-rated floor-ceiling or roof-ceiling assembly can be supported by independent support wires attached to the ceiling assembly. The independent support wires must be distinguishable from the suspended-ceiling support wires by color, tagging, or other effective means.

(2) Nonfire-Rated Ceiling Assembly. Wiring in a nonfire-rated floor-ceiling or roof-ceiling assembly can be supported by independent support wires attached to the ceiling assembly. The independent support wires must be distinguishable from the suspended-ceiling support wires by color, tagging, or other effective means. Figure 300–45

(B) Raceways Used for Support. Raceways must not be used as a means of support for other raceways, cables, or nonelectrical equipment, except as permitted in (1) through (3). Figure 300–46

(1) Identified. If the raceway or means of support is identified as a means of support.

Figure 300–46

(2) Class 2 and 3 Circuits. Class 2 and 3 cable can be supported by the raceway that supplies power to the equipment controlled by the Class 2 or 3 circuit. Figure 300–47

(3) Boxes Supported by Raceways. Raceways are permitted as a means of support for threaded boxes and conduit bodies in accordance with 314.23(E) and (F), or to support luminaires in accordance with 410.36(E).

(C) Cables Not Used as Means of Support. Cables must not be used to support other cables, raceways, or nonelectrical equipment. Figure 300–48

Figure 300–47

Figure 300–49

Figure 300–48

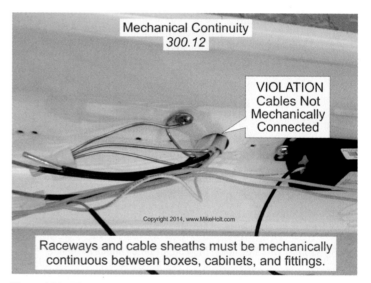

Figure 300–50

300.12 Mechanical Continuity

Raceways and cable sheaths must be mechanically continuous between boxes, cabinets, and fittings. Figures 300–49 and 300–50

Ex 1: Short sections of raceways used to provide support or protection of cable from physical damage aren't required to be mechanically continuous [250.86 Ex 2 and 300.10 Ex 1]. Figure 300–51

Ex 2: Raceways at the bottom of open-bottom equipment, such as switchboards, motor control centers, and transformers, aren't required to be mechanically secured to the equipment. Figure 300–52

Author's Comment:

■ When raceways are stubbed into an open-bottom switch-board, the raceway, including the end fitting, can't rise more than 3 in. above the bottom of the switchboard enclosure [408.5].

Mechanical Continuity
300.12 Ex 1

Short sections of raceways used to provide support or protection of cable from physical damage aren't required to be mechanically continuous.

Copyright 2014, www.MikeHolt.com

Figure 300–51

Splices in Raceway
300.13(A)

VIOLATION

Splices or taps aren't permitted within a raceway.

Copyright 2014, www.MikeHolt.com

Figure 300–53

Mechanical Continuity
Open-Bottom Equipment
300.12 Ex 2

Open-Bottom Equipment

Copyright 2014, www.MikeHolt.com

Raceways and cables installed into the bottom of open-bottom equipment aren't required to be mechanically secured to the equipment.

Figure 300–52

Device Removal
Neutral Continuity
300.13(B)

Multiwire Circuit
Pigtail Required for Neutral

Conductor Pigtail not Required

Copyright 2014, www.MikeHolt.com

Continuity of the neutral conductor of a multiwire branch circuit must not be interrupted by the removal of a wiring device.

Figure 300–54

300.13 Splices and Pigtails

A) Conductor Splices. Splices must be in enclosures as per 300.15 and aren't permitted in raceways, except as permitted by 376.56, 386.56, or 388.56. Figure 300–53

B) Device Removal–Neutral Continuity. Continuity of the neutral conductor of a multiwire branch circuit must not be interrupted by the removal of a wiring device. In these applications the neutral conductors must be spliced together, and a pigtail provided for the wiring device. Figure 300–54

Author's Comment:

■ The opening of the ungrounded conductors, or the neutral conductor of a 2-wire circuit during the replacement of a device, doesn't cause a safety hazard, so pigtailing these conductors isn't required [110.14(B)].

⚠ **CAUTION:** *If the continuity of the neutral conductor of a multiwire circuit is interrupted (opened), the resultant over- or undervoltage can cause a fire and/or destruction of electrical equipment.*

Hazard of Open Neutral

Example: *A 3-wire, single-phase, 120/240V multiwire circuit supplies a 1,200W, 120V hair dryer and a 600W, 120V television.* Figure 300–55

If the neutral conductor of the multiwire circuit is interrupted, it'll cause the 120V television to operate at 160V and consume 1,067W of power (instead of 600W) for only a few seconds before it burns up. Figure 300–56

Step 1: *Determine the resistance of each appliance:*

$$R = E^2/P$$

R of the hair dryer = 120V2/1,200W
R of the hair dryer = 12 ohms

R of the television = 120V2/600W
R of the television = 24 ohms

Step 2: *Determine the current of the circuit:*

$$I = E/R$$

E = 240V

R = 36 ohms (12 ohms + 24 ohms)

I = 240V/36 ohms

I = 6.70A

Step 3: *Determine the operating voltage for each appliance:*

$$E = I \times R$$

I = 6.70A

R = 12 ohms for hair dryer and 24 ohms for TV

Voltage of hair dryer = 6.70A x 12 ohms
Voltage of hair dryer = 80V

Voltage of television = 6.70A x 24 ohms
Voltage of television = 160V

Figure 300–55

Figure 300–56

WARNING: *Failure to terminate the ungrounded conductors to separate phases can cause the neutral conductor to become overloaded, and the insulation can be damaged or destroyed by excessive heat. Conductor overheating is known to decrease the service life of insulating materials, which creates the potential for arcing faults in hidden locations, and can ultimately lead to fires. It isn't known just how long conductor insulation lasts, but heat does decrease its life span.* Figure 300–57

Miswired Multiwire Circuit - Overload on Neutral

Figure 300–57

Caution: If the ungrounded conductors of a multiwire circuit aren't terminated to different phases or lines, the currents on the neutral conductor won't cancel, but will add, which can cause a dangerous overload on the neutral conductor.

300.14 Length of Free Conductors

At least 6 in. of free conductor, measured from the point in the box where the conductors enter the enclosure, must be left at each outlet, junction, and switch point for splices or terminations of luminaires or devices. Figure 300–58

Figure 300–58

Boxes with openings less than 8 in. must have at least 6 in. of free conductor and at least 3 in. of free conductor outside the box opening.

Boxes that have openings less than 8 in. in any dimension, must have at least 6 in. of free conductor, measured from the point where the conductors enter the box, and at least 3 in. of free conductor outside the box opening. Figure 300–59

At least 6 in. of free conductor is required at each box. Where the box opening is less than 8 in., conductors must extend at least 3 in. outside the box opening.

Figure 300–59

Author's Comment:

■ The following text was the Panels' Statement when it rejected my proposal to require the free conductor length to be unspliced in the 2008 *NEC*. "The purpose of Section 300.14 is to permit access to the end of the conductor. Whether this conductor is spliced or unspliced doesn't affect the length of this free end of the conductor. Many conductors originate inside the box and are spliced to other conductors within the box but extend out of the box for connection to a device of some kind. Making this change wouldn't permit this very common application. Even the exception to this section states that unspliced or unterminated conductors don't have to comply with 300.14."

Ex: Six inches of free conductor isn't required for conductors that pass through a box without a splice or termination.

300.15 Boxes or Conduit Bodies

Fittings can only be used with the specific wiring methods for which they're listed and designed. For example, Type NM cable connectors must not be used with Type AC cable, and electrical metallic tubing fittings must not be used with rigid metal conduit or intermediate metal conduit, unless listed for the purpose. Figure 300–60

Figure 300–60

Author's Comment:

■ PVC conduit couplings and connectors are permitted with electrical nonmetallic tubing if the proper glue is used in accordance with manufacturer's instructions [110.3(B)]. See 362.48.

A box or conduit body must be installed at each splice or termination point, except as permitted for by 310.15(A) through (L): Figure 300–61

- Cabinets, 312.8
- Luminaires, 410.64
- Surface Raceways, 386.56 and 388.56
- Wireways, 376.56

Author's Comment:

■ Boxes aren't required for the following signaling and communications cables or raceways: Figure 300–62

  ☐ CATV, 90.3

Figure 300–61

A box isn't required for communications, signal, control, and optical fiber conductors/cables [90.3, 725.3, and 770.3].

Figure 300–62

  ☐ Class 2 and 3 Control and Signaling, 725.3
  ☐ Communications, 90.3
  ☐ Optical Fiber, 770.3

(C) Raceways for Support or Protection. When a raceway is used for the support or protection of cables, a fitting to reduce the potential for abrasion must be placed at the location the cables enter the raceway. Figure 300–63

Raceways for Support or Protection
300.15(C)

When a raceway is used for the support or protection of cables, a fitting to reduce the potential for abrasion must be placed at the location the cables enter the raceway.

Copyright 2014, www.MikeHolt.com

Figure 300–63

(F) Fitting. A fitting is permitted in lieu of a box or conduit body where conductors aren't spliced or terminated within the fitting if it's accessible after installation. Figure 300–64

Fitting in Lieu of Box
300.15(F)

A fitting is permitted in lieu of a box or conduit body where the conductors aren't spliced or terminated within the fitting and the fitting is accessible after installation.

Copyright 2014, www.MikeHolt.com

Figure 300–64

(G) Underground Splices. A box or conduit body isn't required where a splice is made underground if the conductors are spliced with a splicing device listed for direct burial. See 110.14(B) and 300.5(E).

Author's Comment:

■ See the definition of "Conduit Body" in Article 100.

(H) NM Cable Interconnection Devices. A box or conduit body is not required where a listed nonmetallic-sheathed cable interconnector device is used in existing buildings for exposed and concealed locations in accordance with 334.40(B). Figure 300–65

NM Cable Interconnection Devices
334.40(B)

A box or conduit body isn't required where a listed NM cable interconnector device is used in existing building for exposed and concealed locations in accordance with 300.15(H).

Figure 300–65

(I) Enclosures. A box or conduit body isn't required where a splice is made in a cabinet containing switches or overcurrent devices if the splices or taps don't fill the wiring space at any cross section to more than 75 percent, and the wiring at any cross section doesn't exceed 40 percent. See 312.8 and 404.3(B). Figure 300–66

Splice and Termination Points
Switch/Circuit Breaker Enclosure
300.15(I)

An enclosure can be used as a raceway if the conductor fill doesn't exceed 40%, and splices are permitted if the fill doesn't exceed 75% [312.8 and 404.3].

Copyright 2014, www.MikeHolt.com

Figure 300–66

(L) Handhole Enclosures. A box or conduit body isn't required for conductors installed in a handhole enclosure. Splices must be made in accordance with 314.30. Figure 300–67

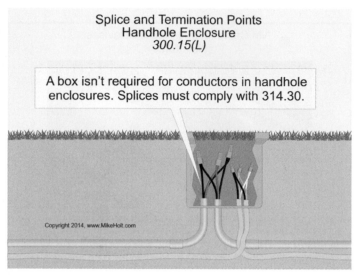

**Splice and Termination Points
Handhole Enclosure
300.15(L)**

A box isn't required for conductors in handhole enclosures. Splices must comply with 314.30.

Copyright 2014, www.MikeHolt.com

Figure 300–67

Author's Comment:

- Splices or terminations within a handhole must be accomplished by the use of fittings listed as suitable for wet locations [110.14(B) and 314.30(C)].

300.16 Raceway or Cable to Open or Concealed Wiring

(B) Bushing. A bushing is permitted in lieu of a box or terminal where the conductors emerge from a raceway and enter or terminate at equipment such as open switchboards, unenclosed control equipment, or similar equipment.

300.17 Raceway Sizing

Raceways must be large enough to permit the installation and removal of conductors without damaging the conductor's insulation.

Author's Comment:

- When all conductors in a raceway are the same size and of the same insulation type, the number of conductors permitted can be determined by Annex C.

Question: How many 12 THHN conductors can be installed in trade size ¾ electrical metallic tubing? Figure 300–68

(a) 12   (b) 13   c) 14   (d) 16

Answer: (d) 16 conductors [Annex C, Table C1]

**Raceway Sizing
300.17**

¾ EMT

Sixteen 12 THHN conductors
[Annex C, Table C.1]

When all conductors in a raceway are the same size and insulation type, the number of conductors permitted can be determined by Annex C.

Copyright 2014, www.MikeHolt.com

Figure 300–68

Author's Comment:

- When different size conductors are installed in a raceway, conductor fill is limited to the percentages in Table 1 of Chapter 9. Figure 300–69

Table 1, Chapter 9	
Number	Percent Fill
1 Conductor	53%
2 Conductors	31%
3 or more	40%

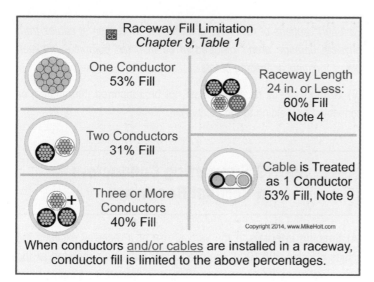

Figure 300–69

The above percentages are based on conditions where the length of the conductor and number of raceway bends are within reasonable limits [Chapter 9, Table 1, Note 1].

Step 1: *When sizing a raceway, first determine the total area of con ductors (Chapter 9, Table 5 for insulated conductors and Chapter 9, Table 8 for bare conductors).* Figure 300–70

Figure 300–70

Step 2: *Select the raceway from Chapter 9, Table 4, in accordance with the percent fill listed in Chapter 9, Table 1.* Figure 300–71

Figure 300–71

Question: *What trade size Schedule 40 PVC conduit is required for the following conductors?* Figure 300–72

3—500 THHN
1—250 THHN
1—3 THHN

(a) 2   *(b) 3*   *(c) 4*   *(d) 6*

Answer: *(b) 3*

Step 1: *Determine the total area of conductors [Chapter 9, Table 5]:*

500 THHN	*0.7073 x 3 =*	*2.1219 in.^{2}*
250 THHN	*0.3970 x 1 =*	*0.3970 in.^{2}*
3 THHN	*0.0973 x 1 =*	*+ 0.0973 in.^{2}*
Total Area =		*2.6162 in.^{2}*

Step 2: *Select the raceway at 40 percent fill [Chapter 9, Table 4]:*

Trade size 3 Schedule 40 PVC = 2.907 sq in. of conductor fill at 40%.

Step 1. Determine the conductor area, Chapter 9, Table 5.

500 kcmil = 0.7073 in.^{2} x 3 conductors = 2.1219 in.^{2}
250 kcmil = 0.3970 in.^{2} x 1 conductor = 0.3970 in.^{2}
3 AWG = 0.0973 in.^{2} x 1 conductor = 0.0973 in.^{2}
Total area of the conductors = 2.6162 in.^{2}

Step 2. Size the raceway at 40% fill, Chapter 9, Table 4.

Trade Size 3 PVC at 40 percent fill = 2.907 in.^{2} Copyright 2014 www.MikeHolt.com

Figure 300–72

300.18 Inserting Conductors in Raceways

(A) Complete Runs. To protect conductor insulation from abrasion during installation, raceways must be mechanically completed between the pulling points before conductors are installed. See 300.10 and 300.12. Figure 300–73

Figure 300–73

Ex: Short sections of raceways used for the protection of cables from physical damage aren't required to be installed complete between outlet, junction, or splicing points.

(B) Welding. Metal raceways must not be supported, terminated, or connected by welding to the raceway.

300.19 Supporting Conductors in Vertical Raceways

(A) Spacing Intervals. If the vertical rise of a raceway exceeds the values of Table 300.19(A), the conductors must be supported at the top, or as close to the top as practical. Intermediate support must also be provided in increments that don't exceed the values of Table 300.19(A). Figure 300–74

Figure 300–74

Author's Comment:

- The weight of long vertical runs of conductors can cause the conductors to actually drop out of the raceway if they aren't properly secured. There have been many cases where conductors in a vertical raceway were released from the pulling "basket" or "grip" (at the top) without being secured, and the conductors fell down and out of the raceway, injuring those at the bottom of the installation.

300.20 Induced Currents in Ferrous Metal Enclosures and Raceways

(A) Conductors Grouped Together. To minimize induction heating of ferrous metal raceways and ferrous metal enclosures for alternating-current circuits, and to maintain an effective ground-fault current path, all conductors of a circuit must be installed in the same raceway, cable, trench, cord, or cable tray. See 250.102(E), 300.3(B), 300.5(I), and 392.8(D). Figure 300–75

Figure 300–75

Author's Comment:

■ When alternating current (ac) flows through a conductor, a pulsating or varying magnetic field is created around the conductor. This magnetic field is constantly expanding and contracting with the amplitude of the ac current. In the United States, the frequency is 60 cycles per second (Hz). Since ac reverses polarity 120 times per second, the magnetic field that surrounds the conductor also reverses its direction 120 times per second. This expanding and collapsing magnetic field induces eddy currents in the ferrous metal parts that surround the conductors, causing the metal parts to heat up from hysteresis heating.

Magnetic materials naturally resist the rapidly changing magnetic fields. The resulting friction produces its own additional heat—hysteresis heating—in addition to eddy current heating. A metal which offers high resistance is said to have high magnetic "permeability." Permeability can vary on a scale of 100 to 500 for magnetic materials; nonmagnetic materials have a permeability of one.

Simply put, the molecules of steel and iron align to the polarity of the magnetic field and when the magnetic field reverses, the molecules reverse their polarity as well. This back-and-forth alignment of the molecules heats up the metal, and the more the current flows, the greater the heat rises in the ferrous metal parts. Figure 300–76

When conductors of the same circuit are grouped together, the magnetic fields of the different conductors tend to cancel each other out, resulting in a reduced magnetic field around the conductors. The lower magnetic field reduces induced currents in the ferrous metal raceways or enclosures, which reduces the hysteresis heating of the surrounding metal enclosure.

Figure 300–76

⚠️ **WARNING:** *There's been much discussion in the press on the effects of electromagnetic fields on humans. According to the Institute of Electrical and Electronics Engineers (IEEE), there's insufficient information at this time to define an unsafe electromagnetic field level.*

(B) Single Conductors. When single conductors are installed in non-metallic raceways as permitted in 300.5(I) Ex 2, the inductive heating of the metal enclosure must be minimized by the use of aluminum locknuts and by cutting a slot between the individual holes through which the conductors pass. Figure 300–77

Figure 300–77

Note: Because aluminum is a nonmagnetic metal, aluminum parts don't heat up due to hysteresis heating.

Author's Comment:

■ Aluminum conduit, locknuts, and enclosures carry eddy currents, but because aluminum is nonferrous, it doesn't heat up [300.20(B) Note].

300.21 Spread of Fire or Products of Combustion

Electrical circuits and equipment must be installed in such a way that the spread of fire or products of combustion won't be substantially increased. Openings into or through fire-rated walls, floors, and ceilings for electrical equipment must be fire-stopped using methods approved by the authority having jurisdiction to maintain the fire-resistance rating of the fire-rated assembly. Figure 300–78

Figure 300–78

Author's Comment:

■ Fire-stopping materials are listed for the specific types of wiring methods and the construction of the assembly that they penetrate.

Note: Directories of electrical construction materials published by qualified testing laboratories contain listing and installation restrictions necessary to maintain the fire-resistive rating of assemblies. Outlet boxes must have a horizontal separation not less than 24 in. when installed in a fire-rated assembly, unless an outlet box is listed for closer spacing or protected by fire-resistant "putty pads" in accordance with manufacturer's instructions. Figure 300–79

Figure 300–79

Author's Comment:

- Boxes installed in fire-resistance-rated assemblies must be listed for the purpose. If steel boxes are used, they must be secured to the framing member, so cut-in type boxes aren't permitted (UL White Book, *Guide Information for Electrical Equipment,* www.ul.com/regulators/2008_WhiteBook.pdf).

- This rule also applies to control, signaling, and communications cables or raceways.

  - CATV, 820.26
  - Communications, 800.26
  - Control and Signaling, 725.25
  - Fire Alarm, 760.3(A)
  - Optical Fiber, 770.26
  - Sound Systems, 640.3(A)

Figure 300–80

300.22 Wiring in Ducts and Plenums Spaces

 Scan this QR code for a video of this *Code* rule. See page xix for information on how to use the QR codes.

The provisions of this section apply to the installation and uses of electrical wiring and equipment in ducts used for dust, loose stock, or vapor removal; ducts specifically fabricated for environmental air, and spaces used for environmental air (plenums).

(A) Ducts Used for Dust, Loose Stock, or Vapor. Ducts that transport dust, loose stock, or vapors must not have any wiring method installed within them. Figure 300–80

(B) Ducts Specifically Fabricated for Environmental Air. If necessary for direct action upon, or sensing of, the contained air, Type MC cable that has a smooth or corrugated impervious metal sheath without an overall nonmetallic covering, electrical metallic tubing, flexible metallic tubing, intermediate metal conduit, or rigid metal conduit without an overall nonmetallic covering can be installed in ducts specifically fabricated to transport environmental air. Flexible metal conduit in lengths not exceeding 4 ft can be used to connect physically adjustable equipment and devices within the fabricated duct.

Equipment is only permitted within the duct specifically fabricated to transport environmental air if necessary for the direct action upon, or sensing of, the contained air. Equipment, devices, and/or illumination are only permitted to be installed in the duct if necessary to facilitate maintenance and repair. Figure 300–81

Figure 300–81

(C) Other Spaces Used for Environmental Air (Plenums). This section applies to spaces used for air-handling purposes, but not fabricated for environmental air-handling purposes. This requirement doesn't apply to habitable rooms or areas of buildings, the prime purpose of which isn't air handling. Figure 300–82

> **Note 1:** The spaces above a suspended ceiling or below a raised floor used for environmental air are examples of the type of space to which this section applies. Figure 300–83

Figure 300–82

Figure 300–84

Figure 300–83

Note 2: The phrase "other space used for environmental air (plenums)" correlates with the term "plenum" in NFPA 90A, *Standard for the Installation of Air-Conditioning and Ventilating Systems*, and other mechanical codes where the ceiling is used for return air purposes, as well as some other air-handling spaces.

Ex: In a dwelling unit, this section doesn't apply to the space between joists or studs where the wiring passes through that space perpendicular to the long dimension of that space. Figure 300–84

(1) Wiring Methods. Electrical metallic tubing, rigid metal conduit, intermediate metal conduit, armored cable, metal-clad cable without a nonmetallic cover, and flexible metal conduit can be installed in plenum spaces. If accessible, surface metal raceways or metal wireways with metal covers can be installed in a plenum space. Figure 300–85

Figure 300–85

Cable ties for securing and supporting must be listed as having adequate fire resistant and low smoke producing characteristics. Figure 300–86

Figure 300–86

Author's Comment:

- PVC conduit [Article 352], electrical nonmetallic tubing [Article 362], liquidtight flexible conduit, and nonmetallic cables aren't permitted to be installed in plenum spaces because they give off deadly toxic fumes when burned or superheated.

- Plenum-rated control, signaling, and communications cables and raceways are permitted in plenum spaces: Figure 300–87

Figure 300–87

- CATV, 820.179(A)
- Communications, 800.21
- Control and Signaling, Table 725.154
- Fire Alarm, 760.7
- Optical Fiber Cables and Raceways, 770.113(C)
- Sound Systems, 640.9(C) and Table 725.154

■ Any wiring method suitable for the condition can be used in a space not used for environmental air-handling purposes. Figure 300–88

Figure 300–88

(2) Cable Tray Systems.

(a) Metal Cable Tray Systems. Metal cable tray systems can be installed to support the wiring methods and equipment permitted by this section. Figure 300–89

(3) Equipment. Electrical equipment with metal enclosures is permitted to be installed in plenum spaces. Figure 300–90

Author's Comment:

■ Examples of electrical equipment permitted in plenum spaces are air-handlers, junction boxes, and dry-type transformers; however, transformers must not be rated over 50 kVA when located in hollow spaces [450.13(B)]. Figure 300–91

Metal Cable Tray Systems in a Plenum Space
300.22(C)(2)(a)

Plenum Space

Cable Tray

Metal cable tray systems are permitted in plenum spaces to support wiring methods and cable types permitted in plenum spaces.

Copyright 2014, www.MikeHolt.com

Figure 300–89

Space Used for Environmental Air (Plenum) - Equipment
300.22(C)(3)

Suspended Ceiling

Plenum Space

Electrical equipment with metal enclosures is permitted in a plenum space.

Copyright 2014, www.MikeHolt.com

Figure 300–90

Other Space Used as a Plenum Space
300.22(C)(3)

Plenum Space

Transformers rated over 50 kVA are not permitted in hollow spaces [450.13(B)].

Electrical equipment with metal enclosures are permitted in plenum space.

Suspended Ceiling

Copyright 2014, www.MikeHolt.com

Figure 300–91

(D) Information Technology Equipment. Wiring methods beneath raised floors for information technology equipment can be as permitted in Article 645. Figure 300–92

Information Technology Equipment Rooms
300.22(D)

Nonplenum Cables Permitted

Copyright 2014
www.MikeHolt.com

Wiring methods beneath raised floors for information technology equipment is permitted in accordance with Article 645.

Figure 300–92

300.23 Panels Designed to Allow Access

Wiring, cables, and equipment installed behind panels must be located so the panels can be removed to give access to electrical equipment. Figure 300–93

Author's Comment:

■ Access to equipment must not be hindered by an accumulation of cables that prevent the removal of suspended-ceiling panels. Control, signaling, and communications cables must be located and supported so the suspended-ceiling panels can be moved to provide access to electrical equipment.

  □ CATV Coaxial Cable, 820.21
  □ Communications Cable, 800.21
  □ Control & Signaling Cable, 725.21
  □ Fire Alarm Cable, 760.21
  □ Optical Fiber Cable, 770.21
  □ Audio Cable, 640.5

Figure 300–93

Notes

ARTICLE
310

CONDUCTORS FOR GENERAL WIRING

Introduction to Article 310—Conductors for General Wiring

This article contains the general requirements for conductors, such as insulation markings, ampacity ratings, and conditions of use. Article 310 doesn't apply to conductors that are part of flexible cords, fixture wires, or to conductors that are an integral part of equipment [90.7 and 300.1(B)].

People often make mistakes in applying the ampacity tables contained in Article 310. If you study the explanations carefully, you'll avoid common errors such as applying Table 310.15(B)(17) when you should be applying Table 310.15(B)(16).

Why so many tables? Why does Table 310.15(B)(17) list the ampacity of 6 THHN as 105 amperes, while Table 310.15(B)(16) lists the same conductor as having an ampacity of only 75 amperes? To answer that, go back to Article 100 and review the definition of ampacity. Notice the phrase "conditions of use." These tables set a maximum current value at which premature failure of the conductor insulation shouldn't occur during normal use, under the conditions described in the tables.

The designations THHN, THHW, RHH, and so on, are insulation types. Every type of insulation has a limit to how much heat it can withstand. When current flows through a conductor, it creates heat. How well the insulation around a conductor can dissipate that heat depends on factors such as whether that conductor is in free air or not. Think about what happens when you put on a sweater, a jacket, and then a coat—all at the same time. You heat up. Your skin can't dissipate heat with all that clothing on nearly as well as it dissipates heat in free air. The same principal applies to conductors.

Conductor insulation also fails with age. That's why we conduct cable testing and take other measures to predict failure and replace certain conductors (for example, feeders or critical equipment conductors) while they're still within design specifications. But conductor insulation failure takes decades under normal use—and it's a maintenance issue. However, if a conductor is forced to exceed the ampacity listed in the appropriate table, and as a result its design temperature is exceeded, insulation failure happens much more rapidly—often catastrophically. Consequently, exceeding the allowable ampacity of a conductor is a serious safety issue.

Part I. General

310.1 Scope

(A) Installations. Article 310 contains the general requirements for conductors, such as insulation markings, ampacity ratings, and their use.

(B) Integral Parts of Equipment. This article doesn't apply to conductors that are an integral part of equipment [90.7 and 300.1(B)]. Figure 310–1

Figure 310–1

Part II. Installation

310.10 Uses Permitted

Conductors described in 310.104 can be used in any of the wiring methods recognized in Chapter 3 as permitted in this *Code [110.8]*.

(B) Dry and Damp Locations. Insulated conductors typically used in dry and damp locations include THHN, THHW, THWN, or THWN-2.

Author's Comment:

■ Refer to Table 310.104 for a complete list of conductors that may be installed in dry or damp locations.

(C) Wet Locations. Insulated conductors typically used in wet locations include:

(2) Types THHW, THWN, THWN-2, XHHW, or XHHW-2

Author's Comment:

■ Refer to Table 310.104 for a complete list of conductors that may be installed in wet locations.

(D) Locations Exposed to Direct Sunlight. Insulated conductors and cables exposed to the direct rays of the sun must be:

(1) Listed as sunlight resistant or marked as being sunlight resistant. Figure 310–2

Figure 310–2

Author's Comment:

■ SE cable and the conductors contained in the cable are listed as sunlight resistant. However, according to the UL listing standard, the conductors contained in SE cable aren't required to be marked as sunlight resistant.

(2) Covered with insulating material, such as tape or sleeving materials that are listed as being sunlight resistant or marked as being sunlight resistant.

(G) Corrosive Conditions. Conductor insulation must be suitable for any substance to which it may be exposed that may have a detrimental effect on the conductor's insulation, such as oil, grease, vapor, gases, fumes, liquids, or other substances. See 110.11.

(H) Conductors in Parallel.

(1) General. Ungrounded and neutral conductors can be connected in parallel, only in sizes 1/0 AWG and larger where installed in accordance with (H)(2) through (H)(6). Figure 310–3

Figure 310–3

(2) Conductor and Installation Characteristics. When circuit conductors are installed in parallel, the conductors must be connected so that the current will be evenly distributed between the individual parallel conductors by requiring all circuit conductors within each parallel set to: Figure 310–4

Figure 310–4

(1) Be the same length.

(2) Consist of the same conductor material (copper/aluminum).

(3) Be the same size in circular mil area (minimum 1/0 AWG).

(4) Have the same type of insulation (like THHN).

(5) Terminate in the same method (set screw versus compression).

Author's Comment:

■ Conductors aren't required to have the same physical characteristics as those of another ungrounded or neutral conductor to achieve balance.

■ When installed in raceways or enclosures, paralleled conductors must be grouped to prevent inductive heating. Figure 310–5

Figure 310–5

(3) Separate Raceways or Cables. Raceways or cables containing parallel conductors must have the same electrical characteristics and the same number of conductors. Figure 310–6

Figure 310–6

Figure 310–7

Author's Comment:

■ If one set of parallel conductors is installed in a metallic raceway and the other conductors are installed in PVC conduit, the conductors in the metallic raceway will have an increased opposition to current flow (impedance) as compared to the conductors in the nonmetallic raceway. This results in an unbalanced distribution of current between the parallel conductors.

Parallel sets of conductors aren't required to have the same physical characteristics as those of another set to achieve balance.

Author's Comment:

■ For example, a 400A feeder with a neutral load of 240A can be paralleled as follows: Figure 310–7

  □ Phase A, Two—250 kcmil THHN aluminum, 100 ft

  □ Phase B, Two—3/0 THHN copper, 104 ft

  □ Phase C, Two—3/0 THHN copper, 102 ft

  □ Neutral, Two—1/0 THHN aluminum, 103 ft

  □ Equipment Grounding Conductor, Two—3 AWG copper, 101 ft*

  *The minimum 1/0 AWG requirement doesn't apply to equipment grounding conductors [310.10(H)(5)].

(4) Conductor Ampacity Adjustment. Each current-carrying conductor of a paralleled set of conductors must be counted as a current-carrying conductor for the purpose of conductor ampacity adjustment, in accordance with Table 310.15(B)(3)(a). Figure 310–8

Figure 310–8

(5) Equipment Grounding Conductors. The equipment grounding conductors for circuits in parallel must be sized in accordance with 250.122(F). Figure 310–9

Conductors in Parallel
Equipment Grounding Conductor
310.10(H)(5)

600A Protection

Parallel Conductors

600A Protection

Copyright 2014, www.MikeHolt.com

The equipment grounding conductor in each raceway is sized to 250.122(F) based on the rating of the overcurrent device. 600A = 1 AWG [Table 250.22]

Figure 310–9

Ampacity
Article 100 Definition

3 THWN-2 Rated 115A at 90°C
115A x 1.00 x 1.00 = 115A

• 3 current-carrying conductors
• Ambient Temperature 86°F

Copyright 2014, www.MikeHolt.com

3 THWN-2 Rated 115A at 90°C
115A x 0.87 x 0.80 = 80A

• 5 current-carrying conductors
• Ambient Temperature 110°F

The maximum current, in amperes, a conductor can carry continuously, under the conditions of use [310.15] without exceeding its temperature rating.

Figure 310–10

Author's Comment:

- The minimum 1/0 AWG parallel conductor size rule of 310.10(H) doesn't apply to equipment grounding conductors.

(6) Bonding Jumpers. Equipment bonding jumpers and supply-side bonding jumpers are sized in accordance with 250.102.

Author's Comment:

- The equipment bonding jumper isn't required to be larger than the largest ungrounded circuit conductors supplying the equipment.

310.15 Conductor Ampacity

 Scan this QR code for a video of this *Code* rule. See page xix for information on how to use the QR codes.

Author's Comment:

- According to Article 100, "ampacity" means the maximum current, in amperes, a conductor can carry continuously, where the temperature of the conductor won't be raised in excess of its insulation temperature rating. Figure 310–10

(A) General Requirements.

(1) Tables for Engineering Supervision. The ampacity of a conductor can be determined either by using the tables in accordance with 310.15(B), or under engineering supervision as provided in 310.15(C).

Note 1: Ampacities provided by this section don't take voltage drop into consideration. See 210.19(A) Note 4, for branch circuits and 215.2(D) Note 2, for feeders.

(2) Conductor Ampacity—Lower Rating. Where more than one ampacity applies for a given circuit length, the lowest value must be used. Figure 310–11

Conductor Ampacity - Lower Rating
310.15(A)(2)

Higher Ampacity on Wall
12 THWN-2 = 30A

Lower Ampacity on Roof
12 THWN-2 = 17.40A (30A x 0.58)

Copyright 2014
www.MikeHolt.com

Where more than one ampacity rating applies to a single conductor length, the lower ampacity must be used for the entire circuit. Entire circuit is rated 17.40A.

Figure 310–11

Ex: When different ampacities apply to a length of conductor, the higher ampacity is permitted for the entire circuit if the reduced ampacity length doesn't exceed 10 ft and its length doesn't exceed 10 percent of the length of the higher ampacity. Figures 310–12 *and* 310–13

**Conductor Ampacity
Higher Rating**
310.15(A)(2) Ex

60 ft

55 ft — 5 ft

Higher Ampacity
◄— 8 AWG = Rated 55A at 90°C —►
[Tbl 310.15(B)(16)]

Lower Ampacity
◄ 8 AWG = 31.9A ►
(55A x 0.58)

Entire Circuit
Ampacity = 55A

Copyright 2014, www.MikeHolt.com

The higher ampacity can be used if the length of the lower ampacity isn't more than 10 ft, and it isn't longer than 10 percent of the higher ampacity length.

Figure 310–12

Conductor Ampacity - Higher Rating
310.15(A)(2) Ex

Higher Ampacity on Wall
8 THWN-2 = 55A

Lower Ampacity on Roof
8 THWN-2 = 31.90A (55A x 0.58)

Copyright 2014
www.MikeHolt.com

The higher ampacity can be used if the length of the lower ampacity isn't more than 10 ft, and it isn't longer than 10 percent of the higher ampacity length.

Figure 310–13

(3) Insulation Temperature Limitation. Conductors must not be used where the operating temperature exceeds that designated for the type of insulated conductor involved.

Note 1: The insulation temperature rating of a conductor [Table 310.104(A)] is the maximum temperature a conductor can withstand over a prolonged time period without serious degradation. The main factors to consider for conductor operating temperature include:

(1) Ambient temperature may vary along the conductor length as well as from time to time [Table 310.15(B)(2)(a)].
(2) Heat generated internally in the conductor—load current flow.
(3) The rate at which generated heat dissipates into the ambient medium.
(4) Adjacent load-carrying conductors have the effect of raising the ambient temperature and impeding heat dissipation [Table 310.15(B)(3)(a)].

Note 2: See 110.14(C)(1) for the temperature limitation of terminations.

(B) Ampacity Table. The allowable conductor ampacities listed in Table 310.15(B)(16) are based on conditions where the ambient temperature isn't over 86°F, and no more than three current-carrying conductors are bundled together. Figure 310–14

Conductor Ampacity - Correction and Adjustment
310.15(B) and Table 310.15(B)(16)

This raceway contains only 3 current-carrying conductors.

3/0 THHN
3/0 THHN
3/0 THHN

Table 310.15(B)(16) ampacity is based on an ambient temperature of 86°F and no more than 3 current-carrying conductors bundled together.

Conductor Ampacity Adjustment

Ambient Temperature

Conductor Bundling

If the ambient temperature is above 86°F or below 78°F, the conductor ampacity changes. [Table 310.15(B)(2)(a)].

If the number of current-carrying conductors exceeds 3, the conductor ampacity decreases [Table 310.15(B)(3)(a)].

Copyright 2014, www.MikeHolt.com

Figure 310–14

The temperature correction and adjustment factors apply to the conductor ampacity, based on the temperature rating of the conductor insulation in accordance with Table 310.15(B)(16). Figure 310–15

Conductor Ampacity - Temperature Correction Adjustment
310.15(B)(2)

Raceway on roof with four 10 THWN-2. The ambient temperature is 150°F (90°F + 60°F) [310.15(B)(3)(c)].

10 THWN-2 rated 40A, Tbl 310.15(B)(16) at 90°C
Ampacity = 40A x 0.58 x 0.80
Ampacity = 18.56A

Figure 310–15

(2) Conductor Ampacity Ambient Temperature Correction. When conductors are installed in an ambient temperature other than 78°F to 86°F, the ampacities listed in Table 310.15(B)(16) must be corrected in accordance with the multipliers listed in Table 310.15(B)(2)(a). Figure 310–16

Conductor Ampacity - Ambient Temperature
Table 310.15(B)(2)(a)

Three
12 THHN
Rated 30A

Ambient Temperature 50°F	Ambient Temperature 86°F (30°C)	Ambient Temperature 150°F
90°C Table Ampacity	90°C Table Ampacity	90°C Table Ampacity
Correction Factor = 115% (1.15)	Correction Factor = 100% (1.00)	Correction Factor = 58% (0.58)
30 Table amps x 1.15 Ampacity = 34.5A	30 Table amps x 1.00 Ampacity = 30A	30 Table amps x 0.58 Ampacity = 17.4A
Ambient Temperature Below 86°F, *Ampacity is Higher*	Ambient Temperature 86°F, *Ampacity Remains the Same*	Ambient Temperature Over 86°F, *Ampacity is Lower*

Figure 310–16

Table 310.15(B)(2)(a) Ambient Temperature Correction

Ambient Temperature °F	Ambient Temperature °C	Correction Factor 75°C Conductors	Correction Factor 90°C Conductors
50 or less	10 or less	1.20	1.15
51–59°F	11–15°C	1.15	1.12
60–68°F	16–20°C	1.11	1.08
69–77°F	21–25°C	1.05	1.04
78–86°F	26–30°C	1.00	1.00
87–95°F	31–35°C	0.94	0.96
96–104°F	36–40°C	0.88	0.91
105–113°F	41–45°C	0.82	0.87
114–122°F	46–50°C	0.75	0.82
123–131°F	51–55°C	0.67	0.76
132–140°F	56–60°C	0.58	0.71
141–149°F	61–65°C	0.47	0.65
150–158°F	66–70°C	0.33	0.58
159–167°F	71–75°C	0.00	0.50
168–176°F	76–80°C	0.00	0.41
177–185°F	81–85°C	0.00	0.29

Question: What's the corrected ampacity of 3/0 THHN conductors if the ambient temperature is 108°F?

(a) 173A   (b) 196A   (c) 213A   (d) 241A

Answer: (b) 196A

Conductor Ampacity [90°C] = 225A
Correction Factor [Table 310.(B)(2)(a)] = 0.87

Corrected Ampacity = 225A x 0.87
Corrected Ampacity = 196A

Question: What's the corrected ampacity of 3/0 THWN conductors if the ambient temperature is 108°F?

(a) 164A (b) 196A (c) 213A (d) 241A

Answer: (a) 164A

Conductor Ampacity [75°C] = 200A
Correction Factor [Table 310.(B)(2)(a)] = 0.82

Corrected Ampacity = 200A x 0.82
Corrected Ampacity = 164A

(3) Conductor Ampacity Adjustment.

(a) Four or More Current-Carrying Conductors. Where four or more current-carrying power conductors are in a raceway longer than 24 in. [310.15(B)(3)(a)(3)], or where cables are bundled for a length longer than 24 in., the ampacity of each conductor must be reduced in accordance with Table 310.15(B)(3)(a).

Table 310.15(B)(3)(a) Conductor Ampacity Adjustment for More Than Three Current–Carrying Conductors	
Number of Conductors1	Adjustment
4–6	0.80 or 80%
7–9	0.70 or 70%
10–20	0.50 or 50%
21–30	0.45 or 45%
31–40	0.40 or 40%
41 and above	0.35 or 35%

[1]Number of conductors is the total number of conductors, including spare conductors, _including spare conductors,_ adjusted in accordance with 310.15(B)(5) and (B)(6). _It doesn't include conductors that can't be energized at the same time._

Author's Comment:

■ Conductor ampacity reduction is required when four or more current-carrying conductors are bundled because heat generated by current flow isn't able to dissipate as quickly as when there are three or fewer current-carry conductors. Figures 310–17 and 310–18

Figure 310–17

Figure 310–18

(1) Conductor ampacity adjustment of Table 310.15(B)(3)(a) doesn't apply to conductors installed in cable trays, 392.80 applies.

(2) Conductor ampacity adjustment of Table 310.15(B)(3)(a) doesn't apply to conductors in raceways having a length not exceeding 24 in. Figure 310–19

(4) Conductor ampacity adjustment of Table 310.15(B)(3)(a) doesn't apply to conductors within Type AC or Type MC cable under the following conditions: Figure 310–20

   a. The cables don't have an outer jacket,

   b. Each cable has no more than three current-carrying conductors,

Figure 310–19

Figure 310–20

c. The conductors are 12 AWG copper, and

d. No more than 20 current-carrying conductors (ten 2-wire cables or six 3-wire cables) are installed without maintaining spacing for a continuous length longer than 24 in.

(5) Ampacity adjustment of 60 percent applies to conductors within Type AC or Type MC cable without an overall outer jacket under the following conditions:

b. The number of current-carrying conductors exceeds 20.

c. The cables are stacked or bundled longer than 24 in. without spacing being maintained.

(c) Raceways and Cables Exposed to Sunlight on Rooftops. When applying ampacity adjustment correction factors, the ambient temperature adjustment contained in Table 310.15(B)(3)(c) is added to the outdoor ambient temperature for conductors installed in raceways or cables exposed to direct sunlight on or above rooftops to determine the applicable ambient temperature for ampacity correction factors in Table 310.15(B)(2)(a) or Table 310.15(B)(2)(b). Figures 310–21 and 310–22

Figure 310–21

Figure 310–22

Ex: The ampacity adjustment isn't required for conductors that are type XHHW-2.

Note 1: See the *ASHRAE Handbook—Fundamentals* (www.ashrae.org) as a source for the ambient temperatures in various locations.

Note 2: The temperature adders in Table 310.15(B)(3)(c) are based on the measured temperature rise above local climatic ambient temperatures due to sunlight heating.

Table 310.15(B)(3)(c) Ambient Temperature Adder for Raceways or Cables On or Above Rooftops		
Distance of Raceway or Cable Above Roof	C°	F°
0 to ½ in.	33	60
Above ½ in. to 3½ in.	22	40
Above 3½ in. to 12 in.	17	30
Above 12 in. to 36 in.	14	25

Author's Comment:

- This rule requires the ambient temperature used for ampacity correction to be adjusted where conductors or cables are installed in a raceway or cable on or above a rooftop and the raceway is exposed to direct sunlight. The reasoning is that the air inside raceways and cables that are in direct sunlight is significantly hotter than the surrounding air, and appropriate ampacity corrections must be made in order to comply with 310.10.

(5) Neutral Conductors.

(a) The neutral conductor of a 3-wire, single-phase, 120/240V system, or 4-wire, three-phase, 120/208V or 277/480V wye-connected system, isn't considered a current-carrying conductor for conductor ampacity adjustment of 310.15(B)(3)(a). Figure 310–23

(b) The neutral conductor of a 3-wire circuit from a 4-wire, three-phase, 120/208V or 277/480V wye-connected system is considered a current-carrying conductor for conductor ampacity adjustment of 310.15(B)(3)(a).

Neutral Conductors From the Same Circuit
310.15(B)(5)(a)

NOT Counted

Neutral conductors that carry only unbalanced current from other conductors from the same circuit aren't considered current-carrying conductors.

Figure 310–23

Author's Comment:

- When a 3-wire circuit is supplied from a 4-wire, three-phase, 120/208V or 277/480V wye-connected system, the neutral conductor carries approximately the same current as the ungrounded conductors. Figure 310–24

Neutral Conductor of a 3-Wire Circuit From a Wye 4-Wire System
310.15(B)(5)(b)

Current-Carrying Conductor

The neutral conductor of a 3-wire circuit from a 4-wire, wye system is considered a current-carrying conductor.

Determine the neutral current.

$$I_{NEUTRAL} = \sqrt{(L_2^2 + L_3^2) - (L_2 \times L_3)}$$

$$I_{NEUTRAL} = \sqrt{(100^2 + 100^2) - (100 \times 100)}$$

$$I_{NEUTRAL} = 100A$$

Figure 310–24

(c) The neutral conductor of a 4-wire, three-phase, 120/208V or 277/480V wye-connected system is considered a current-carrying conductor for conductor ampacity adjustment of 310.15(B)(3)(a) if more than 50 percent of the neutral load consists of nonlinear loads.

Author's Comment:

■ Nonlinear loads supplied by a 4-wire, three-phase, 120/208V or 277/480V wye-connected system can produce unwanted and potentially hazardous odd triplen harmonic currents (3rd, 9th, 15th, and so on) that can add on the neutral conductor. To prevent fire or equipment damage from excessive harmonic neutral current, the designer should consider increasing the size of the neutral conductor or installing a separate neutral for each phase. For more information, visit .MikeHolt.com, click on the "Technical" link, then the "Power Quality" link. Also see 210.4(A) Note, 220.61 Note 2, and 450.3 Note 2. Figure 310–25

Neutral Conductor of a Wye 4-Wire Circuit
Supplying Nonlinear Loads
310.15(B)(5)(c)

Odd triplen harmonic currents from nonlinear loads add on the neutral conductor and the actual current can be twice the ungrounded conductor's current.

Figure 310–25

(6) Grounding Conductors. Grounding and bonding conductors aren't considered current carrying. Figure 310–26

Conductor Ampacity - Grounding and Bonding Conductors
310.15(B)(6)

Equipment grounding and bonding conductors aren't current-carrying and aren't counted when applying the provisions of Table 310.15(B)(3)(a).

Figure 310–26

(7) 120/240V, Single-Phase Dwelling Services and Feeders. For one-family dwellings and individual dwelling units of two-family and multifamily dwellings, service and feeder conductors supplied by a single phase, 120/240V system can be sized using 310.15(B)(7)(1) through (4). Figure 310–27

Service/Feeder Conductor Sizing for
120/240V Dwelling Unit
310.15(B)(7)

Service Conductors

Feeder Conductors

Service and feeder conductors for a single dwelling unit supplied by 120/240V 1-phase can be sized using 310.15(B)(7)(1) through (4).

Figure 310–27

(1) Service conductors supplying the entire load of a one-family dwelling or an individual dwelling unit in a two-family or multi-family dwelling can have an ampacity of 83 percent of the service rating.

Question: *What size service conductors are required if the calculated load for a dwelling unit equals 195A, and the service disconnect is rated 200A?* Figure 310–28

(a) 1/0 AWG   *(b) 2/0 AWG*   *(c) 3/0 AWG*   *(d) 4/0 AWG*

Answer: *(b) 2/0 AWG*

Service Conductor: 2/0 AWG rated 175A at 75°C [Table 310.15(B)(16)] (200A rated circuit breaker multiplied by 83% = 166A).

Figure 310–29

Figure 310–28

Author's Comment:

- 310.15(B)(7) can't be used for service conductors for two-family or multifamily dwelling buildings. Figure 310–29

(2) For a feeder rated 100A through 400A, feeder conductors supplying a one-family dwelling, or an individual dwelling unit in a two-family or multifamily dwelling, can have an ampacity of 83 percent of the feeder rating, but only if the feeder supplies the entire load of the dwelling. Figure 310–30

Author's Comment:

- 310.15B(7)(2) can't be used to size feeder conductors where a feeder doesn't carry the entire load of the dwelling unit. Figure 310–31

Figure 310–30

Question: *What size feeder conductors are required if the calculated load for a dwelling unit equals 195A, the service disconnect is rated 200A, and the feeder conductors carry the entire load of the dwelling unit?* Figure 310–32

(a) 1/0 AWG   *(b) 2/0 AWG*   *(c) 3/0 AWG*   *(d) 4/0 AWG*

Answer: *(b) 2/0 AWG*

Feeder Conductor: 2/0 AWG rated 175A at 75°C [Table 310.15(B)(16)] (200A rated circuit breaker multiplied by 83% = 166A).

Feeder Conductor Sizing for 120/240V Dwelling Unit 310.15(B)(7)(2)

Where the conductors carry the entire load of an individual dwelling unit, they can be sized using 83% of the feeder rating.

Figure 310–31

Feeder Conductor Sizing for Dwelling Unit 310.15(B)(7)(2)

120/208V

A   B   C

200 Amps

200 Amps

200 Amps

L1

L2

N

A 3-wire feed from a 4-wire, three-phase wye system.

The 83% rule [310.15(B)(7)(2)] doesn't apply to 3-wire, 1-phase, 120/208V circuits, because the neutral conductor in these circuits carries neutral current even when the phases are balanced [310.15(B)(5)(b)].

Figure 310–33

Feeder Conductor Sizing for 120/240V Dwelling Unit 310.15(B)(7)(2)

Feeder Rated 200A
200A x 0.83 = 166A
Table 310.15(B)(16)
2/0 rated 175A at 75°C

Figure 310–32

Service/Feeder Neutral Conductor Sizing for 120/240V Dwelling Unit 310.15(B)(7)(4)

Neutral conductors are sized using 220.61 and 230.42 for services, and 220.61 and 215.2 for feeders.

Figure 310–34

⚠ **WARNING:** *310.15(B)(7) doesn't apply to 3-wire service or feeder conductors connected to a three-phase, 120/208V system, because the neutral conductor in these systems always carries neutral current, even when the load on the phases is balanced [310.15(B)(5)(b)]. For more information on this topic, see 220.61(C)(1).* Figure 310–33

(3) Feeders for an individual dwelling unit are never required to be larger than the conductors in 310.15(B)(7)(1) or (2).

(4) Neutral conductors are sized using 220.61 and 230.42 for services and 220.61 and 215.2 for feeders. Figure 310–34

⚠ **CAUTION:** *Because the service neutral conductor is required to serve as the effective ground-fault current path, it must be sized so it can safely carry the maximum fault current likely to be imposed on it [110.10 and 250.4(A)(5)]. This is accomplished by sizing the neutral conductor in accordance with Table 250.102(C), based on the area of the largest ungrounded service conductor [250.24(C)(1)].*

Question: *What size neutral conductor is required if the calculated load for a dwelling unit equals 195A, the maximum unbalanced load is 100A, and the service disconnect is rated 200A with 2/0 AWG conductors?* Figure 310–35

(a) 6 AWG   (b) 3 AWG   (c) 2 AWG   (d) 1 AWG

Answer: *(b) 3 AWG*

Neutral Conductor: 3 AWG is rated 100A at 75°C in accordance with Table 310.15(B)(16), and 310.15(B)(7)(3) doesn't allow for the 83 percent deduction for neutral conductors. In addition, 250.24(C) requires the neutral conductor to be sized no smaller than 4 AWG based on 2/0 AWG service conductors in accordance with Table 250.102(C).

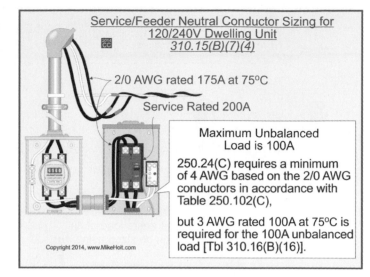

Service/Feeder Neutral Conductor Sizing for 120/240V Dwelling Unit
310.15(B)(7)(4)

2/0 AWG rated 175A at 75ºC

Service Rated 200A

Maximum Unbalanced Load is 100A

250.24(C) requires a minimum of 4 AWG based on the 2/0 AWG conductors in accordance with Table 250.102(C),

but 3 AWG rated 100A at 75ºC is required for the 100A unbalanced load [Tbl 310.16(B)(16)].

Copyright 2014, www.MikeHolt.com

Figure 310–35

Table 310.15(B)(16) Allowable Ampacities of Insulated Conductors
Based on Not More Than Three Current–Carrying Conductors and Ambient Temperature of 30°C (86°F)*

Size	60°C (140°F)	75°C (167°F)	90°C (194°F)	60°C (140°F)	75°C (167°F)	90°C (194°F)	Size
AWG kcmil	TW UF	RHW THHW THW THWN XHHW USE	RHH RHW-2 THHN THHW THW-2 THWN-2 USE-2 XHHW XHHW-2	TW UF	THHN THW THWN XHHW	THHN THW–2 THWN–2 THHW XHHW XHHW–2	AWG kcmil
	Copper			Aluminum/Copper–Clad Aluminum			
14*	15	20	25				14*
12*	20	25	30	15	20	25	12*
10*	30	35	40	25	30	35	10*
8	40	50	55	35	40	45	8
6	55	65	75	40	50	55	6
4	70	85	95	55	65	75	4
3	85	100	115	65	75	85	3
2	95	115	130	75	90	100	2
1	110	130	145	85	100	115	1
1/0	125	150	170	100	120	135	1/0
2/0	145	175	195	115	135	150	2/0
3/0	165	200	225	130	155	175	3/0
4/0	195	230	260	150	180	205	4/0

(continued)

Table 310.15(B)(16) Allowable Ampacities of Insulated Conductors Based on Not More Than Three Current–Carrying Conductors and Ambient Temperature of 30°C (86°F)* (continued)

Size							Size
	60°C (140°F)	75°C (167°F)	90°C (194°F)	60°C (140°F)	75°C (167°F)	90°C (194°F)	
AWG kcmil	TW UF	RHW THHW THW THWN XHHW USE	RHH RHW-2 THHN THHW THW-2 THWN-2 USE-2 XHHW XHHW-2	TW UF	THHN THW THWN XHHW	THHN THW–2 THWN–2 THHW XHHW XHHW–2	AWG kcmil
	Copper			Aluminum/Copper–Clad Aluminum			
250	215	255	290	170	205	230	250
300	240	285	320	195	230	260	300
350	260	310	350	210	250	280	350
400	280	335	380	225	270	305	400
500	320	380	430	260	310	350	500

*See 240.4(D)

Part III. Construction Specification

310.104 Conductor Construction and Application

Only conductors in Tables 310.104(A) though 310.104(G) can be installed, and only for the application identified in the tables.

Author's Comment:

■ The following explains the lettering on conductor insulation: Figures 310–36 and 310–37

- □ F   Fixture wires (solid or 7 strands) [Table 402.3]
- □ FF   Flexible fixture wire (19 strands) [Table 402.3]
- □ No H   60°C insulation rating [Table 310.104(A)]
- □ H   75°C insulation rating [Table 310.104(A)]
- □ HH   90°C insulation rating [Table 310.104(A)]
- □ N   Nylon outer cover [Table 310.104(A)]
- □ R   Thermoset insulation [Table 310.104(A)]
- □ T   Thermoplastic insulation [Table 310.104(A)]
- □ U   Underground [Table 310.104(A)]
- □ W   Wet or damp locations [Table 310.104(A)]
- □ X   Cross-linked polyethylene insulation [Table 310.104(A)]

Table 310.104(A) contains conductor insulation information, such as operating temperature and applications. These conductors can be used in any Chapter 3 wiring method.

Figure 310–36

Table 310.104(A) Conductor Applications and Insulations

Type Letter	Column 2 Insulation	Column 3 Max. Operating Temperature	Column 4 Application	Column 5 Sizes Available AWG or kcmil	Column 6 Outer Covering
RHH	Flame-retardant	90°C	Dry and damp locations	14 – 2,000	Moisture-resistant, flame-retardant, nonmetallic
RHW	Flame-retardant, moisture-resistant thermoset	75°C	Dry and wet locations	14 – 2,000	Moisture-resistant, flame-retardant, nonmetallic
RHW-2	Flame-retardant, moisture-resistant thermoset	90°C	Dry and wet locations	14 – 2,000	Moisture-resistant, flame-retardant, nonmetallic
THHN	Flame-retardant, heat-resistant thermoplastic	90°C	Dry and damp locations	14 – 1,000	Nylon jacket or equivalent
THHW	Flame-retardant, moisture- and heat-resistant thermoplastic	75°C 90°C	Wet locations Dry and damp locations	14 – 1,000	None
THW	Flame-retardant, moisture- and heat-resistant thermoplastic	75°C	Dry and wet locations	14 – 2,000	None
THW-2	Flame-retardant, moisture- and heat-resistant thermoplastic	90°C	Dry and wet locations	14 – 1,000	None
THWN	Flame-retardant, moisture- and heat-resistant thermoplastic	75°C	Dry and wet locations	14 – 1,000	Nylon jacket or equivalent
THWN-2	Flame-retardant, moisture- and heat-resistant thermoplastic	90°C	Dry and wet locations	14 – 1,000	Nylon jacket or equivalent
TW	Flame-retardant, moisture-resistant thermoplastic	60°C	Dry and wet locations	14 – 2,000	None
USE	Heat- and moisture-resistant	75°C	See Article 338	14 – 2,000	Moisture-resistant nonmetallic
USE-2	Heat- and moisture-resistant	90°C	See Article 338	14 – 2,000	Moisture-resistant nonmetallic

Understanding Conductor Insulation Markings
Table 310.104(A)

R - Rubber (Thermoset)
H - (one H) 75°C Insulation
W - Wet, Dry, or Damp Locations

10 RHW-2 600V

-2 - 90°C Insulation Rating

Copyright 2014, www.MikeHolt.com

Figure 310–37

310.106 Conductors

(A) Minimum Size Conductors. The smallest conductor permitted for branch circuits for residential, commercial, and industrial locations is 14 AWG copper, except as permitted elsewhere in this *Code*.

Author's Comment:

■ There's a misconception that 12 AWG copper is the smallest conductor permitted for commercial or industrial facilities. Although this isn't true based on *NEC* rules, it may be a local *Code* requirement.

(C) Stranded Conductors. Conductors 8 AWG and larger must be stranded when installed in a raceway. Figure 310–38

Figure 310–38

Author's Comment:

- Solid conductors are often used for the grounding electrode conductor [250.62] and for the bonding of pools, spas, and outdoor hot tubs [680.26(C)].

(D) Insulated. Conductors must be insulated except where specific permission allows them to be covered or bare. Figure 310–39

Figure 310–39

Author's Comment:

- Equipment grounding conductors are permitted to be bare, see 250.118(1). Figure 310–40

Figure 310–40

310.110 Conductor Identification

(A) Grounded [Neutral] Conductor. Grounded [Neutral] conductors must be identified in accordance with 200.6.

(B) Equipment Grounding Conductor. Equipment grounding conductors must be identified in accordance with 250.119.

(C) Ungrounded Conductors. Ungrounded conductors must be clearly distinguishable from neutral and equipment grounding conductors. Figure 310–41

Author's Comment:

- If the premises wiring system has branch circuits or feeders supplied from more than one nominal voltage system, each ungrounded conductor of the branch circuit or feeder, if accessible, must be identified by system. The means of identification can be by separate color coding, marking tape, tagging, or other means approved by the authority having jurisdiction. Such identification must be permanently posted at each panelboard [210.5(C) and 215.12].

Ungrounded Conductor Identification
310.110(C)

Ungrounded conductors must be clearly distinguishable from neutral and equipment grounding conductors.

Copyright 2014
www.MikeHolt.com

Figure 310–41

■ The *NEC* doesn't require color coding of ungrounded conductors, except for the high-leg conductor when a neutral conductor is present [110.15 and 230.56]. Although not required, electricians often use the following color system for power and lighting conductor identification:

☐ 120/240V, single-phase—black, red, and white

☐ 120/208V, three-phase—black, red, blue, and white

☐ 120/240V, three-phase, delta-connected system— black, orange, blue, and white

☐ 277/480V, three-phase, wye-connected system— brown, orange, yellow, and gray; or, brown, purple, yellow, and gray

ARTICLE 312

CABINET AND CUTOUT BOXES

Introduction to Article 312—Cabinet and Cutout Boxes

This article addresses the installation and construction specifications for the items mentioned in its title. In Article 310, we observed that the conditions of use have an effect on the ampacity of a conductor. Likewise, the conditions of use have an effect on the selection and application of cabinet. For example, you can't use just any enclosure in a wet location or in a hazardous location. The conditions of use impose special requirements for these situations.

For all such enclosures, certain requirements apply—regardless of the use. For example, you must cover any openings, protect conductors from abrasion, and allow sufficient bending room for conductors.

Notice that Article 408 covers switchboards and panelboards, with primary emphasis on the interior, or "guts," while the cabinet that'd be used to enclose a panelboard is covered here in Article 312. Therefore you'll find that some important considerations such as wire-bending space at terminals of panelboards are included in this article.

Article 312 covers the installation and construction specifications for cabinets and cutout boxes. [312.1].

Part I. Scope and Installation

312.1 Scope

Article 312 covers the installation and construction specifications for cabinet and cutout boxes. Figure 312–1

Author's Comment:

■ A cabinet is an enclosure for either surface mounting or flush mounting and provided with a frame in which a door may be hung.

Figure 312–1

312.2 Damp or Wet Locations

Enclosures in damp or wet locations must prevent moisture or water from entering or accumulating within the enclosure, and must be weatherproof. When the enclosure is surface mounted in a wet location, the enclosure must be mounted with not less than a ¼ in. air space between it and the mounting surface. See 300.6(D).

If raceways or cables enter above the level of uninsulated live parts of an enclosure in a wet location, a fitting listed for wet locations must be used for termination.

Author's Comment:

- A fitting listed for use in a wet location with a sealing locknut is suitable for this application.

Ex: The ¼ in. air space isn't required for nonmetallic equipment, raceways, or cables.

312.3 Installed in Walls

Cabinets installed in walls of noncombustible material must be installed so that the front edge of the enclosure is set back no more than ¼ in. from the finished surface. In walls constructed of wood or other combustible material, cabinets must be flush with the finished surface or project outward.

312.4 Repairing Gaps

Gaps around cabinets that are recessed in noncombustible surfaces (plaster, drywall, or plasterboard) having a flush-type cover, must be repaired so that there will be no gap more than ⅛ in. at the edge of the cabinet. Figure 312–2

312.5 Enclosures

(A) Unused Openings. Openings in cabinet and cutout boxes intended to provide entry for conductors must be <u>closed in an approved manner</u>. Figure 312–3

Figure 312–2

Figure 312–3

Author's Comment:

- Unused openings for circuit breakers must be closed by means that provide protection substantially equivalent to the wall of the enclosure [408.7]. **Figure 312–4**

(C) Cable Termination. Cables must be secured to the cabinet or cutout box with fittings designed and listed for the cable. See 300.12 and 300.15. Figure 312–5

Figure 312–4

Figure 312–5

Author's Comment:

■ Cable clamps or cable connectors must be used with only one cable, unless that clamp or fitting is identified for more than one cable. Some Type NM cable clamps are listed for two Type NM cables within a single fitting (UL White Book, *Guide Information for Electrical Equipment,* www.ul.com/regulators/2008_WhiteBook.pdf).

Ex: Cables with nonmetallic sheaths aren't required to be secured to the cabinet if the cables enter the top of a surface-mounted cabinet through a nonflexible raceway not less than 18 in. or more than 10 ft long, if all of the following conditions are met: Figure 312–6

Figure 312–6

(a) Each cable is fastened within 1 ft from the raceway.

(b) The raceway doesn't penetrate a structural ceiling.

(c) Fittings are provided on the raceway to protect the cables from abrasion.

(d) The raceway is sealed.

(e) Each cable sheath extends not less than ¼ in. into the panelboard.

(f) The raceway is properly secured.

(g) Conductor fill is limited to Chapter 9, Table 1 percentages.

312.6 Deflection of Conductors

Cabinets and cutout boxes for conductors must be sized to allow conductors to be deflected in accordance with Table 312.6(A).

Table 312.6(A) Minimum Wire–Bending Space

Wire Size (AWG or kcmil)	Inches
8–6	1½
4–3	2
2	2½
1	3
1/0–2/0	3½
3/0–4/0	4
250	4½
300–350	5
400–500	6
600–700	8

312.8 Cabinets and Cutout Boxes Containing Splices, Taps, and Feed-Through Conductors

Cabinets and cutout boxes can be used for conductors feeding through, spliced, or tapping off to other enclosures, switches, or overcurrent devices where all of the following conditions are met:

(1) The total area of the conductors at any cross section doesn't exceed 40 percent of the cross-sectional area of the space. Figure 312–7

An enclosure can be used as a raceway if the conductors don't fill the wiring space to more than 40%.

Figure 312–7

(2) The total area of conductors, splices, and taps installed at any cross section doesn't exceed 75 percent of the cross-sectional area of that space. Figure 312–8

Splices and taps can be installed in a cabinet if the splices or taps don't fill the wiring space to more than 75%.

Figure 312–8

(3) A warning label that's not **handwritten, must be permanently affixed, be of sufficient durability to withstand the environment involved** [110.21(B)] on the cabinet or cutout box identify the location of the disconnecting means for the feed-through conductors. Figure 312–9

A warning label that complies with 110.21(B) applied to the cabinet must identify the closest disconnect for feed-through conductors.

Figure 312–9

ARTICLE 314

OUTLET, DEVICE, PULL, AND JUNCTION BOXES; CONDUIT BODIES; AND HANDHOLE ENCLOSURES

Introduction to Article 314—Outlet, Device, Pull, and Junction Boxes; Conduit Bodies; and Handhole Enclosures

Article 314 contains installation requirements for outlet boxes, pull and junction boxes, conduit bodies, and handhole enclosures. As with the cabinet covered in Article 312, the conditions of use have a bearing on the type of material and equipment selected for a particular installation. If a raceway is installed in a wet location, for example, the correct fittings and the proper installation methods must be used.

The information here will help you size an outlet box using the proper cubic-inch capacity as well as calculating the minimum dimensions for larger pull boxes. There are limits on the amount of weight that can be supported by an outlet box and rules on how to support a device or outlet box to various surfaces. Article 314 will help you understand these types of rules so that your installation will be compliant with the *NEC*. As always, the clear illustrations in this article will help you visualize the finished installation.

Part I. Scope and General

314.1 Scope

Article 314 contains the installation requirements for outlet boxes, conduit bodies, pull and junction boxes, and handhole enclosures. Figure 314–1

314.3 Nonmetallic Boxes

Nonmetallic boxes can only be used with nonmetallic cables and raceways.

Ex 1: Metal raceways and metal cables can be used with nonmetallic boxes if all raceways are bonded together in the nonmetallic box. Figure 314–2

Outlet Boxes, Conduit Bodies, Pull/Junction Boxes, and Handhole Enclosures
314.1

Junction Box

Outlet Boxes

Conduit Body

Handhole Enclosure

Copyright 2014
www.MikeHolt.com

Article 314 contains the installation requirements for outlet boxes, conduit bodies, pull and junction boxes, and handhole enclosures.

Figure 314–1

Nonmetallic Boxes - Metal Raceways
314.3 Ex 1

Metal raceways can terminate to a nonmetallic box where internal bonding means are provided between all entries.

Figure 314–2

314.4 Metal Boxes

Metal boxes containing circuits that operate at 50V or more must be connected to an equipment grounding conductor of a type listed in 250.118 [250.112(I) and 250.148]. Figure 314–3

Metal Boxes
314.4

Metal boxes containing circuits that operate at 50V or more must be connected to an equipment grounding conductor.

Figure 314–3

Part II. Installation

314.15 Damp or Wet Locations

Boxes, conduit bodies, and fittings in damp or wet locations must prevent moisture or water from entering or accumulating within the enclosure. Figure 314–4

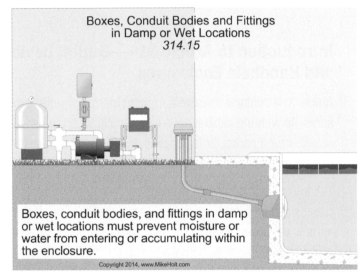

Boxes, Conduit Bodies and Fittings
in Damp or Wet Locations
314.15

Boxes, conduit bodies, and fittings in damp or wet locations must prevent moisture or water from entering or accumulating within the enclosure.

Figure 314–4

Boxes, conduit bodies, and fittings installed in wet locations must be listed for use in wet locations.

Drainage openings can be installed in the field if they aren't larger than ¼ in. For listed drainage fittings, the holes can be larger, but must be in accordance with the manufacturer's instructions. Figure 314–5

Author's Comment:

■ If handhole enclosures without bottoms are installed, all enclosed conductors and any splices or terminations must be listed as suitable for wet locations [314.30(C)].

Figure 314–5

Figure 314–6

314.16 Number of 6 AWG and Smaller Conductors in Boxes and Conduit Bodies

Boxes containing 6 AWG and smaller conductors must be sized in an approved manner to provide free space for all conductors, devices, and fittings. In no case can the volume of the box, as calculated in 314.16(A), be less than the volume requirement as calculated in 314.16(B).

Conduit bodies must be sized in accordance with 314.16(C).

Author's Comment:

- The requirements for sizing boxes and conduit bodies containing conductors 4 AWG and larger are contained in 314.28. The requirements for sizing handhole enclosures are contained in 314.30(A).

(A) Box Volume Calculations. The volume of a box includes the total volume of its assembled parts, including plaster rings, extension rings, and domed covers that are either marked with their volume in cubic inches (cu in.), or are made from boxes listed in Table 314.16(A). Figure 314–6

(B) Box Fill Calculations. The calculated conductor volume determined by (1) through (5) and Table 314.16(B) are added together to determine the total volume of the conductors, devices, and fittings. Raceway and cable fittings, including locknuts and bushings, aren't counted for box fill calculations. Figure 314–7

Figure 314–7

Table 314.16(B) Volume Allowance Required per Conductor

Conductor AWG	Volume cu in.
18	1.50
16	1.75
14	2.00
12	2.25
10	2.50
8	3.00
6	5.00

(1) Conductor Volume. Each unbroken conductor that runs through a box, and each conductor that terminates in a box, is counted as a single conductor volume in accordance with Table 314.16(B). Figure 314–8

Figure 314–8

Each loop or coil of unbroken conductor having a length of at least twice the minimum length required for free conductors in 300.14 must be counted as two conductor volumes. Conductors that originate and terminate within the box, such as pigtails, aren't counted at all. Figure 314–9

Figure 314–9

Author's Comment:

■ According to 300.14, at least 6 in. of free conductor, measured from the point in the box where the conductors enter the enclosure, must be left at each outlet, junction, and switch point for splices or terminations of luminaires or devices.

Ex: Equipment grounding conductors, and up to four 16 AWG and smaller fixture wires, can be omitted from box fill calculations if they enter the box from a domed luminaire or similar canopy, such as a ceiling paddle fan canopy. Figure 314–10

Figure 314–10

(2) Cable Clamp Volume. One or more internal cable clamps count as a single conductor volume in accordance with Table 314.16(B), based on the largest conductor that enters the box. Cable connectors that have their clamping mechanism outside of the box aren't counted. Figure 314–11

(3) Support Fitting Volume. Each luminaire stud or luminaire hickey counts as a single conductor volume in accordance with Table 314.16(B), based on the largest conductor that enters the box. Figure 314–12

Author's Comment:

■ Luminaire stems don't need to be counted as a conductor volume.

Figure 314–11

Figure 314–13

Figure 314–12

Figure 314–14

(4) Device Yoke Volume. Each single-gang device yoke (regardless of the ampere rating of the device) counts as two conductor volumes, based on the largest conductor that terminates on the device in accordance with Table 314.16(B). Figure 314–13

Each multigang-device yoke counts as two conductor volumes for each gang, based on the largest conductor that terminates on the device in accordance with Table 314.16(B). Figure 314–14

Author's Comment:

■ A device that's too wide for mounting in a single-gang box, as described in Table 314.16(A), is counted based on the number of gangs required for the device.

(5) Equipment Grounding Conductor Volume. All equipment grounding conductors in a box count as a single conductor volume in accordance with Table 314.16(B), based on the largest equipment grounding conductor that enters the box. Insulated equipment grounding conductors for receptacles having insulated grounding terminals (isolated ground receptacles) [250.146(D)], count as a single conductor volume in accordance with Table 314.16(B). Figure 314–15

Figure 314–15

Author's Comment:

- Conductor insulation isn't a factor that's considered when determining box volume calculations.

Question: How many 14 AWG conductors can be pulled through a 4 in. square x 2½ in. deep box with a plaster ring with a marking of 3.60 cu in.? The box contains two receptacles, five 12 AWG conductors, and two 12 AWG equipment grounding conductors. Figure 314–16

(a) 3   (b) 5   (c) 7   (d) 9

Answer: (b) 5

Step 1: Determine the volume of the box assembly [314.16(A)]:

Box 30.30 cu in. + 3.60 cu in. plaster ring = 33.90 cu in.

A 4 x 4 x 2⅛ in. box will have a gross volume of 34 cu in., but the interior volume is 30.30 cu in., as listed in Table 314.16(A).

(continued)

Step 2: Determine the volume of the devices and conductors in the box:

Two—receptacles	4—12 AWG
Five—12 AWG	5—12 AWG
Two—12 AWG Grounds	1—12 AWG

Total 10—12 AWG x 2.25 cu in. = 22.50 cu in.

Step 3: Determine the remaining volume permitted for the 14 AWG conductors:

33.90 cu in. − 22.50 cu in. = 11.40 cu in.

Step 4: Determine the number of 14 AWG conductors permitted in the remaining volume:

14 AWG = 2.00 cu in. each [Table 314.16(B)]

11.40 cu in./2.00 cu in. = 5 conductors

Step 1. Volume of box/ring: 30.3 + 3.6 cu in. = 33.9 cu in.
Step 2. Volume of existing conductors/devices = 22.5 cu in.
Step 3. Space remaining: 33.9 - 22.5 = 11.4 cu in.
Step 4. Number of 14 AWG added: 11.4/2.0 cu in. = 5

Figure 314–16

(C) Conduit Bodies.

(2) Splices. Splices are permitted in conduit bodies that are legibly marked by the manufacturer with their volume and the maximum number of conductors permitted in a conduit body is limited in accordance with 314.16(B).

Question: *How many 12 AWG conductors can be spliced in a 15 cu in. conduit body?* **Figure 314–17**

(a) 4   (b) 6   (c) 8   (d) 10

Answer: *(b) 6 conductors (15 cu in./2.25 cu in.)*

12 AWG = 2.25 cu in. [Table 314.16(B)]
15 cu in./2.25 cu in. = 6

Figure 314–17

(3) Short-Radius Conduit Bodies. Capped elbows, handy ells, and service-entrance elbows aren't permitted to contain any splices. Figure 314–18

314.17 Conductors That Enter Boxes or Conduit Bodies

(A) Openings to Be Closed. Unused openings through which cables or raceways enter must be **closed in an approved manner**. Figure 314–19

Author's Comment:

■ Unused cable or raceway openings in electrical equipment must be effectively closed by fittings that provide protection substantially equivalent to the wall of the equipment [110.12(A)].

Figure 314–18

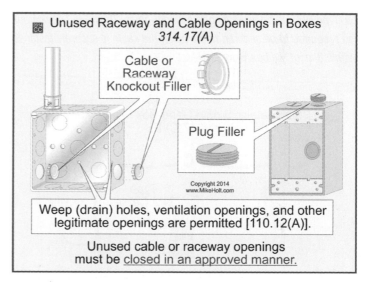

Figure 314–19

(C) Nonmetallic Boxes and Conduit Bodies. Raceways and cables must be securely fastened to nonmetallic boxes or conduit bodies by fittings designed for the wiring method [300.12 and 300.15]. Figure 314–20

The sheath of type NM cable must extend not less than ¼ in. into the nonmetallic box.

Author's Comment:

■ Two Type NM cables can terminate in a single cable clamp, if the clamp is listed for this purpose.

Conductors That Enter
Nonmetallic Boxes and Conduit Bodies
314.17(C)

Raceways and cables must be securely fastened to nonmetallic boxes or conduit bodies by fittings designed for the wiring method.

Figure 314–20

Ex: Type NM cable terminating to a single-gang (2¼ x 4 in.) device box isn't required to be secured to the box if the cable is securely fastened within 8 in. of the box. Figure 314–21

Nonmetallic Single Gang Box - NM Cable
314.17(C) Ex

Type NM Cable

Metal Studs

NM cable terminating to a single-gang (2 ¼ in. x 4 in.) device box isn't required to be secured to the box if the cable is securely fastened within 8 in. of the box.

Figure 314–21

314.20 Boxes Recessed in Walls or Ceilings

Boxes having flush-type covers that are recessed in walls or ceilings of noncombustible material must have the front edge of the box, plaster ring, extension ring, or listed extender set back no more than ¼ in. from the finished surface. Figure 314–22

Boxes Recessed in Walls or Ceilings
314.20

Noncombustible Finished Surface

Maximum of ¼ in. From the Finished Surface

Figure 314–22

In walls or ceilings that are constructed of wood or other combustible material, boxes must be installed so the front edge of the enclosure, plaster ring, extension ring, or listed extender is flush with, or projects out from, the finished surface. Figure 314–23

Boxes Recessed in Walls or Ceilings
314.20

Combustible Finished Surface

Flush With or Project Out From the Surface

Boxes, plaster rings, extension rings, or listed extenders must have the front edge flush with, or project out from, the combustible finished surface.

Figure 314–23

Author's Comment:

■ Plaster rings and extension rings are available in a variety of depths to meet the above requirements.

314.21 Repairing Noncombustible Surfaces

Gaps around boxes with flush-type covers that are recessed in non-combustible surfaces (such as plaster, drywall, or plasterboard) must be repaired so there will be no gap more than ⅛ in. at the edge of the box. Figure 314–24

Figure 314–24

314.22 Surface Extensions

Surface extensions can only be made from an extension ring mounted over a flush-mounted box. Figure 314–25

Ex: A surface extension can be made from the cover of a flush-mounted box if the cover is designed so it's unlikely to fall off if the mounting screws become loose. The surface extension wiring method must be flexible to permit the removal of the cover and provide access to the box interior, and equipment grounding continuity must be independent of the connection between the box and the cover. Figure 314–26

314.23 Support of Boxes and Conduit Bodies

Boxes must be securely supported by one of the following methods:

Figure 314–25

Figure 314–26

(A) Surface. Boxes can be fastened to any surface that provides adequate support.

(B) Structural Mounting. Boxes can be supported from any structural member, or they can be supported from grade by a metal, plastic, or wood brace.

(1) Nails and Screws. Nails or screws can be used to fasten boxes, provided the exposed threads of screws are protected to prevent abrasion of conductor insulation.

(2) Braces. Metal braces no less than 0.02 in. thick and wood braces not less than a nominal 1 in. x 2 in. can support a box.

(C) Finished Surface Support. Boxes can be secured to a finished surface (drywall or plaster walls, or ceilings) by clamps, anchors, or fittings identified for the purpose. Figure 314–27

Boxes can be secured to a finished surface by clamps, anchors, or fittings identified for the purpose.

Figure 314–27

(D) Suspended-Ceiling Support. Outlet boxes can be supported to the structural or supporting elements of a suspended ceiling, if securely fastened by one of the following methods:

(1) Ceiling-Framing Members. An outlet box can be secured to suspended-ceiling framing members by bolts, screws, rivets, clips, or other means identified for the suspended-ceiling framing member(s). Figure 314–28

Outlet boxes can be secured to suspended-ceiling members by bolts, screws, rivets, clips, or other means identified for the purpose.

Figure 314–28

Author's Comment:

- If framing members of suspended-ceiling systems are used to support luminaires, they must be securely fastened to each other and must be securely attached to the building structure at appropriate intervals. In addition, luminaires must be attached to the suspended-ceiling framing members with screws, bolts, rivets, or clips listed and identified for such use [410.36(B)].

(2) Independent Support Wires. Outlet boxes can be secured, with <u>identified</u> fittings, to the ceiling-support wires. If independent support wires are used for outlet box support, they must be taut and secured at both ends [300.11(A)]. Figure 314–29

Outlet boxes can be secured with <u>identified</u> fittings to the ceiling and independent support wires that are taut and secured at both ends.

Figure 314–29

Author's Comment:

- See 300.11(A) on the use of independent support wires to support raceways and cables.

(E) Raceway—Boxes and Conduit Bodies Without Devices or Luminaires. Two intermediate metal or rigid metal conduits, threaded wrenchtight into the enclosure, can be used to support an outlet box that doesn't contain a device or luminaire, if each raceway is supported within 36 in. of the box or within 18 in. of the box if all conduit entries are on the same side. Figure 314–30

Ex: Conduit bodies are permitted to be supported by any of the following wiring methods: Figure 314–31

Figure 314–30

Figure 314–32

Figure 314–31

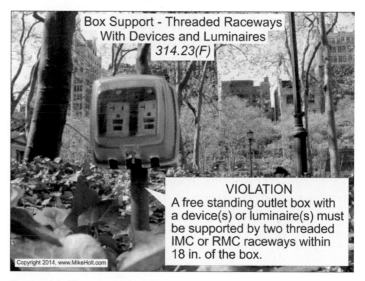

Figure 314–33

(1) Intermediate metal conduit, Type IMC

(2) Rigid metal conduit, Type RMC

(3) Rigid polyvinyl chloride conduit, Type PVC

(4) Reinforced thermosetting resin conduit, Type RTRC

(5) Electrical metallic tubing, Type EMT

(F) Raceway—Boxes and Conduit Bodies with Devices or Luminaires. Two intermediate metal or rigid metal conduits, threaded wrenchtight into the enclosure, can be used to support an outlet box containing devices or luminaires, if each raceway is supported within 18 in. of the box. Figures 314–32 and 314–33

(H) Pendant Boxes.

(1) Flexible Cord. Boxes containing a hub can be supported from a cord connected to fittings that prevent tension from being transmitted to joints or terminals [400.10]. Figure 314–34

Author's Comment:

■ Only cords identified for use as pendants in Table 400.4 may be used for pendants.

Figure 314–34

314.25 Covers and Canopies

When the installation is complete, each outlet box must be provided with a cover or faceplate, unless covered by a fixture canopy, lampholder, or similar device. Figure 314–35

Figure 314–35

Screws used for attaching covers or other equipment to the box must be machine screws that match the thread gage or size of the screw holes in the box or they must be in accordance with the manufacturer's instructions. Figure 314–36

Figure 314–36

(A) Metallic Covers. Metal covers are only permitted if they can be connected to an equipment grounding conductor of a type recognized in 250.118 [250.110]. Figure 314–37

Figure 314–37

Author's Comment:

- Metal switch faceplates [404.9(B)] and metal receptacle faceplates [406.6(A)] must be connected to an equipment grounding conductor.

314.27 Outlet Box

(A) Boxes at Luminaire Outlets.

(1) Luminaire Outlets in <u>or on Vertical Surfaces</u>. Boxes for a luminaire in <u>or on</u> a wall <u>or other vertical surface</u> must be <u>identified and be</u> marked on the interior of the box to indicate the maximum weight of the luminaire if other than 50 lb. Figure 314–38

Figure 314–38

Ex: A <u>vertically</u> mounted luminaire weighing no more than 6 lb can be supported to a device box or plaster ring secured to a device box. Figure 314–39

(2) Luminaire Outlets in the Ceiling. Boxes for a luminaire in a ceiling must be designed to support a luminaire weighing a minimum of 50 lb. Luminaires weighing more than 50 lb must be supported independently of the outlet box unless the outlet box is listed and marked <u>on the interior of the box to indicate</u> the maximum weight <u>the box is permitted to support</u>. Figure 314–40

A luminaire mounted in <u>or on a vertical surface</u> weighing no more than 6 lb can be supported to a device box or plaster ring.

Figure 314–39

Figure 314–40

(B) Floor Box. Floor boxes must be specifically listed for the purpose. Figure 314–41

Figure 314–41

(C) Ceiling Paddle Fan Box. Outlet boxes for a ceiling paddle fan must be listed and marked as suitable for the purpose, and must not support a fan weighing more than 70 lb. Outlet boxes for a ceiling paddle fan that weighs more than 35 lb must include the maximum weight to be supported in the required marking. Figure 314–42

Figure 314–42

Author's Comment:

■ If the maximum weight isn't marked on the box, and the fan weighs over 35 lb, it must be supported independently of the outlet box. Ceiling paddle fans over 70 lb must be supported independently of the outlet box.

Where spare, separately switched, ungrounded conductors are provided to a ceiling-mounted outlet box, in a location acceptable for a ceiling-suspended (paddle) fan in single-<u>family, two-family</u> or multi-family dwellings, the outlet box or outlet box system must be listed for the support of a ceiling-suspended (paddle) fan. Figure 314–43

Figure 314–43

(D) Utilization Equipment. Boxes used for the support of utilization equipment must be designed to support equipment that weighs a minimum of 50 lb [314.27(A)].

Ex: Utilization equipment weighing 6 lb or less is permitted to be supported by any box or plaster ring secured to a box, provided the equipment is secured with no fewer than two No. 6 or larger screws. Figure 314–44

Figure 314–44

314.28 Boxes and Conduit Bodies for Conductors 4 AWG and Larger

Boxes and conduit bodies containing conductors 4 AWG and larger that are required to be insulated must be sized so the conductor insulation won't be damaged. Figure 314–45

Figure 314–45

Author's Comment:

■ The requirements for sizing boxes and conduit bodies containing conductors 6 AWG and smaller are contained in 314.16.

■ If conductors 4 AWG and larger enter a box or other enclosure, a fitting that provides a smooth, rounded, insulating surface, such as a bushing or adapter, is required to protect the conductors from abrasion during and after installation [300.4(G)]. Figure 314–46

Figure 314–46

(A) Minimum Size. For raceways containing conductors 4 AWG and larger, the minimum dimensions of boxes and conduit bodies must comply with the following:

(1) Straight Pulls. The minimum distance from where the conductors enter the box or conduit body to the opposite wall must not be less than eight times the trade size of the largest raceway. Figure 314–47

(2) Angle Pulls, U Pulls, or Splices.

Angle Pulls. The distance from the raceway entry of the box or conduit body to the opposite wall must not be less than six times the trade size of the largest raceway, plus the sum of the trade sizes of the remaining raceways on the same wall and row. Figure 314–48

Pull Box or Conduit Body Sizing - Straight Pull
Insulated 4 AWG or Larger
314.28(A)(1)

Straight Pull

8 Times Largest Raceway
8 x 3 = 24 in.

Copyright 2014
www.MikeHolt.com

The distance from the conductors' entry to the opposite wall must not be less than 8 times the trade size of the largest raceway.

Figure 314–47

Pull Box Sizing - U Pull
Insulated 4 AWG or Larger
314.28(A)(2)

Opposite Wall

A

21 in.

Entry Wall

A: U Pull Sizing:
The distance must not be less than 6 times the largest raceway, plus the sum of the other raceways on the same wall and row.
A = (6 x 3) + 3 = 21 in.

Copyright 2014, www.MikeHolt.com

Figure 314–49

Pull Box or Conduit Body Sizing - Angle Pull
Insulated 4 AWG or Larger
314.28(A)(2)

A = (6 x 3) + 2, A = 20 in.

B = (6 x 3) + 2, B = 20 in.

Copyright 2014
www.MikeHolt.com

The distance (measured from the conductor wall entry to the opposite wall) must not be less than 6 times the trade size of the largest raceway, plus the sum of the diameters of the remaining raceways on the same wall and row.

Figure 314–48

Splices in Pull Boxes
or Conduit Bodies
314.28(A)(2)

18 in.

A

B

24 in.

A = 6 x 3 = 18 in.

B = (6 x 3) + 3 + 3 = 24 in.

Copyright 2014, www.MikeHolt.com

When conductors are spliced, the distance from where the raceways enter to the opposite wall must not be less than six times the trade size of the largest raceway plus the sum of all other raceways on the same wall and row.

Figure 314–50

U Pulls. When a conductor enters and leaves from the same wall of the box, the distance from where the raceways enter to the opposite wall must not be less than six times the trade size of the largest raceway, plus the sum of the trade sizes of the remaining raceways on the same wall and row. Figure 314–49

Splices. When conductors are spliced, the distance from where the raceways enter to the opposite wall must not be less than six times the trade size of the largest raceway, plus the sum of the trade sizes of the remaining raceways on the same wall and row. Figure 314–50

Rows. If there are multiple rows of raceway entries, each row is calculated individually and the row with the largest distance must be used. Figure 314–51

Distance Between Raceways. The distance between raceways enclosing the same conductor must not be less than six times the trade size of the largest raceway, measured from the raceways' nearest edge-to-nearest edge. Figure 314–52

Sizing Junction/Pull Boxes for Angle Conductor Pulls
Determining the Largest Row
314.28(A)(2)

Three 1 EMT Raceways
1½ EMT
1½ EMT
3 EMT
Row A1
Row A2

A 21 in.
B

Copyright 2014, www.MikeHolt.com

When there's more than one row of conduit entries on the same wall, each row must be calculated separately and the larger answer used.
Row A1 = (6 x 3) + 1½ + 1½ = 21 in.
Row A2 = (6 x 1) + 1 + 1 = 8 in. (omit)
Dimension A = 21 in.

Figure 314–51

Distance Between Raceways
Containing the Same Conductor
314.28(A)(2)

A
3 EMT
Angle Pulls
C
18 in.
3 EMT

B
U Pulls
12 in. C
2 EMT
2 EMT

Example A:
C = 6 x 3 = 18 in.
Copyright 2014 www.MikeHolt.com
Example B:
C = 6 x 2 = 12 in.

The distance between raceways containing the same conductor must not be less than 6 times the trade size of the larger raceway entry.

Figure 314–52

Ex: When conductors enter an enclosure with a removable cover, the distance from where the conductors enter to the removable cover must not be less than the bending distance as listed in Table 312.6(A) for one conductor per terminal. Figure 314–53

(3) Smaller Dimensions. Boxes or conduit bodies smaller than those required in 314.28(A)(1) and 314.28(A)(2) are permitted, if the enclosure is permanently marked with the maximum number and maximum size of conductors.

Pull Box and Conduit Body Sizing - Depth
314.28(A)(2) Ex

Dimension D
500 kcmil = 6 in.
D
D

Copyright 2014 www.MikeHolt.com

The distance from where the conductors enter to the removable cover can't be less than the bending distance listed in Table 312.6(A) for one wire per terminal.

Figure 314–53

(B) Conductors in Pull or Junction Boxes. Pull boxes or junction boxes with any dimension over 6 ft must have all conductors cabled or racked in an approved manner.

(C) Covers. Pull boxes, junction boxes, and conduit bodies must have a cover suitable for the conditions. Metal covers must be connected to an equipment grounding conductor of a type recognized in 250.118, in accordance with 250.110 [250.4(A)(3)]. Figure 314–54

Pull Box, Junction Box, and Conduit Body Covers
314.28(C)

Copyright 2014 www.MikeHolt.com

The metal raceway and enclosure is the equipment grounding conductor to which the covers connect.

Metal covers for pull boxes, junction boxes, and conduit bodies must be connected to an equipment grounding conductor in accordance with 250.110.

Figure 314–54

(E) Power Distribution Block. Power distribution blocks installed in junction boxes over 100 cu in. must comply with the following: Figure 314–55

Figure 314–55

(1) Installation. Be listed as a power distribution block.

(2) Size. Be installed in a box not smaller than required by the installation instructions of the power distribution block.

(3) Wire-Bending Space. The junction box is sized so that the wire-bending space requirements of 312.6 can be met.

(4) Live Parts. Exposed live parts on the power distribution block aren't present when the junction box cover is removed.

(5) Through Conductors. Where the junction box has conductors that don't terminate on the power distribution block(s), the through conductors must be arranged so the power distribution block terminals are unobstructed following installation.

314.29 Wiring to be Accessible

Boxes, conduit bodies, and handhole enclosures must be installed so that the wiring is accessible without removing any part of the building or structure, sidewalks, paving, or earth. Figure 314–56

Figure 314–56

Ex: Listed boxes and handhole enclosures can be buried if covered by gravel, light aggregate, or noncohesive granulated soil, and their location is effectively identified and accessible for excavation.

314.30 Handhole Enclosures

Handhole enclosures must be identified for underground use, and be designed and installed to withstand all loads likely to be imposed on them. Figure 314–57

Figure 314–57

(A) Size. Handhole enclosures must be sized in accordance with 314.28(A). For handhole enclosures without bottoms, the measurement to the removable cover is taken from the end of the raceway or cable assembly. When the measurement is taken from the end of the raceway or cable assembly, the values in Table 312.6(A) for one wire to terminal can be used [314.28(A)(2) Ex].

(B) Mechanical Raceway and Cable Connection. Underground raceways and cables entering a handhole enclosure aren't required to be mechanically connected to the handhole enclosure. Figure 314–58

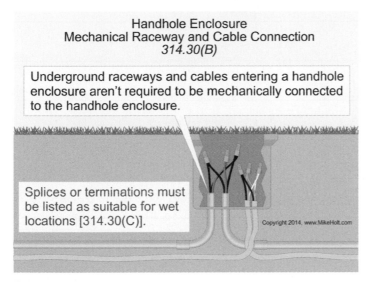

**Handhole Enclosure
Mechanical Raceway and Cable Connection
314.30(B)**

Underground raceways and cables entering a handhole enclosure aren't required to be mechanically connected to the handhole enclosure.

Splices or terminations must be listed as suitable for wet locations [314.30(C)].

Copyright 2014, www.MikeHolt.com

Figure 314–58

(C) Enclosure Wiring. Splices or terminations within a handhole must be listed as suitable for wet locations [110.14(B)].

(D) Covers. Handhole enclosure covers must have an identifying mark or logo that prominently identifies the function of the enclosure, such as "electric." Handhole enclosure covers must require the use of tools to open, or they must weigh over 100 lb.

Metal covers and exposed conductive surfaces of handhole enclosures containing branch circuit or feeder conductors must be connected to an equipment grounding conductor sized in accordance with 250.122, based on the rating of the overcurrent device [250.102(D)]. Figure 314–59

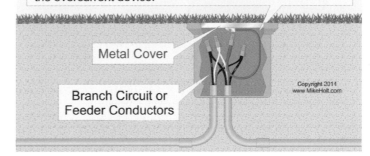

**Handhole Enclosure
Bonding Exposed Conductive Surfaces
314.30(D)**

Metal covers and exposed conductive surfaces of handhole enclosures containing branch circuit or feeder conductors must be connected to an equipment grounding conductor sized in accordance with 250.122, based on the rating of the overcurrent device.

Metal Cover

Branch Circuit or Feeder Conductors

Copyright 2014
www.MikeHolt.com

Figure 314–59

Metal covers and exposed conductive surfaces of handhole enclosures containing service conductors must be connected to a supply-side bonding jumper sized in accordance with Table 250.102(C)(1), based on the size of service conductors [250.92 and 250.102(C)].

Notes

ARTICLE 320

ARMORED CABLE (TYPE AC)

Introduction to Article 320—Armored Cable (Type AC)

Armored cable is an assembly of insulated conductors, 14 AWG through 1 AWG, individually wrapped within waxed paper and contained within a flexible spiral metal sheath. The outside appearance of armored cable looks like flexible metal conduit as well as metal-clad cable to the casual observer. This cable has been referred to as "BX®" cable over the years and used in residential wiring in some areas of the country.

Part I. General

320.1 Scope

This article covers the use, installation, and construction specifications of armored cable, Type AC.

320.2 Definition

Armored Cable (Type AC). A fabricated assembly of conductors in a flexible interlocked metal armor with an internal bonding strip in intimate contact with the armor for its entire length. See 320.100. Figure 320–1

Author's Comment:

- The conductors are contained within a flexible metal sheath that interlocks at the edges, with an internal aluminum bonding strip, giving the cable an outside appearance similar to that of flexible metal conduit. Many electricians call this metal cable "BX®." The advantages of any flexible cables, as compared to raceway wiring methods, are that there's no limit to the number of bends between terminations and the cable can be quickly installed.

Armored Cable - Type AC
320.2 Definition

Waxed Paper Jute

Interlocked Spiral Metal Sheath

Bonding Strip

A fabricated assembly of conductors in a flexible interlocked metal armor with an internal bonding strip in intimate contact with the armor for its entire length.

Copyright 2014, www.MikeHolt.com

Figure 320–1

Part II. Installation

320.10 Uses Permitted

Type AC cable is permitted as follows:

(1) Feeders and branch circuits in both exposed and concealed installations.

(2) Cable trays.

(3) Dry locations.

(4) Embedded in plaster or brick, except in damp or wet locations.

(5) Air voids where not exposed to excessive moisture or dampness.

Note: The "Uses Permitted" isn't an all-inclusive list, which indicates that other suitable uses are permitted if approved by the authority having jurisdiction.

Author's Comment:

■ Type AC cable is also permitted to be installed in a plenum space [300.22(C)(1)].

320.12 Uses Not Permitted

Type AC cable must not be installed in any of the following locations:

(1) If subject to physical damage.

(2) In damp or wet locations.

(3) In air voids of masonry block or tile walls where such walls are exposed or subject to excessive moisture or dampness.

(4) Where exposed to corrosive conditions.

320.15 Exposed Work

Exposed Type AC cable must closely follow the surface of the building finish or running boards. Type AC cable installed on the bottom of floor or ceiling joists must be secured at every joist, and must not be subject to physical damage. Figure 320–2

320.17 Through or Parallel to Framing Members

Type AC cable installed through, or parallel to, framing members or furring strips must be protected against physical damage from penetration by screws or nails by maintaining 1¼ in. of separation, or by installing a suitable metal plate in accordance with 300.4(A), (C), and (D).

AC Cable - Exposed Work
320.15

Type AC cable run on the bottom of floor or ceiling joists must be secured at every joist and not be subject to physical damage.

Copyright 2014, www.MikeHolt.com

Figure 320–2

320.23 In Accessible Attics or Roof Spaces

(A) Cables Run Across the Top of Floor Joists. Where run across the top of floor joists, or across the face of rafters or studding within 7 ft of floor or floor joists, the cable must be protected <u>by guard</u> strips that are at least as high as the cable. If this space isn't accessible by permanent stairs or ladders, protection is required only within 6 ft of the nearest edge of the scuttle hole or attic entrance. Figure 320–3

Accessible Attics or Roof Spaces
Cables Run Across the Top of Joist or Rafters
320.23(A)

Where run across the top of floor joists and within 6 ft of the nearest edge of the scuttle hole or attic entrance, the cable must be protected <u>by guard</u> strips that are at least as high as the cable.

Guard Strip

Copyright 2014
www.MikeHolt.com

Figure 320–3

(B) Cable Installed Parallel to Framing Members. Where Type AC cable is installed on the side of rafters, studs, ceiling joists, or floor joists, no protection is required if the cable is installed and supported so the nearest outside surface of the cable or raceway is at least 1¼ in. from the nearest edge of the framing member [300.4(D)].

320.24 Bends

Type AC cable must not be bent in a manner that'll damage the cable. This is accomplished by limiting bending of the inner edge of the cable to a radius of not less than five times the diameter of the cable. Figure 320–4

Type AC Cable - Bending Radius
320.24

The radius of the inner edge of the curve must not be less than 5 times the diameter of the cable.

Figure 320–4

320.30 Securing and Supporting

(A) General. Type AC cable must be supported and secured by staples, cable ties, straps, hangers, or similar fittings, designed and installed so as not to damage the cable.

(B) Securing. Type AC cable must be secured within 12 in. of every outlet box, junction box, cabinet, or fitting, and at intervals not exceeding 4½ ft. Figure 320–5

Author's Comment:

■ Type AC cable is considered secured when installed horizontally through openings in wooden or metal framing members [320.30(C)].

AC Cable - Securing
320.30(B)

Type AC cable must be secured within 12 in. of termination and every 4½ ft.

Figure 320–5

(C) Supporting. Type AC cable must be supported at intervals not exceeding 4½ ft. Cables installed horizontally through wooden or metal framing members are considered supported if support doesn't exceed 4½ ft. Figure 320–6

AC Cable - Horizontal Support
320.30(C)

AC cable run horizontally through steel or wood framing members is considered supported where such support doesn't exceed 4½ ft.

Metal Studs   Wood Studs

Figure 320–6

(D) Unsupported Cables. Type AC cable can be unsupported where the cable is:

(1) Fished through concealed spaces in finished buildings, if support is impracticable; or

(2) Not more than 2 ft long at terminals where flexibility is necessary; or

(3) Not more than 6 ft long from the last point of cable support to the point of connection to a luminaire or other piece of electrical equipment within an accessible ceiling. Type AC cable fittings are permitted as a means of cable support. Figure 320–7

An insulating anti-short bushing, sometimes called a "redhead," must be installed at all Type AC cable terminations. The termination fitting must permit the visual inspection of the anti-short bushing once the cable has been installed. Figure 320–9

Figure 320–7

Figure 320–9

320.40 Boxes and Fittings

Type AC cable must terminate in boxes or fittings specifically listed for Type AC cable to protect the conductors from abrasion [300.15]. Figure 320–8

Figure 320–8

Author's Comment:

- The internal aluminum bonding strip within the cable serves no electrical purpose once outside the cable, and can be cut off, but many electricians use it to secure the anti-short bushing to the cable. See 320.108.

- Conductors 4 AWG and larger that enter an enclosure must be protected from abrasion during and after installation by a fitting that provides a smooth, rounded, insulating surface, such as an insulating bushing unless the design of the box, fitting, or enclosure provides equivalent protection in accordance with 300.4(G).

320.80 Conductor Ampacity

(A) Thermal Insulation. Conductor ampacity is calculated on the 90°C insulation rating of the conductors, however the conductors must be sized to the termination temperature rating in accordance with 110.14(C)(1). Figure 320–10

Type AC Cable
Ampacity in Thermal Insulation
320.80(A)

AC cable in thermal insulation must have conductors with a 90°C insulation rating, but the ampacity of those conductors must not exceed that of 60°C rated conductors.

Copyright 2014, www.MikeHolt.com

Figure 320–10

Question: What's the ampacity of four 12 THHN current-carrying conductors installed in Type AC cable?

(a) 18A   (b) 24A   (c) 27A   (d) 30A

Answer: (b) 24A

Table 310.15(B)(16) ampacity if 12 THHN is 30A

Conductor Adjusted Ampacity = 30A x 0.80 [Table 310.15(B)(3)(a)]
Conductor Adjusted Ampacity = 24A

Part III. Construction Specifications

320.100 Construction

Type AC cable has an armor of flexible metal tape with an internal aluminum bonding strip in intimate contact with the armor for its entire length.

Author's Comment:

■ The best method of cutting Type AC cable is to use a tool specially designed for the purpose, such as a rotary armor cutter.

■ When cutting Type AC cable with a hacksaw, be sure to cut only one spiral of the cable and be careful not to nick the conductors; this is done by cutting the cable at an angle. Breaking the cable spiral (bending the cable very sharply), then cutting the cable with a pair of dikes isn't a good practice.

320.108 Equipment Grounding Conductor

Type AC cable can serve as an equipment grounding conductor [250.118(8)]. Figure 320–11

AC Cable - Equipment Grounding Conductor
320.108

Type AC cable provides an adequate path for fault current to act as an equipment grounding conductor in accordance with 250.118(8).

The bonding strip can be cut off at the termination or it can be used to secure the anti-short bushing.

Copyright 2014, www.MikeHolt.com

Figure 320–11

Author's Comment:

■ The internal aluminum bonding strip isn't an equipment grounding conductor, but it allows the interlocked armor to serve as an equipment grounding conductor because it reduces the impedance of the armored spirals to ensure that a ground fault will be cleared. It's the combination of the aluminum bonding strip and the cable armor that creates the equipment grounding conductor. Once the bonding strip exits the cable, it can be cut off because it no longer serves any purpose. The effective ground-fault current path must be maintained by the use of fittings specifically listed for Type AC cable [320.40]. See 300.12, 300.15, and 300.10.

ARTICLE
330

METAL-CLAD CABLE (TYPE MC)

Introduction to Article 330—Metal-Clad Cable (Type MC)

Metal-clad cable encloses insulated conductors in a metal sheath of either corrugated or smooth copper or aluminum tubing, or spiral interlocked steel or aluminum. The physical characteristics of Type MC cable make it a versatile wiring method that you can use in almost any location, and for almost any application. The most commonly used Type MC cable is the interlocking kind, which looks similar to armored cable or flexible metal conduit. Traditional interlocked Type MC cable isn't permitted to serve as an equipment grounding conductor, therefore this cable must contain an equipment grounding conductor in accordance with 250.118(1). There's a fairly new product available called interlocked Type MC^{AP} cable that contains a bare aluminum grounding/bonding conductor running just below the metal armor, which allows the sheath to serve as an equipment grounding conductor [250.118(10)(b)].

Part I. General

330.1 Scope

Article 330 covers the use, installation, and construction specifications of metal-clad cable.

330.2 Definition

Metal-Clad Cable (Type MC). A factory assembly of insulated circuit conductors, with or without optical fiber members, enclosed in an armor of interlocking metal tape, or a smooth or corrugated metallic sheath. Figure 330–1

Author's Comment:

■ Because the outer sheath of interlocked Type MC cable isn't listed as an equipment grounding conductor, it contains an equipment grounding conductor [330.108].

Metal-Clad Cable (Type MC Cable)
330.2 Definition

Type MC

Interlocking Metal Sheath

ARMOR SUITABLE AS EGC

Type MC^{AP}®

Copyright 2014, www.MikeHolt.com

A factory assembly of one or more insulated circuit conductors enclosed in an armor of interlocking metal tape, or a smooth or corrugated metallic sheath.

Figure 330–1

Part II. Installation

330.10 Uses Permitted

(A) General Uses.

(1) In branch circuits, feeders, and services

(2) In power, lighting, control, and signal circuits

(3) Indoors or outdoors

(4) Exposed or concealed

(5) Directly buried (if identified for the purpose)

(6) In a cable tray

(7) In a raceway

(8) As aerial cable on a messenger

(9) In hazardous locations as permitted in 501.10(B), 502.10(B), and 503.10

(10) Embedded in plaster or brick

(11) In wet locations, where a corrosion-resistant jacket is provided over the metal sheath and any of the following are met: Figure 330–2

Figure 330–2

a. The metallic covering is impervious to moisture.

b. A jacket is provided under the metal covering that's moisture resistant.

c. The insulated conductors under the metallic covering are listed for use in wet locations.

(12) If single-conductor cables are used, all circuit conductors must be grouped together to minimize induced voltage on the sheath [300.3(B)].

(B) Specific Uses.

(1) Cable Tray. Type MC cable installed in a cable tray must comply with 392.10, 392.12, 392.18, 392.20, 392.22, 392.30, 392.46, 392.56, 392.60(C), and 392.80

(2) Direct Buried. Direct-buried cables must be protected in accordance with 300.5.

(3) Installed as Service-Entrance Cable. Type MC cable is permitted for service entrances, when installed in accordance with 230.43.

(4) Installed Outside of Buildings. Type MC cable installed outside of buildings must comply with 225.10, 396.10, and 396.12.

> **Note:** The "Uses Permitted" isn't an all-inclusive list, which indicates that other suitable uses are permitted if approved by the authority having jurisdiction.

330.12 Uses Not Permitted

Type MC cable must not be used where:

(1) Subject to physical damage.

(2) Exposed to the destructive corrosive conditions in (a) or (b), unless the metallic sheath or armor is resistant or protected by material resistant to the conditions:

a. Direct burial in the earth or embedded in concrete unless identified for the application.

b. Exposed to cinder fills, strong chlorides, caustic alkalis, or vapors of chlorine or of hydrochloric acids.

330.17 Through or Parallel to Framing Members

Type MC cable installed through or parallel to framing members or furring strips must be protected against physical damage from penetration of screws or nails by maintaining a 1¼ in. separation, or by installing a suitable metal plate in accordance with 300.4(A) and (D).

330.23 In Accessible Attics or Roof Spaces

Type MC cable installed in accessible attics or roof spaces must comply with 320.23.

Author's Comment:

■ **On the Surface of Floor Joists, Rafters, or Studs**. In attics and roof spaces that are accessible, substantial guards must protect cables installed across the top of floor joists, or across the face of rafters or studding within 7 ft of floor or floor joists. If this space isn't accessible by permanent stairs or ladders, protection is required only within 6 ft of the nearest edge of the scuttle hole or attic entrance [320.23(A)].

■ **Along the Side of Framing Members [320.23(B)].** When Type MC cable is installed on the side of rafters, studs, or floor joists, no protection is required if the cable is installed and supported so the nearest outside surface of the cable or raceway is at least 1¼ in. from the nearest edge of the framing member where nails or screws are likely to penetrate [300.4(D)].

330.24 Bends

Bends must be made so that the cable won't be damaged, and the radius of the curve of any bend at the inner edge of the cable must not be less than what's dictated in each of the following instances:

(A) Smooth-Sheath Cables.

(1) Smooth-sheath Type MC cables must not be bent so the bending radius of the inner edge of the cable is less than 10 times the external diameter of the metallic sheath for cable up to ¾ in. in external diameter.

(B) Interlocked or Corrugated Sheath. Interlocked- or corrugated-sheath Type MC cable must not be bent so the bending radius of the inner edge of the cable is less than seven times the external diameter of the cable. Figure 330–3

The radius of the inner edge of the curve must not be less than 7 times the diameter of the cable.

Figure 330–3

330.30 Securing and Supporting

(A) General. Type MC cable must be supported and secured by staples, cable ties, straps, hangers, or similar fittings designed and installed so as not to damage the cable.

(B) Securing. Type MC cable with four or less conductors sized no larger than 10 AWG, must be secured within 12 in. of every outlet box, junction box, cabinet, or fitting and at intervals not exceeding 6 ft. Figure 330–4

Listed cables with ungrounded conductors 250 kcmil and larger can be secured at 10-foot intervals when installed vertically.

(C) Supporting. Type MC cable must be supported at intervals not exceeding 6 ft. Cables installed horizontally through wooden or metal framing members are considered secured and supported if such support doesn't exceed 6-foot intervals. Figure 330–5

(D) Unsupported Cables. Type MC cable can be unsupported if the cable is:

(1) Fished through concealed spaces in finished buildings, if support is impracticable, or

Figure 330–4

Figure 330–6

Figure 330–5

Figure 330–7

(2) Not more than 6 ft long from the last point of cable support to the point of connection to luminaires or other electrical equipment within an accessible ceiling. Type MC cable fittings are permitted as a means of cable support. Figure 330–6

(3) Of the interlocked armor type in lengths not longer than 3 ft from the last point where it's securely fastened. This applies only where the cable is used to provide flexibility for equipment that requires movement after installation, or to connect equipment where flexibility is necessary to minimize the transmission of vibration from the equipment. Figure 330–7

330.40 Fittings

Fittings used to secure Type MC cable to boxes or other enclosures must be listed and identified for such use [300.15]. Figure 330–8

Author's Comment:

■ The *NEC* doesn't require anti-short bushings (red heads) at the termination of Type MC cable, but if they're supplied it's considered by many to be a good practice to use them.

Figure 330–8

- Conductors 4 AWG and larger that enter an enclosure must be protected from abrasion during and after installation by a fitting that provides a smooth, rounded, insulating surface, such as an insulating bushing unless the design of the box, fitting, or enclosure provides equivalent protection in accordance with 300.4(G).

330.80 Conductor Ampacities

Conductor ampacity is calculated on the 90°C insulation rating of the conductors; however, the conductors must be sized to the termination temperature rating in accordance with 110.14(C)(1).

Part III. Construction Specifications

330.108 Equipment Grounding Conductor

If Type MC cable is to serve as an equipment grounding conductor, it must comply with 250.118 and 250.122.

Author's Comment:

- The outer sheath of:

  □ Traditional interlocked Type MC cable isn't permitted to serve as an equipment grounding conductor, therefore

this cable must contain an insulated equipment grounding conductor in accordance with 250.118(1). Figure 330–9

□ Interlocked Type MC[AP] cable containing an aluminum grounding/bonding conductor running just below the metal armor is listed to serve as an equipment grounding conductor [250.118(10)(b)]. Figure 330–10

□ Smooth or corrugated-tube Type MC cable is listed to serve as an equipment grounding conductor [250.118(10)(c)].

Figure 330–9

Figure 330–10

Notes

ARTICLE 334

NONMETALLIC-SHEATHED CABLE (TYPES NM AND NMC)

Introduction to Article 334—Nonmetallic-Sheathed Cable (Types NM and NMC)

Nonmetallic-sheathed cable is flexible, inexpensive, and easily installed. It provides very limited physical protection for the conductors, so the installation restrictions are strict. Its low cost and relative ease of installation make it a common wiring method for residential and commercial branch circuits. In the field, Type NM cable is typically referred to as "Romex®."

Part I. General

334.1 Scope

Article 334 covers the use, installation, and construction specifications of nonmetallic-sheathed cable.

334.2 Definition

Nonmetallic-Sheathed Cable (Types NM and NMC). A wiring method that encloses two or more insulated conductors, 14 AWG through 2 AWG, within a nonmetallic jacket. Figure 334–1

- NM cable has insulated conductors enclosed within an overall nonmetallic jacket.
- NMC cable has insulated conductors enclosed within an overall, corrosion resistant, nonmetallic jacket.

Author's Comment:

- It's the generally accepted practice in the electrical industry to call Type NM cable "Romex®," a registered trademark of the Southwire Company.

Nonmetallic-Sheathed Cable
(Types NM and NMC Cable)
334.2 Definition

14/2 w/G   NM-B   600V

A wiring method that encloses two, three, or four insulated conductors (14 AWG to 2 AWG) within an outer nonmetallic jacket.

Copyright 2014, www.MikeHolt.com

Figure 334–1

334.6 Listed

Types NM and NMC cables must be listed.

Part II. Installation

334.10 Uses Permitted

 Scan this QR code for a video of this *Code* rule. See page xix for information on how to use the QR codes.

Type NM and Type NMC cables can be used in the following, <u>except as prohibited in 334.12</u>:

(1) One- and two-family dwellings of any height, and their attached/detached garages or storage buildings. Figures 334–2 and 334–3

NM Cable - One- and Two-Family Dwelling Units
334.10(1)

NM cable can be installed in one- and two-family dwelling units of any height.

Figure 334–2

NM Cable - One- and Two-Family Dwelling Units
334.10(1)

NM cable can be installed in one- and two-family dwelling unit attached/detached garages or storage buildings.

Figure 334–3

(2) Multifamily dwellings permitted to be of Types III, IV, and V <u>construction</u>. Figure 334–4

NM Cable - Multifamily Dwellings
334.10(2)

NM cable can be installed in multifamily buildings of Type III, IV, and V <u>construction</u>.

Figure 334–4

(3) Other structures permitted to be of Types III, IV, and V <u>construction</u>. Cables must be concealed within walls, floors, or ceilings that provide a thermal barrier of material with at least a 15-minute finish rating, as identified in listings of fire-rated assemblies. Figure 334–5

NM Cable - Other Structures
334.10(3)

In other than dwelling units, NM cable can be installed in Type III, IV, and V <u>construction</u>, provided the cables are concealed within a 15-minute finish rating.

Figure 334–5

Author's Comment:

- See the definition of "Concealed" in Article 100.

Note 1: Building constructions are defined in NFPA 220-2006, *Standard on Types of Building Construction*, the applicable building code, or both.

Note 2: See Annex E for the determination of building types [NFPA 220, Table 3-1].

334.12 Uses Not Permitted

(A) Types NM and NMC. Types NM and NMC cables aren't permitted.

(1) In any dwelling or structure not specifically permitted in 334.10(1), (2), (3), **and (5)**.

(2) Exposed in dropped or suspended ceilings in other than one- and two-family and multifamily dwellings. Figure 334–6

NM Cable - Suspended Ceilings
334.12(A)(2)

Suspended Ceiling

VIOLATION

In other than a dwelling unit, NM cable isn't permitted to be run exposed within a suspended ceiling.

Copyright 2014
www.MikeHolt.com

Figure 334–6

(3) As service-entrance cable.

(4) In commercial garages having hazardous locations, as defined in 511.3.

(5) In theaters and similar locations, except where permitted in 518.4(B).

(6) In motion picture studios.

(7) In storage battery rooms.

(8) In hoistways, or on elevators or escalators.

(9) Embedded in poured cement, concrete, or aggregate.

(10) In any hazardous location, except where permitted by other sections in the *Code*.

(B) Type NM. Type NM cables must not be used under the following conditions, or in the following locations:

(1) If exposed to corrosive fumes or vapors.

(2) If embedded in masonry, concrete, adobe, fill, or plaster.

(3) In a shallow chase in masonry, concrete, or adobe and covered with plaster, adobe, or similar finish.

(4) In wet or damp locations. Figure 334–7

NM Cable - Wet Location
334.12(B)(4)

Direct-Buried
Cable or Raceway

Exposed to
Weather

Concrete in direct
contact with earth.

Copyright 2014
www.MikeHolt.com

VIOLATION
Type NM cable isn't suitable for
use in wet or damp locations.

Figure 334–7

Author's Comment:

- Type NM cable isn't permitted in ducts or plenum spaces [300.22], or for wiring in patient care spaces [517.13].

334.15 Exposed

(A) Surface of the Building. Exposed Type NM cable must closely follow the surface of the building.

(B) Protected from Physical Damage. Nonmetallic-sheathed cable must be protected from physical damage by rigid metal conduit, intermediate metal conduit, Schedule 80 PVC conduit, Type RTRC-XW conduit, electrical metallic tubing, guard strips, or other means approved by the authority having jurisdiction.

Author's Comment:

- When installed in a raceway, the cable must be protected from abrasion by a fitting installed on the end of the raceway [300.15(C)].

Type NMC cable installed in shallow chases in masonry, concrete, or adobe, must be protected against nails or screws by a steel plate not less than 1/16 in. thick [300.4(F)] and covered with plaster, adobe, or similar finish.

Author's Comment:

- If Type NM cable is installed in a metal raceway, the raceway isn't required to be connected to an equipment grounding conductor [250.86 Ex 2 and 300.12 Ex].

(C) In Unfinished Basements and Crawl Spaces. If Type NM cable is installed at angles with joists in unfinished basements and crawl spaces, it's permissible to secure cables containing conductors not smaller than two 6 AWG or three 8 AWG conductors directly to the lower edges of the joists. Smaller cables must be installed through bored holes in joists or on running boards. Figure 334–8

Figure 334–8

Type NM cable installed on a wall of an unfinished basement or crawl space subject to physical damage must be protected in accordance with 300.4, or be installed in a raceway with a nonmetallic bushing or adapter at the point where the cable enters the raceway, and the NM cable must be secured within 12 in. of the point where the cable enters the raceway. Figure 334–9

Figure 334–9

334.17 Through or Parallel to Framing Members

Type NM cable installed through or parallel to framing members or furring strips must be protected against physical damage from penetration by screws or nails by 1¼ in. of separation or by a suitable metal plate [300.4(A) and (D)].

334.23 Attics and Roof Spaces

Type NM cable installed in accessible attics or roof spaces must comply with 320.23. Figure 334–10

Figure 334–10

The radius of the inner edge of the curve must not be less than 5 times the diameter of the cable.

Figure 334–11

Author's Comment:

- On the Surface of Floor Joists, Rafters, or Studs. In attics and roof spaces that are accessible, substantial guards must protect cables installed across the top of floor joists, or across the face of rafters or studding within 7 ft of the floor or floor joists. If this space isn't accessible by permanent stairs or ladders, protection is required only within 6 ft of the nearest edge of the scuttle hole or attic entrance [320.23(A)].

- Along the Side of Framing Members [320.23(B)]. When Type NM cable is installed on the side of rafters, studs, or floor joists, no protection is required if the cable is installed and supported so the nearest outside surface of the cable or raceway is at least 1¼ in. from the nearest edge of the framing member if nails or screws are likely to penetrate [300.4(D)].

334.24 Bends

When the cable is bent, it must not be damaged and the radius of the curve of the inner edge of any bend must not be less than five times the diameter of the cable. Figure 334–11

334.30 Securing and Supporting

Staples, straps, cable ties, hangers, or similar fittings must secure Type NM cable in a manner that won't damage the cable. Type NM cable must be secured within 12 in. of every box, cabinet, enclosure, or termination fitting, except as permitted by 314.17(C) Ex or 312.5(C) Ex, and at intervals not exceeding 4½ ft.

Two-wire (flat) Type NM cable isn't permitted to be stapled on edge. Figure 334–12

Type NM cable must be secured within 12 in. of termination and at intervals not exceeding 4¹/₂ ft.

Figure 334–12

Type NM cable installed in a raceway isn't required to be secured within the raceway. Figure 334–13

Figure 334–13

(A) Horizontal Runs. Type NM cable installed horizontally in bored or punched holes in wood or metal framing members, or notches in wooden members is considered secured and supported, but the cable must be secured within 1 ft of termination. Figure 334–14

Figure 334–14

Note: See 314.17(C) for support where nonmetallic boxes are used.

(B) Unsupported. Type NM cable can be unsupported in the following situations:

(1) If Type NM cable is fished between concealed access points in finished buildings, and support is impracticable.

(2) Not more than 4½ ft of unsupported cable is permitted from the last point of support within an accessible ceiling for the connection of luminaires or equipment.

Author's Comment:

■ Type NM cable isn't permitted as a wiring method above accessible ceilings, except in dwellings [334.12(A)(2)].

334.40 Boxes and Fittings

(B) NM Cable Interconnection Devices. A box or conduit body is not required where a listed nonmetallic-sheathed cable interconnector device is used in existing buildings for exposed and concealed locations in accordance with 300.15(H). Figure 334–15

Figure 334–15

Author's Comment:

- According to UL (QAAV), Interconnection devices have been investigated for equivalency to Type NM cable in insulation and temperature rise, and for capability to withstand fault currents, vibration and mechanical shock that may occur during transport. The interconnects are intended for use with 14 and 12 AWG solid or stranded copper conductors.

334.80 Conductor Ampacity

Conductor ampacity is calculated on the 90°C insulation rating of the conductor in accordance with Table 310.15(B)(16), however the conductors must be sized to the termination temperature rating of 60°C.

Figure 334–16

Question: What size Type NM cable is required to supply a 9.60 kW, 240V, single-phase fixed space heater with a 3A blower motor? Figure 334–16

(a) 2 AWG   (b) 4 AWG   (c) 6 AWG   (d) 8 AWG

Answer: (c) 6 AWG

Step 1: Determine the total load in amperes:

$$I = VA/E$$

$I = 9,600W/240V + 3A$
$I = 40A + 3A$
$I = 43A$

Step 2: Conductor and Protection Size [424.3(B)]. Size the ungrounded conductors and overcurrent device at no less than 125 percent of the total heating load.

Conductor/Protection Size = Load x 1.25

Conductor/Protection Size = 43A x 1.25
Conductor/Protection Size = 53.75A

According to Table 310.15(B)(16), a 6 AWG conductor rated 55A at 60°C, protected with a 60A overcurrent device [240.6(A)].

If multiple Type NM cables pass through the same wood framing opening that's to be sealed with thermal insulation, caulking, or sealing foam, the allowable ampacity of each conductor must be adjusted in accordance with Table 310.15(B)(3)(a). Figure 334–17

Figure 334–17

Author's Comment:

- This requirement has no effect on conductor sizing if you bundle no more than nine current-carrying 14 or 12 AWG conductors together. For example, three 14/2 cables and one 14/3 cable (eight current-carrying 14 THHN conductors) are bundled together in a dry location, the ampacity for each conductor (25A at 90°C, Table 310.15(B)(16)) is adjusted by a 70 percent adjustment factor [Table 310.15(B)(3)(a)].

  □ Adjusted Conductor Ampacity = 25A x 0.70
  □ Adjusted Conductor Ampacity = 17.50A

Where more than two NM cables are installed in contact with thermal insulation without maintaining spacing between cables, the allowable ampacity of each conductor must be adjusted in accordance with Table 310.15(B)(3)(a). Figure 334–18

NM Cable - Bundled in Thermal Insulation
334.80

Where multiple Type NM cables are installed in contact with thermal insulation without maintaining spacing between cables, the allowable ampacity of each conductor must be adjusted [Table 310.15(B)(3)(a)].

Copyright 2014
www.MikeHolt.com

Figure 334–18

Part III. Construction Specifications

334.100 Construction

The outer cable sheath of Type NM cable must be constructed with nonmetallic material.

334.104 Conductors

The conductors must be 14 AWG through 2 AWG copper, or 12 AWG through 2 AWG aluminum or copper-clad aluminum.

334.108 Equipment Grounding Conductor

Type NM cable must have an insulated, covered, or bare equipment grounding conductor.

334.112 Insulation

NM conductor insulation must be rated 90°C (194°F).

Note: Types NM cable identified by the markings NM-B meet this requirement.

ARTICLE 338

SERVICE-ENTRANCE CABLE (TYPES SE AND USE)

Introduction to Article 338—Service-Entrance Cable (Types SE and USE)

Service-entrance cable is a single conductor or multiconductor assembly with or without an overall moisture-resistant covering. This cable is used primarily for services, but can also be used for feeders and branch circuits when the limitations of this article are observed.

Part I. General

338.1 Scope

Article 338 covers the use, installation, and construction specifications of service-entrance cable, Types SE and USE.

338.2 Definitions

Service-Entrance Cable. Service-entrance cable is a single or multi-conductor assembly, with or without an overall covering, used primarily for services. Figure 338–1

Type SE. SE and SER cables have a flame-retardant, moisture-resistant covering and are permitted only in aboveground installations. These cables are permitted for branch circuits or feeders when installed in accordance with 338.10(B).

Author's Comment:

- SER cable is SE cable with an insulated neutral, resulting in three insulated conductors with an uninsulated equipment grounding conductor. SER cable is round, while 2-wire SE cable is flat.

Service-Entrance Cable
338.2 Definition

Aboveground

SE cable is permitted only in aboveground installations and is permitted for branch circuits or feeders when installed according to 338.10(B).

Underground Only

USE cable is identified for underground use. Its covering is moisture resistant but not required to be flame retardant, and it isn't suitable for use within a premises.

A single or multiconductor assembly with or without an overall covering used primarily for services not over 600V.

Figure 338–1

Type USE. USE cable is identified as a wiring method permitted for underground use; its covering is moisture resistant, but not flame retardant.

Author's Comment:

- USE cable isn't permitted to be installed indoors [338.10(B)], except single-conductor USE dual rated as RHH/RHW.

Part II. Installation

338.10 Uses Permitted

(A) Service-Entrance Conductors. Service-entrance cable used as service-entrance conductors must be installed in accordance with Article 230.

(B) Branch Circuits or Feeders.

(1) Insulated Conductor. Type SE service-entrance cable is permitted for branch circuits and feeders where the circuit conductors are insulated.

(2) Uninsulated Conductor. SE cable is permitted for branch circuits and feeders if the insulated conductors are used for circuit wiring, and the uninsulated conductor is only used for equipment grounding purposes. Figure 338–2

SE Cable - Use of Uninsulated Conductor
338.10(B)(2)

Proper Installation

VIOLATION

SE and SER cable can be used for branch circuits and feeders, but the uninsulated conductor can only be used for equipment grounding.

Copyright 2014, www.MikeHolt.com

Figure 338–2

Ex: In existing installations, uninsulated conductors may be used for the neutral conductor if the uninsulated neutral conductor of the cable originates in service equipment.

(3) Temperature Limitations. SE cable must not be subjected to conductor temperatures exceeding its insulation rating.

(4) Installation Methods for Branch Circuits and Feeders. SE cable used for branch circuits or feeders must comply with (a) and (b).

(a) Interior Installations. SE cable used for interior branch circuit or feeder wiring must be installed in accordance with the same requirements as Type NM Cable—Article 334, excluding 334.80. Figure 338–3

SE Cable - Interior Installations
338.10(B)(4)(a)

10 kW Heat
3A Fan

(42A + 3A) = 45A
45A x 1.25 = 56A
6 AWG Rated 65A at 75°C
Table 310.15(B)(16)

75°C Terminals

240V

Conductors can be sized to the terminal ratings of equipment in accordance with 110.14(C)(1).

Copyright 2014
www.MikeHolt.com

Figure 338–3

The maximum conductor temperature rating can be used [310.15(B)(2)] for ampacity adjustment and correction purposes.

⚠️ **CAUTION:** *Underground service-entrance cable (USE) is not permitted for interior wiring because it doesn't have a flame-retardant insulation. It would only be permitted in interior wiring when dual listed as wire type in accordance with Table 310.104, such as RHW.*

(b) Exterior Installations. The cable must be supported in accordance with 334.30 and where run underground the cable must comply with Part II of Article 340.

Ex: Single conductor and multi-rated USE conductors aren't restricted to the 60°C rating required by 340.80. Figure 338–4

338.12 Uses Not Permitted

(A) Service-Entrance Cable. SE cable isn't permitted under the following conditions or locations:

(1) If subject to physical damage unless protected in accordance with 230.50(A).

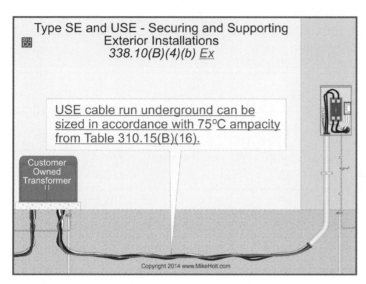

Figure 338–4

(2) Underground with or without a raceway.

(B) Underground Service-Entrance Cable. USE cable isn't permitted:

(1) For interior wiring.

(2) Above ground, except where protected against physical damage in accordance with 300.5(D). Figure 338–5

Figure 338–5

338.24 Bends

Bends in cable must be made so the protective coverings of the cable aren't damaged, and the radius of the curve of the inner edge is at least five times the diameter of the cable. Figure 338–6

Figure 338–6

Notes

ARTICLE 340

UNDERGROUND FEEDER AND BRANCH-CIRCUIT CABLE (TYPE UF)

Introduction to Article 340—Underground Feeder and Branch-Circuit Cable (Type UF)

UF cable is a moisture-, fungus-, and corrosion-resistant cable suitable for direct burial in the earth.

Part I. General

340.1 Scope

Article 340 covers the use, installation, and construction specifications of underground feeder and branch-circuit cable, Type UF.

340.2 Definition

Underground Feeder and Branch-Circuit Cable (Type UF). A factory assembly of insulated conductors with an integral or an overall covering of nonmetallic material suitable for direct burial in the earth. Notice that Type UF is not allowed as a service cable. Figure 340–1

Author's Comment:

- UF cable is a moisture-, fungus-, and corrosion-resistant cable suitable for direct burial in the earth. It comes in sizes 14 AWG through 4/0 AWG [340.104]. The covering of multi-conductor Type UF cable is molded plastic that encases the insulated conductors.

- Because the covering of Type UF cable encapsulates the insulated conductors, it's difficult to strip off the outer jacket to gain access to the conductors, but this covering provides excellent corrosion protection. Be careful not to damage the conductor insulation or cut yourself when you remove the outer cover.

Underground Feeder and Branch-Circuit Cable
Type UF Cable
340.2 Definition

14/2 w/G   UF   600V

Type UF

A factory assembly of one or more insulated conductors with an integral or an overall covering of nonmetallic material suitable for direct burial in the earth.

Copyright 2014, www.MikeHolt.com

Figure 340–1

340.6 Listing Requirements

Type UF cable must be listed.

Part II. Installation

340.10 Uses Permitted

(1) Underground, in accordance with 300.5.

(2) As a single conductor in the same trench or raceway with circuit conductors.

(3) As interior or exterior wiring in wet, dry, or corrosive locations.

(4) As Type NM cable, when installed in accordance with Article 334.

(5) For solar PV systems, in accordance with 690.31.

(6) As single-conductor cables for nonheating leads for heating cables, as provided in 424.43.

(7) Supported by cable trays.

340.12 Uses Not Permitted

(1) As services [230.43].

(2) In commercial garages [511.3].

(3) In theaters [520.5].

(4) In motion picture studios [530.11].

(5) In storage battery rooms [Article 480].

(6) In hoistways [Article 620].

(7) In hazardous locations, except as specifically permitted by other articles in the *Code*.

(8) Embedded in concrete.

(9) Exposed to direct sunlight unless identified.

(10) If subject to physical damage. Figure 340–2

(11) As overhead messenger-supported wiring.

Author's Comment:

- UF cable isn't permitted in ducts or plenum spaces [300.22], or in patient care spaces [517.13].

Figure 340–2

340.24 Bends

Bends in cables must be made so that the protective coverings of the cable aren't damaged, and the radius of the curve of the inner edge must not be less than five times the diameter of the cable.

340.80 Ampacity

The ampacity of conductors contained in UF cable is based on the 60°C insulation rating listed in Table 310.15(B)(16).

340.112 Insulation

The conductors of UF cable must be one of the moisture-resistant types listed in Table 310.104(A) suitable for branch-circuit wiring. If installed as a substitute wiring method for Type NM cable, the conductor insulation must be rated 90°C (194°F).

ARTICLE 342

INTERMEDIATE METAL CONDUIT (TYPE IMC)

Introduction to Article 342—Intermediate Metal Conduit (Type IMC)

Intermediate metal conduit (IMC) is a circular metal raceway with an outside diameter equal to that of rigid metal conduit. The wall thickness of intermediate metal conduit is less than that of rigid metal conduit (RMC), so it's a greater interior cross-sectional area for containing conductors. Intermediate metal conduit is lighter and less expensive than rigid metal conduit, but it can be used in all of the same locations as rigid metal conduit. Intermediate metal conduit also uses a different steel alloy that makes it stronger than rigid metal conduit, even though the walls are thinner. Intermediate metal conduit is manufactured in both galvanized steel and aluminum; the steel type is much more common.

Part I. General

342.1 Scope

Article 342 covers the use, installation, and construction specifications of intermediate metal conduit and associated fittings.

342.2 Definition

Intermediate Metal Conduit (Type IMC). A listed steel raceway of circular cross section that can be threaded with integral or associated couplings. It's listed for the installation of electrical conductors, and is used with listed fittings to provide electrical continuity. Figure 342–1

Author's Comment:

- The type of steel from which intermediate metal conduit is manufactured, the process by which it's made, and the corrosion protection applied are all equal, or superior, to that of rigid metal conduit.

Figure 342–1

342.6 Listing Requirements

Intermediate metal conduit and its associated fittings, such as elbows and couplings, must be listed.

Part II. Installation

342.10 Uses Permitted

(A) All Atmospheric Conditions and Occupancies. Intermediate metal conduit is permitted in all atmospheric conditions and occupancies.

(B) Corrosion Environments. Intermediate metal conduit, elbows, couplings, and fittings can be installed in concrete, in direct contact with the earth, or in areas subject to severe corrosive influences if provided with corrosion protection and judged suitable for the condition in accordance with 300.6.

(C) Cinder Fill. IMC can be installed in or under cinder fill subject to permanent moisture when protected on all sides by 2 in. of noncinder concrete; where the conduit isn't less than 18 in. under the fill; or where protected by corrosion protection judged suitable for the condition.

(D) Wet Locations. Support fittings, such as screws, straps, and so forth, installed in a wet location must be made of corrosion-resistant material, or be protected by corrosion-resistant coatings in accordance with 300.6.

⚠ **CAUTION:** *Supplementary coatings for corrosion protection haven't been investigated by a product testing and listing agency, and these coatings are known to cause cancer in laboratory animals. There's a documented case where an electrician was taken to the hospital for lead poisoning after using a supplemental coating product (asphalted paint) in a poorly ventilated area. As with all products, be sure to read and follow all product instructions, including material data safety sheets, particularly when petroleum-based chemicals (volatile organic compounds) may be in the material.*

342.14 Dissimilar Metals

If practical, contact with dissimilar metals should be avoided to prevent the deterioration of the metal because of galvanic action. Aluminum fittings and enclosures, however, are permitted with steel intermediate metal conduit.

342.20 Trade Size

(A) Minimum. Intermediate metal conduit smaller than trade size ½ must not be used.

(B) Maximum. Intermediate metal conduit larger than trade size 4 must not be used.

342.22 Number of Conductors

The number of conductors in IMC isn't permitted to exceed the percentage fill specified in Table 1, Chapter 9. Raceways must be large enough to permit the installation and removal of conductors without damaging the conductor insulation. When all conductors in a raceway are the same size and insulation, the number of conductors permitted can be found in Annex C for the raceway type.

Question: *How many 10 THHN conductors can be installed in trade size 1 IMC?*

(a) 12   (b) 14   (c) 16   (d) 18

Answer: *(d) 18 conductors [Annex C, Table C4]*

Author's Comment:

- See 300.17 for additional examples on how to size raceways when conductors aren't all the same size.

Cables can be installed in intermediate metal conduit, as long as the number of cables doesn't exceed the allowable percentage fill specified in Table 1, Chapter 9.

342.24 Bends

Raceway bends must not be made in any manner that'd damage the raceway, or significantly change its internal diameter (no kinks). The radius of the curve of the inner edge of any field bend must not be less than shown in Table 2, Chapter 9.

Author's Comment:

- This is usually not a problem, because benders are made to comply with this table. However, when using a hickey bender (short-radius bender), be careful not to over-bend the raceway.

342.26 Number of Bends (360°)

To reduce the stress and friction on conductor insulation, the maximum number of bends (including offsets) between pull points must not exceed 360°. Figure 342–2

IMC - Number of Bends
342.26

90°   90°

To reduce the stress and friction on conductor insulation, the total number of bends (including offsets) between pull points can't exceed 360°.

15°   15°

15°   There's no maximum   15°
distance between pull points.

Pull Points

Copyright 2014, www.MikeHolt.com

Figure 342–2

Author's Comment:

- There's no maximum distance between pull boxes because this is a design issue, not a safety issue.

342.28 Reaming

When the raceway is cut in the field, reaming is required to remove the burrs and rough edges.

Author's Comment:

- It's a commonly accepted practice to ream small raceways with a screwdriver or the backside of pliers. However, when the raceway is cut with a three-wheel pipe cutter, a reaming tool is required to remove the sharp edge of the indented raceway. When conduits are threaded in the field, the threads must be coated with an electrically conductive, corrosion-resistant compound approved by the authority having jurisdiction, in accordance with 300.6(A).

342.30 Securing and Supporting

Intermediate metal conduit must be installed as a complete system in accordance with 300.18 [300.10 and 300.12], and it must be securely fastened in place and supported in accordance with (A) and (B).

(A) Securely Fastened. IMC must be secured in accordance with one of the following:

(1) Fastened within 3 ft of each outlet box, junction box, device box, cabinet, conduit body, or other conduit termination. Figure 342–3

IMC - Securely Fastened
342.30(A)(1)

3 ft   3 ft
Termination   Termination

Intermediate metal conduit must be securely fastened within 3 ft of every box, cabinet, or termination fitting.

Copyright 2014, www.MikeHolt.com

Figure 342–3

Author's Comment:

- Fastening is required within 3 ft of terminations, not within 3 ft of each coupling.

(2) When structural members don't permit the raceway to be secured within 3 ft of a box or termination fitting, the raceway must be secured within 5 ft of the termination. Figure 342–4

Figure 342–4

(3) Conduits aren't required to be securely fastened within 3 ft of the service head for an above-the-roof termination of a mast.

(B) Supports.

(1) General. Intermediate metal conduit must generally be supported at intervals not exceeding 10 ft.

(2) Straight Horizontal Runs. Straight horizontal runs made with threaded couplings can be supported in accordance with the distances listed in Table 344.30(B)(2). Figure 342–5

Table 344.30(B)(2)	
Trade Size	Support Spacing
½ – ¾	10 ft
1	12 ft
1¼ – 1½	14 ft
2 – 2½	16 ft
3 and larger	20 ft

Figure 342–5

(3) Vertical Risers. Exposed vertical risers for fixed equipment can be supported at intervals not exceeding 20 ft, if the conduit is made up with threaded couplings, firmly supported, securely fastened at the top and bottom of the riser, and if no other means of support is available. Figure 342–6

Figure 342–6

(4) Horizontal Runs. Conduits installed horizontally in bored or punched holes in wood or metal framing members, or notches in wooden members are considered supported, but the raceway must be secured within 3 ft of termination.

Author's Comment:

■ IMC must be provided with expansion fittings if necessary to compensate for thermal expansion and contraction [300.7(B)]. The expansion characteristics for metal raceways are determined by multiplying the values from Table 352.44 by 0.20, and the expansion characteristics for aluminum raceways is determined by multiplying the values from Table 352.44 by 0.40 [300.7 Note].

342.42 Couplings and Connectors

(A) Installation. Threadless couplings and connectors must be made up tight to maintain an effective ground-fault current path to safely conduct fault current in accordance with 250.4(A)(5), 250.96(A), and 300.10.

Author's Comment:

■ Loose locknuts have been found to burn clear before a fault was cleared because loose termination fittings increase the impedance of the fault current path.

If buried in masonry or concrete, threadless fittings must be the concrete-tight type. If installed in wet locations, fittings must be listed for use in wet locations in accordance with 314.15(A).

Threadless couplings and connectors must not be used on threaded conduit ends unless listed for the purpose.

(B) Running Threads. Running threads aren't permitted for the connection of couplings, but they're permitted at other locations. Figure 342–7

342.46 Bushings

To protect conductors from abrasion, a metal or plastic bushing must be installed on conduit termination threads, regardless of conductor size, unless the box, fitting, or enclosure is designed to provide this protection.

Running threads aren't permitted for the connection of couplings, but they're permitted at other locations.

Figure 342–7

Note: Conductors 4 AWG and larger that enter an enclosure must be protected from abrasion, during and after installation, by a fitting that provides a smooth, rounded, insulating surface, such as an insulating bushing, unless the design of the box, fitting, or enclosure provides equivalent protection, in accordance with 300.4(G). **Figure 342–8**

Conductors 4 AWG and larger must be protected by a fitting that provides a smooth, rounded, insulating surface, such as an insulating bushing [300.4(G)].

Figure 342–8

Notes

ARTICLE 344

RIGID METAL CONDUIT (TYPE RMC)

Introduction to Article 344—Rigid Metal Conduit (Type RMC)

Rigid metal conduit, commonly called "rigid," has long been the standard raceway for providing protection from physical impact and from difficult environments. The outside diameter of rigid metal conduit is the same as intermediate metal conduit. However, the wall thickness of rigid metal conduit is greater than intermediate metal conduit; therefore the interior cross-sectional area is smaller. Rigid metal conduit is heavier and more expensive than intermediate metal conduit, and it can be used in any location. Rigid metal conduit is manufactured in both galvanized steel and aluminum; the steel type is much more common.

Part I. General

344.1 Scope

Article 344 covers the use, installation, and construction specifications of rigid metal conduit and associated fittings.

344.2 Definition

Rigid Metal Conduit (Type RMC). A listed metal raceway of circular cross section with integral or associated couplings, listed for the installation of electrical conductors, and used with listed fittings to provide electrical continuity. Figure 344–1

Author's Comment:

■ When the mechanical and physical characteristics of rigid metal conduit are desired and a corrosive environment is anticipated, a PVC-coated raceway system is commonly used. This type of raceway is frequently used in the petrochemical industry. The common trade name of this coated raceway is "Plasti-bond®," and it's commonly referred to as

Figure 344–1

"Rob Roy conduit." The benefits of the improved corrosion protection can be achieved only when the system is properly installed. Joints must be sealed in accordance with the manufacturer's instructions, and the coating must not be damaged with tools such as benders, pliers, and pipe wrenches. Couplings are available with an extended skirt that can be properly sealed after installation.

344.6 Listing Requirements

Rigid metal conduit, elbows, couplings, and associated fittings must be listed.

Part II. Installation

344.10 Uses Permitted

(A) Atmospheric Conditions and Occupancies.

(1) Galvanized Steel and Stainless Steel. Galvanized steel and stainless steel rigid metal conduit is permitted in all atmospheric conditions and occupancies.

(2) Red Brass. Red brass rigid metal conduit is permitted for direct burial and swimming pool applications.

(3) Aluminum. Rigid aluminum conduit is permitted if judged suitable for the environment.

(B) Corrosion Environments.

(1) Galvanized Steel and Stainless Steel. Rigid metal conduit fittings, elbows, and couplings can be installed in concrete, in direct contact with the earth, or in areas subject to severe corrosive influences judged suitable for the condition.

(2) Aluminum. Rigid aluminum conduit must be provided with supplementary corrosion protection approved by the authority having jurisdiction if encased in concrete or in direct contact with the earth.

(C) Cinder Fill. Galvanized steel, stainless steel, and red brass RMC is permitted in or under cinder fill subject to permanent moisture, when protected on all sides by a layer of noncinder concrete not less than 2 in. thick; where the conduit isn't less than 18 in. under the fill; or where protected by corrosion protection judged suitable for the condition.

(D) Wet Locations. Support fittings, such as screws, straps, and so forth, installed in a wet location must be made of corrosion-resistant material or protected by corrosion-resistant coatings in accordance with 300.6.

⚠ **CAUTION:** *Supplementary coatings (asphalted paint) for corrosion protection haven't been investigated by a product testing and listing agency, and these coatings are known to cause cancer in laboratory animals.*

344.14 Dissimilar Metals

If practical, contact with dissimilar metals should be avoided to prevent the deterioration of the metal because of galvanic action. Aluminum fittings and enclosures are permitted, however, with rigid metal conduit.

344.20 Trade Size

(A) Minimum. Rigid metal conduit smaller than trade size ½ must not be used.

(B) Maximum. Rigid metal conduit larger than trade size 6 must not be used.

344.22 Number of Conductors

Raceways must be large enough to permit the installation and removal of conductors without damaging the conductors' insulation. When all conductors in a raceway are the same size and insulation, the number of conductors permitted can be found in Annex C for the raceway type.

Question: *How many 8 THHN conductors can be installed in trade size 1½ RMC?*

(a) 16   *(b) 18*   *(c) 20*   *(d) 22*

Answer: *22 conductors [Annex C, Table C8]*

Author's Comment:

- See 300.17 for additional examples on how to size raceways when conductors aren't all the same size.

Cables can be installed in rigid metal conduit, as long as the number of cables doesn't exceed the allowable percentage fill specified in Table 1, Chapter 9.

344.24 Bends

Raceway bends must not be made in any manner that'd damage the raceway, or significantly change its internal diameter (no kinks). The radius of the curve of the inner edge of any field bend must not be less than shown in Table 2, Chapter 9.

Author's Comment:

- This is usually not a problem because benders are made to comply with this table. However, when using a hickey bender (short-radius bender), be careful not to over-bend the raceway.

344.26 Number of Bends (360°)

To reduce the stress and friction on conductor insulation, the maximum number of bends (including offsets) between pull points must not exceed 360°. Figure 344–2

Figure 344–2

Author's Comment:

- There's no maximum distance between pull boxes because this is a design issue, not a safety issue.

344.28 Reaming

When the raceway is cut in the field, reaming is required to remove the burrs and rough edges.

Author's Comment:

- It's a commonly accepted practice to ream small raceways with a screwdriver or the backside of pliers. However, when the raceway is cut with a three-wheel pipe cutter, a reaming tool is required to remove the sharp edge of the indented raceway. When conduit is threaded in the field, the threads must be coated with an electrically conductive, corrosion-resistant compound approved by the authority having jurisdiction, in accordance with 300.6(A).

344.30 Securing and Supporting

Rigid metal conduit must be installed as a complete system in accordance with 300.18 [300.10 and 300.12], and it must be securely fastened in place and supported in accordance with (A) and (B).

(A) Securely Fastened. RMC must be secured in accordance with one of the following:

(1) Fastened within 3 ft of each outlet box, junction box, device box, cabinet, conduit body, or other conduit termination. Figure 344–3

Figure 344–3

Author's Comment:

- Fastening is required within 3 ft of terminations, not within 3 ft of each coupling.

(2) When structural members don't permit the raceway to be secured within 3 ft of a box or termination fitting, the raceway must be secured within 5 ft of the termination. Figure 344–4

Figure 344–4

(3) Conduits aren't required to be securely fastened within 3 ft of the service head for an above-the-roof termination of a mast. Figure 344–5

Figure 344–5

(B) Supports.

(1) General. Rigid metal conduit must be supported at intervals not exceeding 10 ft.

(2) Straight Horizontal Runs. Straight horizontal runs made with threaded couplings can be supported in accordance with the distances listed in Table 344.30(B)(2). Figure 344–6

Figure 344–6

Table 344.30(B)(2)	
Trade Size	Support Spacing
½–¾	10 ft
1	12 ft*
1¼–1½	14 ft
2–2½	16 ft
3 and larger	20 ft

(3) Vertical Risers. Exposed vertical risers for fixed equipment can be supported at intervals not exceeding 20 ft, if the conduit is made up with threaded couplings, firmly supported, securely fastened at the top and bottom of the riser, and if no other means of support is available. Figure 344–7

(4) Horizontal Runs. Conduits installed horizontally in bored or punched holes in wood or metal framing members, or notches in wooden members, are considered supported, but the raceway must be secured within 3 ft of termination.

Figure 344–7

Author's Comment:

- Rigid metal conduit must be provided with expansion fittings if necessary to compensate for thermal expansion and contraction [300.7(B)]. The expansion characteristics for metal raceways are determined by multiplying the values from Table 352.44 by 0.20, and the expansion characteristics for aluminum raceways is determined by multiplying the values from Table 352.44 by 0.40 [300.7 Note].

344.42 Couplings and Connectors

(A) Installation. Threadless couplings and connectors must be made up tight to maintain an effective ground-fault current path to safely conduct fault current in accordance with 250.4(A)(5), 250.96(A), and 300.10.

Author's Comment:

- Loose locknuts have been found to burn clear before a fault was cleared because loose connections increase the impedance of the fault current path.

If buried in masonry or concrete, threadless fittings must be the concrete-tight type. If installed in wet locations, fittings must be listed for use in wet locations, in accordance with 314.15(A).

Threadless couplings and connectors must not be used on threaded conduit ends, unless listed for the purpose.

(B) Running Threads. Running threads aren't permitted for the connection of couplings, but they're permitted at other locations. Figure 344–8

Figure 344–8

344.46 Bushings

To protect conductors from abrasion, a metal or plastic bushing must be installed on conduit threads at terminations, regardless of conductor size, unless the box, fitting, or enclosure is designed to provide this protection.

Note: Conductors 4 AWG and larger that enter an enclosure must be protected from abrasion, during and after installation, by a fitting that provides a smooth, rounded, insulating surface, such as an insulating bushing, unless the design of the box, fitting, or enclosure provides equivalent protection, in accordance with 300.4(G). Figure 344–9

RMC - Bushings
344.46 Note

Threaded Termination	Fitting Termination		Hub or Boss Termination
Any Size Conductor	4 AWG and Larger	6 AWG and Smaller	Any Size Conductor
Bushing Required	Bushing Required	Bushing Not Required	Bushing Not Required

Copyright 2014
www.MikeHolt.com

Conductors 4 AWG and larger must be protected by a fitting that provides a smooth, rounded, insulating surface, such as an insulating bushing [300.4(G)].

Figure 344–9

Part III. Construction Specifications

344.100 Construction

RMC is constructed as one of the following:

(1) Steel (with or without protective coatings)

(2) Aluminum

(3) Red brass

(4) Stainless steel.

344.130 Standard Lengths

The standard length of RMC is 10 ft including an attached coupling, and each end must be threaded. Longer or shorter lengths with or without a coupling and threaded or unthreaded are permitted.

ARTICLE 348
FLEXIBLE METAL CONDUIT (TYPE FMC)

Introduction to Article 348—Flexible Metal Conduit (Type FMC)

Flexible metal conduit (FMC), commonly called "Greenfield" or "flex," is a raceway of an interlocked metal strip of either steel or aluminum. It's primarily used for the final 6 ft or less of raceways between a more rigid raceway system and equipment that moves, shakes, or vibrates. Examples of such equipment include pump motors and industrial machinery.

Part I. General

348.1 Scope

Article 348 covers the use, installation, and construction specifications for flexible metal conduit and associated fittings.

348.2 Definition

Flexible Metal Conduit (Type FMC). A raceway of circular cross section made of a helically wound, formed, interlocked metal strip. Figure 348–1

348.6 Listing Requirements

Flexible metal conduit and associated fittings must be listed.

Part II. Installation

348.10 Uses Permitted

Flexible metal conduit is permitted exposed or concealed.

Figure 348–1

348.12 Uses Not Permitted

(1) In wet locations.

(2) In hoistways, other than as permitted in 620.21(A)(1).

(3) In storage battery rooms.

(4) In any hazardous location, except as permitted by 501.10(B).

(5) Exposed to material having a deteriorating effect on the installed conductors.

(6) Underground or embedded in poured concrete.

(7) If subject to physical damage.

348.20 Trade Size

(A) Minimum. Flexible metal conduit smaller than trade size ½ must not be used, except trade size ⅜ can be used for the following applications:

(1) For enclosing the leads of motors.

(2) Not exceeding 6 ft in length: Figure 348–2

    a. For utilization equipment,

    b. As part of a listed assembly, or

    c. For luminaire tap connections, in accordance with 410.117(C).

FMC - Size
348.20(A)(2)

Trade size 3/8 can be used in lengths not exceeding 6 ft for utilization equipment or tap connections to luminaires.

Copyright 2014, www.MikeHolt.com

Figure 348–2

(3) In manufactured wiring systems, 604.6(A).

(4) In hoistways, 620.21(A)(1).

(5) As part of a listed luminaire assembly in accordance with 410.137(C).

(B) Maximum. Flexible metal conduit larger than trade size 4 must not be used.

348.22 Number of Conductors

Trade Size ½ and Larger. Flexible metal conduit must be large enough to permit the installation and removal of conductors without damaging the conductors' insulation. When all conductors in a raceway are the same size and insulation, the number of conductors permitted can be found in Annex C for the raceway type.

> *Question:* How many 6 THHN conductors can be installed in trade size 1 flexible metal conduit?
>
> (a) 2   (b) 4   (c) 6   (d) 8
>
> *Answer:* (c) 6 conductors [Annex C, Table C3]

Author's Comment:

- See 300.17 for additional examples on how to size raceways when conductors aren't all the same size.

Trade Size ⅜. The number and size of conductors in trade size ⅜ flexible metal conduit must comply with Table 348.22.

> *Question:* How many 12 THHN conductors can be installed in trade size ⅜ flexible metal conduit that uses outside fittings?
>
> (a) 1   (b) 3   (c) 5   (d) 7
>
> *Answer:* (b) 3 conductors [Table 348.22]

One insulated, covered, or bare equipment grounding conductor of the same size is permitted with the circuit conductors. See the "*" note at the bottom of Table 348.22.

Cables can be installed in flexible metal conduit as long as the number of cables doesn't exceed the allowable percentage fill specified in Table 1, Chapter 9.

348.24 Bends

Bends must be made so that the conduit won't be damaged, and its internal diameter won't be effectively reduced. The radius of the curve of the inner edge of any field bend must not be less than shown in Table 2, Chapter 9 using the column "Other Bends."

348.26 Number of Bends (360°)

To reduce the stress and friction on conductor insulation, the maximum number of bends (including offsets) between pull points must not exceed 360°.

Author's Comment:

- There's no maximum distance between pull boxes because this is a design issue, not a safety issue.

348.28 Trimming

The cut ends of flexible metal conduit must be trimmed to remove the rough edges, but this isn't necessary if fittings are threaded into the convolutions.

348.30 Securing and Supporting

(A) Securely Fastened. Flexible metal conduit must be securely fastened by a means approved by the authority having jurisdiction within 1 ft of termination, and it must be secured and supported at intervals not exceeding 4½ ft. Figure 348–3

Figure 348–3

Ex 1: Flexible metal conduit isn't required to be securely fastened or supported where fished between access points through concealed spaces and supporting is impracticable.

Ex 2: If flexibility is necessary after installation, unsecured lengths from the last point the raceway is securely fastened must not exceed: Figure 348–4

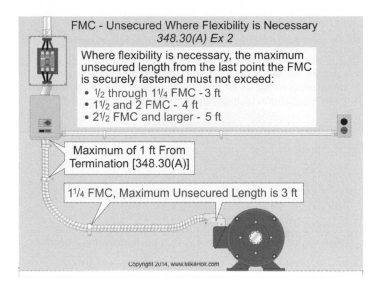

Figure 348–4

(1) 3 ft for trade sizes ½ through 1¼

(2) 4 ft for trade sizes 1½ through 2

(3) 5 ft for trade sizes 2½ and larger

Ex 4: FMC to a luminaire or electrical equipment within an accessible ceiling is permitted to be unsupported for not more than 6 ft from the last point where the raceway is securely fastened. For the purposes of this exception listed fittings are considered support. Figure 348–5

(B) Horizontal Runs. Flexible metal conduit installed horizontally in bored or punched holes in wood or metal framing members, or notches in wooden members, is considered supported, but the raceway must be secured within 1 ft of terminations. Figure 348–6

348.42 Fittings

Angle connectors must not be concealed.

Figure 348–5

Figure 348–6

348.60 Grounding and Bonding

If flexibility is necessary to minimize the transmission of vibration from equipment or to provide flexibility for equipment that requires movement after installation, an equipment grounding conductor of the wire type must be installed with the circuit conductors in accordance with 250.118(5), sized in accordance with 250.122, based on the rating of the overcurrent device. Figure 348–7

Figure 348–7

If flexibility isn't necessary after installation, and vibration isn't a concern, the metal armor of flexible metal conduit can serve as an equipment grounding conductor if the circuit conductors contained in the raceway are protected by an overcurrent device rated 20A or less, and the combined length of the flexible metal raceway in the same ground-fault return path doesn't exceed 6 ft [250.118(5)]. Figure 348–8

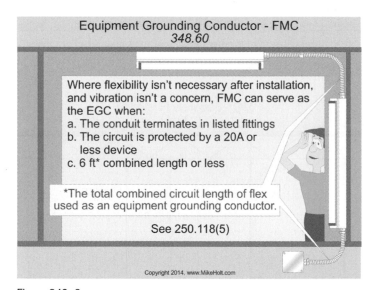

Figure 348–8

If an equipment bonding jumper is installed outside of a raceway, the length of the equipment bonding jumper must not exceed 6 ft, and it must be routed with the raceway or enclosure in accordance with 250.102(E)(2).

ARTICLE 350
LIQUIDTIGHT FLEXIBLE METAL CONDUIT (TYPE LFMC)

Introduction to Article 350—Liquidtight Flexible Metal Conduit (Type LFMC)

Liquidtight flexible metal conduit (LFMC), with its associated connectors and fittings, is a flexible raceway commonly used for connections to equipment that vibrates or is required to move occasionally. Liquidtight flexible metal conduit is commonly called "Sealtight®" or "liquidtight." Liquidtight flexible metal conduit is of similar construction to flexible metal conduit, but it also has an outer liquidtight thermoplastic covering. It has the same primary purpose as flexible metal conduit, but it also provides protection from moisture and some corrosive effects.

Part I. General

350.1 Scope

Article 350 covers the use, installation, and construction specifications of liquidtight flexible metal conduit and associated fittings.

350.2 Definition

Liquidtight Flexible Metal Conduit (Type LFMC). A raceway of circular cross section, having an outer liquidtight, nonmetallic, sunlight-resistant jacket over an inner flexible metal core, with associated connectors and fittings for the installation of electric conductors. Figure 350–1

Liquidtight Flexible Metal Conduit (Type LFMC)
350.2 Definition

A circular raceway having an outer liquidtight, nonmetallic, sunlight-resistant jacket over an inner flexible metal core.

Copyright 2014, www.MikeHolt.com

Figure 350–1

Part II. Installation

350.10 Uses Permitted

(A) Permitted Use. Listed liquidtight flexible metal conduit is permitted, either exposed or concealed, at any of the following locations:

(1) If flexibility or protection from liquids, vapors, or solids is required.

350.6 Listing Requirements

Liquidtight flexible metal conduit and its associated fittings must be listed.

(2) In hazardous locations, as permitted in 501.10(B), 502.10(A)(2), 502.10(B)(2), or 503.10(A)(2).

(3) For direct burial, if listed and marked for this purpose. Figure 350–2

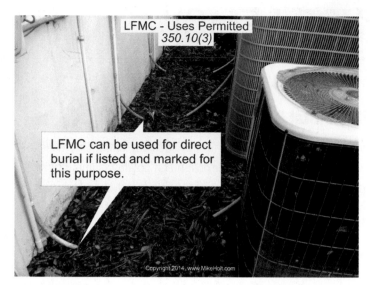

Figure 350–2

350.12 Uses Not Permitted

(1) If subject to physical damage.

(2) If the combination of the ambient and conductor operating temperatures exceeds the rating of the raceway.

350.20 Trade Size

(A) Minimum. Liquidtight flexible metal conduit smaller than trade size ½ must not be used.

Ex: Liquidtight flexible metal conduit can be smaller than trade size ½ if installed in accordance with 348.20(A).

Author's Comment:

■ According to 348.20(A), LFMC smaller than trade size ½ is permitted for the following:

(1) For enclosing the leads of motors.

(2) Not exceeding 6 ft in length:

  a. For utilization equipment,

  b. As part of a listed assembly, or

  c. For tap connections to luminaires as permitted by 410.117(C).

(3) In manufactured wiring systems, 604.6(A).

(4) In hoistways, 620.21(A)(1).

(5) As part of a listed assembly to connect wired luminaire sections, 410.137(C).

(B) Maximum. Liquidtight flexible metal conduit larger than trade size 4 must not be used.

350.22 Number of Conductors

(A) Raceway Trade Size ½ and Larger. Raceways must be large enough to permit the installation and removal of conductors without damaging the insulation. When all conductors in a raceway are the same size and insulation, the number of conductors permitted can be found in Annex C for the raceway type.

> **Question:** *How many 6 THHN conductors can be installed in trade size 1 LFMC?* Figure 350–3
>
> (a) 3   (b) 5   (c) 7   (d) 9
>
> **Answer:** *(c) 7 conductors [Annex C, Table C.7]*

Author's Comment:

■ See 300.17 for additional examples on how to size raceways when conductors aren't all the same size.

Cables can be installed in liquidtight flexible metal conduit as long as the number of cables doesn't exceed the allowable percentage fill specified in Table 1, Chapter 9.

(B) Raceway Trade Size ⅜. The number and size of conductors in a trade size ⅜ liquidtight flexible metal conduit must comply with Table 348.22.

A maximum of seven 6 THHN conductors can be installed in 1 LFMC [Table C.7].

When all conductors in a raceway are the same size and insulation, the number of conductors permitted can be found in Annex C.

Figure 350–3

Question: How many 12 THHN conductors can be installed in trade size ⅜ LFMC that uses outside fittings?

(a) 1   (b) 3   (c) 5   (d) 7

Answer: (b) 3 conductors [Table 348.22]

One insulated, covered, or bare equipment grounding conductor of the same size is permitted with the circuit conductors. See the "*" note at the bottom of Table 348.22.

350.24 Bends

Bends must be made so that the conduit won't be damaged and the internal diameter of the conduit won't be effectively reduced. The radius of the curve of the inner edge of any field bend must not be less than shown in Table 2, Chapter 9 using the column "Other Bends."

350.26 Number of Bends (360°)

To reduce the stress and friction on conductor insulation, the maximum number of bends (including offsets) between pull points must not exceed 360°.

Author's Comment:

- There's no maximum distance between pull boxes because this is a design issue, not a safety issue.

350.30 Securing and Supporting

Liquidtight flexible metal conduit must be securely fastened in place and supported in accordance with (A) and (B).

(A) Securely Fastened. Liquidtight flexible metal conduit must be securely fastened by a means approved by the authority having jurisdiction within 1 ft of termination, and must be secured and supported at intervals not exceeding 4½ ft. Figure 350–4

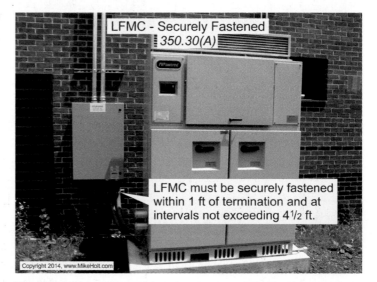

Figure 350–4

Ex 1: Liquidtight flexible metal conduit isn't required to be securely fastened or supported where fished between access points through concealed spaces and supporting is impracticable.

Ex 2: If flexibility is necessary after installation, unsecured lengths from the last point where the raceway is securely fastened must not exceed: Figure 350–5

  (1) 3 ft for trade sizes ½ through 1¼

  (2) 4 ft for trade sizes 1½ through 2

  (3) 5 ft for trade sizes 2½ and larger

Figure 350–5

Figure 350–6

Ex 4: Lengths not exceeding 6 ft from the last point where the raceway is securely fastened can be unsecured within an accessible ceiling for luminaire(s) or other equipment. For the purposes of this exception, listed fittings are considered support.

(B) Horizontal Runs. Liquidtight flexible metal conduit installed horizontally in bored or punched holes in wood or metal framing members, or notches in wooden members, is considered supported, but the raceway must be secured within 1 ft of termination.

350.42 Fittings

Fittings used with LFMC must be listed. Angle connectors must not be concealed. Straight fittings can be buried where marked as suitable for direct burial. Figure 350–6

350.60 Grounding and Bonding

If flexibility is necessary to minimize the transmission of vibration from equipment or to provide flexibility for equipment that requires movement after installation, an equipment grounding conductor of the wire type must be installed with the circuit conductors in accordance with 250.118(6), sized in accordance with 250.122, based on the rating of the overcurrent device. Figure 350–7

Figure 350–7

If flexibility isn't necessary after installation, and vibration isn't a concern, the metal armor of flexible metal conduit can serve as an equipment grounding conductor if the circuit conductors contained in the raceway are protected by an overcurrent device rated 20A or less, and the combined length of the flexible metal raceway in the same ground-fault return path doesn't exceed 6 ft [250.118(6)].

If an equipment bonding jumper is installed outside of a raceway, the length of the equipment bonding jumper must not exceed 6 ft, and it must be routed with the raceway or enclosure in accordance with 250.102(E)(2).

RIGID POLYVINYL CHLORIDE CONDUIT (TYPE PVC)

Introduction to Article 352—Rigid Polyvinyl Chloride Conduit (Type PVC)

Rigid polyvinyl chloride conduit (PVC) is a rigid nonmetallic conduit that provides many of the advantages of rigid metal conduit, while allowing installation in areas that are wet or corrosive. It's an inexpensive raceway, and easily installed. It's lightweight, easily cut and glued together, and relatively strong. However, conduits manufactured from polyvinyl chloride (PVC) are brittle when cold, and they sag when hot. This type of conduit is commonly used as an underground raceway because of its low cost, ease of installation, and resistance to corrosion and decay.

Part I. General

352.1 Scope

Article 352 covers the use, installation, and construction specifications of PVC conduit and associated fittings.

352.2 Definition

Rigid Polyvinyl Chloride Conduit (PVC). A rigid nonmetallic <u>raceway</u> of circular cross section with integral or associated couplings, listed for the installation of electrical conductors and cables. Figure 352–1

Part II. Installation

352.10 Uses Permitted

Note: In extreme cold, PVC conduit can become brittle, and is more susceptible to physical damage.

Figure 352–1

(A) Concealed. PVC conduit can be concealed within walls, floors, or ceilings, directly buried or embedded in concrete in buildings of any height. Figure 352–2

(B) Corrosive Influences. PVC conduit is permitted in areas subject to severe corrosion for which the material is specifically approved by the authority having jurisdiction.

Figure 352–2

Figure 352–3

Author's Comment:

■ If subject to exposure to chemical solvents, vapors, splashing, or immersion, materials or coatings must either be inherently resistant to chemicals based upon their listing, or be identified for the specific chemical reagent [300.6(C)(2)].

(D) Wet Locations. PVC conduit is permitted in wet locations such as dairies, laundries, canneries, car washes, and other areas frequently washed or in outdoor locations. Support fittings such as straps, screws, and bolts must be made of corrosion-resistant materials, or must be protected with a corrosion-resistant coating, in accordance with 300.6(A).

(E) Dry and Damp Locations. PVC conduit is permitted in dry and damp locations, except where limited in 352.12.

(F) Exposed. Schedule 40 PVC conduit is permitted for exposed locations where not subject to physical damage. If PVC conduit is exposed to physical damage, the raceway must be identified for the application. Figure 352–3

> **Note:** PVC Schedule 80 conduit is identified for use in areas subject to physical damage. Figure 352–4

(G) Underground. PVC conduit installed underground must comply with the burial requirements of 300.5.

(H) Support of Conduit Bodies. PVC conduit is permitted to support nonmetallic conduit bodies that aren't larger than the largest trade size of an entering raceway. These conduit bodies can't support luminaires or other equipment, and aren't permitted to contain devices, other than splicing devices permitted by 110.14(B) and 314.16(C)(2).

Figure 352–4

(I) Insulation Temperature Limitations. Conductors rated at a temperature higher than the listed temperature rating of PVC conduit must not be operated at a temperature above the raceway's listed temperature rating. Figure 352–5

352.12 Uses Not Permitted

(A) Hazardous Locations. PVC conduit isn't permitted to be used in hazardous locations except as permitted by 501.10(A)(1)(a) Ex, 503.10(A), 504.20, 514.8 Ex 2, and 515.8.

Figure 352–5

(2) In Class I, Division 2 locations, except as permitted in 501.10(B)(7).

(B) Support of Luminaires. PVC conduit must not be used for the support of luminaires or other equipment not described in 352.10(H).

Author's Comment:

■ PVC conduit is permitted to support conduit bodies in accordance with 314.23(E) Ex.

(C) Physical Damage. Schedule 40 PVC conduit must not be installed if subject to physical damage, unless identified for the application. Figure 352–6

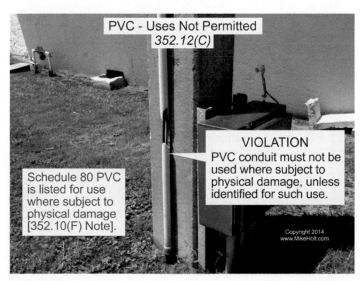

Figure 352–6

Author's Comment:

■ PVC Schedule 80 conduit is identified for use in areas subject to physical damage [352.10(F) Note].

(D) Ambient Temperature. PVC conduit must not be installed if the ambient temperature exceeds 50°C (122°F).

352.20 Trade Size

(A) Minimum. PVC conduit smaller than trade size ½ must not be used.

(B) Maximum. PVC conduit larger than trade size 6 must not be used.

352.22 Number of Conductors

Raceways must be large enough to permit the installation and removal of conductors without damaging the conductors' insulation, and the number of conductors must not exceed that permitted by the percentage fill specified in Table 1, Chapter 9.

When all conductors in a raceway are the same size and insulation, the number of conductors permitted can be found in Annex C for the raceway type.

> **Question:** How many 4/0 THHN conductors can be installed in trade size 2 Schedule 40 PVC?
>
> (a) 2   (b) 4   (c) 6   (d) 8
>
> **Answer:** (b) 4 conductors [Annex C, Table C10]

Author's Comment:

■ Schedule 80 PVC conduit has the same outside diameter as Schedule 40 PVC conduit, but the wall thickness of Schedule 80 PVC conduit is greater, which results in a reduced interior area for conductor fill.

Question: How many 4/0 THHN conductors can be installed in trade size 2 Schedule 80 PVC conduit?

(a) 3   (b) 5   (c) 7   (d) 9

Answer: (a) 3 conductors [Annex C, Table C9]

Author's Comment:

- See 300.17 for additional examples on how to size raceways when conductors aren't all the same size.

Cables can be installed in PVC conduit, as long as the number of cables doesn't exceed the allowable percentage fill specified in Table 1, Chapter 9.

Figure 352–7

352.24 Bends

Raceway bends must not be made in any manner that'd damage the raceway, or significantly change its internal diameter (no kinks). The radius of the curve of the inner edge of any field bend must not be less than shown in Table 2, Chapter 9.

Author's Comment:

- Be sure to use equipment designed for heating the nonmetallic raceway so it's pliable for bending (for example, a "hot box"). Don't use open-flame torches.

352.26 Number of Bends (360°)

To reduce the stress and friction on conductor insulation, the maximum number of bends (including offsets) between pull points must not exceed 360°. Figure 352–7

352.28 Trimming

The cut ends of PVC conduit must be trimmed (inside and out) to remove the burrs and rough edges.

Author's Comment:

- Trimming PVC conduit is very easy; most of the burrs will rub off with fingers, and a knife will smooth the rough edges.

352.30 Securing and Supporting

PVC conduit must be securely fastened and supported in accordance with (A) and (B). Figure 352–8

Figure 352–8

(A) Secured. PVC conduit must be secured within 3 ft of every box, cabinet, or termination fitting, such as a conduit body.

(B) Supports. PVC conduit must be supported at intervals not exceeding the values in Table 352.30, and the raceway must be fastened in a manner that permits movement from thermal expansion or contraction.

Table 352.30

Trade Size	Support Spacing
½–1	3 ft
1¼–2	5 ft
2½–3	6 ft
3½–5	7 ft
6	8 ft

PVC conduit installed horizontally in bored or punched holes in wood or metal framing members, or notches in wooden members, is considered supported, but the raceway must be secured within 3 ft of termination.

352.44 Expansion Fittings

If PVC conduit is installed in a straight run between securely mounted items, such as boxes, cabinets, elbows, or other conduit terminations, expansion fittings must be provided to compensate for thermal expansion and contraction of the raceway in accordance with Table 352.44, if the length change is determined to be ¼ in. or greater. Figure 352–9

Figure 352–9

Author's Comment:

■ Table 352.44 in the *NEC* was created based on the following formula: Figure 352–10

Expansion/Contraction Inches = Raceway Length/100 x [(Temp Change/100) x 4.00]

Expn-Cont In. = (Length/100) x (Temp Change/100 x 4.0)

Figure 352–10

Expansion Calculation Example

Example: *How much contraction will a 25-foot run of PVC conduit experience if it's located on the roof, where the ambient temperature range is between 10°F and 150°F?*

(a) 0.50 in.   (b) 0.60 in.   (c) 0.70 in.   (d) 1.40 in.

Answer: *(d) 1.40 in.*

Expansion/Contraction Inches = Raceway Length/100 x ((Temp °F Change/100) x 4.00)

Expansion/Contraction Inches = (25/100) x ((140°F/100) x 4.00)

Expansion/Contraction Inches = 1.40 in.

352.46 Bushings

Where a conduit enters a box, fitting, or other enclosure, the wire must be protected from abrasion.

Note: Conductors 4 AWG and larger that enter an enclosure must be protected from abrasion, during and after installation, by a fitting that provides a smooth, rounded insulating surface, such as an insulating bushing, unless the design of the box, fitting, or enclosure provides equivalent protection, in accordance with 300.4(G). **Figure 352–11**

Conductors 4 AWG and larger require a fitting that provides a smooth, rounded, insulating surface to protect the wire during and after installation. See 300.4(G).

Figure 352–11

Author's Comment:

- When PVC conduit is stubbed into an open-bottom switchboard, the raceway, including the end fitting (bell-end), must not rise more than 3 in. above the bottom of the switchboard enclosure [300.16(B) and 408.5].

352.48 Joints

Joints, such as couplings and connectors, must be made in a manner approved by the authority having jurisdiction.

Author's Comment:

- Follow the manufacturer's instructions for the raceway, fittings, and glue. Some glue requires the raceway surface to be cleaned with a solvent before the application of the glue. After applying glue to both surfaces, a quarter turn of the fitting is required.

352.60 Equipment Grounding Conductor

If equipment grounding is required, a separate equipment grounding conductor of the wire type must be installed within the conduit [300.2(B)]. **Figure 352–12**

Figure 352–12

Ex 2: An equipment grounding conductor isn't required in PVC conduit if the neutral conductor is used to ground service equipment, as permitted in 250.142(A) [250.24(C)]. Figure 352–13

A supply-side bonding jumper isn't required in PVC if the service neutral conductor is connected to the service equipment via the main bonding jumper.

Figure 352–13

ARTICLE 356

LIQUIDTIGHT FLEXIBLE NONMETALLIC CONDUIT (TYPE LFNC)

Introduction to Article 356—Liquidtight Flexible Nonmetallic Conduit (Type LFNC)

Liquidtight flexible nonmetallic conduit (LFNC) is a listed raceway of circular cross section having an outer liquidtight, nonmetallic, sunlight-resistant jacket over an inner flexible core with associated couplings, connectors, and fittings.

Part I. General

356.1 Scope

Article 356 covers the use, installation, and construction specifications of liquidtight flexible nonmetallic conduit and associated fittings.

356.2 Definition

Liquidtight Flexible Nonmetallic Conduit (Type LFNC). A listed raceway of circular cross section, having an outer liquidtight, nonmetallic, sunlight-resistant jacket over a flexible inner core, with associated couplings, connectors, and fittings, listed for the installation of electrical conductors. Figure 356–1

(1) Type LFNC-A (orange color). A smooth seamless inner core and cover having reinforcement layers between the core and cover.

(2) Type LFNC-B (gray color). A smooth inner surface with integral reinforcement within the raceway wall.

(3) Type LFNC-C (black color). A corrugated internal and external surface without integral reinforcement.

Liquidtight Flexible Nonmetallic Conduit (Type LFNC)
356.2 Definition

Listed Liquidtight

Listed LFNC Fittings

A circular raceway having an outer liquidtight, sunlight-resistant jacket over a flexible inner core.

Copyright 2014, www.MikeHolt.com

Figure 356–1

356.6 Listing Requirement

Liquidtight flexible nonmetallic conduit, and its associated fittings, must be listed.

Part II. Installation

356.10 Uses Permitted

Listed liquidtight flexible nonmetallic conduit is permitted, either exposed or concealed, at any of the following locations:

(1) If flexibility is required.

(2) If protection from liquids, vapors, or solids is required.

(3) Outdoors, if listed and marked for this purpose.

(4) Directly buried in the earth, if listed and marked for this purpose.

(5) LFNC-B (gray color) is permitted in lengths over 6 ft if secured according to 356.30.

(6) LFNC-B (black color) as a listed manufactured prewired assembly.

(7) Encasement in concrete if listed for direct burial.

356.12 Uses Not Permitted

(1) If subject to physical damage.

(2) If the combination of ambient and conductor temperature will produce an operating temperature above the rating of the raceway.

(3) Longer than 6 ft, except if approved by the authority having jurisdiction as essential for a required degree of flexibility.

(4) In any hazardous location, except as permitted by 501.10(B), 502.10(A) and (B), and 504.20.

356.20 Trade Size

(A) Minimum. Liquidtight flexible nonmetallic conduit smaller than trade size ½ isn't permitted, except as permitted in the following:

(1) Enclosing the leads of motors, 430.245(B).

(2) For tap connections to lighting fixtures as permitted by 410.117(C).

(B) Maximum. Liquidtight flexible nonmetallic conduit larger than trade size 4 isn't permitted.

356.22 Number of Conductors

Raceways must be large enough to permit the installation and removal of conductors without damaging the insulation. When all conductors in a raceway are the same size and insulation, the number of conductors permitted can be found in Annex C for the raceway type.

> **Question:** How many 8 THHN conductors can be installed in trade size ¾ LFNC-B? Figure 356–2
>
> **Answer:** Six conductors [Annex C, Table C5]

LFNC - Number of Conductors
356.22

A maximum of six 8 THHN conductors can be installed in ¾ LFNC-B [Table C.5].

When all conductors in a raceway are the same size and insulation, the number of conductors permitted can be found in Annex C.

Figure 356–2

Author's Comment:

■ See 300.17 for additional examples on how to size raceways when conductors aren't all the same size.

Cables can be installed in liquidtight flexible nonmetallic conduit, as long as the number of cables doesn't exceed the allowable percentage fill specified in Table 1, Chapter 9.

356.24 Bends

Raceway bends must not be made in any manner that'd damage the raceway or significantly change its internal diameter (no kinks). The radius of the curve of the inner edge of any field bend must not be less than shown in Table 2, Chapter 9 using the column "Other Bends."

356.26 Number of Bends (360°)

To reduce the stress and friction on conductor insulation, the maximum number of bends (including offsets) between pull points must not exceed 360°.

Author's Comment:

■ There's no maximum distance between pull boxes because this is a design issue, not a safety issue.

356.30 Securing and Supporting

LFNC-B (gray color) must be securely fastened and supported in accordance with one of the following:

(1) The conduit must be securely fastened at intervals not exceeding 3 ft, and within 1 ft of termination when installed in lengths longer than 6 ft. Figure 356–3

Figure 356–3

(2) Securing or supporting isn't required if it's fished, installed in lengths not exceeding 3 ft at terminals if flexibility is required, or installed in lengths not exceeding 6 ft for tap conductors to luminaires, as permitted in 410.117(C).

(3) Horizontal runs of liquidtight flexible nonmetallic conduit installed horizontally in bored or punched holes in wood or metal framing members, or notches in wooden members, are considered supported, but the raceway must be secured within 1 ft of termination.

(4) Securing or supporting of LFNC-B (gray color) isn't required if installed in lengths not exceeding 6 ft from the last point where the raceway is securely fastened for connections within an accessible ceiling to luminaire(s) or other equipment. For the purposes of this allowance, listed fittings are considered support. Figure 356–4

Figure 356–4

356.42 Fittings

Only fittings listed for use with liquidtight flexible nonmetallic conduit can be used [300.15]. Angle connector fittings must not be used in concealed raceway installations. Straight liquidtight flexible nonmetallic conduit fittings are permitted for direct burial or encasement in concrete.

Author's Comment:

- Conductors 4 AWG and larger that enter an enclosure must be protected from abrasion, during and after installation, by a fitting that provides a smooth, rounded, insulating surface, such as an insulating bushing, unless the design of the box, fitting, or enclosure provides equivalent protection, in accordance with 300.4(G).

356.60 Equipment Grounding Conductor

If equipment grounding is required, a separate equipment grounding conductor of the wire type must be installed within the conduit [250.134(B)]. Figure 356–5

If an equipment bonding jumper is installed outside of a raceway, the length of the equipment bonding jumper must not exceed 6 ft, and it must be routed with the raceway or enclosure in accordance with 250.102(E)(2).

Figure 356–5

ARTICLE 358

ELECTRICAL METALLIC TUBING (TYPE EMT)

Introduction to Article 358—Electrical Metallic Tubing (Type EMT)

Electrical metallic tubing (EMT) is a lightweight raceway that's relatively easy to bend, cut, and ream. Because it isn't threaded, all connectors and couplings are of the threadless type and provide quick, easy, and inexpensive installation when compared to other metallic conduit systems, which makes it very popular. Electrical metallic tubing is manufactured in both galvanized steel and aluminum; the steel type is used the most.

Part I. General

358.1 Scope

Article 358 covers the use, installation, and construction specifications of electrical metallic tubing.

358.2 Definition

Electrical Metallic Tubing (Type EMT). A metallic tubing of circular cross section used for the installation and physical protection of electrical conductors when joined together with fittings. Figure 358–1

358.6 Listing Requirement

Electrical metallic tubing, elbows, and associated fittings must be listed.

Figure 358–1

Part II. Installation

358.10 Uses Permitted

(A) Exposed and Concealed. Electrical metallic tubing is permitted exposed or concealed.

(B) Corrosion Protection. Electrical metallic tubing, elbows, couplings, and fittings can be installed in concrete, in direct contact with the earth, or in areas subject to severe corrosive influences if protected by corrosion protection and approved as suitable for the condition [300.6(A)].

Author's Comment:

- Galvanized electrical metallic tubing can be installed in concrete at grade level and in direct contact with the earth, but supplementary corrosion protection is usually required (UL White Book, *Guide Information for Electrical Equipment*). Electrical metallic tubing can be installed in concrete above the ground floor slab generally without supplementary corrosion protection. Figure 358–2

Figure 358–2

(C) Wet Locations. Support fittings, such as screws, straps, and so on, installed in a wet location must be made of corrosion-resistant material, or a corrosion-resistant coating must protect them in accordance with 300.6.

Author's Comment:

- Fittings used in wet locations must be listed for the application (wet location) [314.15]. For more information, visit www.etpfittings.com.

358.12 Uses Not Permitted

EMT must not be used under the following conditions:

(1) Where, during installation or afterward, it'll be subject to severe physical damage.

(2) If protected from corrosion solely by enamel.

(3) In cinder concrete or cinder fill where subject to permanent moisture, unless encased in not less than 2 in. of concrete.

(4) In any hazardous location, except as permitted by 502.10, 503.10, and 504.20.

(5) For the support of luminaires or other equipment (like boxes), except conduit bodies no larger than the largest trade size of the tubing that can be supported by the raceway. Figure 358–3

Figure 358–3

(6) If practical, contact with dissimilar metals must be avoided to prevent the deterioration of the metal because of galvanic action.

Ex: Aluminum fittings are permitted on steel electrical metallic tubing, and steel fittings are permitted on aluminum EMT.

358.20 Trade Size

(A) Minimum. Electrical metallic tubing smaller than trade size ½ isn't permitted.

(B) Maximum. Electrical metallic tubing larger than trade size 4 isn't permitted.

358.22 Number of Conductors

Raceways must be large enough to permit the installation and removal of conductors without damaging the conductor insulation. When all conductors in a raceway are the same size and insulation, the number of conductors permitted can be found in Annex C for the raceway type.

Question: *How many 12 THHN conductors can be installed in trade size 1 EMT?* Figure 358–4

(a) 26   *(b) 28*   *(c) 30*   *(d) 32*

Answer: *(a) 26 conductors [Annex C, Table C.1]*

EMT - Number of Conductors
358.22

A maximum of twenty-six 12 THHN conductors can be installed in 1 EMT [Table C.1].

When all conductors in a raceway are the same size and insulation, the number of conductors permitted can be found in Annex C.

Figure 358–4

Author's Comment:

- See 300.17 for additional examples on how to size raceways when conductors aren't all the same size.

Cables can be installed in electrical metallic tubing, as long as the number of cables doesn't exceed the allowable percentage fill specified in Table 1, Chapter 9.

358.24 Bends

Raceway bends must not be made in any manner that'd damage the raceway, or significantly change its internal diameter (no kinks). The radius of the curve of the inner edge of any field bend must not be less than shown in Chapter 9, Table 2 for one-shot and full shoe benders.

Author's Comment:

- This typically isn't a problem, because most benders are made to comply with this table.

358.26 Number of Bends (360°)

To reduce the stress and friction on conductor insulation, the maximum number of bends (including offsets) between pull points can't exceed 360°. Figure 358–5

EMT - Number of Bends
358.26

90°   90°

To reduce the stress and friction on conductor insulation, the total number of bends (including offsets) between pull points can't exceed 360°.

15°   15°
15°   15°

Pull Points

There's no maximum distance between pull points.

Figure 358–5

Author's Comment:

- There's no maximum distance between pull boxes because this is a design issue, not a safety issue.

358.28 Reaming and Threading

(A) Reaming. Reaming to remove the burrs and rough edges is required when the raceway is cut.

Author's Comment:

- It's considered an accepted practice to ream small raceways with a screwdriver or the backside of pliers.

(B) Threading. Electrical metallic tubing must not be threaded.

358.30 Securing and Supporting

Electrical metallic tubing must be installed as a complete system in accordance with 300.18 [300.10 and 300.12], and it must be securely fastened in place and supported in accordance with (A) and (B).

(A) Securely Fastened. Electrical metallic tubing must generally be securely fastened within 3 ft of every box, cabinet, or termination fitting, and at intervals not exceeding 10 ft. Figure 358–6

EMT - Securely Fastened
358.30(A)

EMT must be securely fastened within 3 ft of termination fittings and at intervals not exceeding 10 ft.

Copyright 2014, www.MikeHolt.com

Figure 358–6

Author's Comment:

- Fastening is required within 3 ft of termination, not within 3 ft of a coupling.

Ex 1: When structural members don't permit the raceway to be secured within 3 ft of a box or termination fitting, an unbroken raceway can be secured within 5 ft of a box or termination fitting. Figure 358–7

EMT - Securely Fastened to Structural Members
358.30(A) Ex 1

VIOLATION
EMT must be unbroken
between termination in this case.

Maximum 5 ft   Maximum 5 ft

Where structural members don't permit fastening within 3 ft of the termination, EMT must be secured within 5 ft.

Copyright 2014, www.MikeHolt.com

Figure 358–7

(B) Horizontal Runs. Electrical metallic tubing installed horizontally in bored or punched holes in wood or metal framing members, or notches in wooden members, is considered supported, but the raceway must be secured within 3 ft of termination.

358.42 Couplings and Connectors

Couplings and connectors must be made up tight to maintain an effective ground-fault current path to safely conduct fault current in accordance with 250.4(A)(5), 250.96(A), and 300.10.

If buried in masonry or concrete, threadless electrical metallic tubing fittings must be of the concrete-tight type. If installed in wet locations, fittings must be listed for use in wet locations in accordance with 314.15(A).

Author's Comment:

- Conductors 4 AWG and larger that enter an enclosure must be protected from abrasion, during and after installation, by a fitting that provides a smooth, rounded, insulating surface, such as an insulating bushing, unless the design of the box, fitting, or enclosure provides equivalent protection, in accordance with 300.4(G). Figure 358–8

Conductors 4 AWG and larger must be protected by a fitting that provides a smooth, rounded, insulating surface, such as an insulating bushing [300.4(G)].

Figure 358–8

358.60 Grounding

EMT is permitted to serve as an equipment grounding conductor [250.118(4)]. Figure 358–9

Figure 358–9

ARTICLE 362
ELECTRICAL NONMETALLIC TUBING (TYPE ENT)

Introduction to Article 362—Electrical Nonmetallic Tubing (Type ENT)

Electrical nonmetallic tubing (ENT) is a pliable, corrugated, circular raceway made of polyvinyl chloride. In some parts of the country, the field name for electrical nonmetallic tubing is "Smurf Pipe" or "Smurf Tube," because it was only available in blue when it originally came out at the time the children's cartoon characters "The Smurfs" were most popular. Today, the raceway is available in many colors such as white, yellow, red, green, and orange, and is sold in both fixed lengths and on reels.

Part I. General

362.1 Scope

Article 362 covers the use, installation, and construction specifications of electrical nonmetallic tubing and associated fittings.

362.2 Definition

Electrical Nonmetallic Tubing (Type ENT). A pliable corrugated raceway of circular cross section, with integral or associated couplings, connectors, and fittings listed for the installation of electrical conductors. Figure 362–1

Electrical nonmetallic tubing can be bent by hand with a reasonable force, but without other assistance.

Part II. Installation

362.10 Uses Permitted

Definition of First Floor. The first floor of a building is the floor with 50 percent or more of the exterior wall surface area level with or above

Electrical Nonmetallic Tubing (Type ENT)
362.2 Definition

Listed ENT Fittings

A pliable corrugated circular raceway with integral or associated couplings, connectors, and fittings listed for the installation of electrical conductors.

Copyright 2014, www.MikeHolt.com

Figure 362–1

finished grade. If one additional level not designed for human habitation and used only for vehicle parking, storage, or similar use is at ground level, then the first of the three permissible floors can be the next higher floor.

(1) In buildings not exceeding three floors. Figure 362–2

    a. Exposed, where not prohibited by 362.12.

    b. Concealed within walls, floors, and ceilings.

Figure 362–2

Figure 362–4

(2) In buildings exceeding three floors, electrical nonmetallic tubing can be installed concealed in walls, floors, or ceilings that provide a thermal barrier having a 15-minute finish rating, as identified in listings of fire-rated assemblies. Figure 362–3

Figure 362–3

Ex to (2): If a fire sprinkler system is installed on all floors, in accordance with NFPA 13, Standard for the Installation of Sprinkler Systems, electrical nonmetallic tubing is permitted exposed or concealed in buildings of any height. Figure 362–4

(3) Electrical nonmetallic tubing is permitted in severe corrosive and chemical locations, when identified for this use.

(4) Electrical nonmetallic tubing is permitted in dry and damp concealed locations, if not prohibited by 362.12.

(5) Electrical nonmetallic tubing is permitted above a suspended ceiling, if the suspended ceiling provides a thermal barrier having a 15-minute finish rating, as identified in listings of fire-rated assemblies. Figure 362–5

Figure 362–5

Ex: If a fire sprinkler system is installed on all floors, in accordance with NFPA 13, Standard for the Installation of Sprinkler Systems, electrical nonmetallic tubing is permitted above a suspended ceiling that doesn't have a 15-minute finish rated thermal barrier material. Figure 362–6

Figure 362–6

(6) Electrical nonmetallic tubing can be encased or embedded in a concrete slab provided fittings identified for the purpose are used.

Author's Comment:

■ Electrical nonmetallic tubing isn't permitted in the earth [362.12(5)].

(7) Electrical nonmetallic tubing is permitted in wet locations indoors, or in a concrete slab on or below grade, with fittings listed for the purpose.

(8) Listed prewired electrical nonmetallic tubing with conductors is permitted in trade sizes ½, ¾, and 1.

(9) Conductors rated at a temperature higher than the listed temperature rating of ENT must not be operated at a temperature above the raceway's listed temperature rating. Figure 362–7

Figure 362–7

362.12 Uses Not Permitted

(1) In any hazardous location, except as permitted by 504.20 and 505.15(A)(1).

(2) For the support of luminaires or equipment. See 314.2.

(3) If the ambient temperature exceeds 50°C (122°F).

(4) For direct earth burial.

Author's Comment:

■ Electrical nonmetallic tubing can be encased in concrete [362.10(6)].

(5) As a wiring method for systems over 600V.

(6) Exposed in buildings over three floors, except as permitted by 362.10(2) and (5) Ex.

(7) In assembly occupancies or theaters, except as permitted by 518.4 and 520.5.

(8) Exposed to the direct rays of the sun for an extended period, unless listed as sunlight resistant.

Author's Comment:

- Exposing electrical nonmetallic tubing to the direct rays of the sun for an extended time may result in the product becoming brittle, unless it's listed to resist the effects of ultraviolet (UV) radiation. Figure 362–8

Figure 362–8

(9) If subject to physical damage.

Author's Comment:

- Electrical nonmetallic tubing is prohibited in ducts, plenum spaces [300.22(C)], and patient care space circuits in health care facilities [517.13(A)].

362.20 Trade Sizes

(A) Minimum. Electrical nonmetallic tubing smaller than trade size ½ isn't permitted.

(B) Maximum. Electrical nonmetallic tubing larger than trade size 2 isn't permitted.

362.22 Number of Conductors

Raceways must be large enough to permit the installation and removal of conductors without damaging the conductors' insulation, and the number of conductors must not exceed that permitted by the percentage fill specified in Table 1, Chapter 9.

When all conductors in a raceway are the same size and insulation, the number of conductors permitted can be found in Annex C for the raceway type.

> **Question:** How many 12 THHN conductors can be installed in trade size ½ ENT?
>
> (a) 5   (b) 7   (c) 9   (d) 11
>
> **Answer:** (b) 7 conductors [Annex C, Table C2]

Author's Comment:

- See 300.17 for additional examples on how to size raceways when conductors aren't all the same size.

Cables can be installed in electrical nonmetallic tubing, as long as the cables don't exceed the allowable percentage fill specified in Table 1, Chapter 9.

362.24 Bends

Raceway bends must not be made in any manner that'd damage the raceway, or significantly change its internal diameter (no kinks). The radius of the curve to the centerline of any field bend must not be less than shown in Chapter 9, Table 2, using the column "Other Bends."

362.26 Number of Bends (360°)

To reduce the stress and friction on conductor insulation, the maximum number of bends (including offsets) between pull points can't exceed 360°.

Author's Comment:

- There's no maximum distance between pull boxes because this is a design issue, not a safety issue.

362.28 Trimming

The cut ends of electrical nonmetallic tubing must be trimmed (inside and out) to remove the burrs and rough edges.

Trimming electrical nonmetallic tubing is very easy; most of the burrs rub off with fingers, and a knife can be used to smooth the rough edges.

362.30 Securing and Supporting

Electrical nonmetallic tubing must be installed as a complete system in accordance with 300.18 [300.10 and 300.12], and it must be securely fastened in place and supported in accordance with (A) and (B).

(A) Securely Fastened. Electrical nonmetallic tubing must be secured within 3 ft of every box, cabinet, or termination fitting, such as a conduit body, and at intervals not exceeding 3 ft. Figure 362–9

Figure 362–9

Ex 2: Lengths not exceeding 6 ft from the last point if the raceway is securely fastened within an accessible ceiling to luminaire(s) or other equipment.

Ex 3: If fished between access points through concealed spaces and supporting is impractical.

(B) Horizontal Runs. Electrical nonmetallic tubing installed horizontally in bored or punched holes in wood or metal framing members, or notches in wooden members, is considered supported, but the raceway must be secured within 3 ft of terminations.

362.46 Bushings

Conductors 4 AWG and larger that enter an enclosure from a fitting must be protected from abrasion, during and after installation, by a fitting that provides a smooth, rounded, insulating surface, such as an insulating bushing, unless the design of the box, fitting, or enclosure provides equivalent protection, in accordance with 300.4(G).

362.48 Joints

Joints, such as couplings and connectors, must be made in a manner approved by the authority having jurisdiction.

Author's Comment:

- Follow the manufacturer's instructions for the raceway, fittings, and glue. According to product listings, PVC conduit fittings are permitted with electrical nonmetallic tubing.

⚠ **CAUTION:** *Glue used with electrical nonmetallic tubing must be listed for ENT. Glue for PVC conduit must not be used with electrical nonmetallic tubing because it damages the plastic from which ENT is manufactured.*

362.60 Equipment Grounding Conductor

If equipment grounding is required, a separate equipment grounding conductor of the wire type must be installed within the raceway. Figure 362–10

Where equipment grounding is required, a separate equipment grounding conductor of the wire type must be installed in the raceway.

Figure 362–10

ARTICLE 376

METAL WIREWAYS

Introduction to Article 376—Metal Wireways

Metal wireways are commonly used where access to the conductors within a raceway is required to make terminations, splices, or taps to several devices at a single location. High cost precludes their use for other than short distances, except in some commercial or industrial occupancies where the wiring is frequently revised.

Author's Comment:

- Both metal wireways and nonmetallic wireways are often incorrectly called "troughs," "auxiliary gutters," "auxiliary wireways," or "gutters" in the field.

Part I. General

376.1 Scope

Article 376 covers the use, installation, and construction specifications of metal wireways and associated fittings.

376.2 Definition

Metal Wireway. A sheet metal trough with hinged or removable covers for housing and protecting electric conductors and cable, and in which conductors are placed after the <u>raceway</u> has been installed. Figure 376–1

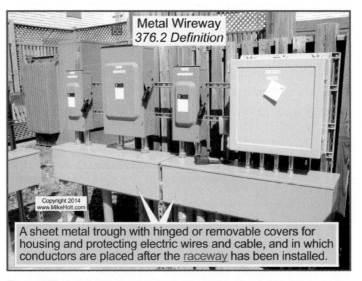

A sheet metal trough with hinged or removable covers for housing and protecting electric wires and cable, and in which conductors are placed after the <u>raceway</u> has been installed.

Figure 376–1

Part II. Installation

376.10 Uses Permitted

(1) Exposed.

(2) In any hazardous locations, as permitted by other articles in the *Code*.

(3) Wet locations where listed for the purpose.

(4) Unbroken through walls, partitions, and floors.

Author's Comment:

- See 501.10(B), 502.10(B), and 504.20 for metal wireways used in hazardous locations.

376.12 Uses Not Permitted

(1) Where subject to severe physical damage.

(2) Where subject to corrosive environments.

376.21 Conductors—Maximum Size

The maximum size conductor permitted in a wireway must not be larger than that for which the wireway is designed.

376.22 Number of Conductors and Ampacity

The number of conductors and their ampacity must comply with 376.22(A) and (B).

(A) Number of Conductors. The maximum number of conductors permitted in a wireway is limited to 20 percent of the cross-sectional area of the wireway. Figure 376–2

The maximum number of conductors permitted in a wireway is limited to 20 percent of the cross-sectional area of the wireway.

Figure 376–2

Author's Comment:

- Splices and taps must not fill more than 75 percent of the wiring space at any cross section [376.56].

(B) Conductor Ampacity Adjustment Factors. When more than 30 current-carrying conductors are installed in <u>any cross-sectional area of the wireway</u>, the conductor ampacity, as listed in Table 310.15(B)(16), must be adjusted in accordance with Table 310.15(B)(3)(a). Figure 376–3

Wireway - Conductor Ampacity
376.22(B)

When more than 30 current-carrying conductors are installed in <u>any cross-sectional area of the wireway</u>, the conductor ampacity, as listed in Table 310.15(B)(16), must be adjusted in accordance with 310.15(B)(3)(a).

Figure 376–3

Signaling and motor-control conductors between a motor and its starter used only for starting duty aren't considered current carrying for conductor ampacity adjustment.

376.23 Wireway Sizing

(A) Sizing for Conductor Bending Radius. Where conductors are bent within a metal wireway, the wireway must be sized to meet the bending radius requirements contained in Table 312.6(A), based on one wire per terminal. Figure 376–4

Figure 376–4

Figure 376–5

376.30 Supports

Wireways must be supported in accordance with (A) and (B).

(A) Horizontal Support. If installed horizontally, metal wireways must be supported at each end and at intervals not exceeding 5 ft.

(B) Vertical Support. If installed vertically, metal wireways must be securely supported at intervals not exceeding 15 ft, with no more than one joint between supports.

376.56 Splices, Taps, and Power Distribution Blocks

(A) Splices and Taps. Splices and taps in metal wireways must be accessible, and they must not fill the wireway to more than 75 percent of its cross-sectional area. Figure 376–5

Author's Comment:

■ The maximum number of conductors permitted in a metal wireway is limited to 20 percent of its cross-sectional area at any point [376.22(A)].

(B) Power Distribution Blocks.

(1) Installation. Power distribution blocks installed in wireways must be listed, and if they're installed on the supply side of the service disconnect they must be listed specifically for that application. Figure 376–6

Figure 376–6

(2) Size of Enclosure. In addition to the wiring space requirements [376.56(A)], the power distribution block must be installed in a metal wireway not smaller than specified in the installation instructions of the power distribution block.

(3) Wire-Bending Space. Wire-bending space at the terminals of power distribution blocks must comply with 312.6(B).

(4) Live Parts. Power distribution blocks must not have uninsulated exposed live parts in the metal wireway after installation, whether or not the wireway cover is installed. Figure 376–7

(5) Conductors. Conductors must be installed so that the terminals of the power distribution block aren't obstructed. Figure 376–8

Figure 376–7

Figure 376–8

ARTICLE 380

MULTIOUTLET ASSEMBLIES

Introduction to Article 380—Multioutlet Assemblies

A multioutlet assembly is a surface, flush, or freestanding raceway designed to hold conductors and receptacles, and is assembled in the field or at the factory [Article 100]. It's not limited to systems commonly referred to by the trade names "Plugtrak®" or "Plugmold®."

Part I. General

380.1 Scope

Article 380 covers the use, installation, and construction specifications of multioutlet assemblies.

Author's Comment:

- A multioutlet assembly is a surface, flush or freestanding raceway designed to hold conductors and receptacles assembled in the field or at the factory [Article 100]. Figure 380–1

A surface, flush, or freestanding raceway designed to hold conductors and receptacles assembled in the field or at the factory.

Figure 380–1

Part II. Installation

380.10 Uses Permitted

Multioutlet assemblies are only permitted in dry locations.

380.12 Uses Not Permitted

(1) Concealed.

(2) If subject to severe physical damage.

(3) If the voltage is 300V or more between conductors, unless the metal has a thickness not less than 0.04 in.

(4) If subject to corrosive vapors.

(5) In hoistways.

(6) In any hazardous location, except as permitted by 501.10(B).

380.76 Through Partitions

Metal multioutlet assemblies can pass through a dry partition provided no receptacle is concealed in the wall, and the cover of the exposed portion of the system can be removed.

SURFACE METAL RACEWAYS

Introduction to Article 386—Surface Metal Raceways

A surface metal raceway is a common method of adding a raceway when exposed traditional raceway systems aren't acceptable, and concealing the raceway isn't economically feasible. It comes in several colors, and is now available with colored or real wood inserts designed to make it look like molding rather than a raceway. A surface metal raceway is commonly known as "Wiremold®" in the field.

Part I. General

386.1 Scope

This article covers the use, installation, and construction specifications of surface metal raceways and associated fittings.

386.2 Definition

Surface Metal Raceway. A metallic raceway intended to be mounted to the surface, with associated accessories, in which conductors are placed after the raceway has been installed as a complete system [300.18(A)]. Figure 386–1

Author's Comment:

- Surface metal raceways are available in different shapes and sizes and can be mounted on walls, ceilings, or floors. Some surface metal raceways have two or more separate compartments, which permit the separation of power and lighting conductors from low-voltage or limited-energy conductors or cables (control, signal, and communications cables and conductors) [386.70].

Surface Metal Raceways
386.2 Definition

A raceway intended to be mounted to the surface, in which conductors are placed after the raceway has been installed as a complete system.

Copyright 2014, www.MikeHolt.com

Figure 386–1

386.6 Listing Requirements

Surface metal raceways and associated fittings must be listed.

Author's Comment:

■ Enclosures for switches, receptacles, luminaires, and other devices are identified by the markings on their packaging, which identify the type of surface metal raceway that can be used with the enclosure.

Part II. Installation

386.10 Uses Permitted

(1) In dry locations. Figure 386–2

Figure 386–2

(2) In Class I, Division 2 locations, as permitted in 501.10(B)(3).

(3) Under raised floors, as permitted in 645.5(E)(2).

(4) Run through walls and floors, if access to the conductors is maintained on both sides of the wall, partition, or floor.

386.12 Uses Not Permitted

(1) If subject to severe physical damage, unless otherwise approved by the authority having jurisdiction.

(2) If the voltage is 300V or more between conductors, unless the metal has a thickness not less than 0.04 in.

(3) If subject to corrosive vapors.

(4) In hoistways.

(5) If concealed, except as permitted in 386.10.

386.21 Size of Conductors

The maximum size conductor permitted in a surface metal wireway must not be larger than that for which the wireway is designed.

Author's Comment:

■ Because partial packages are often purchased, you may not always receive this information.

386.22 Number of Conductors

The number of conductors or cables installed in a surface metal raceway must not be more than the number for which the raceway is designed. Cables can be installed in surface metal raceways as long as the number of cables doesn't exceed the allowable percentage fill specified in Table 1, Chapter 9.

The ampacity adjustment factors of 310.15(B)(3)(a) don't apply to conductors installed in surface metal raceways if all of the following conditions are met: Figure 386–3

(1) The cross-sectional area of the raceway exceeds 4 sq in.

(2) The number of current-carrying conductors doesn't exceed 30, and

(3) The sum of the cross-sectional areas of all contained conductors doesn't exceed 20 percent of the interior cross-sectional area of the raceway.

Surface Raceway - Conductor Fill
386.22

The ampacity adjustment factors of 310.15(B)(3)(a) don't apply where all of the following conditions are met:

(1) The cross-sectional area exceeds 4 sq in.,
(2) The number of current-carrying conductors doesn't exceed 30, and
(3) The conductor fill doesn't exceed 20% of the cross-sectional area of the raceway.

Copyright 2014, www.MikeHolt.com

Figure 386–3

386.30 Securing and Supporting

Surface metal raceways **and fittings** must be **supported in** accordance with the manufacturer's installation instructions. Figure 386–4

Surface Metal Raceway - Securing and Supporting
386.30

Surface metal raceways and fittings must be supported in accordance with manufacturer's instructions.

Copyright 2014
www.MikeHolt.com

Figure 386–4

386.56 Splices and Taps

Splices and taps must be accessible, and must not fill the raceway to more than 75 percent of its cross-sectional area.

386.60 Equipment Grounding Conductor

Surface metal raceway fittings must be mechanically and electrically joined together in a manner that doesn't subject the conductors to abrasion. Surface metal raceways that allow a transition to another wiring method, such as knockouts for connecting raceways, must have a means for the termination of an equipment grounding conductor. A surface metal raceway is considered suitable as an equipment grounding conductor, in accordance with 250.118(14).

386.70 Separate Compartments

If surface metal raceways have separate compartments within a single raceway, power and lighting conductors can occupy one compartment, and the other compartment may contain control, signaling, or communications wiring. Stamping, imprinting, or color coding of the interior finish must identify the separate compartments, and the same relative position of compartments must be maintained throughout the premises.

Author's Comment:

■ Separation from power conductors is required by the *NEC* for the following low-voltage and limited-energy systems:

  □ CATV, 820.44(F)(1)
  □ Communications, 800.133(A)(1)
  □ Control and Signaling, 725.136(B)
  □ Fire Alarms, 760.136(B)
  □ Intrinsically Safe Systems, 504.30(A)(2)
  □ Instrumentation Tray Cable, 727.5
  □ Radio and Television, 810.18(C)
  □ Sound Systems, 640.9(C)

■ Nonconductive optical fiber cables can occupy the same cable tray or raceway as conductors for electric light, power, Class 1, or nonpower-limited fire alarm circuits [770.133(A)].

Notes

_____

_____

_____

_____

_____

_____

_____

_____

_____

_____

_____

_____

_____

_____

_____

_____

_____

_____

_____

ARTICLE 392

CABLE TRAYS

Introduction to Article 392—Cable Trays

A cable tray system is a unit or an assembly of units or sections with associated fittings that forms a structural system used to securely fasten or support cables and raceways. A cable tray isn't a raceway.

Cable tray systems include ladder, ventilated trough, ventilated channel, solid bottom, and other similar structures. Cable trays are manufactured in many forms, from a simple hanger or wire mesh to a substantial, rigid, steel support system. Cable trays are designed and manufactured to support specific wiring methods, as identified in 392.10(A).

Part I. General

392.1 Scope

Article 392 covers cable tray systems, including ladder, ventilated trough, ventilated channel, solid bottom, and other similar structures. Figure 392–1

392.2 Definition

Cable Tray System. A unit or assembly of units or sections with associated fittings forming a rigid structural system used to securely fasten or support cables, raceways, and boxes. Figure 392–2

Author's Comment:

■ Cable tray isn't a type of raceway. It's a support system for cables and raceways.

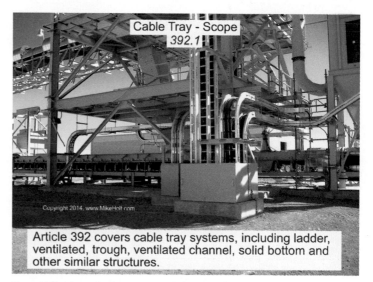

Article 392 covers cable tray systems, including ladder, ventilated, trough, ventilated channel, solid bottom and other similar structures.

Figure 392–1

A unit or assembly of units or sections with associated fittings forming a rigid structural system used to securely fasten or support cables and raceways.

Figure 392–2

Part II. Installation

392.10 Uses Permitted

Cable trays can be used as a support system for service, feeder, or branch-circuit conductors, as well as communications circuits, control circuits, and signaling circuits. Figure 392–3

Cable trays can be used as a support system for:

• Service Conductors • Communications Circuits
• Feeders   • Control Circuits
• Branch Circuits • Signaling Circuits

Copyright 2014, www.MikeHolt.com

Figure 392–3

Author's Comment:

■ Cable trays used to support service-entrance conductors must contain only service-entrance conductors unless a solid fixed barrier separates the service-entrance conductors from other conductors [230.44].

Author's Comment:

■ Cable tray installations aren't limited to industrial establishments.

■ If exposed to the direct rays of the sun, insulated conductors and jacketed cables must be identified as being sunlight resistant. The manufacturer must identify cable trays and associated fittings for their intended use.

(A) Wiring Methods. Any wiring methods listed in Table 392.10(A) can be installed in a cable tray.

Author's Comment:

■ Control, signal, and communications cables must be separated from the power conductors by a barrier or maintain a 2 in. separation.

☐ Coaxial Cables, 820.133(A)(1)(b) Ex 1
☐ Class 2 and 3 Cables, 725.136(B) and 725.136(I)
☐ Communications Cables, 800.133(A)(2) Ex 1
☐ Fire Alarm Cables, 760.136(G)
☐ Optical Fiber Cables, 770.133(B)
☐ Intrinsically Safe Systems Cables, 504.30(A)(2) Ex 1
☐ Radio and Television Cables, 810.18(B) Ex 1

Table 392.10(A) Wiring Methods

Wiring Method	Article/Section
Armored Cable	320
CATV cables	820
CATV raceways	820
Class 2 & 3 cables	725
Communications cables	800
Communications raceways	725, 770, and 800
Electrical metallic tubing	358
Electrical nonmetallic tubing	362
Fire alarm cables	760
Flexible metal conduit	348
Instrumentation tray cable	727
Intermediate metal conduit	342
Liquidtight flexible metal conduit	350
Liquidtight flexible nonmetallic conduit	356
Metal–clad cable	330
Nonmetallic–sheathed cable	334
Nonpower–limited fire alarm cable	760
Polyvinyl chloride PVC conduit	352
Power and control tray cable	336
Power–limited fire alarm cable	760
Power–limited tray cable	Table 725.154 and 725.179(E) and 725.71(F)
Rigid metal conduit	344
Service–entrance cable	338
Signaling raceway	725
Underground feeder and branch–circuit cable	340

(B) In Industrial Establishments. Figure 392–4

(1) Where conditions of maintenance and supervision ensure that only qualified persons service the installed cable tray system, single conductor cables can be installed in accordance with the following:

(a) 1/0 AWG and larger listed and marked for use in cable trays.

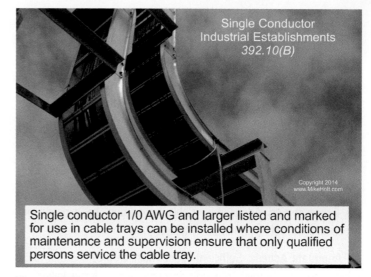

Single conductor 1/0 AWG and larger listed and marked for use in cable trays can be installed where conditions of maintenance and supervision ensure that only qualified persons service the cable tray.

Figure 392–4

(c) Equipment grounding conductors must be 4 AWG and larger.

(C) Hazardous Locations. Cable trays in hazardous locations must contain only the cable types and raceways permitted by the *Code* for the application

Author's Comment:

- For permitted cable types, see 501.10, 502.10, 503.10, 504.20, and 505.15.

(D) Nonmetallic Cable Trays. In addition to the uses permitted elsewhere in Article 392, nonmetallic cable trays can be installed in corrosive areas, and in areas requiring voltage isolation.

392.12 Uses Not Permitted

Cable tray systems aren't permitted in hoistways, or where subject to severe physical damage.

392.18 Cable Tray Installations

(A) Complete System. Cable trays must be installed as a complete system, except mechanically discontinuous segments between cable tray runs, or between cable tray runs and equipment are permitted. The system must provide for the support of the cables and raceways in accordance with their corresponding articles.

A bonding jumper, sized in accordance with 250.102 and installed in accordance with 250.96, must bond the sections of cable tray, or the cable tray and the raceway or equipment.

(B) Completed Before Installation. Each run of cable tray must be completed before the installation of cables or conductors.

(D) Through Partitions and Walls. Cable trays can extend through partitions and walls, or vertically through platforms and floors if the installation is made in accordance with the firestopping requirements of 300.21.

(E) Exposed and Accessible. Cable trays must be exposed and accessible, except as permitted by 392.18(D).

(F) Adequate Access. Sufficient space must be provided and maintained about cable trays to permit adequate access for installing and maintaining the cables.

(G) Raceways, Cables, and Boxes Supported from Cable Trays. In industrial facilities where conditions of maintenance and supervision ensure only qualified persons will service the installation, and if the cable tray system is designed and installed to support the load, cable tray systems can support raceways, cables, boxes, and conduit bodies. Figure 392–5

Figure 392–5

For raceways terminating at the tray, a listed cable tray clamp or adapter must be used to securely fasten the raceway to the cable tray system. The raceway must be supported in accordance with the appropriate raceway article.

Raceways or cables running parallel to the cable tray system can be attached to the bottom or side of a cable tray system. The raceway or cable must be fastened and supported in accordance with the appropriate raceway or cable's *Code* article.

Boxes and conduit bodies attached to the bottom or side of a cable tray system must be fastened and supported in accordance with 314.23.

392.20 Cable and Conductor Installation

(C) Connected in Parallel. To prevent unbalanced current in the parallel conductors due to inductive reactance, all circuit conductors of a parallel set [310.10(H)] must be bundled together and secured to prevent excessive movement due to fault current magnetic forces.

(D) Single Conductors. Single conductors of a circuit not connected in parallel must be installed in a single layer, unless the conductors are bound together.

392.22 Number of Conductors or Cables

(A) Number of Multiconductor Cables in Cable Trays. The number of multiconductor cables, rated 2,000 volts or less, permitted in a single cable tray must not exceed the requirements of this section. The conductor sizes herein apply to both aluminum and copper conductors.

(1) Any Mixture of Cables. If ladder or ventilated trough cable trays contain multiconductor power or lighting cables, the maximum number of cables must conform to the following:

(a) If all of the cables are 4/0 AWG and larger, the sum of the diameters of all cables must not exceed the cable tray width, and the cables must be installed in a single layer.

392.30 Securing and Supporting

(A) Fastened Securely. Cables installed vertically must be securely fastened to transverse members of the cable tray.

(B) Support. Supports for cable trays must be provided to prevent stress on cables where they enter raceways or other enclosures from cable tray systems. Cable trays must be supported in accordance with the manufacturer's installation instructions.

392.46 Bushed Raceway

A box isn't required where cables or conductors exit a bushed raceway used for the support or protection of the conductors. Figure 392–6

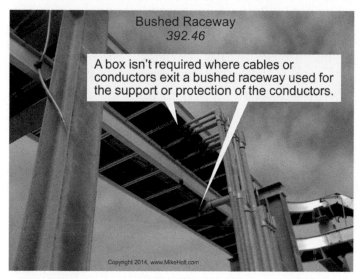

Figure 392–6

392.56 Cable Splices

Splices are permitted in a cable tray if the splice is accessible and insulated by a method approved by the authority having jurisdiction. Splices can project above the side rails of the cable tray if not subject to physical damage. Figure 392–7

Figure 392–7

392.60 Equipment Grounding Conductor

(A) Metal Cable Trays. Metal cable trays can be used as equipment grounding conductors where continuous maintenance and supervision ensure that only qualified persons service the cable tray system. Figure 392–8

Figure 392–8

The metal cable trays containing single conductors must be bonded together to ensure that they have the capacity to conduct safely any fault current likely to be imposed in accordance with 250.96(A).

Metal cable trays containing communications, data, and signaling conductors and cables must be electrically continuous through approved connections or the use of a bonding jumper. Figure 392–9

(B) Serve as Equipment Grounding Conductor. Metal cable trays can serve as equipment grounding conductors where the following requirements have been met [392.10(C)]:

(1) Metal cable trays and fittings can serve as an equipment grounding conductor if identified for this purpose. Figure 392–10

(4) Cable tray sections, fittings, and connected raceways are effectively bonded to each other to ensure electrical continuity and the capacity to conduct safely any fault current likely to be imposed on them [250.96(A)]. This is accomplished by using bolted mechanical connectors or bonding jumpers sized in accordance with 250.102.

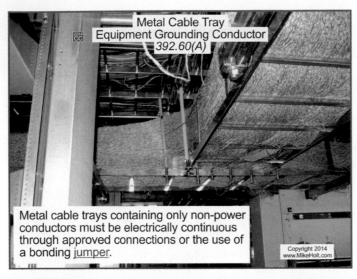

Metal Cable Tray
Equipment Grounding Conductor
392.60(A)

Metal cable trays containing only non-power conductors must be electrically continuous through approved connections or the use of a bonding jumper.

Copyright 2014
www.MikeHolt.com

Figure 392–9

Metal Cable Tray
Equipment Grounding Conductor
392.60(B)(1)

Copyright 2014
www.MikeHolt.com

Metal cable trays and fittings can serve as an equipment grounding conductor if identified for this purpose.

Figure 392–10

392.80 Ampacity of Conductors

(A) Ampacity in Cable Trays.

(1) The allowable ampacity of multiconductor cables installed according to the requirements of 392.22(A) must be as given in Table 310.15(B)(16) and Table 310.15(B)(18).

(a) The conductor ampacity adjustment factors of 310.15(B)(3) (a) apply to a given cable if it contains more than three current-carrying conductors. The conductor adjustment factors only apply to the number of current-carrying conductors in the cable and not to the number of conductors in the cable tray.

LOW VOLTAGE SUSPENDED CEILING POWER DISTRIBUTION SYSTEMS

Introduction to Article 393—Low Voltage Suspended Ceiling Power Distribution Systems

Low-voltage suspended ceiling power distribution systems use the ceiling grid members as electrical conductors. This allows the ceiling grid to provide power to a variety of electrical equipment; but, because of the obvious danger of energizing the ceiling grid, the voltage and current are limited to Class 2 power levels. This limitation provides safety while allowing for low energy-consuming equipment, such as speakers and audio/video equipment, to be used.

Those systems operating at 30 volts ac or less, or 60 volts dc or less, must be listed as a complete system or assembly of listed parts, with the utilization equipment, power supply, and fittings as part of the same identified system [393.6]. Figure 393-1

Low-Voltage Suspended Ceiling Power System
Article 393

Copyright 2014
www.MikeHolt.com

Those systems operating at 30V ac or less, or 60V dc or less, must be listed as a complete system or assembly of listed parts, with the utilization equipment, power supply, and fittings as part of the same identified system [393.6].

Figure 393–1

Scan this QR code for a video of this *Code* rule. See page xix for information on how to use the QR codes.

CHAPTER 3 PRACTICE QUESTIONS

Please use the 2014 *Code* book to answer the following questions.

1. When installed under metal-corrugated sheet roof decking, cables, raceways, and enclosures are permitted in concealed locations of metal-corrugated sheet decking type roofing if they are at least 2 in. away from a structural support member.

   (a) True
   (b) False

2. When installed under metal-corrugated sheet roof decking, the rules for spacing from roof decking apply equally to rigid metal conduit and intermediate metal conduit.

   (a) True
   (b) False

3. Where direct-buried conductors and cables emerge from grade, they shall be protected by enclosures or raceways to a point at least _____ ft above finished grade.

   (a) 3
   (b) 6
   (c) 8
   (d) 10

4. Direct-buried service conductors that are not encased in concrete and that are buried 18 in. or more below grade shall have their location identified by a warning ribbon placed in the trench at least _____ in. above the underground installation.

   (a) 6
   (b) 10
   (c) 12
   (d) 18

5. Which of the following metal parts shall be protected from corrosion?

   (a) Ferrous metal raceways.
   (b) Ferrous metal elbows.
   (c) Ferrous boxes.
   (d) all of these

6. Ferrous metal raceways, boxes, fittings, supports, and support hardware can be installed in concrete or in direct contact with the earth or other areas subject to severe corrosive influences, where _____ approved for the conditions.

   (a) the soil is
   (b) made of material
   (c) the qualified installer is
   (d) none of these

7. Raceways, cable assemblies, boxes, cabinets, and fittings shall be securely fastened in place.

   (a) True
   (b) False

8. Electrical wiring within the cavity of a fire-rated floor-ceiling or roof-ceiling assembly shall not be supported by the ceiling assembly or ceiling support wires.

   (a) True
   (b) False

9. A box or conduit body shall not be required where cables enter or exit from conduit or tubing that is used to provide cable support or protection against physical damage.

   (a) True
   (b) False

10. A box or conduit body shall not be required for splices and taps in direct-buried conductors and cables as long as the splice is made with a splicing device that is identified for the purpose.

    (a) True
    (b) False

11. Electrical installations in hollow spaces, vertical shafts, and ventilation or air-handling ducts shall be made so that the possible spread of fire or products of combustion is not _____.

    (a) substantially increased
    (b) allowed
    (c) inherent
    (d) possible

12. Openings around electrical penetrations into or through fire-resistant-rated walls, partitions, floors, or ceilings shall _____ to maintain the fire-resistance rating.

    (a) be documented
    (b) not be permitted
    (c) be firestopped using approved methods
    (d) be enlarged

13. Parallel conductors shall have the same _____.

    (a) length
    (b) material
    (c) size in circular mil area
    (d) all of these

14. Where conductors in parallel are run in separate raceways, the raceways shall have the same electrical characteristics.

    (a) True
    (b) False

15. A _____ conductor that carries only the unbalanced current from other conductors of the same circuit shall not be required to be counted when applying the provisions of 310.15(B)(3)(a).

    (a) neutral
    (b) ungrounded
    (c) grounding
    (d) none of these

16. On a three-phase, 4-wire, wye circuit, where the major portion of the load consists of nonlinear loads, the neutral conductor shall be counted when applying 310.15(B)(3)(a) adjustment factors.

    (a) True
    (b) False

17. In walls constructed of wood or other _____ material, electrical cabinets shall be flush with the finished surface or project there from.

    (a) nonconductive
    (b) porous
    (c) fibrous
    (d) combustible

18. Noncombustible surfaces that are broken or incomplete shall be repaired so there will be no gaps or open spaces greater than _____ in. at the edge of a cabinet or cutout box employing a flush-type cover.

    (a) $\frac{1}{32}$
    (b) $\frac{1}{16}$
    (c) $\frac{1}{8}$
    (d) $\frac{1}{4}$

19. According to the *NEC*, the volume of a 3 x 2 x 2 in. device box is _____ cu in.

    (a) 8
    (b) 10
    (c) 12
    (d) 14

20. When counting the number of conductors in a box, a conductor running through the box with an unbroken loop or coil not less than twice the minimum length required for free conductors shall be counted as _____ conductor(s).

    (a) one
    (b) two
    (c) three
    (d) four

21. In noncombustible walls or ceilings, the front edge of a box, plaster ring, extension ring, or listed extender employing a flush-type cover, shall be set back not more than _____ in. from the finished surface.

    (a) ⅛
    (b) ¼
    (c) ⅜
    (d) ½

22. In walls or ceilings constructed of wood or other combustible surface material, boxes, plaster rings, extension rings, or listed extenders shall _____.

    (a) be flush with the surface
    (b) project from the surface
    (c) a or b
    (d) be set back no more than ¼ in.

23. A vertically mounted luminaire weighing not more than _____ can be supported to a device box or plaster ring with no fewer than two No. 6 or larger screws.

    (a) 4 lb
    (b) 6 lb
    (c) 8 lb
    (d) 10 lb

24. Boxes used at luminaire or lampholder outlets in a ceiling shall be designed so that a luminaire or lampholder can be attached and the boxes shall be required to support a luminaire weighing a minimum of _____ lb.

    (a) 20
    (b) 30
    (c) 40
    (d) 50

25. Where the junction box contains a power distribution block, and it has conductors that don't terminate on the power distribution block(s), the through conductors must be arranged so the power distribution block terminals are _____ following installation.

    (a) unobstructed
    (b) above the through conductors
    (c) visible
    (d) labeled

26. _____ shall be installed so that the wiring contained in them can be rendered accessible without removing any part of the building or structure or, in underground circuits, without excavating sidewalks, paving, or earth.

    (a) Boxes
    (b) Conduit bodies
    (c) Handhole enclosures
    (d) all of these

27. Exposed runs of Type AC cable can be installed on the underside of joists where supported at each joist and located so it is not subject to physical damage.

    (a) True
    (b) False

28. Type AC cable installed through, or parallel to, framing members shall be protected against physical damage from penetration by screws or nails.

    (a) True
    (b) False

29. Type _____ cable is a factory assembly of insulated circuit conductors within an armor of interlocking metal tape, or a smooth or corrugated metallic sheath.

    (a) AC
    (b) MC
    (c) NM
    (d) b and c

30. Type MC cable shall not be _____ unless the metallic sheath or armor is resistant to the conditions, or is protected by material resistant to the conditions.

    (a) used for direct burial in the earth
    (b) embedded in concrete
    (c) exposed to cinder fill
    (d) all of these

31. Type NM cable shall be _____.

    (a) marked
    (b) approved
    (c) identified
    (d) listed

32. Type NM cables shall not be used in one- and two-family dwellings exceeding three floors above grade.

    (a) True
    (b) False

33. Flat Type NM cables shall not be stapled on edge.

    (a) True
    (b) False

34. Where more than two Type NM cables are installed through the same opening in wood framing that is to be sealed with thermal insulation, caulk, or sealing foam, the allowable ampacity of each conductor shall be _____.

    (a) no more than 20A
    (b) adjusted in accordance with Table 310.15(B)(3)(a)
    (c) limited to 30A
    (d) calculated by an engineer

35. The radius of the curve of the inner edge of any bend, during or after installation, shall not be less than _____ times the diameter of Type USE or SE cable.

    (a) five
    (b) seven
    (c) 10
    (d) 12

36. Materials such as straps, bolts, screws, and so forth, which are associated with the installation of IMC in wet locations shall be _____.

    (a) weatherproof
    (b) weathertight
    (c) corrosion resistant
    (d) none of these

37. Where practicable, contact of dissimilar metals shall be avoided in an IMC raceway installation to prevent _____.

    (a) corrosion
    (b) galvanic action
    (c) shorts
    (d) none of these

38. Galvanized steel, stainless steel and red brass RMC can be installed in concrete, in direct contact with the earth, or in areas subject to severe corrosive influences when protected by _____ and judged suitable for the condition.

    (a) ceramic
    (b) corrosion protection
    (c) backfill
    (d) a natural barrier

39. Galvanized steel, stainless steel, and red brass RMC shall be permitted in or under cinder fill subject to permanent moisture, when protected on all sides by a layer of noncinder concrete not less than _____ in. thick.

    (a) 2
    (b) 4
    (c) 6
    (d) 18

40. The standard length of RMC shall _____.

    (a) be 10 ft
    (b) include a coupling on each length
    (c) be threaded on each end
    (d) all of these

41. In an FMC installation, _____ connectors shall not be concealed.

    (a) straight
    (b) angle
    (c) grounding-type
    (d) none of these

42. When FMC is used where flexibility is necessary to minimize the transmission of vibration from equipment or to provide flexibility for equipment that requires movement after installation, _____ shall be installed.

    (a) an equipment grounding conductor
    (b) an expansion fitting
    (c) flexible nonmetallic connectors
    (d) none of these

43. Extreme _____ may cause PVC conduit to become brittle, and therefore more susceptible to damage from physical contact.

    (a) sunlight
    (b) corrosive conditions
    (c) heat
    (d) cold

44. Joints between PVC conduit, couplings, fittings, and boxes shall be made by _____.

    (a) the authority having jurisdiction
    (b) set screw fittings
    (c) an approved method
    (d) expansion fittings

45. EMT shall not be threaded.

    (a) True
    (b) False

46. EMT couplings and connectors shall be made up _____.

    (a) of metal
    (b) in accordance with industry standards
    (c) tight
    (d) none of these

47. Unbroken lengths of electric nonmetallic tubing shall not be required to be secured where fished between access points for _____ work in finished buildings or structures and supporting is impractical.

    (a) concealed
    (b) exposed
    (c) hazardous
    (d) completed

48. Power distribution blocks installed in metal wireways shall _____.

    (a) allow for sufficient wire-bending space at terminals
    (b) not have uninsulated exposed live parts
    (c) a or b
    (d) a and b

49. The ampacity adjustment factors of 310.15(B)(3)(a) shall not apply to conductors installed in surface metal raceways where the _____.

    (a) cross-sectional area exceeds 4 sq in.
    (b) current-carrying conductors do not exceed 30 in number
    (c) total cross-sectional area of all conductors does not exceed 20 percent of the interior cross-sectional area of the raceway
    (d) all of these

50. Each run of cable tray shall be _____ before the installation of cables.

    (a) tested for 25 ohms resistance
    (b) insulated
    (c) completed
    (d) all of these

CHAPTER 4

EQUIPMENT FOR GENERAL USE

Introduction to Chapter 4—Equipment for General Use

With the first three chapters behind you, the final chapter in the *NEC* necessary for building a solid foundation in general work is Chapter 4. This chapter helps you apply the first three to installations involving general equipment. These first four chapters follow a natural sequential progression. Each of the next four chapters—5, 6, 7, and 8—build upon the first four, but in no particular order. You need to understand all of the first four chapters to properly apply any of the next ones.

As in the preceding chapters, Chapter 4 is also arranged logically. Here are the groupings:

- Flexible cords and cables, and fixture wires.
- Switches and receptacles.
- Switchboards, switchgear, and panelboards.
- Lamps and luminaires.
- Appliances and space heaters.
- Motors, refrigeration equipment, generators, and transformers.
- Batteries, capacitors, and other components.

This logical arrangement of the *NEC* is something to keep in mind when you're searching for a particular item. You know, for example, that transformers are general equipment. So you'll find the *Code* requirements for them in Chapter 4. You know they're wound devices, so you'll find transformer requirements located somewhere near motor requirements.

- **Article 400—Flexible Cords and Flexible Cables.** Article 400 covers the general requirements, applications, and construction specifications for flexible cords and flexible cables.

- **Article 402—Fixture Wires.** This article covers the general requirements and construction specifications for fixture wires.

- **Article 404—Switches.** The requirements of Article 404 apply to switches of all types. These include snap (toggle) switches, dimmer switches, fan switches, knife switches, circuit breakers used as switches, and automatic switches such as time clocks, timers, and switches and circuit breakers used for disconnecting means.

- **Article 406—Receptacles, Cord Connectors, and Attachment Plugs (Caps).** This article covers the rating, type, and installation of receptacles, cord connectors, and attachment plugs (cord caps). It also covers flanged surface inlets.

■ **Article 408—Switchboards, Switchgear, and Panelboards.** Article 408 covers specific requirements for switchboards, panelboards, switchgear, and distribution boards that supply lighting and power circuits.

Author's Comment:

■ See Article 100 for the definitions of "Panelboard," "Switchboard," and "Switchgear."

■ **Article 410—Luminaires, Lampholders, and Lamps.** This article contains the requirements for luminaires, lampholders, and lamps. Because of the many types and applications of luminaires, manufacturer's instructions are very important and helpful for proper installation. Underwriters Laboratories produces a pamphlet called the *Luminaire Marking Guide*, which provides information for properly installing common types of incandescent, fluorescent, and high-intensity discharge (HID) luminaires.

■ **Article 411—Lighting Systems Operating at 30V or Less and Lighting Equipment Connected to Class-2 Power Sources.** Article 411 covers lighting systems, and their associated components, that operate at 30V or less, or that are connected to a Class-2 power source.

■ **Article 422—Appliances.** This article covers electric appliances used in any occupancy.

■ **Article 424—Fixed Electric Space-Heating Equipment.** Article 424 covers fixed electric equipment used for space heating. For the purpose of this article, heating equipment includes heating cable, unit heaters, boilers, central systems, and other fixed electric space-heating equipment. Article 424 doesn't apply to process heating and room air-conditioning.

■ **Article 430—Motors, Motor Circuits, and Controllers.** This article contains the specific requirements for conductor sizing, overcurrent protection, control circuit conductors, motor controllers, and disconnecting means. The installation requirements for motor control centers are covered in Article 430, Part VIII.

■ **Article 440—Air-Conditioning and Refrigeration Equipment.** Article 440 applies to electrically driven air-conditioning and refrigeration equipment with a motorized hermetic refrigerant compressor. The requirements in this article are in addition to, or amend, the requirements in Article 430 and others.

■ **Article 445—Generators.** Article 445 contains the electrical installation requirements for generators and other requirements, such as where they can be installed, nameplate markings, conductor ampacity, and disconnecting means.

■ **Article 450—Transformers.** This article covers the installation of transformers.

■ **Article 480—Batteries.** Article 480 covers stationary installations of storage batteries.

ARTICLE 400

FLEXIBLE CORDS AND FLEXIBLE CABLES

Introduction to Article 400—Flexible Cords and Flexible Cables

This article covers the general requirements, applications, and construction specifications for flexible cords and flexible cables. The *NEC* doesn't consider flexible cords to be wiring methods like those defined in Chapter 3.

Always use a cord (and fittings) identified for the application. Table 400.4 will help you in that regard. For example, use cords listed for a wet location if you're using them outdoors. The jacket material of any cord is tested to maintain its insulation properties and other characteristics in the environments for which it's been listed. Tables 400.5(A)(1) and 400.5(A)(2) are also important tables to turn to when looking for the ampacity of flexible cords and cables.

 Scan this QR code for a video of this *Code* rule. See page xix for information on how to use the QR codes.

400.1 Scope

Article 400 covers the general requirements, applications, and construction specifications for flexible cords and flexible cables as contained in Table 400.4. Figure 400–1

Author's Comment:

■ Article 400 doesn't apply to "power supply cords" or "cord sets" constructed in accordance with UL 817. Figure 400–2

400.3 Suitability

Flexible cords and flexible cables, as well as their fittings, must be suitable for the use and location. Figure 400–3

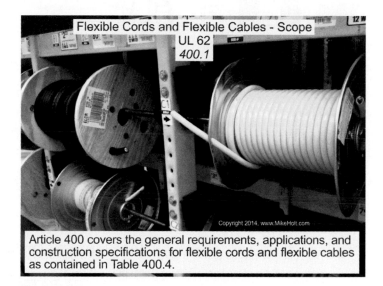

Flexible Cords and Flexible Cables - Scope
UL 62
400.1

Article 400 covers the general requirements, applications, and construction specifications for flexible cords and flexible cables as contained in Table 400.4.

Figure 400–1

400.4 Types of Flexible Cords and Flexible Cables

The use of flexible cords and flexible cables must conform to the descriptions contained in Table 400.4.

Figure 400–2

Figure 400–3

Author's Comment:

- The suffix "W" at the end of a cord type designates that the cord is water and sunlight resistant [Table 400.4, Note 15].

400.5 Ampacity of Flexible Cords and Flexible Cables

(A) Ampacity Tables. Table 400.5(A)(1) lists the allowable ampacity for copper conductors in flexible cords and flexible cables and Table 400.5(A)(2) lists the allowable ampacity for copper conductors

in flexible cords and flexible cables with not more than three current-carrying conductors at an ambient temperature of 86°F.

Where the number of current-carrying conductors in a cable or raceway exceeds three, the allowable ampacity of each conductor must be adjusted in accordance with the following multipliers: Figure 400–4

Figure 400–4

Table 400.5 Adjustment Factor	
Current Carrying	**Ampacity Multiplier**
4–6 Conductors	0.80
7–9 Conductors	0.70
10–20 Conductors	0.50

If the ambient temperature is other than 86°F, the flexible cord or flexible cable ampacity, as listed in Table 400.5(A)(1) or 400.5(A)(2), must be adjusted by using the ambient temperature correction factors listed in Table 310.15(B)(2)(a).

Author's Comment:

- Temperature ratings for flexible cords and flexible cables aren't contained in the *NEC*, but UL listing standards state that flexible cords and flexible cables are rated for 60°C unless marked otherwise.

- See 400.13 for overcurrent protection requirements for flexible cords and flexible cables.

400.7 Uses Permitted

(A) Uses Permitted. Flexible cords and flexible cables within the scope of this article can be used for the following applications:

(1) Pendants [210.50(A) and 314.23(H)].

Author's Comment:

■ Only cords identified for use as pendants in Table 400.4 may be used for pendants.

(2) Wiring of luminaires [410.24(A) and 410.62(B)].

(3) Connection of portable luminaires, portable and mobile signs, or appliances [422.16].

(4) Elevator cables.

(5) Wiring of cranes and hoists.

(6) Connection of utilization equipment to facilitate frequent interchange [422.16]. Figure 400–5

Flexible Cords - Uses Permitted
400.7(A)(6)

A flexible cord can be used to connect utilization equipment to facilitate frequent interchange.

Pendant [400.7(A)(1)]

Copyright 2014
www.MikeHolt.com

VIOLATION [400.7(B)]

Utilization equipment supplied by a flexible cord must have an attachment plug [400.7(B)]. There's no maximum length requirement for cords.

Figure 400–5

(7) Prevention of the transmission of noise or vibration [422.16].

(8) Appliances where the fastening means and mechanical connections are specifically designed to permit ready removal for maintenance and repair, and the appliance is intended or identified for flexible cord connections [422.16].

(9) Connection of moving parts.

Author's Comment:

■ Flexible cords and flexible cables are permitted for fixed permanent wiring by 501.10(A)(2) and (B)(2), 501.140, 502.4(A)(1)(e), 502.4(B)(2), 503.3(A)(2), 550.10(B), 553.7(B), and 555.13(A)(2).

(B) Attachment Plugs. Attachment plugs are required for flexible cords used in any of the following applications:

- Portable luminaires, portable and mobile signs, or appliances [400.7(A)(3)].
- Stationary equipment to facilitate its frequent interchange [400.7(A)(6) and 422.16].
- Appliances specifically designed to permit ready removal for maintenance and repair, and identified for flexible cord connection [400.7(A)(8)].

Author's Comment:

■ An attachment plug can serve as the disconnecting means for stationary appliances [422.33] and room air conditioners [440.63].

400.8 Uses Not Permitted

Unless specifically permitted in 400.7:

(1) Flexible cords must not be used as a substitute for the fixed wiring of a structure.

(2) Flexible cords must not be run through holes in walls, structural ceilings, suspended or dropped ceilings, or floors.

Author's Comment:

■ Article 400 requirements only apply to flexible cords [UL 62]; power supply cords [UL817] don't fall within the scope of Article 400, therefore a power supply cord is permitted to run through a cabinet wall for an appliance. Figure 400–6

(3) Flexible cords must not be run through doorways, windows, or similar openings.

(4) Flexible cords must not be attached to building surfaces.

(5) Flexible cords must not be concealed by walls, floors, or ceilings, or located above suspended or dropped ceilings. Figure 400–7

Figure 400–6

Figure 400–7

Author's Comment:

- Flexible cords are permitted under a raised floor (with removable panels) not used for environmental air, because this area isn't considered a concealed space. See the definition of "Exposed" in Article 100.

- Article 400 requirements only apply to flexible cords [UL 62]; power supply cords [UL817] do not fall within the scope of Article 400, therefore a power supply cord is permitted to run through or be located above a suspended ceiling. Figure 400–8

Figure 400–8

(6) Flexible cords must not be installed in raceways, except as permitted by 400.14 for industrial establishments where the conditions of maintenance and supervision ensure that only qualified persons will service the installation.

(7) Flexible cords must not be subject to physical damage.

Author's Comment:

- Even cords listed as "extra-hard usage" must not be used where subject to physical damage.

400.10 Pull at Joints and Terminals

Flexible cords must be installed so tension won't be transmitted to the conductor terminals. Figure 400–9

Note: This can be accomplished by knotting the cord, winding the cord with tape, or by using support or strain relief fittings.

Author's Comment:

- When critical health and economic activities are dependent on flexible cord-supplied equipment, the best method is a factory-made, stress-relieving, listed device, not an old-timer's knot.

Cord - No Tension at Terminals
400.10

Types of Cable
Strain-relief

Flexible cords must be installed so that tension
won't be transmitted to the conductor terminals.

Copyright 2014, www.MikeHolt.com

Figure 400–9

400.14 Protection from Damage

Flexible cords must be protected by bushings or fittings where passing through holes in covers, outlet boxes, or similar enclosures.

In industrial establishments where the conditions of maintenance and supervision ensure that only qualified persons will service the installation, flexible cords or flexible cables not exceeding 50 ft can be installed in aboveground raceways.

400.23 Equipment Grounding Conductor Identification

A conductor intended to be used as an equipment grounding conductor must have a continuous green color or a continuous identifying marker distinguishing it from the other conductor(s). Conductors with green insulation, or green with one or more yellow stripes must not be used for an ungrounded or neutral conductor [250.119].

Notes

ARTICLE 402

FIXTURE WIRES

Introduction to Article 402—Fixture Wires

This article covers the general requirements and construction specifications for fixture wires. One such requirement is that no fixture wire can be smaller than 18 AWG. Another requirement is that fixture wires must be of a type listed in Table 402.3. That table makes up the bulk of Article 402. Table 402.5 lists the allowable ampacity for fixture wires.

402.1 Scope

Article 402 covers the general requirements and construction specifications for fixture wires.

402.3 Types

Fixture wires must be of a type contained in Table 402.3.

402.5 Allowable Ampacity of Fixture Wires

The allowable ampacity of fixture wires is as follows:

Table 402.5 Allowable Ampacity for Fixture Wires	
Wire AWG	Wire Ampacity
18	6A
16	8A
14	17A
12	23A
10	28A

402.6 Minimum Size

Fixture wires must not be smaller than 18 AWG.

402.7 Raceway Size

Raceways must be large enough to permit the installation and removal of conductors without damaging conductor insulation. The number of fixture wires permitted in a single raceway must not exceed the percentage fill specified in Table 1, Chapter 9.

Author's Comment:

■ When all conductors in a raceway are the same size and insulation, the number of conductors permitted can be found in Annex C for the raceway type.

Question: How many 18 TFFN conductors can be installed in trade size ½ electrical metallic tubing? **Figure 402–1**

(a) 12   (b) 14   (c) 19   (d) 22

Answer: (d) 22 conductors [Annex C, Table C.1]

Figure 402–1

Figure 402–2

Author's Comment:

■ See 300.17 for additional examples on how to size raceways when conductors aren't all the same size.

402.8 Neutral Conductor

Fixture wire used as a neutral conductor must be identified by continuous white stripes.

Author's Comment:

■ To prevent electric shock, the screw shell of a luminaire or lampholder must be connected to the neutral conductor [200.10(C) and 410.50]. Figure 402–2

402.10 Uses Permitted

(2) Fixture wires are permitted for the connection of luminaires. Figure 402–3

Figure 402–3

Author's Comment:

■ Fixture wires can also be used for elevators and escalators [620.11(C)], Class 1 control and power-limited circuits [725.49(B)], and nonpower-limited fire alarm circuits [760.49(B)].

402.11 Uses Not Permitted

Fixture wires must not be used for branch-circuit wiring, except as permitted elsewhere in the *Code*. Figure 402-4

Figure 402-4

402.12 Overcurrent Protection

Fixture wires must be protected against overcurrent according to the requirements contained in 240.5.

Author's Comment:

■ Fixture wires used for motor control circuit taps must have overcurrent protection in accordance with 430.72(A), and Class 1 remote-control circuits must have overcurrent protection in accordance with 725.43.

Notes

ARTICLE 404

SWITCHES

Introduction to Article 404—Switches

The requirements of Article 404 apply to switches of all types, including snap (toggle) switches, dimmer switches, fan switches, knife switches, circuit breakers used as switches, and automatic switches, such as time clocks and timers.

404.1 Scope

The requirements of Article 404 apply to all types of switches, switching devices, and circuit breakers used as switches. Figure 404–1

Switches - Scope
404.1

The requirements of Article 404 apply to all types of switches, such as snap (toggle) switches, knife switches, circuit breakers used as switches, and automatic switches such as time clocks.

Copyright 2014, www.MikeHolt.com

Figure 404–1

404.2 Switch Connections

 Scan this QR code for a video of this *Code* rule. See page xix for information on how to use the QR codes.

(A) Three-Way and Four-Way Switches. Wiring for 3-way and 4-way switching must be done so that only the ungrounded conductors are switched. Figure 404–2

Switch Connections - 3- and 4-Way
404.2(A)

Copyright 2014
www.MikeHolt.com

White Conductor
Used as Traveler

All 3-way and 4-way switching must
be done with the ungrounded conductor.

Figure 404–2

Author's Comment:

- In other words, the neutral conductor must not be switched. The white insulated conductor within a cable assembly can be used for single-pole, 3-way, or 4-way switch loops if it's permanently reidentified to indicate its use as an ungrounded conductor at each location where the conductor is visible and accessible [200.7(C)(2)].

If a metal raceway or metal-clad cable contains the ungrounded conductors for switches, the wiring must be arranged to avoid heating the surrounding metal by induction. This is accomplished by installing all circuit conductors in the same raceway in accordance with 300.3(B) and 300.20(A), or ensuring that they're all within the same cable.

Ex: A neutral conductor isn't required in the same raceway or cable with travelers and switch leg (switch loop) conductors. Figure 404–3

Switch Connections - Single Pole
404.2(B)

White Colored Conductor (not neutral) Supply to Switch

All switching must be done with the ungrounded conductor.

Copyright 2014
www.MikeHolt.com

Switch Leg

A permanently reidentified white conductor within a cable can be used as an ungrounded conductor for switching purposes [200.7(C)(1)].

Figure 404–4

Neutral Conductor - Travelers and Switch Loops
404.2(A) Ex

Travelers

A neutral conductor isn't required to a switch box.

A neutral conductor isn't required to be in the same raceway or cable with travelers and switch legs.

Copyright 2014, www.MikeHolt.com

Figure 404–3

Neutral at Switch Boxes - Cable
Habitable Rooms and Bathrooms - Dwelling
404.2(C)

The neutral conductor for the controlled lighting circuit must be provided at the switch location.

Copyright 2014, www.MikeHolt.com

Figure 404–5

(B) Switching Neutral Conductors. Only the ungrounded conductor is permitted to be used for switching, and the grounded [neutral] conductor must not be disconnected by switches or circuit breakers. Figure 404–4

Ex: A switch or circuit breaker is permitted to disconnect a grounded circuit conductor where it disconnects all circuit conductors simultaneously.

(C) Switches Controlling Lighting Loads. Switches controlling line-to-neutral lighting loads must have a neutral provided at the switch location, **other than in the following locations**: Figure 404–5

(1) Where the conductors for switches enter the device box through a raceway that has sufficient cross-sectional area to accommodate a neutral conductor. Figure 404–6

(2) Where the switch box can be accessed to add or replace a cable containing a neutral without damaging the finish of the building. Figure 404–7

(3) Snap switches with integral enclosures [300.15(E)].

(4) Nonhabitable rooms and bathrooms.

Figure 404–6

Figure 404–7

Figure 404–8

Figure 404–9

Author's Comment:

- A habitable space is a space in a building for living, sleeping, eating, or cooking. Bathrooms, toilet rooms, closets, halls, storage, or utility space and similar areas aren't considered habitable spaces. Therefore the current 2014 rule doesn't apply to commercial occupancies. **Figure 404–8**

(5) **For 3-way and 4-way switches, but only if the entire floor area is visible from the switches' location(s).** Figure 404–9

(6) **Where the lighting is controlled automatically.**

(7) **Switches controlling receptacles.** Figure 404–10

Note: The purpose of the neutral conductor is to complete a circuit path for electronic lighting control devices.

404.3 Switch Enclosures

(A) General. Switches and circuit breakers used as switches must be of the externally operable type mounted in an enclosure listed for the intended use.

Figure 404–10

Figure 404–12

(B) Used for Raceways or Splices. Switch or circuit-breaker enclosures can contain splices and taps if the splices and/or taps don't fill the wiring space at any cross section to more than 75 percent. Switch or circuit-breaker enclosures can have conductors feed through them if the wiring doesn't fill the wiring space at any cross section to more than 40 percent in accordance with 312.8. Figures 404–11 and 404–12

404.4 Damp or Wet Locations

(A) Surface-Mounted Switches or Circuit Breakers. Surface-mounted switches and circuit breakers in a damp or wet location must be installed in a weatherproof enclosure. The enclosure must be installed so not less than ¼ in. of airspace is provided between the enclosure and the wall or other supporting surface [312.2]. Figure 404–13

Figure 404–11

Figure 404–13

(B) Flush-Mounted Switches or Circuit Breakers. A flush-mounted switch or circuit breaker in a damp or wet location must have a weatherproof cover. Figure 404–14

Figure 404–14

(C) Switches in Bathtub or Shower Spaces. Switches can be located next to but not within a bathtub, hydromassage bathtub, or shower space unless installed as part of a listed tub or shower assembly. Figure 404–15

Figure 404–15

404.6 Position of Knife Switches

(A) Single-Throw Knife Switch. Single-throw knife switches must be installed so gravity won't tend to close them.

(C) Connection of Switches. Single-throw knife switches, molded case switches, and circuit breakers used as switches must have the terminals supplying the load deenergize when the switch is in the open position.

Ex: The blades and terminals supplying the load can be energized when the switch is in the open position. For such installations, a permanent label that is not handwritten, be of sufficient durability to withstand the environment involved *[110.21(B)] must on the switch enclosure or immediately adjacent to open switch is required to read:*

**WARNING — LOAD SIDE TERMINALS MAY
BE ENERGIZED BY BACKFEED.**

404.7 Indicating

Switches, motor circuit switches, and circuit breakers used as switches must be marked to indicate whether they're in the "on" or "off" position. When the switch is operated vertically, it must be installed so the "up" position is the "on" position [240.81]. Figure 404–16

Figure 404–16

Ex 1: Double-throw switches, such as 3-way and 4-way switches, aren't required to be marked "on" or "off."

Ex 2: On busway installations, tap switches employing a center-pivoting handle can be open or closed with either end of the handle in the up or down position. The switch position must be clearly indicated and must be visible from the floor or from the usual point of operation.

404.8 Accessibility and Grouping

(A) Location. Switches and circuit breakers used as switches must be capable of being operated from a readily accessible location. They must also be installed so the center of the grip of the operating handle of the switch or circuit breaker, when in its highest position, isn't more than 6 ft 7 in. above the floor or working platform [240.24(A)]. Figure 404–17

Figure 404–17

Author's Comment:

■ The disconnecting means for a mobile home must be installed so the bottom of the enclosure isn't less than 2 ft above the finished grade or working platform [550.32(F)]. Figure 404–18

Ex 1: On busways, fusible switches and circuit breakers can be located at the same level as the busway where suitable means is provided to operate the handle of the device from the floor.

Figure 404–18

Ex 2: Switches and circuit breakers used as switches can be mounted above 6 ft 7 in. if they're next to the equipment they supply, and are accessible by portable means [240.24(A)(4)]. Figure 404–19

Figure 404–19

(B) Voltage Between Devices. Snap switches must not be grouped or ganged in enclosures with other snap switches, receptacles, or similar devices if the voltage between devices exceeds 300V, unless the devices are separated by barriers. Figures 404–20 and 404–21

Figure 404-20

Figure 404-21

404.9 Switch Faceplates

(A) Mounting. Faceplates for switches must be installed so they completely cover the outlet box opening and, where flush mounted, the faceplate must seat against the wall surface.

(B) Grounding. The metal mounting yokes for switches, dimmers, and similar control switches, regardless of whether a metal faceplate is installed, must be connected to an equipment grounding conductor by one of the following means:

(1) Metal Boxes. The switch is mounted with metal screws to a metal box or a metal cover that's connected to an equipment grounding conductor in accordance with 250.148. Figure 404-22

The switch is mounted with metal screws to a metal box or a metal cover that's connected to an equipment grounding conductor in accordance with 250.148.

Snap switches, dimmers, and similar control switches must be connected to an equipment grounding conductor whether or not a metal faceplate is installed [404.9(B)].

Figure 404-22

Author's Comment:

- Direct metal-to-metal contact between the device yoke of a switch and the box isn't required. Figure 404-23

Figure 404-23

(2) Nonmetallic Boxes. The grounding terminal of the switch yoke must be connected to the circuit equipment grounding conductor. Figure 404–24

Figure 404–24

Ex 1: The metal mounting yoke of a replacement switch isn't required to be connected to an equipment grounding conductor if the wiring at the existing switch doesn't contain an equipment grounding conductor and the switch faceplate is nonmetallic with nonmetallic screws, or the replacement switch is GFCI protected.

Ex 2: Listed assemblies aren't required to be connected to an equipment grounding conductor if all of the following conditions are met:

(1) The device is provided with a nonmetallic faceplate that can't be installed on any other type of device,

(2) The device doesn't have mounting means to accept other configurations of faceplates,

(3) The device is equipped with a nonmetallic yoke, and

(4) All parts of the device that are accessible after installation of the faceplate are manufactured of nonmetallic material.

Ex 3: A snap switch with an integral nonmetallic enclosure complying with 300.15(E).

404.10 Mounting Snap Switches

(B) Mounting of Snap Switches. Snap switches installed in recessed boxes must have the ears of the switch yoke seated firmly against the finished wall surface. <u>Screws for attaching a snap switch to a box must be machine screws matching the thread gage or size of the screw holes in the box, unless otherwise allowed by the manufacturer's instructions, or unless part of a listed assembly.</u> Figure 404–25

Figure 404–25

Author's Comment:

■ In walls or ceilings of noncombustible material, such as drywall, boxes must not be set back more than ¼ in. from the finished surface. In combustible walls or ceilings, boxes must be flush with, or project slightly from, the finished surface [314.20]. There must not be any gaps more than 1⁄8 in. at the edge of the box [314.21].

404.11 Circuit Breakers Used as Switches

A manually operable circuit breaker used as a switch must show when it's in the "on" (closed) or "off" (open) position [404.7]. Figure 404–26

Circuit Breakers Used as Switches
404.11

A manually operable circuit breaker used as a switch must show when it's on the "On" or "Off" position.

Copyright 2014, www.MikeHolt.com

Figure 404–26

Author's Comment:

■ Circuit breakers used to switch fluorescent lighting must be listed and marked "SWD" or "HID." Circuit breakers used to switch high-intensity discharge lighting must be listed and must be marked "HID" [240.83(D)]. **Figure 404–27**

Circuit Breakers Used as Switches
240.83(D)

SWD Breaker

HID Breaker

Circuit breakers used to switch 120V or 277V fluorescent lighting circuits must be listed and marked "SWD" or "HID." Circuit breakers used to switch high-intensity discharge lighting circuits must be listed and marked "HID."

Copyright 2014, www.MikeHolt.com

Figure 404–27

404.12 Grounding of Enclosures

Metal enclosures for switches and circuit breakers used as switches must be connected to an equipment grounding conductor of a type recognized in 250.118 [250.4(A)(3)]. Nonmetallic boxes for switches must be installed using a wiring method that includes an equipment grounding conductor.

404.14 Rating and Use of Snap Switches

(A) Alternating-Current General-Use Snap Switches. Alternating-current general-use snap switches can control:

(1) Resistive and inductive loads, including electric-discharge lamps that don't exceed the ampere rating of the switch, at the voltage applied.

(2) Tungsten-filament lamp loads not exceeding the ampere rating of the switch at 120V.

(3) Motor loads rated 2 hp or less that don't exceed 80 percent of the ampere rating of the switch. See 430.109(C).

(B) Alternating-Current or Direct-Current General-Use Snap Switch. A form of general-use snap switch suitable for use on either alternating-current or direct-current circuits for controlling:

(1) Resistive loads not exceeding the ampere rating of the switch at the voltage applied.

(2) Inductive loads not exceeding 50 percent of the ampere rating of the switch at the applied voltage or rated in horsepower for motor loads.

(3) Tungsten-filament lamp loads not exceeding the ampere rating of the switch at the applied voltage if T-rated.

(C) CO/ALR Snap Switches. Snap switches rated 20A or less connected to aluminum wire must be marked CO/ALR. See 406.3(C).

Author's Comment:

■ According to UL listing requirements, aluminum conductors must not terminate in screwless (push-in) terminals of a snap switch (UL White Book, *Guide Information for Electrical Equipment*, www.ul.com/regulators/2008_WhiteBook.pdf).

(E) Dimmers. General-use dimmer switches are only permitted to control permanently installed incandescent luminaires. Figure 404–28

Figure 404–28

404.15 Switch Marking

(A) Markings. Switches must be marked with the current, voltage, and if horsepower rated, the maximum rating for which they're designed.

(B) Off Indication. If in the off position, a switching device with a marked "off" position must completely disconnect all ungrounded conductors of the load it controls.

Author's Comment:

■ If an electronic occupancy sensor is used for switching, voltage will be present and a small current of 0.05 mA can flow through the circuit when the switch is in the "off" position. This small amount of current can startle a person, perhaps causing a fall. To solve this problem, manufacturers have simply removed the word "off" from the switch. **Figure 404–29**

Figure 404–29

ARTICLE 406

RECEPTACLES, CORD CONNECTORS, AND ATTACHMENT PLUGS (CAPS)

Introduction to Article 406—Receptacles, Cord Connectors, and Attachment Plugs (Caps)

This article covers the rating, type, and installation of receptacles, cord connectors, and attachment plugs (cord caps). It also addresses their grounding requirements. Some key points to remember include:

- Following the grounding requirements of the specific type of device you're using.
- Providing GFCI protection where specified by 406.4(D)(3).
- Mounting receptacles according to the requirements of 406.5, which are highly detailed.

406.1 Scope

Article 406 covers the rating, type, and installation of receptacles, cord connectors, and attachment plugs (cord caps).

406.2 Definitions

Child Care Facility. A building or portions thereof used for educational, supervision, or personal care services for five or more children seven years in age or less.

406.3 Receptacle Rating and Type

(C) Receptacles for Aluminum Conductors. Receptacles rated 20A or less for use with aluminum conductors must be marked CO/ALR.

Author's Comment:

- According to UL listing requirements, aluminum conductors must not terminate in screwless (push-in) terminals of a receptacle (UL White Book, *Guide Information for Electrical Equipment,* www.ul.com/regulators/2008_WhiteBook.pdf).

(D) Isolated Ground Receptacles. Receptacles of the isolated grounding conductor type must be identified by an orange triangle marking on the face of the receptacle. Figure 406–1

Isolated Ground Receptacle (IGR)
406.3(D)

Face of IGR Can be Any Color

An IGR is identified by an orange triangle (▲) marking on the face of the receptacle.

Copyright 2014, www.MikeHolt.com

Figure 406–1

(1) Receptacles must have the grounding contact connected to an insulated equipment grounding conductor installed with the circuit conductors, in accordance with 250.146(D). Figure 406–2

Figure 406–2

(2) Receptacles installed in nonmetallic boxes must be covered with a nonmetallic faceplate because a metal faceplate secured to an isolated ground receptacle isn't connected to an equipment grounding conductor.

(E) Controlled Receptacle Marking. All nonlocking, 125V, 15A and 20A receptacles that have an automatic means to remove power from the outlet for energy management or building automation must be marked with the following symbol. The symbol must be placed on the receptacle in a location that's visible after installation. Figure 406–3

Figure 406–3

Ex: The marking isn't required for wall switch-controlled receptacles used for lighting in a dwelling [210.70(A)(1) Ex 2].

406.4 General Installation Requirements

(A) Grounding Type. Receptacles installed on 15A and 20A branch circuits must be of the grounding type, unless used for replacements as permitted in (D)(2). Figure 406–4

Figure 406–4

Receptacles must be installed on circuits for which they are rated, except as permitted in Table 210.21(B)(2) and Table 210.21(B)(3). Figures 406–5 and 406–6

Table 210.21(B)(3) Receptacle Ratings	
Circuit Rating	Receptacle Rating
15A	15A
20A	15A or 20A
30A	30A
40A	40A or 50A
50A	50A

Figure 406–5

Figure 406–7

Figure 406–6

(C) Methods of Equipment Grounding. The grounding contacts for receptacles must be connected to an equipment grounding conductor supplied with the branch-circuit wiring. Figure 406–7

Author's Comment:

- See 250.146 for the specific requirements on connecting the grounding terminals of receptacles to the circuit equipment grounding conductor.

(D) Receptacle Replacement. Arc-fault circuit-interrupter type and ground-fault circuit interrupter type receptacles must be installed at a readily accessible location.

(1) Grounding-Type Receptacles. If an equipment grounding conductor exists, grounding-type receptacles must replace nongrounding-type receptacles and the receptacle's grounding terminal must be connected to the circuit equipment grounding conductor in accordance with 250.130(C) or 406.4(C).

(2) Nongrounding-Type Receptacles. If an equipment grounding conductor doesn't exist in the outlet box, the existing nongrounding-type receptacles can be replaced with: Figure 406–8

Figure 406–8

(a) A nongrounding-type receptacle.

(b) A GFCI-type receptacle marked "No Equipment Ground."

(c) A grounding-type receptacle, if GFCI protected and marked "GFCI Protected" and "No Equipment Ground."

Author's Comment:

■ GFCI protection functions properly on a 2-wire circuit without an equipment grounding conductor because the circuit equipment grounding conductor serves no role in the operation of the GFCI-protection device. See the definition of "Ground-Fault Circuit Interrupter" for more information. Figure 406–9

Figure 406–9

⚠ **CAUTION:** *The permission to replace nongrounding-type receptacles with GFCI-protected grounding-type receptacles doesn't apply to new receptacle outlets that extend from an existing outlet box that's not connected to an equipment grounding conductor. Once you add a receptacle outlet (branch-circuit extension), the receptacle must be of the grounding type and it must have its grounding terminal connected to an equipment grounding conductor of a type recognized in 250.118, in accordance with 250.130(C).* Figure 406–10

Figure 406–10

(3) GFCI Protection Required. When existing receptacles are replaced in locations where GFCI protection is currently required, the replacement receptacles must be GFCI protected.

Author's Comment:

■ See 210.8 for specific GFCI-protection requirements.

(4) Arc-Fault Circuit Interrupters. Effective January 1, 2014, where a receptacle outlet is supplied by a branch circuit that requires arc-fault circuit-interrupter protection [210.12(A)], a replacement receptacle at this outlet must be one of the following:

(1) A listed (receptacle) outlet branch-circuit type arc-fault circuit-interrupter receptacle.

(2) A receptacle protected by a listed (receptacle) outlet branch-circuit type arc-fault circuit-interrupter type receptacle.

(3) A receptacle protected by a listed combination type arc-fault circuit interrupter type circuit breaker.

(5) Tamper-Resistant Receptacles. Listed tamper-resistant receptacles must be provided where replacements are made at receptacle outlets that are required to be tamper resistant in accordance with 406.12 for dwelling units, guest rooms and guest suites, and child care facilities.

(6) Weather-Resistant Receptacles. Weather-resistant receptacles must be provided where replacements are made at receptacle outlets that are required to be so protected in accordance with 406.9(A) and (B).

406.5 Receptacle Mounting

Receptacles must be installed in **identified** outlet boxes. The box must be securely fastened in place in accordance with 314.23.

Author's Comment:

- Boxes containing a hub can be supported from a cord connected to fittings that prevent tension from being transmitted to joints or terminals [400.10 and 314.23(H)(1)]. **Figure 406–11**

Figure 406–11

Screws for attaching receptacles to a box must be machine screws matching the thread gage or size of the holes in the box, or must be part of a listed assembly. Figure 406–12

Author's Comment:

- The position of the ground terminal of a receptacle isn't specified in the *NEC*. The ground terminal can be up, down, or to the side. Proposals to specify the mounting position of the ground terminal have been rejected through many *Code* cycles. For more information on this subject, visit www.Mike-Holt.com. **Figure 406–13**

Figure 406–12

Figure 406–13

(A) Boxes Set Back. Receptacles in outlet boxes that are set back from the finished surface, as permitted by 314.20, must be installed so the mounting yoke of the receptacle is held rigidly to the finished surface or outlet box. Figure 406–14

Author's Comment:

- In walls or ceilings of noncombustible material, such as drywall, outlet boxes must not be set back more than ¼ in. from the finished surface. In walls or ceilings of combustible material, outlet boxes must be flush with the finished surface [314.20]. There must not be any gaps more than 1/8 in. at the edge of the outlet box [314.21].

Receptacle Mounting - Boxes Set Back
406.5(A)

Rigid to Drywall

Rigid to Box

Receptacles in outlet boxes must be installed so that the mounting yoke (strap) of the receptacle is held rigidly to the finished surface or to the outlet box.

Copyright 2014, www.MikeHolt.com

Figure 406–14

(B) Boxes Flush with the Surface. Receptacles mounted in outlet boxes that are flush with the finished surface must be installed so the mounting yoke of the receptacle is held rigidly against the outlet box or raised box cover.

(C) Receptacles Mounted on Covers. Receptacles supported by a cover must be held rigidly to the cover with at least two screws. Figure 406–15

Receptacles Mounted on Covers
406.5(C)

Okay

Okay

VIOLATION

Copyright 2014 www.MikeHolt.com

Receptacles supported by a cover must be held rigidly to the cover with more than one screw.

Figure 406–15

(D) Position of Receptacle Faces. Receptacles must be flush with, or project from, the faceplates.

(E) Receptacles in Countertops and Similar Work Surfaces. Receptacles must not be installed in a face-up position in countertops or similar work surface areas, unless they're part of a listed assembly for countertop surfaces. Figure 406–16

Receptacle Mounted in Countertops and Similar Surfaces
406.5(E)

VIOLATION

Copyright 2014, www.MikeHolt.com

Receptacles can't be installed in the face-up position in countertops or similar areas unless part of an assembly listed for countertop applications.

Figure 406–16

Author's Comment:

- Receptacle outlet assemblies listed for the application can be installed in dwelling unit kitchen and bathroom countertops [210.52(C)(5) and 210.52(D)].

(F) Receptacles in Seating Areas and Similar Surfaces. Receptacles must not be installed in a face-up position in seating areas or similar surfaces, unless the receptacle is:

(1) Part of a listed furniture power distribution unit,

(2) Part of a listed furnishing,

(3) Listed for use in countertops, or Figure 406–17

(4) Installed in a listed floor box.

(H) Voltage Between Devices. Receptacles must not be in enclosures with other switches or receptacles if the voltage between the devices exceeds 300V, unless the devices are installed in enclosures equipped with barriers identified for the purpose, that are securely installed between adjacent devices. Figure 406–18

Figure 406–17

Figure 406–19

Figure 406–18

406.6 Receptacle Faceplates

Faceplates for receptacles must completely cover the outlet openings. Figure 406–19

(B) Grounding. Metal faceplates for receptacles must be connected to the circuit equipment grounding conductor.

Author's Comment:

■ The *NEC* doesn't specify how this is accomplished, but 517.13(B) Ex 1 for health care facilities permits the metal mounting screw(s) securing the faceplate to a metal outlet box or wiring device to be suitable for this purpose. Figure 406–20

Figure 406–20

406.7 Attachment Plugs, Cord Connectors, and Flanged Surface Devices

Attachment plugs and cord connectors must be listed for the purpose and marked with the manufacturer's name or identification and voltage and ampere ratings.

(A) Exposed Live Parts. Attachment plugs, cord connectors, and flanged surface devices must have no exposed current-carrying parts, except the prongs, blades, or pins.

(B) No Energized Parts. Attachment plugs must be installed so their prongs, blades, or pins aren't energized unless inserted into an energized receptacle or cord connector. Figure 406–21

Figure 406–21

(D) Flanged Surface Inlet. A flanged surface inlet must be installed so the prongs, blades, or pins aren't energized unless an energized cord connector is inserted into it.

Author's Comment:

- The use of flanged "inlets," such as those on computers, transfer switches, and so forth, for detachable power cords is increasing.

406.9 Receptacles in Damp or Wet Locations

(A) Damp Locations. Receptacles installed in a damp location must be installed in an enclosure that's weatherproof when an attachment plug cap isn't inserted, and the receptacle cover is closed, or an enclosure that's weatherproof when an attachment plug is inserted. All nonlocking 15A and 20A, 125V and 250V receptacles in a damp location must be listed as weather resistant. Figure 406–22

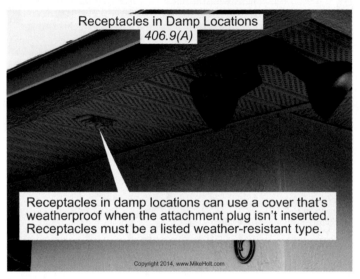

Figure 406–22

Author's Comment:

- Damp locations include locations protected from weather and not subject to saturation with water or other liquids, as well as locations partially protected under canopies, marquees, roofed open porches, and interior locations that are subject to moderate degrees of moisture, such as some basements, barns, and cold-storage warehouses [Article 100].

(B) Wet Locations.

(1) 15A and 20A Receptacles. All 15A and 20A receptacles installed in a wet location must be within an enclosure that's weatherproof when an attachment plug is inserted. Figure 406–23

Outlet box hoods must be listed <u>and must be identified for</u> "extra-duty" use. Figure 406–24

Figure 406–23

Figure 406–24

All nonlocking type 15A and 20A, 125V and 250V receptacles in a wet location must be listed as weather resistant. Figure 406–25

Author's Comment:

■ Exposed plastic surface material of weather-resistant receptacles must have UV resistance to ensure that deterioration from sunlight doesn't take place, or that it's minimal. In testing, receptacles are subjected to temperature cycling from very cold to very warm conditions, and then subjected to additional dielectric testing. The rapid transition from the cold to warm temperatures will change the relative humidity

Figure 406–25

and moisture content on the device, and the dielectric test ensures that this won't create a breakdown of the insulation properties.

Ex: Receptacles rated 15A and 20A that are subjected to routine high-pressure washing spray may have an enclosure that's weatherproof when the attachment plug is removed.

Author's Comment:

■ A wet location is an area subject to saturation with water, as well as unprotected locations that are exposed to weather [Article 100].

(2) Other Receptacles. Receptacles rated 30A or more installed in a wet location must comply with (a) or (b).

(a) Wet Location Covers. A receptacle that's in a wet location, where the load isn't attended while in use, must be installed in an enclosure that's weatherproof when an attachment plug is inserted.

(b) Damp Location Covers. A receptacle installed in a wet location that will only be used while someone is in close proximity to it, such as one used with portable tools, can have an enclosure that's weatherproof when the attachment plug is removed and the cover is closed.

(C) Bathtub and Shower Space. Receptacles must not be installed within or directly over a bathtub or shower stall. Figure 406–26

Figure 406–26

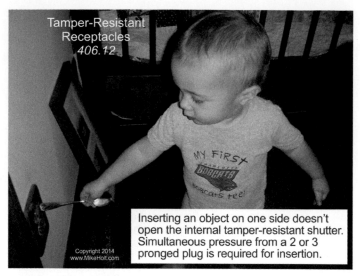

Figure 406–27

(E) Flush Mounting with Faceplate. The enclosure for a receptacle installed in an outlet box that's flush-mounted on a finished surface must be made weatherproof by a weatherproof faceplate that provides a watertight connection between the plate and the finished surface.

406.11 Connecting Receptacle Grounding Terminal to Equipment Grounding Conductor

The grounding terminal of receptacles must be connected to an equipment grounding conductor in accordance with 250.146.

406.12 Tamper-Resistant Receptacles

Tamper-resistant receptacles must be installed in the following areas:

Author's Comment:

- On a tamper-resistant receptacle, inserting an object into one side of the receptacle doesn't open the internal tamper-resistant shutter. Simultaneous pressure from a two or three pronged plug is required for insertion. Figure 406–27

(A) Dwelling Units. All nonlocking type 15A and 20A, 125V receptacles in the following areas of a dwelling unit [210.52] must be listed as tamper resistant. Figure 406–28

Figure 406–28

- Wall Space—210.52(A)
- Small-Appliance Circuit—210.52(B)
- Countertop Space—210.52(C)
- Bathroom Area—210.52(D)
- Outdoors—210.52(E)
- Laundry Area—210.52(F)
- Garage and Outbuildings—210.52(G)
- Hallways—210.52(H)

(B) Hotel and Motel Guest Rooms and Guest Suites. All Nonlocking type 15A and 20A, 125V receptacles in guest rooms and guest suites must be listed as tamper resistant.

(C) Child Care Facilities. Nonlocking type 15A and 20A, 125V receptacles in child care facilities must be listed as tamper resistant.

Author's Comment:

- A child care facility is a building or portions thereof used for educational, supervision, or personal care services for five or more children seven years in age or less [406.2].

Ex: Receptacles in the following locations aren't required to be tamper resistant:

(1) *Receptacles located more than 5½ ft above the floor.* Figure 406–29

(2) *Receptacles that are part of a luminaire or appliance.*

(3) *A receptacle located within dedicated space for an appliance that in normal use isn't easily moved from one place to another.*

(4) *Nongrounding receptacles used for replacements as permitted in 406.4(D)(2)(a).*

Figure 406–29

406.15 Dimmer-Controlled Receptacles

 Scan this QR code for a video of this *Code* rule. See page xix for information on how to use the QR codes.

Receptacles supplying lighting loads must not be connected to a dimmer switch unless the plug/receptacle combination is a nonstandard configuration type specifically listed and identified for each such unique combination. Figure 406–30

Figure 406–30

Notes

SWITCHBOARDS, SWITCHGEAR, AND PANELBOARDS

Introduction to Article 408—Switchboards, Switchgear, and Panelboards

Article 408 covers the specific requirements for switchboards, switchgear, and panelboards that control power and lighting circuits.

There's a tendency among some people in the industry to use the terms switchboard and switchgear interchangeably. Switchgear is manufactured and tested to more exacting standards and is configured differently than switchboards. For example, in switchgear there are physical barriers between breakers, and between the breakers and the bus. Switchgear is more durable and fault resistant, and is commonly selected for larger applications where low-voltage power circuit breakers and selective coordination are applied, such as computer data centers, manufacturing, and process facilities [Source NCCER].

As you study this article, remember some of these key points:

- One objective of Article 408 is that the installation prevents contact between current-carrying conductors and people or equipment.
- The circuit directory of a panelboard must clearly identify the purpose or use of each circuit that originates in the panelboard.
- You must understand the detailed grounding and overcurrent protection requirements for panelboards.

Part I. General

408.1 Scope

Article 408 covers the specific requirements for switchboards, switchgear, and panelboards that control power and lighting circuits. Figure 408–1

Switchboards, Switchgear, and Panelboards
408.1

Cabinet

Switchboard

Switchgear

Panelboard

Copyright 2014, www.MikeHolt.com

Article 408 contains the requirements for switchboards, switchgear, and panelboards for light and power.

Figure 408–1

408.3 Arrangement of Busbars and Conductors

(D) Terminals. In switchboards, switchgear, and panelboards, terminals for neutral and equipment grounding conductors must be located so it's not necessary to reach beyond uninsulated live parts in order to make connections.

(E) Bus Arrangement

(1) AC Phase Arrangement. Panelboards supplied by a 4-wire, delta-connected, 3-phase (high-leg) system must have the high-leg conductor (which operates at 208V to ground) terminate to the "B" phase of the panelboard. Figure 408–2

Figure 408–3

Figure 408–2

Ex: The high-leg conductor can terminate to the "C" phase when the meter is located in the same section of a switchboard or panelboard.

Note: Orange identification, or some other effective means, is required for the high-leg conductor [110.15 and 230.56]. Figure 408–3

⚠️ **WARNING:** *The ANSI standard for meter equipment requires the high-leg conductor (208V to neutral) to terminate on the "C" (right) phase of the meter socket enclosure. This is because the demand meter needs 120V and it gets it from the "B" phase.* Figure 408–4

Figure 408–4

⚠️ **WARNING:** *When replacing equipment in existing facilities that contain a high-leg conductor, use care to ensure that the high-leg conductor is replaced in the original location. Prior to 1975, the high-leg conductor was required to terminate on the "C" phase of panelboards and switchboards. Failure to re-terminate the high leg in accordance with the existing installation can result in 120V circuits being inadvertently connected to the 208V high leg, with disastrous results.*

(F) Switchboard, <u>Switchgear</u>, or Panelboard Identification. <u>Caution labels</u> that aren't <u>handwritten, must be permanently affixed, be of sufficient durability to withstand the environment involved</u> [110.21(B)] as follows must be installed<u>:</u>

(1) High-Leg Identification. A switchboard, <u>switchgear</u>, or panelboard containing a 4-wire, delta-connected system where the midpoint of one phase winding is grounded must be legibly and permanently field marked as follows: Figure 408–5

"CAUTION _____ PHASE HAS _____ VOLTS TO GROUND"

Figure 408–6

Switchboard or Panelboard
High-Leg Identification
408.3(F)(1)

Switchboards, <u>switchgear</u>, or panelboards containing a delta 4-wire system where the midpoint of one phase is grounded must be marked with the following:

CAUTION
B Phase Has 208 Volts to Ground

Figure 408–5

408.4 Field Identification

(A) Circuit Directory or Circuit Identification. All circuits, and circuit modifications, must be legibly identified as to their clear, evident, and specific purpose. Spare positions that contain unused overcurrent devices must also be identified. Identification must include <u>an approved amount of detail to allow</u> each circuit to be distinguished from all others, and the identification must be on a circuit directory located on the face or inside of the door of the panelboard. See 110.22. Figure 408–6

Author's Comment:

■ Circuit identification must not be based on transient conditions of occupancy, such as Brittney's bedroom. Figure 408 7

Circuit identification can't be based on transient conditions of occupancy.

Figure 408–7

(B) Source of Supply. All switchboards, <u>switchgear</u>, and panelboards supplied by a <u>feeder</u> in other than one- or two-family dwellings must be marked as to the device or equipment where the <u>power supply originates</u>. Figure 408–8

Figure 408–8

Figure 408–9

408.5 Clearance for Conductors Entering Bus Enclosures

If raceways enter a switchboard, **switchgear**, floor-standing panelboard, or similar enclosure, the raceways, including end fittings, must not rise more than 3 in. above the bottom of the enclosure.

408.7 Unused Openings

Unused openings for circuit breakers and switches must be closed using identified closures, or other means approved by the authority having jurisdiction, that provide protection substantially equivalent to the wall of the enclosure. Figure 408–9

Part III. Panelboards

408.36 Overcurrent Protection of Panelboards

Each panelboard must be provided with overcurrent protection located within, or at any point on the supply side of, the panelboard. The overcurrent device must have a rating not greater than that of the panelboard, and it can be located within or on the supply side of the panelboard. Figure 408–10

Figure 408–10

Ex 1: Individual overcurrent protection isn't required for panelboards used as service equipment where the service disconnecting means consists of up to six circuit breakers mounted in a single enclosure in accordance with 230.71. Figure 408–11

(B) Panelboards Supplied Through a Transformer. When a panelboard is supplied from a transformer, as permitted in 240.21(C), the overcurrent protection for the panelboard must be on the secondary side of the transformer. The required overcurrent protection can be in a separate enclosure ahead of the panelboard, or it can be in the panelboard. Figure 408–12

Figure 408–11

Figure 408–13

Figure 408–12

(D) Back-Fed Devices. Plug-in circuit breakers that are back-fed from field-installed conductors must be secured in place by an additional fastener that requires other than a pull to release the breaker from the panelboard. Figure 408–13

Author's Comment:

■ The purpose of the breaker fastener is to prevent the circuit breaker from being accidentally removed from the panelboard while energized, thereby exposing someone to dangerous voltage.

⚠ **CAUTION:** *Circuit breakers marked "Line" and "Load" must be installed in accordance with listing or labeling instructions [110.3(B)]; therefore, these types of devices must not be back-fed.*

408.37 Panelboards in Damp or Wet Locations

The enclosures (cabinets) for panelboards must prevent moisture or water from entering or accumulating within the enclosure, and they must be weatherproof when located in a wet location. When the enclosure is surface mounted in a wet location, the enclosure must be mounted with not less than ¼ in. air space between it and the mounting surface [312.2].

408.40 Equipment Grounding Conductor

Metal panelboard cabinets and frames must be connected to an equipment grounding conductor of a type recognized in 250.118 [215.6 and 250.4(A)(3)]. Where a panelboard cabinet contains equipment grounding conductors, a terminal bar for the equipment grounding conductors must be bonded to the metal cabinet or be connected to the feeder equipment grounding conductor. Figure 408–14

Panelboard - Equipment Grounding Conductor
408.40

Grounding Terminal Bar

Copyright 2014, www.MikeHolt.com

Where a panelboard cabinet contains equipment grounding conductors, a terminal bar for the equipment grounding conductors must be bonded to the metal cabinet.

Figure 408–14

Ex: Insulated equipment grounding conductors for receptacles having insulated grounding terminals (isolated ground receptacles) [250.146(D)] are permitted to pass through the panelboard without terminating onto the equipment grounding terminal of the panelboard cabinet.

Equipment grounding conductors aren't permitted to terminate on the neutral terminal bar, and neutral conductors aren't permitted to terminate on the equipment grounding terminal bar, except as permitted by 250.142 for services and separately derived systems. Figure 408–15

Panelboard - Equipment Grounding Conductor
408.40

Grounding Terminal Bar Bonded to the Panelboard Cabinet

Copyright 2014, www.MikeHolt.com

VIOLATION

Equipment grounding conductors must not terminate on the same terminal bar with the neutral conductor, except as permitted by 250.142 for services and separately derived systems.

Figure 408–15

Author's Comment:

- See the definition of "Separately Derived System" in Article 100.

⚠ **CAUTION:** *Most panelboards are rated as suitable for use as service equipment, which means they're supplied with a main bonding jumper [250.28]. This screw or strap must not be installed except when the panelboard is used for service equipment [250.24(A)(5)] or separately derived system [250.30(A)(1)]. In addition, a panelboard marked "suitable only for use as service equipment" means the neutral bar or terminal of the panelboard has been bonded to the case at the factory, and this panelboard is restricted to being used only for service equipment or on separately derived systems according to 250.142(A).*

408.41 Neutral Conductor Terminations

Each neutral conductor within a panelboard must terminate to an individual terminal. Figure 408–16

Neutral Conductor Terminations
408.41

VIOLATION

Each neutral conductor must terminate to an individual terminal in the panelboard.

Copyright 2014, www.MikeHolt.com

Figure 408–16

Author's Comment:

- If two neutral conductors are connected to the same terminal, and someone removes one of them, the other neutral conductor might unintentionally be removed as well. If that happens to the neutral conductor of a multiwire circuit, it can result in excessive line-to-neutral voltage for one of the circuits, as well as undervoltage for the other circuit. See 300.13(B) of this textbook for details. Figure 408–17

Figure 408–17

This requirement doesn't apply to equipment grounding conductors, because the voltage of a circuit isn't affected if an equipment grounding conductor is accidentally removed. Figure 408–18

Figure 408–18

Part IV. Construction Specifications

408.54 Maximum Number of Overcurrent Devices

A panelboard must prevent the installation of more overcurrent devices than the number for which the panelboard was designed, rated, and listed. When applying this rule, a 2-pole circuit breaker is considered to be two overcurrent devices, and a 3-pole circuit breaker is considered to be three overcurrent devices.

Notes

ARTICLE 410

LUMINAIRES, LAMPHOLDERS, AND LAMPS

Introduction to Article 410—Luminaires, Lampholders, and Lamps

This article covers luminaires, lampholders, lamps, decorative lighting products, and lighting accessories for temporary seasonal and holiday use, including portable flexible lighting products, and the wiring and equipment of such products and lighting installations. Even though Article 410 is highly detailed, it's broken down into 16 parts. The first five are sequential, and apply to all luminaires, lampholders, and lamps:

- **Part I. General**
- **Part II. Location**
- **Part III. Boxes and Covers**
- **Part IV. Supports**
- **Part V. Equipment Grounding Conductors**

The first five parts contain mostly mechanical information, and aren't hard to follow or absorb. Part VI, Wiring, ends the sequence. The seventh, ninth, and tenth parts provide requirements for manufacturers to follow—use only equipment that conforms to these requirements. Part VIII provides requirements for installing lampholders. The rest of Article 410 addresses specific types of lighting.

Author's Comment:

- Article 411 addresses "Lighting Systems Operating at 30 Volts or Less."

Part I. General

410.1 Scope

This article covers luminaires, lampholders, lamps, decorative lighting products, lighting accessories for temporary seasonal and holiday use, portable flexible lighting products, and the wiring and equipment of such products and lighting installations. Figure 410–1

Author's Comment:

- Because of the many types and applications of luminaires, manufacturers' instructions are very important and helpful for proper installation. UL produces a pamphlet called the Luminaire Marking Guide, which provides information for properly installing common types of incandescent, fluorescent, and high-intensity discharge (HID) luminaires.

Article 410 covers the wiring and equipment for luminaires, lampholders, and lamps for permanent, decorative, temporary, and flexible lighting products.

Figure 410–1

410.2 Definitions

Closet Storage Space. Storage space is defined as a volume bounded by the sides and back closet walls, extending from the closet floor vertically to a height of 6 ft or the highest clothes-hanging rod at a horizontal distance of 2 ft from the sides and back of the closet walls. Storage space continues vertically to the closet ceiling for a distance of 1 ft or the width of the shelf, whichever is greater. Figure 410–2

Figure 410–2

Author's Comment:

- This definition consists of approximately 125 words in one sentence, perhaps the longest sentence in the *Code*. Take a breath and don't get lost when reading it!

410.6 Listing Required

Luminaires, lampholders, **and retrofit kits** must be listed. Figure 410–3

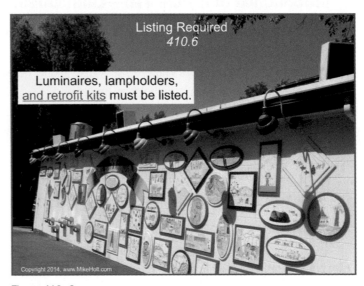

Figure 410–3

Part II. Luminaire Locations

410.10 Luminaires in Specific Locations

(A) Wet or Damp Locations. Luminaires in wet or damp locations must be installed in a manner that prevents water from accumulating in any part of the luminaire. Luminaires marked "Suitable for Dry Locations Only" must be installed only in a dry location; luminaires marked "Suitable for Damp Locations" can be installed in either a damp or dry location; and luminaires marked "Suitable for Wet Locations" can be installed in a dry, damp, or wet location. Figures 410–4 and 410–5

Author's Comment:

- A dry location can be subjected to occasional dampness or wetness. See the definition of "Location, Dry" in Article 100.

Figure 410–4

Figure 410–6

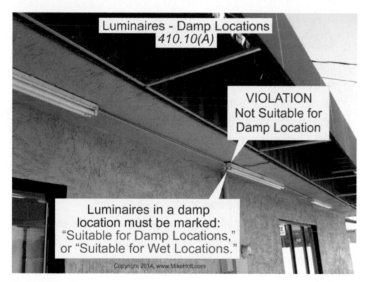

Figure 410–5

(B) Corrosive Locations. Luminaires installed in corrosive locations must be suitable for the location.

(C) In Ducts or Hoods. Luminaires can be installed in commercial cooking hoods if all of the following conditions are met: Figure 410–6

(1) The luminaire is identified for use within commercial cooking hoods.

(2) The luminaire is constructed so that all exhaust vapors, grease, oil, or cooking vapors are excluded from the lamp and wiring compartment.

(3) The luminaire is corrosion resistant, or protected against corrosion, and the surface must be smooth so as not to collect deposits and to facilitate cleaning.

(4) Wiring methods and materials supplying the luminaire must not be exposed within the cooking hood.

Author's Comment:

■ Standard gasketed luminaires must not be installed in a commercial cooking hood because accumulations of grease and oil can result in a fire caused by high temperatures on the glass globe.

(D) Bathtub and Shower Areas. No part of chain-, cable-, or cord-suspended luminaires, track luminaires, or ceiling paddle fans can be located within 3 ft horizontally and 8 ft vertically from the top of the bathtub rim or shower stall threshold. Figure 410–7

Author's Comment:

■ See 404.4 for switch requirements and 406.9(C) for receptacle requirements within or near bathtubs or shower stalls.

Luminaires located within the actual outside dimensions of a bathtub or shower to a height of 8 ft from the top of the bathtub rim or shower threshold must be marked for damp locations. If subject to shower spray, the luminaires must be marked for wet locations. Figure 410–8

Figure 410–7

Figure 410–8

(E) Luminaires in Indoor Sports, Mixed-Use, and All-Purpose Facilities. Luminaires using a mercury vapor or metal halide lamp that are subject to physical damage and are installed in playing and spectator seating areas of indoor sports, mixed-use, or all-purpose facilities must be of the type that has a glass or plastic lamp shield. Such luminaires can have an additional guard. Figure 410–9 .

Figure 410–9

WARNING: *Metal halide lamps can cause serious skin burns and eye inflammation from shortwave ultraviolet radiation if the outer envelope of the lamp is broken or punctured. They shouldn't be used where people will remain more than a few minutes unless adequate shielding or other safety precautions are used. Lamps that will automatically extinguish when the outer envelope is broken are commercially available. If a metal halide or mercury vapor lamp is broken during use:*

- *Turn off the light immediately,*
- *Move people out of the area as quickly a possible, and*
- *Advise people exposed to the damaged lamp to see a doctor if symptoms of skin burns or eye irritation occur.*

(F) Luminaires Installed in or Under Roof Decking. Luminaires installed under metal-corrugated sheet roof decking must be installed at least 1½ in. from the lowest surface of the roof decking measured from the bottom of the decking to the top of the luminaire.

410.11 Luminaires Near Combustible Material

Luminaires must be installed or be equipped with shades or guards so that combustible material isn't subjected to temperatures in excess of 90°C (194°F).

410.16 Luminaires in Clothes Closets

(A) Luminaire Types Permitted. Only the following types of luminaires are permitted to be installed in a clothes closet:

(1) Surface or recessed incandescent or LED luminaires with an enclosed light source.

(2) Surface or recessed fluorescent luminaires.

(3) Surface-mounted or recessed LED luminaires identified for use within the closet storage space.

(B) Luminaire Types Not Permitted. Incandescent luminaires with open or partially open lamps and pendant-type luminaires must not be installed in a clothes closet. Figure 410–10

Figure 410–10

(C) Installation of Luminaires. Luminaires must maintain a minimum clearance from the closet storage space as follows:

(1) 12 in. for surface-mounted incandescent or LED luminaires with an enclosed light source. Figure 410–11

(2) 6 in. for surface-mounted fluorescent luminaires.

(3) 6 in. for recessed incandescent or LED luminaires with an enclosed light source. Figure 410–12

(4) 6 in. for recessed fluorescent luminaires.

Figure 410–11

Figure 410–12

(5) Surface-mounted fluorescent or LED luminaires are permitted within the closet storage space if identified for this use. Figure 410–13

410.18 Space for Cove Lighting

Coves must have adequate space so that lamps and equipment can be properly installed and maintained.

Figure 410–13

Part III. Luminaire Outlet Boxes and Covers

410.22 Outlet Boxes to be Covered

Outlet boxes for luminaires must be covered with a luminaire, lampholder, or blank faceplate. See 314.25. Figure 410–14

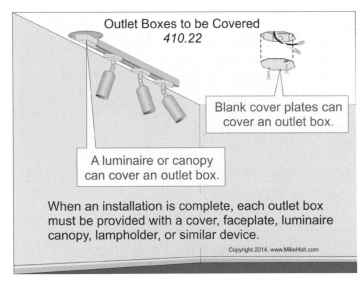

Figure 410–14

410.24 Connection of Electric-Discharge and LED Luminaires

(A) Luminaires Supported Independently of the Outlet Box. Electric-discharge and LED luminaires supported independently of the outlet box must be connected to the branch circuit with a raceway, or with Types MC, AC, or NM cable. Figure 410–15

Figure 410–15

Electric-discharge luminaires can be cord-connected if the luminaires are provided with internal adjustments to position the lamp [410.62(B)].

Electric-discharge luminaires can be cord-connected if the cord is visible for its entire length and is plugged into a receptacle, and the installation complies with 410.62(C).

(B) Access to Outlet Box. When an electric-discharge luminaire or LED luminaire is surface mounted over a concealed outlet box, and not supported by the outlet box, the luminaire must be provided with suitable openings that permit access to the branch-circuit wiring within the outlet box. Figure 410–16

Electric-Discharge and LED Luminaire Over Outlet Box
410.24(B)

Bottom View of Above Fixture

Copyright 2014
www.MikeHolt.com

OKAY

When an electric-discharge luminaire or LED is mounted over an outlet box, the luminaire must permit access to the branch-circuit wiring within the outlet box.

Figure 410–16

Poles Supporting Luminaires
Used as a Raceway
410.30(B)

Communications
Cables Only
OKAY

Power Only
OKAY

M-MART

Copyright 2014, www.MikeHolt.com

VIOLATION
820.133(A)(1)(d) prohibits the mixing of power and communications conductors in the same raceway.

Figure 410–17

Part IV. Luminaire Supports

410.30 Supports

(A) General Support Requirements. Luminaires and lampholders must be securely supported.

(B) Poles.

Author's Comment:

- With security being a high priority, many owners want to install security cameras on existing parking lot poles. However, 820.133(A)(1)(b) prohibits the mixing of power and communications conductors in the same raceway. Figure 410–17

In addition, they must comply with the following requirements:

(1) The pole must have an accessible 2 in. x 4 in. handhole with a cover suitable for use in wet locations that provides access to the supply conductors within the pole. Figure 410–18

Ex 1: The handhole isn't required for a pole that's 8 ft or less in height, if the supply conductors for the luminaire are accessible by removing the luminaire. Figure 410–19

Ex 2: The handhole can be omitted on poles that are 20 ft or less in height, if the pole is provided with a hinged base.

(2) When the supply raceway or cable doesn't enter the pole, a threaded fitting or nipple must be welded, brazed, or attached to the pole opposite the handhole opening for the supply conductors.

Poles Supporting Luminaires
Used as a Raceway
410.30(B)(1)

Copyright 2014
www.MikeHolt.com

The pole must have an accessible 2 x 4 in. handhole with a cover suitable for use in wet locations that provices access to the supply conductors within the pole.

Figure 410–18

(3) A metal pole must have an equipment grounding terminal accessible from the handhole.

Ex: A grounding terminal isn't required in a pole that's 8 ft or less in height above grade if the splices are accessible by removing the luminaire.

(5) Metal poles used for the support of luminaires must be connected to an equipment grounding conductor of a type recognized in 250.118 [250.4(A)(5)]. Figure 410–20

Figure 410–19

Figure 410–20

Figure 410–21

DANGER: *Because the contact resistance of an electrode to the earth is so high, very little fault current returns to the power supply if the earth is the only fault current return path. Result—the circuit overcurrent device won't open and clear the ground fault, and the metal pole will become and remain energized by the circuit voltage.* Figure 410–21

(6) Conductors in vertical metal poles must be supported when the vertical rise exceeds 100 ft [Table 300.19(A)].

Author's Comment:

■ When provided by the manufacturer of roadway lighting poles, so-called J-hooks must be used to support conductors, as they're part of the listing instructions [110.3(B)].

410.36 Means of Support

(A) Outlet Boxes. Outlet boxes designed for the support of luminaires must be supported by one of the following methods:

- Fastened to any surface that provides adequate support [314.23(A)].
- Supported from a structural member of a building or from grade by a metal, plastic, or wood brace [314.23(B)].
- Secured to a finished surface (drywall or plaster walls or ceilings) by clamps, anchors, or fittings identified for the application [314.23(C)].
- Secured to the structural or supporting elements of a suspended ceiling [314.23(D)].
- Supported by two intermediate metal conduits or rigid metal conduits threaded wrenchtight [314.23(E) and (F)].
- Embedded in concrete or masonry [314.23(G)].
- Outlet boxes for luminaires can support a luminaire that weighs up to 50 lb, unless the box is listed for the luminaries' actual weight [314.27(A)(2)].

(B) Suspended-Ceiling Framing Members. If framing members of suspended-ceiling systems are used to support luminaires, they must be securely fastened to each other and they must be securely attached to the building structure at appropriate intervals. Luminaires must be attached to the suspended-ceiling framing members with screws, bolts, rivets, or clips that are listed and identified for such use. Figure 410–22

Figure 410–22

Author's Comment:

■ The *NEC* doesn't require independent support wires for suspended-ceiling luminaires that aren't installed in a fire-rated ceiling; however, building codes often do. Figure 410–23

Figure 410–23

■ Raceways and cables within a suspended ceiling must be supported in accordance with 300.11(A). Outlet boxes can be secured to the ceiling-framing members by bolts, screws, rivets, clips, or independent support wires that are taut and secured at both ends [314.23(D)].

(G) Luminaires Supported by Trees. Trees can be used to support luminaires, but they must not be used to support overhead conductor spans [225.26]. Figure 410–24

Figure 410–24

Part V. Grounding (Bonding)

410.44 Methods of Grounding

The metal parts of luminaires must be connected to an equipment grounding conductor of a type recognized in 250.118. If the equipment grounding conductor is of the wire type, the conductor must be sized in accordance with 250.122, based on the rating of the overcurrent device. Figure 410–25

Ex 1: If an equipment grounding conductor isn't present in the outlet box, the luminaire must be made of insulating material and not have any exposed conductive parts.

Ex 2: Replacement luminaires can be installed in an outlet box that doesn't contain an equipment grounding conductor if the luminaire is connected to one of the following [250.130(C)]:

(1) The grounding electrode system [250.50]

Figure 410–25

(2) The grounding electrode conductor

(3) The panelboard equipment grounding terminal

(4) An equipment grounding conductor that's part of a different circuit, if both circuits originate from the same panel.

(5) The service neutral conductor

Ex 3: GFCI-protected replacement luminaires aren't required to be connected to an equipment grounding conductor if no equipment grounding conductor exists at the outlet box.

Author's Comment:

■ This is similar to the rule for receptacle replacements in locations where an equipment grounding conductor isn't present in the outlet box [406.4(D)(3)].

Part VI. Wiring of Luminaires

410.50 Polarization of Luminaires

Luminaires must have the neutral conductor connected to the screw shell of the lampholder [200.10(C)], and the neutral conductor must be properly identified in accordance with 200.6.

410.62 Cord-Connected Luminaires

(B) Adjustable Luminaires. Luminaires that require adjusting or aiming after installation can be cord connected, with or without an attachment plug, provided the exposed cord is of the hard usage or extra-hard usage type. The cord must not be longer than necessary for luminaire adjustment, and it must not be subject to strain or physical damage [400.10]. Figure 410–26

Figure 410–26

(C) Electric-Discharge and LED Luminaires.

(1) Cord-Connected Installation. A luminaire can be cord connected if: Figure 410–27

(1) The luminaire is mounted directly below the outlet box, and

(2) The flexible cord:

   a. Is visible for its entire length,

   b. Isn't subject to strain or physical damage [400.10], and

   c. Terminates in an attachment plug, canopy with strain relief, or manufactured wiring system connector in accordance with 604.6(C).

Author's Comment:

■ The *Code* doesn't require twist-lock receptacles for this application.

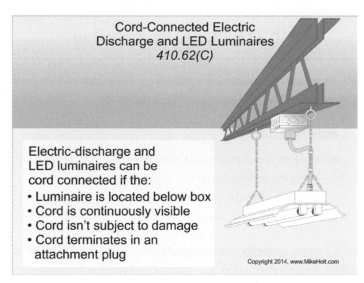

Figure 410–27

410.64 Luminaires as Raceways

(A) Listed. Luminaires aren't permitted to be used as a raceway for circuit conductors unless listed and marked for use as a raceway. Figure 410–28

Figure 410–28

(B) Through-Wiring. Luminaires with an outlet box that's an integral part of a luminaire can be used as a conductor raceway.

(C) Luminaires Connected Together. Luminaires designed for end-to-end assembly, or luminaires connected together by recognized wiring methods, can contain a 2-wire branch circuit, or one multiwire branch circuit, supplying the connected luminaires. One additional 2-wire branch circuit supplying a night light is permitted. Figure 410–29

Figure 410–29

410.68 Conductors and Ballasts

Conductors within 3 in. of ballast, LED driver, power supply, or transformer must have an insulation temperature rating not lower than 90°C.

Part VIII. Installation of Lampholders

410.90 Screw-Shell Lampholders

Lampholders of the screw-shell type must be installed for use as lampholders only.

Author's Comment:

■ A receptacle adapter that screws into a lampholder is a violation of this section. Figure 410–30

Figure 410–30

410.96 Lampholders in Wet or Damp Locations

Lampholders installed in wet locations must be listed for use in wet locations and lampholders installed in damp locations must be listed for damp or wet locations.

410.97 Lampholders Near Combustible Material

Lampholders must be constructed, installed, or equipped with shades or guards so that combustible material isn't subjected to temperatures in excess of 90°C (194°F).

Part X. Recessed Luminaires

410.110 General

Luminaires installed in recessed cavities in walls or ceilings, including suspended ceilings, must comply with this Part (X. Recessed Luminaires).

410.115 Thermally Protected

(C) Recessed Incandescent Luminaires. Recessed incandescent luminaires must be identified as thermally protected.

Author's Comment:

- When higher-wattage lamps or improper trims are installed, the lampholder contained in a recessed luminaire can overheat, activating the thermal overcurrent device and causing the luminaire to cycle on and off.

Ex 2: Thermal protection isn't required for recessed Type IC luminaires whose design, construction, and thermal performance characteristics are equivalent to a thermally protected luminaire.

410.116 Recessed Luminaire Clearances

(A) Clearances From Combustible Materials.

(1) Non-Type IC Luminaires. A recessed luminaire that isn't identified for contact with insulation must have all recessed parts, except the points of supports, spaced not less than ¼ in. from combustible materials. Figure 410–31

Figure 410–31

(2) Type IC Luminaires. A Type IC luminaire (identified for contact with insulation) can be in contact with combustible materials. Figure 410–32

Recessed Luminaires Clearance from
Combustible Materials - Type IC Luminaire
410.116(A)(2)

Thermal Insulation

Wood Ceiling

TYPE IC

Copyright 2014
www.MikeHolt.com

A Type IC luminaire (identified for contact with insulation)
can be in contact with combustible materials.

Figure 410–32

(B) Installation. Thermal insulation must not be installed above a recessed luminaire or within 3 in. of the luminaries' enclosure, wiring compartment, or ballast, transformer, LED driver, or power supply unless identified for contact with insulation, Type IC.

410.117 Wiring

(C) Tap Conductors. Fixture wires installed in accordance with Article 402 and protected against overcurrent in accordance with 240.5(B)(2), are permitted to run from the luminaire to an outlet box located at least 1 ft away from the luminaire, as long as the conductors aren't over 6 ft long. Figure 410–33

Part XII. Electric-Discharge Lighting

410.130 General

(F) High-Intensity Discharge Luminaires.

Recessed Luminaires - Tap Conductors
410.117(C)

Tap Conductors in a Suitable
Raceway, or Types AC or MC Cable

Minimum 18 in. Long
Maximum 6 ft Long

TYPE IC   TYPE IC

Tap conductors can be run from the luminaire termination to an outlet box located at least 1 ft from the fixture. Tap conductors must be at least 18 in. long but not more than 6 ft in length.

Copyright 2014, www.MikeHolt.com

Figure 410–33

(5) Metal Halide Lamp Containment. Luminaires containing a metal halide lamp, other than a thick-glass parabolic reflector lamp (PAR), must be provided with a containment barrier that encloses the lamp, or the luminaire must only allow the use of a Type "O" lamp that has an internal arc-tube shield. Figure 410–34

Metal Halide Lamp Containment
410.130(F)(5)

Open
Luminaires

Enclosed
Luminaires

Luminaires with a metal halide lamp must have a containment barrier such as a lens unless the fixture only accepts Type O lamps.

Luminaires with PAR type metal halide lamps don't require a lens.

Copyright 2014
www.MikeHolt.com

Figure 410–34

Author's Comment:

- Fires have resulted from arc lamps exploding on start-up, shattering the lamp globe and showering glass and hot quartz fragments from metal halide lamp failures. The possibility of failure increases significantly as the lamp approaches and exceeds its rated life. It's projected that one violent rupture occurs in every 100,000 failures.

- "O-rated" lamps, which have an internal arc-tube shield, have been designed to meet ANSI containment standards for the installation of a metal halide lamp in an open fixture.

(G) Disconnecting Means.

(1) General. In indoor locations, other than dwellings and associated accessory structures, fluorescent luminaires that utilize double-ended lamps (typical fluorescent lamps) and contain ballasts that can be serviced in place must have a disconnecting means. Figure 410–35

Disconnect for Electrical-Discharge Lighting
410.130(G)(1)

In indoor locations, other than dwellings and associated accessory structures, fluorescent luminaires that utilize double-ended lamps and contain ballasts must have a disconnecting means.

Figure 410–35

For existing installed luminaires, a disconnecting means must be added at the time the ballast is replaced. Figure 410– 36

Author's Comment:

- Changing the ballast while the circuit feeding the luminaire is energized has become a regular practice because a local disconnect isn't available.

Disconnect for Electrical-Discharge Lighting
Existing Fluorescent Luminaire
410.130(G)(1)

For existing installed fluorescent luminaires without disconnecting means, a disconnecting means must be added when a ballast is replaced.

Figure 410–36

Ex 2: A disconnecting means isn't required for the emergency illumination required in 700.16.

Ex 3: For cord-and-plug-connected luminaires, an accessible separable connector, or an accessible plug and receptacle, is permitted to serve as the disconnecting means.

Ex 4: If more than one luminaire is installed and is supplied by a branch circuit that isn't of the multiwire type, a disconnecting means isn't required for every luminaire; but, only when the light switch for the space ensures that some of the luminaires in the space will still provide illumination.

(2) Multiwire Branch Circuits. When connected to multiwire branch circuits, the fluorescent luminaire disconnect must simultaneously break all circuit conductors of the ballast, including the neutral conductor.

Author's Comment:

- This rule requires the disconnecting means to open "all circuit conductors of a multiwire branch circuit," including the neutral conductor. If the neutral conductor in a multiwire circuit isn't disconnected at the same time as the ungrounded conductors, a false sense of security can result in an unexpected shock from the neutral conductor.

(3) Location. The fluorescent luminaire disconnecting means must be accessible to qualified persons, and if the disconnecting means is external to the luminaire, it must be a single device and must be located in sight from the luminaire.

Part XIV. Track Lighting

410.151 Installation

(A) Track Lighting. Track lighting must be permanently installed and permanently connected to the branch-circuit wiring. Lampholders for track lighting are designed for lamps only, so a receptacle adapter isn't permitted [410.90].

(B) Circuit Rating. The connected load on a lighting track must not exceed the rating of the track, and an overcurrent device whose rating exceeds the rating of the track must not supply the track. Figure 410–37

Track Lighting - Circuit Rating
410.151(B)

A 15A lighting track can't be connected to a 20A circuit.

The connected load on lighting track must not exceed the rating of the track, and the track must not be supplied by a circuit whose rating exceeds that of the track.

Copyright 2014, www.MikeHolt.com

Figure 410–37

The feeder or service load calculations of 220.43(B) don't limit the number of feet of track on a circuit, nor do they limit the number of luminaires mounted on an individual track. Figure 410– 38

(C) Locations Not Permitted. Track lighting must not be installed:

(1) If it's likely to be subjected to physical damage.

(2) In wet or damp locations.

(3) If subject to corrosive vapors.

(4) In storage battery rooms.

Track Lighting - Circuit Rating
410.151(B)

The feeder or service load calculations, based on 220.43(B), don't limit the number of feet of track on a single branch circuit or the number of luminaires on an individual track.

Copyright 2014, www.MikeHolt.com

Figure 410–38

(5) In any hazardous location.

(6) If concealed.

(7) If extended through walls, partitions, or floors.

(8) Less than 5 ft above the finished floor, except where protected from physical damage or where the track operates below 30V open-circuit voltage.

(9) Within 3 ft horizontally and 8 ft vertically from the top of a bathtub rim or shower space [410.4(D)].

410.154 Fastening

Track lighting must be securely mounted to support the weight of the luminaires. A single track section 4 ft or shorter in length must have two supports, and, where installed in a continuous row, each individual track section of not more than 4 ft in length must have one additional support.

Figure 422–4

- Equipment fastened in place must not be rated more than 50 percent of the branch-circuit ampere rating, if the circuit supplies both luminaires and receptacles [210.23(A)(2)]. Figure 422–5

Figure 422–5

422.11 Overcurrent Protection

(A) Branch-Circuits. Branch-circuit conductors must have overcurrent protection in accordance with 240.4, and the overcurrent device rating must not exceed the rating marked on the appliance.

(E) Nonmotor Appliances. The appliance overcurrent device must:

(1) Not exceed the rating marked on the appliance.

(2) Not exceed 20A if the overcurrent device rating isn't marked, and the appliance is rated 13.30A or less, or

(3) Not exceed 150 percent of the appliance rated current if the overcurrent device rating isn't marked, and the appliance is rated over 13.30A. Where 150 percent of the appliance rating doesn't correspond to a standard overcurrent device ampere rating listed in 240.6(A), the next higher standard rating is permitted.

> **Question:** What's the maximum size overcurrent protection device for a 4,500W, 240V water heater? Figure 422–6
>
> (a) 20A   (b) 30A   (c) 40A   (d) 50A
>
> **Answer:** (b) 30A
>
> Protection Size = 4,500W/240V
> Protection Size = 18.75A x 1.50
> Protection Size = 28A, next size up, 30A [240.6(A)]

Figure 422–6

422.12 Central Heating Equipment (Furnaces)

An individual branch circuit must supply central heating equipment, such as gas, oil, or coal furnaces.

Author's Comment:

■ This rule isn't intended to apply to a listed wood-burning fireplace with a fan, since the fireplace isn't central heating equipment.

Ex 1: Auxiliary equipment to the central heating equipment, such as pumps, valves, humidifiers, and electrostatic air cleaners, can be connected to the central heater circuit.

Author's Comment:

■ Electric space-heating equipment must be installed in accordance with Article 424—Electric Space-Heating Equipment.

Ex 2: Permanently connected air-conditioning equipment can be connected to the individual branch circuit that supplies central heating equipment.

422.13 Storage Water Heaters

An electric water heater having a capacity of 120 gallons or less is considered a continuous load, for the purpose of sizing branch circuits.

Author's Comment:

■ Branch-circuit conductors must have a rating of at least 125 percent of the ampere rating of a continuous load [422.10] and the overcurrent protection is sized to 422.11(E)(3). Figure 422–7

422.15 Central Vacuums

(A) Circuit Loading. Central vacuum systems must be on a separate circuit if the rating of the equipment exceeds 50 percent of the ampere rating of the circuit [210.23(A)(2)].

Water Heater
Branch Circuit Conductor Sizing
422.13

Water Heater
4.50 kW, 240V

4,500/240V = 18.75A
18.75A x 1.25 = 23.40A [210.19(A)]
10 AWG rated 35A at 75°C
[Table 310.15(B)(16)]

A water heater with a capacity of 120 gallons or less is considered a continuous load for the purpose of sizing branch circuits.

Copyright 2014
www.MikeHolt.com

Figure 422–7

Author's Comment:

■ 210.23(A)(2) specifies that equipment fastened in place, other than luminaires, must not be rated more than 50 percent of the branch-circuit ampere rating if this circuit supplies both luminaires and receptacles. Due to this requirement, a separate 15A circuit is required for a central vacuum receptacle outlet if the rating of the central vacuum exceeds 7.50A. A separate 20A circuit is required for a central vacuum receptacle outlet if the rating of the central vacuum exceeds 10A, but not 16A [210.23(A)(2)]. Figure 422–8

Appliance - Central Vacuum Outlet
422.15(A)

A separate circuit isn't required for a central vacuum outlet if the rating of the equipment doesn't exceed 50% of the ampere rating of the circuit. See 210.23(A).

Copyright 2014
www.MikeHolt.com

Figure 422–8

422.16 Flexible Cords

(A) General. Flexible cords are permitted to:

(1) Facilitate frequent interchange, or to prevent the transmission of noise and vibration [400.7(A)(6) and 400.7(A)(7)].

(2) Facilitate the removal of appliances fastened in place, where the fastening means and mechanical connections are specifically designed to permit ready removal [400.8(A)(8)].

Author's Comment:

- Flexible cords must not be used for the connection of water heaters, furnaces, and other appliances fastened in place, unless the appliances are specifically identified to be used with a flexible cord.

(B) Specific Appliances.

(1) In-Sink Waste (Garbage) Disposals. A flexible cord is permitted for an in-sink waste disposal if:

(1) The cord has a grounding-type attachment plug.

(2) The cord length is at least 18 in. and no longer than 3 ft.

(3) The in-sink waste disposal receptacle is located to avoid damage to the cord.

(4) The in-sink waste disposal receptacle is accessible.

(2) Dishwashers and Trash Compactors. A cord is permitted for a dishwasher or trash compactor if:

(1) The cord has a grounding-type attachment plug.

(2) The cord length is at least 3 ft and not longer than 4 ft, measured from the rear plane of the appliance.

(3) The appliance receptacle is located to avoid damage to the cord.

(4) The receptacle is located in the space occupied by the appliance or in the space adjacent to the appliance.

(5) The receptacle is accessible.

Author's Comment:

- According to an article in the International Association of Electrical Inspectors magazine (IAEI News), a cord installed through a cabinet for an appliance isn't considered as being installed through a wall.

(3) Wall-Mounted Ovens and Counter-Mounted Cooking Units. Wall-mounted ovens and counter-mounted cooking units can be cord-and-plug-connected for ease in servicing for installation.

(4) Range Hoods. Range hoods can be cord-and-plug-connected if all of the following conditions are met: Figure 422–9

Figure 422–9

(1) The flexible cord terminates with a grounding-type attachment plug.

(2) The length of the cord must not be less than 18 in. or longer than 36 in.

(3) The range hood receptacle must be located to avoid physical damage to the flexible cord.

(4) The range hood receptacle must be accessible.

(5) The range hood receptacle must be supplied by an individual branch circuit.

Author's Comment:

- An above the range microwave that contains a fan listed as a range hood must comply with this section, if it's cord-and-plug-connected.

422.18 Support of Ceiling Paddle Fans

Ceiling paddle fans must be supported by a listed fan outlet box, or outlet box system, in accordance with 314.27(C). Figure 422–10

Figure 422–10

422.19 Space for Conductors

Canopies of ceiling-suspended (paddle) fans and their outlet boxes must comply with the free space requirements of 314.16. Figure 422–11

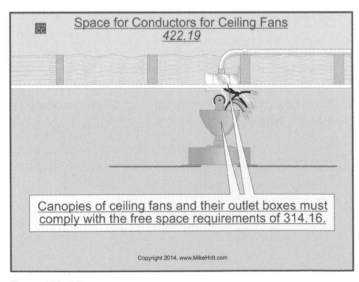

Figure 422–11

422.20 Outlet Boxes to Be Covered

In a completed installation, fan outlet boxes must have a cover unless covered by a ceiling-suspended (paddle) fan canopy. Figure 422–12

Figure 422–12

422.21 Covering of Combustible Material at Outlet Boxes

Any combustible ceiling finish exposed between the edge of a ceiling-suspended (paddle) fan canopy or fan and an outlet box must be covered with noncombustible material. Figure 422–13

422.23 Tire Inflation and Automotive Vacuum Machines

Tire inflation machines and automotive vacuum machines that are provided for public use must be GFCI protected. Figure 422–14

Figure 422–13

Figure 422–14

Part III. Disconnect

422.30 General

Each appliance must have a means that disconnects simultaneously all ungrounded circuit conductors.

422.31 Permanently Connected Appliance Disconnects

(A) Appliances Rated at Not Over 300 VA or 1/8 Horsepower. The branch-circuit overcurrent device, such as a plug fuse or circuit breaker, can serve as the appliance disconnect.

(B) Appliances Rated Over 300 VA. A switch or circuit breaker can serve as the disconnect means if it's located within sight of the appliance, or the switch or circuit breaker is lockable, as described in 110.25. Figure 422–15

Figure 422–15

Author's Comment:

- According to Article 100, within sight means that it's visible and not more than 50 ft from one to the other.

(C) Motor-Operated Appliances Rated Over 1/8 Horsepower. The disconnecting means must comply with 430.109 and 430.110, and meet (1) or (2):

(1) A switch or circuit breaker located within sight from the motor-operated appliance can serve as the appliance disconnect.

Ex: An appliance containing a unit switch that complies with 422.34.

422.33 Cord-and-Plug-Connected Appliance Disconnects

(A) Attachment Plugs and Receptacles. An accessible plug and receptacle can serve as the disconnecting means for a cord-and-plug-connected appliance. Figure 422–16

Figure 422–16

(B) Cord-and-Plug-Connected Ranges. The plug and receptacle of a cord-and-plug-connected household electric range can serve as the range disconnecting means, if the plug is accessible from the front of the range by the removal of a drawer. Figure 422–17

422.34 Unit Switches as Disconnects

A unit switch with a marked "off" position that's a part of the appliance can serve as the appliance disconnect, if it disconnects all ungrounded conductors. Figure 422–18

Figure 422–17

Figure 422–18

422.51 Vending Machines

(A) Cord-and-Plug-Connected. Cord-and-plug-connected vending machines must include a GFCI that's identified for portable use as an integral part of the attachment plug, or within 12 in. of the attachment plug. Older machines that aren't so equipped must be connected to a GFCI-protected outlet. Figure 422–19

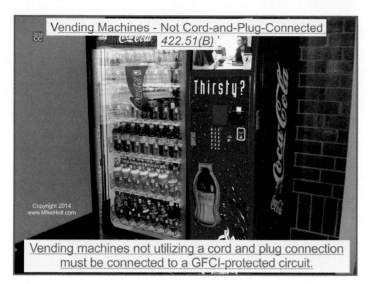

Figure 422–19

(B) Other than Cord-and–Plug-Connected. Vending machines that aren't cord-and-plug-connected must be GFCI protected. Figure 422–20

Figure 422–20

Author's Comment:

■ Because electric vending machines are often located in damp or wet locations in public places, and are used by people standing on the ground, reliance on an equipment grounding conductor for protection against electrocution is insufficient.

422.52 Electric Drinking Fountains

Electric drinking fountains must be GFCI protected. Figure 422–21

Figure 422–21

Notes

ARTICLE 424

FIXED ELECTRIC SPACE-HEATING EQUIPMENT

Introduction to Article 424—Fixed Electric Space-Heating Equipment

Many people are surprised to see how many pages Article 424 has. This is a nine-part article on fixed electric space heaters. Why so much text for what seems to be a simple application? The answer is that Article 424 covers a variety of applications—heaters come in various configurations for various uses. Not all of these parts are for the electrician in the field—the requirements in Part IV are for manufacturers.

Fixed space heaters (wall-mounted, ceiling-mounted, or free-standing) are common in many utility buildings and other small structures, as well as in some larger structures. When used to heat floors, space-heating cables address the thermal layering problem typical of forced-air systems—so it's likely you'll encounter them. Duct heaters are very common in large office and educational buildings. These provide a distributed heating scheme. Locating the heater in the ductwork, but close to the occupied space, eliminates the waste of transporting heated air through sheet metal routed in unheated spaces, so it's likely you'll encounter those as well.

Part I. General

424.1 Scope

Article 424 contains the installation requirements for fixed electrical equipment used for space heating, such as heating cables, unit heaters, boilers, or central systems.

Author's Comment:

- Wiring for fossil-fuel heating equipment, such as gas, oil, or coal central furnaces, must be installed in accordance with Article 422, specifically 422.12.

424.3 Branch Circuits

(B) Branch-Circuit Sizing. For the purpose of sizing branch-circuit conductors, fixed electric space-heating equipment and motor(s) are to be considered a continuous load.

Author's Comment:

- The branch-circuit conductors and overcurrent devices for fixed electric space-heating equipment must have an ampacity not less than 125 percent of the total heating load [210.19(A)(1) and 210.20(A)].

Question: *What size conductor and overcurrent device are required for a 9.60 kW, 240V fixed electric space heater that has a 3A blower motor with 75°C terminals?* Figure 424–1

(a) 10 AWG, 30A   (b) 8 AWG, 40A
(c) 6 AWG, 60A   (d) 4 AWG, 80A

Answer: *(c) 6 AWG, 60A*

Step 1: *Determine the total load:*

$$I = VA/E$$

I = 9,6000 VA/240V
I = 40A + 3A = 43A

(continued)

Step 2: *Size the conductors at 125 percent of the total current load [110.14(C)(1), 210.19(A)(1), and Table 310.15(B)(16)]:*

Conductor = 43A x 1.25

Conductor = 53.75A, 6 AWG, rated 65A at 75°C

Step 3: *Size the overcurrent device at 125 percent of the total current load [210.20(A), 240.4(B), and 240.6(A)]:*

Overcurrent Protection = 43A x 1.25

Overcurrent Protection = 53.75A, next size up is 60A

Branch-Circuit Sizing for
Fixed Electric Space-Heating Equipment and Motors
424.3(B)

6 AWG Rated
65A at 75°C,
Tbl 310.15(B)(16)

60A Protection
[240.6(A)]

Copyright 2014, www.MikeHolt.com

Heat 9.6 kW,
Blower 3A,
240V

40A + 3A = 43A x 1.25 = 53.75A

Fixed electric space heating is a continuous load. The branch-circuit conductors and overcurrent device must be sized no smaller than 125% of the total load (heat & motor).

Figure 424–1

424.9 Permanently Installed Electric Baseboard Heaters with Receptacles

If a permanently installed electric baseboard heater has factory-installed receptacle outlets, the receptacles must not be connected to the heater circuits.

Note: Listed baseboard heaters include instructions that prohibit their installation below receptacle outlets.

Part III. Electric Space-Heating Equipment

424.19 Disconnecting Means

Means must be provided to simultaneously disconnect the heater, motor controller, and supplementary overcurrent devices of all fixed electric space-heating equipment from all ungrounded conductors.

The disconnecting means must be capable of being locked in the open position. The provision for locking or adding a lock to the disconnecting means must be on the switch or circuit breaker, and it must remain in place with or without the lock installed. Figure 424–2

Electric Heat - Disconnect
424.19

When the disconnect isn't within sight from equipment, it must be capable of being locked in the open position. The locking means must remain in place with or without the lock installed.

Copyright 2014
www.MikeHolt.com

Figure 424–2

(A) Heating Equipment with Supplementary Overcurrent Protection. The disconnecting means for fixed electric space-heating equipment with supplementary overcurrent protection must be within sight from the supplementary overcurrent devices.

Author's Comment:

■ According to Article 100, within sight means that it's visible and not more than 50 ft from one to the other.

(2) The disconnecting means for fixed electric space-heating equipment with a motor(s) rated more than ⅛ horsepower and a single unit switch can have a disconnecting means that isn't within sight from the equipment. That disconnect must be capable of being locked in the open position, and the locking means must remain in place with or without the lock installed. Figure 424–3

Figure 424–3

Figure 424–4

Author's Comment:

- According to Article 100, within sight means that it's visible and not more than 50 ft from one to the other.

(B) Heating Equipment Without Supplementary Overcurrent Protection. For fixed electric space-heating equipment, the branch-circuit circuit breaker is permitted to serve as the disconnecting means if the circuit breaker is within sight from the heater or it's capable of being locked in the open position.

(C) Unit Switch as Disconnect. A unit switch with a marked "off" position that's an integral part of the equipment can serve as the heater disconnecting means, if it disconnects all ungrounded conductors of the circuit. Figure 424–4

Part V. Electric Space-Heating Cables

424.36 Clearances of Wiring in Ceilings

Wiring located above heated ceilings must be spaced not less than 2 in. above the heated ceiling and is considered as operating at an ambient temperature of 50°C.

424.38 Area Restrictions

(A) Must not Extend Beyond the Room or Area. Heating cables must not extend beyond the room or area in which they originate.

(B) Uses Prohibited. Heating cables must not be installed:

(1) In closets.

(2) Over walls.

(3) Over partitions that extend to the ceiling.

424.39 Clearance from Other Objects and Openings

Heating elements of cables must be separated at least 8 in. from the edge of outlet boxes and junction boxes used for mounting surface luminaires and 2 in. from recessed luminaires and their trims.

424.44 Installation of Cables in Concrete or Poured Masonry Floors

(G) GFCI Protection. GFCI protection is required for electric space-heating cables that are embedded in concrete or poured masonry floors of bathrooms, kitchens, and hydromassage bathtub locations. Figure 424–5

Author's Comment:

- See 680.27(C)(3) for restrictions on the installation of radiant-heating cables for spas and hot tubs installed outdoors.

Figure 424–5

Figure 424–6

Part VI. Duct Heaters

424.65 Disconnect for Electric Duct Heater Controllers

Means must be provided to disconnect the heater, motor controller, and supplementary overcurrent devices from all ungrounded conductors of the circuit. The disconnecting means must be within sight from the equipment, or it must be capable of being locked in the open position [424.19(A)]. The provision for locking or adding a lock to the disconnecting means must be on the switch or circuit breaker, and must remain in place with or without the lock installed. A portable locking means doesn't meet the "locked in the open position" requirement. Figure 424–6

Author's Comment:

- The disconnecting means for a duct heater isn't required to be readily accessible. Therefore, it can be located within a suspended ceiling area adjacent to the duct heater as long as it's accessible by portable means [240.24(A)(4) and 404.8(A) Ex 2].

424.66 Installation

(B) Limited Access. Where a duct heater is located above a suspended ceiling, all of the following must apply:

(1) The duct heater must be accessible through the lay-in type ceiling or access panel(s).

(2) The width of the working space for the duct heater must be no less than 30 in.

(3) Doors or hinged panels must open at least 90 degrees.

(4) The space in front of the duct heater must comply with Table 110.26(A)(1), yet a horizontal ceiling T-bar can be in this space.

ARTICLE
430

MOTORS, MOTOR CIRCUITS, AND CONTROLLERS

Introduction to Article 430—Motors, Motor Circuits, and Controllers

Article 430 contains the specific rules for conductor sizing, overcurrent protection, control circuit conductors, controllers, and disconnecting means for electric motors. The installation requirements for motor control centers are covered in Part VIII, and air-conditioning and refrigeration equipment are covered in Article 440.

Article 430 is one of the longest articles in the *NEC*. It's also one of the most complex, but motors are also complex equipment. They're electrical and mechanical devices, but what makes motor applications complex is the fact that they're inductive loads with a high-current demand at start-up that's typically six, or more, times the running current. This makes overcurrent protection for motor applications necessarily different from the protection employed for other types of equipment. So don't confuse general overcurrent protection with motor protection—you must calculate and apply them differently using the rules in Article 430.

You might be uncomfortable with the allowances for overcurrent protection found in this article, such as protecting a 10 AWG conductor with a 60A overcurrent protection device, but as you learn to understand how motor protection works, you'll understand why these allowances aren't only safe, but necessary.

Part I. General

430.1 Scope

Article 430 covers motors, motor branch-circuit and feeder conductors and their protection, motor overload protection, motor control circuits, motor controllers, and motor control centers. This article is divided into many parts, the most important being: Figure 430–1

- General—Part I
- Conductor Size—Part II
- Overload Protection—Part III
- Branch Circuit Short-Circuit and Ground-Fault Protection—Part IV
- Feeder Short-Circuit and Ground-Fault Protection—Part V
- Motor Control Circuits—Part VI
- Motor Controllers—Part VII
- Motor Control Centers—Part VIII
- Disconnecting Means—Part IX

Figure 430–1

Note 1: Article 440 contains the installation requirements for electrically driven air-conditioning and refrigeration equipment [440.1]. Also see 110.26(E) for dedicated space requirements for motor control centers.

430.2 Definitions

Controller. A switch or device used to start and stop a motor by making and breaking the motor circuit current. Figure 430–2

Figure 430–2

Author's Comment:

■ A controller can be a horsepower-rated switch, snap switch, or circuit breaker. A pushbutton that operates an electromechanical relay isn't a controller because it doesn't meet the controller rating requirements of 430.83. Devices such as start-stop stations and pressure switches are control devices, not motor controllers. Figure 430–3

■ Controllers discussed in Article 430 are those that meet this definition, not the definition of "Controller" in Article 100.

430.6 Table FLC versus Motor Nameplate Current Rating

(A) General Requirements. Figure 430–4

Figure 430–3

These devices often control the coil of a motor starter but they usually don't carry all of the current of the motor branch circuit.

Figure 430–4

(1) Table Full-Load Current (FLC). The motor full-load current ratings listed in Tables 430.247, 430.248, and 430.250 are used to determine the conductor ampacity [430.22], the branch-circuit short-circuit and ground-fault overcurrent device size [430.52 and 430.62], and the ampere rating of disconnecting switches [430.110].

Author's Comment:

■ The actual current rating on the motor nameplate full-load amperes (FLA) [430.6(A)(2)] isn't permitted to be used to determine the conductor ampacity, the branch-circuit short-circuit and ground-fault overcurrent device size, nor the ampere rating of disconnecting switches.

Motors built to operate at less than 1,200 RPM or that have high torques may have higher full-load currents, and multispeed motors have full-load current varying with speed, in which case the nameplate current ratings must be used.

Ex 3: For a listed motor-operated appliance, the actual current marked on the nameplate of the appliance must be used instead of the horse-power rating on the appliance nameplate to determine the ampacity or rating of the disconnecting means, the branch-circuit conductors, the controller, and the branch-circuit short-circuit and ground-fault protection.

(2) Motor Nameplate Current Rating (FLA). Overload devices must be sized based on the motor nameplate current rating in accordance with 430.31.

Author's Comment:

- The motor nameplate full-load ampere rating is identified as full-load amperes (FLA). The FLA rating is the current in amperes the motor draws while producing its rated horse-power load at its rated voltage, based on its rated efficiency and power factor. Figure 430–5

Figure 430–5

The actual current drawn by the motor depends upon the load on the motor and on the actual operating voltage at the motor terminals. That is, if the load increases, the current also increases, or if the motor operates at a voltage below its nameplate rating, the operating current will increase.

⚠️ **CAUTION:** *To prevent damage to motor windings from excessive heat (caused by excessive current), never load a motor above its horsepower rating, and be sure the voltage source matches the motor's voltage rating.*

430.8 Marking on Controllers

A controller must be marked with the manufacturer's name or identification, the voltage, the current or horsepower rating, the short-circuit current rating, and other necessary data to properly indicate the applications for which it's suitable.

Ex 1: The short-circuit current rating isn't required for controllers applied in accordance with 430.81(A), 430.81(B), or 430.83(C).

Ex 2: The short-circuit rating isn't required on the controller when the short-circuit current rating of the controller is marked elsewhere on the assembly.

Ex 3: The short-circuit rating isn't required on the controller when the assembly into which it's installed has a marked short-circuit current rating.

Ex 4: A short-circuit rating isn't required on controllers rated less than 2 hp at 300V or less, if they're listed for use on general-purpose branch circuits.

430.9 Motor Controller Terminal Requirements

(B) Copper Conductors. Motor controllers and terminals of control circuit devices must be connected with copper conductors.

(C) Torque Requirements. Motor control conductors 14 AWG and smaller must be torqued at a minimum of 7 lb-in. for screw-type pressure terminals, unless identified otherwise. See 110.3(B) and 110.14 Note.

430.14 Location of Motors

(A) Ventilation and Maintenance. Motors must be located so adequate ventilation is provided and maintenance can be readily accomplished.

430.17 The Highest Rated Motor

When sizing motor circuit conductors, the highest rated motor is the motor with the highest rated full-load current rating (FLC).

Question: *Which of the following motors has the highest FLC rating?* Figure 430–6

(a) 10 hp, three-phase, 208V   (b) 5 hp, single-phase, 208V

(c) 3 hp, single-phase, 120V   (d) none of these

Answer: *(c) 3 hp, single-phase, 120V*

10 hp = 30.80A [Table 430.250]
5 hp = 30.80A [Table 430.248]
3 hp = 34.00A [Table 430.248]

Figure 430–6

Part II. Conductor Size

430.22 Single Motor Conductor Size

Conductors to a single motor must be sized not less than 125 percent of the motor FLC rating as listed in Table 430.247 Direct-Current Motors, Table 430.248 Single-Phase Motors, or Table 430.250 Three-Phase Motors. Figure 430–7

Figure 430–7

Question: *What size branch-circuit conductor is required for a 7½ hp, 230V, three-phase motor with 75°C terminals?* Figure 430–8

(a) 14 AWG   (b) 12 AWG   (c) 10 AWG   (d) 8 AWG

Answer: *(c) 10 AWG*

Motor FLC = 22A [Table 430.250]

Conductor's Size = 22A x 1.25
Conductor's Size = 27.50A, 10 AWG, rated 35A at 75°C
[Table 310.15(B)(16)]

Note: The branch-circuit short-circuit and ground-fault protection device using an inverse time breaker is sized at 60A according to 430.52(C)(1) Ex 1:

Circuit Protection = 22A x 2.50
Circuit Protection = 55A, next size up 60A [240.6(A)]

Figure 430–8

430.24 Several Motors—Conductor Size

Circuit conductors that supply several motors must not be sized smaller than the sum of the following:

(1) 125 percent of the full-load current of the highest rated motor

(2) The full-load current ratings of other motors

Question: What size feeder conductor is required for two 7½ hp, 230V, three-phase motors, if the terminals are rated for 75°C? Figure 430–9

(a) 14 AWG   (b) 12 AWG   (c) 10 AWG   (d) 8 AWG

Answer: (d) 8 AWG

Motor FLC = 22A [Table 430.250]

Motor Feeder Conductor = (22A x 1.25) + 22A
Motor Feeder Conductor = 49.50A, 8 AWG rated 50A at 75°C
 [Table 310.15(B)(16)]

Author's Comment:

■ The feeder overcurrent device (inverse time circuit breaker) must comply with 430.62 as follows:

(continued)

Step 1: Determine the largest branch-circuit overcurrent device rating [240.6(A) and 430.52(C)(1) Ex 1]:

22A x 2.50 = 55A, next size up 60A

Step 2: Size the feeder overcurrent device in accordance with 240.6(A) and 430.62:

Feeder Inverse Time Breaker: 60A + 22A = 82A, next size down, 80A

Author's Comment:

■ The "next size up protection" rule for branch circuits [430.52(C)(1) Ex 1] doesn't apply to motor feeder short-circuit and ground-fault protection device sizing.

Figure 430–9

430.28 Motor Feeder Taps

Motor circuit conductors tapped from a feeder must have an ampacity in accordance with 430.22, and the tap conductors must terminate in a branch-circuit short-circuit and ground-fault protection device sized in accordance with 430.52. In addition, one of the following requirements must be met:

(1) 10 ft Tap. Tap conductors not over 10 ft long must have an ampacity not less than one-tenth the rating of the feeder protection device.

---

(2) 25 ft Tap. Tap conductors over 10 ft, but not over 25 ft, must have an ampacity not less than one-third the ampacity of the feeder conductor.

(3) Ampacity. Tap conductors must have an ampacity not less than the feeder conductors.

Part III. Overload Protection

Part III contains the requirements for overload devices. Overload devices are intended to protect motors, motor control equipment, and motor branch-circuit conductors against excessive heating due to motor overloads and failure to start.

Overload is the operation of equipment in excess of the normal, full-load current rating, which, if it persists for a sufficient amount of time, will cause damage or dangerous overheating of the equipment.

Author's Comment:

- Article 100 defines overcurrent as "current in excess of the rated current of equipment or the ampacity of a conductor from an overload, a short circuit, or a ground fault." Because of the difference between starting and running current, the overcurrent protection for motors is generally accomplished by having the overload device separate from the motor's short-circuit and ground-fault protection device (Article 430 Part IV). Figure 430–10

Figure 430–10

430.31 Overload

Overload devices (sometimes called "heaters") are intended to provide overload protection, and come in a variety of configurations; they can be conventional or electronic. In addition, a fuse sized in accordance with 430.32 can be used for circuit overload protection [430.55]. Figure 430–11

Figure 430–11

Note 2: An overload is a condition where equipment is operated above its current rating, or where current is in excess of the conductor ampacity. When an overload condition persists for a sufficient length of time, it could result in equipment failure or a fire from damaging or dangerous overheating. A fault, such as a short circuit or ground fault, isn't an overload [Article 100]. Figure 430–12

Author's Comment:

- Motor overload protection sizing is usually accomplished by installing the correct "heater" or setting the overload device in accordance with the controller's instructions, based on the motor nameplate current rating.

- The intended level of protection required in Article 430 Part III is for overload and failure-to-start protection only, in order to protect against the motor becoming a fire hazard.

Overload protection isn't required if it might introduce additional or increased hazards, as in the case of fire pumps.

Overload Types
430.31

Magnetic Contactor (Starter)

Overload Relay

Heaters

Solid State Overload

Fuses and breakers can provide overload protection [430.55].

Copyright 2014, www.MikeHolt.com

Overloads protect the motor, conductors, and associated equipment from excessive heat due to motor overloads. They're not intended to protect against short circuits and ground faults.

Figure 430–12

Note: See 695.7 for the protection requirements for fire pump supply conductors.

Overload Protection
430.32(A)(1)

A service factor of 1.15 means the motor is designed to operate periodically at up to 115 percent of its rated horsepower without damage to the motor.

Copyright 2014, www.MikeHolt.com

Figure 430–13

430.32 Overload Sizing for Continuous-Duty Motors

(A) Motors Rated More Than One Horsepower. Motors rated more than 1 hp, used in a continuous-duty application without integral thermal protection, must have an overload device sized as follows:

(1) Separate Overload Device. A separate overload device must be selected to open at no more than the following percent of the motor nameplate full-load current rating:

Service Factor. Motors with a marked service factor (SF) of 1.15 or more on the nameplate must have the overload device sized no more than 125 percent of the motor nameplate current rating. Figures 430–13 and 430–14

Author's Comment:

- Motor service factors are safety factors; they indicate how much the motor capacity can be exceeded for short periods without overheating. For example a motor with a service factor of 1.15 can operate at 15% greater than its rated output without overheating. This is important for motors where loads vary and may peak slightly above the rated torque.

Sizing Overload Protection
430.32(A)(1)

35A DE Fuses

Copyright 2014 www.MikeHolt.com

Nameplate value [430.6(A)(2)]
28 FLA x 1.25 = 35A [240.6(A)]

Figure 430–14

Temperature Rise. Motors with a nameplate temperature rise of 40°C or less must have the overload device sized no more than 125 percent of the motor nameplate current rating. Figures 430–15 and 430–16

Author's Comment:

- A motor with a nameplate temperature rise of 40°C means the motor is designed to operate so that it won't heat up more than 40°C above its rated ambient temperature when operated at its rated load and voltage. Studies have shown that when the operating temperature of a motor is increased 10°C above its rating, the motor winding insulating material's anticipated life is reduced by 50 percent.

Figure 430–15

Figure 430–17

Figure 430–16

All Other Motors. No more than 115 percent of the motor "nameplate current rating." Figure 430–17

430.36 Use of Fuses for Overload Protection

If fuses are used for overload protection, one must be provided for each ungrounded conductor of the circuit.

Author's Comment:

■ If remote control isn't required for a motor, considerable savings can be achieved by using dual-element fuses (eliminate a motor controller) sized in accordance with 430.32 to protect the motor and the circuit conductors against overcurrent, which includes overload, short circuit, and ground faults. See 430.55 for more information.

430.37 Number of Overload Devices

An overload device must be installed in the ungrounded conductor(s) in accordance with Table 430.37. Figure 430–18

Part IV. Branch-Circuit Short-Circuit and Ground-Fault Protection

430.51 General

A branch-circuit short-circuit and ground-fault protective device protects the motor, the motor control equipment, and the conductors against short circuits or ground faults, but not against overload. Figure 430–19

Number of Overload Devices
430.37

2 Ungrounded Conductors, 1 Heater

3 Ungrounded Conductors, 3 Heaters

Blank

Copyright 2014 www.MikeHolt.com

An overload device must be installed in the ungrounded conductor(s) in accordance with Table 430.37.

Figure 430–18

Starting versus Running Current

Starting Current
Peak
RMS

LRC

Full Load Current (Running Current)
Peak
RMS

Overload protection is sized between 115% and 125% of the nameplate running current rating.

Short-circuit and ground-fault protection is sized between 150% and 300% of the motor FLC.

Copyright 2014 www.MikeHolt.com

Figure 430–20

Short-Circuit and Ground-Fault Protection
430.51

Short-circuit and ground-fault protection is sized between 150% and 300% of the motor FLC [430.52].

Short-circuit or ground-fault protection is designed for:
• Fast current rise
• Short duration
• Fast response time

Overload protection (OL) is designed for:
• Slow current rise
• Long duration
• Slow response time

A

24 Amps

16A FLA

B

1200 Amps

Copyright 2014, www.MikeHolt.com

Figure 430–19

Author's Comment:

■ Overload protection must comply with the requirements contained in 430.32.

Motor-Starting Current. When voltage is first applied to the field winding of an induction motor, only the conductor resistance opposes the flow of current through the motor winding. Because the conductor resistance is so low, the motor will have a very large inrush current. Figure 430–20

Motor-Running Current. Once the rotor reaches rated speed the starting current reduces to running current due to the counter-electromotive force (CEMF). See Figure 430–20

Motor Locked-Rotor Current (LRC). If the rotating part of the motor winding (armature) becomes jammed so it can't rotate, no counter-electromotive force (CEMF) will be produced in the motor winding. This results in a decrease in conductor impedance to the point that it's effectively a short circuit. Result—the motor operates at locked-rotor current (LRC), often six times the full-load ampere rating, depending on the motor *Code* letter rating [430.7(B)], and this'll cause the motor winding to overheat and be destroyed if the current isn't quickly reduced or removed.

Author's Comment:

■ The *National Electrical Code* requires that most motors be provided with overcurrent protection to prevent damage to the motor winding because of locked-rotor current.

430.52 Branch-Circuit Short-Circuit and Ground-Fault Protection

(A) General. The motor branch-circuit short-circuit and ground-fault protective device must comply with 430.52(B) and 430.52(C).

(B) All Motors. A motor branch-circuit short-circuit and ground-fault protective device must be capable of carrying the motor's starting current.

(C) Rating or Setting.

(1) Table 430.52. Each motor branch circuit must be protected against short circuit and ground faults by a protective device sized no greater than the following percentages listed in Table 430.52.

Table 430.52

Motor Type	Nontime Delay	Dual-Element Fuse	Inverse Time Breaker
Wound Rotor	150%	150%	150%
Direct Current	150%	150%	150%
All Other Motors	300%	175%	250%

Question: What size conductor and inverse time circuit breaker are required for a 2 hp, 230V, single-phase motor with 75°C terminals? Figure 430–21

(a) 14 AWG, 30A breaker
(b) 14 AWG, 35A breaker
(c) 14 AWG, 40A breaker
(d) 14 AWG, 45A breaker

Answer: (a) 14 AWG, 30A breaker

Step 1: Determine the branch-circuit conductor [Table 310.15(B)(16), 430.22, and Table 430.248]:

12A x 1.25 = 15A, 14 AWG, rated 20A at 75°C [Table 310.15(B)(16)]

Step 2: Determine the branch-circuit protection [240.6(A), 430.52(C)(1), and Table 430.248]:

12A x 2.50 = 30A

Author's Comment:

- I know it bothers many in the electrical industry to see a 14 AWG conductor protected by a 30A circuit breaker, but branch-circuit conductors are protected against overloads by the overload device, which is sized between 115 and 125 percent of the motor nameplate current rating [430.32]. The small conductor rule contained in 240.4(D) which limits 15A protection for 14 AWG doesn't apply to motor circuit protection. See 240.4(D) and 240.4(G).

Figure 430–21

Ex 1: If the motor short-circuit and ground-fault protective device values derived from Table 430.52 don't correspond with the standard overcurrent device ratings listed in 240.6(A), the next higher overcurrent device rating can be used. Figure 430–22

Figure 430–22

Question: *What size conductor and inverse time circuit breaker are required for a 7½ hp, 230V, three-phase motor with 75°C terminals?* Figure 430–23

(a) 10 AWG, 50A breaker   *(b) 10 AWG, 60A breaker*
(c) a or b   *(d) none of these*

Answer: *(b) 10 AWG, 60A breaker*

Step 1: *Determine the branch-circuit conductor [Table 310.15(B)(16), 430.22, and Table 430.250]:*

22A x 1.25 = 27.50A, 10 AWG, rated 35A at 75°C [Table 310.15(B)(16)]

Step 2: *Determine the branch-circuit protection [240.6(A), 430.52(C)(1) Ex 1, and Table 430.250]:*

22A x 2.50 = 55A, next size up = 60A

430.55 Single Overcurrent Device

A motor can be protected against overload, short circuit, and ground fault by a single overcurrent device sized to the overload requirements contained in 430.32.

Question: *What size dual-element fuse is permitted to protect a 5 hp, 230V, single-phase motor with a service factor of 1.15 and a nameplate current rating of 28A?* Figure 430–24

(a) 20A   *(b) 25A*   *(c) 30A*   *(d) 35A*

Answer: *(d) 35A*

Overload Protection [430.32(A)(1)]
28A x 1.25 = 35A

Motor Branch-Circuit Short-Circuit Ground-Fault Protection
430.52(C)(1) Ex 1

60A Inverse Time Breaker

10 AWG Rated
35A at 75°C
[Tbl 310.15(B)(16)]

Protection Size:
FLC x 250%
22A x 2.50 = 55A
Next size up, 60A
[240.6(A)]

7½ hp,
230V, 3-Ph
22A FLC

Copyright 2014
www.MikeHolt.com

Where the value determined from Table 430.52 doesn't correspond with a standard device rating, the next size up overcurrent device can be used.

Figure 430–23

Single Protective Device
430.55

35A Fuse

Mike's Motors
SERIAL NO. A61234   FRAME OPEN
SF 1.15
PHASE 1   VOLTS 230   FLA 28.0
CYCLE 60   RPM 1725   °C RISE 40
DUTY CONT   HP 5   CODE LETTER D   TYPE ML
THERMAL PROTECTION NO   IMPEDANCE PROTECTION NO

Overload Protection Size [430.32]
Nameplate Amperes x 125%
28A x 1.25 = 35A

5 hp, 230V, SF 1.15,
28A Nameplate

Copyright 2014
www.MikeHolt.com

A motor can be protected against overload, short circuit, and ground faults by a single overcurrent device sized in accordance with the overload rules of 430.32.

Figure 430–24

Part V. Feeder Short-Circuit and Ground-Fault Protection

430.62 Feeder Protection

(A) Motors Only. Feeder conductors must be protected against short circuits and ground faults by a protective device sized not more than the largest rating of the branch-circuit short-circuit and ground-fault protective device for any motor, plus the sum of the full-load currents of the other motors in the group.

Question: What size feeder protection (inverse time breakers with 75°C terminals) and conductors are required for the following two motors? Figure 430–25

Motor 1—20 hp, 460V, three-phase = 27A FLC [Table 430.250]
Motor 2—10 hp, 460V, three-phase = 14A FLC

(a) 8 AWG, 70A breaker   *(b) 8 AWG, 80A breaker*
(c) 8 AWG, 90A breaker   *(d) 10 AWG, 90A breaker*

Answer: (b) 8 AWG, 80A breaker

Step 1: Determine the feeder conductor size [430.24]:

   (27A x 1.25) + 14A = 48A

   8 AWG rated 50A at 75°C [110.14(C)(1) and
   Table 310.15(B)(16)]

Step 2: Feeder protection [430.62(A)] isn't greater than the largest branch-circuit ground-fault and short-circuit protective device plus the other motor FLC.

Step 3: Determine the largest branch-circuit ground-fault and short-circuit protective device [430.52(C)(1) Ex]:

   20 hp Motor = 27A x 2.50 = 68, next size up = 70A
   10 hp Motor = 14A x 2.50 = 35A

Step 4: Determine the size feeder protection:

   Not more than 70A + 14A, = 84A,
   next size down = 80A [240.6(A)]

Author's Comment:

■ The "next size up protection" rule for branch circuits [430.52(C)(1) Ex 1] doesn't apply to a motor feeder protection device rating.

Figure 430–25

Part VI. Motor Control Circuits

430.72 Overcurrent Protection for Control Circuits

(A) Class 1 Control Conductors. Motor control conductors that aren't tapped from the branch-circuit protective device are classified as a Class 1 remote-control circuit, and they must have overcurrent protection in accordance with 725.43.

Author's Comment:

■ Section 725.43 states that overcurrent protection for conductors 14 AWG and larger must comply with the conductor ampacity from Table 310.15(B)(16). Overcurrent protection for 18 AWG must not exceed 7A, and a 10A device must protect 16 AWG conductors. Figure 430–26

(B) Motor Control Conductors.

(2) Branch-Circuit Overcurrent Device. Motor control circuit conductors tapped from the motor branch-circuit protection device that extends beyond the tap enclosure must have overcurrent protection as follows:

Overcurrent protection for 14 AWG and larger is according to conductor ampacity without applying ampacity adjustment and correction. The maximum for 18 AWG is 7A and the maximum for 16 AWG is 10A.

Figure 430–26

Conductor Size	Overcurrent Protection
18 AWG	7A
16 AWG	10A
14 AWG	45A
12 AWG	60A
10 AWG	90A

Author's Comment:

- The above limitations don't apply to the internal wiring of industrial control panels listed in UL *508 Standard for Practical Application Guidelines.*

(C) Control Circuit Transformer Protection. Transformers for motor control circuit conductors must have overcurrent protection on the primary side in accordance with 430.72(C)(1) through (6).

Author's Comment:

- Many control transformers have small iron cores, which result in very high inrush (excitation) current when the coil is energized. This high inrush current can cause standard fuses to blow, so you should only use the fuses recommended by the control transformer manufacturer.

430.73 Protection of Conductors from Physical Damage

If physical damage would result in a hazard, the conductors of a remote motor control circuit installed outside the control device must be protected by installing the conductors in a raceway or be protected from physical damage.

430.75 Disconnect for Control Circuits

(A) Control Circuit Disconnect. Motor control circuit conductors must have a disconnecting means that simultaneously opens all sources of supply when the disconnecting means is in the open position. If the control circuit conductors are tapped from the controller disconnect, the controller disconnecting means can serve as the disconnecting means for the control circuit conductors [430.102(A)].

If the control circuit conductors aren't tapped from the controller disconnect, a separate disconnecting means is required for the control circuit conductors, and it must be located adjacent to the controller disconnect. Figure 430–27

Figure 430–27

Part VII. Motor Controllers

430.83 Controller Rating

(A) General. The controller must have one of the following ratings:

(1) Horsepower Rating. Controllers, other than circuit breakers and molded case switches, must have a horsepower rating not less than that of the motor.

(2) Circuit Breakers. A circuit breaker can serve as a motor controller [430.111].

> **Author's Comment:**
>
> ■ Circuit breakers aren't required to be horsepower rated.

(3) Molded Case Switch. A molded case switch, rated in amperes, can serve as a motor controller.

> **Author's Comment:**
>
> ■ A molded case switch isn't required to be horsepower rated.

(C) Stationary Motors of Two Horsepower or Less. For stationary motors rated at 2 hp or less, the controller can be:

(2) General-Use Snap Switch. A general-use alternating-current snap switch, where the motor full-load current rating isn't more than 80 percent of the ampere rating of the switch. Figure 430–28

Figure 430–28

> **Author's Comment:**
>
> ■ A general-use snap switch is a general-use switch constructed for installation in device boxes or on box covers [Article 100].

430.84 Need Not Open All Conductors of the Circuit

The motor controller can open only as many conductors of the circuit as necessary to start and stop the motor.

> **Author's Comment:**
>
> ■ The controller is only required to start and stop the motor; it isn't a disconnecting means. See the disconnecting means requirement in 430.103 for more information.

430.87 Controller for Each Motor

Each motor must have its own individual controller.

Part IX. Disconnecting Means

430.102 Disconnect Requirement

(A) Controller Disconnect. A disconnecting means is required for each motor controller, and it must be located within sight from the controller. Figures 430–29 and 430–30

> **Author's Comment:**
>
> ■ According to Article 100, within sight means that it's visible and not more than 50 ft from one to the other.

(B) Motor Disconnect. A motor disconnect must be provided in accordance with (B)(1) or (B)(2). Figure 430–31

(1) Separate Motor Disconnect. A disconnecting means is required for each motor, and it must be located in sight from the motor location and the driven machinery location.

Figure 430–29

Figure 430–31

Figure 430–30

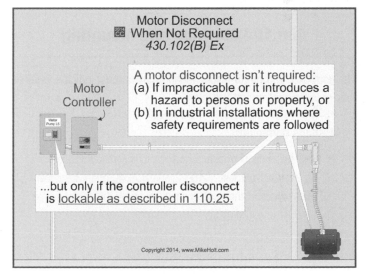

Figure 430–32

(2) Controller Disconnect. The controller disconnecting means [430.102(A)] can serve as the disconnecting means for the motor, if the disconnect is located in sight from the motor location.

Ex to (1) and (2): A motor disconnecting means isn't required under either condition (a) or (b), if the controller disconnecting means [430.102(A)] is lockable, as described in 110.25. Figure 430–32

(a) If locating the disconnecting means is impracticable or introduces additional or increased hazards to persons or property.

(b) In industrial installations, with written safety procedures, where conditions of maintenance and supervision ensure only qualified persons will service the equipment.

Note 2: For information on lockout/tagout procedures, see NFPA 70E, *Standard for Electrical Safety in the Workplace.*

430.103 Operation of Disconnect

The disconnecting means for the motor controller and the motor must open all ungrounded supply conductors simultaneously, and it must be designed so that it won't close automatically. Figure 430–33

Figure 430–33

Figure 430–34

430.104 Marking and Mounting

The controller and motor disconnecting means must indicate whether they're in the "on" or "off" position.

Author's Comment:

- The disconnecting means must be legibly marked to identify its intended purpose [110.22 and 408.4], and when operated vertically, the "up" position must be the "on" position [240.81 and 404.6(C)].

430.107 Readily Accessible

Either the controller disconnecting means or the motor disconnecting means required by 430.102 must be readily accessible. Figure 430–34

430.109 Disconnecting Means Rating

(A) General. The disconnecting means for the motor controller and/or the motor must be a:

(1) Motor-Circuit Switch. A listed horsepower-rated motor-circuit switch.

(2) Molded Case Circuit Breaker. A listed molded case circuit breaker.

(3) Molded Case Switch. A listed molded case switch.

(6) Manual Motor Controller. A listed manual motor controller marked "Suitable as Motor Disconnect."

(B) Stationary Motors of ⅛ Horsepower or Less. For stationary motors of ⅛ hp or less, the branch-circuit overcurrent device is permitted to serve as the disconnecting means.

(C) Stationary Motors of Two Horsepower or Less.

(2) General-Use Snap Switch. A general-use alternating-current snap switch, where the motor full-load current rating isn't more than 80 percent of the ampere rating of the switch. Figure 430–35

(F) Cord-and-Plug-Connected Motors. A horsepower-rated attachment plug and receptacle, flanged surface inlet and cord connector, or attachment plug cord connector having a horsepower rating not less than the motor rating can be used as the motor disconnecting means. Figure 430–36

430.111 Combination Controller and Disconnect

A horsepower-rated attachment plug and receptacle, flanged surface inlet and cord connector, or attachment plug cord connector can be used as the motor disconnecting means.

Switch as Motor Disconnecting Means
430.109(C)(2)

An ac snap switch is permitted as the disconnecting means.

2 hp
Sump
Pump

Copyright 2014
www.MikeHolt.com

A general-use ac snap switch is permitted as the motor disconnecting means for ac motors rated 2 hp or less and 300V or less [430.83(C)].

Figure 430–35

Table 430.248 FLC Single–Phase AC Motors				
	115V	200V	208V	230V
½ hp	9.80	5.60	5.40	4.90
¾ hp	13.80	7.90	7.60	6.90
1 hp	16.00	9.20	8.80	8.00
1½ hp	20.00	11.50	11.00	11.00
2 hp	24.00	13.90	13.20	12.00
3 hp	34.00	19.60	18.70	17.00
5 hp	56.00	32.20	30.80	28.00
7½ hp	80.00	46.00	44.00	40.00
10 hp	100.00	57.50	55.00	50.00

Cord-and-Plug-Connected Motors
430.109(F)

A horsepower-rated attachment plug and receptacle, flanged surface inlet and cord connector, or attachment plug cord connector can be used as the motor disconnecting means.

Copyright 2014, www.MikeHolt.com

Figure 430–36

Part XIV. Tables

Table 430.248 Full-Load Current, Single-Phase Motors

Table 430.248 lists the full-load current for single-phase alternating-current motors. These values are used to determine motor conductor sizing, ampere ratings of disconnects, controller rating, and branch-circuit and feeder protection, but not overload protection [430.6(A)(1) and 430.6(A)(2)].

Table 430.250 Full-Load Current, Three-Phase Motors

Table 430.250 lists the full-load current for three-phase alternating-current motors. The values are used to determine motor conductor sizing, ampere ratings of disconnects, controller rating, and branch-circuit and feeder protection, but not overload protection [430.6(A)(1) and 430.6(A)(2)].

Table 430.250 FLC Three–Phase AC Motors				
	200V	208V	230V	460V
½ hp	2.50	2.40	2.20	1.10
¾ hp	3.70	3.50	3.20	1.60
1 hp	4.80	4.60	4.20	2.10
1½ hp	6.90	6.60	6.00	3.00
2 hp	7.80	7.50	6.80	3.40
3 hp	11.00	10.60	9.60	4.00
5 hp	17.50	16.70	15.20	7.60
7½ hp	25.30	24.20	22.00	11.00
10.00	32.20	30.80	28.00	14.00
15.00	48.30	46.20	42.00	21.00
20.00	62.10	59.40	54.00	27.00
25.00	78.20	74.80	68.00	34.00

Table 430.251 Locked-Rotor Currents

Table 430.251(A) lists the locked-rotor current for single-phase motors, and Table 430.251(B) contains the locked-rotor current for three-phase motors. These values are used in the selection of controllers and disconnecting means when the horsepower rating isn't marked on the motor nameplate.

AIR-CONDITIONING AND REFRIGERATION EQUIPMENT

Introduction to Article 440—Air-Conditioning and Refrigeration Equipment

This article applies to electrically driven air-conditioning and refrigeration equipment. The rules in this article add to, or amend, the rules in Article 430 and other articles.

Each equipment manufacturer has the motor for a given air-conditioning unit built to its own specifications. Cooling and other characteristics are different from those of nonhermetic motors. For each motor, the manufacturer has worked out all of the details and supplied the correct protection, conductor sizing, and other information on the nameplate. So when wiring an air conditioner, trust the information on the nameplate and don't try to over-complicate the situation. The math for sizing the overcurrent protection and conductor minimum ampacity has already been done for you.

Part I. General

440.1 Scope

Article 440 applies to electrically driven air-conditioning and refrigeration equipment.

440.2 Definitions

Rated-Load Current. The current resulting when the motor-compressor operates at rated load and rated voltage.

440.3 Other Articles

(B) Equipment with No Hermetic Motor-Compressors. Air-conditioning and refrigeration equipment that don't have hermetic refrigerant motor-compressors, such as furnaces with evaporator coils, must comply with Article 422 for appliances, Article 424 for electric space heating, and Article 430 for motors.

(C) Household Refrigerant Motor-Compressor Appliances. Household refrigerators and freezers, drinking water coolers, and beverage dispensing machines are listed as appliances, and their installation must also comply with Article 422 for appliances. Figure 440–1

Figure 440–1

440.4 Marking on Hermetic Refrigerant Motor-Compressors and Equipment

(B) Multimotor and Combination-Load Equipment. Multimotor and combination-load equipment must have a visible nameplate marked with the maker's name, rating in volts, number of phases, minimum conductor ampacity, and the maximum rating of the branch-circuit short-circuit and ground-fault protective device.

Author's Comment:

- The minimum conductor ampacity is calculated in accordance with 440.33 and the branch circuit short-circuit and ground-fault protective device rating is sized with 440.22(B)(1).

440.6 Ampacity and Rating

(A) Hermetic Refrigerant Motor-Compressor. For a hermetic refrigerant motor-compressor, the rated-load current marked on the nameplate of the equipment is to be used in determining the rating of the disconnecting means, the branch-circuit conductors, the controller, and the branch-circuit short-circuit and ground-fault protection.

Part II. Disconnecting Means

440.12 Rating and Interrupting Capacity

(A) Hermetic Refrigerant Motor-Compressor.

(1) Ampere Rating. The ampere rating must be at least 115 percent of the nameplate rated-load current or branch-circuit selection current, whichever is greater.

440.13 Cord-Connected Equipment

An attachment plug and receptacle can serve as the disconnecting means for cord-connected room air conditioners, household refrigerators and freezers, drinking water coolers and beverage dispensers.

440.14 Location

A disconnecting means for air-conditioning or refrigeration equipment must be located within sight from and readily accessible from the equipment. Figures 440–2 and 440–3

Air-Conditioning and Refrigeration Equipment
Disconnecting Means
440.14

The disconnect must be within sight and readily accessible from equipment.

Copyright 2014, www.MikeHolt.com

Figure 440–2

Air-Conditioning and Refrigeration Equipment
Disconnecting Means
440.14

The disconnect must be within sight of the equipment.

VIOLATION

Copyright 2014, www.MikeHolt.com

Figure 440–3

Author's Comment:

- According to Article 100, "within sight" means that it's visible and not more than 50 ft from one to the other.

The disconnecting means can be mounted on or within the air-conditioning equipment, but it must not be located on panels designed to allow access to the equipment, or where it'll obscure the equipment nameplate. Figure 440–4

The disconnect can be installed on or within the equipment, but not over panels designed to allow access to internal wiring or over the nameplate.

Figure 440–4

Ex 1: A disconnecting means isn't required to be within sight from the equipment, if the disconnecting means is <u>lockable, as described in 110.25</u>, and if the equipment is essential to an industrial process in a facility that has written safety procedures, and where the conditions of maintenance and supervision ensure only qualified persons service the equipment.

Ex 2: An accessible attachment plug and receptacle can serve as the disconnecting means.

Author's Comment:

- The receptacle for the attachment plug isn't required to be readily accessible.

Part III. Overcurrent Protection

440.21 General

The branch-circuit conductors, control equipment, and circuits supplying hermetic refrigerant motor-compressors must be protected against short circuits and ground faults in accordance with 440.22.

Author's Comment:

- If the equipment nameplate specifies "Maximum Fuse Size," then a one-time or dual-element fuse must be used.

440.22 Short-Circuit and Ground-Fault Overcurrent Device Size

(A) Single Motor-Compressors. The short-circuit and ground-fault protective device must not be more than 175 percent of the motor-compressor current rating. If the protective device sized at 175 percent isn't capable of carrying the starting current of the motor-compressor, the next size larger protective device can be used, but in no case can it exceed 225 percent of the motor-compressor current rating.

> **Question:** What size conductor and protection are required for an 18A motor-compressor with 75°C terminals connected to a 240V circuit? Figures 440–5 and 440–6
>
> (a) 30-40A   (b) 35-45A
> (c) a or b   (d) none of these
>
> **Answer:** (a) 30-40A
>
> Determine the branch-circuit protection [240.6(A) and 440.22(A)]:
>
> 18A x 1.75 = 31.50A, next size down = 30A
>
> If the 30A short-circuit and ground-fault protective device isn't capable of carrying the starting current, then the protective device can be sized up to 225 percent of the equipment load current rating. 18A x 2.25 = 40.50A, next size down is 40A

Air-Conditioning and Refrigeration Equipment
Short-Circuit and Ground-Fault Protection
440.22(A)

30A Protection
18A x 1.75 = 31.50A

The next size up
rule doesn't apply.

18A
Compressor

A short-circuit and ground-fault protection device must not
be greater than 175% of the equipment load current rating.

Figure 440–5

Air-Conditioning and Refrigeration Equipment
Short-Circuit and Ground-Fault Protection
440.22(A)

40A Protection
18A x 2.25 = 40.50A

The next size up
rule doesn't apply.

12 AWG
Rated 25A at 75ºC
[440.32]

Copyright 2014, www.MikeHolt.com

Nameplate

If 175% can't carry the starting current, the overcurrent
device can be sized at a maximum of 225%.

Figure 440–6

(B) Multimotor and Combination-Load Equipment. If the equipment incorporates more than one hermetic refrigerant motor-compressor, or a hermetic refrigerant motor-compressor and other motors or other loads, the equipment must have a visible nameplate containing the maximum rating of the branch-circuit short-circuit and ground-fault protective device.

Author's Comment:

- The branch-circuit conductors are sized at 125 percent of the largest motor-compressor current, plus the sum of the rated-load currents of the other compressors [440.33].

Part IV. Conductor Sizing

440.32 Conductor Size for Single Motor-Compressors

Branch-circuit conductors to a single motor-compressor must have an ampacity not less than 125 percent of the motor-compressor rated-load current or the branch-circuit selection current, whichever is greater.

Author's Comment:

- Branch-circuit conductors for a single motor-compressor must have short-circuit and ground-fault protection sized between 175 percent and 225 percent of the rated-load current [440.22(A)].

Question: What size conductor and overcurrent device are required for an 18A motor compressor with 75ºC terminals? Figure 440–7

(a) 12 AWG, 30A   (b) 10 AWG, 50A
(c) a or b   (d) 10 AWG, 60A

Answer: (a) 12 AWG, 30A

Step 1: Determine the branch-circuit conductor [Table 310.15(B)(16) and 440.32]:

18A x 1.25 = 22.50A, 12 AWG, rated 25A at 75°C [Table 310.15(B)(16)]

Step 2: Determine the branch-circuit protection [240.6(A) and 440.22(A)]:

18A x 1.75 = 31.50A, next size down = 30A

If the 30A short-circuit and ground-fault protection device isn't capable of carrying the starting current, then the protective device can be sized up to 225 percent of the equipment load current rating. 18A x 2.25 = 40.50A, next size down 40A

Author's Comment:

- A 30A or 40A overcurrent device is permitted to protect a 12 AWG conductor for an air-conditioning circuit. See 240.4(G) for details.

Figure 440–7

Figure 440–8

Part VII. Room Air Conditioners

The requirements in this Part apply to a cord-and-plug-connected room air conditioner of the window or in-wall type that incorporates a hermetic refrigerant motor-compressor rated not over 40A, 250V, single-phase [440.60].

440.62 Branch-Circuit Requirements

(A) Sizing Conductors and Protection. Branch-circuit conductors for a cord-and-plug-connected room air conditioner must have an ampacity not less than 125 percent of the rated-load current [440.32].

(B) Separate Circuit. If the room air conditioner is the only load on a circuit, the marked rating of the air conditioner must not exceed 80 percent of the rating of the circuit overcurrent device.

(C) Other Loads on Circuit. The total rating of a cord-and-plug-connected room air conditioner must not exceed 50 percent of the rating of a branch circuit where lighting outlets, other appliances, or general-use receptacles are also supplied. Figure 440–8

440.63 Disconnecting Means

An attachment plug and receptacle or cord connector can serve as the disconnecting means for a room air conditioner, provided: Figure 440–9

Figure 440–9

(1) The manual controls on the room air conditioner are readily accessible and within 6 ft of the floor, or

(2) A readily accessible disconnecting means is within sight from the room air conditioner.

440.64 Supply Cords

If a flexible cord is used to supply a room air conditioner, the cord must not exceed 10 ft for 120V units, or 6 ft for 208V or 240V units.

440.65 Leakage Current Detector-Interrupter and Arc-Fault Circuit Interrupter

Single-phase cord-and-plug-connected room air conditioners must be provided with a factory-installed leakage current detector, or with an arc-fault circuit-interrupter (AFCI).

ARTICLE 445

GENERATORS

Introduction to Article 445—Generators

This article contains the electrical installation, and other requirements, for generators. These requirements include such things as where generators can be installed, nameplate markings, conductor ampacity, and disconnecting means.

Generators are basically motors that operate in reverse—they produce electricity when rotated, instead of rotating when supplied with electricity. Article 430, which covers motors, is the longest article in the *NEC*. Article 445, which covers generators, is one of the shortest. At first, this might not seem to make sense. But you don't need to size and protect conductors to a generator. You do need to size and protect them to a motor.

Generators need overload protection, and it's necessary to size the conductors that come from the generator. But these considerations are much more straightforward than the equivalent considerations for motors. Before you study Article 445, take a moment to read the definition of "Separately Derived System" in Article 100.

445.1 Scope

Article 445 contains the installation and other requirements for generators.

Author's Comment:

- Generators, associated wiring, and equipment must be installed in accordance with the following requirements depending on their use:

  □ Article 695, Fire Pumps
  □ Article 700, Emergency Systems
  □ Article 701, Legally Required Standby Systems
  □ Article 702, Optional Standby Systems

445.11 Marking

Each generator must be provided with a nameplate indicating the manufacturer's name, rated frequency, number of phases, rating in kilowatts or kilovolt amperes, volts and amperes corresponding to the rating, RPM, insulation class and rated ambient temperature or rated temperature rise, and time rating.

Nameplates for portable generators rated more than 15 kW and for all stationary generators must also give the power factor, the subtransient and transient impedances, insulation system class, and time rating.

All generators must be marked by the manufacturer indicating whether or not the generator neutral is bonded to the generator frame. Where the bonding of a generator is modified in the field, additional marking must be provided to indicate whether or not the generator neutral is bonded to the generator frame. Figure 445–1

Generator - Nameplate Marking
445.11

Generators must be marked by the manufacturer indicating whether or not the generator neutral is bonded to the generator frame. If the bonding of a generator is modified in the field, additional marking must be provided to indicate whether or not the generator neutral is bonded to the generator frame.

Copyright 2014
www.MikeHolt.com

Figure 445–1

Ampacity of Generator Conductors
445.13

Transfer Switch

Generator

Copyright 2014
www.MikeHolt.com

The ampacity of the conductors from the generator winding to the line side of the generator overcurrent device must not be less than 115 percent of the nameplate current rating of the generator.

Figure 445–2

445.12 Overcurrent Protection

(A) Generators. Generators must be protected from overload by inherent design, circuit breakers, fuses, or other identified overcurrent protective means.

445.13 Ampacity of Conductors

 Scan this QR code for a video of this *Code* rule. See page xix for information on how to use the QR codes.

The ampacity of the conductors from the generator winding to the line-side of the generator overcurrent protection device must not be less than 115 percent of the nameplate current rating of the generator. Figure 445–2

Author's Comment:

■ Since the overcurrent protection device is typically part of the generator, this rule applies to the generator manufacturer, not the installer.

■ Conductors from the load-side of the generator overcurrent protection device to the transfer switch are sized in accordance with 240.4.

Example: *What size conductor is required from a 100A overcurrent protection device on 20 kW 120/240V single-phase generator to a 200A service rated transfer switch?* Figure 445–3

(a) 4 AWG   (b) 3 AWG   (c) 2 AWG   (d) 1 AWG

Answer: *(b) 3 AWG, Table 310.15(B)(16), rated 100A at 75°C [110.14(C)(1)(b)].*

Ampacity of Generator Conductors
Load Side of Generator Overcurrent Device
445.13

3 AWG Rated
100A at 75°C
Table 310.15(B)(16)

100A Generator Overcurrent Device

Copyright 2014
www.MikeHolt.com

Conductors from the generator overcurrent device to the transfer switch are sized in accordance with 240.4.

Figure 445–3

Generators that aren't a separately derived system must have the neutral conductor sized to carry the maximum unbalanced current as determined by 220.61 and serve as part of the effective ground-fault current path and be not smaller than required by 250.30. Figure 445–4

Generator - Neutral Conductor Size
445.13

The neutral conductor must be sized to carry the neutral and fault current [250.30(A)(1) and 220.61].

Figure 445–4

445.18 Disconnecting Means

Generators must have one or more lockable disconnecting means that disconnects all power, except where:

(1) The generator is portable with a cord-and-plug connection, or

(2) Where both of the following apply:

(a) The driving means for the generator can be readily shut down, rendered unable to start, and is lockable in accordance with 110.25, and

(b) The generator isn't arranged to operate in parallel with another generator or other source of voltage.

⚠ **CAUTION:** *If one generator is used to supply emergency, legally required, as well as optional standby power, then there must be at least two transfer switches; one for emergency power, another for legally required, and one for optional stand-by power [700.5(D)].*

445.20 Ground-Fault Circuit Interrupter Protection for Receptacles on 15 kW or Smaller Portable Generators

Portable generators rated 15 kW or smaller manufactured or remanufactured after January 1, 2015 containing a 125/250V locking receptacle must have 15A, 20A, and 30A, 125V receptacles GFCI protected, or have a feature that will disable the 125V receptacle when the 125/250V locking receptacle is in use. Figure 445–5

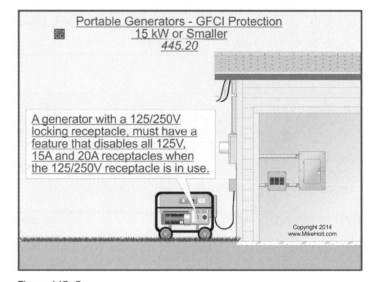

Figure 445–5

Author's Comment:

■ This rule was revised via a Tentative Interim Amendment 14-2 effective November 11, 2013.

Notes

ARTICLE 450

TRANSFORMERS

Introduction to Article 450—Transformers

Article 450 opens by saying, "This article covers the installation of all transformers." Then it lists eight exceptions. So what does Article 450 really cover? Essentially, it covers power transformers and most kinds of lighting transformers.

A major concern with transformers is preventing overheating. The *Code* doesn't completely address this issue. Article 90 explains that the *NEC* isn't a design manual, and it assumes that the person using the *Code* has a certain level of expertise. Proper transformer selection is an important part of preventing it from overheating.

The *NEC* assumes you've already selected a transformer suitable to the load characteristics. For the *Code* to tell you how to do that would push it into the realm of a design manual. Article 450 then takes you to the next logical step—providing over-current protection and the proper connections. But this article doesn't stop there; 450.9 provides ventilation requirements, and 450.13 contains accessibility requirements.

Part I of Article 450 contains the general requirements such as guarding, marking, and accessibility, Part II contains the requirements for different types of transformers, and Part III covers transformer vaults.

Part I. General

450.1 Scope

Article 450 covers the installation requirements of transformers and transformer vaults. Figure 450–1

450.3 Overcurrent Protection

Note 2: Nonlinear loads on 4-wire, wye-connected secondary wiring can increase heat in a transformer without operating the primary overcurrent device. Figure 450–2

Figure 450–1

Figure 450–2

In 3-phase, 4-wire delta/wye transformers, odd triplen harmonic currents from nonlinear loads can cause excessive heating of the primary winding.

(B) Overcurrent Protection for Transformers Not Over 600V. The primary winding of a transformer must be protected against overcurrent in accordance with the percentages listed in Table 450.3(B) and all applicable notes.

Table 450.3(B) Primary Protection Only

Primary Current Rating	Maximum Protection
9A or More	125%, see Table Note 1
Less Than 9A	167%
Less Than 2A	300%

Note 1. *If 125 percent of the primary current doesn't correspond to a standard rating of a fuse or nonadjustable circuit breaker, the next higher rating is permitted [240.6(A)].*

Question: *What's the primary overcurrent device rating and conductor size required for a 45 kVA, three-phase, 480V transformer that's fully loaded? The terminals are rated 75°C.* Figure 450–3

(a) 8 AWG, 40A   *(b) 6 AWG, 50A*
(c) 6 AWG, 60A   *(d) 4 AWG, 70A*

Answer: *(d) 4 AWG, 70A*

(continued)

Step 1: *Determine the primary current:*

$$I = VA/(E \times 1.732)$$

I = 45,000 VA/(480V x 1.732)
I = 54A

Step 2: *Determine the primary overcurrent device rating [240.6(A)]:*
54A x 1.25 = 68A, next size up 70A, Table 450.3(B), Table Note 1

Step 3: *The primary conductor must be sized to carry 54A continuously (54A x 1.25 = 68A) [215.2(A)(1)] and be protected by a 70A overcurrent device [240.4(B)]. A 4 AWG conductor rated 85A at 75°C meets all of the requirements [110.14(C)(1) and 310.15(B)(16)].*

Figure 450–3

450.9 Ventilation

Transformers must be installed in accordance with the manufacturer's instructions, and their ventilating openings must not be blocked [110.3(B)].

Note 2: Transformers can become excessively heated above their rating because nonlinear loads can increase heat in a transformer without operating its overcurrent protective device [450.3 Note].

Author's Comment:

■ The heating from harmonic currents is proportional to the square of the harmonic frequency. This means the 3rd order harmonic currents (180 Hz) will heat at nine times the rate of 60 Hz current. Figure 450–4

Figure 450–4

450.10 Grounding and Bonding

(A) Dry-Type Transformer Enclosures. Where separate equipment grounding conductors and supply-side bonding jumpers are installed, a terminal bar for these conductors must be installed inside the enclosure. The terminal bar must not cover any ventilation openings. Figure 450–5

Ex: Where a dry-type transformer is equipped with wire-type connections (leads), the terminal bar isn't required.

450.11 Marking

(A) General. Transformers must have a nameplate that provides the following information:

(1) The name of the manufacturer

(2) Rated kilovolt-amperes

(3) Frequency

Figure 450–5

(4) Primary and secondary voltage

(5) The impedance of transformers 25 kVA and larger

(6) Required clearances for transformers with ventilating openings

(7) The amount and kind of insulating liquid where used

(8) For dry-type transformers, the temperature class for the insulation system.

(B) Source Marking. A transformer can be supplied at the secondary voltage if allowed in the manufacturer's instructions.

450.13 Transformer Accessibility

Transformers must be readily accessible to qualified personnel for inspection and maintenance, except as permitted by (A) or (B).

(A) Open Installations. Dry-type transformers can be located in the open on walls, columns, or structures. Figure 450–6

(B) Suspended Ceilings. Dry-type transformers, rated not more than 50 kVA, are permitted above suspended ceilings or in hollow spaces of buildings, if not permanently closed in by the structure. Figure 450–7

Author's Comment:

■ Dry-type transformers not exceeding 50 kVA with a metal enclosure can be installed above a suspended-ceiling space used for environmental air-handling purposes (plenum) [300.22(C)(3)].

Figure 450–6

Figure 450–7

Figure 450–8

Figure 450–9

Author's Comment:

- Within sight means that it's visible and not more than 50 ft from one to the other [Article 100].

450.14 Disconnecting Means

A disconnect is required to disconnect all transformer ungrounded primary conductors, unless the transformer is Class 2 or Class 3. The disconnect must be located within sight of the transformer, unless the location of the disconnect is field marked on the transformer and the disconnect is lockable, as described in 110.25. Figures 450–8 and 450–9

ARTICLE 480

STORAGE BATTERIES

Introduction to Article 480—Storage Batteries

The stationary battery is the heart of any uninterruptible power supply. Article 480 addresses stationary batteries for commercial and industrial grade power supplies, not the small, "point of use," UPS boxes.

Stationary batteries are also used in other applications, such as emergency power systems. Regardless of the application, if it uses stationary batteries, Article 480 applies.

Lead-acid stationary batteries fall into two general categories: flooded, and valve regulated (VRLA). These differ markedly in such ways as maintainability, total cost of ownership, and scalability. The *NEC* doesn't address these differences, as they're engineering issues and not fire safety or electrical safety matters [90.1].

The *Code* doesn't address such design issues as optimum tier height, distance between tiers, determination of charging voltage, or string configuration. Nor does it address battery testing, monitoring, or maintenance. All of these involve highly specialized areas of knowledge, and are required for optimizing operational efficiency. Standards other than the *NEC* address these topics.

What the *Code* does address, in Article 480, are issues related to preventing electrocution and the ignition of the gases that all stationary batteries (even "sealed" ones) emit.

480.1 Scope

The provisions of Article 480 apply to stationary storage battery installations.

Note: The following standards are frequently referenced for the installation of stationary batteries:

(1) IEEE 484, *Recommended Practice for Installation Design and Installation of Vented Lead-Acid Batteries for Stationary Applications.*

(2) IEEE 485, *Recommended Practice for Sizing Vented Lead-Acid Storage Batteries for Stationary Applications.*

(3) IEEE 1145, *Recommended Practice for Installation and Maintenance of Nickel-Cadmium Batteries for Photovoltaic (PV) Systems.*

(4) IEEE 1187, *Recommended Practice for Installation Design, and Installation of Valve-Regulated Lead-Acid Batteries for Stationary Applications.*

(5) IEEE 1375, *IEEE Guide for the Protection of Stationary Battery Systems.*

(6) IEEE 1578, *Recommended Practice for Stationary Battery Spill Containment and Management.*

(7) IEEE 1635/ASHRAE 21, *Guide for the Ventilation and Thermal Management of Stationary Battery Installations.*

480.2 Definitions

Cell. The basic electrochemical unit, consisting of an anode and a cathode, which receives, stores, and delivers electrical energy.

Author's Comment:

■ A battery is made up of one or more cells.

Container. An object that holds the elements of a single unit in a battery.

Note: Containers can be single-cell or multi-cell and are often called "jars."

Intercell Connector. A conductive bar or cable that connects adjacent cells.

Intertier Connector. An electrical conductor that connects two cells on different tiers of the same rack, or different shelves of the same rack.

Nominal Voltage (Battery or Cell). The value assigned to a cell or battery for conveniently designating the voltage class. The operating voltage of the cell or battery can be higher or lower than the nominal voltage.

Note: The most common nominal cell voltages are 2V per cell for lead-acid, 1.20V per cell for alkali, and 3.60V to 3.80V per cell for lithium-ion. Figure 480–1

The most common nominal cell voltages are 2V per cell for the lead-acid type, 1.20V per cell for alkali type, and 3.60 to 3.80V per cell for lithium-ion systems.

Figure 480–1

Author's Comment:

■ The voltage of a battery will decrease below the nominal voltage while it's being used (discharged) and the actual voltage will often be higher than nominal when the battery is fully charged.

Sealed Cell or Battery. A cell or battery with no provision for the routine addition of water or electrolyte.

Storage Battery. A battery consisting of one or more rechargeable cells.

480.3 Battery and Cell Terminations

(A) Dissimilar Metals. Where connections between dissimilar metals occur, antioxidant material must be used.

Note: The manufacturer's instructions may have guidance for acceptable materials.

(B) Intercell and Intertier Conductors and Connections. The ampacity of field-assembled intercell and intertier connectors and conductors must be sized so that the temperature rise under maximum load conditions and at maximum ambient temperature doesn't exceed the safe operating temperature of the conductor insulation.

Note: IEEE 1375, *Guide for the Protection of Stationary Battery Systems* provides guidance for overcurrent protection and associated cable sizing. Typical voltage-drop considerations for ac circuits might not be adequate for battery systems.

480.4 Wiring and Equipment Supplied from Batteries

Wiring and equipment supplied from storage batteries must be in accordance with Chapters 1 through 4 unless otherwise permitted by 480.5.

480.8 Racks and Trays

Racks and trays must be:

(A) Racks. Racks (rigid frames designed to support battery cells or trays) must be made of one of the following: Figure 480–2

Battery Racks
480.8(A)

VIOLATION
Racks must be:
(1) Treated metal, or
(2) Fiberglass or a
    suitable nonconductive
    material

Copyright 2014, www.MikeHolt.com

Figure 480–2

(1) Metal, treated to be resistant to deteriorating action by the electrolyte and provided with nonconducting or continuous insulating material members directly supporting the cells.

(2) Fiberglass or other suitable nonconductive materials.

(B) Trays. Trays (boxes of nonconductive material) must be constructed or treated so as to be resistant to deteriorating action by the electrolyte. Figure 480–3

(C) Accessible. The terminals of all cells or multi-cell units must be readily accessible for readings, inspection, and cleaning as necessary. Transparent battery containers must have one side of the container readily accessible for inspection of the internal components.

480.9 Battery Locations

(A) Ventilation. Provisions must permit sufficient diffusion and ventilation of battery gases to prevent the accumulation of an explosive mixture. Figure 480–4

Battery Trays
480.8(B)

Photo by Ryan Arne   Copyright 2014, www.MikeHolt.com

Trays (boxes of nonconductive material) must be constructed or treated so as to be resistant to deteriorating action by the electrolyte.

Figure 480–3

Battery Locations
Ventilation
480.9(A)

Provisions must permit sufficient diffusion and ventilation of battery gases to prevent the accumulation of an explosive mixture.

Photo by Ryan Arne   Copyright 2014, www.MikeHolt.com

Figure 480–4

(B) Live Parts. Live parts of battery systems must be protected in accordance with 110.27.

Author's Comment:

■ According to 110.27, electrical equipment must not be installed where subject to physical damage, unless enclosures or guards are arranged and of such strength as to prevent damage [110.27(B)]. In addition, entrances to rooms and other guarded locations containing exposed live parts must be marked with conspicuous signs forbidding unqualified persons to enter [110.27(C)].

(C) Working <u>Space for Battery Racks</u>. A minimum clearance of 1 in. is required between a cell container and any wall or structure on the side not requiring access for maintenance. Battery stands can make contact with adjacent walls or structures.

> **Note:** Additional space is often needed to accommodate battery hoisting equipment, tray removal, or spill containment.

(D) Top Terminal Batteries. Where top terminal batteries are installed on tiered racks, working space in accordance with the battery manufacturer's instructions must be provided between the highest point on a cell and the row or ceiling above that point.

> **Note:** Battery manufacturer's installation instructions typically define how much top working space is necessary for a particular battery model.

(E) Egress. A personnel door(s) intended for entrance to, and egress from, rooms designated as battery rooms must open in the direction of egress and be equipped with listed panic hardware.

(F) Piping in Battery Rooms. Gas piping isn't permitted in a dedicated battery room.

(G) Illumination. The working space must have illumination that isn't controlled by automatic means only and that doesn't:

(1) Expose personnel to energized battery components while performing maintenance on the luminaires; or

(2) Create a hazard to the battery upon failure of the luminaire.

CHAPTER 4 PRACTICE QUESTIONS

Please use the 2014 *Code* book to answer the following questions.

1. HPD cord shall be permitted for _____.

   (a) not hard usage
   (b) hard usage
   (c) extra-hard usage
   (d) all of these

2. Flexible cords and cables shall not be concealed behind building _____, or run through doorways, windows, or similar openings.

   (a) structural ceilings
   (b) suspended or dropped ceilings
   (c) floors or walls
   (d) all of these

3. Flexible cords and cables shall be connected to fittings so that tension will not be transmitted to joints or terminal screws by _____.

   (a) knotting the cord
   (b) winding the cord with tape
   (c) fittings designed for the purpose
   (d) any of these

4. Fixture wires are used to connect luminaires to the _____ conductors supplying the luminaires.

   (a) service
   (b) branch-circuit
   (c) feeder
   (d) none of these

5. Fixture wires shall not be used for branch-circuit wiring, except as permitted in other articles of the *Code*.

   (a) True
   (b) False

6. Surface-mounted switches or circuit breakers in a damp or wet location shall be enclosed in a _____ enclosure or cabinet that complies with 312.2.

   (a) weatherproof
   (b) rainproof
   (c) watertight
   (d) raintight

7. Switches shall not be installed within tubs or shower spaces unless installed as part of a listed tub or shower assembly.

   (a) True
   (b) False

8. Snap switches are considered to be part of the effective ground-fault current path when _____.

   (a) the switch is connected to the intersystem bonding termination
   (b) the switch is mounted with metal screws to a metal box or a metal cover that's connected to an equipment grounding conductor
   (c) an equipment grounding conductor or equipment bonding jumper is connected to the equipment grounding termination of the snap switch
   (d) b or c

9. A snap switch that does not have means for connection to an equipment grounding conductor shall be permitted for replacement purposes only where the wiring method does not include an equipment grounding conductor and the switch is _____.

   (a) provided with a faceplate of nonconducting, noncombustible material with nonmetallic screws
   (b) GFCI protected
   (c) a or b
   (d) none of these

10. Alternating-current general-use snap switches are permitted to control _____.

   (a) resistive and inductive loads that do not exceed the ampere and voltage rating of the switch
   (b) tungsten-filament lamp loads that do not exceed the ampere rating of the switch at 120V
   (c) motor loads that do not exceed 80 percent of the ampere and voltage rating of the switch
   (d) all of these

11. AC or dc general-use snap switches may be used for control of inductive loads not exceeding _____ percent of the ampere rating of the switch at the applied voltage.

   (a) 50
   (b) 75
   (c) 90
   (d) 100

12. Receptacles rated _____ or less directly connected to aluminum conductors shall be listed and marked CO/ALR.

   (a) 15A
   (b) 20A
   (c) 25A
   (d) 30A

13. Receptacles incorporating an isolated grounding conductor connection intended for the reduction of electrical noise shall be identified by _____ on the face of the receptacle.

   (a) an orange triangle
   (b) a green triangle
   (c) the color orange
   (d) the engraved word ISOLATED

14. Receptacles mounted in boxes set back from the wall surface shall be installed so that the mounting _____ of the receptacle is held rigidly at the finished surface.

   (a) screws or nails
   (b) yoke or strap
   (c) faceplate
   (d) none of these

15. Receptacles mounted in boxes flush with the finished surface or projecting beyond it shall be installed so that the mounting yoke or strap of the receptacle is _____.

   (a) held rigidly against the box or box cover
   (b) mounted behind the wall surface
   (c) held rigidly at the finished surface
   (d) none of these

16. Receptacles installed outdoors, in a location protected from the weather or other damp locations, shall be in an enclosure that is _____ when the receptacle is covered.

   (a) raintight
   (b) weatherproof
   (c) rainproof
   (d) weathertight

17. A receptacle is considered to be in a location protected from the weather when located under roofed open porches, canopies, marquees, and the like, where it will not be subjected to _____.

   (a) spray from a hose
   (b) a direct lightning hit
   (c) beating rain or water runoff
   (d) falling or wind-blown debris

18. A receptacle shall not be installed within, or directly over, a bathtub or shower space.

   (a) True
   (b) False

19. A receptacle installed in an outlet box flush-mounted in a finished surface in a damp or wet location shall be made weatherproof by means of a weatherproof faceplate assembly that provides a _____ connection between the plate and the finished surface.

    (a) sealed
    (b) weathertight
    (c) sealed and protected
    (d) watertight

20. In switchboards and panelboards, load terminals for field wiring shall be so located that it is not necessary to reach across or beyond a(n) _____ ungrounded line bus in order to make connections.

    (a) insulated
    (b) uninsulated
    (c) grounded
    (d) high impedance

21. Panelboards supplied by a three-phase, 4-wire, delta-connected system shall have the phase with higher voltage-to-ground (high-leg) connected to the _____ phase.

    (a) A
    (b) B
    (c) C
    (d) any of these

22. A panelboard shall be protected by an overcurrent device within the panelboard, or at any point on the _____ side of the panelboard.

    (a) load
    (b) supply
    (c) a or b
    (d) none of these

23. Plug-in-type circuit breakers that are backfed shall be _____ by an additional fastener that requires more than a pull to release.

    (a) grounded
    (b) secured in place
    (c) shunt tripped
    (d) none of these

24. A luminaire marked "Suitable for Wet Locations" _____ be permitted to be used in a damp location.

    (a) shall
    (b) shall not
    (c) a or b
    (d) none of these

25. Luminaires can be installed in a commercial cooking hood if the luminaire is identified for use within a _____ cooking hood.

    (a) nonresidential
    (b) commercial
    (c) multifamily
    (d) all of these

26. In clothes closets, recessed incandescent or LED luminaires with a completely enclosed light source can be installed in the wall or the ceiling, provided there is a minimum clearance of _____ in. between the luminaire and the nearest point of a storage space.

    (a) 3
    (b) 6
    (c) 9
    (d) 12

27. Luminaires must maintain a minimum clearance from the closet storage space of _____.

    (a) 12 in. for surface-mounted incandescent or LED luminaires with a completely enclosed light source
    (b) 6 in. for surface-mounted fluorescent luminaires
    (c) 6 in. for recessed fluorescent luminaires or recessed incandescent or LED luminaires with a completely enclosed light source
    (d) all of these

28. Handholds in poles supporting luminaires shall not be required for poles _____ ft or less in height above finished grade, if the pole is provided with a hinged base.

    (a) 5
    (b) 10
    (c) 15
    (d) 20

29. Poles over 20 ft in height above grade, without a hinged base, that support luminaires shall _____.

    (a) have an accessible handhole (sized 2 x 4 in.) with a cover suitable for use in wet locations
    (b) have an equipment grounding terminal that is accessible from the handhole
    (c) a and b
    (d) none of these

30. Replacement luminaires aren't required to be connected to an equipment grounding conductor if no equipment grounding conductor exists at the outlet box and the luminaire is _____.

    (a) more than 20 years old
    (b) mounted to the box using nonmetallic fittings and screws
    (c) mounted more than 6 ft above the floor
    (d) GFCI protected

31. Luminaires shall be wired so that the _____ of each lampholder is connected to the same luminaire or circuit conductor or terminal.

    (a) stem
    (b) arm
    (c) supplemental protection
    (d) screw shell

32. Lampholders of the screw-shell type shall be installed for use as lampholders only.

    (a) True
    (b) False

33. Lampholders installed in wet locations shall be listed for use in _____ locations.

    (a) damp
    (b) wet
    (c) dry
    (d) any of these

34. Thermal insulation shall not be installed above a recessed luminaire or within _____ in. of the recessed luminaire's enclosure, wiring compartment, ballast, transformer, LED driver, or power supply unless it is identified as a Type IC luminaire.

    (a) ½
    (b) 3
    (c) 6
    (d) 12

35. When connected to multiwire branch circuits, the fluorescent luminaire disconnect must simultaneously break all circuit conductors of the ballast, including the grounded conductor.

    (a) True
    (b) False

36. Lighting track shall have two supports for a single section of _____ ft or shorter in length and each individual section of not more than 4 ft attached to it shall have one additional support, unless the track is identified for supports at greater intervals.

    (a) 2
    (b) 4
    (c) 6
    (d) 8

37. A vending machine is defined as any self-service device that dispenses products or merchandise without the necessity of replenishing the device between each vending operation and designed to require insertion of a _____.

    (a) coin or paper currency
    (b) token or card
    (c) key or payment by other means
    (d) all of these

38. An in-sink waste disposer can be cord-and-plug-connected, but the cord shall not be less than 18 in. or more than _____ in. in length.

    (a) 30
    (b) 36
    (c) 42
    (d) 48

39. For cord-and-plug-connected household electric ranges, an attachment plug and receptacle connection at the rear base of the range can serve as the disconnecting means, if it is _____.

    (a) less than 40A
    (b) a flush-mounted receptacle
    (c) GFCI-protected
    (d) accessible from the front by the removal of a drawer

40. A unit switch with a marked _____ position that is part of a fixed space heater, and disconnects all ungrounded conductors, shall be permitted to serve as the required disconnecting means.

    (a) on
    (b) closed
    (c) off
    (d) none of these

41. For general motor applications, the motor branch-circuit short-circuit and ground-fault protection device shall be sized based on the _____ values.

    (a) motor nameplate
    (b) NEMA standard
    (c) *NEC* Table
    (d) Factory Mutual

42. The motor _____ currents listed in Tables 430.247 through 430.250 shall be used to determine the ampacity of motor circuit conductors and short-circuit and ground-fault protection devices.

    (a) nameplate
    (b) full-load
    (c) power factor
    (d) service factor

43. A separate overload device used to protect continuous-duty motors rated more than 1 hp shall be selected to trip at no more than _____ percent of the motor nameplate full-load current rating if marked with a service factor of 1.15 or greater.

    (a) 110
    (b) 115
    (c) 120
    (d) 125

44. Motor control circuit conductors that extend beyond the motor control equipment enclosure shall have short-circuit and ground-fault protection sized not greater than _____ percent of value specified in Table 310.15(B)(16) for 60°C conductors.

    (a) 100
    (b) 150
    (c) 300
    (d) 400

45. The motor disconnecting means shall not be required to be in sight from the motor and the driven machinery location, provided _____.

    (a) the controller disconnecting means is lockable, in accordance with 110.25
    (b) locating the motor disconnecting means within sight of the motor is impractical
    (c) locating the motor disconnecting means within sight of the motor introduces additional or increased hazards to people or property
    (d) all of these

46. A horsepower-rated _____ having a horsepower rating not less than the motor rating shall be permitted to serve as the disconnecting means.

    (a) attachment plug and receptacle
    (b) flanged surface inlet and cord connector
    (c) automatic controller
    (d) a or b

47. The disconnecting means for air-conditioning and refrigerating equipment shall be _____ from the air-conditioning or refrigerating equipment.

    (a) readily accessible
    (b) within sight
    (c) a or b
    (d) a and b

48. Article 445 contains installation and other requirements for generators.

    (a) True
    (b) False

49. Transformers with ventilating openings shall be installed so that the ventilating openings are _____.

    (a) a minimum 18 in. above the floor
    (b) not blocked by walls or obstructions
    (c) aesthetically located
    (d) vented to the exterior of the building

50. A disconnecting means is required within sight of the storage battery for all ungrounded battery system conductors operating at over _____ nominal.

    (a) 20V
    (b) 30V
    (c) 40V
    (d) 50V

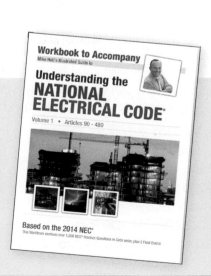

Need Additional Practice?

The *Workbook to Accompany Mike Holt's Understanding the 2014 National Electrical Code, Volume 1* contains more than 1,300 *NEC* Practice questions in *Code* order, along with two random order final exams that follow the *2014 Understanding the NEC, Volume 1* textbook. A two-part Final Exam is also available.

To order call 888.632.2633.

INDEX

Index

Description	Rule	Page

S *(continued)*

Surge Protection

Listing	285.5	288
Location	285.11	289
Number Required	285.4	288
Routing of Conductors	285.12	289
Scope	285.1	288
Short-Circuit Current Rating	285.6	289
Type 1 SPD—Line Side of Service Equipment	285.23	289
Type 2 SPD—Feeder Circuits	285.24	290
Type 3 SPDs—Branch Circuits	285.25	291
Type 4 and Other Component Type SPDs	285.13	289
Uses Not Permitted	285.3	288

Switches

Accessibility and Grouping	404.8	484
Circuit Breakers Used as Switches	404.11	486
Damp or Wet Locations	404.4	482
Grounding of Enclosures	404.12	487
Indicating	404.7	483
Mounting Snap Switches	404.10	486
Position of Knife Switches	404.6	483
Rating and Use of Snap Switches	404.14	487
Scope	404.1	479
Switch Connections	404.2	479
Switch Enclosures	404.3	481
Switch Faceplates	404.9	485
Switch Marking	404.15	488

T

Track Lighting

Fastening	410.154	523
Installation	410.151	523

Transformers

Disconnecting Means	450.14	574
Grounding and Bonding	450.10	573
Marking	450.11	573
Overcurrent Protection	450.3	571
Scope	450.1	571
Transformer Accessibility	450.13	573
Ventilation	450.9	572

U

Underground Feeder Cable

Ampacity	340.80	402
Bends	340.24	402
Definition	340.2	401
Insulation	340.112	402
Listing Requirements	340.6	401
Scope	340.1	401
Uses Not Permitted	340.12	402
Uses Permitted	340.10	401

W

Wireways

Conductors—Maximum Size	376.21	446
Definition	376.2	445
Number of Conductors and Ampacity	376.22	446
Scope	376.1	445
Splices, Taps, and Power Distribution Blocks	376.56	447
Supports	376.30	447
Uses Not Permitted	376.12	446
Uses Permitted	376.10	445
Wireway Sizing	376.23	446

Take Your Training to the next level

& Save 25%

2014 Master & Journeyman Comprehensive Exam Preparation Library

A complete course designed for your success. In-depth instruction for Theory and Code, with step-by-step instructions for solving electrical calculations. The DVDs are a vital component to learning, and the Practice Questions are key to reinforcing what you learn.

Electrical Exam Preparation textbook
Electrical Theory textbook
Understanding the National Electrical Code® Volumes 1 & 2 textbooks
Simulated Exam
Code Review (10 DVDs)
Theory Review (3 DVDs)
Calculations Review (Masters - 8 DVDs; Journeyman - 5 DVDs)

Product Code: 14MACODVD   List Price: $1025.00   Now only $768.75
Product Code: 14JRCODVD   List Price: $925.00   Now only $693.75

2014 Detailed Code Library

There isn't a better way to learn the Code than Mike's Detailed Code Library.
Understanding the National Electrical Code® Volume 1 textbook
Understanding the National Electrical Code® Volume 2 textbook
NEC® Exam Practice Questions workbook
General Requirements DVD
Wiring and Protection DVD
Grounding vs. Bonding (2 DVDs)
Wiring Methods and Materials (2 DVDs)
Equipment for General Use DVD
Special Occupancies DVD
Special Equipment DVD
Limited Energy and Communications Systems DVD

Product Code: 14DECODVD   List Price: $569.00   Now only $426.75

Electrical Estimating DVD Package

Mike Holt's Electrical Estimating DVD Program will give you the skills and the knowledge to get more jobs and to make sure that those jobs will be profitable. This program will also give you a comprehensive understanding of the Estimating process as well as help you understand how Electrical Estimating software can improve your process.

Electrical Estimating textbook
Electrical Estimating (4 DVDs)

Product Code: EST2DVD   List Price: $299.00   Now only $224.25

Call Now 888.NEC.CODE (632.2633)

Mike Holt Enterprises, Inc.

GREYSCALE

BIN TRAVELER FORM

Cut By _Sandy_ Qty _42_ Date _09/19/24_

Scanned By _____ Qty _____ Date _____

Scanned Batch IDs

_____ _____ _____

Notes / Exception

_____

_____

_____

_____

_____